CLIMBING

CLIMBING

The Complete
Reference to
Rock, Ice and
Indoor Climbing

Compiled by Greg Child

☑®

Facts On File, Inc.

Climbing: The Complete Reference to Rock, Ice and Indoor Climbing

Copyright © 1995 by Greg Child

Facts On File, Inc.
11 Penn Plaza
New York NY 10001

Library of Congress Cataloging-in-Publication Data
Child, Greg.
 Climbing: the complete reference / Greg Child.
  p. cm.
 Includes bibliographical references and index.
 ISBN 0-8160-3653-5 (alk. paper)
 1. Mountaineeriing—Encyclopedias. I. Title.
GV200.C44 1995
796.5'22—dc20   94-33254

Facts On File books are available at special discounts when purchased in bulk quantities for businesses, associations, institutions, or sales promotions. Please call our Special Sales Department in New York at 212/967-8800 or 800/322-8755.

Jacket design by Carla Weise

Front cover photo: Allsport, USA

Sketches by John McMullen

Appendixes by Marc Greene

Printed in the United States of America

VB VCS

First paperback printing April 1997

This book is printed on acid-free paper.

CONTENTS

ACKNOWLEDGMENTS

Many writers contributed to this work first begun in 1990. In the United States, thanks are due to the editors at *Climbing* magazine who reviewed early stages of the encyclopedia, especially Alison Osius, editor of many of my stories and a cranking contender in many sport-climbing contests, who wrote the biographies on sport climbers. Jon Waterman, author of Alaskan climbing guidebooks and stories, wrote the Alaskan entries. Sally Greenwood, author of a book on women's climbing, contributed many bios on female climbers. Writer-photographer and author of books on Patagonia Alan Kearney wrote entries about that South American region. H. Adams Carter, editor of the *American Alpine Journal*, reviewed sections of the manuscript. South America was covered by Evelio Echevarria, a professor of foreign languages at Colorado State University with a deep knowledge of the Andes and its history. Thanks are due to Mark Wilford for helping with Colorado and midwestern United States, and for being a fine climbing partner besides. Andy de Klerk compiled information on his native South Africa, and provided some good days on the local crags too. Also helpful with entries and information were writer Gary Speer; John Harlin III, editor of *Summit* magazine; adventure columnist for *Penthouse* magazine Geoff Tabin; journalist John Thackray; Jeff Smoot, author of climbing guidebooks; writer-photographer Andy Selters, for writing about regions from California to Asia; legendary American climbing writer Pat Ament;

Charlie Fowler, pioneer of countless climbs in America and across the world; John Middendorf, for help with reviewing the manuscript; and artist John McMullen, whose illustrations adorn the encyclopedia.

Writers Chick Scott and Greg Horne provided expertise on Canadian climbing history, and party expert and entrepreneur Mike Mortimer's comments on the manuscript were entertaining and helpful. Bernard Mailhot helped with eastern Canadian climbing.

In Britain, I am indebted to the talented writer and winner of the Boardman Tasker Award for Climbing Literature Jim Perrin, for his biographies of British climbers; and to journalist Ed Douglas, for the mammoth task of synthesizing the climbing areas of Britain, Scotland and the European Alps.

Elsewhere across the world, I wish to thank Dolfi Rotovnik for sharing his knowledge of Greenland; the late Romain Vogler, climber and guidebook writer, for helping with French topics; the great Czech climber Jiri Novak helped with Czech subjects; and in Germany, writers Tilmann Hepp, Elmar Landes and the incomparable *Bergsteiger* Kurt Diemberger were of great help.

Finally, I wish to thank Online Press, of Kirkland, Washington, creators of the Quick Course series of computer books, whose computer expertise helped me in a thousand ways.

Greg Child

ABALAKOV, VITALY MIKHAILOVICH (1906–1986) (USSR) "The Father of Soviet Mountaineering," Abalakov pioneered mountaineering in the Soviet Pamirs, Altai, Caucasus and TIEN SHAN ranges in the 1930s. Through his work as an engineer, he developed climbing devices like the "Abalakov cam," a passive CAMMING DEVICE that presaged modern devices. As laboratory director of the Central Scientific Research Institute for Sport, he developed equipment to monitor athletic performance. In later years he was a delegate to the Union Internationale des Association d'Alpinisme (UIAA), and a member of the first Soviet climbing exchange to the United States. The socialist system bestowed him with many honors, including the Soviet Master of Sport (1943), Order of Lenin (1957) and Order of Friendship Among Peoples (1982). He was made an honorary member of the AMERICAN ALPINE CLUB in 1976.

Abalakov began rock climbing around his Siberian birthplace, Krasnoyarsk. He made the first TRAVERSE of Beluhka (1934), the highest peak in the Soviet Altai, and the first Russian ascent of Pik Lenin (1935). His partners included his brother, Evegeny (who made the first ascent of Pik Kommunizma, highest peak in the USSR, in 1933), and his wife, Valentina. In 1936 on an ascent of Khan Tengri in the Tien Shan, Abalakov suffered FROSTBITE, resulting in the amputation of one-third of his left foot and many fingers. Over the next nine years he trained rigorously to adapt to this handicap, by using no gloves in winter to season his hands against cold, performing gymnastics and ski racing.

After World War II he led many high-altitude ascents, such as the FIRST ASCENT of Pik Pobeda (1956), the highest peak in the Tien Shan, and a seven-peak traverse over Pik Lenin, Pik 19 and others in the Pamirs, as well as numerous north faces in the Caucasus. He led the Russian team on the British-Soviet Pamirs Expedition (1962), on which Wilfrid Noyce and Robin Smith were killed. This expedition is recounted in Malcolm Slessor's *Red Peak* (1964). He was also an organizer of the tragic 1974 International Camp in the Pamirs.

Further reading: Robert W. Craig, *Storm and Sorrow* (1977).

ABOMINABLE SNOWMAN See YETI.

ABRUZZI, DUKE OF THE (1873–1933) (Italy) Prince Luigi Amedeo of Savoy, Duke of the Abruzzi, grand-son of King Victor Emmanuel II of Italy, launched meticulously planned climbing and scientific expeditions to the great ranges. His name is synonymous with the Abruzzi Ridge of K2, onto which he ventured in 1909. He served as Chief Admiral of the Italian Fleet in charge of all Allied fleets in the Adriatic Sea during World War I.

This wealthy adventurer made the FIRST ASCENT of Mount SAINT ELIAS in ALASKA (1897) with a team that included American porters carrying his brass bed to base camp. In 1899 he tried to reach the North Pole, but a blizzard halted progress 200 miles (322 km) from its goal. This point (reached by one of his men) was the farthest north anyone had reached, and the Duke lost several fingers to FROSTBITE. In 1906 he penetrated the RUWENZORI mountains of tropical Africa. His expedition mapped and surveyed the range, and climbed most of the main summits, reaching nearly 17,000 ft (5,183 m). His work proved that the snows of the Ruwenzori fed lakes that were the source of the Nile.

His most famous venture was the 1909 KARAKORAM expedition into the Baltoro Muztagh and his attempts on K2 and neighboring peaks. The scientific work on this expedition—photographic panoramas by Vittorio Sella and mapping and observations on glacial movement and meteorology by Filippo de Filippi and Frederico Negrotto—were of lasting importance to science and mountaineering. It was also a breakthrough for equipment design, with sleeping bags made from layers of camel's hair, down, goatskin and waterproof canvas.

The expedition began in Bombay with 13,280 lb (5,976 kg) goods. With some 500 BALTI porters (carrying 500 lb/ 225 kg of rupee coins) they reached K2. They investigated the northeast ridge, attempted in 1902 by Oscar ECKENSTEIN, and reached a point near the Savoia Pass on the northwest ridge above the Savoia Glacier (named by the Duke after his family estate). Declaring both routes impossible, he turned to the southeast ridge, reaching approximately 19,680 ft (6,000 m), and identifying the route the 1954 Italian ascent would follow. The Duke then shifted camp and, with Swiss guides Joseph Petigax and the Brocherel brothers, reached 21,650 ft (6,601 m) on Skyang Kangri (24,750 ft/7,546 m) and 24,600 ft (7,500 m) on CHOGOLISA (25,110 ft/7,655 m)—the latter an altitude record that lasted until the 1922 British attempt on EVEREST.

Further reading: Torino, *From the Pole to K2: The Accomplishments of the Duke of the Abruzzi* (Italian text) (1984).

ABSEIL   The British and Australian term for RAPPEL.

ACCIDENTS   Climbing accidents in the United States are reported annually in *Accidents in North America*, published by the AMERICAN ALPINE CLUB.

ACCLIMATIZATION   The gradual adaptation of the human body to increased altitude and a key element on climbs or mountain treks above 8,000 ft (2,439 m). Important biochemical, ventilatory and circulatory events during acclimatization include: an increase in the breathing rate and/or breathing depth to bring the composition of alveolar air closer to that of the outside environment; a decrease in oxygen pressure between the alveolus and pulmonary capillary; an increase in hemoglobin to allow the blood to carry more oxygen; redirected bloodflow from less important tissues and organs to more important ones (i.e. from skin to the heart); and an adjustment in the metabolic activity of cells to use less oxygen more efficiently. The result of acclimatization is that the oxygen pressure of body tissues is restored to normal sea level values despite a lowered atmospheric pressure.

Successful acclimatization cannot be achieved overnight. The higher the objective, the longer the acclimatization period. Unacclimatized persons who venture above 8,000 ft (2,439 m) too quickly usually suffer symptoms of ACUTE MOUNTAIN SICKNESS (AMS), such as headache, loss of appetite, nausea, lethargy, restless sleep, depression and disorientation. AMS commonly occurs when individuals who dwell at low elevations travel quickly to alpine areas, ski resorts or mountain passes. Descent to low altitude is the best remedy for AMS. Overly rapid or prolonged exposure to higher elevations, particularly above 16,000 ft (4,878 m), may cause high altitude PULMONARY EDEMA (HAPE), or high altitude CEREBRAL EDEMA (HACE), which are potentially fatal altitude-induced maladies. Treatment includes supplementary OXYGEN, decompression (using devices like the GAMOW BAG) and drug therapy, but immediate descent is the best treatment.

The concept of acclimatization was noted as early as the 1800s. Himalayan explorers dreaded the rigors of crossing high passes, but they also knew that the initial unpleasantness of altitude diminished with time spent in the mountains. Explorers, physicians and researchers in the mid-1800s knew that people who live permanently at high elevations, like Nepali Sherpas or Andean natives, are better adapted to altitude than visitors. One of the earliest acclimatization investigations was in 1911, when Yandell Henderson, Erling Schneider, J. S. Haldane and C. G. Douglas camped for several weeks at 14,000 ft (4,268 m) on PIKES PEAK in Colorado and conducted physiological tests. They observed that they all suffered symptoms of altitude sickness with different degrees of severity, and that the rate of acclimatization varied among them.

Subsequent scientific studies observed acclimatization more closely. During Operation Everest in 1947 and Operation Everest II in 1985, subjects spent 35 days inside a decompression chamber, while the pressure was adjusted to the approximate height of Mount EVEREST. In the 1947 experiment, one subject, unaided by supplementary oxygen, rode an exercise bicycle at an altitude pressure of 29,100 ft (8,872 m)—six years before the first ascent of Everest, and 31 years before Reinhold MESSNER and Peter HABELER made the first oxygenless ascent of the peak.

Adequate acclimatization for the highest Himalayan peaks may take 30–50 days, with 16,000 (4,878), 18,000 (5,881), 21,000 (6,412), 23,000 (7,012), 25,000 (7,622) and 26,000 ft (7,927 m) being key acclimatization levels. The maxim "climb high, sleep low" should be the guideline during early phases of acclimatization. Many modern ascents of high peaks cover great distances in short time, but usually such climbers balance the considerable risk by understanding their acclimatization capabilities. Drugs that reduce the problems of acclimatization are gaining acceptance by physicians and climbers. The drug ACETAZOLAMIDE (Diamox) is a respiratory stimulant that reduces unpleasant altitude symptoms, possibly by decreasing the severity of oxygen desaturation during sleep. It is prescribed frequently for skiers and trekkers.

Further reading: Charles S. Houston, *Going Higher: The Story of Man and Altitude* (1987).

ACETAZOLAMIDE (Diamox)   A nonantibacterial sulfonamide drug useful to persons who have difficulty with ACCLIMATIZATION, or who must rapidly ascend from sea level to 12,000 (3,659) to 14,000 ft (4,268 m). It promotes renal bicarbonate excretion, thus reducing the increase in pH (respiratory alkalosis) resulting from carbon dioxide loss caused by the fast, deep breathing usual at high altitude. Acetazolamide is beneficial but does not eliminate all acclimatization problems, nor is it a preventative of high altitude PULMONARY EDEMA. An important benefit of acetazolamide is relief of sleep problems at high altitude. By decreasing the severity of oxygen desaturation and thus severe HYPOXIA during sleep, altitude may be better tolerated during waking hours. Side effects associated with this drug include tingling sensations in lips and fingertips, blurred vision and alteration of taste. Acetazolamide is helpful only in the early stages of acclimatization and at moderate altitudes (to about 20,000 ft/6,098 m). Use of this drug for too long, or at too high an altitude, or using it when one is already acclimatized has caused unfavorable side effects. Used correctly, it has prevented ACUTE MOUNTAIN SICKNESS in many climbers and trekkers.

A CHEVAL   A French mountaineering term, meaning to climb a sharp, horizontal ridge crest by straddling it and shimmying along.

ACONCAGUA (Argentina)   A sky-filling pyramid, Aconcagua is the highest mountain outside Asia. Its summit affords an unobstructed panoramic view of some 230 miles (368 km) of South American territory. Originally volcanic, crowned by marine sediments, it rises above stony valleys 118 miles (190 km) west of Mendoza, 9 miles (15 km) east of the Chilean border. The Incas named it "The White Sentinel" (*acon-* being a corruption of *anco-*, "white"). The thermal spas and the curious rock formation called Puente (bridge) del Inca are located near the settlement of the same name, the starting point for expeditions. Aconcagua's height 22,835 ft (6,960 m), was determined in 1986 by Chilean engineer Luis RISO PATRON. Exaggerated figures have appeared every so often, such as Fitzgerald's 23,080 ft (7,035 m).

Did the Incas ascend the mountain? In 1984, an Inca mummy was excavated at 17,800 ft (5,427 m) in the southwest ridge, a place not easy to reach, and, at 22,700 ft (6,921 m) the corpse of a *guanaco* (a ruminant related to the llama) was found under the ridge between the twin points of the mountain. The Inca mummy has one explanation: OROLATRY. The guanaco has none. Paul Gussfeldt with some Chilean hillmen was the first sportsman to tackle Aconcagua. They reached 21,517 ft (6,560 m). Aconcagua was climbed in 1897, when a richly financed expedition led by Edward Fitzgerald besieged the mountain for two months until guide Matthias ZURBRIGGEN summited on January 14. A month later it was reclimbed and thereafter ascended sporadically by the same (northwest) route, which became known as the *Ruta Normal.* In 1934, four Poles climbed the northeast glacier, today called Glacier de los Polacos.

Routes opened since then include the southwest ridge, by F. Grajales, F. Ibanez, and Dorly and Frederic MARMILLOD (1953); south face, by Frenchmen under Rene Ferlet (1954); southeast face and ridge by Argentinians under G. Vieiro (1978); north side by Italian G. Schranz, solo (1985); west face by Argentinians D. Alsessio and D. Rodriguez (1988).

For an evaluation of routes, especially on the dangerous south face, the *American Alpine Journal 1987* is informative. Aconcagua, today frequently guided, has exacted a toll of victims. In 1944, the Link expedition was almost wholly wiped out by the fearful *viento blanco,* the "white wind" of the region. The Argentinian government then had several huts erected along the Ruta Normal, thus reducing storm victims. To the present, 57 have perished on Aconcagua. The mountain has been benign in other respects, accommodating stunts like high-altitude canine records, paragliding and parachute descents, a mountain-bike ascent and descent, and a motorcycle attempt. The first WINTER ASCENT was made by three Argentinians in 1952 and the first ski ascent (to near the summit) by Catalonians in 1984. Spaniard Fernando Garrido broke the survival record at high altitude by camping for 66 days just under the summit (December 1985–February 1986).

In 1984, the government of the Province of Mendoza created the Aconcagua Mountain Park. A fee of US$80 is now charged to park visitors. Mules, obtained at Puente del Inca, are used for the two-day approach march to base camp, Plaza de Mulas (14,000 ft/4,268 m), at the foot of the normal route.

Guidebooks: Carles Capellas, et al, *Aconcagua* (1982); Alfredo Magnani, et al, *Aconcagua-Argentina* (1981).

Evelio Echevarria
Colorado State University

ACUTE MOUNTAIN SICKNESS (AMS) The most common high-altitude malady, sometimes afflicting climb-

ers as low as 7,000 ft (2,134 m) following a rapid ascent. Symptoms include headache, nausea, vomiting, shortness of breath, disturbed sleep, lethargy and confusion. Victims may exhibit blue-tinged lips and cheeks from cyanosis, which is the presence in circulating blood of amounts of nonoxygenated hemoglobin. Symptoms usually disappear with descent. Slow ACCLIMATIZATION is the best prevention of AMS. Evidence suggests AMS is linked to acute DEHYDRATION, so consuming large quantities of water at high-altitude is beneficial. AMS is not believed to be a dangerous condition, but those suffering from it should be monitored to ensure their condition does not worsen into high-altitude PULMONARY EDEMA or high-altitude CEREBRAL EDEMA. The respiratory stimulant ACETAZOLAMIDE (Diamox) has proved successful in preventing or alleviating AMS.

ADIABATIC WINDS Localized winds caused by the daily warming and cooling by the sun of mountain and valley slopes, and characterized by the up-valley and down-valley "breathing" phenomenon of mountain valleys. The phenomenon begins when air near the ground on a sun-warmed slope rises uphill, and draws the wind up-valley. As the sun sets, the wind reverses when cooled, dense air flows down the mountain slopes and out of the valley. (See WEATHER.)

ADIRONDACKS (United States) A mountain range in upstate New York containing a vast area of mainly granite cliffs in wilderness settings. The range contains the state's highest point, Mount Marcy (5,344 ft/1,629 m), climbed in 1837 by a survey team. Most CRAGS are within Adirondack State Park. Principal cliffs include POK-O-MOONSHINE, Chapel Pond Slab and Spider's Web areas, Wallface, Moss Cliff and Washbowl Cliffs. On these some of the earliest rock climbing in America was practiced, beginning in 1870 when Newell Martin made ropeless ascents of Sawteeth and Gothic mountains. Later, John Case (AMERICAN ALPINE CLUB president from 1944 to 1946) brought roped climbing to these parts; then Fritz WIESSNER, Jim Goodwin and others made climbs. The 1950s and early 1960s were dominated by British expatriate John Turner, who left hard routes on Pok-O-Moonshine and elsewhere. Jim MCCARTHY, John STANNARD, Dick Williams, Art Gran and also Henry BARBER developed the region into the 1970s. Activity continues to produce climbs of all ratings. Winter ice climbing abounds here.
Guidebook: Don Mellor, *Climbing in the Adirondacks* (1986).

ADZE The wide cutting edge of an ICE AXE.

AGOSTINI, ALBERTO DE (1883–1960) (Italy) De Agostini introduced PATAGONIA and Tierra del Fuego, in South America, to the mountaineering world. A missionary, he was sent to Patagonia in 1910. As an explorer and climber, de Agostini was known as "Padre Patagonia." He strove to protect and educate the remaining Selcnam, Alacalufe and Yagan Indians of the southernmost Andes. He also climbed, usually accompanied by alpine guides and Chilean porters. He first climbed in Argentinian Tierra del Fuego (1913) and attempted Cerro SARMIENTO (7,372 ft/ 2,234 m). He perhaps preferred exploration and photography to climbing. By the late 1920s, moving south to north, he began to explore systematically every major glaciated area in Patagonia. Several times he traversed the Patagonian Ice Cap east to west, although he was never able to descend to the Pacific shore. His main ascents were Cerro Electrico (7,200 ft/2,182 m) and Cerro Mayo (8,022 ft/2,431 m). A master photographer famous for his panoramics, he produced superbly illustrated books. His pictures made FITZROY and CERRO TORRE famous. Unfortunately, he liberally sprinkled the southernmost Andes with unacceptable Italian names, afterward recognized in Argentina but rejected in Chile. His major accomplishments came later. In 1943 (he was 60), with two Argentinian guides he won the summit of San Lorenzo (12,229 ft/3,706 m), second highest in Patagonia. And in 1956, as nominal leader of the Italian expedition to Tierra del Fuego, he saw his alpine guides at last climbing Sarmiento and Italia (7,755 ft/2,350 m). The Chilean government named Tierra del Fuego's major inlet "Seno de Agostini" after him. An honorary member of many mountain clubs and geographical societies, he died in Torino, Italy.

Evelio Echevarria
Colorado State University

AHLFELD, FEDERICO (1892–1982) (Germany) Bolivia's most illustrious mountain explorer was a German geologist who visited the country in 1923 to inspect mines and stayed there for good. From 1924 to 1942 as head of Bolivia's geological and mining explorations, he explored the ranges south of La Paz, climbing several peaks over 17,000 ft (5,183 m), at times alone. In 1926, he made the FIRST ASCENT of Chile's active Volcan Huallatire (19,913 ft/6,071 m), and on Hans Pfann's 1928 Austrian-German expedition climbed firsts in the CORDILLERA REAL. In 1939, he founded the Club Andino Boliviano. In the remote Lipez district of southern Bolivia he climbed the highest peak, Uturunco (19,352 ft/5,900 m). He didn't leave records, but his mountaineering is revealed in his scientific writings. Ahlfeld received many distinctions from the Bolivian government.

Evelio Echevarria
Colorado State University

AID CLIMBING   When gymnastic FREE CLIMBING cannot overcome extremely steep or blank rock (or ice), rock-climbing equipment may be used as "aid" for the climber to hang from. Because aid climbing is dependent upon equipment, aid climbing is also called "artificial," or "mechanical," climbing.

A typical aid climbing sequence is as follows: The LEADER places a piece of equipment (i.e., a PITON hammered into a CRACK), clips as CARABINER to this PLACEMENT, then from this suspends an ETRIER (a lightweight ladder made of WEBBING, having three to five steps). The leader may climb with two pairs of etriers, or one pair. Stepping up the etrier(s) to the highest step (topstepping), the leader then

clips directly into the placement with a short SLING connected to the HARNESS. This sling, called a COW'S TAIL, or DAISY CHAIN, affords stability on steep terrain. Reaching above, the leader then makes another placement. Etriers are clipped to this, and the process is repeated. The rope is attached to each placement with a carabiner as the climber moves on.

At the end of the PITCH, the leader makes a BELAY, and ties off the lead rope. The SECOND climber ascends the rope on ASCENDERS, cleaning the pitch (removing equipment) and carrying it up to the belay.

Aid climbing as practiced today arose from primitive techniques using rope tension developed early this century in Europe and Britain. Viewed as a clumsy procedure, aid climbing was known in Britain as "whack and dangle" technique. During the 1950s and 1960s spectacular rock formations long regarded as unclimbable—like the great limestone ROOFS of the DOLOMITES in Italy and the desert sandstone towers in the American Southwest—succumbed to aid climbing techniques and technology. However, in the 1960s to 1980s the huge granite walls of YOSEMITE VALLEY in CALIFORNIA became the crucible in which aid climbing standards, equipment and BIG WALL CLIMBING techniques reached their zenith. The world's most dense concentration of long and technically difficult aid climbs lie on the rock walls of EL CAPITAN and HALF DOME, in Yosemite.

Early aid climbing equipment, like soft steel pitons and wooden wedges, or tactics like using PRUSIK slings to ascend ropes, was crude. The appearance of Yvon CHOUINARD's tough chromolly steel pitons in the 1950s was a breakthrough in American aid climbing. Chouinard's pitons came in a range of sizes, from the six-inch (15 cm) BONG, to the RURP, a piton small enough to fit a hair-line crack. When JUMARS—mechanical rope-ascending devices from Europe—appeared in 1962, many aid climbing procedures were made faster and safer. During the 1960s and 1970s American climbers like Royal ROBBINS made pitoncraft an art, but the advent of the COPPERHEAD changed the face of aid climbing. Suddenly, tiny seams could be filled with these maleable-metal cabled devices. In the 1960s NUTS and STOPPERS, and in the 1970s FRIENDS and other SPRING LOADED CAMMING DEVICES (SLCD) further revolutionized aid climbing, especially in climbing EXPANDING FLAKES (fragile flakes that widen when weighted). SKYHOOKS, which are perched on tiny edges, became part of the modern aid climber's rack and increased the possibilities for overcoming seemingly blank terrain.

Whenever nuts, stoppers and SLCDs (or any hand-placed device that does not need to be hammered into or out of a crack) are used exclusively, the ascent is called "hammerless" or CLEAN CLIMBING. However, most aid climbs call for use of hammer and piton, and hand-drills for drilling RIVET or BOLT LADDERS through blank sections of rock, or to drill bolt belays.

RATING SYSTEMS (in the United States, ranging from A1 to A5) rate the difficulty of aid climbs. This system reflects security as well as technical difficulty. A1 indicates a placement capable of holding massive forces (a piton driven deep into a horizontal crack, for example. Such a piton is said to be BOMBPROOF); A2 is more difficult to place and holds less; A3 will hold a short fall; A4 holds only body weight (a skyhook perched over a fragile FLAKE, for example); A5 entails enough A4 placements to risk a 50-foot fall. Intermediate ratings like A3+, A4+ and A5+ are frequently used in American aid climbing.

A class system was introduced by the Sierra Club (USA) in the 1950s:

Class 1: a hiking scramble. Steep walking.
Class 2: steeper walking, with use of hands on rock occasionally.
Class 3: frequent use of hands on rock.
Class 4: actual climbing with a rope and belay.
Class 5: mandatory need for roped tactics.
Class 6: same as Class 5, but with multiple days/nights spent on the climb.

Advances in aid climbing standards are expressed in a greater willingness by climbers to risk long falls on continuously difficult ground. This ethic was developed during the 1970s, especially by the American climber Jim BRIDWELL, who reasoned that an aid pitch should follow the natural features of the rock, no matter how subtle or tenuous, and that bolts should not be used to "tame" a serious pitch. Bridwell's elegantly conceived routes on El Capitan, Pacific Ocean Wall (VI A5, 5.10) and Sea of Dreams (VI A5, 5.10) took this concept to the limit. These and many other modern routes on El Capitan involved entire pitches of body-weight-only placements on which a fall at any point is likely to rip an entire string of aid placements back to the belay. Such individual pitches may take an entire day to lead and require great psychological stamina.

AID ELIMINATION To FREE CLIMB a PITCH or a sequence of moves previously ascended by AID CLIMBING tactics, thereby replacing "artificial" movement with gymnastic movement. Such an ascent is called a "free" ascent. Guidebooks sometimes note the "first free ascent" of a rock route, indicating that a climber has eliminated aid moves used by earlier parties. FIXED equipment from aided ascents, like BOLTS or PITONS, are often left in place and clipped for protection by free ascensionists. Aid eliminations enjoyed a heyday of popularity in America and Britain during the 1970s–1980s.

AIDERS Another name for ETRIERS. Also known as AID LADDERS. Aiders is typically an American term.

AID LADDERS This term refers to both BOLT LADDERS and to the sewn ladders that AID CLIMBING uses (see AIDERS).

AID RATINGS The A1, A2, A3, A4 and A5 system for rating AID CLIMBING. (See RATING SYSTEMS.)

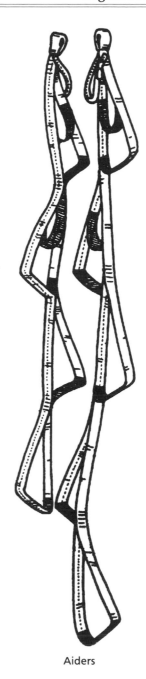

Aiders

AIGUILLE A French word meaning "needle" that is used to describe a sharp, pointed peak. The aiguille peaks surrounding MONT BLANC in the French ALPS are the best example.

AIGUILLE DE ROCHEFORT (France) There are in fact three peaks forming this westward continuation of the Jorasses chain; the Aiguille de Rochefort (13,123 ft/4,001 m) sits in the middle with the elegant Rochefort Arête, first climbed in 1900 by E. Allegra et al, leading to its summit. The other summits are the Dent du Géant (13,163 ft/4,013 m) to its west and the Dôme de Rochefort (13,169 ft/4,015 m) to its east. Ascents usually start from the easily accessible Rifugio Torino.

AIGUILLE VERTE (France) First climbed in 1865 by Edward WHYMPER less than a month before his tragic MATTERHORN ascent, the Aiguille Verte (13,520 ft/4,122 m) is one of the most demanding mountains in the range. In bad weather even the most straightforward approach can trap the climber, and a number of accidents have occurred after parties were caught out too low on the mountain at sunrise. Routes start from the Charpoua and Couvercle Huts above the Mer de Glace and from the Argentière Glacier and Hut. The Whymper Couloir is the most popular way to the summit, but because of the variance in conditions, it should not be underestimated, and parties should be fit enough to escape its walls as quickly as possible. The Moine Ridge is also not demanding technically, although snowy conditions can make this mixed route (also climbed in 1865) a much tougher proposition. An approach from the Aiguille sans Nom was made in 1926 by a party that included the great guide Armand Charlet, who also climbed the Nant Blanc Face Direct in 1935—a route that is reputed to be one of the finest in the range. On the northeast side of the mountain, above the Argentière Glacier, are two COULOIRS, the Cordier and the Couturier. The former is the older route, but because of changes in the GLACIER since it was first ascended in 1876, it offers a sterner test than the latter, which was the 1932 route of M. Couturier, A. Charlet and J. Simond. Both these routes require early starts to avoid any chance of avalanche conditions.

An important subsidiary peak of the Verte is the Aiguille sans Nom, which has an impressive north face overlooking the Nant Blanc Glacier with a number of excellent routes.

ALABAMA (United States) A wealth of sandstone offering gymnastic climbing on OVERHANGS, FACES and CRACKS makes Alabama a major U.S. SPORT-CLIMBING center. The great BOULDERER John Gill was born in Tuscaloosa, and he left severe boulder problems at Shades Crest, a popular 50-ft (15-m) CRAG near Birmingham. Later, Alabama climbers adopted sport climbing early in the American scene, developing their cliffs with hard bolted climbs. Northeast Alabama is dotted with a belt of crags that extends from Lookout Mountain in Chattanooga, TENNESSEE. One well-developed Alabama crag is YELLOW CREEK FALLS, though the 1980s saw other crags developed there: Yellow Bluff; Steele (45 miles/72 km north of Birmingham); Jamestown, Sandrock and Griffin Falls (all near the town of Fort Payne); and Bankhead State Forest. This state's highest point is Cheaha Mountain (2,407 ft/734 m), in Cheaha State Park in Lineville. There are climbing outcrops within the park. Nearby, at Chandler Mountain, 16 miles (26 km) southwest of Gadsen, is a 250-ft (76-m) crag.
Guidebook: Jim Detterline, *A Climber's Guide to the Mid-South* (1982).

ALASKA (United States) Alaska, with a rich diversity of climbing areas, is North America's finest playground for the alpinist willing to suffer storm, cold and high altitude. Unclimbed rock walls, ice faces and CORNICED ridges abound. Of the 20 highest mountains in the United States, 17 are in Alaska, including DENALI, North America's highest. Alaska holds 38 major mountain ranges in a land area four times the size of Texas. The most sought-after mountains lie in the ALASKA RANGE and the SAINT ELIAS range. Although mostly known for large glaciated mountains and granite spires, in recent years roadside crag and ICE CLIMBING near Anchorage and Fairbanks have come of age. The Archangel Valley, 60 miles/96 km north of Anchorage in the Talkeetna Mountains, offers granite rock climbing. The traditional climbing season in the glaciated ranges begins in April and extends into July. As daylight wanes in "the land of the midnight sun," few venture into the subzero darkness, with the exception of ice climbers in Valdez and around Anchorage. (See also ARRIGETCH MOUNTAINS, BROOKS RANGE, CHUGACH MOUNTAINS, FAIRWEATHER, FORAKER, HUNTER, HUNTINGTON, KICHATNA SPIRES, LITTLE SWITZERLAND, MOOSES TOOTH, REVELATION MOUNTAINS.)

ALASKA RANGE (United States) The most popular of Alaska's glaciated ranges, largely because of ski touring on the Ruth Glacier and climbing on DENALI. There are myriad other attractive climbing destinations such as the MOOSES TOOTH (10,335 ft/3,151 m), Mt. Russell (11,670 ft/3,558 m), Mount FORAKER (17,400 ft/5,305 m) and Mount HUNTINGTON (12,240 ft/3,732 m). The range is divided into four distinctively different subranges, extending several hundred miles from the interior to the coast. The Central Alaska Range features Mt. Hayes (13,832 ft/4,217 m) and Mt. Deborah (12,339 ft/3,762 m); the Eastern (aka "the Deltas") Range is a smaller area, containing Mt. Kimball (10,350 ft/3,155 m). Both areas are most commonly approached from Fairbanks. The main Alaska Range lies largely within Denali National Park. This popular area is most frequently approached from Talkeetna and is known for its high mountains and granite spires extending from Denali to the KICHATNA SPIRES. The southern Alaska Range is subject to fickle coastal weather, and includes the REVELATION MOUNTAINS, Mt. Spurr (11,070 ft/3,375 m) and various other volcanoes—all most easily approached from Anchorage. The range is famous for its subzero temperatures, high winds and heavy snowstorms originating when wet ocean air hits the southern coast.

ALBERT, KURT (1954–   ) (Germany) This pioneer of modern FREE CLIMBING invented the term and concept of REDPOINT, which he defined in the mid-1970s after experiencing the style of rock climbing in the ELBSANDSTEINGEBIRGE, where climbers progressed from BOLT TO BOLT free, but hung from the BOLTS to rest. On his local CRAGS at the FRANKENJURA, Albert and partners free-climbed without resting on bolts, and marked all technical routes they could climb completely free with a painted red point on the rock at the bottom of the route. He was the first in Germany to climb the eighth grade, with the route Osterweg, VIII-, at the crag Altmuhltal, and he pioneered long free climbs, such as, in 1987 in the Dolomites, the first redpoint ascents of Schweitzer Dach, IX-, at the Westliche Zinne and the Hasse-Brandler Diretissima, VIII+, on the

Grosse Zinne. With partner Wolfgang GULLICH, he was the first to introduce long, hard free climbing of big walls to the KARAKORAM and PATAGONIA. On Nameless Tower in the TRANGO TOWERS of Pakistan they made the FIRST FREE ASCENT of the Yugoslavian route (1988) and opened Eternal Flame (1989), and in 1991 on the central tower of PAINE (Chile), they opened Riders on the Storm. These involved free climbing up to 5.12, high altitude and alpine conditions.

ALBERTA (Canada) Climbing commenced in Alberta in the late 1880s with the coming of the Canadian Pacific Railway. The great peaks of the Rocky mountains that form the jagged southwest border of the province were explored by American and British mountaineers and their European guides from the 1890s up to 1925. The mountain village of Banff, located in Banff National Park, Alberta, is the birthplace of Canadian mountaineering. The Alpine Club of Canada makes its home in Canmore and there are three local chapters of the club: the Rocky Mountain section, Calgary section and Edmonton section. Members of the Calgary Mountain Club between 1960 and 1985 pioneered most of the climbing developments in the province. Canmore and Jasper are also active climbing centers in Alberta. The climate is generally dry in the summer, cold and dry in winter. FROZEN WATERFALLS abound in winter. Much of the mountain area is protected by parks, keeping the mountains unpolluted and accessible. Eighteen huts operated by the mountain clubs provide shelter for climbers. Alberta mountains covered in this volume are Mounts ALBERTA, ASSINIBOINE, COLUMBIA ICEFIELDS, EDITH CAVELL, KITCHENER, NORTH TWIN, ROBSON, ROCKY MOUNTAINS, TEMPLE. For rock climbing, see BOW VALLEY CORRIDOR. (See also CANADIAN WATERFALL ICE CLIMBING.)

ALBERTA, MOUNT (Canada) One of the great challenges of the Canadian Rockies, and the region's last major summit to be climbed. It is a darkly massive mountain, with a vertical 1,968-ft (600-m) rocky wall on the north. Access is via the Icefields Parkway and Woolley Creek trail to the Alberta Hut (ACC operated). The 11,874-ft (3,619-m) summit was first reached in 1925 by six Japanese (Yukomaki, S. Hasimoto, M. Hatano, T. Hayakawa, Y. Mita and N. Oakbe) and their three guides (Heinrich Fuhrer, Hans Kohler and Jean Weber). Their route to the summit via the southeast face and ridge involved climbing rated at 5.6 levels and stood as the hardest route in North America at the time. It was rumored that the Japanese had left a silver ICE AXE, given to them by their emperor, on the summit. In 1948 Americans Fred Ayres and John Oberlin repeated the route and trophied the axe—in reality made of plain steel—and SUMMIT REGISTER, presenting them to the AMERICAN ALPINE CLUB in New York. Canadian climbing historians still lament the loss of these historic mementos. Alberta's north face was first climbed in 1972 by Jock Glidden and George LOWE. It was an inspiring achievement, (5.9 A3 on the rock with steep ICE FIELDS at the start and end), done in impeccable style on the first attempt, and rarely repeated. Mark Wilford (United States) soloed

a variation to the Glidden-Lowe route in 1991. The peak is named for the fourth daughter of Queen Victoria.
Guidebooks: Sean Dougherty, *Selected Alpine Climbs in the Canadian Rockies* (1991); R. Kruszyna and W. L. Putnam, *The Rocky Mountains of Canada North* (1985).

ALLAIN, PIERRE (1904–   ) (France) During the 1930s Allain developed BOULDERING at a time when rock climbing was regarded as mere training for the longer routes of the ALPS. Allain and his peers, who climbed at the famous boulders of FONTAINEBLEAU, near Paris, were derisively called *Bleausards* by French ALPINISTS, meaning bouldering specialists who only climb on OUTCROPS but not mountains. The Bleausards' routes at Fontainebleau are respectable even by modern standards.

Allain did take rock-climbing skills to the Alps, first repeating many classic routes there, then applying FREE-CLIMBING tactics to the Alps' last great unclimbed problems, at a time when most climbers resorted to AID CLIMBING and even lasso techniques. His ascent of the southwest ridge of the Aiguille du Fou (1933), with Robert Latour, was a difficult rock climb that had been attempted by the best French mountaineers. In 1935, with Raymond Leninger, he stunned the alpine community when he climbed the north face of Les DRUS. Other Allain routes that influenced the tide of alpine climbing include the northeast ridge of the Grandes Charmoz (1937) and also its west ridge (1950), and the west face of the Aiguille Blaiteire (1947). His prowess as a rock climber so impressed French alpinists that it was suggested by his peers, in a lighthearted moment, that he had an extra muscle unknown to medical science. He also was a member of the French Himalayan Expedition (1936). He used his background as an engineer to make contributions to climbing, producing the first aluminum alloy CARABINER (1939), which became the first commercially available carabiners in 1947. His PA FRICTION BOOTS appeared in 1948 and were popular all over the world into the 1970s. He participated in the liberation of Chamonix from German forces in World War II.
Further reading: *Alpinism and Competition* (French text) (1979).

ALLALIN GROUP (Austria) South of the Mischabeljoch the ridge crest is less contiguous and the GLACIERS reach farther up the mountains. The big peaks are more accessible and cable cars operate from both valleys. The first mountain south of the Täschhorn, the Alphubel (13,796 ft/4,206 m), has two contrasting faces. From the west it is a buttressed rock peak, from the east a snow face. The west ridge offers an AD (*Assez Difficile*), starting from the Täsch Hut but the most popular method of ascent is from the Längflue cableway reached in turn from Saas Fee.

The Allalinhorn (13,209 ft/4,027 m) itself has been made very straightforward by the Métro Alpin railway, although this modern intrusion does not have the extrusions and noise of cable cars. Many climbers, in order to preserve the impression that they are on a mountain, choose to climb the east ridge above the Hohlaub Glacier from the Britannia Hut before descending via the Feejoch to the Metro station. There are harder routes on the mountain, equally accessible; the northeast face, for example, is TD: *Très Difficile*.

On the south side of the Allalinpass are the Rimpfischhorn (13,769 ft/4,198 m) and the Strahlhorn (13,540 ft/4,128 m), separated by the Allalin Glacier. The Rimpfischhorn was first climbed in 1859 by Leslie Stephen with Melchior Anderegg and Johann Zumtaugwald by the method of ascent most commonly used today: the east ridge from the Flue Hut, reached in half an hour from the Blauherd cableway station above Zermatt. The Strahlhorn's normal routes is a PD snowplod from the Britannia Hut and best avoided unless on skis. Other routes include the northeast ridge (AD), also started from the Britannia, and the south face (AD+), a mixed route starting from the Sella Hut.

ALLEN, JOHN (1960–   ) (Britain) Teenage rock-genius who reactivated the spirit of traditional gritstone climbing with a series of prime routes in the mid-1970s, and inspired perhaps the most fatuous headline ever to appear even in *Mountain* magazine ("John Allen free-climbs Great Wall, but uses chalk!") when he made the FIRST FREE ASCENT of that oft-tried route of CLOGWYN DU'R ARDDU, in North Wales, at age 15 in 1975; the list of climbs he put up between 1975 and 1977 on the Derbyshire outcrops, mostly in company with Steve Bancroft, is formidable: Old Friends, Hairless Heart, Profit of Doom and Reticent Mass Murderer. After a sojourn in the Antipodes, he returned to Britain and continues to produce climbs of extreme technical accomplishment on the gritstone OUTCROPS of Derbyshire.

ALLISON, STACY (1958–   ) (United States) On September 29, 1988, Allison became the first American woman to reach the summit of Mount EVEREST. A carpenter and building contractor from Portland, Oregon, her mountaineering career began in 1980 with an alpine-style ascent of the Cassin Ridge on DENALI. In 1982 she summited on Ama Dablam in Nepal on an all-women's expedition. Climbing Everest and becoming America's first woman to reach its summit became a personal objective for her. Allison tried the direct north face in 1987, but bad weather halted her team at 26,240 ft (8,000 m). Returning to the South Col route in 1988 with the Northwest American Expedition, she summited after 29 days on the mountain. Her summit partner was Pasang Gyalzen Sherpa and she used supplemental oxygen.

ALMSCLIFF (Britain) Almscliff lies near the village of Huby, 10 miles (16 km) north of Leeds. Yorkshire men believe that rock climbing began here in the 1870s. Almscliff is gritstone and dries quickly after rain. The routes are not more than 50 ft high (15 m) and are NATURALLY PROTECTED.

Impressive contributions to Almscliff came from Arthur Dolphin, who after World War II climbed Z Wall (5.7), Overhanging Groove (5.8) and Great Western (5.8). Dolphin was killed in the Alps aged only 28. In the late 1950s,

Allan Austin climbed a string of futuristic leads, including, solo, the overhang of Western Front (5.10c), after he had fallen from high up the route on a previous solo attempt. He later soloed the overhanging Wall of Horrors (5.10d), a route unrepeated for some years. John Syrett solved a major problem in 1973 when he climbed Big Greenie (5.10d).

Guidebook: Yorkshire Mountain Club, *Yorkshire Gritstone* (1989).

ALP In Europe, a grassy mountain pasture high on the valley flank used by shepherds for grazing animals. Early travelers to Europe's mountains applied the word to the mountains as a whole, hence the European ALPS.

ALPAMAYO (Peru) For its graceful shape, Alpamayo is known worldwide as "the most beautiful mountain in the world." It is a white cathedral, ornamented with flutes and furrows and rimmed by CORNICES, in the northern CORDILLERA BLANCA. Originally placed at 20,074 ft (6,120 m), it is now 19,510 ft (5,947 m), or lower. Austrians Hans Kinzl and Erwin SCHNEIDER, with their astonishing pictures, launched Alpamayo to fame. The 1951 French-Belgian expedition claimed its FIRST ASCENT, but shrewd Germans who studied photos in the 1951 book *The Ascent of Alpamayo* thought differently. In 1957, they reached the actual top, well above the north point of their predecessors. Other routes are the east ridge, by Germans (1969), the northeast side to north ridge, by New Zealanders (1970), with posterior variants by Ecuadorians and Yugoslavians. The normal route is the steep northwest side. The actual summit is seldom trodden; climbers content themselves with reaching the summit ridge and seldom risk the topmost cornice, which may change from year to year.

Guidebooks: Jim Bartle and David Sharman, *Trails and Climbs of the Cordillera Blanca of Peru* (1992); John Ricker, *Yuraq Janka* (1981).

Further reading: Georges Kogan, et al. *The Ascent of Alpamayo* (1954).

Evelio Echevarria
Colorado State University

ALPENSTOCK The forerunner of the ICE AXE, being a long wood-shafted pole with a spike at one end and straight ice pick at the other. European shepherds and alpine pioneers of the early 1800s used the alpenstock as a walking stick and tool on glaciers and snowy slopes. By the 1870s the ice axe had replaced the alpenstock.

ALPINE CLIMBING TECHNIQUES A broad heading, but here discussing techniques for climbing moderately steep snow or ice using ICE AXE and CRAMPONS. Finesse on snow and ice is a matter of balance, footwork and familiarity with ICE TOOLS. Even on gentle slopes that do not require crampons, the ice axe is a useful walking stick. Some climbers prefer holding the ice axe with the pick pointing backward, others prefer to point it forward. Either way, a leash tied to the ice axe and worn around the wrist makes the tool ready for SELF ARREST in the event of a slip. On crusty snow or NEVE, crampons may be unnecessary and steps may be kicked directly into the slope, with the ice axe acting like a "third leg" for balance. Steps into snow should be about a third of a boot deep. Whenever the angle of a slope steepens enough to cause consternation, wear crampons.

Prior to the invention of crampons, and even as recently as the 1960s, steep ice faces were climbed by STEP CUT-TING—hacking out footholds in the ice with the ADZE of the ice axe. Modern ice axes and crampons have virtually eliminated step cutting. However, a few swings of the adze can quickly chop out a restful foot ledge when legs are aching from a long PITCH of FRONT POINTING, or if one has broken a crampon. During the 1960s European climbers refined techniques of cramponing. FRENCH TECHNIQUE (flat footing) and front pointing arose from this era of ALPINISM, but contemporary alpinists agree that a combination of styles works better than adopting one to the exclusion of the other.

When cramponing on easy terrain one should walk normally, but mindful of the hazard of catching crampon points in clothing around the legs and ankles. The weight of the body should be centered over the foot, and is shifted from one foot to another. As much as possible, the flats of the feet should be parallel to the slope so that the maximum number of crampon points bite the snow. When climbing snow up to 55 degrees, the feet should sidestep across each other, with the toes angled across the slope or slightly downhill. Avoid standing on edges of boots, but allow ankles to roll so all points bite. When traversing, climb sideways with the feet as flat as possible to the slope. Angling one foot slightly downhill compensates for a lack of flexibility in the ankles.

The ice axe is crucial for balance at steeper angles. It may be gripped in several ways, either by the head and held like a walking stick with the shaft thrust into the snow, or held braced with both hands.

When climbing down face outward, keep the feet flat, pointed downhill, knees bent in a pronounced squat as the angle approaches 45 degrees. The ice axe is held to the side and behind, ready for self arrest. When the angle feels uncomfortable face into the slope and front point down, digging the ice axe pick or shaft into the snow.

On steep slopes climbing directly up becomes stressful on ankles, so a more comfortable zig-zag diagonal path is struck. At changes in direction, care must be taken not to overbalance. The safest way to execute a switch from, say, a right-trending path to a left-trending one is to sink the ice axe shaft (held in left hand while moving rightward) into the snow (or, if on ice or firm neve, sink the pick into the slope); face into the slope, kicking the feet into the snow; change left hand for right on the ice axe head (perhaps bracing the freed hand on the shaft); then bring the inside foot (in this case right) forward to make the next step. The ice axe is always held on the uphill side. Switches from one hand to another are made with care.

Steep, hard ice is climbed largely by front pointing, and may require two ice axes. On moderate terrain this technique is rarely called for, but modern crampons and rigid mountain BOOTS make front pointing advantageous for many situations. True front pointing means climbing by kicking the tips of crampons into water ice. The ice axe(s) may be placed for balance, or, as with vertical ICE CLIMBING, such as on frozen waterfalls, the climber may be literally hanging from the ice axe picks. On moderately steep alpine ice American technique (called *pied troisième* in French technique) combines flat footing with front pointing by front pointing with one foot while the other foot is placed flat. This method eases strain on the legs.

ALPINE CLUB The noted British mountaineering club formed in 1857 and active today.

ALPINE JOURNAL The annual British mountaineering journal, published by the ALPINE CLUB.

ALPINE START A MOUNTAINEERING term that originated in the European ALPS, meaning to start a climb very early in the morning, usually before sunrise, to make use of firm and safe snow conditions.

ALPINE STYLE A MOUNTAINEERING term that describes a lightweight, self-contained and committed style of ascent. The term is derived from the traditional mountaineering style of the European ALPS, in which a party makes their ascent in a single push, with no prior preparation of the mountain. As the term applies to the larger scale of the HIMALAYA, pure alpine style doesn't use FIXED ROPE, fixed camps, preplaced caches of gear, prior physical reconnaisance of the route or SHERPA or HIGH-ALTITUDE PORTER assistance. In contrast, seige style expeditions use all the aforementioned to climb a mountain. (See also CAPSULE STYLE.)

Pure alpine-style ascents of big peaks are rare and the term is loosely used. Some ascents claiming to be alpine style use limited amounts of fixed rope, or stock small camps along the route, moving in alpine style above the level of their highest camp. Such an ascent is sometimes described as LIGHTWEIGHT EXPEDITION style.

Significant examples of pure alpine-style ascents of Himalayan peaks where the climbers simply started at the bottom of a mountain and reached the summit in a single push include: the 1975 ascent by Tyroleans Reinhold MESSNER and Peter HABELER of the northwest face of GASHERBRUM I (26,470 ft/8,068 m) in PAKISTAN; the FIRST ASCENT in 1982 by Britons Roger Baxter-Jones, Alex MACINTYRE and Doug SCOTT of the southwest face of SHISHAPANGMA (26,397 ft/8,046 m), in TIBET; the first complete traverse in 1984 by the Poles Jerzy KUKUCZKA and Wojciech KURTYKA of BROAD PEAK (26,400 ft/8,047 m) in PAKISTAN; and the solo ascents of new routes in 1989 and 1990 by the Yugoslav Tomo CESEN of the north face of Jannu (25,295 ft/7,710 m) and LHOTSE south face (27,939 ft/8,516 m), in Nepal.

Alpine style has practical problems and inherent risks. On big Himalayan peaks, it is usually necessary to ACCLIMATIZE on routes or peaks other than the route intended for an alpine-style ascent. Doing so can cause logistical problems. However, the greatest problem in alpine-style climbing is risk. Without fixed ropes or support to escape a mountain in times of storm, illness or injury, parties will find descent difficult and dangerous. Nonetheless, alpine style is lauded by the climbing fraternity as the state-of-the-art style of ascent, and many of its proponents have written eloquently of its virtues.

ALPINISM Refers to alpine climbing that involves GLA-CIER travel, ROUTE finding on high mountains and MOUN-TAINEERING skills.

ALPS, THE (Europe) Perhaps the best-known mountain range in the world, the Alps form a natural boundary between Italy and France, Switzerland, Austria and Slovenia. They stretch from the hinterland of Nice in the west to near Ljublijana in Slovenia in the east and Vienna in the north. The highest mountain in the Alps and Western Europe is MONT BLANC at 15,767 ft (4,807 m) and there are 51 other mountains over 13,120 ft (4,000 m).

The Alps get their name from the low areas of the mountain used for pasture in summer and not from the whole mountain. Similarly, Mont originally meant a pass, the only feature of the mountains local inhabitants would have had a use for. These passes have been used for the purposes of trade and warfare since prehistoric times.

The area is also famous for its GLACIERS. Indeed, from the air these are the most striking features. The Great Aletsch is the longest at around 12.5 miles (20 km) but most glaciers are in retreat and substantial changes have been noted, even in the last decade. The rock itself is largely igneous, Chamonix granite for example, but there are notable exceptions, especially outlying regions like the Bernese Alps, which are limestone.

While MOUNTAINEERING was initially the most popular activity in the Alps, skiing has vastly outstripped it and a Victorian time-traveler would have great difficulty in finding the quiet valleys devoid of the traffic and ski-lifts that characterize the area today. This explosion in interest for alpine skiing holidays has brought with it tremendous environmental pressures.

This weight of tourism does mean, however, that the area is well served by hotels, guest houses, campsites, mountain huts, restaurants, bars and climbing shops. Mountain rescue techniques reach their zenith in the Alps, and considering the scores of deaths each year, this is hardly surprising.

Climbing in purely objective terms has an indeterminable history, but ascents, for example, of Mont Aiguille in 1492 and Titlis in 1744, illustrate the exploratory interest of mankind. Likewise, Horace-Bénédict de Saussure offered in 1760 a prize for the first ascent of Mont Blanc as a reward for exploration rather than sporting endeavor. The fact that the prize was not collected for 26 years, and success was prompted by the scientific curiosity of Michel-Gabriel Paccard and the opportunism of crystal hunter Jacques Balmat, illustrates the perils that the Alps held in those days.

The start of climbing as a sport in the Alps, or alpinism, is thought to be the ascent in 1854 of the Wetterhorn by Sir Alfred Wills. This was, in fact, only the fourth ascent of the peak and there are records of over a hundred alpine ascents before that date, but Wills's description of his ascent started what became known as the Golden Age.

The Alps are split into three broad areas: the Western Alps, the Central Alps and the Eastern Alps. Within these general headings are specific ranges with notable peaks comprising one of the finest mountaineering locations in the world.

(See also AIGUILLE VERTE; BERNESE ALPS; CHAMONIX AI-GUILLES; COURTES, LES; DAUPHINE ALPS; DOLOMITES; DROITES, LES; DRUS, LES; GRAIAN ALPS; GRANDES JORASSES; HAUTE SAVOIE ALPS; MATTERHORN; MONT BLANC RANGE; ORTLER ALPS.)

ALTERNATE LEADS A term meaning to alternate or switch the leads of PITCHES between two or more climbers. The first climber leads a pitch to its end, BELAYS, then the next climber takes a turn leading the next pitch, and so on, in rotation.

ALTIMETER A small barometer calibrated in altitude instead of pressure, used by mountaineers to determine elevation, for navigating and for forecasting weather. In dense brush, fog or WHITE-OUT, location on a topographic map may be found by comparing contour lines with the altimeter's elevation reading. Navigating with altimeter and compass is often used when descending mountains in low visibility. Like a barometer, an altimeter indicates changing weather. Increased elevation means decreased barometric pressure and bad weather. Conversely, decreased elevation means increased barometric pressure, indicating good weather. Rapid changes in readings indicate the arrival of strong weather fronts. Altimeters may be mechanical (consisting of a hollow metal capsule linked to a rotating needle) or electronic (an electronic sensor linked to circuitry). Temperature change may also affect readings, though sophisticated altimeters are designed to cope with extremes of temperature.

ALTITUDE ILLNESS A general term, usually referring to mountain sickness, or, more accurately ACUTE MOUNTAIN SICKNESS. PULMONARY EDEMA, CEREBRAL EDEMA and RETINAL HEMORRHAGE are more serious types of altitude illness. (See ACCLIMATIZATION, ALTITUDE MEDICINE.)

ALTITUDE MEDICINE The following drugs are regarded as useful in the prevention of high-altitude maladies, and are typically stocked in an expedition base camp:

ACETAZOLAMIDE (Diamox): for prevention of ACUTE MOUNTAIN SICKNESS, and for accelerating ACCLIMATIZATION. Taken orally.

Aspirin: mild analgesic and anti-inflammatory that also thins the blood, possibly beneficial at high altitude. Taken orally.

DEXAMETHAZONE (Decadron): proven useful in treatment of PULMONARY EDEMA and possibly CEREBRAL EDEMA. Taken orally or by injection.

GAMOW BAG: a portable hyperbaric chamber proven useful in treating pulmonary edema and cerebral edema.

Nifedipine: Though little is known of this drug, research indicates it may prevent pulmonary edema. Taken orally.

Oral Rehydration Salts: mixtures of glucose and salt added to water to prevent the profound dehydration common at high altitude.

Oxygen: proven effective when a controlled flow through a respirator is administered to persons suffering from a variety of ALTITUDE ILLNESSES.

ALUMAHEAD An item of equipment used in AID CLIMBING, identical in design to a COPPERHEAD, but swaged with a softer aluminum head instead of copper. When hammered, aluminum adheres to seams more effectively than copper.

AMENT, PAT (1946–   ) (United States) Tom FROST wrote of this climber and writer, "He is a mentor influencing some of the outstanding climbers of three generations." Climbing under the tutelage of Layton KOR in the early 1960s, then with Royal ROBBINS and Chuck PRATT, he climbed in COLORADO, YOSEMITE and the Southwest desert. With John Gill he developed extreme BOULDERING around Boulder in the late 1960s, and opened some of the first 5.11 routes in Colorado. Supremacy Crack, Vertigo, Northwest Corner of the Bastille and Super Slab (ELDORADO CANYON), Country Club Crack (BOULDER CANYON) and, near Estes Park, Crack of Fear are still respected classics. He also pioneered BIG WALL routes on the BLACK CANYON OF THE GUNNISON and in the Royal Gorge. Ament strove to capture the climbing life in his poetry, prose and film. His book *Swaramandel* described the vagabond climber's life of the 1960s. Of the experience of climbing he wrote, "The mountains—their psychic, sonorous, spiritual realities—have a history as venerable as light. They are a dream where beauty wanders its own way, and more interesting than the height that you think you should achieve is the individual strain of revelation into which you are drawn."
Further reading: Pat Ament, *Master of Rock* (1977).

AMERICAN ALPINE CLUB Founded in 1902, the club remains the only national organization in the United States devoted exclusively to MOUNTAINEERING and climbing. With an emphasis on adventure, the club is devoted to the exploration and study of high-mountain elevations of the world, the cultivation of mountaincraft and the preservation of mountain, polar, rock and ice climbing regions. The American Alpine Club is not-for-profit and publishes the annual AMERICAN ALPINE JOURNAL, *Accidents in North American Mountaineering* and the quarterly *American Alpine News*. For more information, contact: The American Alpine Club, 710 Tenth Street—Suite 100, Golden, CO 80401; (303) 384-0110

AMERICAN ALPINE JOURNAL The annual journal published by the AMERICAN ALPINE CLUB, edited by H. Adams CARTER.

AMERICAN BIG WALL TECHNIQUE The BIG WALL technique developed in YOSEMITE in the 1960s and 1970s by people like Royal ROBBINS and Jim BRIDWELL. (See also HAULING, PORTA-LEDGES.)

AMERICAN FORK CANYON (United States) An important SPORT-CLIMBING area of UTAH, in the Wasatch Mountains 25 miles (40 km) south of Salt Lake City. Fifteen 80-foot (24-m) crags, vertical to overhanging, of dark Mississippian limestone are scattered along the road above Timpanogas Cave National Monument. Most routes are bolt-protected with BOLT ANCHORS. Climbing is gymnastic and technical. Although development began during the 1970s, it wasn't until 1989 that Utah climbers like Bill Boyle, Boone Speed and Jeff Pederson began developing the sport-climbing potential here. The bulk of these steep ROUTES are in the 5.10–5.14 category. License to Thrill (5.11c) overhangs 15 ft (4.5 m) in 60 ft (18 m). Other classics include Caress of Steel (5.10a), Beeline (5.12c) × (5.13a). Hell Cave boasts the highest concentration of 5.13s in America, with J. B. TRIBOUT's Cannibals (5.13d/5.14a) being one of the hardest. April through October is the prime season. Rock Canyon is a nearby quartzite CRAG of significance in the foothills behind Provo.
Guidebook: Bret and Stuart Ruckman, *Wasatch Climbing South, American Fork Canyon* (1991).

AMERICAN TECHNIQUE See FRONT POINTING.

ANCHORS Just as an anchor holds a ship fast against storm and current, roped climbing on rock or ice depends on a solid anchor at either end of a PITCH where the lead rope is secured, and to which a BELAY is attached. Anchors are a key part of the system of LEADING, which involves ROPES, PROTECTION and belays. The guideline for anchors is that they must be failsafe even if all protection anchors placed in a pitch are ripped out in the event of a LEADER fall. In such a case the anchor is the last resort for survival and must be strong enough to sustain massive force. Many types of anchor exist for use on rock, ice and snow. Types of SNOW AND ICE ANCHORS are discussed under that heading, but the principles of setting up and loading anchors are the same for rock as for snow and ice.

There are three classes of anchor: natural, artificial and permanent. On rock, natural anchors are created from naturally occurring features, such as the rope tied around a large, firmly rooted tree, or a SLING draped over a HORN of rock. However, natural anchors are not always available, and the climber will need a knowledge of equipment placement to rig safe anchors. Cracks present many possibilities for placing NUTS, STOPPERS, SPRING-LOADED CAMMING DEVICES or PITONS as artificial anchors. In blank rock, drilling a hole and placing a BOLT offers a permanent anchor.

Belay anchors should consist of at least two anchors, but multiple anchors are advisable. Natural anchors should be carefully inspected to ensure they are sturdy. When using artificial anchors in cracks, avoid spreading anchors too widely. Because a falling leader exerts an upward force on an anchor and a falling SECOND exerts a downward force, anchors should be rigged for multidirectional pulls. When placing a nut that will take a downward force, match it

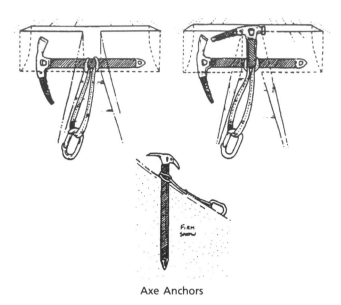

Axe Anchors

with one in OPPOSITION, or one that will take an upward force. Modern bolt anchors using 3/8-inch (1.25-cm) steel bolts are strong, but older 1/4-inch (.75-cm) bolt anchors should be regarded as weak and backed up with additional gear. Anchor components should be connected (with clove hitches) or equalized (with a self-equalizing slider knot) that distributes loading over the whole anchor. A double FIGURE-EIGHT KNOT is tied in the rope to connect the climber to the anchor. The principles of rigging anchors on climbs are essentially the same as for rigging anchors for descent. For discussion of setting up fixed anchors (bolt anchors, chain anchors) and retreat anchors, see RAPPEL ANCHORS.

Equalized Anchors

ANDES (South America) The longest mountain chain on earth, highest outside Asia, and having the highest volcanoes in the world. The chain dominates life along the entire length of western South America, forming the watershed between the Pacific Ocean and the rivers that drain to the Atlantic. The Inca word *anta* means "copper," but the metal is found only in the Andean foothills; the name alludes rather to the rich copper color of the higher rocks. The chain runs north to south, from Lake Maracaibo to Cape Horn, for some 5,000 miles (8,045 km). The peaks of the Antarctic peninsula are a continuation of the southernmost Andes and the Chileans call them the Antartandes. The Andes were perhaps born in the late Cretaceous and seem to be still uplifting, on account of their volcanism. Current glaciation has greatly receded since the era of Pleistocene ice caps. The highest peak is ACONCAGUA (22,835 ft/6,920 m), with glaciers down to 14,300 ft (4,360 m). In the central Andes or Puna (latitude 26° south) volcanoes over 17,000 ft (5,183 m) do not show any permanent snow, but nearing Cape Horn, mere hillocks 4,000 ft (1,220 m) high carry hanging ice.

The Andes are divided according to the boundaries of the seven Andean nations, but orographical studies show four groups: the northern Andes (VENEZUELA, COLOMBIA, and eastern ECUADOR), with a climbing season in January, February and March; the central tropical zone (western Ecuador, PERU and BOLIVIA), with a dry winter between May and August; the Puna or desert zone of northern CHILE and ARGENTINA; and the southern Andes (central Chile and Argentina, down to Cape Horn); the last two areas have a climbing season from December to March. There are hundreds of volcanic peaks, including Nevado OJOS DEL SALADO (22,590 ft/6,885 m), highest volcano in the world, with an active crater at around 21,500 ft (6,555 m). MOUNTAINEERING in the Andes began early. The Incas climbed for religious purposes some 100 summits over 16,000 ft (4,878 m) and even inhabited some of them (see OROLATRIC MOUNTAINEERING). The Andes, at least for Westerners, were discovered by Spanish navigator Juan de la Cosa, who sighted ice peaks from Caribbean shores. First recorded ascent was in Ecuador: In 1582, Quito's city mayor, Jose T. de Ortiguera, and a retinue ascended active Volcan Pichincha (15,718 ft/4,791 m) to inspect its crater. Thus, Andean mountaineering was the child of vulcanology. In 1802, Alexander von Humboldt and companions attempted CHIMBORAZO, a truly sportive effort. During the 19th century, South American governments sent scientific and surveying expeditions to study and chart their mountain lands. Foremost was the work of the Chilean Boundary led by Luis RISO PATRON. At the same time, alpinists of repute like Edward WHYMPER, Paul Gussfeldt, Martin CONWAY and Theodor Herzog explored, climbed and did scientific work. This expeditionary activity was continued after the First World War by parties from Austria, Germany, Italy and Poland. At the same time, local foreign residents, mostly Germans, were active. South American mountain clubs were born between 1909 and 1950. During the Second World War, local climbers started to develop climbing as well as skiing and the construction of mountain huts, particularly in Chile and Argentina. After 1950, French rock experts like Lionel TERRAY brought equipment improvements and technical climbing, and won difficult Andean summits, like FITZROY (also called Chalten) in PATAGONIA and Chacraraju in Peru. Ascents of new peaks reached a high point in the 1960s and was practiced by both Andeans and foreigners. By the late 1970s, expeditionary climbing in the Andes took a downward course, because the mountains of Asia were opened. The search for the most difficult routes, instead of new peaks, is now the fashion.

Locally, climbing is called *andinismo*; climbers, *andinistas*. In the last 10 years, several Andean governments developed mountain tourism, opened national parks, constructed mountain roads and began a tardy defense of mountain ecosystems. The remapping of the high Andes was also undertaken. As a result, heights of several major peaks were lowered or raised. There is still confusion in this respect. Argentinian heights may show a difference of as much as 1,200 ft (400 m) over Chilean official figures. With caution in mind, the following list covers the 15 highest Andean peaks, including the year of first ascent; in the case of an Indian or Pre-Columbian ascent, the year of the first modern climb is added:

1. Cerro Aconcagua (Argentina): 22,835 ft/6,960 m (1897).
2. Nevado Ojos del Salado (Chile-Argentina): 22,590 ft/6,885 m (1937).
3. Nevado de Pissis (Argentina): 22,241 ft/6,780 m (1937).
4. Nevado HUASCARAN Sur (Peru): 22,205 ft/6,769 m (1932).
5. Nevados de Tres Cruces, South Peak (Chile-Argentina): 22,155 ft/6,753 m (1937).
6. Cerro Llullaillaco (Chile-Argentina): 22,110 ft/6739 m (Indian ascents; 1952).
7. Cerro Mercedario (Argentina): 21,884 ft/6,670 m (Indian ascents; 1934).
8. Nevado del Cazadero (Argentina): 21,851 ft/6,660 m (1972).
9. Nevado Huascaran Norte (Peru): 21,830 ft/6,654 m (1908).
10. Nevados de Tres Cruces, Central Peak (Chile): 21,720 ft/6,620 m (1937).
11. Nevado YERUPAYA (Peru): 21,711 ft/6,617 m (1950).
12. Nevado Incahuasi (Chile-Argentina): 21,687 ft/6,610 m (Indian ascents; 1913).
13. Cerro Tupungato (Chile-Argentina): 21,490 ft/6,550 m (1897).
14. Nevado Sajama (Bolivia): 21,463 ft/6,542 m (1939).
15. Cerro Ata (Argentina): 21,326 ft/6,500 m (1955).

From time to time, inflated figures are given to some of these peaks, but they are commonly taken by altimeters, always unreliable. Mathia Rebitsch always gives 21,654 ft (6,600 m) to Cerro Gallan in Argentina, but the mountain has been measured since early this century in only 18,209

ft/5,550 m. No definite figure for most of the highest peaks can be expected until more reliable surveys are performed.

Editor H. Adams Carter of the AMERICAN ALPINE JOURNAL has kept the best information on Andean climbing.
Further reading: Jill Neate, *Mountaineering in the Andes* (1987).

Evelio Echevarria
Colorado State University

ANDINISMO A SOUTH AMERICAN word meaning ANDEAN climbing.

ANDINISTAS SOUTH AMERICAN name for one who climbs in the ANDES.

ANGLE A channel, or V-shaped PITON.

ANNAPURNA (Nepal) The 12th highest mountain in the world rises to 26,545 ft (8,093 m) in the Annapurna Himal of central NEPAL. The highest point, Annapurna I, is at the west end of a 50-mile (80-km) long east-west barrier of mostly 22,960 ft (7,000 m) peaks, including Annapurnas II, III and IV, Gangapurna, and Lamjung. North-south spurs from the main barrier rise to Hiunchuli, Annapurna South, Machhapuchare and Tilicho. The first three of these outliers branch off Annapurna I and almost completely encircle a high basin popular with mountaineers and trekkers—the Annapurna Sanctuary. The north side of the barrier is heavily glaciated and infamous for AVALANCHES, but its easier ROUTES are frequently attempted. The southern aspects are rockier and steeper. The direct relief above the valleys on either side is 12,000 to 15,000 ft (3,659 to 4,573 m).

Annapurna I was the first 26,240-ft (8,000-m) peak climbed, by a 1950 French team including Lionel TERRAY, Gaston REBUFFAT, Maurice HERZOG and Louis LACHENAL. Herzog's epic tale of their success—*Annapurna*—is one of the great mountaineering books. The steep 10,000-foot (3,049-m) rock and ice wall of Annapurna's south face was climbed in 1970 by a British team led by Chris BONINGTON. This historic climb succeeded after a long siege and placed Don WHILLANS and Dougal HASTON on top. Bonington's *Annapurna South Face* (1971) recounts the climb. During the 1980s several climbers opened up routes on the south face, perhaps the most notable being the Spaniards Enric Lucas and Nil Bohigas whose 1984 route was made completely in ALPINE STYLE. The steep west face was first climbed circuitously by Reinhold MESSNER (1985); more direct routes by Swiss in 1986, and a bold solo bid (1990) by Slavc Sveticic (Slovenia) climbed the wall but not to the summit.

ANORAK A windproof, waterproof pullover-style outer garment, having a hood. The word is of Eskimo origin.

ANTARCTICA Though this last great wilderness has countless unclimbed peaks, MOUNTAINEERING in Antarctica has been sporadic, partly because the mountains are guarded by the world's deepest ice cap. Another prohibiting factor is that Antarctica is the most expensive place in the world to climb, due to the high cost of access and travel.

The earliest notable climb in Antarctica was the FIRST ASCENT of Mount Erebus (13,350 ft/4,070 m), the active volcano on Ross Island on the shores of McMurdo Sound, by members of Shackleton's 1908 expedition. The spine of Antarctica, the Transantarctic Mountains, stretches almost continuously from the tip of the Antarctic peninsula to Cape Adare on the other side of the continent. One of the most impressive peaks, Mount Fridtjof Nansen (13,354 ft/4,071 m) just 300 miles (480 km) from the South Pole, was discovered and named by Roald Amundsen.

The highest mountains in Antarctica occur in the Sentinel Range of the Ellsworth Mountains, 2,000 miles (3,200 km) from the tip of SOUTH AMERICA and 800 miles (1,280 km) from the South Pole. VINSON MASSIF (16,850 ft/5,137 m), the highest, is a plateau 15 miles (24 km) long and 10 miles (16 km) wide. Vinson and Mount Tyree (16,290 ft/4,966 m), Antarctica's second highest, were first climbed by Americans in 1966. Though the standard ROUTE is nontechnical, extreme cold, bad weather and remoteness make this a formidable undertaking. Other peaks in the vicinity are now receiving attention. The most notable climb of recent times was the solo ascent of a new route on Tyree by Mugs STUMP.

Vinson is regularly ascended and guided because of the service offered by Adventure Network International (ANI), which runs charter flights in summer (November–January) from South America to a blue-ice runway in the Ellsworth from which smaller aircraft, ski or snowmobile are used to reach Vinson or nearby peaks. The ANI flights originated in climbers' attempts in the 1980s to climb Mount Vinson as part of various campaigns to climb the SEVEN SUMMITS. Early expeditions were supported by the Chilean air force but commercial Antarctic expedition aviation was pioneered by English pilot Giles Kershaw, flying a modified DC3.

The Antarctic peninsula, or Graham Land, is often called the Banana Belt because of the relatively benign climate. It has accessible mountains and has been the focus of many private parties. Some private expeditions have ventured to Antarctica by yacht, such as the Australian Bicentennial Antarctic expedition, which made the first ascent of Mount Minto in the Admiralty Mountains of North Victoria Land.

Most of the Antarctic Treaty nations discourage nonofficial climbing and private expeditions because they do not wish to divert resources from government-funded scientific projects, should rescues be necessary. Mountaineers must be self-sufficient in case of accident or nonarrival of planes or ships, and well insured to pay for evacuation.

ANTHOINE, JULIAN "MO" (1939–1989) (Britain)
Began climbing in the 1950s in North Wales. His new climbs in Snowdonia in the 1960s—Devil's Nordwand in Cwm Idwal and The Groove on Llech Ddu—were notably difficult. Throughout his involvement with climbing, Mo debunked the "professionalism" in British MOUNTAINEER-ING. Such a rebellious attitude to conformity, and his legendary capacity for partying, ribaldry and repartee, earned him, even among the unshockable ranks of the British climbing scene, the reputation of a wild man. In 1961 Mo and a former boxer from Derbyshire known as Fox embarked on a Rabelaisian Grand Tour that left a trail of epic stories across five continents. Tragically, it also involved a spell working in a blue asbestos mine in Australia, which resulted—predictably according to the incubation period—in Mo's death from cancer 21 years later. After 1964, he made important British ascents in the DOLOMITES, including the Comici Route on the Cima Grande di Lavaredo with writer Al Alvarez. The pair survived a storm, and summited in verglassed conditions. Alvarez later paid tribute to Mo's skill in the *New Yorker* magazine with a fictionalized account, "Night Out," that is a minor classic of mountaineering literature. This climb, and an ascent of the Old Brenva Route on MONT BLANC in the great storm of August 1966, established for Mo a reputation of extreme toughness. On the latter climb two of Mo's companions died in enforced bivouacs in snow holes. One of the other survivors, Richard McHardy, later recounted the superstitious dread that Mo aroused in him by strolling around outside the snow hole in the teeth of the storm and jocularly inviting God to do his worst. In 1968 he set up a business—Snowdon Mouldings—in Llanberis making quality mountaineering gear. He participated in the 1973 expedition to the 1,700-foot (518-m) rock PROW of RORAIMA in the Guyanan jungle. In 1977 he joined Clive Rowlands, Chris BONINGTON and Doug SCOTT on the FIRST ASCENT of the KARAKORAM peak, The OGRE. On the descent from the 24,000-foot (7,317-m) summit Scott fell and broke both ankles. A storm came in. Bonington also took a fall, breaking two ribs. Responsibility for retreat devolved to Mo and Rowlands. Their skill in getting the injured pair down is one of the great tales of mountaineering lore. It is recounted in the biographies of Bonington and Scott. He took part in two expeditions to the northeast ridge of EVEREST, one of them only weeks after an operation for removal of a brain tumor. The condition recurred a year later and he died 11 days after his 50th birthday.

Further reading: Al Alvarez, *Feeding the Rat: Profile of a Climber* (1988).

ARAPILES, MOUNT (Australia) One of the finest FREE CLIMBING areas in the world. It sports a few of the harder ROUTES ever done, and its well-featured walls offer some 3,000 quality routes at every level of difficulty. The cliff lies on the Wimmera plains, in western Victoria, near the town of Horsham. The rock is hard orange quartzite sandstone. Unlike most modern hard areas of SPORT CLIMBING, "Araps" still maintains a tradition of mostly natural protection, which abound in perfect CRACKS and fissures. Early climbs were done here by Melbourne climbers in the 1960s, and Bard (12) remains popular from that era. A boom of new routes by climbers like Chris Baxter and Chris Dewhurst appeared in the 1970s. American Henry BARBER opened local eyes when he freed many routes here in 1975, upping grades to 23, as with Taste of Honey. During the

late 1970s and 1980s Australian climbers like Michael LAW, Kim CARRIGAN, Louise SHEPHERD and her brothers Lincoln and Mark, and the brilliant Mark Moorehead, who tragically died on MAKALU in 1984, added scores of hard routes, culminating, at least in terms of difficulty, in Carrigan's Masada (30). Visits by Europeans Wolfgang GULLICH and Stefan GLOWACZ left harder routes still: Gullich's Punks in the Gym (32) was confirmed by England's Jerry MOFFAT, who repeated it in impeccable style in 1992, while Lord of the Rings (31) went to Glowacz. The area is a constant haven for visiting climbers, who camp amid a pine grove beneath the cliffs. Year-round climbing is possible, though summer may be scorching.

Guidebook: Louise Shephard, *The Arapiles Guide* (1994).

ARCH A free-standing rock formation such as those found in the COLORADO PLATEAU. Also used to refer to a large curving ROOF formation found on vertical rock faces.

ARCHES NATIONAL PARK See COLORADO PLATEAU.

ARCO (Italy) One of the finest Italian limestone CRAGS, the town of Arco lies 12 miles (20 km) southwest of Trento, 36 miles (60 km) east-northeast of Milano. Its 15 main cliffs are scattered around the River Sarca, and 14th-century castle ruins cap some crags. Hundreds of climbs of all angles offer both easy ROUTES with hand-placed PROTECTION and extreme SPORT CLIMBS with small edges and POCKET-pulling through OVERHANGS. As well as being an old training ground for DOLOMITE climbers, Arco also was the home of the 1986 and 1987 Sportroccia Competitions, a contest in which the rock was altered to make a climbing competition, on Mount Colodri and Rupe Secca. Routes can be up to 10 PITCHES long, but the hardest climbing is on short crags, like La Gola, the Swing area, Massone and Spiaggio delle Lucertole. Here, Italy's best sport climbers have left their mark, like Manolo and Heinz Mariacher. The climate is benign though hot in summer. TOPOS for the cliffs are sold in Arco's climbing shops.

ARETE On a cliff or mountain, a sharply defined RIDGE or an outside corner, rather like the corner of a building.

ARGENTINA Argentina, like CHILE, belongs not to the tropical patterns of the other five Andean countries but to those of the temperate lands. Both countries have GLACIERS that descend to valleys and four distinct seasons, one of which is the skiing season. Argentina is rather dry, but with a variety of climate systems and vegetation. Argentina's ANDES run north-south for 2,100 miles (3,379 km), reaching at times a width of 80 miles (129 km), from the Chilean borderline to the chains that in the east rise over plateau or *pampa*. There are four major zones. The Northern Andes or Puna contain the highest volcanoes in the world, active or dormant like OJOS DEL SALADO (22,590 ft/6,885 m). The Central Andes, south of 29° south, begin to display glaciers, have only a few scattered volcanoes and are fre-

Arete

quently climbed; the great peaks ACONCAGUA (22,835 ft/6,960 m), Mercedario (21,884 ft/6,670 m) and TUPUNGATO (21,490 ft/6,550 m) are found here. The Southern Andes (south of the town of Malargue), offer few ice volcanoes (like Nevado Domuyo, 15,286 ft/4,660 m) and granite climbing west of the Andean city of BARILOCHE. The last two regions named, unless hit by drought, have a skiing season (June through August). Last zone are the Andes Australes, which include PATAGONIA and Tierra del Fuego, an area well known for its two famous peaks, FITZROY (Chalten) and CERRO TORRE. Its highest point is however Cerro San Lorenzo (12,157 ft/3,706 m), situated on the Chilean border. Throughout the country, rock is unstable andesite, but in contrast, the Fitzroy group offers some of the best granite in the continent. As in all the former Inca mountainlands, Indians were the first mountaineers. Their world altitude record, established on the summit of Llullaillaco (22,110 ft/6,739 m) remained unchallenged by Europeans until 1853. Mummies have been unearthed from the summits of high peaks. (See OROLATRIC MOUNTAINEERING.)

Sportive climbing came to Argentina quite late. Paul Gussfeldt and his Chilean hillmen climbed Volcan Maipo (17,356 ft/5,290 m) and attempted Aconcagua up to 21,700 ft (6,616 m) (1883). The well-financed expedition led by FitzGerald in 1897 made two ascents of Aconcagua and one of Tupungato. First Argentinian mountaineers were the army men who reached the summit of isolated Domuyo, in the far south (1882). Fritz REICHERT then explored the central and Patagonian zones, his being a life almost wholly devoted to the CORDILLERA (1906 to 1941). Argentinians began climbing and skiing around 1925, introduced to the sport by European residents from Mendoza and Bariloche. In the 1930s, strong Polish and Italian groups were successful on very high peaks. In 1952, Lionel TERRAY and Guido Magnone climbed Fitzroy (11,072 ft/3,375 m), at that time rightly hailed as a landmark in technial climbing. And in 1954, (Frenchmen) also scaled the dreaded south face of Aconcagua. But Aconcagua has always remained the great attraction; it has dominated the Argentinian mountaineering scene since 1897.

Nowadays, mountain clubs exist in all Andean cities, with Mendoza and Bariloche leading the way. Buenos

Aires, albeit a seaport, houses important clubs and is the seat of the Federacion Argentina de Ski y Andinismo (Argentinian Ski and Mountaineering National Association). Argentinian mountaineering, like its Chilean counterpart, is unique in that it has developed a cadre of climber-archeologists that ascend summits to rescue Inca relics that, if found, become automatically a national patrimony. A major investigator in this field is Antonio Beorchia, from San Juan. Writers and researchers of importance have been Alfredo Magnani, Marcelo Scanu and Vojslav Arko, the last one concentrating on Patagonian climbing. Local mountaineering journals have been *La Montana* (Buenos Aires), *Antisuyu* (San Juan), *Anuario* (Bariloche) and *Nuestras Montanas* (Mendoza).

Evelio Echevarria
Colorado State University

ARIZONA (United States) Arizona's dry desert climate and varied topography, from deep, cool canyons to high desert plateau, offers year-round climbing. "The Grand Canyon State" is, in its north, a high basaltic plateau intersected by canyon systems cutting through sedimentary rocks. Flagstaff is the rock-climbing hub of northern Arizona. OUTCROPS within reach of this town are volcanic (basalt/dacite) or sedimentary (limestone/sandstone). Canyon-rimmed basalts form beautiful columns with fine CRACKS and ARETES. PARADISE FORKS and Oak Creek Overlook, near the town of Parks, northwest and south of Flagstaff, exemplify columnular basalt cragging. The dacite of the Mount Elden complex, northeast of Flagstaff, forms cracks, FACES and BOULDERING on sharp rock. Grand Canyon, 80 miles (128 km) from Flagstaff, and Canyon de Chelley, east of Flagstaff, are famous Arizona landmarks, offering adventurous climbing in inspiring settings on soft sandstone spires and walls that comprise the Four Corners geologic strata shared with other desert states (for these, see CANYONLANDS). (Monument Valley is a part of this complex, but is legally off limits to climbing and part of a Navaho Indian reservation.) East of Flagstaff more sandstone climbing is available at Oak Creek Canyon and Red Rocks, near SEDONA, and the Winslow Wall near the eponymous town. Limestone areas are exemplified by the recently developed SPORT CLIMBING area Le Petit Verdon ("The Pit"), southeast of Flagstaff. A plutonic batholith running diagonally across Arizona from Kingman to Tucson presents granitic outcrops. Major granite crags include GRANITE MOUNTAIN and the Granite Dells near Prescott, and, by Tucson, Mount LEMMON. Cochise's Stronghold is a backcountry granite area in the Dragoon Mountains, 25 miles (40 km) from Tombstone near the Mexican border. Its walls are up to 900 ft (274 m), the area boasts over 200 routes from 5.8 to 5.11+ and the granite is unusual in that it forms large CHICKENHEADS and POCKETS offering NATURAL PROTECTION. Hulapai Wall, near Kingman, is a 600-ft (183-m) cliff of gneiss. In southern Arizona, near the Mexican border and the town of Ajo, is a 1,000-ft (305-m) granite formation called Baboquivari Peak with several fine long ROUTES. In central Arizona within reach of Phoenix, the Superstition Mountains have become an important sport-

climbing area with POCKET and face routes on volcanic formations similar to SMITH ROCKS (OREGON). Phoenix boasts many semi-urban crags. The 1990s search for European-style limestone unearthed the Virgin River Gorge, 90 miles (144 km) northeast of Las Vegas and beside Interstate 15. Arizona's high point is Humphrey's Peak (12,633 ft/3,851 m), a nontechnical summit of the San Francisco Mountains in north central Arizona.

Guidebooks: Tim Toula, *A Cheap Way to Die: Sedona Area Rock Climbs* (1991); Jim Waugh, *Phoenix Rock: A Guide to Central Arizona Crags* (1987).

ARKANSAS (United States) Short OUTCROPS of sandstone and limestone dot this state, which contains sections of the Ouichita and Ozark mountain ranges. In northwest Arkansas, near the town of Fayetteville and five miles (40 km) from Lurton, is the state's largest sandstone cliff, Sam's Throne, named after a local reverend of old who delivered sermons from atop the cliff. Nearby and also sandstone are Busby Hollow, east of Ponca, and Red Rock Point, near Jasper. Eighteen miles (29 km) southeast of Paris is Mount Magazine (the state's high point, 2,753 ft/839 m) and a 90-ft (27-m) cliff. Blanchard Springs in north-central Arkansas is an area of many small cliffs. Further south near Little Rock is Pinnacle Mountain State Park.

ARM BAR A FREE CLIMBING technique for ascending wide, or offwidth CRACKS. The technique involves wedging one arm into a crack up to the shoulder and flexing the arm into a V. The palm of the hand pushes against one wall of the crack while the elbow and back press against the other. The effect is to form a wedge with the torso. Feet and legs may be braced against the crack also. An arm lock is similar, though the arm is bent more sharply. (See OFFWIDTH.)

ARNOLD, BERND (1947–   ) (Germany) Despite an almost complete lack of climbing equipment, due to East Germany's isolation from mainstream climbing, Arnold dominated the climbing scene of the ELBSANDSTEINGEBIRGE region for 25 years, opening 700 new ROUTES. All his routes—such as Lineal, a poorly protected 5.10+, climbed in 1970, and Garden of Eden, 5.12+, climbed in 1989—were climbed from the ground up and without TOP ROPE inspection, using only hand-drilled ring BOLTS and knotted SLINGS for PROTECTION, the unique rules of "Dresden" sandstone climbing. On the soft rock of his local cliffs, he was well known for barefoot climbing, done largely due to the lack of ROCK SHOES in East Germany. Since German unification he has opened a climbing shop in the Elbsandstein, near the village of Hohnstein.

ARRAN (Scotland) The Isle of Arran is located in the Firth of Clyde, southwest of Glasgow. Its climate is more hospitable than other Scottish mountain areas. The island can be reached by ferry from Ardrossan to the village of Brodick, or from Claonaig arriving in Lochranza. Most crags here are granite. Main areas include A'Chir (pronounced A Keer), north from Brodick, and Cir Mhor (pro-

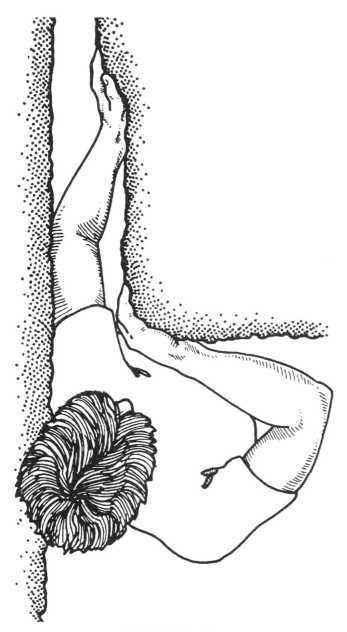

Offwidth Arm Bar

nounced Keer Vor), a 1,000-ft (305-m) crag on which the Rosa Pinnacle is a major formation with some famous ROUTES. The south ridge itself was climbed in 1941 by J. F. Hamilton and D. Patterson and offers one of the finest 5.7s in Britain, following the RIDGE for over 1,000 ft (305 m). Cioch-na-h-Oighe (pronounced Keeok Na Hoyk) emerges from the north ridge of Mullach Buidhe. Here Dave Cuthbertson and Kev Howett climbed the hardest route on Arran, in 1985, the 320-ft (98-m) Token Gesture (5.12a).

The Cobbler, a crag on Ben Arthur, is located 35 miles (56 km) north of Glasgow near the village of Arrochar. The crag, at an altitude of 2,600 ft (793 m), can be seen from across Loch Long in Arrochar. Following World War II, members of the Creagh Dhu climbing club dominated Scottish development. The south face of The Cobbler's

south peak, which overlooks Glen Croe, contains a number of their routes. Robin SMITH's Glueless Groove, from 1957, at 5.9, is notable among these. Of the more modern additions, Dave Griffiths's Osiris is the best at 5.11a, a brilliant one-pitch slab climb. Hamish MACINNES and Bill Smith added Whither Whether, an outstanding and steep 5.7, said to be one of the finest of its grade anywhere, and in 1954 Pat Walsh climbed the Club Crack, at 5.10a one of the hardest in the country. There are a number of modern hard lines here too, like Dave Cuthbertson's Wild Country (5.12a).

The Brack, a crag across Glen Croe from The Cobbler, includes one of the most famous mountain routes in Scotland, Edge of Extinction (5.12a), climbed in 1980 by Pete Whillance and Pete Botterill. It is technical and serious, using a RURP for protection at one point. See SCOTLAND.
Guidebooks: Kevin Howett, *Rock Climbing in Scotland* (1990); A. Walker and K. Crocket, *Climbers' Guide to Arran and Arrochar* (1989).

ARRIGETCH MOUNTAINS (United States) Also known as the Arrigetch Spires, this small orange granite cirque of Tolkienesque spires is tucked away in the center of Alaska's BROOKS RANGE, with the Alatna River to the east and the Noatak River to the west. Although the spires are farther north than any other climbing destination in North America, these low-altitude towers have no snow or ICE CLIMBING to speak of. The climbing potential of the area was brought to the attention of climbers by Chuck Loucks's article on the area in the 1965 AMERICAN ALPINE JOURNAL, and later by Dave ROBERTS's article, "Shot Tower," in the 1972 *American Alpine Journal*. The climbing season here, high in the Arctic Circle, lasts two to three months, although clouds of mosquitoes often beset climbers in June, and snowstorms come in August. BUSH PILOTS are hired from the village of Bettles, which is one hour's flying time from Fairbanks. Climbers are usually dropped off below Arrigetch Creek, a full-day's walk from the main climbing cirque. The range lies within the gates of the Arctic National Park and Preserve.

ARTIFICIAL CLIMBING Another term for AID CLIMBING.

ASCENDERS Mechanical devices with movable, self-locking cams that, when attached to a single strand of rope, slide up but do not slide down. Ascenders are a more efficient solution to PRUSIKING. Originally developed for rescue work, they are used in situations where a free-hanging rope must be climbed, such as seconding an aid-pitch (see AID CLIMBING, BIG WALL CLIMBING). They are valuable for HAULING and CREVASSE RESCUE. An ascender is often called a JUMAR, and the act of ascending is called Jumaring, after the trade name of the first mechanical ascender, which revolutionized big wall climbing in the 1960s.

Ascenders are used in pairs (one for each hand), in conjunction with SLINGS and ETRIERS. They consist of a strong metal handle and a spring-loaded cam. The rope is held in place in a slot by means of a locking device or trigger that engages or disengages the cam. Many brands and designs exist: Jumar, Petzl, Clog, CMI and Gibbs are tried and tested models. Use of ascenders varies between brands, but several safety factors remain constant:

a) The climber must be connected by the harness to each ascender either by slings tied into the harness or secured to the harness with LOCKING CARABINERS. In addition, the climber should be tied to the end of the rope whenever possible in case of ascender failure.

b) When the rope is placed in the ascender's slot it should be checked that the safety catch or trigger is locked. Care should be taken when clipping into a rope tensioned diagonally, as the taut rope may open the trigger and disengage the locking cam. A free-running carabiner on a sling clipped between the climber and the rope can prevent the rope from twisting an ascender, and also add another point of connection between the climber and the rope.

c) Although using ascenders is straightforward, incorrect use can lead to disaster. Using ascenders to cross traverses, pendulums or roofs is awkward. In such cases, in addition to connecting the harness to the ascenders with slings, it is prudent to tie into the rope with short bights at regular intervals.

d) On iced, wet, or muddy ropes the small teeth on the camming device which grip the rope may clog up and cause the device to slip. To guard against injury from sudden slippage, again, the climber should tie into the rope at regular intervals. Fixed ropes should be connected to belays or knotted at the end to prevent an ascender sliding off the end of the rope. Dirt or ice should be cleaned from ascender teeth.

Petzl Ascender

ASSAM HIMALAYA (India, Bhutan, China) Little known and restricted to foreigners, Assam's reputation as being rain-soaked and peopled by unfriendly tribes has caused these mountains to remain largely unexplored. Assam Himalaya originally defined ranges stretching from Pauhunri (23,375 ft/7,125 m) on the Sikkim-TIBET border, eastward across BHUTAN to mysterious NAMCHE BARWA (25,531 ft/7782 m), the world's highest unclimbed peak, in CHINA. However, this broad definition is becoming obsolete; the HIMALAYA extends beyond Namche Barwa, to Yunnan in China, where the peak Kang Karpo is signifi-

cant. Indian climbing historians Mehta and Kapadia explain in *Exploring the Hidden Himalaya* (1990) "the portion of the range lying mainly in Bhutan is now correctly called Bhutan Himalaya, and the erstwhile mega-province of Assam has lost its Himalayan frontier to [the province of] Arunachel Pradesh, recently born out of what was the North-Eastern Frontier Agency (NEFA). So, properly speaking, there is no longer any Assam Himalaya." Nonetheless they agree that the term has a tradition of usage by mountaineers. Assam Himalaya then, as it runs east across Bhutan and INDIA, is comprised of the following transverse ranges bounded north and south by the Tsangpo and Brahmaputra rivers: the Dongkya Range (shared with Sikkim), Chomolhari Range, Lunala Range, Kangto Range, Pachakshiri Range and Namche Barwa Range. It was through the Kangto Range that the Chinese army swept into India in the 1962 border war. Largely because of this war, Assam was included in the "Inner Line" and restricted to Indians and foreigners alike. H. W. TILMAN explored the region in 1939. Namche Barwa, around which the Tsangpo flows in a great bend, remains the great mountaineering objective in this region. Chinese attempts in 1983 and 1984, and multi-million-dollar Japanese attempts in the 1990s failed to climb it.

Further reading: H. W. Tilman, *The Seven Mountain Travel Books (Where Men and Mountains Meet)* (1983).

ASSINIBOINE, MOUNT (Canada) Sometimes called "the Matterhorn of the Canadian Rockies," due to its shape. For the climber it offers several great ridges and faces. Assiniboine (11,870 ft/3,618 m) was first climbed by J. OUTRAM and his two Swiss guides, C. Bohrn and C. Hasler, via the southwest face. The north ridge is considered the normal route, (first climbed by W. Douglas and guides Hasler and Kaufmann in 1903); the north face (first climbed by CHOUINARD, Faint and Jones in 1967); and the east face (V 5.9 A2, first climbed by CHEESMOND and Dick in 1982). The name is derived from the Assiniboine Indians.

Guidebooks: G. Boles, R. Kruszyna and W. L. Putnam, *The Rocky Mountains of Canada South* (1979); Sean Dougherty, *Selected Alpine Climbs in the Canadian Rockies* (1991).

AUSTRALIA This low-lying island continent is dotted with some of the most ancient rock formations on earth. Australia is roughly the same size as the United States, yet the climbing population is small. Nonetheless, Australian climbers have developed their cliffs with enthusiasm. With a high point of 7,313 ft (2,229 m), on Mount KOSCIUSKO in the Snowy Mountains, options for alpine climbing are slim. Nonetheless, as Australasia's highest point Kosciusko is one of the SEVEN SUMMITS, and Australian alpinists have climbed the Himalaya's highest peaks.

Oddly enough, the highest point under Australian control is the ice-clad, active volcano Big Ben (9,009 ft/2,746 m), 2,484 miles (3,997 km) south of Hobart (Tasmania). Its FIRST ASCENT was made in 1964 by Warwick Deacock, G. Budd (Australia), P. Temple, C. Putt (New Zealand) and Bill TILMAN (Britain).

The warm Australian climate makes climbing possible year round, by traveling north during winter (April–September), and migrating to the temperate southern highlands in summer (October–May). Most climbing lies on the eastern seaboard scattered throughout the 1,850-mile (2,977-km) Great Dividing Range, in the states of Queensland, New South Wales, Victoria and South Australia, and in the rugged island state of Tasmania. In vast West Australia, climbers have explored significant sea cliffs at West Cape Howe and Albany. The best-known formation in Australia is Ayer's Rock, now called Uluru, 280 miles (450 km) southwest of Alice Springs. Except for the tourist route, climbing this sacred aboriginal sandstone dome is prohibited, but barely explored quartzite cliffs in outlying areas are of high quality.

Early rock climbing in Australia was shaped by ETHICS imported by expatriate Britons. During the 1960s John EWBANK pioneered hundreds of climbs in the Blue Mountains outside Sydney and devised the Australian open-ended numerical grading system. During the 1970s a whirlwind visit by American climber Henry BARBER pushed standards beyond what Australians dreamed possible. Barber's influence inspired a decade of FREE CLIMBING activity. During the 1980s climbers like Mike LAW opened hundreds of new routes, but Kim CARRIGAN's route at Arapiles— Masada, the first grade 30 (5.13)—was the big breakthrough. During the 1980s bolt-protected FACE CLIMBS ushered in harder grades, but the hardest route in the country remains Punks in the Gym (32), Wolfgang Gullich's 1985 testpiece at ARAPILES. This conservatively rated route was the first 5.14 and remained the hardest route in the world for several years. It is comparable to today's top French rating of 8c. Of interest to visitors is the Australian bolting system of portable keyhole HANGERS, essential equipment with a standard rack.

In Queensland the principal areas of interest lie in the state's southeast corner. Frog Buttress, a 145-ft (44-m) columnular rhyolite cliff 62 miles (99 km) southwest of Brisbane, near Boonah, is the main crag. The volcanic plugs of the Glasshouse Mountains, 56 miles (90 km) north of Brisbane, offer longer climbs. Also of interest are the granite domes of Girraween, south of Brisbane.

Perhaps the most unusual objective in Australia is Ball's Pyramid, a volcanic breccia spire rising 1,850 ft (564 m) out of the Pacific Ocean near Lord Howe Island, off the New South Wales coast. Major sea cliff areas near Sydney are the Sydney Sea Cliffs, which are soft, steep sandstone, and Point Perpendicular, a sandstone area around Jervis Bay, 118 miles (189 km) south of Sydney. Bungonia Gorge is a 650-ft (198-m) limestone gorge with bolt-protected face climbs 155 miles (249 km) southwest of Sydney, near Goulburn. The picturesque Blue Mountains near Katoomba, 62 miles (99 km) west of Sydney, are an extensive sedimentary sandstone escarpment. Among the many cliffs there are Porters Pass, Shipley Rock, Mount Piddington, Mount York and Cosmic County. Similar in rock and scale to the Blue Mountains is the nearby Wolgan Valley, near Lithgow. Also near Lithgow are the granite domes of Tarana. The Warrumbungle Range, 186 miles (299 km) northwest of Sydney, near Coonabarabran is an adventure climbing area of long, steep, moderate-grade volcanic spires.

In the Australian Capital Territory, Booroomba Rocks, 18 miles (29 km) south of Canberra, is Australia's main granite SLAB climbing area.

Victoria contains many of Australia's best crags. The Grampians Range, 124 miles (199 km) west of Melbourne, include the cliffs Mount Rosea, Bundaleer, Mount Stapylton and Redmans Bluff. Characterized by overhanging red quartzite walls, these areas are the sport-climbing center of the country. On a 1990 visit, the famous French free climber Patrick EDLINGER called Mount Stapylton's Taipan Wall "the best rock I've ever climbed on." Mount Arapiles is a complex of quartzite cliffs, 40 to 300 ft (12 to 90 m) high, near the town of Natimuk, 174 miles (280 km) west of Melbourne. Some 3,000 climbs of all grades make this Australia's most popular crag. Although steep faces and roofs characterize the area, Arapiles is also a haven of moderate climbing. Mount Buffalo, a high alpine plateau, offers a midsummer retreat from lowland heat. Buffalo's 1,000-ft (305-m) north wall gorge and surrounding crags have long AID and free routes on coarse granite.

South Australia's main cliff is Moonarie, a sandstone cliff in the midst of a remote desert landscape, 250 miles (402 km) north of Adelaide in the Flinders Ranges.

Tasmania, the island state, has rugged valleys and at times hostile weather, but it is also blessed with grand crags. The most accessible areas are the 300-ft (91-m) dolerite columns of the Organ Pipes on Mount Wellington, 10 miles (16 km) from Hobart and the granite sea cliff slabs of Coles Bay, near Bicheno. Similar columnular formations dot Tasmania and its coastline. Such areas include Mount Geryon, the Acropolis, Ben Lomond and the Tasman peninsula. Frenchman's Cap is a fine 1,000-ft (305-m) quartzite face in a remote setting 124 miles (199 km) from Hobart; near Queenstown is one of Australia's finest walls.

The largest climbing clubs are: Victorian Climbing Club, GPO Box 1725P, Melbourne, Victoria, 3001, and Sydney Rock Climbing Club, PO Box A592, Sydney South, NSW, 2000.

AVALANCHE   A mass of snow, rock and/or ice falling down a mountain. There are many types of avalanche: ice avalanche from falling SERACS; rock avalanches in unstable stone chutes on mountains; and mud slides of loose earth. However, mountaineers associate the term with snow. Temperature, orientation to sun or wind and angle of slope are important factors in avalanches. Slopes of 30 to 45 degrees are at greatest risk, though snow may slide from slopes as gentle as 15 degrees, or as steep as 55 degrees. Accurately predicting avalanches is almost impossible, but avalanche-prone climbs or ski routes should be avoided for several days after heavy snowfall or during sudden warm weather.

Small events, such as minor STONEFALL hitting a snow slope, may begin a snow slide that will gain momentum and material as it descends. Sometimes as dangerous as the avalanche itself is the huge mass of air pushed before an avalanche. Such wind blasts can flatten forests. The worst accident in mountaineering history occurred on July 13, 1990 in the Soviet Pamirs, when a massive avalanche obliterated a camp at 17,000 ft (5,183 m) on the standard

Razdelny route on Pik Lenin (Russia), killing 43 climbers. Serac fall triggered by an earthquake precipitated the slide.

The main types of avalanche are:

Wet-snow avalanches, which occur during warming trends or in spring, and involve masses of heavy, water-laden snow that slide a slow-moving compact mass.

Powder-snow avalanches occur in cold weather and comprise light, loose powder sloughing off a slope or down a gully in billowing clouds. Unless large, they are the least dangerous.

Slab avalanches are the most serious avalanche hazard for mountaineers. They occur when wind- or temperature-compacted snow overlaying unstable or rotten snow cracks loose. Slopes to the lee side of prevailing winds are at great risk to slab formation. Slab avalanches begin when a large mass of cohesive snow begins to slide on a weak layer or on smooth ground. They are marked by a distinct fracture line at the top of the avalanche, called a crown or crown line. They occur most frequently on slopes between 30 and 45 degrees. A test pit dug into a suspect slope may reveal telltale signs of potential slab avalanche, namely a brittle crust overlying a hollow-sounding unconsolidated snow layer.

There are two main types of slab formation:

Soft slabs are comprised of fresh soft snow or powder. They form over wide areas during periods of heavy storm, snow, wind and high humidity. They trigger easily and are most hazardous in cold periods immediately during or after snowfall. When released, soft slabs break up into fine particles. Soft slabs tend to stabilize during warmer temperatures.

Hard slabs (also called **wind slabs**) often form in localized areas, such as the lee side of ridges. Cold temperatures and prolonged strong winds contribute to hard-slab formation. Slopes at risk of hard-slab avalanche are frequently underlaid by a weak layer of DEPTH HOAR. Telltale signs of

avalanche-prone hard slabs are a hollow sound beneath the slab and a noticeable drop of the slab when it is stood upon or disturbed. Large blocks of snow deposited at the bottom of a slope can indicate previous hard-slab avalanches. Even in times of low snowfall, high winds may redeposit snow from one side of a ridge to another and form slab conditions. At higher elevations hard-slab avalanche is an ever-present, unpredictable threat, in that many persons may cross a hard slab before it releases.

Slabs avalanche for several factors. In warmer temperatures wet-snow slab avalanches occur when a layer of snow becomes heavy and lubricated with melt or rain water. The gradual slip of the heavy layer exerts a tensile stress between the layers and causes an area to break away. Dry-slab avalanches occur in cold temperatures. Such avalanches begin when shearing forces literally snap off a brittle, weak layer, which causes tensile failure around the edge of the slab.

Experts advise that if one is caught in an avalanche one should attempt to "swim" on the surface of the snow while the avalanche is a fluid mass by using breast-stroke movements and kicking actions to keep the head above the snow. When snow stops moving, it quickly solidifies. If buried in an avalanche, attempt to guard the face and create an air pocket. Before crossing dangerous terrain, be certain there is no alternative route or that retreat is not a better course of action. Dig a test pit if in any doubt about conditions. Belaying with a rope offers a measure of safety in that a climber may be held in the event of an avalanche. Climbers should tread carefully, in single file across a slope—never cut multiple tracks. Follow the contours of cliffs above a snow slope rather than cross an open slope low. If, carrying avalanche rescue beacons switch them on. Be sure that clothing is closed around neck and wrists to keep snow out, and that an escape route is planned in the event of an avalanche. Avalanche windblasts can lift climbers up and hurl them great distances. Boulders and crevasses can offer protection. Avoiding obvious avalanche

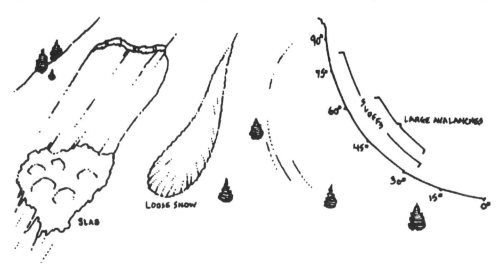

Types of Avalanches

slopes or chutes (i.e., slopes cleared of trees), slopes of deep fresh snow and lee sides of ridges subject to strong winds are also ways to protect oneself from slab avalanche. **Further reading:** Tony Daffern, *Avalanche Safety for Skiers and Climbers* (1983).

AVALANCHE CORD Lightweight, bright-colored cord (or, a climbing rope) sometimes trailed by a climber or skier crossing AVALANCHE terrain. If an avalanche occurs the cord may be followed to locate a buried victim. Ski mountaineers prefer to use AVALANCHE RESCUE BEACONS.

AVALANCHE PROBE A metal rod for probing into AVALANCHE debris to locate buried persons. Two types are common: sectional aluminum tubes that screw together to form long sections, and ski poles with removable grips and baskets that can be connected. They are advisable equipment for ski mountaineering.

AVALANCHE RESCUE While AVALANCHE rescue can be quick and effective in controlled areas like downhill ski resorts, avalanches in mountain areas present great problems for victims and rescuers. Survival of an avalanched person depends upon the immediate actions of those who are unburied. Avalanched snow sets like concrete after it settles. Buried persons have little chance of digging themselves out, and have only a short time before suffocation results in death. Therefore, every available person should immediately assist in locating a victim. AVALANCHE RESCUE BEACONS are the most effective means for locating a victim, but are seldom carried on climbs. AVALANCHE PROBES or makeshift probes of ice axes or tent poles are the next best tools for searching for a victim. AVALANCHE CORD may lead rescuers to a victim, as can a climbing rope, though many climbers resist the temptation to rope together in avalanche terrain because the rope can dangerously entangle victims.

The following is an itinerary for finding an avalanche victim:

1. Assess danger from further avalanche, post a lookout for avalanches and plan an escape route for searchers.
2. Switch on avalanche rescue beacons if carried. Quickly search debris for clues of the victim, mark the spot the victim was last seen and estimate the line the victim has traveled.
3. Probe around rocks or trees where the victim might have lodged, including areas up the line of the avalanche.
4. After all likely locations have been probed, set up an organized probe line of searchers and probe likely areas like large piles of debris in the main deposit and the estimated line the victim has traveled.
5. Probe uphill, in an organized manner, with rescuers close together probing at intervals of one step.
6. Mark areas already probed with skis, packs, etc.
7. Do not litter the area with food or urine as this will cause a rescue dog to lose the victim's scent.
8. Quickly dig the victim out.

Avalanche victims need immediate medical attention, but moving severely injured or unconscious persons is risky. HYPOTHERMIA, fractures, concussion and internal injuries are likely. Helicopter evacuation may be necessary. Victims should be warmed in a sleeping bag or tent until rescue arrives.

AVALANCHE RESCUE BEACONS Also called avalanche tranceivers, these compact battery-powered electronic devices are capable of both transmitting and receiving a radio signal. They are the most effective means of locating persons buried in an avalanche, though they are more commonly used by mountain ski tourers than climbers. During travel in avalanche terrain each person carries a beacon switched to transmit. If someone is buried by an avalanche, their beacon will continue to transmit while the remaining party switch their beacons to receive mode and begin an organized search (see AVALANCHE RESCUE). The signal of a transmitting beacon intensifies as a receiving beacon nears it. Beacons must transmit and receive the same frequency to be useful. Of the types used in the United States and Europe, the Skadi, Echo 1 and 2 and Pieps 1 and 2 operate on a frequency of 2275 kHz; the Autophon VS 68 operates on 457 kHz; and the Ortovox and Pieps 3 operate on both frequencies.

AVON (Britain) The limestone cliffs on Bristol's western edge above the River Avon are among the most popular in southern England. Because of the busy road beneath the CRAGS, which leads out of Bristol toward Avonmouth and the M5, climbing here is noisy and is not recommended for those seeking solitude. There are three principal areas: the Main Wall, the Sea Walls/Unknown Area to its north and the Suspension Bridge Buttress to its south. The latter climbs underneath I. K. Brunel's suspension bridge.

Historic ROUTES include Tony Wilmott's 1971 classic in the Unknown Area, Amanita Muscarina (5.11a) and Yellow Edge (5.10d) on the Exploding Galaxy wall. Tour de France, by Pat LITTLEJOHN is fierce at 5.12a. On the Sea Walls are Ed DRUMMOND's Last Slip (5.10c) climbed in 1966, and Martin Crocker's modern testpiece Edgemaster (5.12b). On the Main Wall, Chris BONINGTON's 1957 classic Malbogies remains a popular if polished 5.8. Pinkginsane (5.12c), climbed in 1980 by Nipper Harrison, and Martin Crocker's 1985 testpiece Polar Reaches (5.12c) are two modern classics. At the 5.8–5.9 level Suspension Bridge Buttress offers three mid-1960s routes of poet-author Ed Drummond: Limbo, Earl of Perth and Hell Gates.

Avon is south-facing and dries quickly after rain. Routes vary from one PITCH to three. There is some fixed gear on many routes and BOLTS on the harder ones. **Guidebook:** Pat Littlejohn, *South West Climbs* (1991).

A VUE A French SPORT-CLIMBING term, literally meaning to climb a ROUTE ON SIGHT, or without prior knowledge of the route. (See STYLE.)

AXE Short term for ICE AXE.

B

BACHAR, JOHN (1957–) (United States) During the mid-1980s this hard-training Californian was recognized as one of the world's best and boldest FREE CLIMBERS. He first climbed at Stony Point, near his birthplace of Los Angeles, in his teens. In the early 1970s, he began a long association with YOSEMITE that produced many breakthrough ascents. In 1975 he was one of the team that free climbed the East Face of Washington Column (now called Astroman, 5.11d), one of the first multi-pitch hard free routes. Also in 1975 he and Ron KAUK climbed one of the first 5.12 routes, Hotline on Elephant Rock; and in 1976 Bachar made perhaps the first 5.11 solo, New Dimensions on Arch Rock. In 1986 with Peter CROFT he made the first one-day link-up of EL CAPITAN (The Nose in 10.05 hrs) and HALF DOME (regular northwest face in 4.03 hrs). Elsewhere, in 1981 in France and Germany he established routes (up to 5.12c). He continued to take bouldering-thinking onto long routes, becoming the first to free solo 5.12 and 5.13, with Baby Apes (5.12b) in 1982, and Father Figure (5.13) in 1985, in JOSHUA TREE. In TUOLOMNE MEADOWS Bachar established bold routes on the knobby faces, and brought to the fore the technique of standing on SKYHOOKS to place BOLTS while leading, as on the frightening Bachar-Yerian (5.11b). In 1984 the AMERICAN ALPINE CLUB awarded him the Underhill Award for achievement. Bachar is a strong advocate of TRADITIONAL ETHICS, always establishing routes from the ground up, never inspecting by RAPPEL, and at times enforcing his views by chopping bolts placed on rappel by other climbers.

BACKING OFF To retreat from a ROUTE. (See RAPPEL.)

BACKPACK Another word, of American origin, for a PACK.

BACK ROPE A ROPE TECHNIQUE for protecting the SECOND climber across a TRAVERSE. If using two ropes, as the second traverses to the BELAY, one rope is clipped into a piece of PROTECTION at the start of the traverse. The LEADER pays out slack on this rope, while taking in rope on the other rope. In the event of a fall, the rope going through the protection at either end prevents the second from swinging. At the end of the traverse, the second unties from the back rope and pulls it through the protection, which must be abandoned. If only one rope is used, the second can still rig a back rope by clipping the single rope

through the protection at the start of the traverse, then clipping a CARABINER from the HARNESS over the rope that leads to the belay.

BACK-UP A secondary ANCHOR added to the main anchor, as a safety precaution in case the main anchor fails.

BAFFIN ISLAND (Canada) These remote mountains with their magnificent granite faces are in Canada's Northwest Territories, on the Cumberland Peninsula of Baffin Island, close to the Arctic Circle. Most climbing lies within Auyuittuq National Park, which encompasses a 2,200-square-mile (5,696-sq-km) ICE CAP, one of the largest in the northern hemisphere. In the eastern tip fjords indent the coast and jagged peaks rise to 6,560 ft (2,000 m). The land is tundra and swampy muskeg.

Developed climbing has concentrated around South and North Pangnirtung fjords, above the Weasel and Owl Valleys. Thousands of square miles of granite peaks and GLACIERS remain unexplored. The peaks are remote, there is no chance of rescue, and Arctic weather can be foul. June through August offer the most stable weather, with 24-hour daylight in July. Spring offers the best snow conditions. Around Pangnirtung Pass it is necessary to plan an itinerary around the ice pack of the South Pangnirtung Fjord, which breaks up in June and moves out to sea. Snowmobiles are used to negotiate the fjord when it is frozen.

Tete Blanche (7,072 ft/2,156 m) is the highest peak. In addition to huge low-angle granite SLABS, there are overhanging 4,000-ft (1,202-m) walls and grade VI ROUTES on Mount Asgard, Mount Thor and Mount Overlord. The first climbing here was by Tom LONGSTAFF in 1934. In the 1950s Pat Baird made many FIRST ASCENTS and in the 1970s BIG WALL climbs were made by Doug SCOTT and Dennis Hennek. Since then the area has attracted a handful of international climbers. Scheduled jet service from Montreal, 1,500 miles (2,414 km) away, delivers expeditions to Pangnirtung, where snowmobiles and boats to the mountains can be arranged. Climbers should contact the Superintendant, Auyuittuq National Park, Pangnirtung, Northwest Teritories, XOA ORO, Canada.

Further reading: John Cleare, *Collins Guide to Mountains and Mountaineering* (1979); M. R. Kelsey, *Climbers and Hikers Guide to the World's Mountains* (1990); Doug Scott, *Big Wall Climbing* (1981).

BAGGY POINT (Britain) The most popular CRAG in DEVON, due to the pleasant SLABS and coastal setting, Baggy Point is just north of Croyde village near the towns of Barnstaple and Ilfracombe. The beach of Croyde Bay with its big waves is a British surfing destination.

Climbing at Baggy has a long history, beginning with the ascent of Scrattling Crack (5.5) in 1898 by Tom LONGSTAFF. Exploration following this climb was sporadic until the late 1960s when the North London Mountaineering Club, began developing Baggy. Ben Wintringham's Twinkletoes (5.7) and Sexilegs (5.8) are notable climbs from this era, as are Tony Wilmott's Heart of the Sun (5.10), freed by Arni Strapcans in 1977, and Dave Johnson's Kinkyboots (5.7). Harder routes include Pete Bull's Inferno (5.11d) and D. Thomas's committing test-piece Embers (5.12a). Most routes are between 150 and 300 ft (46 and 91 m) with the added interest of a sea whose tides can swell 30 ft (9 m) or more.

Guidebooks: Pat Littlejohn, *South West Climbs* (1991); Iain Peters, *North Devon and Cornwall* (1988).

BALLING UP When snow softens in warm temperatures, large clumps may ball up or cling to CRAMPONS. Balling up impedes progress and may cause climbers to lose their footing. A firm tap of the ICE AXE against the boot will dislodge balled-up snow, but on a warm slope every step will ball up. One method for relieving the problem is to affix a shield or gasket of plastic, rubber, tin or duct tape between the base of the crampon and the boot sole.

BALTI The name of the people who inhabit Baltistan, in northern PAKISTAN. Balti PORTERS are often employed for EXPEDITIONS to the BALTORO in the KARAKORAM.

BALTORO The name of the 40-mile- (64-km)-long GLACIER that is trekked to reach the BASE CAMPS of K2, GASHERBRUM Group, TRANGO TOWERS.

BARBER, HENRY (1953–) (United States) American climber who influenced world climbing during the 1970s. Barber was known for his solo climbs and bold leads, his ON-SIGHT FREE ASCENTS of aid routes, his devotion to CLEAN CLIMBING and his appetite for climbing—he climbed on 320 days in a single year. He is America's first professional climber.

Born in Boston, Barber began climbing at east coast areas like Quincy Quarries, the SHAWANGUNKS and CATHEDRAL LEDGE. In 1972 he made the second free ascent of what was then America's hardest FREE CLIMB, a 12-ft (4-m) ROOF called "Foops," freed by John STANNARD in 1968. Stannard's ETHICS, which embodied a willingness to attempt a climb many times until every move could be made free in one continuous effort, were the genesis of Barber's ethics. Like Stannard, Barber rejected the placement of PITONS or BOLTS on free climbs, placing NUTS and STOPPERS instead. When thwarted by a climb and forced to descend, he DOWN-CLIMBED rather than hang on PROTECTION. He would then pull the rope through his protection, and relead the

PITCH to the previous high point without the benefit of the TOP ROPE. Many of Barber's ethics have been absorbed into modern climbing, yet in the 1970s they were innovations.

Barber's peripatetic career was characterized by his ability to visit a new area and leave bold, hard routes. In YOSEMITE VALLEY (California) in 1973 and 1974, his FIRST ASCENTS of the oft-tried 5.11 CRACKS Butterballs and Fish Crack, and his two-and-a-half-hour solo ascent of the 1,800-ft (549 m) Steck-Salathe Route on Sentinel Rock became internationally recognized achievements. The American climber Royal ROBBINS called the latter climb "an act of vision." The British magazine *Mountain* published an interview with Barber, referring to him as "Hot Henry," an appellation that became his trademark. In a 44-day tour of Australia in 1975 Barber visited 27 cliffs and made 60 first or first-free ascents, establishing the hardest grade (23) at that time in Australia. In Britain he soloed hard routes and made a televised solo ascent of the sea-cliff climb The Strand. In East Germany he adapted to the barefoot climbing style and minimal protection of the sandstone towers of the ELBESANDSTEINGEBIRGE.

Barber was also an ALPINIST, involved in first ascents of many FROZEN WATERFALLS. The Ghost, a grade IV ice route on CANNON Mountain (1973), and in NORWAY the first ascent with Rob Taylor of the 1,300-ft (396-m) Vettifossen (1977), were the hardest waterfall climbs of the time. In the TIEN SHAN Mountains in Central Asia in 1976 he soloed a new 2,300-ft (701-m) ice face on Korea Peak. Barber eased out of professional climbing after 1977, following an incident on the then-unclimbed Breach Wall of KILIMANJARO (Africa) in which his partner was severely injured.

Further reading: Chip Lee, *On Edge* (1982).

BARD, DALE (1956–) (United States) Between 1973 and the early-1980s in YOSEMITE VALLEY, Bard climbed many of Yosemite's hardest free climbs—including an early, nearly free ascent of the Nose—but it was his appetite for BIG WALL CLIMBING that set him apart from other Yosemite climbers. On EL CAPITAN he climbed 30 big wall routes. His Yosemite big wall ascents totalled about 50. In one season in 1980 he climbed 18 El Capitan routes, at one point spending 21 out of 30 days on the wall. He was involved in the FIRST ASCENTS of several A5 big walls on El Capitan, the hardest of which were the Sea of Dreams, with Jim BRIDWELL and Dave Diegelman; Iron Hawk, with Ron KAUK; and Sunkist, with Bill Price. On Half Dome, he and Bridwell climbed the overhanging, dangerous walls Bushido, and with Kim Schmitz, Zenith. Bard pioneered many extreme aid PITCHES on these routes, using long sequences of HOOKS, COPPERHEADS and RURPS rather than resort to drilled ladders. He also contributed to the creation of the PORTA-LEDGE.

BARILOCHE (Argentina) Southwest of Buenos Aires by 800 miles (1,287 km) the ski resort of Bariloche lies nestled between glacial lakes and snow-capped peaks. There are two types of climbing in the area: alpine rock climbs on solid granitic spires and snow climbs on volcanoes up to 11,000 ft (3,354 m). The Cathedral (Cerro Catedral) (7,903 ft/2,408 m) is the highest peak in a tight cluster of small, steep rock spires that surround Lake Frey, southwest of Bariloche. The east face of the mountain sports a 13-pitch 5.10a rock route of high quality. Fine climbs abound on nearby Cerro Campanile (7,578 ft/2,310 m), Cathedral South (7,834 ft/2,388 m) and Aguja Frey.

Snow enthusiasts can drive 60 miles (96 km) south and then west of Bariloche to access the three summits of Tronodor, an extinct volcano. Pico Chile is across the border, Pico Internationale at 11,660 ft/3,553 m straddles the border and Pico Argentine at 10,000 ft/3,048 m is in Argentina. The latter is the most accessible and is an enjoyable snow climb from the Otto Meiling hut at 6,000 ft (1,829 m). Since Bariloche is not technically part of PATAGONIA, there is little published in English about climbing there. The hut at Lake Frey has a log book recording rock climbs done in that area. In recent years many bolted sport routes have been climbed here.

BARN-DOOR A characteristic of difficult LIE BACK climbs, in which the position and balance-point of the body creates a tendency for the climber to swing out of balance, like an opening door.

BAROMETER See ALTIMETER.

BASE CAMP In MOUNTAINEERING terminology, the main camp near the base of the mountain, used as a supply depot, headquarters and resting place during efforts on a mountain. In cases where a base camp cannot be situated near the foot of the mountain, an advance base camp is often placed beyond base camp. Camps on the mountain are called camp one, camp two, etc.

BASE JUMPING A parachute jump and free fall from any fixed object, but as it relates to climbing, from a cliff. The activity was named by its pioneer, Carl Boenish, who was killed jumping from the TROLL WALL in NORWAY. BASE is an acronym for Building, Antenna (or tower), Span (or bridge) and Earth (or cliff). To be regarded as a BASE jumper, an individual must make one jump in each category. BASE jumping entered the climbing world when jumpers combined ascents of tall cliffs with parachute descents. BASE jumper Randy LEAVITT coined the term "cliffing" to describe an ascent of a climb combined with a BASE jump from the top of it. (See CLIFFING.)

BASHIE Another name for a COPPERHEAD.

BASS, RICHARD (DICK) (1929–) (United States) Dallas financier and developer of Snowbird ski resort in Utah, Bass was first to climb the highest points on seven continents (SEVEN SUMMITS), finishing with Mount EVEREST, April 30, 1985. He set the goal following his 1981 ascent of DENALI'S west buttress. Frank Wells, then president of Warner Brothers in Hollywood, had had a similiar idea following a KILIMANJARO ascent in 1954. Wells learned of Bass's plan, and they joined forces in 1981 to climb six of the seven peaks together: ACONCAGUA (South America, 22,834 ft/6,962 m); Denali (North America, 20,320 ft/195 m);

Kilimanjaro (Africa, 19,340 ft/5,896 m); Elbrus (Europe, 18,481 ft/5,984 m); Vinson, ANTARCTICA, 16,067 ft/4,820 m); and Kosciusko (AUSTRALIA, 7,316 ft/2,230 m). The book *Seven Summits,* a collaborative effort by Bass with Wells and Rick RIDGEWAY (1986) is an account of the feat. Some regard Canadian Pat MORROW as the first Seven Summiter, calling his ascent of CARSTENZ PYRAMID in Irian Jaya to be the highest in Australasia, rather than Kosciusko on the Australian mainland. Bass differs, saying Australasia is not a continent.

BATES, ROBERT (1901–) (United States) This Harvard graduate climbed through two "golden ages" of climbing: the exploration of ALASKA and the Yukon in the 1930s, and the attempts on the 26,240-ft (8,000-m) peaks in the 1950s. With Bradford WASHBURN in 1935, Bates was the first to explore the 10,000-sq-mile (25,889-sq-km) Saint Elias Ice Field. In 1937 they made the FIRST ASCENT of Mount Lucania (17,147 ft/5,228 m) in the Yukon. On this, he and Washburn became stranded after their plane crash-landed on the Walsh Glacier. They climbed Lucania then escaped by climbing neighboring Mount Steele (16,644 ft/ 5,074 m), descending its east ridge and trekking out 60 miles (96 km).

In 1938 he reached 26,000 ft (7,927 m) on K2 on the first American attempt, then (after developing cold-weather gear for the army in World War II, during which he made the third ascent of DENALI) returned to K2 with Charles HOUSTON's 1954 expedition. On the ABRUZZI Ridge, seven climbers were ready to place an assault camp when a four-day storm and altitude illness in Art Gilkey forced retreat. The harrowing descent and Gilkey's death is told in Houston and Bates's *The Savage Mountain* (1978).

While an English teacher at Phillips Exeter Academy in New Hampshire, Bates participated in surveying expeditions to Nevado in CHILE (1958), and to Ulugh Muztagh (22,922 ft/6,987 m) in CHINA's KUNLUN RANGE (1974). While Chinese made Ulugh Muztagh's first ascent, Bates and colleagues measured the peak and found it 2,500 ft (762 m) lower than previously believed.

BAT HOOK A SKYHOOK filed to a sharp point for tapping into shallow drilled holes. In AID CLIMBING a bat-hook ladder is a ladder of bat-hook holes. The hook is removed as the LEADER moves past. The advantage of bat-hooking over placing BOLTS is that of speed and the conservation of bolts or rivets.

BATURA MUZTAGH (Pakistan) This westerly part of the KARAKORAM RANGE stretches from the Batura Glacier and the Ishkoman River in the west to the Hunza River in the east. In the north lies the Wakhan Corridor, which is the PAKISTAN-Afghanistan border. The Pakistani towns of Gilgit and Karimabad lie to the south. The CREST of the Batura Muztagh, often called the Batura Wall, is a magnificent array of 22,960-ft (7,000-m) peaks. These comprise Kampire Dior (23,431 ft/7,142 m) on the west, Shishpare (24,970 ft/7,611 m), Ghenta (23,260 ft/7,090 m), Bojohagur Duanasir (24,044 ft/7,329 m) and Ultar (24,238 ft/7,388 m).

To the south rise Hachindar Chhish (23,500 ft/7,163 m) and Sangemar Mar (22,798 ft/6,949 m). The northern slopes of the Batura Wall are great ice basins that feed the 35-mile (56-km) Batura Glacier, the eighth largest in the Karakoram. Important ascents include the 8,000-ft (2,439-m) south wall of Shispare, climbed by a Polish-German team in 1974, and the 11,000-ft (3,353-m) north face of Batura V (24,707 ft/7,531 m), climbed by Poles in 1983. Though the main summits of the Batura Wall have been climbed, untapped possibilities abound.

Guidebook and map: Jerzy Wala, *Batura Muztagh, Orographical Sketch Map* (1988).

BECKEY, FRED (1921–   ) (United States) Since his teenage participation in the FIRST ASCENT of Forbidden Peak (WASHINGTON STATE) in 1940, Beckey has been a leading figure in the development of North American ALPINISM. Though never a climber of exceptional technical prowess, Beckey is prolific for his tally of first ascents across America, estimated at around 1,000, though he himself has never counted them.

In the CASCADE RANGE his name is everywhere for first ascents of classic ROUTES—Liberty Bell, Mount SLESSE's north BUTTRESS and Mount RAINIER's Mowich Face—all climbed at a time when the range was largely wilderness. His *Cascade Alpine Guide* (1977–81) guidebook trilogy of Washington State's Cascade Range reveal his encyclopedic acquaintance with that range. He also pioneered some of the first rock routes at INDEX Town Wall.

One of his finest early climbs was the second ascent of Mount WADDINGTON (1942, Canada), when Beckey was age 21, with his 16-year-old brother Helmy. Having trekked for days through remote forests, they climbed the route of Fritz WIESSNER and William HOUSE—the south face—changing out of mountain boots and into tennis shoes with felt overboots to climb the wet summit rocks.

His calling was indeed on big mountains. In Canada he made first ascents like Snowpatch Spire east face (BUGABOOS), north face of EDITH CAVELL, the DEVIL'S THUMB and the first WINTER ASCENT of Mount ROBSON. In ALASKA he made first ascents of Mount HUNTER, Mount Deborah, DENALI's northwest buttress and almost climbed the MOOSES TOOTH. In the NEPAL HIMALAYA, he attempted LHOTSE in the mid-1950s when it was unclimbed, and again returned to high altitude in 1982, at age 61, to organize a successful expedition to Jiazi (21,457 ft/6,540 m) in CHINA. In elder years he shared his knowledge of hidden objectives in America's ranges with fitter, younger climbers and continued to climb new routes every year.

Further reading: Fred Beckey, *Challenge of the North Cascades* (1969); Beckey, *Mountains of North America* (1982).

BEGHIN, PIERRE (1951–1992) (France) Premier Himalayan ALPINIST of France, engineer by profession, and also a hardened alpinist in his own country. He executed hundreds of hard climbs across the ALPS, like the Walker Spur of the GRANDES JORASSES solo, first winter solo of the Pic sans Nom North Face in five days, and Bonatti-Vaucher on the Jorasses in winter. He visited the HIMALAYA first in 1974, beginning a career of LIGHTWEIGHT EXPEDITIONS. His big routes included: west pillar of DHAULAGIRI (1980, though not to the summit); MANASLU west face (1981, new route); KANGCHENJUNGA south face (solo, 1983); Dhaulagiri south spur (1984, ALPINE STYLE, with Jean-Noel Roche); four unsuccessful attempts on EVEREST; the Japanese Route on Jannu (1987, alpine style, with Erik Decamp); MAKALU south face (1989, eventually solo to the top); and K2 in very light style with Christophe PROFIT. On K2 the pair began in PAKISTAN and linked sections of previously climbed routes from the northwest ridge and north face. He was killed while attempting Annapurna south face when an anchor pulled during the retreat.

BELAY The procedure of securing the LEADER or SECOND with the rope. (See BELAYING TECHNIQUES.)

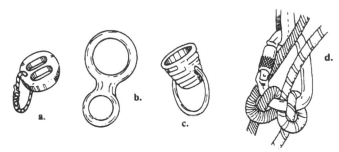

Belay Devices: a. Stitch Plate b. Figure-Eight c. L.A.S. Tuber d. Munter Hitch Knot

BELAYING TECHNIQUES Belaying is the managing of the rope by one climber—the belayer—while the other climber climbs, either leading or seconding. In the event of a fall, the belayer arrests the fall by some friction method and brings the climber to a halt. There are two categories of belay: dynamic and static. Within these categories many belaying techniques exist. Some are regarded as more failsafe than others, but any climber should know a range of techniques. When discussing belaying procedures, the following terms are used: The "live end" or "live rope" is rope between the belayer and the climber; "dead rope" is rope in reserve, not yet in use between belayer and climber; the "guide hand" controls the movement of the live end; the "brake hand" is the opposite hand, and its job is to lock the rope off in the event of a fall; a "bight" of rope is a length of rope.

When catching a fall, belayers arrest considerable energy. This energy is concentrated on the rope and belay device and the anchor. Strong belays and ANCHORS are, therefore, essential.

The body belay, or waist or hip belay, is the basic dynamic belay. Its dynamic quality lies in the fact that in a fall some rope is pulled through the system before the belayer stops the fall, and this slowly decelerates the falling climber. The body belay is set up by positioning the rope so that it runs around the back and over the hips. The guide hand manages the rope and the brake hand locks it off when necessary by bringing the hand sharply around the waist. At all times, both hands must be on their respective ends of the rope. Most important, the rope should pass through a locking CARABINER clipped to the HARNESS at the waist, to keep it from being pulled away in a fall. The disadvantage of this belay is that it is uncomfortable to hold a climber's weight for very long, and that large falls are difficult to arrest and may result in rope burn for the belayer. Gloves ease this problem. The shoulder belay works on the same principle, except the rope is run over the shoulder and around the back. This older-style belay is not recommended because in a fall the belayer is likely to overbalance and lose control of the rope.

Belays using devices are called static belays, and present the safest belay techniques as the rope is locked tightly in a device and is brought to a quick stop. The same principles of rope management apply to belay devices as to the body belay.

The belay plate, or Sticht plate, is a metal disc with one or two holes drilled through it. A bight of rope is pushed through one hole (of matching size to the rope diameter) and clipped through a locking carabiner connected to the harness. The plate has a short keeper-strap that is also clipped to the locking carabiner. This strap prevents the plate from sliding along the rope out of the belayer's grasp. To pass rope to a leader, the belayer simply feeds "dead" rope into the hole, around the carabiner, and out the other side of the hole (where it becomes "live" rope), in one smooth action. In a fall, the rope presses the plate and rope together and the rope locks. The Sticht plate, however, does have a tendency to grab, or lock up unintentionally—a problem for leaders pulling rope up to clip protection. Some plates attempt to prevent this by incorporating a built-in coil-spring, which holds the rope off the plate. A better effect can be achieved by clipping a second carabiner through the bight of rope (but not through the harness or locking carabiner). The Lowe Tuber is a conical device that works on the same principle. A belay link is a piece of chain link. In all belay plate devices, the belayer should hold the dead end of the rope back across the face of the plate, away from the line of pull ready to lock the rope.

A friction hitch called a Munter hitch or Italian hitch, wrapped around a locking carabiner, is a good alternative to belay devices. The Munter hitch locks under the load of a fall and is UIAA approved. A specially shaped carabiner, called a pearabiner, which has no sharp angles to jam the smooth action of the hitch, should only be used.

A figure-eight rappel device can also be used for belaying, though it is not as static as other devices. If using the figure-eight, a bight of rope is passed through the large hole, but is not brought around the stem of the figure-eight, as would be the case in a rappel. Instead the rope is held parallel to the smaller hole and both are clipped into a locking carabiner. The action of rope movement in this method does cause the rope to kink, unlike the Sticht plate or tuber.

A recent mechanical belay device from the French company Petzl is the Gri Gri, which locks off rope that is fed into it via the action of a friction-activated cam, similar in principle to the inertia-reel seat-belt device in cars. Other belay situations are discussed under TOP ROPING.

BELAY PLATE Another name for a STICHT PLATE, used for belaying. (See BELAYING TECHNIQUES.)

BELAY SEAT Sometimes called a butt bag. A lightweight, pocket-size fabric seat that can be suspended from an ANCHOR by WEBBING straps. Useful for HANGING BELAYS on steep rock walls.

BELAY STATION The site chosen for a belay ANCHOR, where the belay is made. A belay station may be a comfortable ledge, a small foot stance or a HANGING BELAY where one is suspended from the anchors. Also called belay stance.

BEN NEVIS (Scotland) One of the few CRAGS in Britain noted more for its ICE CLIMBING than its rock climbing. At 4,406 ft (1,343 m), it is the highest mountain in the British Isles. Located in the Lochaber area to the southeast of Fort William, the Ben has commanding views on rare clear days and a craggy northern aspect. Climbers usually approach by following the Allt a'Mhuilinn from the distillery in Fort William. This path leads in around two hours to the Charles Inglis Clark (CIC) hut, which can be used by prior arrangement. From here the topography of the Ben becomes clear. The head of the glen, Coire Leis, is bounded by the northeast buttress. Between this and the next ridge, Tower, is the Orion Face, and beyond that is the broad expanse of Coire na Ciste, which ends with the huge mass of the Carn Dearg Buttress. Into this framework slip a host of other buttresses and gullies that are evocative to many British climbers of cold, hard and short days. The Ben offers the only true MOUNTAINEERING, with the possible exception of SKYE, in the country.

Unfortunately for the fiercely protective Scottish Mountaineering Club, it was a family from Manchester, the Hopkinsons, who made the earliest forays on the north side of the Ben, climbing the northeast ridge and descending Tower Ridge (5.3), in 1892. The Hopkinsons left little record of their climbs and for many years the SMC assumed they had the FIRST ASCENTS. Other ROUTES worth noting at this end of the Ben are Left-Hand Route, climbed in 1944 by the pacifist Brian Kellet, an 800-ft (244-m) 5.7. Even longer, indeed the longest in the British Isles, is The Long Climb, 1,430 ft (440 m) and climbed in 1940 by the great James Bell. It follows a LINE up the Orion Face on good rock at 5.6. Even better is Minus One Direct, a sustained 860 ft (262 m) 5.8 of the very best quality on perfect rock, climbed by Bob Downes and others in 1956. There are a number of good routes on the Trident Buttresses at the back of Coire na Ciste, including the outstanding Metamorphosis (5.9) that takes a hanging corner on Central Trident and was climbed by Steve Docherty in 1971.

To the modern rock-climber the chief attraction of Ben Nevis is the Carn Dearg Buttress (pronounced Karn Jarrak). It includes routes by many of Britain's most adventurous

climbers and was the venue of some national rivalry. There are easier lines: Alan Hargreaves and George McPhee climbed the classic Route I in 1931, a wandering 5.5, and Brian Kellet added Route II, a brilliant 5.6 in superb positions climbed in 1943. The Rock and Ice caused the Creagh Dhu some heartache by climbing Sassenach (5.8) and then the huge CORNER of Centurion (5.8), the former by Joe BROWN and Don WHILLANS and the latter by Whillans and Bob Downes in 1956. Robin SMITH and Dougal HASTON, with Doug SCOTT, the first Britons to climb EVEREST, solved The Bat (5.10a) in 1959, so called because of the late hour the route was finished, and the Scots' revenge continued in 1961 with Jimmy Marshall Bullroar (5.8) and John McLean and Bill Smith's Torro (5.9) in 1962. Brown and Whillans had beaten Tom PATEY to Sassenach, and in the 1970s Mick Fowler and Phill Thomas beat Dave Cuthbertson and Murray Hamilton to Titan's Wall, a brilliant 5.10d up a previously aided crackline. Hamilton, climbing with Rab Anderson, saved Scottish honor, with The Banana Groove (5.11a) and Anderson with Pete Whillance did much for cross-border relations with Agrippa, the Ben's only 5.12 and considered one of its finest routes. Routes on Carn Dearg vary from 800 ft (244 m) (Torro) to 300 ft (91 m) (Agrippa) in length.
Guidebooks: Donald Bennet, *The Munros* (1991); Kevin Howett, *Rock Climbing in Scotland* (1990); C. Stead and J. Marshall, *Lochaber and Badenoch* (1981).

BERGSCHRUND Also *'schrund*, from the German; *rimaye* in French. In general usage, a CREVASSE separating the uppermost ice of a GLACIER or snow slope from the mountain behind it, often forming a deep, steep-walled gap that is difficult to cross. In correct usage this formation is actually a *randkluft* (German), a *bergschrund* more accurately being a gap between two fields of ice in the upper reaches of a glacier. However, in English usage, *bergschrund* identifies any such gap.

BERNESE ALPS, THE (Switzerland) A range of mountains that extend from Lake Geneva to the Lake of Lucerne and from the Aare Valley in the north to the upper Rhône Valley in the south. It is naturally divided into three areas; the West Bernese is separated from the Bernese Central or Bernese Oberland by the Gemmi Pass and the latter from the East Bernese Alps by the Grimsel Pass. The West Bernese Alps hold the least interest for the mountaineer, the principal summits being the Wildhorn (10,653 ft/3,248 m), Wildstrubel (10,634 ft/3,242 m) and Les Diablerets (10,529 ft/3,210 m).

The East Bernese Alps are more complicated, divided into a northern and southern section by the Susten Pass. To the north is Titlis (10,624 ft/3,239 m), the chief center being Engelberg. In the southern region of the East Bernese is the Sustenhorn (11,493 ft/3,504 m), an easy snow peak, and the rock-climbing area of the Dammastock (11,906 ft/3,630 m). At the eastern end of this area is the Salbitschijen, a granite peak in the Voralp Tal near Goschenan noted for its difficult rock climbs.

The Central Bernese Alps have nine peaks over 13,120 ft (4,000 m) and the area is heavily glaciated—the longest GLACIER in the Alps, the Aletsch, is in the Bernese. There is a good reason for this that is pertinent to mountaineers; while they are not the highest mountains, the Bernese Central lie on the windward side and rise steeply out of the foothills to a significant precipitation. The most commonly used base is Grindelwald, but for outlying peaks Kandersteg and Lötschental prove more practical. There is a useful rail-car link between these two towns. The climbing, like that of the Pennines, is largely mixed snow and rock.

Among the 13,120-ft (4,000-m) peaks is the Aletschhorn (13,760 ft/4,195 m), the second-highest peak in the area, which dominates the largest glacier in the Alps. The north face is especially dramatic and was climbed in 1925 by E. Blanchet with A. Rübi and K. Mooser at TD. Huts in the area include the Oberaletsch Hut and the Mittelkaletsch Bivouac Hut. Other notable peaks in the area are the Dreieckhorn (12,497 ft/3,810 m) to the northeast of the Aletschhorn and the Geisshorn to the south.

BERNINA ALPS (Italy, Switzerland) This range is located on the Swiss-Italian border above the skiing resorts of St. Moritz and Pontresina. It includes the only 13,120-ft (4,000-m) peak outside the western ranges, Piz Bernina (13,281 ft/4,049 m) and other famous mountains like Piz Palü (12,808 ft/3,905 m), Piz Scersen (13,025 ft/3,971 m), Piz Zupo (13,107 ft/3,996 m) and Piz Roseg (12,913 ft/3,937 m). Piz Palü featured in the famous black-and-white film, the WHITE HELL OF PIZ PALÜ and its proximity to the cable car at Diavolezza draws many visitors. The other attractions of the Bernina, Piz Zupo for example, are not so well known and offer a quieter alternative.

BETA A SPORT CLIMBING term, referring to a move-by-move verbal description of a section of a FREE CLIMB. Beta is derived from the video format, and the concept of the instant replay in a televised football game.

BEYER, JIM (1955–) (United States) The most accomplished American BIG WALL soloist, a staunch TRADITIONALIST who bolted only as a last resort, and the first climber to introduce the aid rating A6. Beyer's routes, both ROPED-SOLO and with partners, both multi-pitch AID and short FREE, number in the hundreds, in CANYONLANDS, the TETONS, WIND RIVERS, BLACK CANYON OF THE GUNNISON, YOSEMITE and the KARAKORAM. His aid climbing prowess led him to initiate an aid RATING SYSTEM that subdivided the usual five ratings (A1 to A5) into 14 ratings: A1, A2, A2+, A3, A3+, A4a, A4b, A4c, A4d, A5a, A5b, A5c, A5d, A6. He defined A6 as having "more than two pitches with a potential death fall of 200 feet, cruxes of cutting edge technical difficulty, no bolts, and possibility of ripping lower anchors in the case of fixed ropes below." He began his solo career in 1975, with a route on the DIAMOND, Sunshine, (VI 5.7 A3). In Yosemite on EL CAPITAN in the

1970s he made first solo ascents of Dihedral Wall and The Shield; in the 1980s he achieved the first one-day roped solo of El Cap via the west face; and he added a new route there, Reach for the Sky, 5.11d A4d. Harder still was his route on Leaning Tower, Heading for Oblivion (VI A4+). In 1989 and 1991 he added two grade VI A4+ routes to the Black Canyon, one on the Painted Wall, the other on North Chasm View Wall. He placed no BOLTS. But his most imposing routes are on the fragile 900-ft (270-m) desert spires of the Fisher Towers of Utah. He climbed five routes there during the 1980s, culminating in Intifada (VI 5.10 A6a). In the Tetons his solo route of 1991 on the GRAND TETON, Looking for Trouble (V 5.12 or AO, A3 and ice) is the hardest in the range. In 1989 he visited the Karakoram, soloing in 13 days a new 54 pitch route on Baltoro Cathedral (VII 5.10 A4), then returning in 1990 to the spire Bib-O-li-Motin, soloing the southeast face by a route that had thwarted three expeditions, but missing the actual blocky summit by mere meters.

BHUTAN This tiny kingdom of the eastern HIMALAYA, squeezed between TIBET and INDIA, is one of the least-explored mountain regions in the world. While geography plays a role in its isolation, politics is the key factor as the Royal Government of Bhutan severely restricts tourism and intercourse with foreigners, due to ecological concerns and to preserve the Bhutanese culture, which is the last remaining example of a Tibetan-derived Buddhist culture.

Little climbing has been done in Bhutan despite many peaks up to and above 22,960 ft (7,000 m). The Bhutan Tourist Corporation (Bhutan Tourist Corporation, PO Box 159, Thimphu, Kingdom of Bhutan) limits the number of expeditions attempting peaks over 19,680 ft (6,000 m) and places a very high price on visits to Bhutan, putting climbing there out of reach for all except heavily funded expeditions. Climbing in Bhutan requires a high commitment to adventure, as the mountains are largely unexplored and unmapped. Exact heights and locations of most peaks are unknown.

Most climbing in Bhutan has been done in the far northwestern corner, near Jhomolhari (also called Chomolhari), a peak of over 22,960 ft (7,000 m). A relatively popular trekking route, from the town of Paro to the capital city of Thimphu, provides access to this area in which most peaks rise above 19,680 ft (6,000 m). Jhomolhari is a sacred peak on the Tibetan frontier range and is visible to travelers on the north side of Everest. The peak was climbed in 1937 by Spencer Chapman (Britain), but between then and 1983 (when the BTC opened Bhutan to tourism) Bhutan was virtually closed to climbers.

Kula Kangri (possibly 24,777 ft/7,554 m) is probably Bhutan's highest peak. It was climbed by a Japanese party in 1986, via the west ridge. Located in the far northern corner of Bhutan, this remote area probably contains more unclimbed 22,960-ft (7,000-m) peaks than any part of the Himalaya. Another major ascent made in Bhutan is that of Jitchu Drake (about 22,960 ft/7,000 m), climbed in 1988 via the south face/southeast ridge by a British expedition led by Doug Scott.

Bhutan's mountains experience heavy MONSOON weather from the end of May through August. The postmonsoon season—September till November—may be the best time to climb lower peaks, while spring—March through May—is probably more favorable for climbing higher peaks.

BIAFO GLACIER The name of the GLACIER that is trekked for the approach to LATOK and OGRE peaks.

BIG BRO A modern device for protecting OFFWIDTH CRACKS, up to 12 inches (30 cm) wide. The Big Bro is a spring-loaded adjustable CHOCK that fits a range of crack-widths. The concept was derived from the tube chock, a simple aluminum tube wedged into wide cracks. Manufactured in the United States by Colorado Mountain Hardware.

BIGHT A loop or length of ROPE.

BIG WALL CLIMBING The term was coined during the 1960s in YOSEMITE VALLEY, in CALIFORNIA, to describe a style of multi-day ascent on the huge granite walls there, such as EL CAPITAN's 2,700-ft (823-m) walls. Big wall climbing tends to be synonymous with AID CLIMBING techniques using masses of equipment, though some modern big walls, such as some found in the BLACK CANYON OF THE GUNNISON (COLORADO), are entirely free. Logistics present as many problems as climbing on big walls, as climbers must haul all food, water and bivouac equipment for the duration of their ascent. Loads typically exceed 200 lb (90 kg), and can be as heavy as 400 lb (180 kg) for a 10-day ascent. When natural ledges cannot be found bivouacs are made in hammocks, or, more comfortably, in PORTA-LEDGES (portable hanging tent platforms).

True big wall climbs are multi-day affairs. One of the longest durations climbers have lived on a wall, and one of the world's longest rock climbs, is the Norwegian route on Great Trango Tower (1984), in the TRANGO TOWERS of PAKISTAN in the KARAKORAM RANGE. This 5,000-ft (1,524-m) vertical wall required 22 continuous days of climbing. An even longer duration—40 days—was spent by a Japanese solo climber on the northeast face of Nameless Tower (1990), also in the Trango Towers. Many big walls are so OVERHANGING that descent becomes a real problem after a certain point, committing climbers to the route. Alpine big walls—for example those of BAFFIN ISLAND in the Canadian Arctic—present even greater logistical problems, including cold weather, and the need for stoves to melt ice that is scraped from ledges.

Big wall routes are rated according to a system using Roman numerals. A grade V indicates a climb requiring one BIVOUAC; grade VI indicates a multi-bivouac route; the rarely used grade VII indicates a grade VI made under extreme conditions such as in a remote, high-altitude mountain setting.

Further reading: John Long and John Middendorf, *How to Rock Climb: BIG WALLS* (1994); Doug Scott, *Big Wall Climbing* (1981); Mike Strassman, *Climbing Big Walls* (1991).

BIRDBEAK A thin, hooking-type PITON manufactured by A5 Adventures, Inc. (see Appendices). The Birdbeak can also be used to hook small CRACKS and was largely used on the first CLEAN ascent of the Shield route on EL CAPITAN.

BIVOUAC Any night spent camping on a mountain or cliff during a climb, whether in a TENT, BIVOUAC SACK, SNOW CAVE, HUT, HAMMOCK or PORTA-LEDGE or under the stars. Planned bivouacs can be a joy of climbing. Unplanned or forced, bivouacs in cold conditions are a nightmare. A BIVOUAC SACK or large plastic bag provides portable emergency shelter. Sitting on a small foam pad will insulate against cold, as will sitting on a coiled rope or boots. Sleeping bag, gloves, headwear, additional clothing, food and a stove make a forced bivouac bearable, but climbers sometimes find themselves forced to spend a night wearing only the clothes on their backs. Conserving warmth is an art. Since much heat is lost through the head, wearing a hat or even covering the head with a pack can reduce heat loss. In wind, rain, snow or extreme cold, shelter is essential to avoid HYPOTHERMIA or FROSTBITE. Protection from weather may be found among rocks or trees, or in snow caves or snow holes dug out with ICE AXES and covered with a tarp or pack. Equipment should be carefully stowed when bivouacking.

BIVOUAC SACK A light fabric sack carried by climbers for BIVOUACS in the open, which sometimes are unplanned. Modern GORE-TEX bivouac sacks are waterproof and breathable. Large plastic bags are also used for emergency bivouacs in bad weather.

BIVOUAC TENT Also, bivvy tent. A compact one- or two-person TENT weighing about five lb (two kg), favored by ALPINISTS for bivouacs on mountains.

BJORNSTADT, ERIC (1934–) (United States) Prolific climber from WASHINGTON, now living in Moab, UTAH. Ascents in Washington and the Northwest include FIRST ASCENTS in the BUGABOOS, CASCADES and the COAST range. Bjornstadt frequently climbed with Fred BECKEY. In 1967 Bjornstadt moved to Moab to climb on the COLORADO PLATEAU, and has established many first ascents in the area, including routes on SHIPROCK.
Further reading: Eric Bjornstadt, *Desert Rock* (1988).

BLACK CANYON OF THE GUNNISON (United States) Located in west-central Colorado, 15 miles (24 km) east of Montrose, this forbidding 1,700- to 2,700-ft (518- to 823-m) gorge cut by the Gunnison River offers adventurous BIG WALL CLIMBING to rival that of YOSEMITE VALLEY. However, the granite is laced with loose pegmatite bands, and route-finding is serious. Initial development was by the San Juan Mountaineers in the 1930s, but it was Layton KOR with a host of partners in the 1960s who pioneered some dozen difficult mixed free and aid routes, such as Green Slab. On the imposing Painted Wall—the area's largest—a major grade VI aid route, was climbed by Bill Forrest and

Kris Walker in 1973, then FREE-CLIMBED in 27 PITCHES at 5.11d in 1984 by Randy LEAVITT and Leonard Coyne. They reclimbed the route in a day and renamed it Stratosfear. Other big wall routes appeared in the canyon during the 1980s, such as The Hallucinogin Wall, VI 5.11 A5. Most attention today centers on the long free routes and solid and accessible rock of North Chasm View Wall. Weather in the Black Canyon can be unpredictable and cold in spring, and sweltering in summer.
Guidebooks: Leonard Coyne and Webster, ed, "The Rock and Ice Guide: The Black," *Rock and Ice Magazine #20*, 1987; John Harlin, *Rocky Mountains Rock Climbs* (1985).

BLACKCHURCH (Britain) Blackchurch is part of the dramatic and remote Culm Coast, so called because of the geological formations or "culms" (towers) that project from the sea. While the CRAGS are loose in their natural state, cleaning has made them sound. Blackchurch lies a mile from the fishing village of Clovelly. Classic routes include Mick Fowler's Rude Nude (5.10b) from 1983, and Pete Whillance's 1978 route Godspell (5.11a), the best and boldest route on the crag. Pat LITTLEJOHN, who appears in the new routes lists of DEVON on a virtually continual basis, climbed the contrasting Sacré Coeur (5.10a) on Blackchurch Rock, a particularly dramatic culm. The routes on the main cliff have some dubious rock and reach up to 240 ft (73 m). PROTECTION is natural but sketchy.
Guidebooks: Pat Littlejohn, *South West Climbs* (1991); Iain Peters, *North Devon and Cornwall* (1988).

BLACK ICE Another name for VERGLAS.

BLANC, MONT See ALPS, MONT BLANC.

BLANCHARD, BARRY (1959–) (Canada) A leading Canadian alpinist throughout the 1980s who set Canadian standards in ICE CLIMBING, winter and summer ALPINISM and altitude climbing. In the early 1980s, he made the first one-day ascent of Polar Circus, a WINTER ASCENT of Grand Central Couloir on Mount KITCHENER, as well as hard climbs in Europe and Alaska (all in the company of Kevin Doyle). With David CHEESMOND he created perhaps the hardest alpine ROUTE in North America: the north pillar of NORTH TWIN (1985). Also significant in the Rockies are his new winter climbs on the north face of Howse Peak and east face of Mount Chephren. With Cheesmond he applied the lightweight alpinism they'd perfected in the ROCKY MOUNTAINS to the great ranges, climbing the north ridge of RAKAPOSHI (1984), in PAKISTAN, and later with ALPINE-STYLE tries for EVEREST and NANGA PARBAT.

BLEAKLOW AND KINDER SCOUT (Britain) The moors above Glossop and Hayfield in the PEAK DISTRICT are often buried in cloud, but the CRAGS on Kinder Scout, which lies between Edale to the south and the A57 to the north, and on Bleaklow, to the north again, offer uncrowded gritstone climbing of the highest quality in spells of good weather.

Guidebooks: British Mountain Club, *Kinder* (1990); Paul Nunn, *Rock Climbing in the Peak District* (1987).

BLUE SCAR (Britain) This crag, set in the countryside of Wharfedale just south of Arncliffe, holds some of BRITAIN's boldest limestone routes. Important climbs began appearing here in 1980 when Pete Gomersall climbed Central Wall (5.12a) and the serious Death Wish (5.13a), with its ground-fall potential from the crux at 75 ft (23 m). Two years later, after the memory of Death Wish had sufficiently faded, Gomersall added Hammerhead (5.12b) and The Great White (5.12b) and then in 1984 Blue Water White Death (5.12b). All these ROUTES are on immaculate rock and are in strong contrast to the steeper, bolted LINES found elsewhere in Yorkshire. PROTECTION is from small wires and PEGS. Routes on the central wall reach 120 ft (36 m).
Guidebook: Yorkshire Mountain Club, *Yorkshire Limestone* (1985).

BLUFF A CLIFF or OUTCROP, usually jutting out of a hillside.

BLUM, ARLENE (1945–) (United States) Expedition leader of the first American ascent of ANNAPURNA I (1978). Irene Miller and Vera Komarkova with two SHERPAS reached the summit, followed by Alison Chadwick-Onyszkiewicz and Vera Watson, who died on their way to the top. The expedition was funded in part by selling t-shirts with the slogan, "A Woman's Place Is on Top." She was born in Iowa and began climbing while at Reed College, OREGON. MOUNTAINEERING took her around the world with ascents in MEXICO (1965), PERU (1967), WADDINGTON in BRITISH COLUMBIA (1969) and an ascent of McKinley's west buttress (1970) with the first successful all-women's team. Following completion of her doctorate in biophysical chemistry at the University of California, Berkeley (1971), she organized a 15-month-long Endless Winter expedition (1971–1972) to climb peaks in Ethiopia, the RUWENZORI of Uganda, Kenya, Kashmir (making probable first ascents of Tuliyen, Brama and Vishnu), Afghanistan (including to 23,700 ft/7,226 m on Noshaq), and then crossing the Tesi Lapcha Pass in NEPAL. She reported this expedition in each of the six 1972 issues of *Summit* magazine. She then participated in trips to Peak Lenin in the Pamirs (1974), Trisul (1975), EVEREST (1976), and CHIMBORAZO and Cotopaxi in ECUADOR (1977). Following Annapurna she led a joint Indian-American women's expedition for the first ascent of Bhrigupanth (22,300 ft/6,799 m) in the GARWHAL HIMALAYA (1980). She left her career as a scientist in 1980 to pursue travel and business opportunities. She trekked the length of the HIMALAYA (1981–1982), the first American and first woman to do such a TRAVERSE. Her awards include the Society of Woman Geographers' Gold Medal for Outstanding Achievement (1984), Sierra Club's Francis Farquhar Award for Mountaineering (1982) and honorary memberships in the Appalachian Mountain Club (1984) and Mazamas (1988).

Further reading: Arlene Blum, *Annapurna, A Woman's Place* (1981).

BOARDMAN, PETER (1950–1982) (Britain) Leading British Himalayan climber of the 1970s. Discovery of his body in the remains of a camp on the northeast ridge of EVEREST in 1992 ended speculation about his and Joe TASKER's disappearance 10 years earlier. A gifted natural climber from his early teens, Boardman had completed an impressive list of climbs in the ALPS and HINDU KUSH before his invitation to join the 1975 expedition to the southwest face of Everest, the top of which he reached on the second summit bid. He climbed CHANGABANG (1976), KANGCHENJUNGA (1979), and made the FIRST ASCENT of the south summit of Gaurishankar, in NEPAL (1979). He rose through the ranks of British climbing, from instructor at Glenmore Lodge to National Officer of the British Mountaineering Council to Head of the International School of Mountaineering in Leysin. The role he and Tasker played in the promotion, both politically and by example, of the LIGHTWEIGHT EXPEDITION for high and difficult ROUTES was pivotal. The implicit risks of such ventures were only too well illustrated by their deaths.
Further reading: Peter Boardman, *The Shining Mountain* (1978); Boardman, *Sacred Summits* (1982).

BOARDMAN TASKER AWARD, THE Set up to commemorate Peter BOARDMAN and Joe TASKER, who died on EVEREST in 1982, the Boardman Tasker Prize for Mountaineering Literature is awarded annually at a ceremony held each autumn at the Alpine Club headquarters in London by a panel of three judges appointed to serve for two years by the award's trustees. It started off rather shakily in 1983, when none of the entrants were deemed of sufficient quality. It was shared between two books in 1984 (Scott and MacIntyre's *The Xixapangma Expedition* and Linda Gill's *Living High*), and in 1985 its first outright winner was *Menlove*, Jim Perrin's biography of Menlove EDWARDS. It has made some inspired choices, particularly with the two fiction winners, Mike Harrison's *Climbers* (1989) and Alison Fell's *Mer de Glace* (1991). On the whole, it has certainly encouraged interest in, and production of, climbing literature, and is currently worth about $2,250 to the winner. Entry is open to any book in English containing material published for the first time between the qualifying dates in the year of entry.

BODY BELAY Also, waist belay. A basic DYNAMIC BELAY technique in which the belayer wraps the ROPE around the back and hips. Falls are held by the friction of the rope around the body. See BELAYING TECHNIQUES for a complete discussion.

BOIVIN, JEAN-MARC (1951–1990) (France) Climber and pioneer of BASE-jumping in France, he died after BASE-jumping from Angel Falls in South America, for a French TV series called "Ushuaia." Another jumper had been injured, and when Boivin jumped to reach the stricken parachutist below, he struck the wall and trees and soon died of injuries. For over a decade he had been a talented alpinist and daredevil, setting many FIRST ASCENTS and first descents. He flew off K2 from 24,928 ft (7,600 m) in a hang glider during the French attempt on the south-southwest spur. In 1985 he flew off the summit of GASHERBRUM II. By PARAPENTE, he flew from EVEREST's summit in 1990. As an extreme skier he descended unlikely faces like Les DRU South Face, or the 65-degree Y Gully on AIGUILLE LES VERTE. He was also prolific with linkups. On the MATTERHORN, in a day, he soloed up the north face, skied down the east face, climbed up again by the normal route, then descended by hang glider. While Christophe PROFIT and Eric ESCOFFIER competed for the first winter solo of the "trilogy"—the linkup of the EIGER, GRAND JORASSES and Matterhorn—Boivin came along and scooped them by soloing not three, but four north faces in a row. He pioneered steep ice classics like the Dru Super Couloir and DROITES North Face. On rock, he established some 20 new rock routes in the MONT BLANC RANGE, and three on the Grand Capucin.

Further reading: Jean-Marc Boivin, *Trois Defis au Cervin; L'Abominable Homme des Glaces.*

BOLDNESS When applied to a climb, boldness describes a ROUTE that has scarce PROTECTION. A bold climber is one who has the confidence and technical skill to climb such routes.

BOLIVA The high desert of the 13,000-ft (3,963-m) Bolivian altiplano, around which the Bolivian ANDES rise, is sometimes called "The Tibet of the Americas." Bolivia contains three branches of the Andes—the Cordillera Apolobamba in the north, the CORDILLERA REAL, and in the south the Cordillera Quimsa Cruz. The Cordillera Real is Bolivia's highest and most extensive range, with six peaks above 19,680 ft (6,000 m), including popular peaks like Illimani (21,003 ft/6,402 m or 21,193 ft/6,460 m) and the easily accessible Huayna Potosi (19,973 ft/6,088 m), which lies close to the Bolivian capital, La Paz. Bolivia's highest peak is Sajama (21,423 ft/6,530 m), located 186 miles (298 km) southwest of La Paz, near the village of Sajama. This glaciated volcano presents an expeditionary objective, and is typically climbed by its south-southwest slopes. Like PERU, the dry season from May through August presents the best weather and alpine conditions for climbing in Bolivia.

Guidebooks: Michael Kelsey, *Climber's and Hiker's Guide to the World's Mountains* (3rd ed., 1990); R. Pecher and W. Schmiemann, *Southern Cordillera Real—A Guide for Mountaineers, Skiers, and Walkers* (1977).

BOLLARD A protrusion of rock, such as a knob or rock spike or HORN that can be slung as a runner or ANCHOR for a BELAY or RAPPEL. Care should be taken to ensure bollards are secure for upward-pulling forces as well as downward pulls, as an upward pull can lift a SLING from the bollard. Backing the bollard up with an opposing anchor can solve this problem. (See also ICE BOLLARD, SNOW BOLLARD.)

BOLT HANGER A metal structural member that is attached to a BOLT to allow a CARABINER to be clipped. (See BOLTS.)

BOLT LADDER A line of bolts, DOWELS or RIVETS drilled into a cliff to overcome crackless rock. In AID CLIMBING they are used to connect discontinuous crack systems, and are climbed by clipping ETRIERS from bolt to bolt, like a ladder. On FREE CLIMBS bolts provide PROTECTION only. The term is sometimes used derogatorily, indicating an unsightly overuse of bolts.

BOLTED CLIMB See EURO-STYLE.

BOLTS Industrial-strength masonry anchors placed in drilled holes and used as ANCHORS and PROTECTION on rock. Bolt diameters range from quarter-inch to half-inch (.64 to 1.27 cm), length from one-and-a-quarter inches to over three inches (3.18 to 7.62 cm). Bolting systems comprise bolts, HANGERS and drills. Drill bits must correspond to bolt diameter. Bolting systems specially designed for climbing include equipment by Metolius, Mountain High, and Hurricane Rock Drills in the United States, Mammut and Petzl in Europe.

Drills are divided into two classes: Hand drills are hand-held steel holders into which a drill bit is slotted. The unit is hammered and twisted by hand with each blow. Depending on rock hardness, it may take 10 minutes or hours to hand-drill a hole. The Mammut is an integrated bolt/drill self-driving system used in Europe. Power drills are portable battery-powered rotary hammers that drill a hole in seconds. Sport climbers use Bosch and Hilti drills for rappel bolting. Portable gasoline-powered drills are sometimes used.

Drill bits bore out the hole. Bits may be single-fluted, triple-fluted or without twists, and may have chisel-shaped or pointed tips. Experts feel two-fluted chisel tips drill faster.

Numerous bolts exist. Different systems work better in different rock. Split shank bolts of one-quarter- or five-sixteenths-inch (.64 to 1.28 cm) diameter are usually older (1960s vintage in the United States), weaker and seldom used on modern climbs. However they have the advantage of being light and quick to hand-drill, useful in alpine or remote settings. Sport climbers favor three-eighths and half-inch (1.1 to 1.27 cm) bolts, approximately 4,000 lbs (1,800 kg) strong. Fixed bolt anchors should be minimum three-eights inch (1.1 km). Stainless steel bolts resist corrosion.

Bolts are of three classes:

Hammer-in bolts are pounded into drilled holes. Rawl-drive industrial anchors (quarter- to three-eighths-inch diameter) have split-shank halves that compress, exerting an outward spring force against the surrounding hole. They are suitable for hard rock like granite but not for sandstone. Of the two types (button head and screw-top), the button head tests stronger. The quarter-inch Rawl drive was the staple of United States climbing for decades. When old quarter-inch bolts are encountered they should be treated with care, never re-hammered, and should be backed up with other protection, as over time they loosen and corrode. Wedge-anchors include a variety of industrial stud and self-driving anchors, hammered into a hole then tightened with a wrench. Strong three-eighths-inch (1.1 cm) bolts are common on sport climbs. Common machine bolts filed to a taper to plug a hole are common in Australia. Short unfiled machine bolts are used as RIVETS on AID CLIMBS. Half-inch (1.27 cm) angle pitons are sometimes hammered into three-eighths-inch (1.1 cm) holes in soft sandstone.

Torque bolts are placed in drilled holes, then tightened with a wrench to expand a sleeve or component in the bolt. Three-eighth- and half-inch (1.1 and 1.27 cm) torque bolts resist massive shear and pullout forces and are favored on sport climbs.

Glue-in bolts are threaded rods placed in oversize holes and glued with polyester resin. They are common on European sport climbs, strong and weather-resistant.

Hangers are stainless or chromolly steel plates fixed to a bolt. A hole or eye in the hanger is provided for clipping a CARABINER. Modern steel hangers are rated at strengths over 4,000 lbs (1,800 kg). Alloy hangers are weaker. Eye bolts or ring bolts are bolts with a welded eye or ring integral to the bolt shaft. Homemade mild steel hangers encountered on older climbs should be regarded as weak. Australian climbing uses a troublesome system of removable keyhole hangers, placed by the leader and retrieved by the second.

Placing safe bolts requires a knowledge of drilling technique. Rock that is fractured or too close to an edge should be avoided. Exfoliation flakes should be removed from a hole site by hammer taps. The hole must be drilled perpendicular to the rock. Angling a hole can break a drill bit and cause uneven torque on a bolt. Rock dust must be removed periodically to prevent the drill binding up. All bolts should be placed according to manufacturers' specifications. Even strong bolts are susceptible to fatigue from frequent loading, and should be inspected.

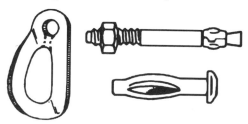

Bolts and Hanger

BOLT TO BOLT   The term used in SPORT CLIMBING to indicate a climber having climbed each move of a climb free, but used the BOLTS in place to rest between sections of the climb. Generally not considered a true FREE ASCENT.

BOMB-BAY   A gaping CHIMNEY that is flared downward, being wider at the bottom than at the top.

BOMBPROOF   Colloquial term meaning a very solid ANCHOR placement.

BONATTI, WALTER (1930–) (Italy) The leading personality in European MOUNTAINEERING for 20 years whose deeds influenced the shape of modern ALPINISM. Bonatti grew up in a working-class family during World War II, and his youth of hardship bred the determination and endurance that were the hallmarks of his climbing. In Europe his first ascents in the MONT BLANC area include the east face of Grand Capucin (1951); the southwest (Bonatti) pillar of the DRU (1955), soloed in six days; and in Switzerland the direct north face of MATTERHORN (1965), soloed in wintertime and after which he announced his retirement from mountaineering. Other noteworthy ascents in the Mont Blanc area include his three new routes on the Grand Piller d'Angle; Pilier Rouge de Brouillard; and the Whymper Spur on the GRANDES JORASSES. In the KARAKORAM his energy contributed to the successful Italian first ascent of K2 in 1953, though he missed the summit after enduring a forced BIVOUAC near the high camp. The FIRST ASCENT of GASHERBRUM IV in 1958, with Carlo Mauri, was perhaps the first "technical" route at high altitude. He also climbed peaks in the ANDES, like Cerro Moreno and Cerro Adele in PATAGONIA, and Rondoy Norte, Paria Norte and Ninashanca in PERU. Since 1965 he has worked as a photojournalist. His books translated into English are *On the Heights* (1964) and *The Great Days* (1974). Other works, in Italian, include *Ho vissuto con gli animali selvaggi* (1980); *Avventura* (1984); *Processo al K2* (1985); *La mia Patagonia* (1986); *Amazzonia* (1988); and *Un modo di Essere* (1989).

BONG   A large angle-type PITON (two to six inches/five to 15 cm wide) made from aluminum. It is named for the metallic sound it makes when hammered. Large CAMMING DEVICES have replaced bongs.

BONINGTON, CHRISTIAN (1934–) (Britain) The public face of British MOUNTAINEERING, Bonington's early career as a climber embraced new climbs in Snowdonia and middle-grade classics on the limestone CRAGS of Bristol's Avon Gorge. His reputation was firmly established by a series of climbs undertaken in company with Don WHILLANS in the late 1950s and early 1960s, when the latter was at the height of his powers. In the 1960s he produced some good par ascents in the LAKE DISTRICT. When the HIMALAYAS once again became open to climbers from other countries in the early 1970s, Bonington used his entrepreneurial skills to mount a series of major and heavily sponsored expeditions to venues such as the south face of ANNAPURNA (1970) and the southwest face of EVEREST (1975), both of these being successful, despite lives lost. In later years he adopted the "small expeditions" creed and managed more trips under this banner, chronicling them in a lengthy series of journalistic volumes. A certain ambivalence is often betrayed about him within the British climbing community, which may be nothing more than an aspect of that nation's habitual dislike of the winner.

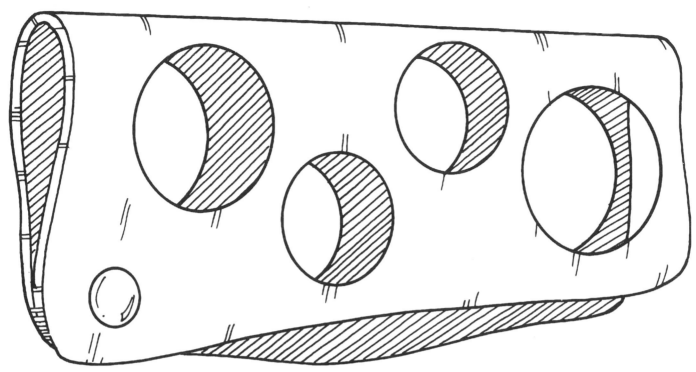

Bong Piton

Bonington's autobiography, *I Chose to Climb* (1966), is the first volume, and by far the best, in the author's ongoing chronicle of his life.

BOOT-AXE BELAY   Also called boot belay, foot brake. A quick, dynamic snow belay technique, not as failsafe as conventional belays but useful for holding a stumble on easy terrain or when other belays are not possible. Performed from a stamped-out platform, the ICE AXE shaft is jammed deeply in snow, perpendicular to the fall line. The belayer braces the uphill foot beside the axe, on its downhill side. The uphill hand holds the axe head. Running up from the belayed climber, the ROPE is arranged in an S shape, over the toe of the BOOT, around the ice axe shaft, then back around the boot instep. The downhill hand controls the rope. Pressure can be applied on the rope by pushing down on the axe and bringing the rope around the instep. (See also SNOW AND ICE BELAYS.)

BOOTS   See PLASTIC BOOTS, ROCK SHOES.

BORROWDALE   (Britain)   This beautiful wooded valley of The Lakes District runs south of Keswick and includes Derwent Water at its bottom. There are many CRAGS here, most close to the road, making the area especially popular. Campsites and facilities abound nearby.

Among Borrowdale's best crags is Upper Falcon, which lies above the southwestern tip of Derwent Water. On this is found a striking 5.10a corner climbed by Paul Ross in 1958, and the harder Dry Gasp, which climbs the wall to its left at 5.10d. Reecastle, near Watendlath village is a steep but short crag with a string of hard 5.12s, including

Torture Board, Remission and Grevious Bodily Arm. Black Crag, located in the tiny valley of Troutdale 20-minutes' walk from the road, has the Matheson and Cleasby 1976 classic Grand Alliance, a 230-ft (70-m) 5.10d.

On Great End Crag, is Nagasaki Grooves, a 5.11c ROPE-SOLOED by Pete LIVESEY in 1974. Goat Crag, located on the hillside southwest of Grange, has the area's best hard routes. Pete Botteril's Tumbleweed Connection (5.10b), Les Brown's 1965 classic Praying Mantis (5.8) and Livesey's Bitter Oasis (5.10d) from 1975 are milestone climbs. But the crag's most famous route is undoubtedly Footless Crow, a tremendous 180-ft (55-m) route up a steep, fingery wall that became even more fingery in 1990 after a crucial hold snapped. It now rates around 5.12d.

Guidebooks: Bill Birkett, et al, *Rock Climbing in the Lake District* (1986); FRCC, *Borrowdale* (1990).

BOSCH DRILL   Also, Bosch Bulldog (Bosch product #11213K). The 7.7-lb (3.47-kg) portable rotary hammer drill used by sport climbers for bolting. Its rechargeable 24-volt battery can drill eight to 12 holes up to half-inch (1.27-cm) diameter in granite, drilling a hole in less than a minute. (See BOLTS.)

BOSIGRAN   (Britain)   The romantic coastline of Bosigran, near St. Just, offers the finest granite cliffs in CORNWALL, usually without the problem of tides common to other sea crags. There is a Climbers' Club hut above the cliffs.

The principal areas at Bosigran are the main face and The Great Zawn. The former is more amenable and nontidal with a wide range of grades. Among the easier classics are Doorpost, an exceptional 5.6 climbed in 1955 by Peter Biven. His fierce Suicide Wall from 1955 ascends the main wall at 5.10a. Bow Wall passes through bristling OVER-HANGS at 5.10a and was put up by Joe BROWN in 1957. Another inspired operator here was Ed DRUMMOND who freed Biven's The Ghost with Tom Proctor in 1973 at 5.10d. Modern greats include the strenuous crackline Kafoozalem, freed at 5.11a by Jim Moran in 1974, and Pat LITTLEJOHN's Evil Eye, a 5.11 groove.

The Great Zawn is an intimidating yawn of rock. Its approach is awkward and the tide is often a problem. One outstanding route is the Dream/Liberator combination that follows an exposed ARETE at 5.10d. It was freed by Ron FAWCETT and Pete LIVESEY in 1976. The routes are generally two or three PITCHES and are rarely more than 200 ft (61 m) high.

Guidebooks: Des Hannigan, *Bosigran* (1991); Pat Littlejohn, *South West Climbs* (1991).

BOULDER (United States) Around the city of Boulder, COLORADO, lie many BOULDERING and rock-climbing areas. Certainly, the most important area is ELDORADO CANYON. BOULDER CANYON to the west is a well-developed granite area. Above Boulder lie sandstone formations like The Maiden, Fern Canyon and Bear Canyon, Green Mountain, Skunk Canyon and the FLATIRONS. Flagstaff Mountain offers richly developed bouldering and cragging on conglomerate sandstone formations.

Guidebooks: John Harlin, *Climber's Guide to North America: Rocky Mountain Rock Climbs* (2nd ed., 1991); Bob Horan, *Front Range Bouldering* (1990); Richard Rossiter, *Boulder Climbs North* (1990); Rossiter, *Boulder Climbs South* (1990).

BOULDER CANYON (United States) A granite canyon immediately west of BOULDER, COLORADO, offering highly developed roadside cragging with CRACK and FACE CLIMBS. Major formations in this 11-mile (18-km) canyon include Elephant Buttress, The Dome, Cob Rock, Boulder Falls and Castle Rock, which is a 250-ft (75-m) cliff.

Guidebook: Richard Rossiter, *Boulder Climbs North* (1988).

BOULDERING A facet of FREE CLIMBING in which short, technically difficult climbs are executed on small boulders or OUTCROPS. Though often just a few feet long, boulder problems can involve extremely difficult sequences that may require multiple attempts and falls before completion. Shorter problems are climbed unroped, longer problems may be TOP-ROPED. From the 1960s to 1970s, the American climber John Gill pushed limits of bouldering to extremes of technical finesse, strength, gymnastics and BOLDNESS. He developed the B1 to B3 bouldering RATING SYSTEM. Important U.S. bouldering areas include HORSETOOTH RESERVOIR (Colorado) and HUECO TANKS (Texas), and, in France, FONTAINEBLEAU.

BOWLINE A KNOT used to tie a loop in the end of a ROPE. Frequently used to tie the rope to a HARNESS.

BOW VALLEY CORRIDOR (Canada) This is the meandering river valley that leads from Lake Louise to Banff and east to the foothills of the Rockies, in ALBERTA, where three major FREE-CLIMBING areas are found: Grotto Canyon, Yamnuska and Lake Louise (Back of the Lake). The Bow Corridor has long been the crucible of Alberta rock climbing, both for long alpine rock routes and SPORT CLIMBS. Limestone mountains around Canmore, like Windtower, Mount Rundle, Mount Louis and Castle Mountain, provided Canadians with spectacular long alpine rock ROUTES, and desperate approaches. In the 1970s and 1980s the steep limestone wall of Yamnuska (Mount John Laurie) (7,850 ft/2,393 m) was developed. This 1,300-ft (396-m) south-facing "big wall" now has over 50 routes, many with aid, most of them committing in a MOUNTAINEERING sense. The cliff lies at the entrance to the Bow Valley. Pioneers of this area include Rockies stalwarts like Brian GREENWOOD, Don Vockeroth, Lloyd Mackay, Dave CHEESMOND, Brian Gross, Brian Wallace, Jeff Marshall and Steve Dimaio. Classic routes of Yamnuska include Red Shirt (5.6), Direttissima (5.7), Forbidden Corner (5.8), Kahl Wall (5.10) and CMC Wall (5.11). By 1984 the small crags at the foot of the Rockies drew attention, and the gray water-worn limestone of Grotto Canyon (6 miles/10 km east of Canmore) was one of the first to see the sport-climbing revolution, complete with local controversies over BOLTING and enhancement of holds. Grotto Canyon offers hard one-pitch free climbs in the modern European style. Other limestone cliffs around Canmore developed in the 1980s include the bulging walls of Carrot Creek, Barrier Mountain in the Kananaskis Valley to the southeast, and the cliffs of Cougar Creek. Simultaneously, quartzite in the picturesque setting of Lake Louise was opened up on the crag called "Back of the Lake." The steep, solid, pink and yellow quartzite is horizontally bedded and peppered with tiny HOLDS, offering both traditionally protected routes and fine sport climbs. The crag lies a short hike from the Banff Springs Hotel and is popular due to its ambience. Modern pioneers include Mark Deleeuw and Sean Dougherty. Barrier Mountain, in the Kananaskis Valley, is also a developing rock-climbing area.

Guidebooks: B. Howatt and C. Zacharias, *The Back of the Lake* (1987); Jon Martin, *Kananaskis Rock* (1989); Chris Perry, John Martin, Sean Dougherty, *Bow Valley Rock, Bow Valley Update* (1988, 1991); Murray Toft, *Banff Rock Climbs* (1985).

BOYSEN, MARTIN (1942–   ) (Britain) German-born Boysen's father, a musician and "intellectual" and therefore in all probability a critic of Hitler's, had been sent to fight on the Russian Front, was captured, spent several years in Soviet prisoner-of-war camps and did not rejoin his family until some years after the war ended. When Martin came to England, he spoke no English, and his nationality was not warmly regarded. Perhaps as a result of this, his childhood was solitary, and he spent much of it wandering the woods and hills of the Kentish Weald, discovering the sandstone OUTCROPS of the region and watching climbers on them. The first ROUTE he did was The Niblick at Harrison's Rocks, a technical and strenuous 5c (5.10) PITCH. After that he progressed rapidly to become perhaps the most precociously gifted technical climber of his generation, with an elegant style. He made many hard new climbs on the sandstone outcrops, which still maintain their reputation for difficulty even after 30 years. On his first visit to Wales he seconded Joe BROWN with ease on perhaps the most technical of his FIRST ASCENTS of the 1950s on CLOGWYN DU'R ARDDU—Woubits and in the 1960s proceeded to add great routes of his own throughout the British Isles. He also excelled in the ALPS, where he repeated many of the hard classics in fast times, FREE-CLIMBED the American Route on the south face of the Aiguille du Fou, and added several significant ascents of his own. He played an important support role on the 1970 ANNAPURNA south face expedition, but was defeated by the loss of a CRAMPON at the very top of the southwest face of EVEREST in 1975. Now a biology teacher in his fifties, he still climbs and puts out new routes to a very high standard in the purest style. (See also TRANGO TOWERS.)

BRAKE BAR The part of a rappel that produces friction, being a metal bar (or additional CARABINERS) fitted across carabiners. (See RAPPELLING.)

BRAZIL This South American nation has much rock climbing, from BIG WALLS to smaller SPORT CLIMBS. In the state of Rio de Janeiro, around the city of Rio lies the birthplace of Brazilian climbing, on the 984-ft (300-m) Sugar Loaf (which has a cable car to its summit) and some 30 similar granite DOMES that rise out of city dwellings and Guanabera Bay. The first ROUTES were done here in 1949. Brazilians are now climbing 5.13 on their cliffs. Visits by foreign climbers have implanted sport-climbing tactics in the Brazilian scene. The sport-climbing center of Rio City is a cliff called Morro da Babilonia. Outside the city lie 1,640-ft (500-m) domes, in the Jacarepagua district. The longest routes are up to 17 PITCHES and require two days to climb. Long adventure climbs lie in Petropolis (38 miles/60 km north of Rio), in Serra dos Orgaos National Park (63 miles/100 km north of Rio), around Friburgo and the Salinas Valley, and at Italtiaia National Park (156 miles/250 km south of Rio) where the rock is syenite. SEA CLIFFS are found around Buzios, in the north.

In the state of Minas Gerais (250 miles/400 km north from Rio) is a 230-ft (70-m) quartzite crag called Serra do Lenheiro that lies near the town of Sao Joao del Rey. Quartzite and marble has been climbed on at the massif around Serra do Cipo National Park (63 miles/100 km north of Belo Horizonte), and at Ouro Preto's popular quartzite spires. Pocketed limestone has been developed at Cerca Grande.

In the state of Espiritu Santo are climbable formations called "fingers."

In the state of Parana a granite range of peaks, Serra do Marumbi, near Curitiba (capital of Parana) offers climbs, while at Vila Velha, the rock is sandstone. The closest rock to Curitiba is a bouldering ground called Anhangava. The idyllic coastline of this state has sea cliffs at Ilha do Mel.

The state of Bahia is distant, yet has one of Brazil's finest areas, the quartzite massif in Chapada Diamantina National Park. This dry region is blessed with many crags to 984 ft (300 m).

Climbing is possible year round in Brazil, but the summer heat is oppressive. Due to the tropical climate the granite is often festooned with vegetation, yet established routes tend to be cleaned. Cleaning the routes is now known to harm fragile ecosystems of cliff-dwelling plants like bromeliads, and the practice has come under revision. Brazil has two clubs with mountaineering sections: Centro Excursionista Guanbara, Rua Washington Luiz 9/coberura, Lapa-Rio de Janeiro-RJ, 20230, Brazil, and Centro Excursionista Brasileiro, Av. Almirante Barroso 2/8 andar, Centro-Rio de Janeiro-RJ, 20031.

BREAKING TRAIL When moving through snow, the climber or skier who goes in front is breaking trail.

BREASHEARS, DAVID (1956–) (United States) As a teenager in BOULDER, COLORADO, Breashears appeared in 1975 as a gifted FREE CLIMBER dedicated to pure and TRADITIONAL rock-climbing ETHICS. His ascents in the Boulder area are many, but his ON-SIGHT FIRST ASCENT of the 5.11 vertical, 150-ft (46-m) unprotected FACE CLIMB Perilous Journey in ELDORADO CANYON (Colorado) was one of the major climbing achievements of the 1970s in the United States. His casual and rapid repeat of the ROUTE Kloberdanz (Eldorado Canyon) earned him the long-standing nickname "Kloberdanz Kid." A LEADER fall onto a ledge during a climb at Estes Park (Colorado) caused a hairline fracture in his spine and slowed his rock climbing, but he passed his recovery MOUNTAINEERING, which he quickly mastered. During the 1980s he climbed summits like Ama Dablam, a new ice route in winter on Kwangde, with Jeff LOWE (1983), and made two ascents of EVEREST. As a documentary cameraman for ABC Sports (United States) on his second Everest ascent he shot the first live video from Everest's summit. He has filmed other mountaineering, such as Catherine DESTIVELLE's ascent with Jeff Lowe of Nameless Tower (TRANGO TOWERS) via the Yugoslav route (1990).

BREGAGLIA (Switzerland, Italy) These sharp granite peaks on the Swiss-Italian border above the Val Bregaglia are extremely popular, because of Ricardo CASSIN's 1937 ROUTE UP the northeast face, achieved with considerable personal cost. Piz Badile is contained in the Sciora Cirque and to the east are two more, the Albigna and Forno Cirques, the latter containing the Cima di Rosso (11,040 ft/3,366 m). The biggest mountain in the area is Monte Disgrazia (12,064 ft/3,678 m), an impressive, almost savage-looking peak. Nearly all the approaches to its summit are difficult although Leslie Stephen, Edward Kennedy et al, found a straightforward though exposed route, called the Preda Rossa, to the summit in 1862. The north face of the mountain offers a fearsome prospect with excellent though demanding climbs.

BREATHABLE FABRICS A term for fabrics that make use of a semipermeable membrane that permits body moisture to pass outward, but prevents larger molecules of rain or snow from penetrating. These fabrics include Entrant, GORE-TEX and Versatech. (See WATERPROOF CLOTHING.)

BRECHE A French word meaning a gap or notch in a RIDGE.

BRIDESTONES (Britain) This collection of grit boulders or "kebs" thrown across the moors in the YORKSHIRE countryside lie above the A646 Burnley-Sowerby road. The rocks are around 12 to 24 ft (four to seven m) high.
Guidebook: Yorkshire Mountain Club, *Yorkshire Gritstone* (1989).

BRIDGING Another term for STEMMING.

BRIDWELL, JIM (1943–   ) (United States) John LONG wrote in *Mountain* magazine of this climber who epitomized the 1960s–1970s heyday of YOSEMITE, "Unlike many pontifical climbers who, having made their mark silently slip into history, Bridwell's initiative has redoubled with each new ROUTE. Indeed, he has maintained a level of motivation unmatched by any climber anywhere." Bridwell first climbed in Yosemite in 1962, with Chuck PRATT, Layton KOR, Frank Sacherer and Kim Schmitz. By the mid-1970s Bridwell was a moving force in FREE CLIMBING, especially long routes, and he enlisted young climbers—like Ron KAUK, John BACHAR and Mark Chapman—for free climbs like Nabisco Wall, Hot Line and Greek Towers, often inspiring them to produce the hardest leads. His article in *Mountain* from 1973, "Brave New World," helped define the direction of U.S. free climbing. Bridwell's forte though, was BIG WALL CLIMBING. He pushed standards with hooks, RURPS and COPPERHEADS to create, between 1975 and 1990, several of the finest A5 big wall climbs: Pacific Ocean Wall, Sea of Dreams, Zenyatta Mondatta on EL CAPITAN, The Big Chill on HALF DOME, with partners like Billy Westbay, Dale BARD and Peter Mayfield. His leadership of Yosemite climbing earned him the title of Admiral, or Commander. While he never turned his back on Yosemite, Bridwell moved toward alpine climbing after his one-day ascent of the Nose in 1975, with Long and Westbay. He made a rapid ascent (with Steve Brewer) of the Maestri Route on CERRO TORRE, becoming the first to summit the tower via Maestri's BOLTS. Later routes include big walls on KITCHATNA SPIRE (with Andy Embick), the MOOSES TOOTH (with Mugs STUMP) and Torre Egger in PATAGONIA. His climbing biography is *Jim Bridwell's Climbing Adventures: A Climber's Passion*, with Keith Peal (1993).

BRIMHAM ROCKS (Britain) This collection of boulder-sized grit OUTCROPS lies near the village of Summerbridge, a few miles northwest of Harrogate. Local theories explaining how these strange-shaped rocks were created include the idea that druids were responsible.

Allan Austin, Doug Verity, Joe "Morty" Smith, Joe BROWN and Dennis Gray established ROUTES here in the 1950s, as did the Barley brothers, Robin and Tony, in the 1960s. Hard climbing arrived in the 1970s, with classic routes like John Syrett's Brutalizer and Hank Pasquill's

Joker's Wall Arete (5.10d) and, later that decade, Jerry Peel's overhanging OFFWIDTH, Gigglin' Crack (5.12c).
Guidebook: Yorkshire Mountain Club, *Yorkshire Gritstone* (1989).

BRITAIN Rock climbing has been practiced in Britain for over a century. The range of climbing is huge, from short GRITSTONE OUTCROPS to towering SEA CLIFFS to long mountain routes to athletic limestone SPORT CLIMBS to winter ice. There are thousands of CRAGS in the United Kingdom, and many thousands of routes. Unlike that of European crags, protection in Britain tends to be naturally placed, with aging and suspect equipment frequently encountered, though sport climbing is popular in Britain too. Crags are often short, easily accessible by car, and with camping, pubs and sometimes climbing huts nearby where the subculture of British climbing has flowered.

For an overview of British climbing, see ALMSCLIFF; AVON; BAGGY POINT; BLACKCHURCH; BLEAKLOW AND KINDER SCOUT; BLUE SCAR; BORROWDALE; BOSIGRAN; BRIDESTONES; BRIMHAM ROCKS; CALEY; CARN GOWLA; CARN KENIDJACK; CASTLE ROCK OF TRIEMAIN; CHAIR LADDER; CHALK; CHEDDAR GORGE; CHEEDALE; CHEW VALLEY; CLOGWYN DU'R ARDDU; CORNWALL; CRATCLIFFE TOR; CURBAR EDGE; DEVON; DEWERSTONE, THE; DOVE CRAG; DOVEDALE; DOW CRAG; ESK BUTTRESS; EXMANSWORTHY CLIFF; FROGGATT EDGE; GABLE CRAG; GIMMER CRAG; GOGARTH; GORDALE SCAR; GRITSTONE; GURNARD'S HEAD; HAY TOR AND LOW MAN; HIGH TOR; ILKLEY; KILNSEY CRAG; LAKE DISTRICT; LAND'S END; LIZARD, THE; LLANBERIS PASS; LLANBERIS SLATE; LLIWEDD; LOWER SHARPNOSE; LUNDY; MALHAM COVE; MILLSTONE; NAPES, THE; NORTH WALES LIMESTONE; OGWEN AND CARNEDDAU; PAVEY ARK; PEAK DISTRICT; PEMBROKE; PENTIRE POINT; RAVEN CRAG; RAVEN TOR; SCAFELL CRAG; SCAFELL EAST BUTTRESS; SENNEN; STAFFORDSHIRE GRIT; STANAGE; STONEY MIDDLETON; SWANAGE; TINTAGEL HEAD; TORBAY; TREMADOG; WATER-CUM-JOLLY; WHITE GHYLL CRAG and YORKSHIRE.

BRITISH COLUMBIA (Canada) This mountainous province is home to all or part of eight major ranges—the COAST MOUNTAINS (see Mount WADDINGTON and WADDINGTON RANGE), Northern CASCADES, INTERIOR RANGES (see SELKIRK RANGE, Mount SIR DONALD, BUGABOO Mountains), ROCKY MOUNTAINS and SAINT ELIAS. The Coast Range also spills onto Vancouver Island, where seldom-visited peaks like Mount Colonel Foster offer large alpine faces. (See also DEVIL'S THUMB.) The city of Vancouver is British Columbia's center of MOUNTAINEERING. Other climbing centers are Golden, Field, Nelson and Revelstoke. Rock climbing is centered on SQUAMISH, and developing CRAGS like Penticton in eastern British Columbia. The oldest operating climbing club in the province is the British Columbia Mountaineering Club. The Alpine Club of Canada has chapters in Vancouver and on Vancouver Island. Kootenay Mountaineering Club in Nelson is also active. The Rogers Pass in the Selkirk Mountains is regarded as the birthplace of Canadian mountaineering. Most mountains and forests in British Columbia are unprotected and are being rapidly ravaged for their resources. Three general guidebooks serve the province: Dick Culbert's *Climber's Guide to the Coastal Ranges of British Columbia* (1965), his *Alpine Guide to SW British Columbia* (1974) and Bruce Fairley's *Guide to Climbing and Hiking in British Columbia* (1986).

BROAD PEAK (Pakistan) Rising above the KARAKORAM Range's Godwin Austen Glacier, the world's 12th highest mountain has three distinct summits: The southernmost main peak (26,402 ft/8,047 m); the central peak (26,247 ft/8,000 m); and the north peak (24,770 ft/7,550 m). British Explorer W. M. CONWAY named the mountain in 1892 for its elongated appearance. Phalchan Ri and Phalchan Kangri have been suggested as BALTI names but are not in use. For all its breadth, few ROUTES penetrate Broad Peak's formidable ice cliffs to its shattered metamorphic summit pyramids.

The FIRST ASCENT was in 1957, up the west spur above the Godwin Austen Glacier by an Austrian Alpine Club expedition of Marcus Schmuck, Fritz Winterstellar, Kurt DIEMBERGER and Hermann BUHL. This expedition was innovative, as neither supplemental oxygen or HIGH-ALTITUDE PORTERS were used. The climbers reached the false summit (26,361 ft/8,035 m), just 30 to 60 minutes before the main peak, on their first attempt. This summit is still the high point of many attempts. Several days later the Austrians returned and summited. Diemberger returned in 1984 at the age of 52 to make his second ascent of his route. He also accompanied Italian and Spanish attempts during the 1990s on the remote eastern faces in Xinjiang CHINA. Broad Peak has seen rapid ascents—16 hours from BASE CAMP to summit—by Krzystof Wielicki (Poland) in 1984, and by Benoit Chamoux (France) in 1986. The first woman's ascent (1983) was by Krystyna Palmowska (Poland).

Poles climbed the rocky central peak in 1975. They followed a more direct variation of the 1957 route to the 25,591-ft (7,802-m) COL between the main and central peaks. K. Glazek and J. Kulis reached the top, while B. Nowaczyk, M. Kesicki and A. Sikorski sheltered below the summit from a building storm. As they descended late in the day, a blizzard broke and they rappelled in darkness. The last man, Nowaczyk, fell down the east face taking the ROPES with him. Without ropes or shelter the others bivouacked on the col. At daybreak they fashioned a makeshift rope from SLINGS and HARNESSES and reached the heavily snowed western slopes. While descending, Sikorski, Kulis and Kesicki fell, and only Kulis survived. After a second night in the open, Kulis and Glazek descended the mountain, with severe FROSTBITE.

The north peak was climbed in 1983, by Renato CASAROTTO (Italy), who soloed the difficult north spur.

Broad Peak's last challenge was the 1.8-mile (3-km) TRAVERSE over all three summits. In 1984, between July 13 and 18, Wojciech KURTYKA and Jerzy KUKUCZKA completed this traverse, in ALPINE STYLE, beginning with the north face of the north peak, and descending the Austrian Route from the main summit.

Further reading: Greg Child, *Thin Air: Encounters in the Himalaya* (1990); Kurt Diemberger, *Summits and Secrets* (1991).

Broad Peak

BROOKS RANGE (United States) The most northerly of ALASKA's ranges, bounded by the Arctic plains on the north, CANADA to the east, and the Chukchi Sea to the west. The Brooks Range is the first geologic link in North America's Rocky Mountain chain. With the exception of the ARRIGETCH spires, there is little of technical interest to modern climbers, although the vast wilderness and abundant wildlife make the Brooks Range a unique destination. Its gentle rounded peaks contrast the higher, actively glaciated peaks in the ALASKA and SAINT ELIAS RANGES. However, one region known as the Romanzof Mountains, within the Arctic National Wildlife Refuge, is heavily glaciated. Mount Chamberlin (9,020 ft/2,750 m) is the Romanzof range's highest peak.

Further reading: Robert Marshall, *Arctic Wilderness* (1973).

BROWER, DAVID (1912–   ) (United States) Brower is best known as an environmentalist, and for his leadership of the Sierra Club, Friends of the Earth and Earth Island Institute. In his youth, he was an accomplished climber. In the 1930s, Brower lived in YOSEMITE and established 19 FIRST ASCENTS. In 1935, he climbed to the northwest summit of Mount WADDINGTON. Brower then made the first ascent of SHIPROCK—an 1,800-ft (549-m) tower in NEW MEXICO, which a 1939 climbing editor called "the finest thing ever done in rock climbing on our continent." Brower drilled the first expansion BOLTS (in the United States) on the climb, and 52 years later at a MOUNTAINEERING conference on North American climbing, he apologized for "being at the root of all this furor about bolting." His climbing life is included in his autobiography, *For Earth's Sake* (1990).

BROWN, BELMORE (1880–1954) (United States) Browne accompanied Frederick COOK during an attempt to climb DENALI in 1906. After Cook later claimed to have reached Denali's summit, Browne returned in 1910, found Cook's Fake Peak (5,360 ft/1,634 m) and took photographs that perfectly matched Cook's fraudulent "summit" photograph. Two years later, during a storm on the upper reaches of the Harper Glacier, Browne crawled on his hands and knees past his companions, but was forced to retreat within 100 ft (30 m) of Denali's summit. Several days later, while resting at BASE CAMP, the great earthquake of 1912 tore apart the upper mountain. Had they remained there, they surely would have perished in an AVALANCHE. During the next five years, Browne and Charles Sheldon did much work to establish Mount McKinley National Park. In Browne's later years, he became a nationally known landscape artist.

Further reading: Robert H. Bates, *Mountain Man; The Story of Belmore Browne* (1988); Belmore Browne, *The Conquest of McKinley* (1956).

BROWN, JOE (1930–) (Britain) The definitive British rock-climber. The seventh child of a poor Catholic family from Manchester during the great depression. His father died when he was eight months old and he grew up in a poor slum area. At the age of 12, he was exploring caves and mines. By his mid-teens he was climbing on the gritstone edges of Derbyshire. His ROUTES of the late 1940s on STANAGE, FROGGATT, Whimberry and elsewhere established a new order of technical difficulty for British climbing, and Brown became recognized as an authentic phenomenon. After a break for National Service between 1949 and 1951, the aura around his routes and the legend of a short, slight youth ascending with ease the past generations' impossible problems grew. In the early 1950s, he teamed up with Don WHILLANS, and reeled off a string of FIRST ASCENTS between 1952 and 1957 that rank among the great classics, particularly of Welsh rock: Cenotaph Corner, Cemetery Gates, Vember, Llithwrig, Octo, The Grooves and The Black Cleft. His gritstone climbs marked a formidable advance too, particularly in OFFWIDTH CRACK and ROOF-climbing, as typified by Right Eliminate on CURBAR EDGE, The Dangler on Stanage, The Overhanging Crack on Dovestones, Ramshaw Crack on the rocks of the same name and The Sloth at the Roaches. He also showed an early aptitude for MOUNTAINEERING in the ALPS and Greater Ranges: In 1955 he was first to climb KANCHENJUNGA, and the following year he made a bold ascent as part of a small expedition to MUZTAGH TOWER.

By the 1960s his interest had focused on technical masterpieces on the crags of Snowdonia—routes like Vector and Pellagra at Tremadog, Ferdinand on Clogwyn y Wenallt and Hardd on Carreg Hyll Drem. His pioneering interest reawakened in 1966 on the newly discovered SEA CLIFFS of Anglesey, where he made climbs like Mousetrap, Dinosaur, Primate, Winking Crack, Red Wall and Wendigo.

Further reading: Joe Brown, *The Hard Years* (1967).

BRUCE, GENERAL CHARLES GRANVILLE (1866–1939) (Britain) Charles Granville Bruce's career was defined by an association with the 5th Gurkha Rifles Regiment that began in 1889. He spent the closing decade of the 19th century fighting alongside the Gurkhas on the Northwest Frontier, distinguishing himself in the 1897 uprising and taking time off to join W. M. CONWAY's expedition to the Hispar and Biafo GLACIERS of 1892, and MUMMERY and COLLIE's expedition to NANGA PARBAT in

1895, on which the former was killed. Bruce himself accompanied LONGSTAFF to Trisul in 1907, and made plans to attempt EVEREST in 1907 and 1910, which were aborted for political reasons. He commanded his Gurkha regiment at Gallipoli in World War I, was severely wounded in the leg in 1915, and retired from the army with the rank of brigadier-general in 1920. Despite his age, he organized and led the British Everest expeditions of 1922 and 1924. Of great physical strength (to keep fit, he used to run up the foothills around the Khyber Pass carrying his orderly on his back) and a playful, gregarious nature, he had a deep sympathy with the native peoples of the HIMALAYAS, learned many of their dialects and, as his enduring contribution to mountain exploration, was first to recruit SHERPA tribesmen as HIGH-ALTITUDE PORTERS.

Further reading: Charles Granville Bruce, *Himalayan Wanderer* (1934).

BUCKET In FREE CLIMBING, a HOLD large enough to hang onto with the entire hand, incut like the lip of a bucket.

BUGABOOS, THE (Canada) These mountains are located in the Purcell Mountains of BRITISH COLUMBIA. They provide alpine rock-climbing on granite spires rising out of glacial ice on some of the best granite in Canada. Access is via a logging road from Brisco and a two-hour hike to the Conrad Kain Hut, which sleeps 50 people. Conrad KAIN visited the range in 1916, and climbed the 10,450-ft (3,186-m) Bugaboo Spire (Kain Route, 5.6), still a popular climb. Latter-day moderate classics include northeast RIDGE of Bugaboo Spire (IV 5.7), the southeast face (IV 5.7) of Snowpatch Spire (10,050 ft/3,064 m), and the superb Beckey-Chouinard Route (IV 5.10a) on the west face of South Howser Tower (11,150 ft/3,399 m). Fred BECKEY climbed the area's first grade V, the east face of Snowpatch Spire (5.9 A3) in 1959. Shortly after, Beckey and Yvon CHOUINARD made an ALPINE-STYLE ascent of the west BUTTRESS of South Howser Tower, an ascent that opened the way for many grade VI routes in the Bugaboos. FREE ASCENTS came in the 1980s, like the south face of Snowpatch Spire and east face of Bugaboo Spire (both V 5.11).

Guidebooks: J. F. Garden, *The Bugaboos: An Alpine History*; R. Green and J. Benson, *Bugaboo Rock, A Climber's Guide* (1990).

BUHL, HERMANN (1925–1957) (Austria) Though his life was brief, this climber from Innsbruck became a hero for generations of alpinists. A master on rock and ice, Buhl pioneered difficult ascents in the Eastern and Western Alps before World War II, such as the EIGER north face, the Watzmann east face in winter and a repeat of the Walker Spur of the GRANDES JORASSES. On July 3, 1953, he reached solo the summit of NANGA PARBAT, a FIRST ASCENT on this oft-tried 26,658-ft (8,125-m) KARAKORAM peak. His book *Nanga Parbat Pilgrimage* (1981, 1987) describes this legendary undertaking. In 1957, with Austrians K. DIEMBERGER, F. Winterstellar and M. Schmuck he climbed the first ascent of BROAD PEAK (26,402 ft/8,047 m), in PAKISTAN.

This ascent was without the usual help of HIGH-ALTITUDE PORTERS or OXYGEN APPARATUS, and with little FIXED ROPE. Buhl called this new lightweight approach *Westalpenstil*—literally "in the style of the Western Alps." It is from this term and that expedition's approach that the modern term ALPINE STYLE was derived. A few days after climbing Broad Peak, Buhl perished when a CORNICE broke while he attempted the first ascent, in pure alpine style with Diemberger, of Chogolisa (25,149 ft/7,665 m).

BUHLER, CARLOS PALTENGHE (1954–) **(United States)** This most accomplished of American Himalayan climbers has summited (26,240-ft/8,000-m) peaks like DHAULAGIRI, CHO OYO and KANCHENJUNGA with small teams without oxygen, and EVEREST, via the Kanshung Face (FIRST ASCENT) with oxygen. Otherwise, he has climbed new routes on Ama Dablam and Baruntse. In PERU, he has established new routes on the west face of Extremo Ausangate, Carhuaco Punco's west face and HUASCARAN Sur's northeast face.

BUILDERING A corruption of the word BOULDERING. Buildering describes climbing on buildings or manmade structures like brick walls as a form of training for rock climbing.

BULGE A rounded OVERHANG or ROOF.

BUOUX (France) This world-famous SPORT CLIMBING area lies in the hills of Luberon, 28 miles (45 km) southeast of Avignon. The limestone is extremely solid, riddled with POCKETS and notorious for BULGES. The texture is less abrasive than other French limestones, yet has excellent friction. Most cliffs face south and are well protected from the Mistral wind. Climbing is possible year-round though winters may be cold. ROUTES reach 328 ft (100 m) on the Pilier des Fourmis. *Moulinettes* (fixed ANCHORS) are common, though some routes require a 197-ft (60-m) ROPE to lower the LEADER off. Until 1980 Buoux was a backwater, but then it became known as the "Laboratory" of hard FREE CLIMBING when people realized that almost any square meter of rock—no matter how steep—was climbable thanks to numerous tiny pockets. Buoux offers the largest choice of extreme routes in France. Landmarks in the quest for new levels of difficulty are Polka des Ringards (7c), Elixir de Violence (8a), Chouca (8a +), Mains Sales (8b), La Rage de Vivre (8b +) and Le Minimum (8c). Famous less-extreme routes include La Beda, Pepsicomane and Buffet Froid (all in the 6 a/b range); T.C.F., Alertez les Bébés, Le Loir and Les Diamants (in the 6c to 7a range); and, one step harder, No Man's Land, Rose des Sables and Viol de Corbea.
Guidebook: D. Gorgeon, S. Javlin, A Lucchesi, *Escalade à Buoux.*

BUSH PILOTS (United States) These pilots of ALASKA and the Yukon are known for their daring in mountain rescues or while flying climbers to their objectives amid the glaciated ranges of the north. One of the earliest pilots, Bob Reeve, built his airplane's skis out of a bartop before flying Bob BATES and Brad WASHBURN into Mount Lucania in 1937. The most famous of all mountain bush pilots was Don Sheldon from Talkeetna, Alaska who, along with his Talkeetna competitor, bush pilot Cliff Hudson, performed innumerable rescues, mountain-climber flights and antics. There are a host of other well-known bush pilots who served or continue to serve climbers: Joe Crosson, Phil Upton, Jack Wilson, Lowell Thomas Jr., Jim Sharp, Cliff and his son Jay Hudson, Doug Geeting, Kittie Banner, Jim Okonek, Mike Ivers and Paul Claus.
Further reading: James Greiner, *Wager with the Wind: The Don Sheldon Story* (1982); John Krakauer, *Eiger Dreams; Ventures Among Men and Mountains* (1990).

BUTT BAG A BELAY SEAT.

BUTTERMILKS, THE (United States) These curiously egg-shaped coarse-grained granitic boulders and 1-pitch OUTCROPS dot the eastern escarpment of the SIERRA NEVADA in CALIFORNIA. Smoke Blanchard first climbed there in the 1940s, developing his "Obstacle Course" of boulder routes. Blanchard, Galen ROWELL, John Fischer, Allen Steck, Doug Robinson and others of a counter-culture group known as the Armadillos further developed the area during the 1960s and 1970s. Tim Harrison first climbed on the monolithic Peabody boulders in the early 1970s. Climbers continue to add new boulder problems of high difficulty. The name comes from a nearby homestead whose milk supposedly churned to buttermilk on the rough road to Bishop, which is some 10 miles (16 km) east.
Guidebook: Alan Bartlett and Errett Allen, *The Sierra Eastside* (1989).

C

CAGOULE A long WATERPROOF pullover outer garment with a hood, similar to an ANORAK. Popular for alpine BIVOUACS up to the 1960s, but less fashionable today.

CAIRN A pile of stones marking a trail or path, a landmark or a summit.

CAIRNGORMS, THE (Scotland) This is the second major mountain group in SCOTLAND and characteristically different from LOCHABER, 50 miles (80 km) to the west. The Cairngorms are split by the valley of Royal Deeside, which runs east to west and includes the village of Braemar. The northern Cairngorms are formed of a high mountain plateau, reaching over 4,000 ft (1,219 m), run through with deep glaciated valleys. The southern range is dominated by two peaks, Broadcairn and Lochnagar, the latter's northeast coire, or gully being especially popular in winter. The principal attraction, however, is the huge mass of Creag an Dubh Loch on Broadcairn.

Loch A'an or Loch Avon is located in the heart of the northern Cairngorms, surrounded by the peaks of Cairn Gorm, Ben Macdui, Cairn Lochan and Beinn Mheadhoin. Around the head of the lake are four cliffs, three of which are described here. Hell's Lum is on the southern flank of Cairn Lochan. The cliff is approached from Aviemore to the north. The principal feature on Hell's Lum is its front face, almost 500 ft (152 m) of clean granite, steepening at its top.

Shelter Stone Crag is a magnificent CRAG beneath Ben Macdui, opposite Hell's Lum. It offers some of the best climbing in Britain, with a wealth of hard routes in a remote setting. The rock is granite and the crag faces northeast, which, at its altitude of 2,000 ft (610 m), makes it a summer venue.

Creagan a'Choire Etchachan is a 350-ft (107-m) granite face on the eastern slopes of Creagan a'Choire Etchachan, to the north of Derry Cairngorm. Approaches can be made from Aviemore.

The southern Cairngorms are a great contrast to the bleak loneliness of the northern corries or gullies. To the south of Royal Deeside and its forests is the broad mass of Lochnagar. The crag is best approached from the Spittal of Glenmuick at the head of Glen Muick to the east of the mountain. Lochnagar is 700 ft (213 m) high and since the crag is at an altitude of some 3,000 ft (915 m) and faces northeast, one of its chief attractions is as a winter climbing

venue. There are a number of worthwhile summer routes, mostly in the easier grades.

Creag an Dubh Loch is another magnificent crag, up to 900 ft (274 m) high, on the northern slopes of Broadcairn. It is the biggest single FACE in the Cairngorms and comprises solid pink and gray granite. The Dubh Loch (black lake), as it is commonly known to climbers, is approached along the northern shore of Loch Muick to Glas-alt-Shiel.
Guidebooks: Donald Bennet, *The Munros* (1991); Allen Fyffe and Andy Nisbet, *Cairngorms* (1985/90); Kevin Howett, *Rock Climbing in Scotland* (1990).

CALANQUES (France) These limestone SEA CLIFFS stretch along the Mediterranean coast between Marseilles and Cassis. The fragrance of the pine trees, the tiny coves and the presence of the sea give the Calanques a unique flavor. From east to west one finds En Vau (reached from Cassis by boat or a one-hour hike), Candelle and Sugiton (near the University of Luminy), Morgiou (near Baumettes Prison), Sormiou (near La Cayde) and Les Goudes. The Calanques form a huge climbing area with 45 main cliffs and hundreds of ROUTES. Climbing is possible year-round. Routes range from one to six PITCHES, and vary in steepness and difficulty. Morgiou boasts SLAB routes and wild TRAVERSES above the water on Cap Norgiou. PROTECTION is a mix of BOLTS and old PITONS. Climbing began here in the 1940s with George Livanos and Gaston REBUFFAT among the pioneers, though the classic Arête de Marseilles on La Candelle was climbed in 1927. Today hard climbers are lured to new areas of the Calanques like the ROOF band of Sugiton. At En Vou famous routes in the 5b/5c category include Super Calanque, Eperon des Americains, Le Doigt de Dieu and Sirene Liotard. On the Candelle, Arête de Cassis (4c) is famous. Important routes at Sugiton include Extreme Onction (6c), Des Enfers Fabuleux (7a) and Le Bol des Sirenes (8a).
Guidebooks: *Sormiou; En Vau;* published by Edisud.

CALEY (Britain) This collection of grit boulders up to 40 ft (12 m) high has been highly developed, especially by boulderers from Leeds. The rocks are located two miles (three km) east of Otley on a steep hillside above the A660. This YORKSHIRE CRAG came into vogue in the mid-1970s. Important ROUTES include Alan Manson's High Noon (5.11a), Adrenalin Rush (5.12a) and Marrow Bone Jelly (5.13c), Ron FAWCETT's Psycho (5.11d) and Craig Smith's Great Flake (5.12a).

Guidebook: Yorkshire Mountain Club, *Yorkshire Gritstone* (1989).

CALHOUN, KITTY (1960–) (United States) With ascents of DHAULAGIRI and MAKALU, Calhoun is America's most respected female Himalayan climber. She was born in South Carolina and started climbing and skiing while attending college in New England. She later moved on to winter climbs in the Rockies of COLORADO and WYOMING and started guiding. On her first trip to the HIMALAYA with Andy Selters in 1986, Calhoun attempted the north face of Thalay Sagar (India) but bad weather forced an eight-day stay in a PORTA-LEDGE before an epic retreat. In 1987 she and now husband Colin Grissom, and John Culberson climbed Dhaulagiri's northeast ridge, despite an AVALANCHE accident. In the spring of 1990 she and John Schutt completed Makalu's west pillar.

CALIFORNIA (United States) See JOSHUA TREE, SEQUOIA-KINGS CANYON NATIONAL PARK, SHASTA, SIERRA NEVADA, TUOLUMNE MEADOWS, YOSEMITE VALLEY.

CAMALOT This SPRING-LOADED CAMMING DEVICE is manufactured by Black Diamond, United States (formerly Chouinard Equipment). Its cams are fitted to double-axles, making it unique from other SLCDs. Like FRIENDS, camalots fit flared and parallel sided CRACKS.

CAMMING DEVICE A piece of climbing equipment that locks into a CRACK by means of one or more metal cams. They may be passive cams with nonmoving parts (HEXENTRICS, TRI-CAMS), or active cams with movable cams mounted on an axle and adjusted to CRACK size by means of a trigger (FRIENDS, TCUS and CAMALOTS). The latter are called SPRING-LOADED CAMMING DEVICES (SLCD), and have the advantage of fitting a range of crack sizes in parallel and flared placements.

CAMP FOUR The famous campground in YOSEMITE VALLEY (CALIFORNIA) where climbers traditionally have camped since the 1950s is now called Sunnyside. The term Camp Four has entered American climbing jargon to describe a gathering of climbers living together.

CANADA Approximately 1 million square miles (1,609,000 sq km) of peaks, passes, GLACIERS, ICE FIELDS and alpine terrain cover the Canadian provinces of BRITISH COLUMBIA, ALBERTA, QUEBEC, ONTARIO and the Yukon and Northwest Territories. Terrain and climbing opportunities range from roadside cragging to wilderness expedition MOUNTAINEERING. Factors of Canadian mountaineering include frigid winters, possible encounters with dangerous animals like bears and difficult access. Canadian climbing sprang from British and American alpinists with European clients who climbed big, easy peaks in the 1880s, and who were aided by the westward expansion of the Canadian Pacific Railway (1884) into the ROCKY MOUNTAINS. The Alpine Club of Canada (Box 1026, Banff, Alberta, TOL OCO) formed in 1906 and today operates eighteen moun-

tain huts, a clubhouse in Canmore and an alpine center at Lake Louise. Other important clubs include Federation Québecois de la Montagne (4545 Ave Pierre de Coubertin, C.P. 1000, Succursale M, Montreal, Quebec, HIV 3RZ); Federation of Mountain Clubs of British Columbia (#336, 1367 West Broadway, Vancouver, BC); Association of Canadian Mountain Guides (Box 1537, Banff, Alberta, TOL OCO). Eastern Canada enjoys easy access to large peaks, little snow, ICE CLIMBING from December through March, and fairly dry summers from May through September. Western Canada is warmer, with higher rainfall and often difficult access. Alberta's Rocky Mountains (see Mounts ALBERTA, ASSINIBOINE, CANADIAN WATERFALL ICE CLIMBING, COLUMBIA ICE FIELDS, EDITH CAVELL, KITCHENER, NORTH TWIN, ROBSON, TEMPLE), are well known to climbers and have been explored for over 100 years, but most of these mountains have rarely felt the foot of man (see SELKIRK RANGE, Mount SIR DONALD). Alberta has also developed rock climbing (see BOW VALLEY). In the Yukon and Northwest Territories the SAINT ELIAS Range offers a wilderness of ice while the CIRQUE OF THE UNCLIMBABLES and BAFFIN ISLAND offer BIG WALL granite. In British Columbia the COAST MOUNTAINS (see WADDINGTON RANGE, Mount WADDINGTON) are in wilderness areas though accessible technical climbing is found in the BUGABOO Range and SQUAMISH. See also INTERIOR RANGES and DEVIL'S THUMB. In Eastern Canada, the Torngats in Labrador, and the huge walls of the Long Range on Newfoundland's west coast are largely unexplored, while rock climbing and ice climbing in Quebec and Ontario are well developed.

Further reading: Randy Morse, *The Mountains of Canada* (1978).

CANADIAN ROCKIES See ROCKY MOUNTAINS (Canada).

CANADIAN WATERFALL ICE CLIMBING The ROCKY MOUNTAINS of Western CANADA (ALBERTA) are the birthplace of waterfall climbing, a sport that reached its 25th anniversary in 1990. Mountains around Banff and Jasper, with their giant walls and abundant flow of water combined with cold Canadian winters, produce thousands of frozen climbs, some 3,280 ft (1,000 m) long. Many are close to the Ice Fields Parkway highway. In the early 1970s when Hamish MACINNES's terradactyl ICE TOOLS reached Canada, climbers like Bugs McKeith, Rob Wood and Tim Auger (all British) tackled the region's abundant ice, beginning in the winter of 1972–73. Ascents of Rogan's Gully (grade 2) and Bow Falls (grade 3) paved the way for harder routes like Borgeau Right-hand (grade 4). AID CLIMBING by attaching SLINGS to terradactyls (devised by McKeith) led to the first grade-6 routes. Grade-5 routes like Weeping Wall (in Banff), Pilsner Pillar and Carlsberg Column (in Yoho Park), and grade 6 routes like Takakaw Falls (Yoho Park), Borgeau Left-hand (Banff) and Nemesis (Kootenay Park), were first climbed on aid, but have since been freed. It is not unheard of, especially in Jasper, for the temperature to plunge to −58 degrees F (−50 degrees C), with lows hovering at −4 degrees F to −22 degrees F

(−20 degrees C to −30 degrees C) for a week or more. The Alpine Club of Canada's clubhouse in Canmore and youth hostels in Banff and Jasper provide accommodation to shelter ice climbers during 16-hour nights. In recent years most of the waterfalls beside the highways have been climbed, leading to the development of backcountry ice combined with ski touring. Thin ice smears and drips that form below SERACS and ICE CAPS, like the Columbia Ice Field, led to spectacular yet potentially suicidal grade seven climbs during the 1980s, like American Marc Twight's Reality Bath, and Riptide by Jeff Marshall and Larry Ostrander. Of the ice cap run-off formations, Slipstream (VI grade 4) on the east face of Snowdome is immensely popular, as is Polar Circus (grade 6). Ice climbing in the Ghost River Valley is also significant.

Climbers must assess cold, length of climbs and objective hazards like AVALANCHE, technical grades and difficulty of descent whenever contemplating any ice routes.

QUEBEC also is noted for waterfall ice climbing. In the Malbaie region, the Pomme d'Or is a classic grade 5 and Mont Morency Falls near Quebec City is popular.
Guidebook: Albi Sole, *Waterfall Ice* (2nd ed., 1988).

CANNON CLIFF　(United States) This granite cliff in NEW HAMPSHIRE is a 1,000-ft (300-m) exfoliated SLAB that lies 45 miles (72 km) east of North Conway in the alpine setting of White Mountains National Forest. The cliff is a mile and a half (2 1/2 km) wide and its main feature is a sharp RIDGE. This, the Whitney-Gilman Ridge (5.8), was climbed without protection by the 1929 first ascensionists. The central Big Wall Section, is a steep slab sporting locally famed routes like VMC Direct (5.11), Labyrinth Wall (5.11), Moby Grape (5.8) and Vertigo (5.9 A0). Historic routes of the Cannon Slabs are Lakeview (5.5), Consolation Prize (5.8) and the Wiessner Corner (5.5), which dates back to Fritz WIESSNER and Robert UNDERHILL, in 1933. Spring through fall are the prime climbing months here.
Guidebook: Ed Webster, *Rock Climbs in the White Mountains of New Hampshire* (1987).

CANYONLANDS　(United States) See COLORADO PLATEAU.

CAPSULE STYLE A style of expedition MOUNTAINEERING (usually used in the HIMALAYA), capsule style makes progress by leap-frogging a single camp or pair of camps up a mountain. First, FIXED ROPE is pushed up the mountain to a suitable campsite. This camp is supplied and occupied and the fixed rope is removed, brought up and pushed ahead until a second campsite is found. The first camp is then dismantled to make the second campsite, and the rope is again pushed ahead. The process continues until the summit is within reach.

Although capsule style uses less ROPE and equipment than heavier expedition styles, it requires a similar expenditure of energy to seige style. Also, on extremely high peaks it commits climbers to spending much time at altitude without a way down. Consequently it is seldom used. However, capsule style has been used successfully on small

peaks of considerable technical difficulty. Capsule style originated during the 1970s. (See ALPINE STYLE, LIGHTWEIGHT EXPEDITION.)

CARABINER Also karabiner, biner. A carabiner is a lightweight aluminum alloy (early carabiners were steel) snaplink with a spring-gate. Essential for many climbing procedures, carabiners are used to clip climbers to BELAYS and ANCHORS, to clip ROPES to PROTECTION, and to suspend climbers from DIRECT AID points. Several shapes and weights are used. They are strong, with breaking strengths of 3,500 to 5,000 pounds (1,575 to 2,250 kg). Locking carabiners, used for belaying and RAPPELLING, have a screw-sleeve that locks the gate shut. The German rock climber Otto Herzog is credited with making the first climbing carabiner in 1910, adapting them from firemen's *karabiners*.

Carabiners

CARN GOWLA　(Britain) These extensive and serious Cornish SEA CLIFFS are located one mile (1.6 km) west of the village of St. Agnes and close to St. Agnes Head, just off the A30 between Bodmin and Redruth. Carn Gowla includes the crags America Buttress, Red Walls, Baptist Cliff and Triple Buttress.

America Buttress holds three fine LINES, Pat LITTLEJOHN's 1973 classic America (5.11a); the more demanding Guernica, a 5.12d wall that he climbed in 1987; and Mausoleum (5.10c), which takes a striking corner and was climbed by Keith Darbyshire and Littlejohn in 1973. On the Baptist Cliff are two ROUTES that typify the area's atmosphere: Rowland Edwards's 1985 route Crystal Voyage, an exposed and remote 5.9, and the huge arch of Mercury, a sobering line that follows a huge groove and is approached by ABSEILS to an inescapable position, especially when the sea is high. Littlejohn's 1974 classic is 5.9. Carn Gowla contains a variety of good rock. Routes can reach 300 ft (91 m).
Guidebooks: Pat Littlejohn, *South West Climbs* (1991); Iain Peters, *North Devon and Cornwall* (1988).

CARN KENIDJACK　(Britain) This 150-foot (46-m) Cornish CRAG near St. Just, beneath the site of a pre-Roman fort, is a SLAB of killas slate. The most popular LINE is Saxon, a sustained 5.8 climbed by Pat LITTLEJOHN in 1974. In great contrast to the delicate slab routes is Stormbringer, a steep 5.10c at the back of the ZAWN climbed in 1979 by Rowland Edwards.
Guidebooks: Des Hannigan, *Bosigran* (1991); Pat Littlejohn, *South West Climbs* (1991).

CARRIGAN, KIM (1958–) (Australia) Carrigan heralded the modern wave of extreme FREE CLIMBING in AUSTRALIA and the world in the late 1970s, and was among the earliest of the world's globetrotting SPORT CLIMBERS, repeating and establishing hard routes across the United States and Europe. His finest contributions came between 1978 and 1984 at Mount ARAPILES (Australia), where he systematically freed most of the AID routes on this cliff and added several hundred new routes. At Arapiles, he opened Australia's first grade 26, Procul Harum; then extended the rating system with the first 27, Denim; the first 28, Yesterday; the first 29, India (named by a local climber who, astounded that Carrigan was contemplating free climbing this overhanging wall, commented wryly that the climber, like the nation India, could not exist without aid); and the first 30, Masada. He also opened long routes across the world, such as the Swiss alpine rock route Kein Wasser, Kein Mond, 5.13b, which he established while working for the Swiss rope manufacturer Arova Mammut.

CARSTENZ PYRAMID (Irian Jaya) At 16,503 ft/5,030 m (or, on some maps, 16,023 ft/4,884 m) this peak is the highest point in Australasia. It is also called Puncak Jaya in Indonesian. Irian Jaya was formerly called Dutch New Guinea. This giant rock flake of prickly limestone is a glaciated massif rising out of the equatorial forests of the Sudirman Range. Some regard it as one of the SEVEN SUMMITS (the highest point on each continental land mass), but others hold that Mount Kosciusko (AUSTRALIA) is Australasia's (or Oceania's) legitimate high point. Difficulties in obtaining permission from Indonesian authorities for this peak, sporadic Papuan nationalist rebel uprisings and travel restrictions imposed by local mining operations make expeditions to this region infrequent. Typically, expeditions fly to Illagu, a village populated by the primitive Dani tribe who were until recently reputed to be cannibals. Dani porters are used to reach a BASE CAMP at 14,500 ft (4,420 m) beneath the north face, above which lie the 31 summits of Carstenz Pyramid. The FIRST ASCENT was in 1963 by a party led by Heinrich HARRER. His book *I Come from the Stone Age* (1964) describes the first ascent, and Peter BOARDMAN's *Sacred Summits, A Climber's Year* (1982) recounts a more recent EXPEDITION. In 1981 an American expedition climbed a direct rock route on the 3,000-ft (915-m) north face. The easiest routes lie on the south face. The dry season lasts from May to November.
Guidebook: Joe Kelsey, *Guidebook to the World's Mountains*, (3rd ed., 1990).

CARTER, H. ADAMS (1914–1995) (United States) A veteran of three dozen EXPEDITIONS to formerly unexplored mountain regions of South America, the HIMALAYA and ALASKA, Carter made the FIRST ASCENT of Mount Crillon in Alaska in 1934. In 1936, he accompanied the team that first climbed India's NANDA DEVI. From Milton, Massachusetts, Carter is best known for his skillful editorship (since 1959) of AMERICAN ALPINE JOURNAL, the most respected annual climbing publication in the world.

CARTER, HARVEY THORTON (1930–) (United States) Noted desert climber famous for his climbs on the COLORADO PLATEAU.

CASAROTTO, RENATO (1948–1986) (Italy) One of the most accomplished soloists of technical mountains, Casarotto began climbing in 1968 while in the alpine regiment of the Italian military. From 1974 into the 1980s he made ROPED-SOLO ascents of many ROUTES in the DOLOMITES: the Simon-Rossi route on the north face of Monte Pelmo (winter), the Andre-Fae route on Punta Civetta (winter), a new route on the Spiz del Lagunaza in the Pale di San Lucano, and the Fachiri route on Cima Scotoni, and the Cozzolino Diedre of the Piccolo Mangart di Coritenza (winter). On these steep routes he refined his strategy of self-BELAYING, fixing rope and load hauling that he used on his ascents in the ANDES and the HIMALAYA.

In the Peruvian Andes in 1976, while climbing with others on a new route on the south face of Huandoy South he saw the imposing cliffs of the north face of HUASCARAN. In 1977 he returned and climbed it during a 17-day solo push, hugging the repulsive overhanging middle section because it offered the only protection from falling debris. In 1979 he soloed the north pillar of FITZROY, which he named the Goretta Pillar, after his wife who accompanied him on every expedition. Outstanding among his many ascents in Europe during the 1980s is his 15-day ENCHAINMENT in the ALPS of the Ratti-Vitale route on the Aiguille Noire, the Gervasutti-Boccalatte on the Gugliermina and the central pillar of Freney (1982).

By 1982 he quit his job as a nurse to become a professional climber. That year he attempted the unclimbed north ridge of BROAD PEAK (PAKISTAN), completing the route on a seven-day push on a second expedition the next year. In 1985, again in Pakistan, he and Goretta climbed GASHERBRUM II, on which Goretta set an altitude record for Italian women. In 1984 he soloed the FIRST ASCENT of the southeast ridge of DENALI. In 1986 he tackled one of the hardest routes anywhere: the then-unclimbed south-southwest pillar of K2. Casarotto had attempted K2 in 1979 on Reinhold MESSNER's EXPEDITION, but in 1986 he climbed solo on the world's second-highest peak. After several attempts on which he reached 27,250 ft (8,175 m) he turned back. At the foot of the mountain, a short distance from base camp, he fell into a CREVASSE. He died of internal injuries shortly after being rescued.

CASCADE RANGE (United States) The dominant mountain chain of WASHINGTON and OREGON, it was so-named by explorers in the early 1800s because the Columbia River formed a cascade where it cut through this range. The Cascades comprise hundreds of peaks, some ice-clad volcanos and hundreds of GLACIERS. The range extends from near Lassen peak in the south into BRITISH COLUMBIA where the Fraser River divides the Cascades from the COAST RANGE. The east limit is at the Columbia and Okanaogan rivers. Puget Sound, around which Seattle is built, forms the west boundary. The North Cascades Range is north of Stevens Pass or Snoqualmie Pass.

The Cascades present a rugged array of jagged peaks in a wilderness setting, with many objectives for mountaineers. Main valley floors are typically around 3,000 ft (915 m), with great rises to summits. From the summit of Bonanza Peak to Lake Chelan beneath it is a drop of 8,430 ft (2,570 m). Rainfall is high, at 150 inches (381 cm) per year on the western slopes, and snowfall in winter can be heavy. July and August are the driest months. Glaciers comprise a major feature in this range, one estimate giving Washington 77% of the glaciers in the United States outside of ALASKA. The highest peak is the volcano Mount RAINIER (14,411 ft/4,394 m). Other major volcanoes include Mounts SAINT HELENS and HOOD. Challenging peaks are SHUKSAN, LIBERTY BELL, SLESSE and STUART. A major player whose name appears everywhere in Cascade guidebooks is Fred BECKEY.

Guidebooks: Fred Beckey, *Cascade Alpine Guide*, Vol. I, II, III.

CASSIN, RICCARDO (1990–   ) (Italy) One of Italy's most distinguished alpinists, Cassin was born in Friul, a poor region of Italy. He started climbing in his youth around Lecco, on the limestone of the Grigna. Learning the use of PITONS from Emilio Comici, Cassin established new ROUTES in the DOLOMITES like the southeast face of Cima Piccolissima di Lavaredo, the north spur of Cimone della Bagozza, the southwest spur di Torre Trieste and the north face of the Cima Ovest di Lavaredo (1934 and 1935). He solved two "great problems" in the Alps: the northeast face of the Piz Badile (1937, with Ratti and Esposito), and the Walker Spur of the GRANDES JORASSES (1938, with Esposito and Tizzoni). In 1957, he lead the Italian EXPEDITION to GASHERBRUM IV that placed W. BONATTI and C. Mauri on the summit. In 1961 he and his whole party climbed to the top of DENALI along the south ridge, which is now called the Cassin Ridge. After leading two ambitious attempts to the west face of Jirishanca in the Peruvian ANDES (1969) and to the south face of LHOTSE in NEPAL (1975), Cassin retired from extreme alpinism. In 1985, at the age of 78 he celebrated the 50th anniversary of his FIRST ASCENT on the northeast face of Piz Badile by climbing it again. Cassin narrated his experiences in four books: *Dove la Parete Strapiomba; La Sud del McKinley; Lhotse '75;* and *Cinquant'anni di Alpinismo,* translated into English as *50 Years of Alpinism.* His biography is *Cassin—Il etait une foix le sixième degré,* by Georges Livanos (1983).

CASTLE ROCK OF TRIEMAIN (Britain) This CRAG lies at the northern end of Thirlmere, a few miles southeast of Keswick, and offers excellent steep climbing at an amenable grade. Camping is available at Dale Bottom, a small village on the A591 between Keswick and Thirlmere.

Overhanging Bastion is rated among the best 5.7s in the LAKE DISTRICT. It was climbed in 1939 by Jim Birkett. After the war Birkett added Harlot Face at 5.9, a steep and fingery face ROUTE, and Paul Ross climbed Thirlmere Eliminate, also 5.9. North Crag Eliminate (5.9), climbed in 1952 by Harold Drasdo and Dennis Gray, is Castle Rock's most

famous route, having been included in Ken Wilson's book, *Hard Rock.*

Across the valley on the eastern side is Raven Crag, a common name in the Lakes, which has one or two outstanding hard routes through some very steep territory. Chris BONINGTON's 1964 classic Totalitarian (5.10c) and Martin BOYSEN's Medlar (5.10d) are two of the older LINES, but The Gates of Delirium, which climbs through an obvious cave, is the best at 5.11d.

Guidebooks: Bill Birkett, et al, *Rock Climbing in the Lake District* (1986); FRCC, *Buttermere and Eastern Crags* (1987).

CASTLETON TOWER (United States) A famous 500-ft (152-m) spire on the COLORADO PLATEAU that was climbed by Layton KOR and Huntley Ingalls in 1961. Formerly known as Castle Rock.

CATHEDRAL LEDGE (United States) Located in the Mount WASHINGTON valley, near North Conway in the White Mountains, this 450-foot (137-m) cliff is the centerpiece of NEW HAMPSHIRE climbing. The well-featured granite of this cliff led it to become a focal point for the best northeast FREE CLIMBERS in the 1970s and 1980s, though British expatriate John Turner's Recompense (5.9), from 1959, was a landmark. The 1970s ROUTES include Women in Love (5.11+) by Henry BARBER and Ed WEBSTER in 1978; The Prow (5.11+), Paul Ross's route, freed by Jim Dunn and Jay Wilson in 1977; and Stage Fright (5.12+), a very dangerous lead of Hugh HERR's in 1985. Jimmy Surette brought 5.13 to New Hampshire in 1897 when he climbed the rather bold Liquid Sky (5.13b). Alongside Cathedral Ledge is a granite SLAB called Whitehorse. Here, hard friction routes coexist with easier classics like Children's Crusade (5.8), which follows a dike. Spring through fall are the best seasons here. In winter ice routes form on sections of the walls.

Guidebook: Ed Webster, *Rock Climbs in the White Mountains of New Hampshire* (1986).

CATHEDRAL RANGE (United States) Another name for the KICHATNA SPIRES in the southwest tip of the ALASKA RANGE.

CEILING The smooth underside of a ROOF or OVERHANG.

CENTRAL HIGHLANDS (Scotland) A general heading for areas near Fort William or the CAIRNGORMS. Creag Dubh is a broad mass a few miles west of Newtonmore. The rock is compact mica-schist and protection is often well spaced, providing some of the boldest ROUTES in Scotland. Craig-a-Barns is a group of mica-schist CRAGS above the village of Dunkeld. Here, Cave Crag has become a favorite with young Scottish sport climbers.

Guidebooks: Dave Cuthbertson, *Creagh Dubh and Craig-a-Barns* (1983); Kevin Howett, *Rock Climbing in Scotland* (1990).

CEREBRAL EDEMA (HACE) More correctly called High Altitude Cerebral Edema, this is the accumulation of fluid on the brain brought on by lack of oxygen at high altitudes. The resulting increase in pressure in the brain causes serious problems. Most cases occur above 12,000 ft (3,659 m). HACE is insidious and attacks suddenly, even among fit, acclimatized mountaineers. Severe headache, mental dysfunction like memory loss, confusion, psychosis and hallucinations, as well as ataxia (lack of muscle coordination) are the initial symptoms. Inability to walk, coma and death may follow rapidly. Descent to lower elevation is the best treatment. OXYGEN and DEXAMETHAZONE have been used with success, as has the GAMOW BAG (a portable hyperbaric chamber), as a means of returning a victim to low-altitude pressures. It is common to find HACE occurring with PULMONARY EDEMA, but the conditions also occur independently.

CERRO Spanish term for peak, or summit used in South America.

CERRO TORRE (Argentina) This legendary spire (in English, Tower Mountain) is, at 10,262 ft/3,127 m, the highest in a trilogy of difficult PATAGONIA summits that also include Torre Egger (9,511 ft/2,899m) and Cerro Stanhardt (9,183 ft/2,799m). Ice encrustations and ICE MUSHROOMS formed by storms, adorn it. The superb granite that comprises the spires is part of the Patagonian Batholith. FREE CLIMBING consists of jamming perfect CRACKS or FACE CLIMBING UP solid crystals on coarse rock. Situated 280 miles (448 km) north of the Strait of Magellan and bordering the eastern edge of the South Patagonian Ice Cap, Cerro Torre has anything but good weather. In fact, its raging winds and ice-caked walls repulsed climbing attempts for 16 years until an Italian EXPEDITION led by Casimiro Ferrari claimed the undisputed FIRST ASCENT of the summit by the icy west face in 1974.

Among those attempts to reach Cerro Torre's summit were those of the Italian Cesare MAESTRI, whose adventures on Cerro Torre have become one of the enduring mysteries of MOUNTAINEERING. Maestri's attempts began in 1959 when he and Austrian Toni Egger spent five days climbing the mountain's northeast ridge. The climb ended in Egger's death in an AVALANCHE on the descent. Lost with Egger was the camera and the record of their reaching the summit. Over the years, Maestri's ascent has come under close scrutiny. The majority of climbers throughout the world have questioned the accuracy of his account, although it is accepted in ARGENTINA as the first. Maestri returned to Cerro Torre in 1970 to clear his name but brought additional derision by establishing a route up the southeast ridge and claiming the first ascent without climbing the final ice mushroom that caps the summit. With regard to the top he stated, "the mushroom was not really part of the mountain and would fall off someday." Maestri used a gas-powered air compressor to place 300 BOLTS up the climb (see COMPRESSOR ROUTE). Although scorned by many for being so extensively bolted, the southeast ridge, which is frequently climbed today, can be very challenging. Jim BRIDWELL and Steve Brewer (United States) completed this route to the summit in 1979. Several

parties have attempted to repeat the mysterious northeast ridge without success.

In addition to the southeast ridge, Cerro Torre has three other completed routes: the east face (Slovene, 1986); south face (Slovene, 1987); and the west face. The latter is an ice climb above the ICE CAP.
Further reading: Alan Kearney, *Mountaineering in Patagonia* (1992).

Cerro Torre, Argentina

CESEN, TOMO (1960–) (Yugoslavia) When Cesen claimed his solo ascents of Jannu north face and LHOTSE south face he redefined the notion of "impossible" in Himalayan climbing. He also found himself at the center of a controversy in Europe when his claims of climbing those last great problems were disputed.

Born in Kranj, in the Yugoslav Julian Alps, Cesen's solo career began in 1985 when he surprised the alpine community with his four-day winter "trilogy" of the EIGER, GRANDES JORASSES and MATTERHORN north faces. Other Alps solos include the Pilier Rouge of the Brouillard, in winter.

Cesen made impressive ascents of Himalayan and Karakoram climbs from 1985 to 1987. These included Yalung Kang north face (27,903 ft/8,507 m) in NEPAL (1985), on

Tomo Cesen

which his summit partner Borut Bergant fell to his death while descending; BROAD PEAK (26,402 ft/8,049 m) solo; a solo attempt on K2 south spur (1986); and in 1987 a traditional attempt on Lhotse Shar (27,514 ft/8,388 m).

He staggered climbing circles in 1989 by soloing the north face of Jannu (25,294 ft/7,712 m): 23.5 hours up, 18 down. Previous efforts by the French had deemed Cesen's route an unlikely possiblity (see KANGCHENJUNGA HIMAL). The climb involved complex route finding, 5.11a rock climbing and total commitment. For this climb he was presented with the Snow Lion award, a $10,000 prize created by Reinhold MESSNER.

Equally incredible was his 1990 two-day solo of the south face of Lhotse (27,892 ft/8,504 m), a FACE dubbed by Messner as "a problem for the year 2000," and one tried by the world's best climbers. Cesen said that he bivouacked at 24,600 and 27,000 ft (7,500 and 8,232 m) and summited at 2:20 P.M. on April 24. He had no witnesses. The feat received international recognition, but six months later a Russian team who had climbed Lhotse by a different route claimed the first ascent of the face, ignoring Cesen's climb. The Russians based their claim on disbelief of Cesen's summit photo, which showed the western CWM of EVEREST; a view not possible from the summit, they claimed. Moreover, the Russians had suffered terribly in their ascent. Six members sustained FROSTBITE, and one climber lost both his hands and feet to amputations. They doubted a lone climber could escape the face unscathed. Cesen's lack of

witnesses and photographic proof of this and his other solo climbs caused skeptics to question all his ascents. The controversy became front page news in Europe. Cesen insisted his word was proof enough. Notable alpinists defended him and in 1991 the elite French climbing association, Groupe de Haute Montagne (GHM), sided with Cesen, acknowledged his ascents, and made him a member. His autobiography *Alone,* was published in Yugoslavia and France.

Then, in 1993, the Slovenian climber Viki Groselj divulged that photos from Lhotse that Cesen had advanced as proof of his ascent, and which had been printed in the French climbing magazine *Vertical,* were, in fact, not Cesen's, but his. Groselj had taken the photos during different attempts of his own on Lhotse, and Cesen had borrowed them. Cesen admitted the photos were not his, and blamed *Vertical* for an editorial error. *Vertical* denied any mistake, and Groselj's revelation again placed Cesen's claim in question. Strangely, Cesen changed his statements from 1990, when he affirmed that he took photos on Lhotse, saying in 1993 that he did not take photos on Lhotse. Messner retracted his Snow Lion award and withdrew his support of Cesen's climb. As of 1994 Cesen still maintained he had climbed Lhotse, though many questions remain unanswered.

CEUSE (France) This limestone CRAG has been called the crag of the year 2000. At an elevation of over 5,904 ft (1,800 m), Ceuse is snowed in winter and hot in summer, making spring and fall the best seasons for climbing. It is eight miles (14 kilometers) southwest of Gap. There are over 100 routes with miles of cliffline still untouched. The cliff, between 196 and 393 ft (60 and 120 m) high, faces east and south. The rock is superb, featuring SLABS, CRACKS and OVERHANGS pitted with POCKETS. Ceuse went unnoticed until the late 1970s. Now it has earned a nationwide reputation, but due to its mountainous location is not as crowded as BUOUX or VERDON, and offers a quiet, uncrowded mountain atmosphere and fine BOULDERING. Long routes requiring gear include the classic Natilik (6a). Sustained one-PITCH BULGES include Tenere (7c+) or Le Privilège du Serpent (7c+). One of Ceuse's hardest SPORT CLIMBS is Patience (8c) by J. C. Lafaille.

CHAIR LADDER (Britain) This blocky 200-ft (61-m) CRAG on West Penwith's south coast epitomizes Cornish granite climbing and offers mid-grade climbers an adventurous setting. The cliffs drop dramatically into the sea, but the majority of routes are low angle, and start from large platforms. There are four principal sections, Bulging Wall, Main Cliff, Wolf Buttress and Bishop Buttress. The crags lie near Porthgwarra, a tiny village near Penzance.

John "Zeke" Deacon made a considerable contribution here in the mid-1950s, including the brilliant 5.6 Pegasus on the Bulging Wall and Bishop's Rib, a bold 5.9 on Bishop's Buttress. Bishop's Buttress's finest route is undoubtedly Diocese, which follows an OFFWIDTH before breaking across a SLAB to a 5.7 crack system. Modern LINES include Rowland Edwards's 1984 classic Animated Wall

(5.11a), and Pat LITTLEJOHN's thin crack, The Spire (5.10d). **Guidebooks:** Pat Littlejohn, *South West Climbs* (1991); Pete O'Sullivan, *West Penwith* (1983).

CHALK White powdered gymnast's chalk (carbonate of magnesia) is used by rock climbers to maximize friction against rock by drying moisture on hands and fingertips. It is carried in a chalk bag.

Chalk appeared in the United States during the early 1970s. Initially it was used by a few top climbers but as its benefits became apparent, chalk use spread among climbers everywhere. When chalk reached Britain in the 1970s, the editor of *Mountain* magazine, Ken Wilson, wrote editorials condemning chalk as a form of pollution: "Chalk usage not only diminishes one of the principal pleasures of rock climbing—the primitive delight in the feel of the rock—it also interferes in the mental sphere: chalked holds stand out from below, indicating many of the secrets of a route in advance, and thereby removing its technical mystery. Finally, it is aesthetically insulting to find the visual balance of a cliff destroyed by chalk-dusted routes." (*Mountain* 45, 1975.)

Editors of climbing magazines in the United States and elsewhere called chalked ascents aided, and chalk "courage in a bag." But with the explosion of hard climbing during the 1970s, and the 1980s popularization of SPORT CLIMBING, chalk use became universal and the controversy faded. Regardless, a few areas, like the ELBSANDSTEINGEBIRGE region of Germany still ban chalk.

CHALK BAG A small sack for carrying powdered CHALK, into which hands or fingers can be dipped. Usually worn around the waist and positioned at the back.

CHAMONIX (France) The world-famous mountain range of MONT BLANC above the town of Chamonix has magnificent granite rock climbing. The Aiguille du Midi, Helbronner or Grands Montets télépheriques or the train of Montenvers are typically used to reach these high-altitude cliffs. For most cliffs the usual procedure is to hike two to four hours to a hut in the afternoon and then climb the next day, though on less remote cliffs the télépheriques allow town-to-town one-day ascents. There are about 100 excellent cliffs scattered in the Mont Blanc Range, ranging from 492 to 3,280 ft (150 to 1,000 m). Most cliffs are accessible but require basic MOUNTAINEERING skills to reach them. ROUTES are usually rappel-descended and thus have excellent belay ANCHORS. A standard rack of NUTS, FRIENDS and QUICK DRAWS is required, as are two 164-ft (50-m) ROPES. A helmet is recommended though there is little rockfall. The common climbing season extends from June to September with peak crowds from July 15th to August 15th. On sunny windless days it is possible to climb as early as March and as late as November. Whatever the season, weather can change quickly. The DRUS, for instance, is infamous for its thunderstorms. Challenging rock routes first appeared in the 1950 by W. BONATTI, G. REBUFFAT, Contamine and others, who used PITONS for protection. In the 1970s, more crack lines were explored by

people like G. Bettembourg or P. Cordier. In 1979 Michel Piola ventured on the blank SLABS, placing BOLTS on the lead. Bolts and a new focus on quality climbing (not necessarily to summits) opened a new generation of routes. Piola has put up hundreds of fine routes and inspired other pathfinders, like Romain Vogler who discovered over 70 new lines.

On the CHAMONIX AIGUILLES some major cliffs and their famous routes include: Pilier Cordier on Grandes Charmoz; L'eau Rance d'Arbie and Fidel Fiasco at Blaitière; Ticket, Vaucher and Postcriptone on LePeigne. On the back side of the Aiguilles are Marchand de Sable, George V, Pyramid on the Fou south face. In the Mont Blanc du Tacul area are Rebuffat, Super Dupont or Ballade pour Aurelia on the Aiguille du Midi; Contamine and Bon Filon at Lachenal; Totem on Trois Pointes; Bonatti, Gulliver and Echo des Alpages on the Grand Capucin; and Lepinoy on Trident. In the Charpoval Talefre area are American Direct and Bonatti on Les DRUS, Coloriages on Moine and Anouk on Petites Jorasses. In the Argentière basin are Pirate, Verssantsatanique and Defense d'Obéir on the south face of Argentière, and Rêve de Singe on La Verge.

CHAMONIX AIGUILLES (France) From the center of CHAMONIX, the Aiguilles are the dramatically beautiful spires of rock to the left of MONT BLANC and the right of the Mer de Glace. They stretch in a largely continuous chain from the Aiguille du Midi in the west to the Aiguille de l'M in the east. Aiguille means needle, and the steep rock faces of these peaks offer a lower but more technical alternative to the ROUTES on Mont Blanc. While most routes in the area are rock climbs, there are some interesting ice climbs as well, including the north face of the Plan. Below the Aiguilles is the Plan de l'Aiguille, a flat area that is readily accessible by cable car and the starting point for many of the routes. It offers the option of a more permanent base. Climbs are also approached from the Montenvers train station—huts include the charming Envers Hut above the Mer de Glace and the Requin on the Tacul Glacier. For climbs on the Aiguille du Midi, the highest cable-car station in the Alps offers an instant approach to the Vallée Blanche and the Midi's south face, as well as the south side of Mont Blanc du Tacul, the Tour Ronde and its north face and the Géant Glacier. The recently constructed Cosmiques Hut has largely curtailed the less pleasant alternatives such as the Abri Simond bivouac hut or sleeping in the téléphérique station.

First climbed in 1818, the Aiguille du Midi (12,602 ft/ 3,842 m) now sports some of the hardest rock climbs in the Alps on excellent Chamonix granite. Routes include the south-southwest ridge, first climbed in 1911 by George Finch of Everest fame and a good introduction to the mixed climbing in the area. On the southeast pillar, often referred to as the south face, is the classic Rébuffat Route, climbed in 1956 with some aid but now often climbed free at around VI. In a more modern vein, and illustrative of the recent explosion in technical rock climbs, is Ma Dalton that takes a dramatic roof crack at IX- and was climbed by G. Hopfgartner and M. Piola. The north side of the Midi has a number of excellent mixed routes, the most famous and most obvious from Chamonix being the Frendo Spur. At around 3,280 ft (1,000 m) long with rock to Grade V and 55° ice, this classic from 1941 offers an intermediary step between easier climbs and the *grandes courses*.

The Aiguille du Plan (12,047 ft/3,673 m) has a number of modern classics, but the most famous route is that climbed in 1929 by A. Charlet, J. Simond and P. Dillemann up the hanging GLACIER of its north face (TD-). Joe BROWN and Tom PATEY climbed the renowned but surprisingly unfrequented Central Pillar Direct (TD-) in 1963 and Patrick Gabarrou climbed the Grand West Couloir with J. Picard-Deyme in 1975 at ED+. Perhaps the most impressive LINE in the area is the Lagarde-Segogne Couloir on the Dent du Caiman. Climbed in 1926, the route went unrepeated for fifty years and still rates TD+. There is a very popular TRAVERSE between the Midi and the Plan.

The Dent du Requin (11,290 ft/3,442 m) offers some excellent rock climbs and some of the smaller peaks around the Requin Hut now have a large number of modern routes. The classic route on the Requin itself was climbed in 1945 by Jean Couttet and Gaston Rébuffat at TD. The Aiguille des Pélerins (10,883 ft/3,318 m) has a number of contrasting routes, from the novices' classic south face or normal route to a winter ascent of the north face, first climbed in 1975 by Al Rouse and Rab Carrington at ED+. Another hard modern classic here is Michel Piola's Nostradamus on the north pillar. Graded ED+, RPs are said to be useful.

The Aiguille du Peigne (10,470 ft/3,192 m) is one the most popular of the Aiguilles with a large number of excellent rock routes that are readily accessible. Among the better known are the Papillons or west ridge and the Vaucher Route on the southwest face. The Aiguille du Fou (11,483 ft/3,501 m) can be ascended by its north-northeast ridge and is best combined with an ascent of the Aiguille de Blatière (11,552 ft/3,522 m). The south face of the Fou is especially well known, being the work of Tom FROST, John HARLIN, Gary HEMMING and Steve Fulton. Climbed in 1963, it remains a serious undertaking, rarely done free and exposed to STONEFALL in its lower parts. On the Blatière, the Spencer offers an easy (AD) but lengthy approach to the summit, while the west face has a number of hard rock climbs, especially on the Red Pillar. The classic remains Joe Brown and Don WHILLANS's route from 1954. This features the Fissure Brown, a unique OFFWIDTH experience if done free. Among the more modern rock routes, Michel Piola's Majorette Thatcher and Williamine Dada are especially recommended.

The Aiguille du Grépon (11,421 ft/3,482 m) is the most famous of the Aiguilles and its FIRST ASCENT by Albert MUMMERY with his guides Burgener and Venetz in 1881 is one of the great achievements of alpinism. The Mer de Glace face is another great classic on perfect rock and less frequented now that shorter, more technical routes have become popular. It was first climbed in 1911 by H. Jones, R. Todhunter and G. Young with J. Knubel and H. Brocherel. The shorter routes that have usurped such classics,

often with bolted protection, feature strongly on the Aiguille de Roc's east face, above the Envers Hut and the Mer de Glace. Michel Piola was busy here as elsewhere, climbing Children of the Moon (VI), which offers a good introduction to other similar routes in the area. The Aiguille des Grands Charmoz (11,300 ft/3,445 m), often climbed in conjunction with the Grépon, has a number of excellent climbs on its west face including the highly recommended Cordier Pillar, climbed in 1970 at TD. The north face climbed by Willy MERKL and Willo WELZENBACH in two attempts in 1931 is also noteworthy. Finally in the Aiguilles, the Aiguille de l'M (9,328 ft/2,844 m) has two or three short routes that make a pleasant introduction to the harder lines hereabouts, including the north-northeast ridge and the Couzy and Ménégaux routes on the northwest face. A traverse of the Aiguilles, usually undertaken from the Charmoz and ending at the Midi over two days, is a unique experience and highly recommended.

CHANGABANG (India) This granite peak of the GARWHAL Range, regarded as INDIA's hardest, has captivated climbers for generations. Frank SMYTHE described it in 1937 as "a peak that falls from crest to glacier in a wall that might have been sliced in a single cut of a knife." Changabang's sheer walls and 22,520-ft (6,864-m) summit present great challenges to climbers, perhaps more so today because since 1982 environmental concerns have prohibited entry to the NANDA DEVI Sanctuary. The approach to this peak is difficult, either up the rugged Rishi Ganga Gorge or from Lata, via Dharansi Pass. Although Englishman W. Murray claimed he climbed Changabang in the 1800s (a claim discounted by the Alpine Club), the FIRST ASCENT was in 1974. A strong British team, led by Chris BONINGTON included Dougal HASTON, Doug SCOTT and Martin BOYSEN as well as Indians Balwant Sandhu and SHERPA Tashi. They intended to climb the west face, but upon seeing this wall Boysen remarked that "the vertical and overhanging rock, plated here and there by ludicrously steep ice . . . was obviously so difficult it was laughable." They shifted their efforts to the other side of the peak over Shipton's Col, and climbed the snowy face below Kalanka east face (22,741 ft/6,931 m) and then the northeast ridge. This expedition is described in *Changabang* by Bonington, Scott, et al (1975).

In 1976 six Japanese made a FIXED ROPE ascent of the southwest ridge. Later that year five Britons made an ALPINE-STYLE route on the east face. At the same time, on the other side of Changabang one of the milestones in Himalayan climbing was underway: The two-man ascent of the formidable west face by Peter BOARDMAN and Joe TASKER, which was the first major climb done CAPSULE STYLE and is described in Boardman's acclaimed book *The Shining Mountain, Two Men on Changabang's West Wall* (1978). An equally bold alpine-style ascent of the direct south face was made by Wojciech KURTYKA, Alex MACINTYRE and John Porter in 1978. The last major route on Changabang was by a large Italian expedition in 1981, which climbed the south ridge with fixed rope.

CHARLET, ARMAND (1900–1975) (France) One of the greatest prewar French guides, Charlet was also mayor of Argentière, Officer of the Légion d'Honneur, President of the Compagne des Guides of CHAMONIX and from 1945 to 1957 Technical Director of the Ecole Nationale de Ski et d'Alpinisme (ENSA) in Chamonix. In World War II he smuggled people across frontiers at personal risk from the Gestapo. But Charlet was best known for his 3,000 guided ascents around Chamonix, with 1,200 different clients, some of whom were Robert and Miriam UNDERHILL (United States), and Wilfred Noyce and Sir Douglas Busk (BRITAIN). His ascents include 100 ascents of the AIGUILLE VERTE by 14 routes (seven of them new), 72 ascents of the Grepon, 39 ascents of MONT BLANC, and 22 of Les DRUS, including its first WINTER ASCENT. He was fast even by modern standards: he climbed the Aiguille Verte by the Moigne Ridge in three hours, and the Peuterey Ridge from the Gamba Hut in 10 hours, both climbed by cutting steps in nailed boots or primitive 10-point CRAMPONS. He never used artificial aids. A sometimes prickly but loyal teetotaller and nonsmoker, Charlet timed every ascent and took his pulse on the summits. In his role at ENSA he demanded excellence from aspirant guides, reportedly remarking once that "in this profession you must learn to suffer."
Further reading: Sir Douglas Busk, *Armand Charlet* (1975).

CHEDDAR GORGE (Britain) This geological phenomenon is cut into Somerset's Mendip Hills, a narrow cleft surrounded by steep limestone walls. The B3135 road runs from Cheddar village through the middle of the gorge. The loose rock and the area's environmental importance have presented access problems in recent years as tourists have been peppered by falling rock and rare plants have been trampled. The proviso to climbing here is that the access situation must be ascertained before a visit.

Cheddar comprises many walls and BUTTRESSES that are loose in some areas, though popular ROUTES are usually sound. On Spacehunter Wall at Castle Rocks, Martin Crocker climbed two outstanding 5.12cs in the mid-1980s: Spacehunter, a bold PITCH above stepped OVERHANGS, and Star Spangled Banner, a BOLT-protected line. On Sunset Buttress, he also freed the AID route Bird of Paradise at 5.12c. Described by guidebook-author Pat LITTLEJOHN as "mind-blowing," these routes illustrate Crocker's dominance in this area during the last decade.

West of Sunset Buttress is 350-ft (107-m) tall High Rock, of which Coronation Street (5.9) is the obvious classic. Climbed in 1965 by Chris BONINGTON, John Cleare and Tony Greenbank, it gives five pitches up the middle of the CRAG, directly above the road. Also long is Pat Littlejohn's The Crow (5.10c) from 1970. A one-pitch modern route is Martin Crocker's Wishing Wall (5.12a), left of Crow.
Guidebook: Pat Littlejohn, *South West Climbs* (1991).

CHEEDALE (Britain) This charming dale, with the River Wye running through its heart, is near Miller's Dale and the A6 in the heart of the PEAK DISTRICT. STONEY MIDDLETON or Hathersage provide services or campsites.

There are a number of isolated BUTTRESSES along the length of the valley including Sirplum and Two Tier, but the main CRAG is Chee Tor, a one-pitch limestone incline close to the river. Like other Peak limestone areas, it was used for winter AID-CLIMBING initially, but as the loose rock was removed, interest in FREE-CLIMBING grew.

As at Stoney Middleton, Tom Proctor instigated the new, powerful climbing style. His Mortlock's Arete (5.11a) from 1976 remains a classic LINE. In 1980, Pete LIVESEY climbed The Golden Mile (5.11d), and his protegé Ron FAWCETT took things a stage further in 1982 with Tequila Mockingbird (5.12b), which controversially used a couple of BOLTS. Even more controversially, it was later retro-bolted to better protect the start. Cheedale became the testing ground for bolting in the United Kingdom and the principle that steep limestone could rarely be climbed without bolts was established. This was emphasized by Ben Masterson's Boo (5.12c) in 1985 and Chris Gore's The Ogre (5.13a) in 1986.
Guidebooks: British Mountain Club, *Peak Limestone—Cheedale* (1987); Paul Nunn, *Rock Climbing in the Peak District* (1987).

CHEESMOND, DAVID (1952–1987) (Canada) An inspired climber from Durban, South Africa, Cheesmond moved to ALBERTA, CANADA, in 1981 and became a one-man revolution in ALPINISM there. In Africa he made hard rock-climbs, and climbed KILIMANJARO by a new LINE on the Breach Wall. He repeated the great north faces of the European Alps, FITZROY in PATAGONIA, and soloed the Cassin Ridge on DENALI. In the CANADIAN ROCKIES he pushed alpine standards, inspiring a clique of alpinists who became known as "The Wild Boys." His achievments include five of the hardest firsts in the Rockies: Mount ROBSON Emperor face, by a new line, (1981); Mount ASSINIBOINE east face (1982) with Tony Dick; the 6,000-ft (1,829-m) north face of Mount Goodsir (1983) with Kevin Doyle; Mount Andromeda (The Andromeda Strain) in 1983; north pillar of NORTH TWIN (1985), a five-day rock route with Barry Blanchard. Cheesmond also developed the Alberta crag Yamnuska with high caliber routes. In ALASKA, he climbed the east ridge of Mount Deborah and the west face of Mount Hayes with Carl Tobin. In the HIMALAYA he led a successful Canadian expedition to RAKAPOSHI (with Doyle and Blanchard) that repeated the north ridge, alpine style. Attempts on K2 and EVEREST were less successful. In 1987 he disappeared, with Catherine Freer, on the Hummingbird Ridge of Mount LOGAN.

CHEST HARNESS Also body harness. A harness worn around the torso in addition to a waist HARNESS. Though seldom worn by modern climbers, a chest harness is the safest harness because it supports the back in long falls or in AID CLIMBING. They are commercially made, or may be improvised from WEBBING.

CHEW VALLEY (Britain) The area northeast of Manchester and immediately east of the village of Greenfield contains excellent gritstone CRAGS. Above Dove Stone Reservoir is Wimberry. Routes there include Dougie Hall's Appointment with Fear (5.12d), climbed in 1986 and Wrist-cutter's Lullaby (5.12d), climbed by Nick Plishko in 1988. Other crags in the area worth attention are Running Hill Pits with Hall's Scoop de Grace (5.13d), Dovestones Quarries with Steve Bancroft's 1970s classic Bob Hope (5.11a) and Ravenstones.

Guidebooks: British Mountain Club, *Moorland Gritstone— Chew Valley* (1988); Paul Nunn, *Rock Climbing in the Peak District* (1987).

CHEYNE-STOKES BREATHING Periodic breathing common in some individuals at altitudes above 13,000 ft (3,963 m), but occurring as low as 8,000 ft (2,394 m). It is most prominent during sleep. Cheyne-Stoking begins with several shallow breaths leading to deeper, sighing breaths that suddenly fall off in intensity so that it may appear breathing has ceased completely. This period may be marked by restlessness from a feeling of suffocation. After an interval the pattern begins again. Even among experienced high-altitude climbers Cheyne-Stokes respiration is common. It is not considered dangerous, but it does disturb sleep and results in poor performance during the day. It may also indicate problems such as upper-airway obstruction. ACETAZOLAMIDE before sleep may alleviate the condition (but only at low altitude). Sedatives should never be taken at altitude.

CHICKENHEAD A protuberance or knob of intrusive rock on a cliff, providing a positive handhold. Usually found in granitic rock, xenoliths in volcanic rock or pebbles in conglomerate are also called chickenheads. The word originated in the United States.

CHILE This country with a north-south length of 2,800 miles (4,505 km) and a width of 100 miles (160 km), has a range of equal length that rises over 22,000 ft (6,707 m) and has GLACIERS that descend into the Pacific. Length implies variety of setting and climate; and the modern towns of Chile mean resources and comfort. The Chilean mountain land is divided into five regions. The desertic north, or Puna, contains Nevado OJOS DEL SALADO (22,590 ft/ 6,885 m), highest point in the country. The Central ANDES resemble the ALPS or the Caucasus, but much higher, with TUPUNGATO (21,490 ft/6,550 m) at the apex; it is a zone within easy reach of big cities, including Santiago, the capital. The Southern Andes or El Sur is a region quite similar to the American Northwest, with isolated ice volcanic cones that rise to 12,000 ft (3,659 m) above forests and blue lakes. The Andes Australes include PATAGONIA (where the granite BIG WALLS of the PAINE GROUP attract modern alpinists) and Tierra del Fuego, a sort of Chilean ALASKA, stormier, to be sure, but no higher than the 12,828 ft (3,911 m) of SAN VALENTIN. Finally, the Antartandes, or peaks in the Antarctic peninsula are a continuation of the South American mainland and eventually abate at the South Pole. There are volcanoes, some active, in all five regions. The Antartandes have seen only sporadic expeditions. Thus, the national sports of hiking, climbing and skiing

are concentrated on the central and southern zones. Glaciation is strong and the andesitic rock is rather poor. Chile's mountaineering season is from mid-November through March, the southern summer. First climbing was undertaken by the Inca and Atacamenan peoples, who left mummies buried on summits from 17,000 to 22,000 ft (5,183 to 6,707 m). Some climbing was done between 1828 and 1859 by occasional travelers who ascended volcanoes in the rainy south. Then the exploring and surveying commissions followed from 1868 to 1910, charting the Andes and ascending a good many peaks up to 19,500 ft (5,945 m) and realizing in 1898 the first crossing of the Patagonian ICE CAP (Pascua Glacier to Lake San Martin). Foreign expeditions (1883 to 1950), Chilean-Germans (1896 to 1960) and the Chileans themselves (since 1914) made many ascents in all areas, including the Antartandes. Luis RISO PATRON, Francisco J. de San Roman and Fritz REICHERT were well known Chilean climbers. Skiing as a sport began around 1915 and as an industry, in the late 1930s. The first national mountain club was the D.A.V. Chile (1909), still active. The Club Andino de Chile was founded in 1933, and in 1954, the Federacion de Andinismo de Chile (National Mountaineering Association) began to group all mountain clubs under its wings. It embraces today 40 institutions and one climbing school. Local mountaineering publications have been *Andina* (by the German clubs), *Revista Andina* (by the Club Andino de Chile) and *Anuario de Montana*, the Federacion's yearbook. An unusual characteristic of Chilean mountaineering is its connection to two scientific endeavors, high-mountain archeology or OROLATRIC MOUNTAINEERING and glaciology, a field in which some climbers have excelled, particularly Humberto Barrera, the first to study the curious "penitent snow."

Guidebook: Gaston San Roman, *Guia de excursionismo para la cordillera de Santiago* (1977).

Evelio Echevarria
Colorado State University

CHIMBORAZO (Ecuador) For some 60 years, until 1818, when higher peaks were discovered, Chimborazo was considered the highest mountain on earth. It is an inactive volcano, carries 14 GLACIERS and culminates in two DOMES, rising to 20,563 ft (6,267 m). Its Indian name means "Ice Peak of the Other Side." The mountain, highest in ECUADOR, belongs to the Cordillera Occidental and is located some 100 miles (160 km) south-southeast of Quito, the capital. Access is through the city of Ambato. Chimborazo has two huts on its northern and southern slopes, the latter being more commonly used. Alexander von Humboldt made Chimborazo famous by attempting it, up to 18,300 ft (5,579 m), in 1802. Edward WHYMPER, climber of the MATTERHORN, visited Ecuador in 1880 with guides Jean Antoine Carrel and Lois Carrel and climbed Chimborazo's south-southwest side, a history-making FIRST ASCENT. With two Ecuadorians, they reclimbed it six months later, by the northwest side. Nicolas G. MARTINEZ with Indian guide Miguel Tul made the third ascent in 1911. Important new ROUTES have been the south side direct (Totorillas Glacier) by Italians I. Formaggio, P. Ghiglione and German W.

Kuhm (1939), and the north side by Americans under R. Hechtel (1968). Ecuadorian climbers have TRAVERSED the Chimborazo east to southwest (1980, 1990).
Guidebook: Marco Curz, *Die Schneeberge Ecuadors* (1983).
Evelio Echevarria
Colorado State University

CHIMNEY A chimney is a wide CRACK or fissure in a cliff. Chimneying, the technique used to climb chimneys, is awkward yet entertaining to watch. It combines squirming, STEMMING, and back and foot techniques.

CHIMNEY ROCK (United States) This 400-foot (122-m) granite tower is one of the United States' better rock-climbing areas. Situated at an elevation of 7,000 ft (2,134 m) on the SELKIRK Crest, summer and fall are the best months for climbing. A one-and-a-half-hour approach is required. Technical ascents were recorded here as early as 1934. The area is noted for difficult CRACK CLIMBING on impeccable rock. The west face has fine ROUTES like Rappel Chimney (5.6), West Face Direct (5.8) and Sticky Fingers (5.10). The east face offers Magnum Force (5.10b) and Tsunami (5.11d).
Guidebook: Randall Green, *Idaho Rock: A Climbing Guide to the Selkirk Crest and Sandpoint Areas* (1987).

CHINA Permission to climb in China is controlled by several state-appointed offices, the longest established being the Chinese Mountaineering Association (9 Tiyuguan Road, Beijing). Separate mountaineering associations and trekking agencies exist in Xinjiang, Szechuan and in Chinese-controlled TIBET. Chinese teams have climbed 26,240-ft (8,000-m) peaks like Everest, and Chinese made the FIRST ASCENT of Shishapangma. Climbing in China is expensive; Japanese expeditions reportedly paid million-dollar sums to secure permission to climb first ascents on K2 and Everest from the north, and to try to climb Namche Barwa in Szechuan. China's mountains fringe its borderlands in the west, extending from ASSAM and the MINYA KONKA REGION in the moist south in Szechuan, to the Yulongxue Shan Mountains in Yunnan, then northward to the Tibetan Plateau and the northern watersheds of the Himalayan ranges of INDIA and NEPAL (see CHO OYU, EVEREST, GANGOTRI REGION, JANAK HIMAL, KUMAON-GARHWAL, MAHALANGUR HIMAL, NALAKANKAR HIMAL, PAMARI HIMAL, ROLWALING HIMAL, SHISHAPANGMA, TRANSHIMALAYA). Further north, in arid Xinjiang, China has the northern watersheds of the KARAKORAM (see BROAD PEAK, GASHERBRUM I, GASHERBRUM II, K2) and the KUNLUN RANGE (see MUZTAGATA) and TIEN SHAN RANGE.

CHINOOK WIND A warm wind resulting from moist air flowing over a mountain and warming as it descends the lee slope. As moist air rises it cools and condenses, usually falling as rain on windward slopes. When this air mass descends the leeward slope, it is drier and warms quickly due to the LAPSE RATE (the change in air temperature with increase or decrease in altitude). (See ADIABATIC WIND.)

CHIPPING The creation or enhancement of HOLDS on a FREE CLIMB by chisel or drill in order to make the climb possible is called chipping. Chipping has created controversy within the climbing community and much editorializing in climbing publications during the 1980s and 1990s. Chipping is rare and is seldom visible, but its impact on climbing is considerable.

Chipping has few advocates, but the logic behind it says that subtle, undetectable enhancement of holds to connect sequences of hard moves opens otherwise impossible ROUTES, and that the impact on the rock is marginal compared to the athletic benefits gained. This argument has been used in the case of some French limestone SPORT CLIMBS of the 1980s, which were chipped. Such climbs contributed to high standards, but they also encouraged chipping.

Those against chipping call it vandalism, arguing that it negates the fundamental principle of free climbing that regards the rock as an inviolable medium and natural rock architecture the framework within which climbers work. Some climbs chipped several years ago would probably have been feasible in their original states given today's levels of climbing ability. Other chipped routes turn totally blank rock into free climbs. Furthermore, chipping is not always restricted to FIRST-ASCENT parties: Climbs have been altered for subsequent ascents.

The issue of chipping raises moral questions about the use of the environment by climbers, and about the changing ETHICS of climbing. Worldwide, chipping has raised the ire of public-land managers. Chipping presents not only an ethical schism among contemporary climbers, but if land managers restrict climbing due to a perceived misuse of cliffs, it poses a threat to the freedom and access for climbers.

CHOCKS A general name, like NUTS, given to any item of climbing equipment slotted by hand into a crack to create a natural CHOCKSTONE that can be used as an ANCHOR. Active CAMMING DEVICES with movable parts (SLCDs) are not usually regarded as chocks, which are passive camming devices. Chocks include HEXENTRICS, STOPPERS, ROCKS and other tapered wedges. Chocks are examples of CLEAN CLIMBING equipment. (See CRACK PROTECTION.)

CHOCKSTONE A natural stone jammed in a CRACK or CHIMNEY. Chockstones may be slung for protection or used as handholds or footholds.

CHOGOLISA (Pakistan) Sometimes called Bride Peak, this 25,149-ft/7,665-m mountain of perpetual snows lies in the BALTORO Muztagh of the KARAKORAM. Its northern flanks feed the upper Baltoro Glacier, and its southern side drops toward the Kaberi Glacier, reached via the Hushe Valley. Chogolisa actually has two summits, the northeast summit being a lower rocky surmount (25,111 ft/7,654 m), and the slightly higher southwest summit being a razor-edge.

It was first attempted by the Duke of ABRUZZI in 1909 after his expedition failed on K2. On the northeast ridge they reached 24,280 ft (7,402 m)—an altitude record at the time—but quit in low-visibility and AVALANCHE-prone conditions. In 1957 the northeast ridge drew the attention of Hermann BUHL and Kurt DIEMBERGER, who, well acclimatized a few days after their FIRST ASCENT of BROAD PEAK, tackled Chogolisa in alpine style. They climbed to 24,000 ft (7,317 m) but a furious wind turned them back. During the descent Buhl broke through a CORNICE and fell down the north face to his death. Diemberger's books noted below describe this episode. The Academic Alpine Club of Kyoto, Japan, completed this route in 1958, reaching the northeast summit with oxygen.

The true southwest summit was finally climbed in 1975 by Austrians led by Edi Koblmuller. Their approach was arduous, via the Kaberi Glacier. The northwest spur to the main summit (Germans, 1983); the southwest face (French, 1984); and the northeast ridge (Spanish, 1986), on which G. de la Torre made the first hang-glider descent, are Chogolisa's other routes. A variation to the northwest spur was climbed and descended on skis by Europeans (1984). But the coup was by the British-Scottish team of L. Elliot, H. Irvine, S. Lamb and A. Fanshawe, who in alpine style TRAVERSED the twin summits (1986). Their route, via the Vigne Glacier and the southwest ridge, climbed to the southwest summit then crossed the 1,000-ft (305-m) ridge to the northeast summit.

Further reading: Kurt Diemberger, *Summits and Secrets* (1990); Diemberger, *K2: The Endless Knot* (1990); A. Fanshawe, *Coming Through: Expeditions to Chogolisa and Menlungtse* (1990); Jill Neate, *High Asia* (1989).

CHO OYU (Nepal, Tibet) Twenty miles (32 km) northwest of EVEREST, straddling the NEPAL-TIBET border, lies the world's sixth-highest peak, Cho Oyu. The mountain is 26,906 ft/8,201 m high. Loosely translated, its Tibetan name means "Turquoise Demon." The first Cho Oyu expedition (1952) was led by Eric SHIPTON and included Edmund HILLARY. Though unsuccessful, they discovered a promising ROUTE from the northwest, over the Nangpa La (an 18,754-ft/5,718-m trading pass) into forbidden Tibet, and thence up the west BUTTRESS. In 1954 the Austrian Herbert TICHY arrived at the foot of Cho Oyu, intent on proving that a large peak could be climbed without oxygen by a small group. After a foiled summit attempt on which Tichy sustained FROSTBITE, and the arrival of an unexpected French-Swiss team also vying for the FIRST ASCENT, Tichy, Sepp Jochler and SHERPA Pasang Dawa Lama (who accompanied Fritz WIESSNER on the 1939 K2 attempt, and climbed Cho Oyu again in 1958) beat their rivals to the summit via the west buttress.

The Austrian route is regarded as among the easiest of the EIGHT THOUSANDERS. In 1988 Marc Batard and Sundare Sherpa blitzed this route in twenty-one hours from 18,700 ft (5,701 m) and, that winter, Fernando Garrido of Spain soloed the route. Many variations above the Nangpa La have been made: Reinhold MESSNER's alpine-style ascent in 1983 (with Hans Kammerlander and Michl Dacher) rose from the Nangpa La, via the southwest ridge and face, as did the more direct 1986 Polish southwest buttress (.9 mile/1.5 km right of Messner's route). Nevertheless, AVALANCHE and weather have claimed many lives on these slopes. The towering south face was climbed by Edi Koblmuller's Austrian party (1978). The first WINTER ASCENT (1984), via a new route on the 10,000-ft (3,049-m) southeast buttress was by a group of Poles led by Andrej ZAWADA, and included Jerzy KUKUCZKA. Yugoslavs climbed the steep 6,500-ft (1,982-m) north face in 1988. The serious east ridge was climbed by a large Russian-Ukrainian expedition in 1991.

Guidebook: Jan Kielkowski, *Cho Oyu*, Vol. 1 and 2 (German text, 1988).

Further reading: Louis C. Baume, *Sivalaya: Explorations of the 8000-Meter Peaks* (1979); Herbert Tichy, *Cho Oyu: By Favor of the Gods* (1957).

CHOP Slang word meaning to remove BOLTS, as in "The route got chopped."

CHOP ROUTE This colloquial term describes a rock climb with such poor PROTECTION that a fall would be fatal, or an alpine route with serious objective dangers.

CHOSS Choss is a colloquial rock-climbing term that describes dirty or loose climbing. The word originated in BRITAIN during the 1950s and is still used today.

CHOUINARD, YVON (1938–) (United States) In 1964 Chouinard pushed the envelope of rock climbing by pioneering YOSEMITE's North American Wall on EL CAPITAN (with Royal ROBBINS and others). For nearly 20 years his name and ICE-CLIMBING techniques were synonymous with granite crags and ice faces from Korea to PATAGONIA to CANADA. Chouinard also became a virtuoso at designing climbing equipment. He parlayed this expertise from a backyard operation into the multi-million-dollar companies, Chouinard Equipment (now Black Diamond) and Patagonia.

CHUGACH MOUNTAINS (United States) The most accessible of ALASKA's glaciated ranges, bounded by Anchorage on the west and Cordova on the east. "The Ice Fields" as they're also known, are studded with 8,000-ft (26,240-m) peaks. The mountains curve around Prince William Sound, with myriad tidewater GLACIERS, reaching as high as Mount Marcus Baker (13,176 ft/4,017 m). The mountains are beset by a cycle of winds that come off the ocean, pick up speed over the ice fields, and roar back down the Matanuska Valley. Although not a popular expeditionary climbing destination, some climbers opt for "surf and turf," skiing to a kayak and leaving the mountains via one of the many fjords in Prince William Sound.

CHULILLA (Spain) This FREE-CLIMBING area lies 31 miles (50 km) west-northwest of Valencia, and around the village of Chulilla not far from the more developed cliff MONTENEJOS. The cliffs are fine-grained limestone bluffs,

up to 165 ft (50 m) high. Hard SPORT CLIMBS lie on the CRAG Zona de los Perros, while moderate ROUTES lie on the crag Peneta. The best seasons for this crag tend to be spring and fall, with winters also mild.
Guidebook: Nico and Leuehnser Mailander, *Sun Rock.*

CIMAI (France) This SPORT-CLIMBING cliff is located six miles (10 km) northwest of Toulon. It is an OVERHANGING rock band up to 50 ft (80 m) high, facing southeast and protected from the Mistral, a fierce north wind ensuring fair but cool weather in southern France. It is one of the best French winter CRAGS. Most ROUTES are one PITCH long and range from 7a to 8b+. The rock is extremely sharp limestone. The cliff has earned an international reputation and attracts climbers from all over Europe. Among many famous routes are Le Surplomb des Bois (6c+); Rodeo (7a), so named because you must ride an overhanging stalagtite; Le Pilier des Clodos (7b); the finger crack Orange Méca-nique Z(8a); and En un Combat Douteux (8a), hailed as one of the best 8a routes in France. A topo guidebook is available locally.

CIRQUE A cirque is an enclosure of mountains. A cirque lake is one ringed by mountains.

CIRQUE OF THE UNCLIMBABLES (Canada) A remote YOSEMITE-like area of granite spires in the Logan Mountains, on the border of the Northwest and Yukon Territories. The spires rise above four small CIRQUES, and the highest peak is Sir James MacBrien (9,050 ft/2,759 m). Arnold Wexler coined the name "Cirque of the Unclimb-ables" in 1955 because of the 2,000-ft (610-m) cliffs guarding the nine main summits, but most high points were reached via the easiest ways in 1960 by Bill Buckingham's (United States) party. In 1963 Royal ROBBINS, Jim MCCARTHY, Layton KOR and Dick McCracken brought BIG WALL tactics to the wilderness with their ascent of Mount Proboscis' Southeast face. The centerpiece of the Cirque, and the ROUTE that draws most climbers, is a granite spire called Lotus Flower Tower. It was climbed in 1968 by McCarthy, Tom FROST and Sandy Bill, and FREE-CLIMBED in 1977 (V 5.10) by Steve Levin, Mark Robinson and Sandy Stewart. The Cirque is 1,400 miles (2,253 km) from Vancouver via the Alaska Highway. Flights into Glacier Lake originate from the towns of Watson Lake (Yukon Territories), Fort Simpson or Fort Liard (Northwest Territories). July and August offer respite from frequent rains.
Further reading: Allen Steck and Steve Roper, *Fifty Classic Climbs in America* (1979).

CITY OF ROCKS (United States) A complex of mon-zonite granite domes in the high desert of southern IDAHO, 40 miles (64 km) from Burley, 150 miles (240 km) from Salt Lake City, UTAH. The rocks lie in a National Reserve, and on private grazing lands. It was through this maze of rocks that thousands of pioneers traveled in the 1800s, taking wagons along the CALIFORNIA trail. The rocks reach 300 ft (90 m), yet most ROUTES are one PITCH. In the mid-1960s Greg LOWE and friends opened some 400 routes here.

Among them, Crack of Doom (5.11c) and the Lowe Route (B1+) boulder problem on Clam Shell boulder were equal to the hardest climbs in America. In the 1980s climbers pushed grades, and tactics. SPORT CLIMBING arrived in 1987 with RAPPEL-BOLTED routes like Power Tools (5.12b/c), by Tedd Thompson and Darius Azin, and She's the Bosch (5.11a). BOLTED CLIMBS now number in the hundreds, and offer many quality routes even at easy ratings. A morato-rium on bolting imposed by park officials in 1990 has slowed development. In the 1990s Tony YANIRO pushed routes to extremes, with Remora (5.14), on The Dolphin, and The Boogieman, a crack route so extreme (perhaps the hardest crack in the world) that he applied a French rating of 8b to it. The area's high elevation means cold weather from November to March, with extreme heat in mid-summer.
Guidebook: Dave Bingham, *City of Rocks Idaho, A Climber's Guide* (1991).

CLARKE, JOHN (1946–) (Canada) Clarke is a modern legend in Canadian climbing for his largely solo explorations in the COAST MOUNTAINS of BRITISH COLUMBIA. He estimated in 1990 that he had traveled 13,670 miles (21,995 km) on foot during 160 trips. He attended a Bendic-tine missionary school near Vancouver, and turned to MOUNTAINEERING early. His first major solo trip was made in 1971 when he pioneered routes in the Misty Range in Garibaldi Park. Since then he has explored the Coast Range methodically, climbing hundreds of peaks. The Alpine Club of Canada made him an honorary member in 1988. Among his more difficult climbs was Klattasine Ridge, with Peter CROFT in 1986.

CLASSIC An excellent or popular climb is called a clas-sic. The DULFERSITZ rappel is sometimes called the classic rappel. (See RAPPELLING.)

CLEAN CLIMBING Rock climbing (free or aid) using hand-placed CRACK PROTECTION that does not damage rock is clean climbing. Clean climbing arose in the early 1970s when climbers in U.S. areas like YOSEMITE VALLEY noticed the scarring that the repeated hammering of PITONS left on rock. The development of clean-climbing equipment like HEXENTRICS, STOPPERS and CRACK-N-UPS by Yvon CHOUIN-ARD and his company, Chouinard Equipment, and later FRIENDS by Ray JARDINE, and the championing of clean-climbing ETHICS in magazine articles, led climbers to aban-don hammer and pitons on many routes. In 1973 in Yosem-ite the Nose of EL CAPITAN and the northwest face of HALF DOME were climbed clean, using NUTS and fixed pitons encountered on the route. These breakthrough ascents proved that some long, largely free routes could be climbed without further rock damage. Clean ascents became popu-lar during this period throughout the United States, BRIT-AIN (where it already had a traditional ethical presence, especially in gritstone areas) and AUSTRALIA. Clean climb-ing proved practical in soft sandstone areas in the American Southwest such as ZION and CANYONLANDS, where the rock scars easily. Clean-climbing equipment and ethics are accepted as the general basis for modern FREE CLIMBING. However, clean climbing has not totally replaced pitons, which are still essential equipment on most BIG WALL aid routes in areas like Yosemite Valley. Yet more and more routes, such as the Shield route on El Capitan, have now been climbed clean.

CLEANING A PITCH   In rock climbing, to remove PROTECTION or AIDS from a PITCH is referred to as cleaning a pitch. This is done by the second climber after the LEADER has anchored the ROPE. Also, cleaning can mean removing dirt and vegetation from a planned new route.

CLEANING TOOL   This lightweight steel probe about eight inches (20 cm) long is used for poking into cracks to dislodge NUTS that have become stuck, and for cleaning dirt from cracks. Cleaning tools can be improvised from long PITONS. Specially designed stamped-steel versions have a hook-nose for manipulating equipment. Cleaning tools for removing stuck SPRING-LOADED CAMMING DEVICES (like the Friend of a Friend, by Leeper United States) are more elaborate with sliding arms to clasp and retract cam triggers. See CRACK PROTECTION for illustration.

CLIFFHANGER   Another name for a SKYHOOK.

CLIFFING   A term coined by American climber and base jumper Randy LEAVITT, cliffing describes the fusion of ascending a BIG WALL or peak and descending the formation by parachute (see BASE JUMPING). Cliffing is a way in which climbing and parachuting can be combined efficiently to work as complements. It was inaugurated in 1980 when Leavitt jumped the 2,700 ft (823 m) FACE of EL CAPITAN in YOSEMITE VALLEY, CALIFORNIA after a six-day ascent of the route Excalibur. HALF DOME, a 2,200-ft (671-m) wall also in Yosemite, was first climb/jumped in 1982 via the BIG WALL route Tis-sa-ack, by Will Oxx. Parachuting from any rock formation in Yosemite is illegal and carries severe penalties. Cliffing, which uses a parachute and involves freefalling, should not be confused with descent by PARAPENTE. A parapente is inflated by wind prior to flight, and performs like a wing, while a parachute is inflated in midair. Leavitt's article, "Cliffing," in *Mountain* magazine #99 describes the origins and adventures of cliffing during the 1980s.

CLIMBING COMMANDS   Signals called between climbers are climbing commands. Common commands and their meanings are:

"On belay?"
Climber asks if the BELAY is ready.
"Belay on."
Belayer affirms belay is ready, and the climber (LEADER or SECOND) may begin.
"Climbing."
Climber leaves the belay.
"Slack."

Climber requests more ROPE to be let out.
"Watch me."
Climber calls to belayer to belay with care and expect to hold a fall.
"Tight rope" or "Tension."
Climber (in this case the second) calls to belayer to hold the rope tight on the belay. A fall is imminent.
"Falling!" or "Take me!"
Climber calls to belayer to hold a fall.
"How much rope?"
Leader asks belayer how much rope is left, to which the belayer responds with an estimate.
"Belay off" or "Safe."
Leader informs belayer that the next belay has been reached and the leader is safely clipped to it. Belayer may remove belaying device from rope.
"Off belay."
Belayer responds to inform leader that the belay is off.

   When descending by RAPPEL (or ABSEIL), the following commands are commonly used.

"Rope!"
Warning called by descending climbers to anyone below that the end of the rope is about to be dropped. Take cover.
"Rock!"
A warning of falling rocks. Take cover.
"On rappel" or "Rappelling."
Optional command to establish that rappelling is in progress.
"Off rappel" or "Rope clear."
Rappelling climber has reached end of the rappel and has unclipped from rope. Stationary climber may rappel.

   A common BOULDERING command is "Spot me," which indicates that the climber wants someone on the ground to prepare to break a fall or assist in backing off a move.

CLIMBING COMPETITION   A competition for SPORT CLIMBING that often takes place on an indoor CLIMBING WALL. (See also ARCO, COURSE SETTER .)

CLIMBING GYM   Indoor gymnasiums with manmade walls and training facilities are a phenomenon of modern SPORT CLIMBING. The VERTICAL CLUB of Seattle, WASHINGTON, was the first such gym in the United States.

CLIMBING HOLDS   Also known as modular hold, climbing holds are manufactured from polyester resins and are made in a variety of shapes and sizes. Used for CLIMBING WALL.

CLIMBING WALL   A manmade wall built to simulate a rock face. Though brick-wall structures have been a feature of British rock-climbing training and education for decades, during the 1980s and 1990s in Europe and the United States, elaborate indoor and outdoor training walls were built in CLIMBING GYMS and for competitions. Walls built for European WORLD CUP SPORT CLIMBING competitions are elaborate structures of cantilevered steel scaffolding to support OVERHANGING faces and ROOFS on which molded resin panels, textured to feel like rock, are fixed. MODULAR HOLDS are bolted on by COURSE SETTERS to create climbs of varying difficulty.

CLINCH, NICHOLAS (1930–   ) (United States) Clinch coordinated, with Pete Schoening, the only FIRST ASCENT by Americans of an EIGHT THOUSAND METER PEAK (26,240-ft); Andy Kauffman and Pete Schoening reached the 26,480-ft (8,073-m) summit of GASHERBRUM I (Hidden Peak), July 5, 1958. Clinch described the expedition in *A Walk in the Sky* (1983). Born in Illinois and raised in Texas, Clinch's first TECHNICAL climb was the GRAND TETON in 1948. Other climbs include first ascents on Hraundrangi, a lava spire in Iceland (1956), and in the CORDILLERA BLANCA the north summit of Puchajirca with Andy Kauffman (1955) and Nevado San Juan with Rick Tidrick (1957). Clinch also directed expeditions for first ascents of MASHERBRUM (1960) on which William UNSOELD and George Bell summited, followed the next day by Clinch and Javed Akhter; Mounts Vinson and Tyree in the VINSON MASSIF, ANTARCTICA in 1966–1967; and a Chinese-American expedition to Ulugh Muztagh (22,923 ft/6,989 m), 1985. A Stanford Law School graduate, Clinch was active in the Sierra Club, from 1961 to 1981 serving as Executive Director from 1976 to 1981. As AMERICAN ALPINE CLUB president (1968–1970), he orchestrated the establishment of the Climber's Ranch in Grand Teton National Park, WYOMING.

CLINOMETER This device for measuring the angle of a slope is used for judging AVALANCHE hazard. Clinometers designed specifically for avalanche evaluation usually consist of a level and dial that indicates slope angle and a corresponding chart providing information about avalanche likelihood at given angles. Some compasses have built-in clinometers.

CLOGWYN DU'R ARDDU (Britain) This CRAG, affectionately known as Cloggy, is the spiritual home of British climbing. Tucked into Snowdon's north side, the black cliff of the black height, as its name translates, is visible from the Snowdon Mountain Railway and the path that follows it from Llanberis, where services and camping are found. Cloggy divides into the east and west BUTTRESSES, the former comprised of steep walls, the other of layered SLABS. It offers long and demanding climbs from 200 to 600 ft (61 to 183 m). There are no BOLTS and few PEGS. A full RACK is essential.

Cloggy was climbed on prior to World War I, but it was in the late 1920s that the first breakthroughs occurred. Considering their equipment and the poor rock, Alf Pigott's 1927 ROUTE on the east buttress and Jack LONGLAND's (of EVEREST fame) 1928 LINE up the west buttress were remarkable achievements. Both routes rate 5.7 and are still repeated.

In the early 1930s, Colin KIRKUS added Great Slab, Pedestal Crack and Curving Crack, all 5.7. Post-World War II

was Cloggy's heyday, with Joe BROWN and Don WHILLANS dominating the 1950s with a string of lines climbed with minimal equipment. Vember (5.9), The Black Cleft, Pinnacle Flake, Llithrig (5.8) and Whillan's Woubits (5.10a) bear their marks. Others made fine routes here, like Ron Moseley, whose White Slab (5.9) on the west buttress is elegant.

When Pete Crew used aid to breach the Great Wall in 1962, a three-decades-long fascination by British hard men for this impressive and smooth wall began. Crew's route was freed in 1975 by John ALLEN at 5.11a. Ed DRUMMOND used aid on the Great Wall to force A Midsummer Night's Dream in 1973. It was freed by Pete Whillance at 5.12a in 1977. Pat LITTLEJOHN climbed the ARETE of The Axe at 5.11 and four years later Jerry MOFFATT provided one solution to the long-standing problem of the right side of the Great Wall with his Master's Wall (5.13b), a route that completed an earlier effort by John Redhead. In 1986 Johnny DAWES continued up where Moffat had moved right to produce the mind-numbing Indian Face (5.14b), a fall from which would be fatal. It remained unrepeated in 1991.
Guidebooks: Paul Williams, *Clogwyn D'ur Arddu* (1989); Williams, *Rock Climbing in Snowdonia* (1990).

CLOTHING FOR MOUNTAINEERING The guiding principle for dressing in cold weather is layering, which uses multiple layers of fabric to regulate the body's microclimate. Layering controls warmth and perspiration by adding or shedding layers. A typical layering system uses three main layers: one next to the skin, a thicker insulating layer over that and an outer layer that is wind- and waterproof.

Thermal or long underwear is worn against the skin. The goal of this layer is to "wick" or transport perspiration away from the body to avoid the chilled, clammy feeling that comes from sweat-soaked underwear and drains the body of warmth. Therefore, these fabrics must absorb minimal moisture and must dry quickly. Examples of such fabrics are synthetics like polypropylene, capilene and chlorofiber. Nylon or polyester is sometimes blended into these fabrics for their hydrophilic (water-loving) properties, or their propensity to spread moisture over a large area for quick evaporation. Wool, silk and wool-synthetic blends are used, but their fibers absorb more moisture than pure synthetics. Cotton absorbs moisture like a sponge.

A thicker layer of primary insulation, such as fiber pile, is worn over underwear. Wool is a long-standing choice, but synthetics like polyester, polyamide (nylon) and polypropylene are lighter and quick-drying. Unlike wool, synthetics absorb no moisture other than that suspended between fibers, and can be wrung out when wet. Synthetics are woven into fiber pile, a carpetlike fuzzy weave that effectively traps dead air as insulation. Two or three medium-weight layers rather than one thick layer is more versatile for layering.

Very cold climates require a layer of heavy insulation, in the form of a thick insulated garment to be worn next. This insulation may be either natural feather down or synthetics like Hollofil, Quallofil or Thinsulate, which are matted, interwoven microfibers (see SLEEPING BAGS AND INSULATED CLOTHING).

The outer layer protects the body from rain, snow and WIND CHILL. Wind blowing against wet clothing blows away warmth by convection. At zero degrees F (−18 degrees C) with a wind of 10 mph (16 km per hour) the wind chill effect is −22 degrees F (−30 degrees C). Many fabrics are used for the outer layer. In dry conditions noncoated nylon or similar closely woven fabric is enough to prevent wind from compromising insulation. Coated cloths like nylon coated with polyurethane or polyvinylchloride (PVC), or cotton/polyester (Japara, oilskin or 60/40 cloth) treated with wax/polyurethane coatings are waterproof but are also nonbreathable, meaning body moisture collects inside the garment, dampening the wearer's clothing.

Dispersal and removal of body moisture while preventing rain or snow melt from entering has been the object of much research by fabric technologists. Because body vapor molecules are different from rain molecules, it is possible to control the transmission of the two types of moisture. The following fabrics work toward this end:

Microfiber fabrics: Woven micro-threads that are water-repellent and breathable without the use of coatings or laminates, such as Microfine, H2Off and Versatech.

Waterproof/breathable treatments: Nonporous coatings use a polyurethane film that diffuses perspiration.

Branded microporous coatings: These attain waterproof/breathable characteristics through micropores.

Microporous membranes: A polytetrafluroethylene (PTFE) membrane made microporous by a biaxial stretching process. GORE-TEX is the pioneer in its field.

Temperature may be further controlled in outer garments by the use of zippers in the armpits and chest. Overdressing will cause the wearer to overheat and drench clothes with perspiration, so shedding clothes as activity warms the wearer is an essential part of dressing in layers for cold weather.

CLOVE HITCH   An adjustable knot used to secure a ROPE to a CARABINER, especially at a BELAY. (See KNOTS.)

Clove Hitch Knot

CLYDE, NORMAN (1885–1972) (United States)
Clyde was a pioneer of many climbs in the SIERRA NEVADA Range during the 1920s. Originally from Philadelphia, Clyde migrated to CALIFORNIA at age 25 to work as a schoolteacher. When Clyde was 28, after three years of marriage his wife died of tuberculosis. Clyde became a recluse who devoted his life to MOUNTAINEERING, at which

he remained active until the age of 85. Clyde was renowned for his strength and energy. His contemporary David BROWER called him "the pack that walks like a man." In 1923 Clyde visited Glacier National Park in MONTANA, where in a fit of endurance he climbed 36 peaks in as many days, most of them FIRST ASCENTS. His first ascents in the Sierras totalled 160 during the 1920s. Many were climbed solo. Among his more technical routes are the icy U-Notch Couloir on Clyde Minaret, Clyde Couloir on North Palisade, and the East Arete of Mount Humphreys. In 1931 he climbed the last of the Sierra's 14,000-ft (4,268-m) peaks, Thunderbolt Peak. Clyde Minaret, Norman Clyde Peak and Clyde Spires bear his name. He was a prolific writer, publishing over 30 articles on his climbing experiences.

COAST MOUNTAINS   (Canada)   This 500-mile (800-km) wilderness of peaks lies along the west coast of BRITISH COLUMBIA, extending north to the ALASKA panhandle. The full range runs from the Fraser River north to the SAINT ELIAS Range. However, local aficionados regard the core of the Coast Mountains as being between the towns of Pemberton and Bella Coola. No roads penetrate this 219-mile (350-km) stretch, and there are about 100 peaks over 10,000 ft (3,049 m). This area contains great ICE FIELDS such as the Homathko, the Lilooet, the Hai-Iltzuk and the Compton-Toba complex, and peaks like WADDINGTON, Monmouth, Raleigh, Gilbert, Good Hope, Queen Bess, Greenville, Razorback, Silverthrone and Monarch. The area is distinguished by remoteness, difficulty of access, rugged terrain and troublesome weather. Potential for new ROUTES in the area is extensive. August and September offer the best weather. Access is normally via helicopter from either Pemberton, Bluff Lake or Bella Coola. The northernmost region, the Stikine (containing the DEVIL'S THUMB), is normally approached from Petersburg or Wrangell in Alaska.
Guidebooks: Dick Culbert, *Climber's Guide to the Coastal Ranges of British Columbia* (1965, with updates 1969, 1974); Bruce Fairley, *A Guide to Climbing and Hiking in British Columbia* (1986).

COCHITI MESA   (United States)   An escarpment of welded tuff on the Pajarito Plateau of NEW MEXICO. The rock resembles SMITH ROCKS and is peppered with small POCKETS. Early ROUTES here include CRACKS like The Apprentice (5.11c) by Mark Royball and Mark Hesse in the late 1970s. The cliffs' relevance to modern climbing began in 1985 when Doug Pandorf and French expatriate Jean de Lataillade rediscovered it and initiated SPORT CLIMBING there. Currently there are many difficult routes, such as Shadowdancer (5.13a) by de Lataillade and Bertrand Gramont (France).

COL   A saddle or pass, usually between two mountains.

COLD   In cold conditions a poorly protected human body loses more heat to the environment (through conduction, convection, radiation and evaporation) than it can produce. Mechanisms of the body for coping with cold include shivering, which produces heat by increasing metabolism within the muscles, and constricting blood vessels in the skin (around extremities like arms, legs or nose) to reduce blood flow and limit heat loss by letting tissues cool. But it is ingenuity that has allowed humans to adapt to and inhabit cold areas like polar and Himalayan regions. Shelter and clothing are important factors in cold survival. Diet is also important in extreme cold. Polar and Himalayan expeditioners have found that the rigors of cold, combined with altitude and physical exertion, drain the body of 20 to 30% of its body weight. An intake of 5,000 to 6,000 calories per day, eaten in regular snacks, is advised to avoid depletion of muscle tissue. Cold-weather diets favor high-calorie foods like carbohydrates and fats. Eskimos, who inhabit northern latitudes, eat high-protein, high-fat foods like pemmican.

Living in an environment in a state of constant freeze presents many difficulties. Problems include shelter from wind and storm (see BIVOUAC, BIVOUAC SACK, IGLOO, PORTA LEDGE, SNOW CAVE, TENTS, WIND CHILL); cooking and producing water (see DEHYDRATION, STOVES); keeping warm (see CLOTHING FOR MOUNTAINEERING, INSULATION, SLEEPING BAGS, VAPOR BARRIER LINERS); and avoiding maladies like FROSTBITE, HYPOTHERMIA, RAYNAUD'S DISEASE.

COLLIE, JOHN NORMAN (1859–1942) (Britain)

One of the great names in British mountain exploration at the turn of the century, Collie's journeys and discoveries among his native hills of SCOTLAND, SKYE and Cumbria contributed to the mapping and geographical understanding of those regions. In the ALPS, he made the FIRST ASCENT of the Dent du Requin, first TRAVERSE of the Grepon and first guideless ascent of the Old Brenva route on MONT BLANC. In the HIMALAYA, he climbed Diamirai Peak with A.F. MUMMERY in 1895. In the CANADIAN ROCKIES, he made first ascents of Mounts Lefroy, Victoria, Athabasca, Edith, and Forbes, and discovered the COLUMBIA ICE FIELDS. He also climbed in Arctic NORWAY.

His place in British MOUNTAINEERING history is as much a function of character as it is a consequence of his three most famous ascents—of SCAFELL's Moss Ghyll in 1892, Tower Ridge on BEN NEVIS in 1894 and the Cioch on Sron na Ciche in Skye in 1906. The former climb earned Collie notoriety on account of the "Collie Step"—a small foothold chipped with an ICE AXE into the SLAB at the route's crux. When criticized for this he commented "Peccavi!" (Latin, meaning "I have sinned"). Nonetheless he served, in 1920, as president of the ALPINE CLUB of Britain. He was a lifelong, aloof and reclusive bachelor, and a distinguished scientist. He took the first Chair of Organic Chemistry in University College, London. He cooperated with Nobel Prize winner William Ramsay in the discovery of the "noble gases"—argon, helium, krypton, xenon and neon, and pioneered the development of the neon light and X-ray photography. A great conversationalist who lived on whisky, tobacco and little else, Collie claimed to believe in fairies and the Loch Ness monster, and may have originated the myth of the Great Grey Men of Ben MacDhui. He proposed Aleister Crowley to the Alpine Club and cultivated friendships that cut across the social barriers of the time. His most constant companion (by whose side he lies buried in Struan Kirkyard on Skye) was a Highland peasant and Skye mountain guide and ghillie, John Mackenzie.

Further reading: Norman Collie, *Mountaineering on the Himalaya and other Mountain Ranges* (1902); Norman Collie with H. E. M. Stutfield, *Climbs and Explorations in the Canadian Rockies* (1904); Christine Mill, *Norman Collie: A Life in Two Worlds* (1987).

COLOMBIA

The country has three ranges. The northernmost and highest is Sierra Nevada de Santa Marta (with Pico Bolivar, 18,947 ft/5,775 m), the highest coastal mountain range in the world, located 40 miles (64 km) south of the Caribbean beaches. The Cordillera Central (with Nevado del Huila, 17,842 ft/5,439 m), southwest of Bogota, is a string of volcanos that marches south over the Ecuadorian border. The Cordillera Oriental, is near the VENEZUELA border. Its main peaks are in the Sierra Nevada de Cocuy. All three glaciated Colombian ranges rise above torrid valleys. Their proximity to the equator has endowed them with a peculiar environment, comparable to exotic areas like Uganda's RUWENZORI. Vegetation is striking, with giant groundsels ("trailejones" or *espelethias*) growing at over 15,000 ft (4,573 m). The last two ranges named have populated slopes but the Santa Marta district is guarded by the Arhuaco tribes.

MOUNTAINEERING in Colombia was initiated by the country's "Founding Father" Francisco Jose de Caldas (1770–1816), who climbed volcanoes Purace (15,256 ft/4,650 m) and Pan de Azucar (15,322 ft/4,670 m) in 1800. He invented the hypsometer, an instrument to measure altitudes by means of boiling water. Between 1868 and 1870, German vulcanologists Wilhelm Reiss and Alfons Stuebel climbed volcanos in the Cordillera Central, but the major volcanic peaks were climbed by German-Colombian parties: Ruiz (17,145 ft/5,226 m) in 1936; Tolima, a shapely conical volcano (17,108 ft/5,215 m), in 1926; and Santa Isabel (16,703 ft/5,090 m) in 1943. In 1939 a Colombian of German descent, Edwin Kraus, and his friends climbed Pico Bolivar, of the Santa Marta Range, highest in Colombia. The same year Thomas Cabot led an AMERICAN ALPINE CLUB expedition up Pico Colon, barely seven ft (two m) lower than Bolivar.

During the Second World War, Americans under Paul PETZOLDT pioneered El Guardian (17,343 ft/5,285 m), Pico Ojeda (18,012 ft/5,490 m) and La Reina (18,158 ft/5,535 m). The Cocuy chain, between 1938 and 1944, attracted the Swiss Georges Cuenet and August Gansser, who collected the central and northern peaks, while Kraus and comrades seized the southern and eastern ones. Periods of political unrest have retarded the growth of mountaineering in Colombia.

There are in Colombia today 10 mountain clubs, grouped under the Federacion Colombiana de Montanismo (Colombia Mountaineering Association), based in Bogota. TECHNICAL rock-climbing is found 18 miles (30 km) from Bogota, at a sandstone cliff called Suesla.

Further reading: Jose F. Machado, et al, *Frontera Superior de Colombia* (1987).

Evelio Echevarria
Colorado State University

COLORADO (United States) See BOULDER, FLAT-IRONS, FRONT RANGE, INDEPENDENCE PASS, ROCKY MOUNTAIN NATIONAL PARK, SOUTH PLATTE, TURKEY ROCK.

COLORADO ICE CLIMBING (United States) COLORADO has numerous popular ICE-CLIMBING areas. Most notably, the ice on the outskirts of Ouray (in southern Colorado) offers the widest variety of accessible ice in the state, from multi-pitch waterfalls to one-pitch TOP-ROPE SMEARS. Just down the road, Telluride has the two most famous ice climbs: Bridleveil Falls and the Ophir Ice Hose. In recent years, a canyon outside Rifle has become popular for its short but sustained ice. Glenwood and Hidden Falls are also well-known ROUTES, both accessed from Interstate 70, a dozen miles (19 km) east of Glenwood Springs. The fiercely steep Fang and the classic Rigid Designator both form in Vail above the golf course. Otherwise, ice appears sporadically throughout Colorado: near Redstone, in ROCKY MOUNTAIN NATIONAL PARK and deep within the San Juan Mountains.

COLORADO NATIONAL MONUMENT (United States) This rock-climbing area of variable-quality red sandstone is located near the COLORADO-UTAH border, five miles (eight km) west of Grand Junction, Colorado. The area has long CRACK and FACE routes on canyon walls and spectacular spires, such as the six-pitch Independence Monument. Like all desert areas of the American Southwest, seasonal extremes of temperature affect climbing, making spring and fall the best periods.
Guidebook: Eric Bjornstad, *Desert Rock: Climber's Guide to Canyon Country* (1988).

COLORADO PLATEAU (United States) This vast region of the American Southwest desert is one of the world's largest rock-climbing areas, and encompasses areas of UTAH, COLORADO, ARIZONA and NEW MEXICO. Spectacular beauty, strenuous climbing and soft, red-hued sandstone characterize Colorado Plateau climbing. CRACK CLIMBING is found in unlimited quantities, and the most popular cragging site lies along the Potash Road (Scenic Byway 279) near Moab and features BOLT-protected FACE climbs. Although short FREE CLIMBS are the main attraction, the Colorado Plateau is renowned for multi-pitch AID CLIMBS up slender towers.

Climbers first made serious forays into the region in the late 1930s and 1940s. The 1960s were the golden age of Canyonlands climbing, when most of the desert spires were climbed, with Layton KOR leading the way. The area is visited by greater numbers of climbers today, but the solitude and possibilities for adventure have not diminished. The best weather is in the cooler months of spring and fall, although subject to thundershowers.

Most climbing areas are centered around the old mining town of Moab, Utah. The principal areas include:

Arches National Park: 5 miles (eight km) north of Moab, this park is a recent climbing destination. Most activity has been on the desperately soft Entrada Formation. Fine one-pitch free climbs have been accomplished here, but the best routes are multi-pitch aid climbs on intimidating towers.

Canyonlands National Park: This extensive region has seen little action, and most activity is confined to the Island in the Sky. Many classic desert towers are found here, such as the very popular Moses Tower and the towers of Monument Basin.

Castle Valley: About 20 miles (32 km) east of Moab, scenic Castle Valley lies between the La Sal Mountains and the Colorado River. The centerpiece of the area is Castle Rock aka CASTLETON TOWER, one of the most visited towers in the Southwest. To the east lie the Fisher Towers Group, home to some of the longest (900 feet/274 m), softest and most challenging aid climbs in the desert.

Monument Valley: Located within the Navajo Tribal Nation astride the Arizona-Utah boarder, Monument Valley contains some of the most recognizable scenery in America, and some of the most spectacular climbs, such as the precarious-looking Totem Pole. Although climbing is officially limited to those who pay very high fees, clandestine ascents are common in the Tribal Park. Many fine towers are located outside the park.

Indian Creek: The Wingate Canyons in this area of Canyonlands (some of which is private land, the remainder is under the U.S. Bureau of Land Management) offer extensively developed crack-climbing cliffs. Climbs are one to four pitches long, and are known for their relentless difficulty and steepness.

Guidebooks: Eric Bjornstad, *Desert Rock* (1988); Kyle Copeland, *Climbs to Nowhere* (1989).

COLUMBIA ICE FIELDS (Canada) This is a 92-sq-mile (230-sq-km) mass of glacial ice in the central CANADIAN ROCKIES. It is 9,000 ft (2,744 m) high and is big enough to create its own weather. Eight GLACIERS radiate from its central plateau, and meltwater flows from here to the Arctic, Atlantic and Pacific oceans. The Columbia River is fed by this ICE CAP. The ICE FIELD was discovered in 1898 by J. N. COLLIE and H. Woolley. Several great peaks of the Rockies are located nearby. The highest summit, Mount Columbia (12,290 ft/3,747 m) was first climbed in July 1902 by James OUTRAM and Swiss guide Christian Kaufmann. At the time they believed it was the highest point in CANADA. Mount LOGAN, far to the north, was found to be higher. March through May are the popular months for climbing on skis in this region. During the summer skis are still recommended for travel across the ice field. Peaks like Castleguard, Columbia, Snow Dome, Kitchener, East and West Stutfield and NORTH TWIN are popular ski mountaineering objectives. Mount Athabasca and neighboring Mount Andromeda (11,316 ft/3,450 m) are the most accessible snow and ice peaks of the Columbia Ice Field, both having 10 or more routes.

COMBINED TACTICS To stand on one's partner's shoulders, or to receive a boost up to overcome a holdless start on a climb is referred to as combined tactics.

COMBIN GROUP (France) The most westerly outpost of the Pennine Alps, this group is really a separate massif on the frontier crest linking the Mont Blanc group and the higher Pennine peaks. The usual base for this area is the village of Bourg St. Pierre, around 25 miles (40 km) from Martigny. The principal summit in the area is the Grand Combin (14,150 ft/4,314 m). Because it is more remote, it appeals to those interested in exploration. Its routes are not without the element of risk. Ascents most usually start from the Cabane Valsorey and climb to the Col du Meitin. From there the west ridge, first climbed in 1884 by C. Boisviel et al, offers a fine continuation at PD + . Otherwise a traverse can be made under the mountain before climbing the northwest face, a ROUTE put up in 1933 by E. Blanchet and K. Mooser. The south face can be approached from a BIVOUAC shelter on the Plateau du Couloir, reaching the subsidiary summit of the Combin de Valsorey (3,724 ft/4,184 m) and the west ridge of the Grand Combin. There is some danger of stonefall on this route. On the mountain's north ridge is the Aiguille du Croissant (3,940 ft/4,250 m) and to its east is the Combin de Tsessetta (13,582 ft/4,141 m).

COMMITMENT A climb is said to be committing, or a climber is committed to a climb, when there is no way of backing down or reversing the move or section climbed. (See POINT OF NO RETURN.)

COMPASS An instrument that indicates magnetic north, or a compass, is essential for mountain navigation. The Silva design, with a rotating compass housing on a transparent base plate for laying over maps has proved the most functional compass for climbers. Use of a compass is dependent upon basic principles. A compass needle always points to magnetic north (true north is the direction from any point on earth to the geographic North Pole). The magnetic north pole (located in northern Canada) varies from year to year. This variation (or declination) causes compass readings to vary east or west, depending on location. Compasses must be corrected for declination using a map's key.

COMPASS AND ALTIMETER NAVIGATION In WHITE-OUT or foggy conditions one's location on a route may be estimated with map, compass and altimeter by taking elevation readings with an altimeter and matching them to map contours, and by following predetermined compass bearings from point to point. The technique works most effectively if bearings from prominent landmarks are recorded on a map during ascent so they may be followed during descent. On some popular peaks navigation details are provided in guidebooks or at ranger stations.

COMPETITION See CLIMBING COMPETITION.

CONDENSATION Condensation is the buildup of body-driven water vapor (sweat, breathing) on the surface of a nonbreathable fabric such as a rain jacket, tent wall or the inside of a boot. In MOUNTAINEERING situations where temperature differences between outside (cold) and inside a tent or clothing are great, vapor condenses quickly, causing dampness. Thus, over prolonged periods clothing and sleeping bags may become wet, lose their insulating properties and put climbers in danger of HYPOTHERMIA. Solutions to condensation include ventilating or airing out clothing and tentage (modern clothing and TENTS use vent designs and BREATHABLE FABRICS like GORE-TEX to combat condensation); avoiding overdressing; LAYERING clothing by utilizing layers of fabrics with low water-retention properties; and wearing VAPOR BARRIER LINERS close to the skin to keep moisture close to the body and out of clothing.

CONDORIRI (Bolivia) The Aimara highlanders of BOLIVIA explained the birth of this peak with a legend: It was the body of a white condor—a good omen for their people—shot down by the arrow of a prince. Where the bird fell there rose a giant ice peak, resembling a condor with outstretched wings. From the south, this is how Condoriri looks, and the original name, *Cunturchiri*, means "The Frozen Condor." The mountain is 18,531 ft (5,648 m) high and is located about 40 miles (64 km) north of La Paz. It was climbed solo in July 1941 by Wilfred Kuhm (German), by the southwest ridge. Other routes are the east and southeast ridge (Italians, 1968), the north wall (Germans, 1969) and the west side (Germans, 1982). Condoriri's neighbors are also fine peaks. The west "wing" of the Frozen Condor, Cuchillo Cunu (18,150 ft/5,532 m) is a dazzling white wall and the Nevado de Fabulosa (17,618 ft/5,370 m) is a steep pyramid known as Pequeno [smaller] Alpamayo.
Guidebook: Alain Messili, *La Cordillera Real de los Andes, Bolivia* (1984).

Evelio Echevarria
Colorado State University

CONTOUR Lines on a map that mark and connect points of equal height.

CONWAY, WILLIAM MARTIN (1856–1937) (Britain) This Victorian mountaineer and art critic had his first season in the ALPS in 1872. He was not naturally gifted either as athlete or rock-climber, and his bent was insistently toward mountain travel, one of those who ". . . always wants to see what is on the other side of any range of hills, prefers passes to peaks, chooses the easiest and most normal route." This instinct perhaps found its most significant expression in his work of 1892 in mapping the KARAKORAM, for which he was knighted in 1895. In 1896 he made the first crossing of Spitzbergen, and he climbed ACONCAGUA and other ANDEAN peaks in 1898. He wrote several important books on mountaineering, in a fine, precise yet evocative descriptive style: "He looked at peaks and glaciers with the trained eye of a connoisseur of colour and form, quick to note not only the more dramatic effects, but also the elusive beauty of some apparently featureless snowfield." By profession, he was a professor of fine art and a reputable late-Victorian art critic. His *Early Flemish Artists* of 1887 is still an important work on the period. In later life he served as a member of Parliament for the combined universities until his elevation to the peerage by Prime Minister Ramsay MacDonald in 1931. Conway also traveled widely in the newly created Soviet Union in his sixties, and wrote *The Art Treasures in Soviet Russia* (1925). After being made a baron, he took the title Lord Conway of Allington. He was remarkable in his time for being so amiable that he was impossible to quarrel with—a useful attribute on his many expeditions. With W. A. B. Coolidge, he edited the first series of alpine guidebooks, which eventually, despite their dire warnings against a practice Conway himself frequently followed, were to result in the spread of guideless climbing.

Further reading: William M. Conway, *Mountain Memories* (1920).

COOK, FREDERICK (1856–1940) (United States)

Cook achieved notoriety for his fraudulent claim to have climbed DENALI. A few years later, he also fraudulently claimed to have reached the North Pole. In 1903, Cook and several others climbed to 10,000 ft (3,049 m) on Denali and then completed their epic circumnavigation. He returned to New York and obtained sponsorship for another try at Denali from *Harpers* magazine. After abortive attempts to climb Denali from the south in 1906, his companions Parker and Browne left the expedition and returned to the States. Cook pressed on up the Ruth Glacier with only a horsepacker, Edward Barrill, and after a two-week trip, told the press that he had climbed Denali. Three years later, Barrill testified that they had climbed no higher than 10,000 ft (3,049 m). After Cook's ensuing North Pole debacle, he was jailed in Texas for mail fraud.

COOK, MOUNT (New Zealand)

Located on NEW ZEALAND's South Island, Mount Cook (12,346 ft/3,764 m) is the highest peak in that country. Its slopes are visited by numerous climbers who are often guided. The mountain can be subject to harsh winds and deep snows blowing from the Tasman Sea, 15 miles (24 km) away. AVALANCHES also sweep the faces—in 1992 one of the greatest avalanches ever known fell from the summit of Cook, scoured the 5,000-ft (1,524-m) east face, and traveled four miles (six km) to cross the Tasman Glacier, dropping 9,000 ft (2,744 m) by the end. The summit was reduced in height by some 30 to 70 ft (nine to 21 m). Climbers have since reached the summit area, but found it unstable.

Attempts to climb Cook began in 1882. It was first successfully climbed in 1894 (north ridge) by New Zealanders George Graham, Tom Fyfe and Jack Clark on Christmas Day. They had been spurred to action by news of a planned visit by E. A. Fitgerald (BRITAIN) and his guide Mathias ZURBRIGGEN, who in 1895 made the second ascent by a new route (northeast ridge), Zurbriggen summiting alone.

Cook is a triple-summited mountain, and the Grand Traverse of Cook came in 1913, by Peter Graham, Darby Thompson and Freda du Fuar, who had made the first female ascent of Cook in 1910. This is now recognized as a CLASSIC alpine TRAVERSE. Du Fuar also made first ascents of Mount Dampier and second ascents of Mount Tasman.

The major ridges of Cook were climbed in the decades following, the last being the south ridge, in 1948, by a party including Edmund HILLARY, of EVEREST fame. The faces of Cook then became sought after, with the Hooker Face going in 1956, followed by the east face (1961) and the south face (1962). The longest and steepest, the Caro-

Mount Cook, New Zealand

line Face, went to two parties; Peter Gough and John Glasgow, and Graeme Dingle and George Harris.

COPPERHEAD

An item of climbing equipment used for BIG WALL and AID CLIMBING, a copperhead consists of a lump of malleable metal crimped to the end of a short length of steel cable, with a swagged loop at the end which is clipped into. The head is copper, though aluminum is sometimes used. This softer variety is called an ALUMA-HEAD. Copperheads range in size from one-eighth inch to one-half inch (one-third to one-and-a-quarter cm). They are regarded as body-weight-only placements, and typify difficult aid climbing. A variation in design is the circle head, also known as Mashheads, for placement under arches or in ceilings.

Copperheads can be placed where PITONS, NUTS or other devices will not work, especially in shallow grooves and seams of incipient cracks. A copperhead is placed by positioning it in a groove and striking the head repeatedly with a hammer until the metal softens and bites into the texture of the rock. Placement is complete when the copperhead is well set, or "pasted" into the groove. For precise placement, a striking tool is sometimes used, like a piton or a sawed-off nail punch. Copperheads are removed by attaching a sling or chain of CARABINERS between the hammer and the copperhead loop and pulling vigorously outward. Because copperheads must be hammered, they are mainly useful on hard rock like granite.

Forrest Mountaineering (United States) manufactured copperheads during the 1970s and 1980s. They have become an essential tool in the ascents of some of the most difficult aid climbs in America.

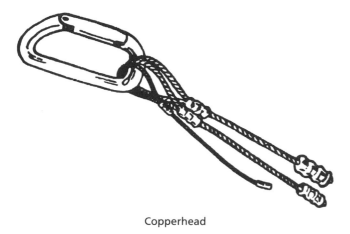

Copperhead

CORDILLERA Spanish for mountain range. Used in the ANDES.

CORDILLERA BLANCA (Peru) The White Cordillera are the highest, perhaps most beautiful alps of the tropical zone and also boast the greatest number of GLACIERS. With a granitic core crowned everywhere by hanging ice, the range runs roughly north to south for a length of some 100 miles (160 km), with an average width of 20 miles (32 km). HUASCARAN Sur (22,205 ft/6,769 m), highest point in the range and in PERU, rises more than 10,000 ft (3,049 m) above the farms of the Santa Valley. The range lies almost entirely within the Huascaran National Park. Its southernmost valleys exhibit the indigenous plant *puya* (*Puya Raimondi*), a bromeliad that rises 15 ft (4.5 m) tall and which, when in bloom, displays the largest inflorescence in the plant world. The northern third of the range, with valleys descending to 6,000 ft (1,829 m), has groves of *quenua* (*Polylepis incana*), a red bark tree. Access to the Cordillera Blanca is easy, a seven-hour bus ride from Lima to Huaras, the starting point. Valleys are usually short and pleasant; glaciers descend to 16,400 ft (5,000 m). Temperatures are benign, causing unstable snow and rockfalls. Safest are the flanks of peaks that face the south or southeast. CORNICES are a permanent danger. Highest unclimbed peak is Puntancuerno II (19,551 ft/5,959 m), in the Chinchey group. Climbing season is from the end of May to mid August. Expeditions use porters and caravans of donkeys to carry equipment and there are professional guides (some trained in Germany and Spain) to be hired at the Casa de Guias (Guides' Quarters) in Huaras. First climb in the range was by Annie PECK (1908). The Austro-Germans that repeatedly climbed in the Cordillera Blanca produced excellent maps, scale 1:100,000 in 1935 and 1942. French, Italian, Peruvians, Germans and Americans (the last ones repeatedly led by Leigh Ortenburger and H. Adams CARTER) won new peaks and great new routes. Best expedition

records for the history of this cordillera have been kept by the *American Alpine Journal* since 1952. In Ricker's famous guidebook, it is stated that to visit the White Range means "to be captive for life."
Guidebooks: Jim Bartle, *Parque Nacional Huascaran. Ancash-Peru* (1985); Philippe Beaud, *The Peruvian Andes* (1988); John Ricker, *Yuraq Janca* (1981).

Evelio Echevarria
Colorado State University

CORDILLERA DE HUAYHUASH (Peru) The Huayhuash impresses the climber for its ferocity. It is composed of some 60 granitic peaks, placed between 16,100 and 21,711 ft (4,900 and 6,617 m). There are two groups of mountains: the northern or main one has Yerupaja, highest in the system, with 21,836 ft (6,617 m), plus Siula (20,813 ft/6,341 m), Sarapo (20,103 ft/6,127 m), Yerupaja Chico (20,082 ft/6,121 m); the southern group runs east to west, with some 20 peaks of which Huacshash is the highest (18,516 ft/5,644 m). The towns of Chiquian and Cajatambo, reached by motor, are the gates to the range. Dry season extends from mid May to August.

Climbing began in 1936 when Austrians Arnold Awerzberg and Erwin SCHNEIDER attempted the incredibly steep YERUPAJA and scaled Siula and Rassac (19,743 ft/6,017 m). Hans Kinzl and Schneider produced then an excellent map, scale 1:50,000, although not including the southern group, which is still imperfectly surveyed. In 1950, American university students climbed Yerupaja. In 1954 and 1957, the Austrians climbed Sarapo, Yerupaja Chico, Jirishhanca, the sharp white needle of Jirishhanca Chico (17,936 ft/5,467 m) and many other peaks. Italians under Bonicelli collected another good harvest in 1964. The American Carter expedition (1975) and the Italian Bulfoni group (1979) climbed in the southern group. Since then nearly all the Huayhuash peaks have been ascended. Choice of new routes has been very easy: They abound. Remarkable endeavors have been the climbing of walls and the crossing of ridges of Yerupaja (Americans, Argentinians, Germans and New Zealanders); ascents of buttresses of Jirishhanca (Italians) and Rondoy (Britons, Czechs); and climbs of north faces on Puscanturpa Norte (17,854 ft/5,442 m) by Italians. Toni Valeruz, another Italian, dared to ski-extreme down the south face of Sarapo.
Guidebook: Jim Bartle and David Sharman, *Trails and Climbs of the Cordillera Blanca of Peru* (1992).
Further reading: Jim Bartle, *Parque Nacional Huascaran* (1985); Philippe Beaud, *Cordillera Blanca. Cordillera Huayash* (1988).

Evelio Echevarria
Colorado State University

CORDILLERA DE VILCABAMBA (Peru) A complex of sharp ice peaks, endowed with CORNICED RIDGES and fluted ice walls, situated 45 miles (72 km) west-north-west of Cuzco, the former Inca capital. The name stands for the lower ALPS and moors around, or *vilca-pampa* (sacred plains). Still not well surveyed, the heights of most of its peaks has been determined by ALTIMETER and figures may eventually prove lower. The highest peak, now well measured, is Nevado Salcantay (20,574 ft/6,271 m). It was first scaled in 1952 by a large French-American group, after a Swiss team had also tried for the summit. In 1956, an American party led by Fred Ayres climbed four peaks between 18,000 and 19,029 ft (5,488 and 5,801 m) of Lasunayoc. The same year, Lionel TERRAY and three companions summited the difficult Nevado Humantay (or Soray) (19,414 ft/5,917 m). In 1957, a party of British university students ascended Pumasillo, probably 19,500 ft (5,945 m) high. A large Swiss expedition went in 1959 to the Panta and Camballa groups, climbing nearly all their peaks (averaging 18,000 ft/5,488 m) and mapping that massif, the only good Vilcabamba map to date. Later large New Zealand and Australian groups traveled to the range, methodically grabbing the majority of the remaining peaks (1962, 1968 and 1969), including Sacsarayoc (19,670 ft/5,996 m). But Salcantay is the great attraction of this district. It has so far yielded nine difficult routes, but the south precipice has seen the boldest enterprises. In 1970, Bavarians climbed the south BUTTRESS, and in 1973 Australians and New Zealanders did the southeast RIDGE. In 1986, British climbers risked their lives up the AVALANCHE-prone southwest face. But since the early 1980s, expeditions to the Vilcabamba have been sporadic. Lacking good maps, it is not possible to tell the number of unclimbed peaks that may remain. The Vilcabamba is a ferocious range, much like its northern sister, the Huayhuash. Access is via the Cuzco-Limatambo road, then by the Soray Pass. Being close to the Amazon, weather during the climbing season (June–August) is unpredictable.

Evelio Echevarria
Colorado State University

CORDILLERA REAL (Bolivia) The Major or Royal Range comprises some 400 peaks rising above the Bolivian plateau on the west and tropical valleys on all other sides. It has roughly a north-south direction, a length of 90 miles (144 km) and a width of 10 miles (16 km). It begins in the north with the mighty massif of Sorata, which includes ILLAMPU (20,893 ft/6,368 m), Anchohuma (21,087 ft/6,427 m) and some 50 peaks averaging 18,000 ft (5,488 m). It continues southward toward La Paz, where CONDORIRI (18,530 ft/5,648 m) and Huayna Potosi (19,975 ft/6,088 m), two favorites of climbers, are found. South of the Bolivian capital the ranges abate below 18,000 ft (5,400 m) but rise again with Mururata (19,290 ft/5,879 m) and ILLIMANI (21,004 ft/6,402 m). The latter, the backdrop of the steep streets of La Paz, signals the end of the range.

Climbing season is from May to September, but cold and wind are constant. Access with a vehicle is so easy that a peak over 19,680 ft (6,000 m) can be climbed from La Paz (11,850 ft/3,612 m) in one day, roundtrip. MOUNTAINEERING history began in 1898 when Martin CONWAY and guides ascended Illimani. Local and visiting Germans then took over until the late 1930s, climbing Ancohuma, Haucana (20,365 ft/6,207 m), Huayna Potosi, Illampu, Condoriri and others. Major TECHNICAL climbs have been on the west faces of Illampu, Huayna Potosi and Tiquimani (18,108

ft/5,519 m), the last one a peak sacred to the Aimaras. In normal years, some skiing takes place (March–April) in Chacaltaya (16,450ft/5,015 m). In 1935, the German and Austrian Alpine Club made a map of the Sorata Massif (revised in 1987), but the area south of La Paz is uncharted. **Further Reading:** Martin Conway, *The Bolivian Andes* (1901); Alain Mesili, *La Cordillera Real de los Andes: Bolivia* (1984).

Evelio Echevarria
Colorado State University

CORDILLERA VILCANOTA (Peru) Highest range in southeast PERU, this cordillera rises 70 miles (112 km) southeast of Cuzco, capital of the vanished Inca empire. *Vilca* means "sacred." The range is composed of two major branches. The main and northern runs east to west and has easy access from Cuzco, via the Ocongate and Tinqui farm districts. The highest mountain is Ausangate, or rather, Asuancati (Peak of Fear), 20,933 ft or 6,372 m high, first climbed in 1953 by three Bavarians. The northern area also has 10 more peaks over 19,500 ft (5,945 m) and in the 1950s and 1960s, international expeditions, mostly German, collected a good harvest. The second group is lower and permanently visible to travelers, since it runs north to south, parallel to the east side of the Cuzco-Juliaca railroad and highway. Its highest peak may be Yanacuchilla (17,780 ft/5,476 m). Peruvian climbers have been active in this group, however the highlands south and east of both groups are largely unsurveyed. Political unrest in the Cuzco area greatly reduced mountaineering after 1980. **Guidebook:** Rob Rachowiecki, *Peru: A Travel Survival Kit* (1987).

Evelio Echevarria
Colorado State University

CORNER On a cliff, a feature shaped like an open book. The word is used in British and U.S. climbing. DIHEDRAL (United States) and DIEDRE (France) are equivalent words.

CORNICE Mountain ridges at any altitude may be capped with cornices of snow. Prevailing winds deposit and sculpt snow into peaked crests that appear as overhanging caps on ridges. The side facing the prevailing wind tends to be smooth and rounded, offering easier climbing terrain. The lee side of a cornice forms an OVERHANG of unstable snow that can fracture under a climber's weight. FACES underneath such formations are at risk of falling cornices, and climbers TRAVERSING a corniced RIDGE often travel across fragile snow and undercut cornices in ignorance of the danger they are in. Atmospheric and temperature conditions affect cornice stability. They may be firm and relatively safe to cross, or they may consist of dangerously soft layered or porous snow. Double cornices, which overhang both sides of a ridge, are especially troublesome and dangerous to cross. At their worst cornices can resemble huge tottering rolls of whipped cream. Such cornices may be impassable. Fatalities of climbers breaking through cornices are common, and cornice crests should be avoided. Instead, traverse on the windward side several feet below the crest, near rocks if any are visible and viable. BELAYS should be used if possible.

CORNWALL (Britain) The southwest tip of the English coast is noted for its SEA CLIFF climbing. See BOSIGRAN; CARN GOWLA; CARN KENIDJACK; CHAIR LADDER; GURNARD'S HEAD; LAND'S END; LIZARD, THE; PENTIRE POINT; SENNEN; TINTAGEL HEAD.

CORRIE Scottish word for an enclosure of mountains at the head of a valley, sometimes surrounding a lake. CIRQUE and CWM have the same meaning.

COULOIR A French word meaning gully, couloir is used in English to describe any cleft running through the flanks of a mountain. They may be snow-, ice- or rubble-filled. Couloirs are natural AVALANCHE chutes and should be regarded as potentially dangerous, especially in warm weather or during daylight hours. Couloirs are often climbed at night by headlamp when conditions are frozen and safer.

COURSE SETTER In CLIMBING COMPETITIONS, a climber who creates ROUTES for contestants by devising MOVES and affixing CLIMBING HOLDS to a CLIMBING WALL, is the course setter.

COURTES, LES (France) This mountain is in the same RIDGE that takes in the AIGUILLE VERTE and Les DROITES, and, despite being 472 ft (144 m) short of the magic 13,120 ft (4,000 m) mark, is frequently climbed. The views from its summit are especially fine. The mountain's FIRST ASCENT is uncertain, but a regular method of ascent is the TRAVERSE of the main ridge, first climbed, at least in part, by O. Schuster and A. Swaine in 1897. Like Les Droites, it is the mountain's northern aspect that holds the most dramatic promise. The northeast slope, first climbed in 1930 by P. Chevalier and G. Labour, offers a good introduction to the steeper snow routes in the area at AD. The Austrian Route on the north face is, perhaps, the second lesson in that introduction at TD-, being long, sustained but relatively safe. The Swiss Route on the north face, first climbed in 1938, is a highly popular prize, although at TD- with an average angle of 55° it is not the hardest LINE in the area. (See RATING SYSTEMS for explanation of French grades AD, TD, etc.)

COW'S TAIL See DAISY CHAIN.

CRACK A split or fissure in a rock face.

CRACK CLIMBING The art of FREE CLIMBING cracks by JAMMING one's hands and feet into the CRACK and pulling upward. (See FINGERLOCK, FIST JAM, HAND JAM, OFF HAND and OFFWIDTH.)

CRACK-N-UP An item of CLEAN CLIMBING equipment developed in the United States during the 1970s by Yvon CHOUINARD and Tom FROST and manufactured by Chouinard Equipment. No longer manufactured, they were in-

tended for AID CLIMBING as an alternative to using PITONS, which scar the rock with repeated placement. Crack-n-ups are chromolly steel anchor-shaped devices consisting of a stem and short hatchetlike blade that slots into pin scars and thin cracks. A bend in the stem twists and cams the blades into a crack when the device is weighted. They can also be used as marginal PROTECTION on FREE CLIMBS. (See NATURAL PROTECTION.)

CRACK PROTECTION See NATURAL PROTECTION.

CRAG A British word meaning a small cliff or rock OUTCROP. Cragging is rock climbing on such cliffs.

CRAMPONS Metal frames strapped or clamped to the soles of boots for foot traction on snow and ice. They consist of 10 or more downward-facing points and, usually, two forward-facing points (front points).

Oscar ECKENSTEIN produced the first climbing CRAMPONS in 1910, though shepherds in the European ALPS had used crude INSTEP CRAMPONS since the 1500s. Crampons quickly replaced nailed boots for ice-work. Since the 1950s crampons have grown increasingly sophisticated in design. No longer hand-forged, they are stamped from light, strong steel and resist cold and constant flexing. Crampons are specialized for different levels of climbing.

Hinged crampons consist of two parts, a heel frame with four points and a front frame with six or eight points. Both frames are linked by an adjustable steel hinge. This type is advantageous for non-rigid-soled boots, and also for MIXED CLIMBING (climbing on iced-over rock) which is stressful on crampon frames. Crampons for novice use are hinged.

Rigid crampons are for TECHNICAL ICE CLIMBING. The one-piece frame gives a stable platform under the boot. Footfangs are a specialized type of rigid crampon for vertical ice.

Front points, the part of the crampon that penetrates ice when the boot is kicked, divide crampons into further categories. Curved front points (also called French) maximize penetration of ice with each kick of the foot. Points are curved downward, and two additional points protruding at approximately 45 degrees below the front points add further stability in NEVE and snow. Standard points are slightly curved but droop less sharply to the frame. The points behind the front points are vertical. They are regarded as very stable in mixed climbing. Inclined points (a variation of standard) protrude 45 degrees to the frame. Vertical points, or 10-point crampons for nontechnical applications like GLACIER travel have no front points, and are archaic. Mono-points, a single front point, are a specialist innovation for climbing FROZEN WATERFALLS. In general, technical ice-climbing crampons have longer front points than general-purpose crampons, while crampons for mixed climbing favor shorter front points to reduce leverage on front points when a point is hooked over a rock edge. Crampons must be regularly sharpened with a file.

Numerous strap systems fix crampons to boots. Modern clip-on or binding designs work like a ski binding, having a toe-bale and heel-clamp that, when clipped on, exert squeeze-fit pressure on a boot. Only rigid boots with distinct recesses or welts at toe and heel accept clip-ons. Straps with buckles are the traditional method of affixing crampons to boots. Neoprene and webbing are the preferred strap fabrics. Many lacing procedures are used for strapping crampons to boots.

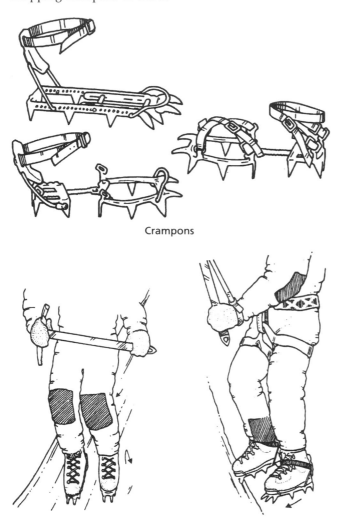

Crampons

Crampon Technique

CRANK A colloquial FREE CLIMBING term, meaning to pull or heave strenuously with fingers or arms.

CRATCLIFFE TOR (Britain) This PEAK DISTRICT CRAG overlooks the B5056 Bakewell to Ashbourne road mile (1.6 km) west of Birchover. It is largely a crag for the accomplished climber with 18 of its 30 ROUTES being 5.9 or more. Famous routes include the 1946 CLASSIC Suicide Wall (5.8) from Peter Harding and a string of excellent crack-lines climbed in the 1970s including Fern Hill (5.10b) from Keith Myhill and Boot Hill (5.10c) from Tom Proctor.

CREVASSE A crevasse is a split or crack in GLACIER ice, caused by glacial movement and compression, and generally running at right angles to the flow of the glacier.

Crevasses may be shallow or hundreds of feet deep; they can be narrow enough to jump across or form impassable chasms. During summer and fall, when glaciers are dry, their presence is obvious, but in winter or spring crevasses may be concealed by snow and pose serious hazards for mountaineers and skiers. Snow-covered crevasses are sometimes indicated by shallow furrows in a snow pack. Climbers traveling on glaciers usually rope together for safety (see ROPING UP), probe the surface of suspect snow fields with their ICE AXE before stepping forward, and BELAY when crossing SNOW BRIDGES spanning crevasses.

CREVASSE RESCUE Several methods of crevasse rescue exist, but four methods involving a minimum of persons and equipment are discussed here. On GLACIERS climbers should always be roped together for safety (see ROPING UP), yet this alone is not protection from falling into concealed CREVASSES. If an unroped climber has fallen into a crevasse, the first task is to establish verbal or visual contact to assess the climber's situation. Next, a rope must be connected to the climber. If the climber is unconscious or wedged tight in the crevasse, it may be necessary for the rescuer to enter the crevasse by RAPPEL. If the climber is conscious, a rope may be lowered from above and the crevassed climber may PRUSIK or use ASCENDERS on the rope to climb out. Rescuers must take care while standing near crevasse edges, which can be undercut and unstable. Therefore, ANCHORS and BELAYS should be set up immediately.

CROFT, PETER (1958–) (Canada) Canadian FREE-CLIMBER Croft elevated free soloing and rapid ENCHAINMENTS of long ROUTES in North America to new heights in the 1980s and 1990s. His appetite for soloing is huge. In 1989 at Mount ARAPILES (AUSTRALIA) he soloed 110 PITCHES in a day. His most famous solo marathon was in 1986 in YOSEMITE VALLEY (CALIFORNIA) when he climbed the multi-pitch routes Astroman (5.11) and the Rostrum (5.11), and numerous routes on the Cookie Cliff—over 30 pitches. Croft is an avowed TRADITIONALIST and a crack specialist. On the lead he has FLASHED the hardest Yosemite cracks—Phoenix and Cosmic Debris (both 5.13). In Squamish in 1987 he freed the original AID line of University Wall (5.13) on Squamish Chief (he previously freed the University Wall by a variation [5.12b], with Greg Foweraker and Hamish Fraser in 1982).

Croft also made fast solo mountain enchainments: In 1983 in 14 hours in the BUGABOOS (CANADA) he soloed the Chouinard-Beckey route on Howser Tower, the McCarthy Route on Snowpatch Spire, the northeast ridge of Bugaboo Spire and the McTech Arete on Crescent Spire. On another one-day marathon in 1985 in the Stuart Range of the CASCADE RANGE (WASHINGTON), he soloed the north ridge of Mount STUART, Sherpa Peak, west ridge of Argonaut, Colchuck Peak, Dragontail Peak and the west ridge of Prussik Peak. In 1987 he made the first TRAVERSE of the Mount WADDINGTON massif in the COAST RANGE of BRITISH COLUMBIA, with Don Serl and Greg Foweraker, and elsewhere in the Coast Range (CANADA), soloed a new route on the 1,500 ft (457-m) BUTTRESS on Klattasine Ridge. His hardest enchainments are on EL CAPITAN. In 1986 he and John BACHAR made a one day roped ascent of the Nose of El Capitan and the northwest face of HALF DOME, and in 1990 Croft and Dave Schultz linked the Nose and the Salathe Wall in 20.5 hours. In 1991 Croft and Schultz broke all existing speed records on the Nose of El Capitan: 4 hours and 48 minutes and in 1992 Croft bettered it with Hans Florine in 4 hours 24 minutes.

CROUCHER, NORMAN (1941–) (Britain) An inspirational character, Croucher has refused to allow the fact that he is a double amputee to stand in the way of his building a fine MOUNTAINEERING record. Raised in CORNWALL, he lost both legs below the knee when he rolled drunkenly down a railway embankment onto the tracks in the path of an oncoming train at the age of 19: "If it had happened in a car accident and had been someone else's fault, perhaps I would've been bitter. But there's never been the reason to allow myself that luxury. I've just had to get on with it, and that's been a good thing." Thereafter, he began to walk and climb, his first training session being a 900-mile (1,440-km) walk from John O'Groats to LAND'S END in BRITAIN. In the ALPS he climbed the MATTERHORN, EIGER and MONT BLANC. His high-altitude peaks include ELBRUS, HUASCARAN, MUZTAGII, ACONCAGUA, and an attempt on BROAD PEAK. He earns a living by lecturing on motivation, and is sponsored in his fundraising activities for charity by a cider manufacturer whose motto is "Legless but smiling."
Further reading: Norman Croucher, *Tales of Many Mountains* (1989).

CRUX The most difficult section of a climb is called a crux.

CURBAR EDGE (Britain) This 50-ft (15-m) crag above the village of Curbar is a natural extension of Froggatt. J. W. Puttrell took the first steps here, and Joe BROWN was active in the 1950s with Avalanche Wall (5.8); the fierce OFFWIDTH of Elder Crack (5.10a), originally graded 5.7; and another OFFWIDTH, Right Eliminate (5.10c). He also climbed the obvious feature of the Peapod (5.8) and the brutish OVERHANG of L'Horla (5.9).

Things developed slowly until the 1970s when John ALLEN climbed Moon Crack (5.11c) and the hanging groove of Profit of Doom (5.11c) in 1975. Still under 20 at that time, Allen's mercurial rise led him to become a British legend. In 1976 Mick Fowler climbed the frightening Linden at 5.12 after Ed DRUMMOND had led it with two chipped hook placements. It was a controversial episode for gritstone purists. Ron FAWCETT opened the 1980s with One Step Beyond (5.12b) and Tim Leech solved the desperate Moonshine (5.12c). In 1984 Neil Foster climbed Ulyses or Bust (5.12b) in preparation for an ascent of Ulysees at STANAGE, on which he broke an ankle. In 1986 Johnny

Dawes climbed several testpieces, the hardest being End Of The Affair (5.13d). Finally, Andy Pollitt climbed the bold wall and slab Knockin' on Heaven's Door (5.13d) in 1988.
Guidebooks: British Mountain Club, *Derwent Gritstone* (1985); Paul Nunn, *Rock Climbing in the Peak District* (1987).

CWM A Welsh word, pronounced "Coomb," meaning an area ringed by mountains, sometimes surrounding a lake or glacier. Corrie (Scottish) and cirque have the same meaning. The term has entered common mountaineering usage.

CZECH REPUBLIC AND SLOVAKIA The most significant mountain range is the High Tatra in Slovakia, with a main ridge 16 miles (27 km) long encompassing 35 separate valleys. The highest peak Gerlachovasky Stit is 8,708 ft (2,655 m). The highest face is the 2,952-ft (900-m) north face of Maly Kezmarsky Stit. Granite predominates the Tatra. There are no GLACIERS. The most important centers for alpinism in the Tatra are Strbske Pleso, Tatranska Lomnica and Stary Smokovec.

There are many limestone cliffs, but the most important rock climbing is on soft sandstone. In these areas rules apply to FREE CLIMBING similar to the rules of the ELBSANDSTEINGEBIRGE in Germany. These rules are intended to preserve the rock: Climbing on wet sandstone and the use of CHALK are forbidden, and metal protection devices are not allowed. Instead, knotted SLINGS are used. Sandstone areas use a local rating system, the hardest rating being XIb (X- in the UIAA system).

The sandstone zones are located in north Bohemia. From west to east, they are Labske Piskovce (Elbsandstein), Cesky Raj (Paradise of Bohemia) and Adrspach-Teplice. The areas are located near the towns of Decin, Turnov, Jicin and Trutnov.

Czech climbing began in the late 1800s and developed under the auspices of clubs like the Czech section of "Planiska sveza Slovenie" (established 1897), IAMES (established 1921) and Czech Alpine Club-KAC (established 1924). As of 1992, there exists a Czech/Slovak Mountaineering Association composed of the Czech Mountain Association, with 7,000 members, and Slovak IAMES, with 2,500 members. In addition there is the Czech Himalayan Club.

Before the 1950s, activities by Czech climbers abroad were rare, but with opportunities to travel since the 1960s Czechs have made many important FIRST ASCENTS in the ALPS, especially in winter, and also in the Caucasus. In the 1970s Czech mountaineering took to the HIMALAYAS in force. Czech Himalayan firsts include MAKALU southeast ridge (1976), NANDA DEVI northeast ridge (1981), LHOTSE Shar south face (1984), DHAULAGIRI west face (1984), Dhaulagiri northwest pillar, alpine style, (1988). Also notable are CHO OYU, by the women's team D. Sterbova and V. Komarkova (United States).

D

DACHSTEINS Mittens made from shrunken wool used in extreme cold. Still popular despite synthetic insulation. (See CLOTHING FOR MOUNTAINEERING.)

DAGGER TECHNIQUE A method of climbing snow or ice in which the ICE AXES are held by the heads and the picks are jabbed into the snow. (See SNOW AND ICE CLIMBING TECHNIQUES.)

DAISY CHAIN Also called cow's tail. Used in AID CLIMBING. A WEBBING SLING, sewn or knotted into short loops into which CARABINERS may be clipped. When attached to the HARNESS a climber may clip it into aid PLACEMENTS or BELAYS, or lean or hang on it for balance or rest. The loops at different intervals allow precise adjustment between the climber and the equipment into which the daisy chain is clipped, to maximize comfort and freedom of movement.

DAUPHINÉ ALPS (France) These mountains are entirely within France and are in fact the western extension of the Cottian Alps, which run east of the Col du Galibier. The Dauphiné Alps contain Monte Viso (12,598 ft/3,841 m), first climbed in 1861 by William Mathews, one of three brothers who were very influential in the early years of alpinism.

The Dauphiné themselves are of more interest to the climber as the region lies between MONT BLANC and the Mediterranean. The highest peak in this starkly beautiful region is the Barre dés Écrins (13,451 ft/4,101 m), first climbed in 1864 by Edward WHYMPER and Adolphus Moore with guide Michel Croz from Chamonix. That year was the great alpine season and these two men were at the height of their powers. The starting point for an ascent of their route is Ailefroide, a popular location for tourists. Other centers in the area include La Grave and La Bérarde. There are numerous huts in the area.

A great number of peaks in the area are worthy of mention. Because they fall below the magic (13,120 ft/4,000 m) and are not served by téléphériques, they offer a more genuine mountain experience than the more famous and higher Mont Blanc Range. Among these peaks is La Meije (13,064 ft/3,983 m), first climbed in 1891 by John Gibson and the guide Ulrich Almer, the TRAVERSE of which is especially recommended. The south face direct of La Meije

is also famous, first climbed in 1934. Among the party was Pierre Allain, the equipment innovator.

Other famous peaks in the area are Ailefroide (12,969 ft/3,954 m), Mont Pelvoux (12,943 ft/3,946 m), Pic sans Nom (12,838 ft/3,914 m) and Le Râteau (12,493 ft/3,809 m). Many of the peaks in the region were not climbed until the latter quarter of the 19th century because of the region's remoteness.

Further reading: Robin Collomb, *Écrins Park: Dauphiné Alps*; Richard Goedeke, *The Alpine 4000m Peaks*; A. W. Moore, *The Alps in 1864*; Edward Whymper, *Scrambles Amongst the Alps in the Years 1860–9* (1936, 1986).

DAWES, JOHNNY (1963–) (Britain) Dawes came to prominence in the early 1980s for his bold and exceptionally difficult climbs on Derbyshire gritstone, the best of which were perhaps Braille Trail on Burbage and Gaea at Black Rocks. He moved his focus to North Wales from 1985 onward, producing many new climbs in that region. Two of his ROUTES from 1986, The Quarryman (E8,7b) at Dinorwig, and The Indian Face (E9,6c) on CLOGWYN DU'R ARDDU, remain unrepeated at the time of writing.

Since 1986 Dawes has continued to produce occasional new climbs of great technical virtuosity like The Very Big and The Very Small (E8,7a) on the Rainbow Slab (1990). His climbs often demand extraordinary whole-body agility in positions of extreme risk. His routes and personality have provided a contrast in terms of technique and courage to the power-oriented SPORTS CLIMBS that began to dominate British and European climbing in the 1980s. His routes carry the same psychological aura as did those of Joe BROWN 30 years before.

DEADMAN A snow ANCHOR useful in a wide range of snow conditions. It consists of a spade-shaped alloy plate approximately 8 × 10 inches (20 × 50 cm) with a cable fixed to the center for clipping the rope into. The deadman is placed in a slot in the snow cut with an ICE AXE. It is hammered into the slot at forty degrees to the snow surface (this angle is very important), and at right angles to the fall line. The deadman should be at least 10 inches beneath the snow surface. The deadman is strongest in hard snow. A correctly placed deadman resists considerable force and digs itself deeper into snow. If placed in soft snow, or at too sharp or too shallow an angle, it may pull out. A deadboy is a small deadman. (See SNOW AND ICE ANCHORS.)

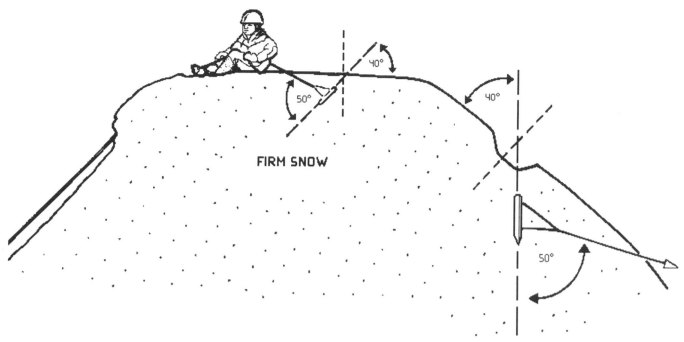

FIRM SNOW

Deadman Placements

DEADPOINT A FREE CLIMBING technique, really an aspect of the dynamic move, or lunge. The deadpoint is the point on an arc of movement or a jump in the air before the body starts to fall and is weightless and motionless for a split second. Free, precise movement—such as a lunge with the hand for a hold—is possible at this point. Immediately after the deadpoint, gravity takes over and the climber starts to drop back down.

DEATH ZONE The region at or above 26,240 ft (8,000 m), found on the 14 Himalayan mountains above that height. In the death zone, the rigors of thin air, HYPOXIA, COLD and extreme weather present serious risks for the survival of climbers. See EIGHT-THOUSAND-METER (26,240 ft) PEAKS.

DEHYDRATION Fluid deficit due to high activity and low fluid intake is common among climbers not only in hot temperatures but also in cold dry air and at high altitude. The human body is approximately 67% water, with much of that volume contained in striated muscle. The body continuously expels and replenishes its fluid content, but in climbing situations fluid replacement is usually inadequate due to increased sweating, respiratory water loss and fewer opportunities for replacement.

At high altitude it is estimated that up to three and a half quarts (three liters) of water per day is lost from the body in expired air from heavy breathing. Excessive sweating caused by the heavy exertion of climbing may leave high-altitude climbers at a constant 7 to 8% loss in body weight, reducing blood plasma volume by 14 to 20%. Such plasma volume reduction (literally thickening of the blood) can seriously impair working capacity and exacerbate symptoms of ACUTE MOUNTAIN SICKNESS, such as

headache, anorexia, confusion, sleeplessness, nausea and apathy. Additional indications of dehydration include muscle cramps and extremely dark brown urine.

In hot temperatures HEAT ILLNESS, or heat stroke, may coincide with dehydration. Symptoms include shivering, headache and dry skin that is warm to the touch. Prevention of dehydration is simple: drink a lot. But thirst is not an adequate gauge of fluid requirements, and active climbers should force themselves to drink up to five and a third quarts (five liters) per day, taken regularly. Since mountaineers may find it impossible to stop to operate a stove and melt snow during a climb, large quantities of water should be consumed at campsites. Rock climbers will find dehydration leads to subdued performance and dulled reflexes. An indication of healthy fluid levels is the passing of clear urine. Sweating due to overdressing may also cause fluid loss, therefore shedding to ventilate the body is important, as is protecting the head from the sun. Electrolyte replacement mixes (Rehydrate, Isostar, Gatorade, etc.) consisting of mineral additives that are lost through sweating are helpful when mixed with water, but salt should never be added to drinking water.

DENALI **(United States)** At 20,320 ft (6,195 m), this is the highest mountain on the North American continent. Its 18,000-ft (5,488-m) rise from the surrounding tundra gives it greater vertical relief than any mountain in the world. Many call it the coldest mountain on earth. Even halfway to the summit the climate is equivalent to that of the North Pole. All other 20,000-ft- (6,098-m)-plus peaks are located between latitude 43 degrees north and 32 degrees south of the Equator; Denali lies at 63 degrees north. The peak was first sighted in 1794 by George Vancouver, who reported two stupendous mountains in the distance, crowned with snow. Some Fairbanks residents refer to its two peaks (the north summit is 19,470 ft/5,936 m) as Churchill Peaks. Other indigenous names exist, but in 1897 William Dickey named it Mt. MCKINLEY after the presidential candidate. The State of ALASKA Board of Geographic Names now refers to the mountain by its native name, Denali, which means "the High One." The mountain hit the front pages of newspapers around the country when Frederick COOK fraudulently claimed to have climbed it in 1906. Four years later, the SOURDOUGHS did succeed in reaching the lower north peak in an 18-hour push from 10,000 ft (3,049 m) on the Muldrow Glacier. In 1912, Belmore BROWNE came within 100 ft (30 m) of the south summit, but was driven back by a storm. The following year, the FIRST ASCENT was claimed by Walter HARPER, Hudson STUCK, Harry Karstens and Robert Tatum. Denali was not climbed again for another 19 years. The next major ascent was Bradford WASHBURN's pioneer ascent of the west buttress. On this he used a ski-plane to reach the mountain. In 1954, the mountain was first climbed by both the south and northwest buttresses. The classic and most difficult route is a granite RIB up the middle of the 9,000-ft (2,744-m) south face, first climbed by Riccardo CASSIN in 1961—the Cassin Ridge remains a testpiece for alpinists around the world, and has now been soloed in 15 hours and climbed in winter. The mountain received its first WINTER ASCENT in 1967, by the west buttress. Today, over 1,000 climbers attempt Denali every year by two dozen different routes; only half succeed. Arctic weather, high altitude, AVALANCHE and crevasse hazards make Denali the most challenging 20,000-ft (6,097-m) mountain in the world. There have been over 50 deaths and hundreds of rescues.

Guidebook: Jonathan Waterman, *High Alaska; A Historical Guide to Denali* (1989).

Further reading: Art Davidson, *Minus 148: The Winter Ascent of Mt. McKinley* (1986); Terris Moore, *The Pioneer Climbs* (1981); Glenn Randall, *Mt. McKinley Climber's Handbook* (1984); Bill Sherwonit, *To the Top of Denali* (1990); Howard Snyder, *The Hall of the Mountain King* (1973); Bradford Washburn, *Mt. McKinley; The Conquest of Denali* (1991); and Jonathan Waterman, *Surviving Denali; A Study of Accidents on Mount McKinley* (1991).

DENT BLANCHE GROUP (France) The Dent Blanche (14,288 ft/4,356 m) is a striking and classical pyramid in the Alps with long ridges leading from its summit oriented exactly to the four points of the compass. The south ridge fell first, to Jean-Baptiste Croz and Johann Kronig with E. S. Kennedy and W. Wigram in 1862. The east ridge or Viereselsgrat was climbed in 1882 by Ulrich Almer and A. Pollinger with Stafford Anderson and G. P. Baker and is still graded D. Pollinger returned in 1889 to climb the west or Ferpècle Ridge, which offers a more technical route to the summit. Ascents begin at the village of Les Haudères five miles (eight km) to the northwest. North of the Dent Blanche is the Glacier du Cornier and above the Grand Cornier (12,992 ft/3,961 m). (See RATING SYSTEMS for explanation of French ratings.)

DEPTH HOAR Fragile ice crystals that form in the snow pack during cold weather. They represent a weak layer and are often the cause of AVALANCHE.

DESCENDEUR French for descender, or RAPPEL device. (See RAPPELLING.)

DESMAISON, RENE (France) A Parisian whose exploits in the ALPS were dogged by media controversy and tragedy, Desmaison is best known for hard "hivernales," or WINTER ASCENTS. His first such effort was the west face of the Petite Dru (with Jean Couzy), his second the northwest face of the Olan, and his third—after summiting with the 1962 French team on Jannu in Eastern Nepal—the Walker Spur. In 1966 Desmaison participated in the rescue of two German climbers off the west face of the DRUS. Ten other climbers also took part, some alongside Desmaison (the American Gary HEMMING and the Britisher Mick Burke), others working at cross purposes. Desmaison did not come out well in the maelstrom of media coverage and Monday morning quarterbacking. He lost his membership in the Bureau des Guides de Chamonix, while the American became an overnight celebrity for his part in the rescue. In 1967 Desmaison climbed the central pillar of Frenay in winter, vindicating his abilities, which had come under a cloud in 1961 on this same route when he lost a race to the summit with a British team. In 1968 Desmaison pulled off another plum hivernale first: the Shroud on the GRANDES JORASSE in the Alps. But three years later, a winter attempt on a new route on the Walker Spur resulted in the death of his partner, Serge Goussault. Once again Desmaison was criticized and blamed. The next year he, Giorgio Bertone and Michel Claret succeeded on this direttissima.

DESTIVELLE, CATHERINE (1960–) (France) One of the best-known climbers worldwide, a champion rock climber and strong alpinist, Destivelle was the first woman to solo the north face of the EIGER. She was climbing on the boulders of FONTAINEBLEAU at the age of 14, and on the 1,500-ft (457-m) walls of the VERDON Gorge at 16. In the Alps at 17 she climbed the American Direct Route on the DRU in a fast seven hours, leading every PITCH.

She originally intended a career as a physical therapist but opted for professional climbing when she won the first CLIMBING COMPETITION she attended, in Bardoneccia, Italy, in 1985. Ten days later she fell 115 ft (35 m) into a CREVASSE in the Alps, and broke her hip and back. Recovered, she dominated world competitions for four years. Destivelle first met America's Lynn HILL at a competition jointly held in Bardoneccia and ARCO, Italy, in 1986, and the two began a grand rivalry, dueling it out for wins. Destivelle won their first showdown, in Bardoneccia. She was second to Hill at a subsequent invitational in Bercy, France, in 1988, and then bested Hill at the International Sport Climbing Championship at Snowbird, Utah, that same summer. That spring she made the hardest ascent yet done by a woman of a rock route, climbing Chouca (8a/b, or 5.13b/c) at BUOUX. Among Destivelle's major competition wins were the Sport

Roccia, a World Cup in Bardoneccia in 1988, and a world event at Vaulx-en-Velin.

In 1990 she completed what is possibly the hardest solo alpine ascent in the Alps by a woman with her solo of the Bonatti Pillar on the Dru, in the MONT BLANC Range. She climbed ropeless on all but a 164-ft (50-m) aid section, and finished the 2,100-ft (640-m) face (V 5.11 A2) in four and a half hours. In 1991 she established a new route in 11 days between the Thomas Gros and Grenier routes, left of the Bonatti Pillar. She made front-page news in 1992, when at 32 she soloed the Eiger Nordwand in winter, in 16 1/2 hours. Destivelle has been featured in several films, including one of an ascent of Nameless Tower in PAKISTAN with Jeff LOWE (United States) in 1990, and another about climbing in Mali, West Africa, in 1987.
Further reading: Catherine Destivelle, *Destivelle: Danseuséen Roche.*

DEVIL'S LAKE   (United States) Located outside Baraboo, Wisconsin, this historic midwest CRAG is 40 to 80 ft (12 to 24 m) high, and of smooth horizontally bedded quartzite. Climbing began here in the 1920s when brothers Joe and Paul Stettner motorcycled from Chicago to train for their historic FIRST ASCENT of the east face of LONG'S PEAK (COLORADO). In the 1960s climbers like Rich Goldstone, John Gill and Pete Cleveland climbed hard routes, often TOP-ROPE but frequently on lead or solo. Gill's Sometimes Crack and Gill Crack were serious efforts. Cleveland left the biggest impact though, leading routes like Son of Great Chimney (5.11) on sight in 1965, Bagatelle (5.12c) in 1969 and Phlogiston (5.13a/b) in 1977. This was possibly the hardest route in the world at the time. Modern contributors have been many, like Dave Groth, who in 1990 top-roped Ice (5.13). The historic atmosphere, excellent rock, loyal following of climbers and fierce technicality of routes have brought climbers from all over America to this area.
Guidebooks: Don Hynek, *Extremists Guide to Devil's Lake;* William Widule and Sven Swartling, *Climber's Guide to Devil's Lake.*

DEVIL'S THUMB   (Canada) This 9,077-ft (2,767-m) spire dominates the GLACIERS of the Stikine Wilderness, along the ALASKA panhandle and BRITISH COLUMBIA border. There are no easy ROUTES. The approach is difficult and weather can be atrocious. Its striking summit was first climbed by Fred BECKEY, Bob Craig and Cliff Schmidtke (1946). Principal routes are the airy east ridge (Culbert, Starr and Douglas, 1970); the beautiful rock of the south face (George LOWE, Chris Jones and Lito Tejada Flores, 1973); and the forbidding northeast and northwest faces (Stutzman and Plumb, 1978; Pilling and Bebie, 1991).
Further reading: Steve Roper and Allen Steck, *Fifty Classic Climbs of North America* (1979).

DEVILS TOWER   (United States) A 350-ft (107-m) volcanic plug of columnular basalt rising out of the plains in northeast WYOMING in the Devils Tower National Monument, 60 miles (96 km) from Gillette and near Sundance.

The striking symmetry of Devils Tower became well known as the setting for the movie *Close Encounters of the Third Kind.* FREE CLIMBING at Devils Tower is characterized by difficult STEMMING DIHEDRALS on solid rock with excellent friction. STOPPERS and RPS are useful for protection. Several rappel routes provide descent from the summit. The optimum climbing season is April through October. Most routes at Devils Tower were climbed in the 1970s and 1980s, but the early history of this area is unusual.

Because Devils Tower is surrounded by vertical cliffs it is as inaccessable as a mountain summit. Although the first "true" ascent of the tower was claimed by Fritz WEISSNER, William HOUSE and Lawrence Coveney in 1937, the summit was first reached in a colorful episode during a Fourth of July picnic in 1893 by ranchers Willard Ripley and Will Rogers, who organized a fair at which the main attraction was to be the tower's ascent. Over 1,000 people came from as far away as 125 miles (200 km)—a week's roundtrip by wagon. Willard and Rogers had prepared a route up the tower a month before by hammering numerous 30-inch (76-cm) wooden pegs into the vertical cracks that run up the tower and nailing wooden strips to the pegs, making a 350-ft (107-m) ladder. At the fair Rogers received an invocation from a minister then quickly scaled the ladder, unfurling a U.S. flag on the summit to great applause. When the flag blew down to the ground that afternoon, Ripley and Rogers cut it up and sold the pieces as souvenirs.

In 1941 George Hopkins parachuted onto the summit of Devils Tower as a publicity stunt for a planned altitude jumping record. Intending to lower himself on a long rope, he became marooned on top when he found this technique unviable. Hopkins's predicament attracted national attention. The Goodyear Blimp set out from Ohio for the rescue, and a pilot announced plans to land a plane on the summit, while air drops delivered provisions, coal, hot water bottles and blankets to Hopkins. Few climbers in America were capable of such climbing at the time, so it was fortuitous when Jack Durrance (who had already made the second ascent of Devils Tower) and Paul PETZOLDT arrived with a team from the Dartmouth Mountaineering Club to finally rescue Hopkins five days after he landed atop the tower.
Guidebooks: S. Gardiner and D. Guilmette, *Devils Tower* (1986). Dennis Horning, *Free Climbs of Devils Tower;* (8th ed., 1990).

DEVON   (Britain) The beautiful countryside of Devon offers a broad range of rock, from SEA CLIFFS to moorland CRAGS to limestone desperates. See BAGGY POINT; BLACKCHURCH; DEWERSTONE, THE; EXMANSWORTHY CLIFF; HAYTOR AND LOW MAN; LOWER SHARPNOSE; TORBAY.

DEWERSTONE, THE   (Britain) These granite pinnacles, shrouded by trees and on the banks of the River Plym, lie eight miles (13 km) northeast of Plymouth, near the village of Shaugh Bridge. There are excellent middle-grade ROUTES, like Climbers' Club Direct (5.8), climbed in 1936 by Robin Hodgkin. This steep CRACK is now well protected by modern gear. Tom PATEY climbed here too in the 1950s, adding Leviathan (5.7) and the excellent Spider's Web (5.8), a delicate and intricate climb.

DEXAMETHASONE (Decadron) A drug that has been shown to prevent and treat both mild and severe cases of ACUTE MOUNTAIN SICKNESS, high-altitude PULMONARY EDEMA and high-altitude CEREBRAL EDEMA. It is a steroid drug that may be taken orally or by injection. Precisely how this drug affects edema is still unclear to medical researchers, yet dexamethasone is endorsed by high-altitude researchers as a potential life-saver for persons stricken with edema.

DHAULAGIRI (Nepal) The earth's seventh-highest peak is 26,795 ft/8,167 m. It rises in western NEPAL's DHAULAGIRI HIMAL, above the valley of the mighty Kali Gandaki River. Difficult on all sides, its 14,700-ft (4,482-m) limestone west face ranks with the Rupal Face of NANGA PARBAT and DENALI's Wickersham Wall as the largest wall on earth. The heavily SERACED south face is equally imposing. The mountain has claimed many lives: AVALANCHES off the southeast flanks killed five Americans and two Sherpas in 1969, and six Japanese in 1975. Dhaulagiri was the second to last eight-thousander to be climbed and was tried by six expeditions before the successful 1960 Swiss ascent on the northeast ridge. This expedition did not use oxygen and placed Ernst Forrer, Kurt DIEMBERGER, Peter Diener, Albin Schelbert and Sherpas Nima Dorje and Nawang Dorje on top. It also set an aircraft altitude landing record when a Pilatus-Porter plane supplied a camp on the northeast col at 18,700 ft (5,701 m). Americans settled their long-standing score with Dhaulagiri in 1973 when a team climbed the northeast spur, placing Lou REICHARDT, John ROSKELLEY and Sherpa Nawang Samden on the summit.

Over the years many climbers have contemplated the south face. The margins of this wall were climbed by a Japanese expedition in 1978 (south ridge), and in 1981 Yugoslavs made an ALPINE-STYLE route up the south face to the Japanese ridge and then down the northeast ridge. An important alpine-style ascent came in 1980 when Wojciecch KURTYKA (Poland), Alex MACINTYRE (Britain), Rene Ghillini (France) and Ludwick Wilczycnski (Poland) climbed the east face. Japanese climbed the oft-tried Pear Route (northwest ridge) in 1982. Czechs monopolized the west side of the mountain in the 1980s: In 1984 and 1985 they climbed two extreme routes on the west face, and in 1988 three Czechs completed the oft-tried "French Route" (southwest pillar), making the climb in a 16-day roundtrip alpine-style push. Jiri NOVAK was present on all three climbs.

Further reading: Kurt Diemberger, *Summits and Secrets* (1991); Andrew Thompson and Todd Thompson, *Mountain of Storms: The American Expeditions to Dhaulagiri* (1974).

DHAULAGIRI HIMAL (Nepal) A lofty range in western NEPAL dominated by DHAULAGIRI I (26,788 ft/8,167 m) and the peaks of the Dhaulagiri Group (Dhaulagiri II to VI, Putha Hiunchuli, Churen West, Churen East and Gurja Himal), which form a chain of 22,960-ft (7,000-m) summits, to its west. The region is bounded on the east by the Kali Gandaki River (on which lies the town of Tukche), on the north by the Barbung *Khola,* the *Sangda La* and *Kena Lungpo,* and on the west by the Beri River. Altogether there are 13 peaks above 22,960 ft (7,000 m) here. Dhaulagiri II (25,423 ft/7,751 m) was first climbed in 1971 via the southwest ridge by an Austrian expedition that was led by Franz Huber and included American Ronald Fear. Dhaulagiri III (25,305 ft/7,715 m) was climbed in 1973 via the southwest face by a German team. Two Japanese climbers summited on Dhaulagiri IV (25,128 ft/7,661 m) in 1975 via the west ridge from the Kaphe Glacier, but they fell to their deaths while descending. A Japanese team climbed Dhaulagiri V (24,987 ft/7,618 m) via the south ridge, and Dhaulagiri VI (23,839 ft/7,268 m) by the west spur and south ridge in 1975. A fine alpine-style ascent on the southwest buttress of Dhaulagiri VI was made in 1983 by four Canadians. But perhaps the most significant climb done here was the marathon Japanese TRAVERSE of Dhaulagiri II (via east ridge) and Dhaulagiri V (via south ridge). Both routes were climbed simultaneously, with camps placed on the summits of both peaks. Parties then traversed the two-and-a-half miles (four km) in each direction, surmounting Dhaulagiri III en route.

DIAMOND, THE (United States) The name given to the vertical east face of LONG's PEAK in COLORADO, the Diamond is a granite big wall in an alpine setting. The Diamond itself begins at the ledge system called Broadway, at 13,110 ft (3,997 m), and in a diamond-shaped sweep, rises to the 14,255-ft (4,346-m) summit of Long's Peak. The complete wall, rising from the CIRQUE of the Andrews Glacier, presents a 2,000-ft (610-m) cliff. The nature of the rock is good CRACKS surrounded by sharp-edged HOLDS.

When two Colorado climbers notified the National Park Service of their intention to climb the Diamond in 1954, the NPS forbade the ascent and prohibited climbing there until 1960. The Diamond was thus a coveted prize to Coloradoans, but the first ascent was snatched by two Californians, Dave Rearick and Bob Kamps, in 1960. This route was D-1, rated V 5.7 A4. In 1967 Layton KOR and Wayne Goss made the first WINTER ASCENT. The Diamond was first soloed by Bill Forrest in 1970. The FIRST FREE ASCENT of the wall came in 1975, by Goss and Jim Logan. Numerous grade IV and V free routes up to 5.12 have been made on the Diamond, and several FREE-SOLO ascents of the wall have been made.

Guidebook: Richard Rossiter, *Climber's Guide to Rocky Mountain National Park* (1991).

Further reading: Glenn Randall, *Long's Peak Tales* (1981); Stephen Trimble, *Long's Peak: A Rocky Mountain Chronicle* (1984).

DIAMOX See ACETAZOLAMIDE.

DIEDRE French word meaning a large right-angled corner or DIHEDRAL, shaped like an open book.

DIEMBERGER, KURT (1932–) (Austria) Diemberger's career spans 40 years of climbing, filmmaking and writing and is marked by over 20 expeditions to the mountains of Asia, on which he summited seven times on 26,240 ft (8,000-m) peaks—BROAD PEAK (1957, again 1984); DHAULAGIRI (1960); EVEREST and MAKALU (1978); GASHERBRUM II (1979); and K2 (1986). His were the FIRST ASCENTS of both Broad Peak and Dhaulagiri, and he helped introduce the concept of ALPINE STYLE climbing in the Himalaya with ascents like Broad Peak (with Hermann BUHL), and Tirich West IV (24,074 ft/7,338 m) in 1967.

In the European ALPS in the 1950s Diemberger made ascents of the north faces of the MATTERHORN, EIGER and GRANDES JORASSES, but his 1956 first ascent of the Konigswand Direttissima, with Viennese climber Wolfgang Stefan, was ahead of its time as a difficult snow and ice route. His filming career began with an expedition to the Integral Peuterey Ridge of MONT BLANC. The film of this five-day TRAVERSE won the 1962 Trento Film Festival in Italy. His career as cameraman of the 26,240-ft (8,000-m) peaks began in 1978 when he filmed on Everest's summit with Pierre Mazeaud's French expedition. In 1981 he received an Emmy Award for his documentary of the American attempt on the Kangshung Face of Everest.

He and Julie TULLIS formed in 1983 the "highest film team in the world." Their partnership lasted till 1986 when Tullis died in a blizzard after the pair summited K2. Diemberger survived but was severely FROSTBITTEN. His film K2—Traum und Schicksal won the Grand Prize at Trento in 1989. **Further reading:** Kurt Diemberger, *The Endless Knot–K2, Mountain of Dreams and Destiny* (1991); Diemberger, *Summits and Secrets* (1991).

DIHEDRAL American rock-climbing term meaning an inside corner, shaped like an open book.

DIKE A vein of igneous or intrusive rock, often occurring in granite. Dikes frequently provide a line of holds on otherwise blank rock.

DINNER-PLATING A characteristic of very cold, dense ice, in which large plates fracture and break away during the placement of ICE TOOLS and ICE SCREWS. (See ICE CLIMBING, WATERFALL CLIMBING.)

DIRECT A route on a cliff or mountain that climbs straight up, without wavering from side to side. (See DIRETTISSIMA.)

DIRECT AID To use AID CLIMBING techniques, or to hang from one or several pieces of PROTECTION for assistance while climbing a PITCH.

DIRETTISSIMA Loosely translated, Italian for "direct." Used to indicate the LINE of a route that ascends a mountain or cliff in a straight line. The word entered climbing parlance when Emilio Comici, the Italian who pioneered difficult climbs in the DOLOMITES during the 1930s, wrote, "I wish some day to make a route and from the summit let fall a drop of water and this is where my route will have gone." Direttissimas, or direct routes, are regarded as elegant lines. On serious mountain faces, and also in FREE CLIMBING cliffs, great efforts have been made to emulate Comici's theoretical concept of an unwavering line of ascent. The EIGER Direct in the ALPS is such an example.

DOCTORING Colloquial term in rock climbing for altering HOLDS to make them easier to use. (See CHIPPING.)

DOLOMITES (Italy) This remarkable group of rocky peaks in the northeastern corner of Italy was, until the end of World War I, part of the southern Austrian Tyrol. Political upheavals mean that most of the mountains and villages have both German and Italian names. The peaks are limestone and the highest is the Marmolata (10,962 ft/3,342 m), although height has less relevance here since it is technical interest that draws climbers. Many of the routes rely on AID but climbers continue to put up routes with traditional methods rather than resorting to the bolt drill. There is much scope in the future for long free routes of considerable difficulty. Perhaps the best known climb in the area, is the north face of the Cima Grande, climbed in 1933 by Emilio Comici and G. and A. Dimai and a tremendous breakthrough. Ricardo CASSIN was also active in the Dolomites at that time, climbing the north face of the Cima Ouest in 1935. Other great Dolomite climbers included Emil Solleder who climbed the northwest face of the Civetta in 1925 and a year later the east face of the Saas Mor. Exploration after the war continued to produce a string of demanding, steep climbs including the fearsome Phillipp-Flamm on the Civetta, climbed in 1957 by Walter Philipp and Dieter Flamm. Good bases include Cortina d'Ampezzo and Canazei.

DOME Common in granitic cliff and mountain formation, domes are rounded, dome-shaped batholith formations that often form SLABS of moderate angle. Glaciation can also shape domes. JOSHUA TREE and TUOLOMNE MEADOWS are two examples of American granite dome-climbing areas.

DOUBLE BOOTS A two-part MOUNTAINEERING boot system for cold weather, having a rigid shell and removable insulated inner boot. (See BOOTS.)

DOUBLE FISHERMAN'S KNOT A knot used to join two ropes together, usually for a RAPPEL. (See KNOTS.)

DOUBLE ROPE TECHNIQUE A system of using two .36-in (nine mm) ropes for leading. (See ROPE TECHNIQUES.)

DOVE CRAG (Britain) Forbidding and remote, Dove Crag is tucked away at the end of Dovedale in the LAKE DISTRICT. Its 250-ft (76-m) walls contain some of the best hard routes in the area. There is one excellent 5.8, Hangover, climbed in 1939, and Dove Crag bears one of Don WHILLANS's finest lines, Extol (5.10b). Bill Birkett caused controversy in 1981 by naming a large open groove after a boot company for a sum of money. Asolo is 5.10c. He also bagged the crag's hardest route, Fear and Fascination (5.12a), an overhanging FACE route that climbs 175 ft (53 m) in one PITCH.

Another important crag in this area is Raven Crag at Threshwaite Cove, three-quarters of a mile (1 km) southeast of the village of Hartsop.

Guidebooks: Bill Birkett et al, *Rock Climbing in the Lake District* (1986); FRCC, *Buttermere and Eastern Crags* (1987).

DOVEDALE (Britain) Along the banks of the River Dove between Milldale to the north and Thorpe Cloud to the south are isolated limestone tors. The principal CRAGS along the dale include Ravens Tor (not to be confused with the other, harder RAVEN TOR to the north), Pickering Tor, Ilam Rock, The Watchblock and Tissington Spires. There are services at Tissington.

The Rock and Ice Club, with Joe BROWN and Don WHILLANS, climbed many ROUTES here in the 1950s. Jack Street's ascent of Adjudicator Wall (5.10b) on The Watchblock was notable for 1969. Ed DRUMMOND, who was at the time adding a host of brilliant routes across the peak, added Easter Island (5.9) on Ilam Rock in 1972. When the limestone boom of the early 1980s caught up with Dovedale, the Lee brothers, Dominic and Daniel, added Jungleland (5.12) in 1982, and in the same year Ron FAWCETT added Eye of the Tiger (5.12), Ilam Rock. In 1984 Craig Smith solved one of the few remaining lines when he freed Dove Holes' Pumping Iron, at 5.12.

Routes are usually one pitch. PROTECTION is with wires and the occasional in situ peg. There is also climbing in the Manifold Valley to the west, between the villages of Wetton and Grindon, with Beeston Tor and Thor's Cave being especially fine.

Guidebooks: British Mountain Club, *Peak Limestone— South* (1987); Paul Nunn, *Rock Climbing in the Peak District* (1987).

DOVER (Britain) The tall white cliffs of Dover are a potent symbol in English culture, but in climbing terms they present a hazardous challenge on the fringes of acceptable limits. The rock is chalk, with a consistency varying from that of St. Margaret's Bay, north of Dover, where it is soft enough to accept ICE TOOLS, to areas where more conventional techniques apply such as Beachy Head, west of Eastbourne. Chalk is appallingly loose and requires a confident approach. The Coast Guard must be informed of any climbing activity.

Surprisingly, climbing got underway on chalk in the latter 1800s, providing an alpine training ground for the father of modern alpinism, Albert MUMMERY, who was born in St. Margerat's Bay. But it was the eccentric diabolist Aleister Crowley who made the greatest impression, at Beachy Head. He climbed Ethelreda's Pinnacle (5.7), in 1893, and the more impressive Devil's Chimney, which

collapsed in the 1950s. He also attempted a crackline in the main face but had to be rescued.

Activity ceased until 1979 when Arnie Strapcans reclimbed Ethelreda's Pinnacle. In 1980 Mick Fowler and others finished Crowley's Crack (5.9), 85 years after Crowley's aforementioned attempt. In 1981 Fowler and team ventured onto the cliffs at Dover. Armed with ice tools for the chalk they established Dry Ice (IV), but were hampered by rescue attempts and the interference of a BBC TV crew. Fowler diverted his attention to Beachy Head and climbed Monster Crack. Phil Thornhill arrived in Dover in 1982, beginning a sustained period of exploration, sometimes alone and often taking days to complete ascents. In 1983 he teamed up with Fowler and Chris Watts to climb the stupendous Great White Fright (VI), and with Craig Jones to produce The Ferryman (VI).

Guidebook: Dave Turner, *Southern Sandstone* (1989).

DOW CRAG (Britain) This is the most southerly of the Lakeland mountain crags. Furthermore, the walk-in is short. The towns of Coniston and Ambleside and the M6 are nearby. There are four prominent BUTTRESSES, the left-hand one offering ROUTES up to 375 ft (114 m). Dow is a rhyolite crag with rough, fissured rock that is naturally protected. When wet, however, it responds like VERGLAS.

Among the better classics is the Gordon/Craig Route from 1909, a 5.4 up the first A Buttress. Les Brown added two excellent 5.10a routes here in the early 1960s, Isengard and the serious Sidewalk.

On the B Buttress are some outstanding harder routes, the greatest probably being Rob Matheson's, including the bold Tarkus (5.9), Pink Panther (5.10d) and Holocaust (5.11a). Ed Cleasby solved a longstanding problem when he climbed Close to Critical (5.11d). C Buttress has easier routes dating back to before and just after World War I.

Guidebooks: Al Phizacklea, *Scafell, Dow and Eskdale* (1988); Bill Birkett, et al, *Rock Climbing in the Lake District* (1986).

DOWEL In AID CLIMBING, a short length of aluminum rod stock hammered into a shallow hole as an alternative to a full-length bolt (see BOLTS, RIVETS).

DOWN The fine breast feathers of the goose or duck, used as INSULATION in SLEEPING BAGS and CLOTHING FOR MOUNTAINEERS.

DOWN CLIMBING The act of climbing down a face. (See REVERSE.)

DOWN SUIT A lightweight, down-filled over-suit, baffled or quilted and made of nylon or a breathable fabric. They are usually one-piece but may consist of separate trousers and a jacket with a hood, and are the choice among climbers venturing to high, cold Himalayan peaks. (See CLOTHING FOR MOUNTAINEERS.)

DROITES, LES (France) This is a magnificent mountain, especially when viewed from its north side on the Argentière Glacier. It has two summits, the west summit being 13,067 ft/3,984 m and the east 13,062 ft/4,000 m, both climbed for the first time in 1876. Climbs start from the Couvercle Hut on the south side of the mountain and the Argentière Hut for the north. The south ridge offers a technically straightforward but long and demanding route at AD. The great routes, however, are on the north side of the east summit. The Lagarde Couloir is one such, and its FIRST ASCENT in 1930 by J. Lagarde was an achievement considering the steepness of this face. Other classics include the northeast spur that, despite its magnificent position, MIXED CLIMBING and possible BIVOUAC, is never overly technical at TD+. The direct, climbed by J. Droyer and C. Gaby in 1971, is a fine mixed climb. On the north face proper, P. Cornau and M. Davaille's 1955 ascent stands as out as an impressive ice route although the modern line is somewhat different. Most parties climb the lower section at night to ensure being on the headwall before the sun hits the upper slopes. (See RATING SYSTEMS for French grades.)

DRUS, LES (France) This fin of granite is an outstanding attraction of the MONT BLANC RANGE and many of the area's most historic climbs have been on its southwest face. There are two tops, the Grand Dru (12,313 ft/3,754 m) and the Petit Dru (12,234 ft/3,730 m). The south side is approached from Montenvers and the Charpoua Glacier and Hut. The south face of the Grand Dru has fewer trails compared to the relatively crowded routes on the southwest face of the Petit Dru. Recommended here is the south pillar, climbed in 1952 by M. Bastien and A. Contamine. The traverse of the DRUS follows the route climbed in 1903 by E. Giraud with J. Ravanel and A. Comte. The southwest or Bonatti Pillar of the Petit Dru is one of the finest climbs in the Mont Blanc Range and at the time of its FIRST ASCENT in 1955 the most difficult. Most parties still require two days. Seven years later, American climbers Gary HEMMING and Royal ROBBINS scaled the American Direct and ROBBINS was back three years after that with John HARLIN to add the American Superdirect. Although M. Pedrini freed this line in 1983 with pitches up to VIII+, most parties still resort to a lot of aid and ascents taking three or four days are not uncommon. Catherine DESTIVELLE's route in 1991 illustrates the enduring appeal and importance of the Dru.

DU FAUR, FREDA (1882–1935) (Australia) One of the first women alpinists of Australia, Du Faur achieved the first female ascent of Mount COOK, NEW ZEALAND's highest peak, in 1910. As a teenager she attended Sydney's Church of England Girl's Grammar School and taught herself rock-climbing skills while rambling about the bush near her Sydney home. She failed nursing school, and a photograph of Mount Cook drew her to climbing. Under the instruction of New Zealand guide Peter Graham and after physical conditioning at the Sydney Institute of Physical Education, she and Graham reached Cook's summit in six hours. In 1913 the same pair, and another guide, made the first TRAVERSE of Cook in a grueling 20-hour climb. She repeated other high peaks, and made the first traverse of Mount Sefton. Graham silenced those who thought it

improper for a lady to be climbing by saying she was as good as any man he'd climbed with. Du Faur was, however, unhappy in her life, and committed suicide at the age of 53.

DULFERSITZ A rappel method wherein the rope is wrapped around the body. (See RAPPELLING.)

DUMBARTON ROCK (Scotland) One of several OUTCROPS around Glasgow and Edinburgh. It is a volcanic plug of basalt nailed into the flat plain of the River Clyde, and is easily seen from the A82 north of Glasgow. It reaches a maximum of 220 ft (67 m) and its best feature is the spectacular and overhanging northwest face, giving some fierce one-PITCH routes. The crag is straightforward to reach, either by car or public transport, and begins directly above the parking lot. There are a range of grades here, with a number of excellent 5.8s and a good 5.9, Longbow, all on the northwest face. But Dumbarton is famous for its harder lines like Chemin de Fer (5.11d) and Rock of Ages (5.10d) and Requiem (5.13b). It is one of the hardest routes in SCOTLAND.
Guidebook: Kevin Howett, *Rock Climbing in Scotland* (1990).

DUVET A high-lofting quilted or baffled coat with a hood, and filled with down or synthetic INSULATION. An important component of CLOTHING FOR MOUNTAINEERS.

DYHRENFURTH, DOCTOR GUNTER OSKAR (1886–1975) (Switzerland) One of the most distinguished German mountaineers and scholars, Dyhrenfurth was born in Breslau. He became a professor of geology at the university there, and worked on the geological map of Switzerland. During World War I he was a mountain guide officer with the German Army on the Ortler Front. In 1933 he gave up his chair at the University of Breslau to protest the Nazi seizure of power and moved to Switzerland and gained citizenship. He led two important expeditions: the 1930 international expedition to KANGCHENJUNGA on which he made the FIRST ASCENT of Jongsong Peak (24,501 ft/ 7,470 m) and in 1934, an exploratory visit to the BALTORO Muztagh on which he and his first wife, Hettie, climbed Sia Kangrin's west summit (3,993 ft/7,315 m), setting a woman's altitude record. His explorations in these regions helped future expeditions. For his 1934 expedition he and Hettie received gold medals at the 1936 Olympics in Berlin. He made some 60 first ascents in Europe and Asia, wrote *To the Third Pole* (1952) and *The Third Pole* (1960) and compiled the *Himalayan Chronicles*. After World War II he was granted reparations by the German government for his stand against Nazism. He is the father of Norman DYHRENFURTH.

DYHRENFURTH, NORMAN (1918–   ) (Switzerland) Dyhrenfurth inherited his interest in MOUNTAINEERING from his father, Gunter Oskar DYHRENFURTH and led important Himalayan expeditions that he also filmed. At the outbreak of World War II he was guiding in WYOMING and ALASKA, and remained in the United States to become an officer with the U.S. army. In peacetime he became head of the motion picture division and an associate professor at UCLA. During the second Swiss attempt on EVEREST in 1952 he was both filmmaker and photographer. In 1955 he led an attempt on LHOTSE, and in 1958 was deputy leader of the Slick-Johnson expedition to NEPAL in search of the YETI. In 1960 he produced the film of the Swiss FIRST ASCENT of DHAULAGIRI, and in 1963 he led the first successful American expedition to Everest on which Willi UNSOELD and Tom HORNBEIN pioneered the west ridge and Jim WHITTAKER and Sherpa Gombu repeated the south col route. Dyhrenfurth returned to Everest in 1971, co-leading (with Lt. Col. J. O. M. Roberts) the International Southwest Face expedition. The team reached 27,388 ft (8,350 m). His later films include *Tibetan Death Rites*, which, like many of his others, received international awards.

DYNAMIC BELAY A technique of belaying wherein a small amount of rope is allowed to slip through the belay system to reduce the impact forces generated in a fall, thus stopping the falling climber somewhat gently. (See BELAYING TECHNIQUES.)

DYNAMIC ROPES Ropes that incorporate a degree of stretch into their design to absorb the energy of a fall. All climbing ropes used for leading are dynamic. (See ROPES.)

DYNO A colloquial way of referring to a dynamic move. It is a controlled lunge from one handhold to another initiated by a release of explosive energy. During a dyno a climber's hands and feet may be disengaged from the rock. A dyno requires considerable strength.

E

EB A once-popular rock shoe designed by French boulderer Emile Bordenau in the 1930s and later manufactured in France. During the 1960s and 1970s EBs dominated the world rock shoe market, but the introduction of the Spanish FIRE rock shoe, with its stickier rubber, quickly replaced the EB in the early 1980s. (See ROCK SHOES.)

ECKENSTEIN, OSCAR (1859–1921) (Britain) This British railway engineer and chemist was an early advocate of guideless climbing, invented the first CRAMPONS and the first short ICE AXE (of about 34 inches/85 cm), and was among the first climbers to attempt K2. He also was one of the first climbers to practice BOULDERING, which he did around the Welsh CRAGS. He visited the KARAKORAM and saw K2 on W. M. CONWAY's 1892 expedition, but Eckenstein and Conway quarreled and Eckenstein left the expedition. Their views on climbing were polarized; Eckenstein disliked clubs and believed in climbing for the sake of climbing, while Conway, who became a president of the Alpine Club in 1902, criticized Eckenstein for his guideless ascents. Both wrote accounts of the expedition that make little mention of the other. Eckenstein's is *The Karakorams and Kashmir: An Account of a Journey* (1896).

Eckenstein climbed with Aleister Crowley, the British climber and occultist. Together they climbed in England, the ALPS and on the Mexican volcanoes. In 1902 the pair launched the first K2 expedition. It was troubled from the outset. In Rawalpindi Eckenstein was detained and refused entry into KASHMIR. It is believed his old rival Conway sent word to officials that Eckenstein was a Prussian spy. When entry was permitted (after a journey to see Lord Curzon in Delhi), the team arrived at K2 and attempted the southeast ridge, reaching about 20,000 ft (6,097 m). This ridge became the American route of 1978. The feud with Conway caused Eckenstein's considerable accomplishments to be downplayed in the annals of British climbing.

Further reading: David Dean, "Who was Oscar Eckenstein?" *The Alpine Journal* (1960).

ECUADOR The ANDES of Ecuador are volcanic peaks. There are two parallel systems that run roughly north to south: the Cordillera Occidental, with CHIMBORAZO (20,563 ft/6,267 m), highest in the country; and the Cordillera Oriental, with symmetrical Cotopaxi (the world's highest active volcano) (19,350 ft/5,897 m), its highest. Between both ranges are several basins supporting cities and farming. Quito, the capital (altitude: 9,389 ft/2,863 m; population, 1,300,000) at the base of Pichincha, is the starting point for the peaks and has been called "the most comfortable base camp in Ecuador." Weather is uneven. July and August are the reliable months for the Cordillera Occidental, January and February, for the Oriental. Rain and sleet are common. Snow is usually deep and the ice retreating, unstable. Local climbers usually camp high, set out around 1 A.M., reach summits by sunrise and are back in camp before the noon fog and mist descend.

Vulcanology prompted MOUNTAINEERING in Ecuador. In 1582, an eruption of Pichincha forced Spaniards to inspect its crater (15,616 ft/4,761 m). Savant La Condamine climbed Corazon (same height) in 1738. Alexander von Humboldt attempted Chimborazo, and in his books he made the mountain sound fabulous. Until 1818, Chimborazo was considered the highest mountain on earth. In the 1870s, vulcanologists Wilhelm Reiss and Alfons Stuebel ascended many peaks, including Cotopaxi. In 1880, Edward WHYMPER climbed Chimborazo and 10 other peaks. Ecuadorian pioneer Nicolas MARTINEZ made some new climbs including one up Cotopaxi from the east. In 1939, Italians and Germans climbed Chimborazo up its Totorillas Glacier. Altar, a majestic horseshoe-shaped knot of peaks called by Humboldt "the masterpiece of Creation," attracted Italians under Marino Tremonti, who climbed Obispo, the highest (17,451 ft/5,319 m) in 1963. Italians, Ecuadorians and Germans seized the remaining summits of this wonderful massif. Other popular volcanoes include Tunguraha (16,456 ft/5,016 m), an easy peak bordering the Amazon Basin, and the two Iliniza Peaks, Norte (15,583 ft/4,750 m) and Sur (17,276 ft/5,266 m). El Altar, which defeated Whymper, is a TECHNICAL peak attracting renewed interest.

Today the Ecuadorian heights attract many trekkers and climbers. Ecuador has 11 mountain clubs, grouped under the Federacion de Andinismo (national association). *La Montana* and *Campo Abierto* are Ecuadorian climbing publications.

Guidebooks: Jorge Anhalzer, *Ecuador, tierras altas* (1987); Jorge Anhalzer and Ramiro Navarrete, *Por los Andes del Ecuador* (1983); Bob Rachowiecki, *Climbing and Hiking in Ecuador* (1984).

Evelio Echevarria
Colorado State University

EDGING   A FREE CLIMBING term, meaning to stand with precision on small edges or features on a cliff. (See FACE CLIMBING.)

Edging

EDITH CAVELL, MOUNT   (Canada)   This beautiful 11,033-ft (3,363-m) peak of the ROCKY MOUNTAINS lies southwest of Jasper, ALBERTA. Its quartzite walls rise 7,216 ft (2,200 m) from the valley of the Athabasca River. It was first climbed via the easy slopes from Verdant Pass by A. J. Gilmour and E. W. D. Holway (1915). The blocky east ridge (by J. W. A. Hickson and guide Conrad KAIN in 1924) is the highly recommended standard ROUTE. A side road leads to the base of the north face, making it the most accessible face in the Rockies, but the wall is subject to rock fall and CORNICE collapse, especially in summer. Late August and September are the favored climbing times. At least four routes line the north face, all IV, 5.7, with grade 3 ice, or harder. The first of these routes was a milestone for postwar mountaineering in North America. Over two days in 1961 Yvon CHOUINARD, Fred BECKEY and Dan Doody struggled up the face through rock fall, rain and lightning. The climbing was poorly protected, the rock often rotten. The north face received its FIRST WINTER ASCENT by Barry BLANCHARD and Ward Robinson in 1988.
Guidebooks: Sean Dougherty, *Selected Alpine Climbs in the Canadian Rockies* (1991); Steve Roper and Allen Steck, *Fifty Classic Climbs of North America* (1979).

EDLINGER, PATRICK   (1960–   )   (France)   The French climbing champion who popularized SPORT CLIMBING in France, Edlinger was widely covered by the media. He won a seminal competition, the 1986 Sport Roccia in Bardoneccia and ARCO, Italy. In a magical performance, Edlinger also won the first professional sport-climbing contest held in the United States, the International Sport Climbing Championship at Snowbird, UTAH, in 1988. At Arco in 1988 he tied for first with Stefan GLOWACZ.

On rock, Edlinger established the second 5.13 in France, The Medius (7c+, 5.13a) at St. Victoire. In 1980, he soloed three 7a+ ROUTES, a breakthrough for the time. In 1982, he made the FIRST FREE ASCENTS of the two hardest routes in the VERDON, Chrysalis and Fenrir (both 7c+, or 5.13a). Also in 1982, he ON-SIGHTED routes like La Polka des Ringards (7c or 5.12d) and Parties Carées. In on-sighting at this time, according to Martin Atkinson, a British guidebook author, "he was two years ahead of Jerry MOFFAT and three years ahead of his French contemporaries."

In 1983 he created one of the first 8a routes in France, Ça Glisse aux Pays des Merveilles at BUOUX. During a tour of the United States in 1985, he ticked off the hardest routes of the time in good style, FLASHING, for example, Thunderdome (5.12d) in the SHAWANGUNKS. Among his other achievements are the coveted second ascent of Maginot Line (variously called 8c or 5.14b, or 8b+ or 5.14a) at VOLX in 1990. He also flashed Mirage (7c or 5.12d) in CEUSE, an area he largely developed, and on-sighted L'Autoroute de Soleil (7c+ or 5.13a) at Buoux. At Chateauvert, he put up Are You Ready? (8b/c or 5.14a) in 1989. Edlinger has appeared in climbing films like *Life by the Fingertips*, and co-produced the book *Rock Games*.

EDWARDS, JOHN MENLOVE   (1910–1958) (Britain)   Youngest of a Lancashire clergyman's four children and the greatest rock-climbing innovator of the interwar period in Britain. He began climbing in his late teens on the limestone SEA CLIFFS of Pembroke during family holidays. The sandstone OUTCROP of Helsby, near Liverpool, became the focus of his activities when he went to study medicine at Liverpool University in 1929, and it was there that he met Colin KIRKUS—already established as the outstanding young rock-climber of his generation. By 1931 Menlove was adding numerous new routes to the cliffs of WALES, and his free lead—the first—of Scafell's central buttress in the LAKE DISTRICT in September of that year consolidated a growing reputation and brought him acceptance as Kirkus's peer. Throughout the 1930s he continued to climb new routes in WALES, greatly expanding the concept of what was considered climbable. Of great physical strength, his predilection was for the steep cliffs of Llanberis and the Devil's Kitchen—until that time thought too loose for safety—from which he unearthed a collection of climbs that are now among the popular CLASSICS of Snowdonia, and which at the time of their FIRST ASCENT marked a distinct psychological advance. He also made important first ascents on Lliwedd, CLOGWYN DU'R ARDDU and Tryfan. The period in which he was pioneering new climbs stretched from 1930 to 1957. Aside from climbing, his exploits on water were most remarkable: He swam down the Linn of Dee when it was in spate, and rowed across The Minch to Lewis in a small open boat in midwinter.

A psychiatrist, he practiced in Liverpool, and a homosexual, he proselytised for tolerance years before it was acceptable or legal in BRITAIN. During the Second World War he registered as a conscientious objector, but the isolation occasioned both by this and his sexual orientation brought him to mental breakdown. The last years of his life were spent in suffering from paranoid schizophrenia, with intervals of lucidity in which he continued to add important new routes, particularly in the LLANBERIS PASS. He made several attempts at suicide, and eventually took his own life in February 1958.

As a writer, his small output of guidebooks and essays is the most significant single body of work about rock-climbing yet produced. The essays in particular are of inexhaustible density and resonance, unique in tone, and have been much anthologized.

Further reading: Jim Perrin, *Menlove: The Life and Writings of John Menlove Edwards* (1985).

EIGER (Austria) Beyond the Mönch to the north and overlooking Grindelwald and the village of Kleine Scheidegg is the Eiger (13,022 ft/3,970 m). It is without question one of the world's most famous mountains. The reason lies first in its prominent location and second in the notoriety surrounding various attempts in the 1930s to climb its north (in reality northwest) face. There are, other ROUTES to the summit; the mountain was first climbed in 1858 and the Lauper Route of 1932 takes the RIB separating the Eigerwand from the true north face. The Mittelegi Ridge rises up to the summit from the northeast and had been climbed in 1921.

It is perhaps forgivable, therefore, that when Austrian and German climbers started exploring the Eigerwand, some saw it as a meaningless variation. History, however, says otherwise and not only has the mountain become famous but small sections of it are also well known; Death Bivouac where M. Seldmayer and K. Mehringer perished during the first serious attempt in 1935, the Hinterstoisser Traverse that its progenitor failed to reverse leading to the deaths of himself, Toni Kurz, Eddie Rainer and Willy Angerer in 1936 and the White Spider at the top of the face. The route was eventually climbed in 1938 by Heinrich HARRER, Anderl Heckmair, Fritz Kasparek and W. Vorg. Other climbs have followed, most notably the Harlin Direct climbed in the winter of 1966 and named after American alpinist JOHN HARLIN II who perished during the ascent, but the 1938 route, whose reputation probably outweighs its difficulties, remains the ambition, secret or otherwise, of many climbers.

EIGHT-THOUSAND-METER (26,240 FT) PEAKS
The 14 mountains in the HIMALAYAN and KARAKORAM ranges that stand more than 8,000 m (26,240 ft) above sea

level are the "eight-thousanders." They are the highest mountains on earth.

The term first gained currency in Europe during the 1950s when the highest peaks received their FIRST ASCENTS. In the 1980s, with the increased interest in Himalayan climbing and the focus on the 14 eight-thousanders by climbers like Reinhold MESSNER, who first climbed all 14 (followed a few months later by the Pole Jerzy KUKUCZKA), the term came to suggest the ultimate challenge in MOUNTAINEERING.

The eight-thousand-m (26,240-ft) peaks present serious mountaineering objectives. In addition to being subject to harsh weather and extreme cold, their summits lie near the level of the jet stream that seasonally rises and falls. During periods when the jet stream lowers, near the approach of winter, severe winds may preclude the chance of summiting. Although all the eight-thousand-meter (26,240-ft) peaks have now been climbed without the use of OXYGEN APPARATUS, the rigors of oxygen deprivation present real problems and dangers to humans: Near the summits of EVEREST and K2, the oxygen content is approximately one-third that found at sea level. Many expeditions still use oxygen on the tallest eight-thousand-meter peaks, especially the five highest, sometimes referred to as "the big five." On these peaks, climbers have found that an additional BIVOUAC is often necessary above 8,000 m (26,240 ft), thus increasing the risk of ALTITUDE ILLNESSES like PULMONARY EDEMA and CEREBRAL EDEMA.

Critics of the preoccupation in modern mountaineering with the eight-thousanders cite the fact that the popularity of these peaks is less a function of their difficulty or beauty than a function of the metric measuring system. In the United States, where English measurement is used, 8,000 m converts to an ungainly sounding 26,240 ft. Furthermore, critics point out that a peak of 7,999 m (26,237 ft) is no less significant in real terms than a peak one meter (3.28 ft) higher.

Since some of the eight-thousand-meter peaks are comprised of clusters of summits above 8,000 m (26,240 ft), there are actually a total of 22 distinct summits on earth above 8,000 m (26,240 ft). For instance, KANGCHENJUNGA is comprised of four summits between 8,586 m and 8,476 m (28,162 and 27,801 ft) (for a full list of these peaks see Appendices). Many of these additional summits have come to be regarded by the governments concerned as individual peaks requiring separate climbing permission.

The 15 recognized eight-thousand-meter (26,240-ft) peaks are:

1. EVEREST (also Sagarmatha or chomolungma Feng; China/Nepal border): 29,028 ft/8,848 m
2. K2 (also Godwin Austin or Chogori; Kashmir-Sinkiang border): 28,250 ft/8,611 m
3. KANGCHENJUNGA (India/Nepal border): 28,170 ft/ 8,586 m
4. LHOTSE I (Nepal/Tibet border): 27,923 ft/8,511 m
5. MAKALU (China/Nepal border): 27,766 ft/8,463 m
6. DHAULAGIRI (Nepal): 26,795 ft/8,167 m

7. MANASLU (Nepal): 26,781 ft/8,163 m
8. CHO OYU (Nepal/Tibet): 26,750 ft/8,153 m
9. NANGA PARBAT (Kashmir): 26,657 ft/8,125 m
10. ANNAPURNA (Nepal): 26,545 ft/8,091 m
11. GASHERBRUM I (also Hidden Peak; Pakistan/China border): 26,470 ft/8,068 m
12. BROAD PEAK (Pakistan/China border): 26,400 ft/8,047 m
13. SHISHAPANGMA (Tibet): 26,397 ft/8,046 m
14. GASHERBRUM II (Paskistan/China border): 26,361 ft/8,035 m
15. GOSAINTHAN (Nepal): 26,287 ft/8,012 m

ELBRUS, MOUNT (Republic of Georgia) See SEVEN SUMMITS.

ELBSANDSTEINGEBIRGE (Germany) Also called Elbsandstein, or Dresden, after the city near these historic cliffs on which FREE CLIMBING as we know it today began. In fact, when Fritz WEISSNER, an Elbsandsteingebirge climber, moved to the United States in 1922, he took the idea of free climbing with him and applied it to the SHAWANGUNKS. Elbsandsteinbirge rock is soft sandstone and there are about 12,000 ROUTES. The climbing is often BOLD, with long RUNOUTS between BOLTS or knotted SLINGS.

In 1864 villagers from Schandau climbed the tallest tower of the area, the Falkenstein, using aid. A decade later the area's FIRST FREE ASCENT was made on the tower called the Monchsteins. In 1890 Oscar Schuster and party originated the Elbsandstein's tactic of partially free ascents, by climbing free to a stance, hand-drilling a large ring-bolt on which they hung and rested, then proceeding free to the next bolt. This tradition continued into modern times. Schuster is credited with creating the first RATING SYSTEM for the area, which appeared in 1897 and consisted of three degrees of climbing; I, II and III. Modern ratings range from IV to Xc. Schuster also constructed a climbing shoe with a hemp sole, though many Elbsandstein climbers climbed in bare feet.

In 1913 the rules that govern climbing in the area were formulated by Rudolf Fehrmann. These rules state that FIRST ASCENTS are made from the ground up, and as few ring-bolts as possible are placed; that resting on rings is permissible, as is resting on knotted SLINGS placed in CRACKS and POCKETS; that CHALK is forbidden; and that metal protection like FRIENDS or NUTS are forbidden because they damage the soft sandstone. These rules remained intact during East Germany's isolation from the changes in western climbing. Nonetheless, there are climbs of 5.10 and 5.11 involving perilous runouts that were climbed before World War II. Since the reunification of Germany younger climbers have sought to bring the rules up to modern standards, but TRADITIONALISTS are reluctant to lose the unique heritage of Elbsandstein climbing.

EL CAPITAN (United States) The ultimate BIG WALL CLIMBING monolith on earth, located in the sunny environs of YOSEMITE VALLEY, CALIFORNIA, attracts climbers from all over the world. Its walls—nearly 3,000 ft (914 m) at the highest point—are of especially solid granite. It OVERHANGS throughout, especially on the east FACE, which is drastically steep for some 20 consecutive PITCHES. AID CLIMBING techniques and equipment as we know it today evolved out of ascents of El Capitan. Some 50 ROUTES scale it, and the longest is over 30 pitches. Landmark climbs on it include the East Buttress, done in 1953 by a team including Allen Steck and Willi UNSOELD. The Nose, the first route up the center of the monolith, was seiged over weeks by Warren HARDING, Wayne Merry and G. Whitmore and others in 1958. The climbers placed 125 bolts and FIXED ROPES much of the way. The Salathe Wall, by Royal ROBBINS, Chuck PRATT and Tom FROST, was done three years later, with deliberate efforts to use less fixed rope and fewer bolts. Both routes have been climbed now in just a few hours (see SPEED CLIMBING).

Robbins, Yvon CHOUINARD and others developed PITON work to high standards on El Capitan, and in 1964 they, with Pratt and Frost, climbed the North America Wall. This stood as the hardest wall in the world for many years. Originally rated A5, it is now regarded as A3+, yet it is steep and the rock is delicate. Robbins culminated his Yosemite career in 1968 by soloing the first big wall on El Cap, the Muir Wall. Robbins also raised a controversy when he repeated the Wall of the Early Morning Light, which took Harding and Dean Caldwell 28 days to climb. Robbins, like others, regarded Harding's 300 bolts and rivets excessive, so he chopped the rivets on the lower pitches. His act caused so much furor that, in the early 1990s, the rivets were replaced. During the 1970s full-time climbers inhabited Yosemite and focused on big wall climbing as a lifestyle. Charlie PORTER, with various partners including Canadians Hugh Burton and Steve Sutton, pioneered many walls, with Porter's input on The Shield, Mescalito, Tangerine Trip and Zodiac being key. They are among the most frequently climbed walls on El Cap today. Jim BRIDWELL took up where Porter left off. His routes of the latter 1970s, Pacific Ocean Wall, Sea of Dreams and Zenyatta Mondatta pushed the notion of A5 to new heights, utilizing extensive COPPERHEADING, SKYHOOKING and climbing thin, EXPANDING FLAKES. Sea of Dreams contains a full pitch of hooking. By the 1980s the tradition of living on the walls for days on end was set, and gaps between climbs were filled. Of note in the A5 category are Space, by Charles Cole solo, and Jolly Rodger, by Cole and Steve Grossman; Aurora by Peter Mayfield and Greg Child; Lost in America, by Child and Randy LEAVITT; and, among the most serious, Sheep Ranch of Wyoming, by Rob Slater and John Barbella; and Atlantic Ocean Wall by John Middendorf and John Barbella. Climbers continue to enjoy freedom on El Capitan, with the major rules set by the national park being that no climbers should jettison their haul bag from the summit, and that climbers observe seasonal route closures on the east face during nesting periods of the peregrine falcon.

Guidebook: George Meyers and Don Reid, *Yosemite Climbs* (1987).

El Capitan, United States

ELDORADO CANYON   (United States) One of the wellsprings of American FREE CLIMBING, this fine-grained sandstone area lies 10 miles (16 km) south of BOULDER, COLORADO. Cliffs and tower-like features of orange rock offer steep FACE CLIMBING, occasional CRACKS and at times large ROOFS. Principal formations are The Bastille, Red Garden Wall, West Ridge, Wind Tower, Rincon Wall, Mickey Maus and The Whale's Tale. Development began in 1954, when an army team aided the Bastille Crack, which today is a popular 5.9 free climb. The first notable free climb was made in 1956. Redgarden Wall, a 5.7 climbed by Chuck Marley, Dick Bird, and others was visionary. Milestone ROUTES of the 1950s were the long T2 by Gerry Roach and Layton KOR (the latter of whom opened numerous routes in Eldorado), and the first 5.10—Ray Northcutt's Direct Start to the Bastille. This was the only 5.10 around Boulder until the mid 1960s. The style of climbing in Eldorado Canyon heralded the modern trend focusing on TECHNICAL face climbing and the elimination of aid. Larry Dalke and Pat AMENT led this trend during the 1960s, and Jim Erickson, Duncan Ferguson and Steve WUNSCH were prolific in the 1970s. The most famous route of this era is The Naked Edge, climbed by Kor and Bob Culp in 1962,

then freed at 5.11 by Erickson and Ferguson in 1971. Throughout this time Eldorado remained a bastion of traditional ground-up and CLEAN CLIMBING ETHICS. Landmarks of the traditional era include: Wunsch's 1975 routes Psycho Roof (5.12) and the committing Jules Verne (5.11×) (× denoting seriousness and long-fall potential); the exceptional psychological efforts of Dave BREASHERS's unprotected Perilous Journey (5.11×, in 1975), and Mark Wilford's Spinal Tap (5.13×, in 1986), and in 1979, Jim Collins's FREE ASCENT of Gensis (5.12c). In the mid-1980s ground-up tactics gave way to SPORT CLIMBING. Christian GRIFFITH was largely responsible for sport climbing in Eldorado. Bolted routes like his Paris Girls (5.12+) and Desdichado (5.13 b/c), Bob Horan's Rainbow Wall (5.12) and Dale Goddard's The Sacred and The Profane (5.13a) exemplify this period. The 1990s opened with two significant developments in Eldorado: a backlash to sport-climbing ethics when Park Service managers outlawed bolting, and a potential 5.14 when England's Ben MOON freed the oft-tried Undertaker.

Guidebook: Richard Rossiter, *Boulder Climbs South* (1990).

Further reading: Bob Godfrey and Dudley Chelton, *Climb! Rock Climbing in Colorado* (1977).

ELIMINATE   Archaic British rock-climbing term, meaning a climb that straightens out the line of earlier ROUTES. Also used as "aid eliminate," to FREE CLIMB an existing aid route.

ELLINGWOOD,   ALBERT   (1887–1934)   (United States)   A Rhodes Scholar with a Ph.D. in social and political science, Ellingwood contributed to the development of COLORADO mountaineering when he brought rope techniques and gear from BRITAIN after studying at Merton College, Oxford. He established TECHNICAL rock routes to 5.6 in GARDEN OF THE GODS, and made FIRST ASCENTS in the WIND RIVER RANGE and ROCKY MOUNTAINS. In 1920 he climbed Lizard's Head, a steep peak with 5.7 climbing, and in 1925 he led a party up the 2,000-ft (610-m) east face of Crestone Needle in the Sangre de Cristo Mountains. Both routes were breakthroughs for the period. His frequent rope-partner was Eleanor Davis, an accomplished woman climber of the era.

EMERALDS, THE   (United States)   A sport-climbing area between Nevada City and Truckee, CALIFORNIA, this 80-ft (24-m) gorge, and its surrounding cliffs, was cut by the south fork of the Yuba River through metamorphosed sedimentary and igneous rock. It is named after the green-pools from which the climbs rise. Discovered in 1988, some 100 well-bolted routes up to hard 5.13 on highly featured, overhanging faces have been developed.
Guidebook: Mike Carville, *A Climber's Guide to Tahoe Rock* (1991).

ENCHAINMENT   To link rock climbs or mountain climbs in a continuous movement of climbing. The practice attracted a following in the French Alps in the 1970s and 1980s with efforts to combine the three north faces (GRANDES JORRASSES, MATTERHORN and EIGER) in a day. Frenchmen like Patrick GABBAROU, Jean-Marc BOIVIN, Pierre BEGHIN and Eric ESCOFFIER, the Swiss Erhard LORETAN and Slovene Tomo CESEN have all made impressive enchainments in the Alps, sometimes using PARAPENTE, hang glider, skis, car and helicopter to speed descents from peak to peak. American Terry (Mugs) STUMPS has made grueling enchainments in ALASKA. In YOSEMITE rock climbing, Peter CROFT and climbers like John BACHAR and Dave Schultz have enchained long hard FREE CLIMBS in marathon days.

ERBESFIELD, ROBYN   (1963–   )   (United States)   A top contender on the world SPORT-CLIMBING circuit, Erbesfield burst onto the scene in early 1989 by winning the second world competition she entered, the WORLD CUP at Leeds, England. The climber from Atlanta, Georgia, won two other world events that year, at Massey, France, and in Bulgaria, and placed third overall in the World Cup standings. In 1990 she placed second at the International Escalade at St. Jean de Maurienne, France, and the season continued with consistent high placings, including second at the World Cup in Nuremberg. She placed fourth overall in the UIAA rankings. She had an outstanding season in 1991, winning the World Cup in Tokyo and entering the final competition of the season, in Birmingham, England, in position to take first, though she placed third there and overall. At the time of this writing Erbesfield has ON-SIGHTED nine 5.12ds and a 5.13a called Soupir Pour Pas Dormir in the Vin Grau, France. She has worked routes up to 8b (5.13d). She also did the FIRST ASCENT of an 8b in Switzerland.

ERICKSON,   JAMES   (JIM)   (1948–   )   (United States)   An influential figure in U.S. FREE CLIMBING in the 1970s, Erickson began climbing at DEVIL'S LAKE and continued in BOULDER, COLORADO, where he began studying classical music in 1967. At ELDORADO CANYON between 1967 and 1977 he pioneered aid eliminations, systematically freeing some 100 aid routes and pushing free-climbing limits. In 1971 he achieved a major accomplishment when he, Steve WUNSCH and Duncan Ferguson free-climbed The Naked Edge (5.11b), in Eldorado, a route Erickson had worked on since 1969. After this route he revised his free-climbing tactics, choosing to abandon a climb if he fell or used protection to lower off. He summed up his approach with the words, "I would try to do nothing which a climber who was soloing could not do." In today's vernacular he strived for ON-SIGHT FLASH ascents. He rejected CHALK, for its use tainted an ascent. He relaxed his no-falls philosophy in 1976 to achieve the FIRST FREE ASCENT, with Art Higbee, of the Regular Northwest Face of Half Dome (5.12). The film of this climb—*Freeclimb*—inspired a generation of rock climbers. John STANNARD's concept of clean climbing closely paralleled Erickson's, and both advocated NUTS rather than rock-scarring PITONS for protection.
Further reading: James Erickson, *Rocky Heights: A Guide to Boulder Free Climbs* (1980).

ERTO   (Italy)   This small town and its limestone CRAGS, located near the village of Longaronne in the DOLOMITE area of Northern Italy, is noted for its fine, overhanging SPORT CLIMBING. It is a roadside crag popular in summer due to its high elevation. Camping and services abound in the region.

ESCOFFIER,   ERIC   (1960–   )   (France)   Rock climber, alpinist and expeditioner, PARAPENTE expert and car racer, Escoffier was FREE CLIMBING the hardest VERDON routes in 1982 and then moved on to the ALPS with a one-day enchainment of the American Direct and Bonatti Pillar on Les DRU, a linkup of some 5,904 ft (1,800 m) of steep granite. Escoffier then took to winter enchainments, linking the Croz and Walker Spurs on the GRANDES JORASSES, solo. He also made several attempts at the one-day winter solo of the "trilogy"—a linkup of the MATTERHORN, EIGER and Jorasses, and he made ascents of GASHERBRUM II and K2. A severe car crash jeopardized his climbing career in 1987, though he has participated in French EVEREST expeditions since then.

ESK BUTTRESS   (Britain)   Esk Buttress lies on the south flank of Scafell Pike. A southerly aspect, sound rock and incut holds make Esk a popular venue, despite its long approach. One approach is by walking up Eskdale after driving over the Wrynose and Hardknott Passes from the eastern lakes. The nearest village is Boot.

Of the earlier climbs, Alf Bridge's long 5.6 from 1932 and Arthur Dolphin's Trespasser Groove (5.8) from 1952 are notable, but it wasn't till a decade later that the CRAG matured with good ROUTES like Pete Crew's Central Pillar (5.10b).

Modern routes include Fallout, an imposing 5.11a climbed by Bill Birkett and Andy Hyslop in 1978, but the crag's outstanding desperate is The Cumbrian, first climbed with aid by Rod Valentine and Tut Braithwaite in 1974 and freed by Martin and Bob Berzins at 5.12a.

Guidebooks: Bill Birkett, et al. *Rock Climbing in the Lake District* (1986); Al Phizacklea, *Scafell, Dow and Eskdale* (1988).

ETHICS Climbing ethics reflect changing attitudes toward climbing styles and the behavior of climbers toward cliffs and mountain regions. Because climbing is an individualistic pursuit with no single body dictating policy, ethics have been a matter of choice among climbers from area to area and generation to generation. What constitutes ethical and unethical behavior is a matter of subtle interpretation and provides much debate in climbing circles. However, in response to the increased numbers of climbers in recent years and the potential for impact on areas by climbers and legislation against climbing by land managers, the AMERICAN ALPINE CLUB drew up the following "Ten Commandments of Sustainable Climbing," published in the 1990 AMERICAN ALPINE JOURNAL:

1. Never disturb historically, archeologically or environmentally sensitive areas.
2. Don't scar, chisel, glue holds onto or otherwise deface the rock.
3. Don't place bolts near cracks or other natural protection.
4. Avoid using colored bolt hangers that contrast brightly to the rock.
5. Don't add fixed protection on established routes except to beef up questionable belay or rappel anchors.
6. Don't establish routes in heavy traffic areas such as campgrounds or directly above public trails or roads.
7. If you must leave slings at rappel stations or "back off" gear, use colors that blend in with the surrounding rock.
8. Don't throw anything—rotten slings, trash or even human waste—off climbs; it's simple: Everything you start up with comes off the climb with you, not before.
9. Accept responsibility even for the impact of other climbers on the mountain environment by removing rotten slings and garbage from climbs, bivouac areas and descent routes.
10. Know and follow local regulations on climbing restrictions on bolting, motorized bolting and chalk. Then work to change unfair restrictions through the American Alpine Club Access Committee or local climber organizations.

For further discussion on rock-climbing ethics see CHIPPING, CLEAN CLIMBING, EURO-STYLE, HANGDOGGING, SPORT CLIMBING, STYLE, TRADITIONALIST; for mountaineering ethics see ALPINE STYLE, CAPSULE STYLE.

ETRIERS A French word for a set of foot slings. Also called stirrups, because of their resemblance to stirrups used on a saddle. In the United States they are called aiders. Etriers are short ladders of webbing that a climber stands in during AID CLIMBING. A typical etrier is made of one-inch (2.54 cm) WEBBING, knotted into three to five steps. A loop at the top is used to accommodate a CARABINER that is clipped into PITONS, NUTS, etc. European-style etriers use aluminum rungs. Two etriers are used, one for each foot, but on long or difficult aid routes two pairs of etriers are more convenient.

EURO-STYLE Also called French style, but generally known as SPORT CLIMBING, this term generally refers to BOLTED ROUTES. The style of climbing wherein any form of preparation and practice of the ROUTE is permissible as long as the route is finally RED POINTED, or led without weighting PROTECTION. The style was developed in France in the 1980s and led to dramatic increases in the difficulties of FREE CLIMBING. (See also HANGDOGGING, ON SIGHT, RAPPEL BOLTING.)

EVEREST, MOUNT (Nepal-Tibet) Rightly or wrongly, the world's highest mountain (29,028 ft/8,848 m) has come to symbolize the ultimate in human achievement, and more has been written about it than any other mountain. Reaching its summit carries prestige, and today scores of climbers flock to it, creating crowds (in 1992 37 people reached the top in one day) and trash (expeditions just to remove garbage from Everest were a development of the 1990s). It has been climbed as fast as 22 hours, by Mark Batard (France), and descended via PARAPENTE by J. M. BOIVIN, both feats in 1988.

Its southern flanks face NEPAL, and hill people and SHERPAS call the mountain Sagarmatha. Its northern flanks face TIBET, whose people call it Chomolungma, meaning "Mother Goddess of the District." The Nepal side resembles a huge horseshoe, with Everest, LHOTSE and Nuptse all connected by COLS and RIDGES with the great KHUMBU icefall falling out of the semicircle like a white tongue. The north wall is a huge, moderate-angled slope bounded by long ridges on the north and west.

Britons became intrigued with reaching the top of Everest in the 1890s. Major C. G. BRUCE's 1922 expedition was the first of several British expeditions to the north col. On a 1924 attempt George MALLORY and Andreas Irvine disappeared high up. Perhaps they summited, perhaps not; the answer will probably never be known, although their frozen bodies may have been sighted by Chinese climbers.

In the 1950s entry into Tibet became impractical due to the Chinese takeover, and a route was sought in Nepal, up the Khumbu icefall. In 1952 a Swiss team reached 28,208 ft (8,600 m) on the southeast ridge, but it was a British-led expedition in 1953 that made the first ascent. On that occasion, Edmund HILLARY and Tenzing NORGAY summited via the southeast ridge.

CHINA launched a 214-climber assault from the north col in 1960, placing three men on top. The third new route came in 1963 when Norman DYHRENFURTH's American expedition put Willi UNSOELD and Tom HORNBEIN on top via the west ridge. They descended the southeast ridge (up which Jim WHITTAKER had climbed, a few days earlier to become the first American Everester) thus completing the first full traverse.

The first of four expeditions to the southwest face began in 1971 and succeeded in 1975 when Chris BONINGTON's British team members, Dougal HASTON and Doug SCOTT, became the first to top this wall. Other routes on the south side are the Polish south pillar of 1980 and the 1982 Soviet route on the southwest face, arguably the hardest on Everest and which included tough climbers like V. Balyberdin, S. Bershov and E. Myslovsky. Slovenes climbed the complete west ridge in 1979, and Poles Leszach Cichy and Krzysztof Wielicki made the first WINTER ASCENT in 1980 (southeast ridge), summiting in −40-degree-F (−40-degree-C) cold and high winds.

Reinhold MESSNER and Peter HABELER became the first to climb Everest without oxygen in premonsoon season in 1978. Between then and the spring of 1992, 34 climbers made 44 OXYGENLESS ascents. They include Messner, who returned to make the first solo ascent (north col) during the MONSOON of 1980; Ang Rita Sherpa, who climbed it oxygenless seven times; Larry Nielson, the first American (1983); Lydia Bradey (New Zealand), the first woman, in 1988; and Tim MACARTNEY-SNAPE, whose two oxygenless ascents were by new routes, the north face in 1984, and on foot from the Bay of Bengal to Everest's summit via the south col in 1990.

Lesser-known faces opened up when China opened Tibet in the 1980s. The north wall produced two principal routes up huge COULOIRS; the Great Couloir by Australians in 1984, and another huge couloir near the west ridge climbed by Japanese in 1980. Terrain between the north col and Great Couloir afforded several variations and is regarded as the easiest route.

Everest from the east is a SERAC-covered amphitheater bounded by Lhotse and the northeast ridge. A hazardous route up the Kangshung Face was completed by Americans in 1983 (among whom were George LOWE and Carlos BUHLER), and a route up the east face of the south col by an Anglo-American team in 1988. On the long northeast ridge Englishmen Peter BOARDMAN and Joe TASKER disappeared in 1983. The ridge was later climbed to its junction with the main summit pyramid, but not to the top.

By 1995, Everest has had over 500 people reach the summit. Nepal now changes a $50,000 fee, per expedition, to climb it.

EWBANK, JOHN (1948–) (Australia) Ewbank shaped Australian rock climbing, establishing new standards of FREE and AID CLIMBING in the 1960s and 1970s. Born in Yorkshire, England, he began cragging on gritstone

at the age of 12. After migrating to Australia at 15, he climbed under the tutelage of Bryden Allen, an expatriate Briton and the best climber in AUSTRALIA. Australia's untapped climbing potential inspired Ewbank to embark on a spree of new ROUTES that, for volume, few Australian climbers have equaled even today. He spent the night of his 16th birthday sleeping in SLINGS during the FIRST ASCENT of the 650-ft (198-m) overhanging wall of Echo Point, at Katoomba, in the Blue Mountains.

He believed Australian climbing should exist on its own terms, with its own ethos and ETHICS, free of the dictates of Europe or America. Thus, in 1966 he became founding editor of *Thrutch*, Australia's first climbing magazine. With the publication of *Rockclimbs in the Blue Mountains* in 1968 he introduced his own RATING SYSTEM, soon adopted throughout Australia. Its function was, "to unjam this absurd bottleneck created by this silly ceiling called *exceptionally severe* or 5.9." The open-ended system (from 1 to 21 upon introduction, currently topping out at 32) was also intended, Ewbank wrote, "to free climbers of my generation from the conceit and limitations of believing that the highest standards of our own time are any indication of the possibilities of the future." He advocated CLEAN CLIMBING, and manufactured hexagonal NUTS.

Among his hundreds of first ascents are Totem Pole, and southeast face of Frenchman's Cap in Tasmania; The Crucifixtion on Crater Bluff, and three routes on Bluff Mountain in the Warrumbungle Range (all with Bryden Allen); Old Baldy in the Wolgan Valley; and, in the Blue Mountains, serious aid routes on Dogface, and the crack Janicepts (21) at Mount Piddington, which for years was the hardest route in the country. Ewbank retired from climbing in the late 1970s to pursue a career in contemporary folk music.

EXMANSWORTHY CLIFF (Britain) On the western Culm Coast of DEVON, near the village of Hartland, lies this remote and serious sea CRAG offering fine climbing and generally sound rock. However, the approach is potentially dangerous and careful attention should be paid to the guidebook. Exmansworthy is around 140 ft (42 m) high, and since routes often follow CRACKS, they are well protected. JUMARS and ABSEIL ropes are useful for escapes.

The crag was discovered in 1979. Local expert Pete O'Sullivan climbed two of the crag's finest routes in 1980, Shadow Walker (5.10d) and Cat Burglar (5.10c). Two years later Pete Whillance added Culm Dancing (5.10d) with Murray Hamilton. All are CRACK CLIMBS.

Guidebooks: Pat Littlejohn, *South West Climbs* (1991); Iain Peters, *North Devon and Cornwall Climbers' Club* (1988).

EXPANDING FLAKE An exfoliating flake of rock that widens when PITONS, NUTS or CAMMING DEVICES are placed behind it. When a piece of equipment in such a flake is weighted with a downward force, a corresponding force is exerted outward, widening the flake. Because each successive placement marginally widens an expanding flake, placements below are weakened. This, and the risk of expanding the flake beyond the point of its natural elastic-

ity and breaking it off, mean considerable fall potential for the leader. Expanding flakes are often encountered in granite AID CLIMBING. Techniques for aid climbing on expanding flakes rely on disturbing the flake as little as possible. Pitons widen a flake the most, nuts and STOPPERS less, and SPRING-LOADED CAMMING DEVICES like FRIENDS the least. One way of climbing fragile expanding flakes is to tap a piton behind the flake, lever the flake open, then slip a stopper between the wall and the piton. When the stopper is weighted, the wedging action of the stopper is spread across the greater surface area of the piton. Other techniques include stacking stoppers in opposition to each other (as in one upside down against the other, with the down-wedging stopper weighted).

EXPANSION BOLT A type of bolt used for rock climbing. (See BOLT.)

EXPEDITION General term to describe an undertaking to travel to and climb a large peak in a remote, usually foreign, area. For discussion of expedition styles, see AL-PINE STYLE, CAPSULE STYLE, LIGHTWEIGHT EXPEDITIONS.

EXPOSURE Loss of deep body heat due to severe chilling. Also, an airy or "exposed" position on a climb. (See HYPOTHERMIA.)

EXUM, GLENN (1911–   ) (United States) This American mountaineer climbed and guided in the TETONS (WYOMING) during the 1930s and 1940s. Exum's best-known route, the popular Exum Ridge on the GRAND TETON, was climbed in 1931 when he split off from a guided party led by Paul PETZOLDT and soloed this bristling RIDGE of pinnacles to the top. Exum was an assistant guide and comparative novice at the time. In 1946 Petzoldt and Exum founded the first climbing school in the United States, the Petzoldt/Exum School of American Mountaineering. Exum became its sole owner the following year. The school, now called Exum Mountain Guides, still operates in the Teton Range.

F

FACE The term used to indicate a smooth vertical section of a rock surface or mountain.

FACE CLIMBING FREE CLIMBING on crackless rock walls, using small EDGES or POCKETS as handholds and for balance. The term applies to FACES of all steepness. On low-angle SLABS where cliffs can be devoid of edges, climbers make progress by balance, footwork and pure friction from boot rubber. On vertical and overhanging faces more strenuous demands are placed on fingers and arms. SPORT CLIMBING focuses on extremely steep, THIN faces.

Face Climbing

FAIRWEATHER, MOUNT (United States) One hundred fifty miles (241 km) south of SAINT ELIAS on the southeastern Alaskan panhandle, this 15,300-ft (4,664-m) mountain lies on a peninsula surrounded by the Pacific Ocean and Glacier Bay. Captain James Cook discovered the mountain during his voyage from England in 1778 and named it Fair Weather because the conditions were optimal for sailing if the mountain was visible. Several attempts were made to climb the mountain, before Terris MOORE and Allen Carpe successfully climbed its southern RIB in 1931. Its Carpe Ridge was the most difficult Alaskan route of the era. Since then, eight more of Fairweather's ridges have been pioneered. Fairweather received its FIRST WINTER ASCENT in 1984, by the west ridge. Climbs made from March through May avoid the rain and dangerous snow conditions of summer.

Further reading: Bradford Washburn, *American Alpine Journal* (1981).

FALL ARRESTER A product manufactured by Forrest Mountaineering (United States) in the 1980s. The Fall Arrester was a "QUICK DRAW" of WEBBING and synthetic material intended to be clipped to PROTECTION at a CRUX or before a poorly protected section of a PITCH. If fallen onto, it effectively absorbs the impact, reducing the FALL FACTOR and stress on protection and ROPE, thereby reducing the likelihood of equipment and rope failure. Other concepts followed the lead of this item. One concept relied on bar tacks (lines of sewing) that ripped apart under impact force. Safety problems and a preference among climbers toward better protection from BOLTS led to the demise of these products.

FALL FACTOR A figure, or number, indicating the severity of a leader fall, calculated by dividing the distance of a fall by the amount of rope run out. For example, if the leader is 20 ft (6 m) above the belayer and has no protection between himself and the belay, the fall will be 40 ft (12 m). Length of fall (40 ft/12 m) divided by length of rope (20 ft/6 m) = a fall factor of 2. This is the most severe stress on a rope. If there was a point of protection 10 ft (3 m) above the belayer, with 20 ft (6 m) of rope out, the fall length would be reduced to 20 ft (6 m), the fall factor to 1. (See ROPES.)

FALL LINE A term used to describe the most direct and steepest line down a snow slope.

FANTIN, MARIO (1921–1980) (Italy) A prolific MOUNTAINEERING researcher and writer, Fantin was born in Bologna. He did not begin mountaineering until the age of 27, but he soon became known for ascents at home and abroad, since he took up filmwork, photography and writing to accompany expeditions to the high ranges. In 1954, he was a member of the successful Italian KARAKORAM expedition and made the film *Italia K2*. Between 1954 and 1973 he climbed in every continent. He made several FIRST ASCENTS in the ANDES of PERU and in GREENLAND. He shared a part of his knowledge in books, some of which have become standard treatises (like *Montagne de Groenlandia*, 1969, the product of seven expeditions to the island). He produced 20 books in less than 23 years, and numerous monographs. In 1967, he founded the Italian Center for the Study of Mountaineering Abroad (CISDAE). It housed a library, photography and map collections and historical archives. His last book was *Le Ande* (1979). Argentinians named Cerro Fantin (16,700 ft/5,091 m) after him. His CISDAE became the property of the Club Alpino Italiano.

Mario Mingardi
Evelio Echevarria

FAWCETT, RON (1955–) (Britain) The outstanding figure in the revolution that took place in British rock-climbing in the 1970s, Ron Fawcett was born in YORKSHIRE where he began climbing on gritstone OUTCROPS in 1970. He rapidly progressed to repeat ascents, often in bad weather, of the hardest ROUTES of the day. He teamed up briefly in the mid-1970s with Peter LIVESEY, whom he soon outstripped in ability, going on to open up the blank walls of difficulty's new order: Strawberries on the Vector Buttress headwall (1980); the series of routes in the remaining bare spaces on the walls of Cenotaph Corner, particularly Lord of the Flies (1979); The Cad (1978) beneath Anglesey's North Stack lighthouse; the smooth verticality between Gargoyle and Octo above CLOGWYN DU'R ARDDU'S east gully where Psychokiller (1980) found a way; the technically desperate and ferociously overhanging twin starts to Gordale's Cave Route (1982). And perhaps above all, the soaring lean of Derbyshire's RAVEN TOR—in the words of one magazine writer of the mid-1970s, "the ultimate outcrop [which] defies all attempts at free-climbing it." Fawcett climbed seven routes here between 1976 and 1982, culminating in The Prow, still regarded as one of the desperates, "the ultimate body-pump." Chris Gore, a frontrunner in the pack that began to catch up in 1982, made the following assessment of Ron's contribution in those years:

"After Livesey faded out it was always Ron who was pushing his own standard, and that's the hardest thing in the world to do. In running you have pacemakers, but he had no-one but himself. What he did, despite that handicap, was absolutely brilliant and will be looked on as one of the watersheds."

A bad break to an arm in 1983 put Fawcett out of action at a time when younger climbers—notably Jerry MOFFAT—were seizing the initiative. He recovered quickly, however, and returned at the end of December that year to lead the ARETE right of Green Death on Derbyshire's MILLSTONE Edge, previously TOP-ROPED by Moffat, who had opined that whoever first led it would be the true master. TECHNICAL and protectionless on its CRUX, The Master's Edge is E8, 7a, and has seen very few repeat ascents.

FEBRUARY, ED (1956–) (South Africa) One of a handful of black South African climbers, February is perhaps the world's leading black climber today. His activity and personality made an indelible impression on the isolated South African climbing scene during the 1970s and 1980s. Raised in Wynesberg, Cape Town, he began climbing at the age of 14 with his brother, Rodney, under the auspices of the Western Province Mountain Club, a predominantly "colored" hiking club. His rebellious nature led him to break with the club and climb independently. In 1972 he made the FIRST FREE ASCENT of Roullette, grade 18, on Table Mountain, a breakthrough in FREE CLIMBING for South Africa, and the beginning of a 20-year career during which he made 500 new ROUTES, most in the Western Cape. In 1984 a 100-ft (30-m) fall smashed his ankle and put him out of climbing for two years, but he has since returned to the forefront of South African rock climbing. Trained as an industrial radiographer, he has a master's degree in archeology and is employed by the Museum of South Africa. His achievements in climbing and academia has been testimony to his force of will to overcome apartheid barriers. (See SOUTH AFRICA.)

FELL WALKING British term for NONTECHNICAL mountain and hill walking.

FEUZ, EDWARD, JR. (1884–1981) (Canada) Following in the footsteps of his father, Edward Sr., Swiss-born Feuz became a mountain guide, beginning as an apprentice in CANADA in 1903 at age 19. Over his career, he made FIRST ASCENTS of 78 peaks in the Canadian Rockies. Some of the more prominent of these are Mount Saint Bride, Mount Sir Sandford, Mount Adamant, NORTH TWIN, South Twin and Mount Joffre.
Further reading: A. J. Kaufmann and W. L. Putnam, *The Guiding Spirit* (1986).

FIBER PILE A general name for the fuzzy nylon or polyester fleece fabric used extensively in climbing clothing, especially for mountaineering. It is lightweight, dries quickly and has high thermal properties, although it is not windproof. (See CLOTHING FOR MOUNTAINEERING, LAYERING.)

FIFI HOOK An AID CLIMBING device used in Europe for quickly climbing ladders of fixed PITONS or BOLTS. A fifi hook is a metal hook fitted to the top of an ETRIER, which is clipped directly into the eye of a PITON. A cord tied between the fifi hook and the climber's HARNESS lifts the etriers as the climber moves onto the next piton. A griff fifi incorporates a handle onto the hook. The device is not popular in American aid climbing.

FIGURE-EIGHT DESCENDER A rappel device shaped like the number eight, consisting of two metal rings of different size, cast or welded together, through which the ROPE is passed to create friction. (See RAPPELLING.)

FIGURE-EIGHT KNOT A knot used for tying the rope into the HARNESS. (See KNOTS.)

Figure-Eight Descender

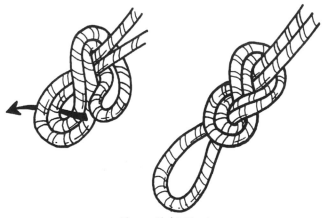

Figure-Eight Knot

FINALE (Italy) Steep POCKETED limestone 300 to 800 ft (91 to 244 m) high and a coastal setting make this one of Italy's most developed SPORT CLIMBING areas. The CRAGS cluster around the towns of Finale Liguria and Finale Borgo, 34 miles (54 km) southwest of Genoa. Hundreds of routes lie on 15 crags around these towns. All are BOLTED. SEA CLIFF climbing is also found here, and a classic offering is a 2,624-ft (800-m) GIRDLE TRAVERSE of the crag Cappo Noli, called The Mixer. Monte Cucco and Rocca di Perti offer concentrations of hard, bolted routes. Climbing is done year round, and services and camping are plentiful.
Guidebooks: Andrea Gallo and Giovanni Massari, *Finale* (Italian text) Martin Lochner, *Finale Auswahlfuhrer* (German text).

FINGERBOARD A training device on which the climber does pull-ups and hang-routines to strengthen the fingers and arms for FREE CLIMBING. Made of resinous material, fingerboards are molded to simulate EDGES, HOLDS and POCKETS of various sizes. (See CLIMBING HOLDS.)

FINGER LOCK Or finger jam. The FREE CLIMBING technique of slotting the fingers into a thin CRACK and forming a grip by twisting and wedging the fingers against the walls of the crack. (See CRACK CLIMBING.)

Finger Lock

FINSTERAARHORN AND OTHER PEAKS (Austria) A little more than 1 mile (2 km) east of the Mönchsjoch are the Gross-Fiescherhorn (13,280 ft/4,049 m) and to its south the Hinter-Fiescherhorn (13,202 ft/4,025 m). To the south of these peaks is the Gross-Grünhorn (13,264 ft/4,044 m). The Finsteraarhorn (14,015 ft/4,273 m) is east of the Fieschergletscher and has a long approach, which can be done by ski in spring, so the peak is quite popular. To the north of the Finsteraarhorn are the Schreckhorn (13,376 ft/4,078 m) and the Lauteraarhorn (13,258 ft/4,042 m), both demanding and remote peaks. The Schreckhorn, despite being climbed as long ago as 1867 by Leslie Stephen et al, is renowned for its mammoth approach.
Further reading: R. Collomb, *Bernese Central*; Peter Gillman and Dougal Haston, *Eiger Direct*; Richard Goedeke, *The Alpine 4000m Peaks*; Heinrich Harrer, *The White Spider* (1989); Leslie Stephen, *The Playground of Europe*.

FIRE The first ROCK SHOE with sticky rubber, made by Boreal of Spain and introduced in the 1980s. Fires contributed to the rise of FREE CLIMBING standards and to modern rock-shoe technology.

FIRN Or firn snow. Snow compacted due to melt and freeze, and the pressure of overlaying snow. In common usage, firn is snow that has survived the spring thaw and marks the level of permanent snow. This level is called the firn line.

FIRNIFICATION The process by which snow changes to GLACIER ice. (See SNOW AND ICE, PROPERTIES OF.)

FIRST ASCENT The first time a route is climbed, pioneered or opened. First-ascent parties are recorded in guidebooks.

FIRST FLASH ASCENT The first time a climber FLASHES a route.

FIRST FREE ASCENT The first time a route is FREE CLIMBED, generally involves a route that was previously AID CLIMBED.

FIRST WINTER ASCENT See WINTER ASCENT.

FISHER TOWERS See COLORADO PLATEAU.

FIST JAM The FREE CLIMBING technique of locking the fist in a wide CRACK by clenching the fist to enlarge the small muscles on the outside of the hand. This technique is strenuous and often awkward. (See CRACK CLIMBING.)

FITZROY (Argentina) At 11,289 ft (3,440 m), Fitzroy is PATAGONIA's highest summit. Named after the British captain of *The Beagle* (of Darwin fame), it lies 2 miles (3 km) northeast of CERRO TORRE, and whereas Cerro Torre is a striking needle of icy rock, Fitzroy is a colossal thrust of ice-coated 5,000-ft (1,524-m) granite walls and hanging GLACIERS, often capped by a wind-driven plume of snow. Nearby peaks include Aguja Poincenot (9,961 ft/3,036 m), Rafael (8,205 ft/2,501 m) and Saint Exupery (8,792 ft/2,780 m) to the south, and Aguja Mermoz (9,035 ft/2,754 m) and Guillaumet (8,507 ft/2,593 m) to the north. All offer challenging climbing on excellent rock and ice.

Between 1916 and 1948 expeditions from ARGENTINA and Italy attempted the mountain from various sides without success. In 1952 a French expedition led by M. A. Azema put two climbers on the summit after a long siege on the southwest face and a last-minute alpine dash. One of the climbers was Lionel TERRAY who later stated that Fitzroy was the hardest climb of his career. Azema's book, *The Conquest of Fitzroy* (1957) recounts that expedition.

Of Fitzroy's 11 routes, the Supercouloir (Argentines 1965), southwest ridge (Americans 1968) and the north pillar (soloed by Italian Renato CASAROTTO in 1979) are the most beautiful and frequently tried LINES.
Further reading: Alan Kearney, *Mountaineering in Patagonia* (1992).

FIXED PROTECTION PITONS, NUTS, BOLTS and ANCHORS left in place on a climb are termed fixed, and are used by future ascents.

FIXED ROPE Rope left in place along the route on long rock climbs or mountains to facilitate a line of supply and escape in storm or emergency, and as a means of regaining a high point after descent. Fixed-rope ascents in Himalayan climbing are often called seige style. On many popular Himalayan routes, fixed rope is abandoned, creating a litter problem.

FLARE A CRACK or CHIMNEY that is wider on the outside than on the inside, and V-shaped in appearance.

FLASH To flash a climbing route is to climb the route on the first try without prior knowledge or experience of the particular route. Distinguished from RED POINT, which involves prior attempts. (See A VUE, ON SIGHT, STYLE.)

FLAT FOOT TECHNIQUE Another term for the French technique of CRAMPONing, in which the climber keeps the feet flat against the ice, achieving foot traction from all the crampon points. (See SNOW AND ICE CLIMBING TECHNIQUES.)

FLATIRONS (United States) These prominent sandstone SLAB formations, shaped like a blacksmith's iron, are located on Green Mountain just west of BOULDER, COLORADO. The strata of these formations are tilted, so that climbs on the east side are low-angle, long, and moderately graded, and routes on the back sides are steep SPORT CLIMBS.
Guidebook: Richard Rossiter, *Boulder Climbs South* (1990).

FLEISCHBANK (Austria) Rising in the Wilder Kaiser Mountains, this 650-ft (198-m) limestone east wall has hard modern routes, yet its earlier climbs illustrate the development of Eastern ALPS climbing. Hans Dulfer and Werner Schaarschmidt climbed it first via the easiest solution in 1912. In 1925 Roland Rossi and Fritz WEISSNER climbed the harder southeast face, using so much equipment that it opened a new phase in climbing. The steeper central east face succumbed in 1930 to Peter Aschenbrenner (who accompanied Heinrich HARRER in his Asian travels) and Hans Luck. In 1943 when Hermann BUHL and Waldemar Gruber set out to repeat the 1930 route they disregarded their predecessors' TRAVERSE and continued directly into a wide CHIMNEY. For this, Buhl suffered a 160-ft (48-m) fall, but the pair survived. In 1949 Marcus Scmuck, Rudi Bardodej and Hardwin Pollack found themselves in the same chimney, but pressed on, climbing simultaneously and unbelayed to reach the north ridge and complete the route. It wasn't repeated until 1960 and retains a serious reputation. Heini Holzer later soloed it; a WINTER ASCENT came in 1970.

FOAM PAD Though rarely regarded as one of alpinism's great technological advances, the introduction of the closed-cell foam pad during the 1970s enabled climbers to sleep comfortably on cold ground and ice, making alpine BIVOUACS easier to bear and making longer, difficult mountain climbs more feasible. Previously, climbers had used air mattresses, which were heavy and ineffective, or open-cell foam, which soaked up moisture. Closed-cell foam insulation resists heat loss because convection currents cannot move between the tiny partitioned cells within the foam. Closed-cell foam pads are of two types: chemically blown and pressure-blown polyvinylacetate. The latter is more durable and has higher insulating properties. Karri-mat and Ensolite are two frequently used brands of pressure-blown pad. Self-inflating open-cell pads, like the Therm-a-rest by Cascade Designs (United States) consist of a slab of open-cell polyurethane covered and bonded to an airtight nylon envelope. Though more comfortable than closed-cell foam, they don't insulate as well and are prone to punctures.

FONTAINEBLEAU (France) The forest of Fontaine-bleau is half an hour by road southeast of Paris, and scattered among the forest are thousands of sandstone boulders. There are no less than 24 BOULDERING areas. The boulders come in all heights and shapes. Wintertime affords the best friction. There are delicate SLABS, acrobatic OVERHANGS and some CRACKS. The HOLDS are usually rounded with an occasional JUG or a sharp edge. Most boulders are done ropeless and are safe thanks to sandy landings. In all the areas, many "circuits" have been painted on the rock with different colors according to their level. Ratings are indicated by color. In order of difficulty, circuits run yellow, orange, green, blue, red, black and white. The boulders were popular between the World Wars when people like Pierre ALLAIN began using the first FRICTION BOOTS. Alpinists of the 1950s like Paragot or Berardini used the technical moves of Fontainebleau as training for the ALPS and DOLOMITES. Bouldering for its own sake became popular in the 1970s. Michel Libert, Alain Michaud, Eddy Bouchet and Jean-Pierre Bouvier were important developers, and Jacky Godoffe's Coup de feel (8a+, at Pas Covier), is one of Fontainebleau's hardest. Other famous boulder problems include Big Boss at Covier Rempart, Le 12 bis at Isatis, La Dame Jeanne (the highest rock, at 49 ft/15 m), La Traverse des Dieux, La Balance, le toit du Col de Chien, L'Etrave, and Le Carnage.
Guidebook: S. Jouty, *Bleau.*

FOOT BRAKE Another term for the BOOT-AXE BELAY.

FOOTFANG A specialized CRAMPON for technical ICE CLIMBING manufactured by Lowe (United States) and Camp (Italy).

FOOTHOLD Any EDGE or bump on rock that is stood on.

FORAKER, MOUNT (United States) At 17,004 ft (5,184 m), Foraker is the sixth-highest peak in North America. The mountain lies within Denali National Park in ALASKA. Like its 10-mile (16-km)-distant neighbor, DENALI, Foraker has a north and south summit. The south summit is smaller at 16,812 ft (5,126 m). The original Tanaina Indian

name, Sultana, meant "woman" or "wife" of Denali. In 1899 Lieutenant Joseph S. Herron renamed the mountain for the Ohio Senator, Joseph B. Foraker, who was later driven from public office for accepting fees and loans from an oil company. In 1934, Charles S. HOUSTON, T. Graham Brown and Chychele Waterston first climbed the mountain by its northwest ridge. Few parties have repeated the route because of its arduous overland access. In 1963, the dangerous and AVALANCHE-prone southeast ridge was successfully climbed. Because of its easy access, this ridge is the most popular route, though the Infinite Spur and the French Ridge are Foraker's true testpieces. To date, 14 routes have been established on the mountain, and the FIRST WINTER ASCENT of Mount Foraker, by the southeast ridge, was completed in 1975. Few climbers attempt Mount Foraker, and most parties fail because of avalanche conditions on the southeast ridge.
Guidebook: Jonathan Waterman, *High Alaska; A Historical Guide to Denali, Mount Foraker and Mount Hunter* (1989).

FOURTEENERS, THE (United States) Refers to the peaks of the Rocky Mountains of COLORADO that are 14,000/ 4,268 m or higher. Every summer, leagues of peak baggers assemble around the state, seeking to climb all 54. Most of these peaks are little more than arduous scrambles. But Crestone Needle, Little Bear, Pyramid, South Maroon and Capitol offer loose rock, knife edges, steep climbing and route-finding challenges. Several thousand climbers have been to the top of all 54 peaks. In 1991, Lou Dawson succeeded in skiing them all, although no one has climbed them all in winter.
Guidebooks: Walter Borneman and Lyndon Lampert, *A Climbing Guide to Colorado's Fourteeners* (1988); Steve Roper and Allen Steck, *Fifty Classic Climbs of North America* (1979).

FRACTURE LINE Or crown line. In an AVALANCHE, the division between a sliding SLAB and the more stable snow surrounding it.

FRAME PACK A type of pack consisting of a padded rectangular metal frame from which a pack bag and shoulder straps are suspended. (See PACKS.)

FRANKENJURA (Germany) Located near Nuremberg, this sprawling limestone area is the most famous and the finest cragging area in Germany. The Frankenjura consist of a 62-mile (100-km) stretch of short CRAGS nestled among forests and rolling hills. It is divided into two regions: in the north is the Nordlicher Frankenjura with the Frankische Schweiz, and in the south is the Sudlicher Frankenjura with the crags Donautal and Altmuhtal. It is in the Frankenjura that RED POINT climbing tactics were devised, largely by Kurt ALBERT, in the 1970s. The bulk of the area's 2,000 routes are BOLT-protected SPORT CLIMBS, of all grades. The area's hardest route is Wolfgang GULLICH's Action Directe, XI (5.14d), climbed in 1991 at the cliff Waldkopf.

FRANKLIN, SCOTT (1966–) (United States) Franklin attracted the American spotlight in 1987 by making the second ascent of To Bolt or Not to Be, the first 5.14 in America, established in 1986 by Jean Baptiste TRIBOUT. He took 16 days to complete the route. As of this writing only three other climbers—Alan WATTS, Ron KAUK and Jerry MOFFAT—have climbed the route. Franklin, originally a New Yorker, was the first American to solo a 5.13, Survival of the Fittest (5.13a), and to ON-SIGHT a 5.13a, Time's Up at SMITH ROCKS. In 1988 he was the first American to establish a 5.14, Scarface at Smith Rocks. In 1989, when he added White Wedding (5.14a) to his ascents, Franklin followed Moffat's suit in doing the "Triple Crown"—the three 5.14s—at Smith Rocks.

In world events, Franklin placed seventh at the International Sport Climbing Championship at Snowbird in 1988, 12th in the 1990 World Cup in Nuremberg, and sixth at Serre Chevalier, France, in 1991. His best-known routes are Blow of Death (5.13d) at AMERICAN FORK; Planet Fresh (5.12d) and Cybernetic Wall (5.13d) in the SHAWANGUNKS; The Edge of the World (5.13c) at CATHEDRAL LEDGE; and Mango Tango (5.13d), NEW RIVER GORGE.

FREE ASCENT   An ascent involving no AID CLIMBING. ROPES and equipment are generally used.

FREE CLIMBING   Gymnastic climbing using hands and feet to grip or stand on natural rock features. ROPE or equipment is used for safety in the event of falling, but not for upward progress. (See CRACK CLIMBING, SPORT CLIMBING.)

FREE SOLOING   To solo a free climb, or climb a rock route free, alone, and without use of ROPE or PROTECTION. Free soloing is practiced only by extremely accomplished climbers. (See BACHAR, John; CROFT, Peter.)

FREMONT CANYON   (United States)   A gorge of pink granite 40 miles (64 km) west of Casper, WYOMING. Access to climbs here is by RAPPEL from the rim, down 300-ft (91-m) walls to the North Platte River, which rises periodically when the floodgates of the Pathfinder Dam open. CRACK CLIMBS predominate in the canyon, ranging from 5.10 to 5.13b/c. Climbing history at Fremont Canyon is of recent vintage. The first climb took place in the 1950s, but most of the canyon's 300 climbs are attributed to local climbers in the 1980s. Summer is the ideal season for climbing in Fremont Canyon.
Guidebook: Steve Petro, *Climber's Guide to Fremont Canyon and Dome Rock in Central Wyoming* (1989).

FRENCH TECHNIQUE   The method of climbing snow and ice by FLAT FOOTING with the CRAMPONED feet pointing downward so that the crampon points bite the snow. The ICE AXE, integral to the technique, acts as an ANCHOR or third point of contact.

FRICTION BOOT   A general term for ROCK SHOES.

FRICTION   CLIMBING   Another term for SLAB climbing.

Footwork During Friction Climbing

FRIENDS™   The trade name for the original SPRING-LOADED CAMMING DEVICE introduced in 1978. Designed by Ray JARDINE (United States) and manufactured by Wild Country of BRITAIN, Friends changed the face of climbing by adding a new dimension to PROTECTION and the ease with which it could be placed. Parallel or flared CRACKS and horizontal breaks previously considered unprotectable with NUTS or HEXENTRICS suddenly offered good protection. Numerous copies and refinements of the Friend have appeared over the years, but all rely on Jardine's principle of retractable sprung cams and a trigger mounted on an axle connected to a stem. (See CAMALOT, SPRING-LOADED CAMMING DEVICE, TCU.)

SLCD Friend

FROGGATT EDGE   (Britain)   The escarpment overlooking the Derwent Valley south of Hathersage includes several 50-ft (15-m) CRAGS of which this is the best known. It is located above the Chequers Inn on the road between Sheffield and Calver Slough. Hathersage and STONEY MIDDLETON provide services.

After some climbs by J. W. Puttrell before World War I, Joe BROWN in the late 1940s began an intense period of exploration with ROUTES like Tody's Wall (5.8), Three Pebble Slab (5.8) and an excellent LINE on the pinnacle, Valkyrie (5.8). After national service Brown returned as a member of the Rock and Ice Club, climbing a BOLD line on the Great Slab (5.10). The 1960s saw sporadic development, but in 1968 Tom Proctor climbed the short but committing Oedipus! Ring Your Mother (5.11c). The 1970s at Froggatt belonged to John ALLEN with Hairless Heart (5.11a) in 1975, an unprotected route on the Great Slab and Strapadictomy (5.11d), a powerful route at the northern end of the crag in 1976. A year later Pete LIVESEY climbed the "chipped" slab of Downhill Racer (5.11a).

In 1982 Johnny Woodward climbed the most inspiring line on the crag, the exposed ARETE of Beau Geste (5.13a). This was an outstanding achievement and its second ascent was a notable prize taken by Johnny Dawes. He also added the SLAB route, Benign Lives (5.13a), in 1984. In 1987 Mark Leach solved the longstanding crack problem Screaming Dream (5.14a), which required weeks of practice. Finally, Jerry MOFFATT TOP-ROPED Slingshot, also 5.14a.

Guidebooks: British Mountain Club, *Derwent Gritstone* (1985); Paul Nunn, *Rock Climbing in the Peak District* (1987).

FRONT POINTING   Also called German technique. The technique of climbing ice by kicking the crampon front points into the ice. (See CRAMPONS, SNOW AND ICE CLIMBING TECHNIQUES, WATERFALL CLIMBING.)

FRONT RANGE (United States)   Front Range is generally considered to comprise COLORADO climbing areas east of the Continental Divide from Colorado Springs in the south to Fort Collins in the north. Principal areas include GARDEN OF THE GODS, SOUTH PLATTE, Morrison (BOULDERING), ELDORADO CANYON, the FLATIRONS, BOULDER CANYON, LUMPY RIDGE and HORSETOOTH RESERVOIR (bouldering).

FROST, TOM (1936–   ) (United States)   This Southern California engineer is a mythic figure in American BIG WALL CLIMBING, ALPINISM and equipment design. The RURP piton, the CRACK-N-UP, the early CHOUINARD crampon, HEXENTRICS and STOPPERS were all co-designed by Frost and Yvon Chouinard. Royal ROBBINS wrote that Frost was "the best AID CLIMBER in the world," but he was also a fine FREE CLIMBER, climbing one of CALIFORNIA's first 5.10 routes, Dave's Deviation, at TAHQUITZ rock (1958). In the 1960s he made many firsts of big walls in YOSEMITE VALLEY (California): the west face of Sentinel Rock and the northwest face of Quarter Dome, with Chouinard; the Salathe Wall on EL CAPITAN (1961), with Robbins and Chuck PRATT; and the frightening north face of Higher Cathedral Spire with Robbins (1962). He also made second ascents of the northwest face of HALF DOME and the Nose of El Capitan, with Robbins (1960). But his hardest wall was the 1964 FIRST ASCENT on El Capitan of the wildly steep North America Wall (VI 5.8 A5), with Robbins, Pratt and Chouinard.

In the TETONS he and Chouinard opened the east face of Disappointment Peak (1962), and in the CIRQUE OF THE UNCLIMBABLES (Canada) he opened Lotus Flower Tower, with Jim McCarthy and Sandy Bill. In 1963 in the KHUMBU region of Nepal, he made the first ascent of Kangtega (22,241 ft/6,781 m) with Dave Dornan, and he supported Don WHILLANS and Dougal HASTON in their summit climb on the British Annapurna south face expedition (1970).

FROSTBITE   A hazard of extreme COLD. Frostbite is a localized cold injury produced by freezing of the tissues, caused when the body constricts blood vessels in extremities and redirects blood to warm the body core. As circulation slows, capillaries leak plasma through their walls, and the exchange of oxygen and nutrients is hampered, leading to thickened blood and susceptibility to freezing of tissues. If ice crystals form within tissues the cells are seriously damaged. Superficial frostbite involves partial skin thickness and usually results in complete recovery. Deep frostbite may penetrate skin into fat, muscle, bones and nerves.

Contact with metal, wetness and wind chill are the main causes of frostbite. Hands, feet, nose and ears are commonly affected as these are furthest from the heart and most exposed to weather. Cold causes loss of feeling, so while frostbite is occurring there is no pain. The only warning may be complete lack of feeling in a foot or hand. Frostbitten parts are pale, firm, numb and if badly frozen, immobile and dull-purple in color. After warming, blisters of fluid appear. If this fluid is clear it is a good sign, as the underlying tissue is alive and frostbite is superficial. Blood-filled blisters indicate dead tissue and deep damage. No blisters at all but a dark purple color indicates exceptionally bad damage. In serious cases as healing occurs blisters shrivel, tips of fingers or toes contract and blacken and may separate after several weeks. Frostbitten tissues often become gangrenous and require amputation. Modern medicine advises waiting as long as possible—several weeks—before amputating.

Prevention of frostbite includes protecting hands and feet from wind, and wearing well-insulated, loose clothing. Avoid getting wet or touching metal with bare skin. Be conscious of numb extremities that are a sign of trouble. Rapid rewarming is the best treatment for frostbite; however, thawing tissue that is already frozen then refreezing severely damages tissues. A rewarmed foot, for example, will swell and become painful and prevent a climber from wearing a boot and walking. Less damage is done by walking on a frozen foot. Warm water between 100–108 degrees F (38–42 degrees C) is used for rewarming. Soaking should continue for up to an hour until feeling, color or some improvement occurs. Pain accompanies thawing, and painkillers may be given. Hot damp cloths may be used to rewarm facial frostbite. Parts should be dried gently, wrapped loosely and elevated slightly to lessen swelling. Every effort to avoid breaking blisters should be made as infection of dead, thawed tissue is a serious risk in remote areas. Antibiotics should be on hand. Hospitalization is imperative. Long-term effects of frostbite include sensitivity to cold, arthritis and excessive sweating of frostbitten areas, especially feet.

FROZEN WATERFALL   See ICE CLIMBING, WATERFALL CLIMBING.

GABARROU, PATRICK (1951–) (France) Across the French and Swiss Alps, hundreds of new ROUTES, especially on ice, bear Gabarrou's name. On MONT BLANC itself he established 14 routes, including rock climbs like Divine Providence or Pilier Rouge du Brouillard. His passion for MOUNTAINEERING is only part of a wider love of the mountains, and the culture and nature within them. A guide by profession, he is also president of the environmental body Mountain Wilderness. He rejects the use of helicopters in the mountains, except in emergencies. To illustrate that climbers can dispense with air transport, he once climbed seven north faces of the Alps in a row, starting from the valley floor of each, on foot.

GABLE CRAG (Britain) Situated on the north side of Great Gable, Gable Crag overlooks the picturesque Ennerdale. The CRAG has a frigid aspect that allows it to hold ice in winter. It is approached from Wasdale and the Sty Head Pass, or from the Honister Pass in BORROWDALE.

The most celebrated ROUTE at Gable Crag is The Engineer's Slabs, climbed in 1934 by F. G. Balcombe, J. A. Shepherd and J. A. Cooper. The route, around 180 ft (55 m) high, is steep and serious, and in bad conditions belies its 5.7 grade. Modern testpieces include The Tomb (5.10b), right of The Engineer's Slab, and Sarchophagus (5.10d), by Pete Whillance and Dave Armstrong.

Guidebooks: Bill Birkett, et al., *Rock Climbing in the Lake District* (1986); FRCC, *Gable and Pillar* (1989).

GAITERS Coverings of nylon or fabric (usually waterproof, sometimes made of GORE-TEX) worn around the lower legs and ankles to protect them from snow and water and to prevent stones from entering the boot. SUPER GAITERS and OVERBOOTS cover the entire boot and are used in subzero conditions.

GAMOW BAG A portable hyperbaric chamber invented by Igor Gamow (United States), a professor of chemical engineering at the University of Colorado, for reversing symptoms of high-altitude maladies like CEREBRAL EDEMA or PULMONARY EDEMA. A Gamow bag weighs 12 lbs (5.4 kg) and consists of a cylindrical nylon-fabric chamber with a foot-operated air pump. An altitude-stricken victim is placed in the bag and the pump is operated to increase air pressure (and introduce breathable air) within the bag to simulate the greater air pressure of lower altitude. At an altitude of 14,000 ft (4,268 m) the bag can simulate the atmospheric pressure of 6,200 ft (1,890 m); theoretically, at the summit of EVEREST (29,028 ft/8,850 m), the bag can simulate an altitude of 20,000 ft (6,098 m). It has been used with success on numerous edema sufferers on treks and mountaineering expeditions in the high ranges of the world. The Gamow bag is distributed in the United States by Portable Hyperbarics Inc., Box 510, Ilion, NY 13357, and Altitude Technologies, Box 622, Avon, CO 81620.

GANESH HIMAL (Nepal) The imposing faces of the five Ganesh peaks, ringed around the Torro Gompa Glacier, dominate this range of central NEPAL. The eastern boundary of the range is the Trisuli-Bhote Kosi. The western boundary is separated from the tiny Serang Himal by a semicircle of mountains beginning at the Taple La and down the Shyar Khola to its junction with the Budhi Gandaki. The Budhi Gandaki also separates Ganesh Himal's western boundary from the Mansiri Himal. Ganesh I (called Yangra, 24,367 ft/7,429 m), II (23,324 ft/7,111 m), III (called Salasungo, 23,320 ft/7,110), IV (called Pabil, 23,130 ft/ 7,052 m) and V (2,914 ft/6,986 m) are the tallest peaks, and over a dozen other peaks in this range exceed 19,680 ft (6,000 m). Ganesh I was attempted several times before it succumbed to a Franco-Swiss expedition in 1954 that included the Frenchwoman Claude KOGAN. Ganesh II was climbed in 1979 via the north face by a Japanese-Nepalese expedition, but the huge and hazardous south face—perhaps the most impressive and difficult facet of the range— was not climbed until 1984 by Britons Rick Allen and Nick Kekus. Ganesh III was attempted six times before two expeditions (German and Japanese) simultaneously succeeded in 1981, climbing the north ridge and face.

GANGOTRI REGION (India) This range of northern INDIA'S GARWHAL HIMALAYA is known to mountaineers for steep TECHNICAL peaks of granite with easy access from Delhi, via Uttarkashi. It has a reputation of being the "Chamonix of the Himalaya." The region is bounded in the north and east by Mana Pass, which crosses into TIBET, and the Saraswati River, which becomes the Alaknanda— sacred source of the Ganges. The rivers forming its western boundary are the Chor Ghad, the Jadh Ganga and the Bhagirathi. The region contains 78 peaks between 23,420 ft/7,138 m and 19,820 ft/6,041 m.

The major GLACIERS of this huge mountain expanse are the Gangotri, Chaturangi and Raktavarn, but the center-piece is certainly the 18-mile (29 km) Gangotri Glacier, which lies nine miles (14 km) beyond the holy village of Gangotri. The snout of this glacier is the destination of Hindu pilgrims, who call the place Gaumukh, or "mouth of the cow," and who bathe in the frigid waters to expiate their sins. Further on, the glacier is flanked by the big walls and sharp ridges of SHIVLING (21,467 ft/6,543 m) and the three Bhagirathi peaks (22,493 ft/6,856 m to 21,175 ft/6,454 m). On the Bhagirathis vertical western faces lie several BIG WALL climbs. Other significnt peaks along the Gangotri Glacier or its tributaries are Kedarnath (22,770 ft/6,940 m); the steep Thelay Sagar (22,650 ft/6,904 m); Bhrigupanth (22,220 ft/6,772 m), which was first climbed by an international women's expedition in 1980; Satopanth (23,212 ft/7,075 m); and the Chaukhamba peaks, of which Chaukhamba I (23,420 ft/7,138 m) is the region's tallest. Climbing here is dictated by the MONSOON.

Further reading: Greg Child, *Thin Air: Encounters in the Himalaya* (1990); S. Mehta and H. Kapadia, *Exploring the Hidden Himalaya* (1990).

GARDEN OF THE GODS (United States)

Located immediately west of Colorado Springs, COLORADO, this cluster of soft red sandstone domes is a popular tourist attraction and semi-urban climbing destination. The climbs lie on a dozen formations—believed to be fossilized sand dunes—some as high as 350 ft (107 m). The area saw some of the first roped climbs in America. Albert ELLINGWOOD's Ellingwood's Ledge (5.6) is a bold ROUTE from the 1920s. The CRACK Anaconda (5.11) was notably hard when freed in 1975 by Earl Wiggins.

Guidebook: Peter Hubbel and Mark Rolofson, *Rock Climbing Guide to the South Platte River Valleys and Garden of the Gods* (1988).

GARWHAL HIMALAYA (India)

Another term for the great range of the Indian Himalaya. (See KUMAON-GARWHAL HIMALAYA.)

GAS

Fuel for lightweight stoves stored as compressed liquid in nonrefillable cylinders. Propane or butane are most commonly used. Propane/butane mix is more efficient in freezing temperatures. See STOVES AND FUEL for a thorough discussion of all fuels.

GASHERBRUM I (Pakistan)

Also called Hidden Peak, this is the highest of the six Gasherbrum peaks that form a semicircle around the South Gasherbrum Glacier of the BALTORO Muztagh. At 26,471 ft/8,068 m it is the 11th-highest point on earth. W. M. Conway coined the name Hidden Peak because it is concealed from view until one reaches the ABRUZZI Glacier at the end of the Baltoro Glacier in the KARAKORAM Range.

Attempts on the southern flanks by Austrians and French in the 1930s encouraged Americans to try the southwest ridge in 1958. The FIRST ASCENT, by Pete Schoening and Andy Kauffman, is the only 26,240-ft (8,000-m) peak ascended first by Americans. Since 1985 this route has been closed due to a large Pakistan army encampment engaged in skirmishes with the Indian Army in a border war.

The mountain was not climbed again until 1975, when Peter HABELER and Reinhold MESSNER climbed the northwest face in ALPINE STYLE. This rapid, lightweight ascent was a pivotal event for Himalayan climbing. A route right of the Messner-Habeler was climbed alpine style in 1985 by Frenchmen Benoit Chamoux and Eric ESCOFFIER. Other routes on Gasherbrum I are the west ridge (Yugoslav, 1978), south-southwest ridge (French, 1980), north face (Germans, 1982) and southwest face (Spanish, 1983). A major addition came in 1983 when Wojciech KURTYKA and Jerzy KUKUCZKA (Poland) climbed the west face, alpine style. In 1985 Messner returned to Gasherbrum I with Hans Kammerlander to link this peak with GASHERBRUM II in the first continuous TRAVERSE of two 26,240-ft (8,000-m) peaks. The mountain's Chinese eastern flanks above the North Gasherbrum Glacier are unclimbed.

GASHERBRUM II AND GASHERBRUM III (Pakistan)

At 26,363 ft/8,035 m this is the lowest of the fourteen 26,240-ft (8,000-m) peaks in the world. It lies in the BALTORO Moztagh, at the head of the South Gasherbrum Glacier and is separated from Gasherbrum I by the pass Gasherbrum La (21,653 ft/6,601 m). G. O. DYHRENFURTH's 1934 International Expedition identified the southwest ridge as the most feasible line, and it was this route that the 1956 Austrian expedition climbed, placing S. Larch, H. Willenpart and F. Moravec on the summit after they TRAVERSED at 24,600 ft (7,500 m) beneath the rocky summit pyramid to the east ridge. Although the 7-mile (11-km) approach up the South Gasherbrum Glacier is heavily crevassed, this route is frequently ascended.

Marc Batard and Yannick Seigneur (French) climbed the prominent southeast ridge in 1975. The same year a Polish men's and women's expedition climbed a variation of the 1956 route, traversing northwest at the base of the summit pyramid to the COL (24,770 ft/7,552 m) between Gasherbrums II and III. From there L. Cichy, J. Onyszkiewicz and K. Zdiowiecki climbed the northwest face of GII. (Later Zdiowiecki; Onyszkiewicz; his wife, Alison Chadwick-Onyszkiewicz [Britain]; and Wanda RUTKIEWICZ, made the FIRST ASCENT of Gasherbrum III [26,091 ft/7,952 m] by the east face. This is the highest peak on which women took part in the first ascent.) Reinhold MESSNER and Hans Kammerlander traversed Gasherbrum II and III in 1984. Frenchmen have skied from the summit (1984), descended the mountain by PARAPENTE (Pierre Gevaux, 1985) and hang glider (Jean-Marc BOIVIN, 1985). The Pakistani HIGH-ALTITUDE PORTER Karim also summited in 1985, carrying Boivin's 34-lb (15.3-kg) hang glider.

GASHERBRUM IV (Pakistan)

This stately KARAKORAM peak—at 26,000 ft/7,925 m—is the world's 17th-highest summit. Its truncated pyramid shape dominates PAKISTAN's upper BALTORO Glacier. Its best-known view is from Concordia, where the sight of the 10,000-ft (3,049-m) west face saturated with alpenglow on clear evenings has inspired generations of climbers and trekkers. This beauty was not lost on BALTI porters, for Gasherbrum means in Balti "beautiful mountain." Gasherbrum IV is steeper and more difficult than its higher namesakes. The mountain is a swirl of geological contact zones, composed of granitic rocks, basalt, marble and limestone on the summit cap. Its unclimbed northern flanks, lie within Xinjiang CHINA.

In 1958 a strong Italian expedition led by Riccardo CASSIN slogged up the South Gasherbrum Glacier and began fixing rope on the northeast ridge. On the fourth of August Walter BONATTI and Carlo Mauri reached the lower north summit, then made the arduous 1,000-ft (305-m) TRAVERSE to the main summit. This difficult route remains unrepeated. Two books describe this expedition: Bonatti's *On The Heights* (1964) and Fosco Mariani's *Karakoram: The Ascent of Gasherbrum IV* (1959). Many years passed before another successful ascent of "G4." In 1985 Wojciech KURTYKA and Robert Schauer climbed the daunting west face in a multiday ALPINE-STYLE effort, but exhaustion and deteriorating weather led them to forsake the true summit and descend the northwest ridge. Although they did not summit, their climb is celebrated as a high point of Himalayan alpinism. Eight expeditions failed on Gasherbrum IV before the peak's second ascent by the northwest ridge. In 1986, an Australian-American expedition approached via the West Gasherbrum Glacier and placed Greg Child, Tim MACART-NEY-SNAPE and Tom Hargis on top. Child's book *Thin Air: Encounters in the Himalayas* (1990) describes this expedition.

GEAR Another name for climbing equipment. (See CAMMING DEVICE, CARABINERS, NUTS, ROPES.)

GEAR SLING Also called racking sling, hardware sling or bandolier. A sling made of WEBBING, sometimes padded and specially sewn, worn over the shoulder and used for carrying equipment arranged on CARABINERS.

GENDARME A French word which can be known as a prominent rock tower or pinnacle on a mountain ridge. The Italian equivalent is *torre*, the German *turme*. Gendarme is accepted in English climbing usage.

GERVASUTTI, GIUSTO (1909–1946) (Italy) One of the great route pioneers of the Western ALPS, Gervasutti is best remembered for FIRST ASCENTS of the Right Frêney Pillar, the south face of the Pointe Gugliermina and the east face of the GRANDES JORASSES. When weather conditions were poor around Courmayeur and CHAMONIX, he climbed in the Dauphiné, putting up major routes on L'Olan and Allefroide. Another notable achievement is his second ascent of the north face of the Grandes Jorasses during a violent storm. At Christmas in 1936 he soloed the MATTERHORN from the Italian side. A resident of Turin, Gervasutti refused to let his climbing be politicized. When asked by the then Fascist-dominated Club Alpino Italiano not to climb with a French friend, Lucien Davies, Gervasutti refused. He died on a rappel accident while attempting a new route on Mont Blanc du Tacul. In the

Introduction to *Gervasutti's Climbs*, first published in English in 1957, 11 years after his death, Lucien Davies wrote: "Everyone who had seen him in action agreed that he was a born climber of quite exceptional quality—one of those rare, outstanding figures who emerge from time to time in every sport. He had a magnificent style, perfect in its simplicity and effectiveness—the style of a conqueror— and his combination of virtuosity and precision inspired absolute confidence."

GHERSEN, ALAIN (1963–   ) (France) Ghersen is an alpinist, SPORT CLIMBER and ENCHAINMENT specialist of the modern French generation. In the 1980s he completed some unusual feats that illustrate the breadth of his adaptation to TECHNICAL climbing: he climbed one of the hardest boulder problems in FONTAINEBLEAU, and then drove to the Alps to solo the Peuterey Ridge on MONT BLANC. In 1990, also in the Alps, he free-soloed, back-to-back, the American Direct on Les DRU, Walker Spur on GRANDES JORASSES and the Peuterey Integral. On the French limestone crag BUOUX he made the second ascent of Le Minimum (8b+). He pushed FREE-CLIMBING standards in the Alps by freeing Divine Providence (7c) on the Pilier d'Angle, and les Ailes du Desir (7c) on the Fou south face.

GIBRALTAR, ROCK OF The peak in Gibraltar (United Kingdom possession). The spectacular north face was first climbed by H. Day, BOYSEN and M. Burke in 1971.

GIMMER CRAG (Britain) This rhyolite, southerly facing CRAG is perhaps the finest around the LAKE DISTRICT. It is located on the southern flank of the Langdale Pikes.

Gimmer has two justly famous ROUTES in the easier grades. Gimmer Crack takes the best LINE on the crag up a magnificent CORNER that bounds the northwest face at 5.7 and was the work of A. B. Reynolds and G. McPhee in 1928. The other classic is Kipling Groove, so called because its "ruddy 'ard," which breaks across the northwest face at 5.8. Kipling was climbed in 1948 by the great Yorkshireman Arthur Dolphin. Gimmer String (5.9) is a well-known route up the ARETE separating the two aforementioned routes. It was the work of Allan Austin.
Guidebooks: D. Armstrong, et al, *Langdale* (1989); Bill Birkett, et al, *Rock Climbing in the Lake District* (1986).

GIRDLE TRAVERSE A route that TRAVERSES across a cliff or face from one end to the other. Especially popular in British climbing.

GLACIER CREAM Another term for SUNSCREEN, worn as protection against ultraviolet radiation that is reflected more harshly off glaciers at higher elevations.

GLACIERS Glaciers, which appear to be tongues of ice flowing along a valley, are actually rivers of ice moving downhill under the influence of gravity. They are fed by permanent snowfields, and form when snowfields swell in size until the weight of the snow begins pushing downhill. Over eons, a glacier scours a path through the mountains, cutting through bedrock, moving masses of rubble (which is deposited as MORAINE) and shaping the mountain land-scape. At lower elevations the surface ice of a glacier melts in a process called ablation. At the snout, terminus, or end of a glacier the buildup of ice is balanced by ablation. Glaciers advance or recede according to climatic change, but most glaciers at present are shrinking. Huge glaciers like the BALTORO in the KARAKORAM are 50 miles (80 km) long and, in places, four miles (six km) wide. ICE CAPS are flat ice sheets similar to a massive glacier found in Polar regions such as ANTARCTICA and GREENLAND, and along PATAGONIA's west side. HANGING GLACIERS or pocket gla-ciers are short glaciers nestled on a mountain flank.

Glaciers move on an underlayer of dense plasticlike ice that lets the glacier flow at slow speeds. This ice may be very deep—the world's deepest glaciers, in Antarctica, are 9,500 ft (2,896 m) deep. Glaciers move constantly. The Mer de Glace, in CHAMONIX, France, is a very fast glacier, moving approximately 10 inches (25 cm) per day. The top layer (200 ft/61 m) of glacier ice is brittle and prone to fracturing into CREVASSES, ICE FALLS, BERGSCHRUNDS and SERACS as the glacier drops in elevation or flows over obstacles. This layer creates considerable hazards for climb-ers. (See CREVASSE RESCUE, GLACIER TRAVEL, ROPING UP.)

GLACIER TABLE A flat boulder on a GLACIER resting on a narrow column or pedestal of ice, and resembling a table or mushroom. It is formed as the level of glacier ice melts down during summer. The ice beneath the boulder, being shaded, melts more slowly than the surrounding ice, leaving the boulder elevated. This is common a feature of rock-strewn glaciers in regions like the KARAKORAM.

GLACIER TRAVEL The art of moving safely along GLACIERS and among CREVASSES. On dry glaciers crevasses are clearly visible, but on snow-covered or wet glaciers they may be hidden. In such cases route-finding skills are essential. When a climber is forced off safe features like terminal or medial MORAINES and onto glacier ice, roping up is necessary for safety. Most accidents on glaciers hap-pen to unroped persons. The more people in a roped party, the stronger the holding power of a team in the event of a crevasse fall. Usually the climber most experi-enced in glacier travel leads, as that climber is more likely to detect signs of hidden crevasses like shallow furrows or hollow-sounding snow. The leader and last climber (or anchoring climber) tie directly into the rope. As much distance as possible should be allowed between the leader and anchoring climber, as stopping time is needed to arrest a falling leader. An anchoring climber dragged into a crevasse is disastrous. See ROPING UP for techniques.

On dangerous terrain the leader's rope is braced or anchored with a BOOT-AXE BELAY. If a fall into a crevasse takes the party by surprise, the anchoring climber can hold the fall by dropping back into a sitting position and digging his heels into the snow. The rope should never be slack between leader and party, nor should loose coils be carried by hand.

Selecting a logical path along a glacier requires common-sense and experience. A path should be picked from a vantage spot if possible. Glacier travel is safer in cold conditions of morning, as sun-warmed snow is soft and can break through. Crevasses usually run across the flow of a glacier, which means climbers walking up a glacier travel perpendicular to crevasses. Approaching crevasses at right angles is better than approaching them obliquely at an angle, but if traveling parallel to crevasses a party may have to travel in staggered formation (en echelon), on opposite sides of a crevasse. This approach is tricky and troublesome and in practice is seldom used. The leader's task is to test the terrain, probing suspicious snow with an ICE AXE, stepping wide or jumping over slots, maneuvering through crevassed areas, crossing SNOW BRIDGES and keep-ing the party away from crevasse edges, which may be undercut.

GLISSADING A technique of descent by sliding over snow that is useful to rapidly lose elevation. Two basic methods are used: The standing glissade adopts an upright stance akin to a skiing position. The climber leans forward and places his body weight directly over the feet, which are planted somewhat apart. Hands are held to the sides, for balance. An ICE AXE is kept at the ready in case SELF ARREST is needed. As in skiing, turns are initiated by weighting and turning the outside, lower foot. The sitting glissade, or bum slide is easier to control and is performed in a sitting position. The ice axe tip is used as a brake. This glissade has the advantage of placing the climber closer to the slope, and the ice axe is more easily used for self arrest. Conditions are not always appropriate for glissading: AVA-LANCHE conditions, obstacles like rocks, CREVASSES, and patches of ice that can lead to dangerous acceleration should all be assessed before glissading. Speed should be checked by frequent braking. Moderately steep slopes easing to level ground offer hospitable terrain for practic-ing glissading.

GLOVES Gloves protect hands from cold and wind. Many systems exist for different needs, but LAYERING com-binations of fabrics over the hand retains thermal warmth and makes drying of components of the glove system easy. A typical three-part system for cold weather consists of a liner glove, the main mitten or glove of heavy insulation and an outer shell of mittens or gloves.

Liner gloves are thin finger gloves. They are made either of wool, synthetics like polypropylene, polyester or nylon, or wool-synthetic blends. They are thin enough to wear when rock climbing. (Fingerless gloves with cutoff finger ends are worn for maximum dexterity on difficult climbs.)

The main insulating layer of mittens or gloves overlays the liner. Mittens offer less dexterity than gloves, but are warmer. The choice is one of personal preference. Insulat-ing materials are many. The weight of insulation depends on the climate. Wool is warm but retains moisture and dries slowly. DACHSTEIN and similar mittens of thick pre-shrunk wool are proven in the coldest climates. In snow, Dachsteins trap a layer of snow on the surface that renders them snowproof and windproof. Fiber-pile (polyester or nylon fleece) is warm, light, retains minimal moisture in fibers and dries quickly. However, synthetic fibers flatten with extended use and lose thermal efficiency. Heavy insulators like Thinsulate or other multi-filament insulations are very warm but also compress. DOWN mittens are coveted for extreme cold, but are bulky and down is useless when wet. The outer shell covering a glove system should be windproof, waterproof and breathable. Fabrics like GORE-TEX and Entrant offer these characteristics. Coated nylon is waterproof but nonbreathable, causing CONDENSATION. Waterproof, nonbreathable Neoprene rubber can also be useful for wet conditions or ice climbing. Stitching lines in glove shells leak unless they are sealed during manufacture. Shell features like cuffs or gauntlets extending up the wrists keep out snow, but cuffs should not be tight enough to constrict circulation. Wrists should be well insulated as, like the back of the neck, temperature sensors are located there.

Rather than rely on a single pair of gloves, alpinists carry spare gloves, changing them as they dampen and drying them against the chest or in sleeping bags at night. Retaining cords made from string attached to the cuff and looped over the wrist prevent the loss of gloves.

GLOWACZ, STEFAN (1965–) (Germany) Top
rock climber and competition champion, Glowacz is the winner of the 1992 Masters Invitational at Chambery, France, a demonstration event held in the presence of International Olympic Committee members in hopes of climbing becoming an Olympic sport. He won the first professional competition ever, in Bardoneccia, Italy, in 1985, and also won the prestigious invitational competition in ARCO, Italy, in 1988 and 1989, although in 1988 he tied with Patrick EDLINGER. Glowacz won the International Frankenjura Sport Kletter Cup, in Nuremburg, Germany, in 1989. In 1991 he won a World Masters Tour event at LaRiba, Spain, in a controversial finish. He and another contestant, François LEGRAND, tied for first, and instead of holding a superfinal round, organizers scored them on speed.

Glowacz is noted for his hard ON SIGHT leads. In Erto, Italy, known as having high standards (even the world's best climbers rarely ON SIGHT 5.12c there), he on-sighted Pole Position (7c+ or 5.13a) and Mr. Rase (5.13b). In 1992 he on-sighted Meatgrinder Arete (5.13b) in YOSEMITE VALLEY, and RED-POINTED Agincourt (8c, or 5.14b) at BUOUX, France. His hardest FIRST ASCENTS were on the climb Wet Willi (8b/c or 5.14a) in VERDON.

Glowacz starred in a feature film about climbing, *A Cry of Stone*, directed by Werner Herzog. In the film his character wins the World Championship in Frankfurt, Germany, then goes mountaineering in PATAGONIA. After the film opened in 1991, Glowacz participated in the World Championships in Frankfurt. Life did not imitate art. He mistakenly stepped on a BOLT in the quarterfinal round and was disqualified.

GMOSER, HANS (1932–) (Austria/Canada)
Gmoser created modern guiding and commercial MOUNTAINEERING in CANADA, and pioneered new climbs in the ROCKY MOUNTAINS. He arrived in Canada from war-ravaged Austria in 1951. In 1952 his FIRST ASCENT of the Grillmair Chimney Route on Yamnuska in the BOW VALLEY ushered in a new era of climbing in Canada. An active period of mountaineering followed, with the first ascent of Mount Blackburn (ALASKA, 1958) and the third ascent of Mount ALBERTA (1958). In 1959 he led a team on a 26-day wilderness journey from Kluane Lake to climb Mount LOGAN's east ridge, returning to civilization via the Donjek Glacier and River. In 1960 he led a long ski TRAVERSE along the ICE FIELDS of the continental divide. He also climbed DENALI (north summit) via a new route up the Wickersham Wall (1963). But it was as a guide and as the creator of Canadian Mountain Holidays (Canada's largest operator of mountain adventures) and of the association of Canadian Mountain Guides, that Gmoser made his mark. Gmoser received the Order of Canada (1987), was elected to the honor roll of Canadian skiing (1989), and was made an honorary member of the Alpine Club of Canada. He received the Summit of Excellence Award in Banff in 1988.

Further reading: Phil Dowling, *The Mountaineers* (1979).

GOGARTH (Britain) This is the name given to the 3
miles (5 km) of limestone cliffs on Holy Island off the coast of Anglesey. Gogarth is an important crucible of British climbing and is one of the foremost SEA-CLIFF climbing areas in the world. Its most famous CRAGS are the South Stack lighthouse, including the Red Walls, Castell Helen and Yellow Wall, and the North Stack, which includes the Main Cliff and the Upper Tier. Camping is plentiful on the island, and LLANBERIS on the mainland is nearby.

Development began in the early 1960s. Alpha Club members Bas Ingle and Martin BOYSEN climbed the first two lines, Gogarth and Shag Rock, 5.9s on the Main Cliff and Upper Tier. Following a live TV show from Gogarth in 1966, interest was renewed and Joe BROWN discovered Wen Slab on which he added Wen (5.8) with Boysen and also Winking Crack (5.10b) on the Upper Tier. Peter Crew, the other dominant force in Welsh climbing at that time, climbed Big Groove (5.10a) on the Main Cliff, before teaming up with Brown on Dinosaur, an imposing line also on the Main Cliff that now goes free at 5.11a.

In 1967 Crew teamed up with the controversial Ed DRUMMOND to climb Mammoth on the Main Wall with six points of aid, a route that would be freed in 1984 by Andy Pollitt at 5.12. Drummond also added The Strand (5.10a) on the Upper Tier and the celebrated A Dream of White Horses with Dave Pearce, a 5.8 girdle of Wen Zawn and one of the finest routes in Britain. In 1969 he climbed T. Rex (5.10c), also in Wen Zawn, with Pearce and Lawrie Holliwell, and in 1971 The Moon (5.10c) on the Yellow Wall.

Climbing genius Al ROUSE fought his way up Positron on the Main Wall, in 1971, with five aids eventually eliminated at 5.11d by Ron FAWCETT. This demanding route was soloed by Stevie Haston in 1985. The mid-1970s produced routes like Fawcett's The Cad, a 5.12a face route on the North Stack that controversially used two BOLTS for protection. It has since been climbed without these, and been soloed. In 1980, John Redhead climbed The Bells, The

Bells, also on North Stack, a 5.13a death route that was repeated on sight by Andy Pollitt in 1986. In the mid-1980s Gogarth produced scores of bold and hard climbs. Among the notables were Johnny Dawes and Paul Pritchard, who added Come To Mother, a 5.13a on the Red Walls; Redhead, who climbed The Demons of Bosch (5.13a); and Pollitt, who added The Hollow Man (5.13c), both on North Stack. Perhaps the finest achievement was Dawes's onsight FIRST ASCENT of Hardback Thesaurus in 1988, another serious 5.13a in Wen Zawn.

Gogarth is a big and serious crag and the climbing often requires a cool head. Protection is with a usual rack. In situ pegs must be treated with caution due to corrosion from the sea.

Guidebooks: Climbers' Club, *Gogarth* (1990); Paul Williams, *Rock-climbing in Snowdonia* (1990).

GOGGLES Used as eye protection in mountain conditions, goggles offer better visibility than sunglasses in foggy or windy conditions. See SUNGLASSES for a discussion of eye protection.

GORDALE SCAR (Britain) The cleft of Gordale Scar with its overhanging limestone walls is a sobering prospect to all but the fittest climbers. The CRAG is in YORKSHIRE, near the village of Malham, between Skipton and Settle. Malham provides services and camping, including a café run by legendary British climber Pete Livesey.

Gordale was initially dominated by AID CLIMBING in the 1960s, and many modern ROUTES follow old aid-lines. In 1964 Eric Wallis and Des Hadlum pioneered an early free exploration with Light (5.9), which climbs a crack through impressive country. Free climbing really got underway when Pete LIVESEY and John Sheard freed Face Route (5.10d) in 1971. Previously they had added the subtle but bold Jenny Wren (5.11a), probably the hardest route in BRITAIN at the time.

In the late 1970s Ron FAWCETT came to the fore, freeing the Cave Routes (both 5.12d) while on honeymoon in 1982. In 1984 Martin Atkinson, a uniquely powerful climber, freed Pierrepoint (5.13a), which ascends the steepest part of the gorge, and in 1985 produced Super Cool (5.13d). Fawcett's iDefcon 3 (5.13) and Greg Rimmer's bold Bliss (5.13a) are also significant.

Gordale is 170 ft (52 m) high. While there are middle-grade routes, the main challenges are harder. The area contains many sport climbs.

Guidebooks: Yorkshire Mountain Club, *Yorkshire Limestone* (1985).

GORE-TEX Trade name for the first waterproof, breathable and windproof fabric developed by W. L. Gore, Inc. It is extensively used in climbing and mountaineering outerwear. (See BREATHABLE FABRICS.)

GRADES Grades are roman numerals used in BIG WALL CLIMBING to indicate the length of ascent. Grade V climbs can take many days to complete. (See RATING SYSTEMS.)

GRADING SYSTEMS See RATING SYSTEMS.

GRAIAN ALPS (France) This large range, split into three groups, lies between the MONT BLANC Range and the Dauphiné. Running north to south and roughly parallel, they comprise the Central Graians, the Tarentaise or Vanoise to the west and the Eastern Graians or Mountains of Cogne. The central area is less frequented. Principal summits include the Pointe de Charbonnel (12,300 ft/3,750 m) and Rochemelon (11,605 ft/3,538 m). The Vanoise are famous for their beauty and while the higher peaks, including Grande Casse (12,635 ft/3,852 m), are straightforward, lower peaks like the Aiguille de Vanoise (9,151 ft/2,790 m) offer good rock climbing. Centers for exploring these ranges include Pralognan and Val d'Isère.

The main interest for the mountaineer lies in the Eastern Graians. The highest mountain is Gran Paradiso (13,320 ft/ 4,061 m) but being the easiest peak above the "magic" 13,120 ft/4,000 m mark can make it unbearably popular. The normal ascent (PD-), first done in 1860 by J. J. Cowell and W. Dundas with the guides J. Payot and J. Tairraz, begins at Pont to the west of the mountain and climbs via the Vittorio Emanuele II Hut. Emanuelle was the founder of the region's national park and savior of the local ibex population. Other routes on Gran Paradiso worth considering are the East Face (D) and the North Ridge Intégral (D). The usual center for the Eastern Graians is Cogne and other peaks in the area include Herbetet (12,392 ft/3,778 m) and Grivola (13,018 ft/3,969 m). (See RATINGS SYSTEMS for explanation of French ratings.)

Further reading: Robin Collomb, *Graians East: Gran Paradiso National Park*; Richard Goedeke, *The Alpine 4000m Peaks*.

GRANDE COURSE A French term meaning a long, classic alpine route.

GRANDES JORASSES (France) Were it positioned at the end of the Mer de Glace rather than at the head of the Leschaux Glacier, the north face would be one of the most famous mountain aspects in the world. As it is, the ROUTES climbed on it have a resonance that bring to mind the great climbers at their pioneering best. The peak, in reality a ridge of jagged points, forms the French-Italian border for almost a mile. The principal tops are Point Whymper (13,723 ft/4,184 m) or the west summit, and Point Walker (13,802 ft/4,208 m) or the east summit. Ascents from the south side of the mountain start at the Grandes Jorasses Hut on the Planpincieux Glacier in Italy. Routes on the north face generally start at the Leschaux Hut on the Leschaux Glacier. The west ridge offers a committing TRAVERSE and a natural continuation to the Rochefort Arête from the Canzio Bivouac on the Col des Jorasses. Giusto GERVASUTTI added one of his finest creations by climbing the east face of the Jorasses, a serious and committing ED which is strafed by stonefall in its lower reaches. The south pillar, climbed in 1948 by Piero Ghiglione, is a remote but good TD, offering an escape from the crowds elsewhere. The northeast or Hirondelles Ridge is also recommended.

The north face, however, offers the most exciting challenges. Working from west to east, the Croz Spur, climbed in 1935 by M. Meier and R. Peters, offers a serious undertaking at ED- and is best considered in winter when the risks from stonefall are minimized. For those seeking only a temporary sojourn on the planet, the Japanese route is ideal with poor rock and fierce stonefall. Climbed in 1972 by a Japanese team, there is no recorded second. Nick Colton and Alex McIntyre added the British route of 1976 to Pointe Walker, which also has its share of objective danger, but the classic to this summit is the Walker Spur. Climbed in 1938 by Riccardo CASSIN on his first visit to the MONT BLANC Range, it remains one of the great routes of all time, safer and with more traffic than its neighbors. While not technically of the highest order, it is nevertheless a long and demanding line and a great monument to its originator. Another alpinist, René DESMAISON, added the second world-famous line in 1968 when he climbed the ICE FIELD to the left of the Walker Spur called The Shroud.

GRAND TETON (United States)

The highest peak of the TETON Range in WYOMING. "The Grand" has figured prominently in the development of alpine climbing in America. Most of the climbing is on gneiss, although icy rock, ice COULOIRS and GLACIER approaches are common. The first confirmed ascent was organized by William Owen and guided by Franklin Spalding in 1898. The ROUTE they followed—the Owen-Spalding—is now climbed by hundreds each year. The first TECHNICAL route climbed was the east ridge, by Robert UNDERHILL and Kenneth Henderson, in 1929. In 1931 this pair climbed the Teton Glacier, and continued up what is regarded as one of the greatest alpine routes in America, the north ridge. Also in 1931 Glen EXUM soloed the now-popular Exum (south) Ridge (5.4). Five years later Jack Durrance and Paul and Eldon PETZOLDT climbed the 3,000-ft (915-m) high north face. Durrance also pioneered the west face (IV, 5.8) in 1940. In 1961 Raymond Jacquot and Herbert Swedlund climbed the Black Ice Couloir, still a famous alpine ice climb. Leigh Ortenburger, the LOWE family, Jim Beyer and Renny Jackson have figured prominently in establishing modern routes on the Grand. In all about three dozen routes, most with variations, ascend the Grand Teton.

Guidebooks: Leigh Ortenburger and Reynold Jackson, *A Climbers Guide to the Teton Range*, Vols I and II; Richard Rossiter, *Teton Classics: Selected Climbs in Grand Teton National Park* (1991).

GRANITE MOUNTAIN (United States)

Situated near the town of Prescott, Granite Mountain is one of ARIZONA's finest CRAGS. The cliff is a single large bluff on the side of a 7,626-ft (2,325-m) mountain. The cliff is 3,000 ft (915 m) wide and 500 ft (152 m) high. Strenuous CRACK routes and steep SLAB climbs typify the climbing. The surroundings consist of arid cactus-covered and boulder-strewn hills. Climbing at Granite Mountain began in 1966, by a club of Prescott and Flagstaff climbers who called themselves "The Syndicato Granitica." CLEAN-CLIMBING ETHICS prevail today at this well-developed cliff. The cli-

mate is extremely hot in summer, with spring and fall presenting the most favorable climbing weather. Ratings span 5.2 to 5.13a. All routes may be done in a day.

Guidebook: Jim Waugh, *Topo Guide to Granite Mountain* (1982).

GRAPEVINE KNOT

Another name for the double fisherman's knot, used to secure two ropes together. (See KNOTS.)

Grapevine Knot

GRAUPEL

A type of snow crystal resembling a ball-shaped pellet. Graupel forms when a snow crystal falls through a layer of air containing water droplets. Water freezes to the crystal, encrusting it with rime. As the rime thickens, the geometric shape of the snow crystal is obscured, resulting in a round ball. When present in the snow pack, graupel can form a weak, AVALANCHE-prone layer.

GREENLAND

The world's largest island is 844,015 sq miles (2,186,000 sq km), of which the Ice Cap covers 666,525 sq. miles (1,726,300 sq km). The coastline of Greenland extends 24,860 miles (40,000 km). From Kap Morris Jesup, at the far north to Kap Farvel in the south, the distance is 1,659 miles (2,670 km). From west to east, the distance is 652 miles (1,050 km) at the widest point. Numerous ski and sled traverses of the ice cap have been made.

Expeditions in Greenland require permission from the Danish Polarcenter, Hausergade 3, Dk-1128 Copenhagen K. Maps of Greenland can be purchased at the National Survey and Cadastre, Rentemestervej 8, DK-2400 Copenhagen, NV. Some expeditions (especially to the west and south coast) can be conducted as tourist activities, if endorsed by The Danish Polar Center. Permission is granted on condition of insurance covering rescue expenses. Expeditions should apply for permission at least six months before the expedition.

Summer temperatures on the coast range from 68 degrees F (20 degrees C) in the south to 32 degrees F (0 degrees C) in the north. Winter temperatures in the south seldom fall below −4 degrees F (−20 degrees C), whereas in the north they can drop to −40 degrees F (−40 degrees C). The best months for climbing in Greenland are July and August when the sun hardly goes down.

Greenland is reached by airplane from Denmark, Canada and Iceland. Local transportation to the climbing areas is by boat or helicopter. The distance from Nanortalik to Tasermiut Fjord (South Greenland) is a few hours by boat. The Angmagssalik area involves a multi-day boat journey. Helicopter costs amount to $3,000 to 4,000 per hour. The Blosseville coast and the Staunings Alps can be reached by small airplanes from Iceland.

For mountaineers, the following five areas are the most interesting: Kap Farvel area in the south with the mountains along the Tasermiut and Lindenow Fjord (Firth); Sukkertoppen and Evighedsfjord area on the west coast; the mountains in the Umanak and Upenavik Area on the northwest coast; the Angmagssalik area on the east coast (the most visited area); and the mountains on the Blosseville Coast with the Staunings Alps in the northeast.

The highest mountain in Greenland is the easy but remote Gunnbjorn Fjeld (12,136 ft/3,700 m), on the Blosseville Coast. British climbed it in 1935. Greenland mountain types vary, including many huge granitic peaks offering big wall alpinism. Technical peaks include Djaevelens Tommelfinger or Devils Thumb (1,902 ft/580 m) north of Upernavik; Snepyramiden (7,334 ft/2,236 m) in Umanak; Ketil (4,756 ft/1,450 m) and Ulamertorssuaq (6,002 ft/1,830 m) in Tassermiut Firth; Apostelens Tommelfinger (7,544 ft/2,300 m) in Lindenow Firth; Ingolffjeld (8,397 ft/2,560 m), Laupersberg (8,462 ft/2,580 m), Rytterknaegten (6,954 ft/2,120 m), Tupilak (7,426 ft/2,264 m), Ice Dome (7,406 ft/2,258 m), Meskeal (6,232 ft/1,900 m), Pharaoe (11,076 ft/3,377 m), Domzale Fjeld (10,955 ft/3,340 m), all in the Angmagssalik area; Ejnar Mikkelsen Fjeld (11,506 ft/3,508 m) on the Blosseville Coast.

Germans were the earliest mountaineers in Greenland, ascending Papyer Spitze (6,986 ft-2,130 m) in the northeast in 1870. In 1872 Edward WHYMPER came to the west coast and climbed Quilertinguit (6,455 ft/1,968 m). It was not until the 1920s that more difficult climbing took place, with the high summits going first. In 1929, Britons climbed Petermann Peak (9,758 ft/2,975 m) in the northeast. Just before the Second World War, E. Wyss-Dynant's Swiss expedition made 14 first ascents, like Mont Forel (11,021 ft/3,360 m).

Italians also put their mark on Greenland. Guido Monzino with Mario Fantin and others, in 1964, climbed Danmarks Tinde (9,610 ft/2,930 m) via the north wall.

Big Wall climbing began in 1971 with a Croatian route on the extremely difficult Ingolffjeld East Ridge. A second climb up the southwest face was made by Britons in 1975 (63 pitches between IV and VI, 5,248 ft/1,600 m) with four bivouacs. South Greenland's Yosemite-like towers attracted Austrians in 1974, who climbed Ketil (4,756 ft/1,450 m) East Ridge. But the 4,428-ft (1,350-m)-high vertical west wall was the great prize, on which French climbers in 1975, then Spanish and again French in 1984, made big wall routes. Full-scale big wall routes have appeared on Ullamertorssuaq (near Ketil), Pyramid Wall, and Apostlens Tommelfinger (7,544 ft/2,300 m) in South Greenland.

Further reading: D. Bennett, *Staunings Alps* Mario Fantin, *Montagne di Groenlandia* (1969); Erik Hoff, "Mountaineering in Greenland 1967–1976," *American Alpine Journal* (1979); Dolfi Rotovnik and Peter Sondergaard, "Mountaineering in Greenland 1977–1986," *American Alpine Journal* (1988).

GREENWOOD, BRIAN (1934–   ) (Canada) This British expatriate helped bring Canadian MOUNTAINEERING in tune with modern standards. When he arrived in CANADA in 1956, Canadian climbing was a backwater, with standards in the ROCKY MOUNTAINS decades behind European standards. His ascent of the Belfry Route on Yamnuska in the BOW VALLEY CORRIDOR (a commiting five-pitch 5.8 rock climb done with CHOCKSTONES and homemade NUTS) paved the way for a new generation of TECHNICAL routes. For 20 years he was the leading climber in the Rockies. He repeated classics like Mount ALBERTA, and discovered and helped develop areas like the Tower of Babel, Yamnuska, Tonquin Valley and the west side of the Howser Towers. On Yamnuska alone he opened nine difficult new routes. In WINTER CLIMBING he made FIRST ASCENTS of Hungabee, Victoria and Tower Castle Mountain, as well as the first winter TRAVERSE of Mount Rundle. Greenwood's first ascent of the north face of Mount Temple remains a classic testpiece of the Rockies. He made the first ascent of the forbidding east face of Mount Babel and during the early 1970s pioneered waterfall climbs like Bow Falls and Borgeau right hand. At the age of 40, he climbed the Salathe route on EL CAPITAN and retired shortly thereafter. He was made an honorary member of the Calgary Mountain Club in 1987.

GRIFFITH, CHRISTIAN (1964–   ) (United States) One of the early proponents of SPORT CLIMBING in the United States, Griffith, of BOULDER, COLORADO, showed early promise as a rock climber, climbing Crimson Cringe (5.12a) in YOSEMITE at the age of 15. He has done some 30 new routes and FIRST FREE ASCENTS, chief among them Red Dihedral (5.12d R); Desdichado, (5.13c/d) in 1985; and Verve (5.13d) in 1986. The latter two were probably the hardest routes in the United States at the time. Griffith is a consistent force at national CLIMBING COMPETITIONS, and a COURSE SETTER at national and world events. He was a member of the first U.S. climbing team, and won the Canadian Open national competition in 1991 and the Phoenix Bouldering Competition in 1988. He has designed several major CLIMBING GYMS in the United States.

GRIP A climber's HOLD on the rock. Also used to refer to a boot's GRIP on the rock.

GRIPPED A colloquialism in climbing, indicating a state of fear, especially of falling or of exposure.

GRITSTONE (Britain) Observed American Pat AMENT in 1986 of the small sedimentary crags of the PEAK DISTRICT, "The short gritstone routes of Britain bear more significance to me than an ascent of Everest or of the Eiger North Wall in winter." (See BLEAKLOW and KINDER SCOUT, CHEW VALLEY, CRATCLIFFE TOR, CURBAR EDGE, FROGGATT EDGE, MILLSTONE, STAFFORDSHIRE GRIT, STANAGE.)

GUIDEBOOK A book containing ROUTE descriptions, maps, access notes and FIRST-ASCENT information to a climbing area.

GUIDES Professional mountaineers or rock climbers who take clients up climbs for a fee.

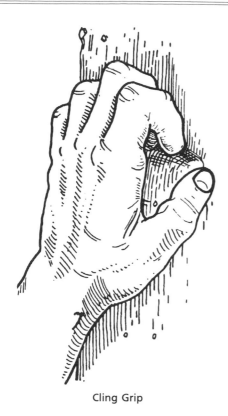

Cling Grip

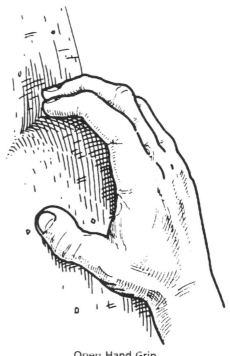

Open Hand Grip

GULLICH, WOLFGANG (1960–1992) (Germany)
Gullich made breakthroughs in FREE CLIMBING from 1978 to 1991, yet shunned Europe's SPORT-CLIMBING competition scene. Among the hardest routes of his career in the limestone of Germany's Sudlicher FRANKENJURA, was in 1984 Germany's first UIAA grade X (the world's first 5.13d) Kanal im Rucken. In 1987 in the Nordlicher Frankenjura he opened Level 52 (X+, 5.14a), followed by Germany's first XI- (5.14b) Wallstreet. The rating has been confirmed by top climbers, including Guido Kostermeyer, one of the few to repeat it. Gullich's visit to Mount ARAPILES in AUSTRALIA in 1985 produced the world's first 5.14a (X+, Australian 32), Punks in the Gym, a feat later confirmed by Didier RABOUTOU. Gullich trained intensively and traveled widely. He once said: "It is important to go to different areas to get a treasury of movements. If you don't ever travel, it is possible to become a 'stupid' climber. A person who climbs only in his own area is very limited and often climbs like a computer." Gullich claimed the first grade VIII in the ALPS Locker vom Hocker in 1981. On his 1982 visit to the United States he repeated America's hardest cracks, like Grand Illusion (5.13c) at The Sugarloaf near TAHOE, while in 1986 his solo of Separate Reality (5.12) impressed even resident Yosemite soloists. But his two ascents of Nameless Tower in the TRANGO TOWERS of PAKISTAN distinguish him as a visionary free climber: In 1988 he made the FIRST FREE ASCENT of the Yugoslav Route (VIII+, 5.12), and in 1989 he climbed Eternal Flame, (IX−, 5.12b). The latter they "worked" on, resting or aiding until PITCHES were RED POINTED. It has 35 pitches, 11 rated 5.11, two rated 5.12, at elevations between 17,000 ft (5,183 m) and the 20,510-ft (6,253-m) summit. Both ascents were

made with Kurt ALBERT. In 1991 he visited the PAINE GROUP in PATAGONIA to climb Riders on the Storm, (IX, 5.12+), a route of 3,000 ft (915 m), but established what may be the world's hardest free climb, Aktion Direkt, in the Frankenjura. Its rating (German XI, French 9a, USA 5.14c/d) opened a new chapter in levels of difficulty. At the peak of his prowess this gifted and respected ambassador of climbing died in a car accident while going to an ISPO trade show.

GULLY A deep fault in a cliff. If snow- or ice-filled it may be called a COULOIR.

GURANS HIMAL (Nepal) An extensive range of western NEPAL that is bounded on the east and north by the Humla Karnali River. The pass known as the Lipu Lekh is its northern limit. The western boundary extends from the Lipu Lekh southwest along the Kali Ganga. The range is divided by the Seti River. The range west of this river is the Yoka Pahar subsection, and the range east of the Seti is the Saipal Himal. The peak Api (23,393 ft/7,132 m), in the northwest tip of Nepal (in the Yoha Pahar), is a frequently visited and imposing peak, first climbed in 1960 by Japanese climbers via the northwest face. The east ridge (Italians, 1978) and northwest ridge (Poles, winter 1983) have also been climbed. Dominating the Saipal Himal is the peak Saipal (23,061 ft/7,031 m), which has been climbed by the south ridge (Japanese, 1963) and by a two-way TRAVERSE by two parties of the west ridge and southwest Face (Spanish, 1985). The Gurans Himal has many peaks above 19,680 ft (6,000 m).

GURNARD'S HEAD (Britain) Unlike the majority of SEA CLIFFS' rock in CORNWALL's West Penwith, Gurnard's

Head is formed of greenstone, a compact, dark-colored rock. The CRAG is located between St. Ives and St. Just, which is more practical a base, on the B3306. The routes are approached by ABSEIL.

Gurnard's Head comprises a huge open-book CORNER and this feature is climbed by an outstanding 5.6, Right Angle, climbed by Iain Peters in 1966. The main attractions though are the 5.10 routes on the right wall. Examples are Pat LITTLEJOHN's Behemoth from 1969, Rowland Edwards's strenuous and direct Black Magic, and from 1978 Mastodon, said to be the best route on the cliff.

Guidebooks: Des Hannigan, *Bosigran* (1991); Pat Littlejohn, *South West Climbs* (1991).

HABELER, PETER (1942–   ) (Austria) With Reinhold MESSNER, Habeler made the FIRST ASCENT of Mount EVEREST without supplemental oxygen (1978), a feat described in *The Lonely Victory: Mt. Everest '78* (1978). Habeler began climbing near Mayrhofen in the Zillertal Alps at the age of six. Certified as a guide and ski instructor in 1963, he worked in the United States (1966–1971). In 1970 he and Briton Doug SCOTT made the first all-European ascent of EL CAPITAN's Salathe Wall. Habeler and Messner climbed a number of routes together, including the GRANDES JORASSES, Walker Spur; YERUPAJA (1969); a 10-hour ascent of the EIGER north face (1974); second ascent of GASHERBRUM I, by a new route, ALPINE STYLE (1975); and an attempt on DHAULAGIRI south face (1977).

HACKETT, PETER, DOCTOR (1947–   ) (United States) Hackett is widely recognized as the premier authority on high-altitude illness and adaptation. Born in Chicago, Hackett got his medical degree and started his mountain medicine career as a consultant for the rescue team in YOSEMITE VALLEY. He worked as trek doctor for Mountain Travel in NEPAL and PAKISTAN, and took on leadership of the Himalayan Rescue Association in KHUMBU, in 1974. There he initiated the first multicase studies of high-altitude illnesses. In 1981 he partook in a medical expedition to Mount EVEREST, and summited (South Col Route). He has continued to study altitude illnesses and medications on DENALI, and is a leading consultant to the Wilderness Medical Association and the American Mountain Guides Association.

HALF DOME (United States) A granite monolith in YOSEMITE. The 2,000-ft (610-m) northwest FACE was first climbed in 1957 by Royal ROBBINS, and is a centerpiece of AMERICAN BIG WALL TECHNIQUE.

HALF-ROPE A rope of one-third inch (nine mm) or less, as used in double rope technique, and which is intended to be used with a second half-rope to create a strong rope system. (See ROPE TECHNIQUES.)

HAMMER See ROCK HAMMER or ICE HAMMER.

HAMMOCK A nylon hammock designed for hanging BIVOUACS on cliffs. Originally, hammocks used on BIG WALL CLIMBS were garden-variety mesh hammocks. In the 1970s Chouinard Equipment (United States) manufactured the Peapod, a ripstop nylon and webbing hammock. This two-point hammock required ANCHORS at either end for suspension. The more versatile single-point hammock by Forrest Mountaineering (United States) consisted of a nylon hammock suspended by six straps connected at a common point, allowing for suspension from one anchor. PORTALEDGES replaced hammocks as big-wall bivouac equipment during the early 1980s.

HAND JAM In FREE CLIMBING, a CRACK technique in which the hand is placed in a crack and flexed to make the hand muscles form a wedge that locks securely in a crack. Cracks of this width (about 2.5 inches/6.35 cm wide) are called hand cracks.

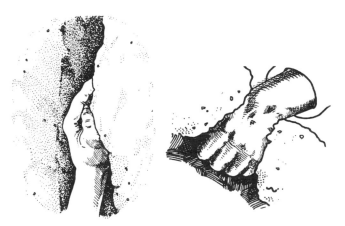

Hand Jams

HAND STACKING In FREE CLIMBING a CRACK CLIMBING technique used on wide cracks in which one hand is locked beside the other (usually clenched as a fist) by squeezing both hands against the sides of the crack.

HAND TRAVERSE A strenuous TRAVERSE with holds for the hands but not for the feet.

HANGDOGGING A FREE CLIMBING and SPORT CLIMBING term originating in the United States in the 1980s. It was originally a derogatory term describing an ascent on which the LEADER hung on PROTECTION to rehearse MOVES. Purists at the time believed this style was a form of aid and hence cheating, but hangdoggers called it an effective way of rehearsing very hard moves for an eventual no-falls (RED POINT) ascent. The debate over the morality of hangdogging versus the traditional ETHIC that every climb should be made from the ground up was the subject of many magazine articles in the United States. The 1987 AMERICAN ALPINE CLUB meeting gathered activists from both ethical standpoints to discuss the subject in "The Great Debate." While the debate raged in the United States, European free climbing standards rapidly rose as a result of widespread hangdogging tactics. This observation, and the desire to excel in CLIMBING COMPETITIONS, led many top U.S. and British climbers to recant TRADITIONALIST beliefs and adopt hangdogging to raise their own standards. By the 1990s the style is widespread throughout the United States if not universally accepted. In current vernacular, to "dog a route" is to climb from BOLT TO BOLT, resting on bolts to work out moves.

HANGER   See BOLT HANGER.

HANGING BELAY   Or hanging stance. A BELAY location with no ledge to stand on, forcing the belayer to hang from the ANCHOR, supported by the HARNESS or a BELAY SEAT.

HANGING BIVOUAC   A BIVOUAC, usually on a BIG WALL, where there is no ledge to sleep on and where HAMMOCKS or PORTA-LEDGES must be suspended from ANCHORS. An airy way to sleep.

HANGING GLACIER   A subsidiary GLACIER set on a mountainside above the main glacier. They are often unstable, having ice cliffs that break away and sweep the valley below.

HANGING STOVE   A stove and pot arrangement that can be suspended by a light chain or cable from an anchor or from the inside of a tent. Useful for alpinists who must BIVOUAC on cramped ledges, in BIVOUAC TENTS or on HANGING BIVOUACS. (See STOVES AND FUEL.)

HARAMOSH RANGE   (Pakistan)   South of the RAKAPOSHI RANGE and sandwiched between the Shigar River in the north and east, and the Indus River Valley in the south is this range of the Lesser Karakoram. The snowy massif of Haramosh (24,301 ft/7,409 m), some 70 miles (112 km) north of the town of Gilgit, dominates the range. Though it was the east ridge of Haramosh that led three Austrians to the top in 1958, a grueling and ill-fated attempt in 1957 by a British–New Zealand team led by Tony Streather was immortalized in Ralph Barker's *The Last Blue Mountain* (1960). Haramosh's west ridge (Japanese, 1978) and the difficult 12,000-ft (3,658-m) southwest face (Polish, 1988) have also been climbed.

HARDMAN   An archaic term popular in BRITAIN and to some degree in the United States in the 1960s and 1970s, meaning a good, or hard, climber.

HARDING, WARREN   **(1924–   )**   **(United States)** In the summer of 1957 Warren Harding and a couple of friends launched themselves on the smooth faces of EL CAPITAN, YOSEMITE, stopping after seven days and 1,000 ft (305 m) of climbing. The 3,000-ft (915-m) route was finished in November of the following year, after Harding rejected a misguided rescue effort. On the final, 11th, day he drilled 28 BOLTS on the headwall, climbing by headlamp in an all-night push. Many regard this FIRST ASCENT of El Cap as the climb that ushered in the era of true BIG WALL CLIMBING in the Yosemite Valley. Until that moment the longest climb was on HALF DOME. In 1970 Harding was back on El Capitan this time on the Wall of Early Morning Light, which he climbed with Dean Caldwell in 27 days, topping out to meet a large crowd and press. He was, briefly, a media star, appearing in ABC's "Wide World of Sports," and publishing *Downward Bound*, an off-beat autobiography. Despite his showmanship, "Batso" Harding was not really cut in the heroic mold. He was perhaps too eccentric, bizarre even. And in the end he was on the wrong side of profound ethical divisions among the Valley climbers of his day. The moral victor of the debate was Royal ROBBINS who ostentatiously removed Harding's bolts on the Wall of the Early Morning Light during a second ascent, which took six days. Robbins's draconian gesture influenced the climbing community against over-bolting. The heat around this single issue has dimmed some of Harding's significant achievements, such as his FREE-CLIMBING skills in cracks during his early days, and the part played by him in the first ascent of the east buttress of Middle Cathedral, Lost Arrow Direct, Half Dome's and Mount Watkins's south face and the Keeler Needle in Yosemite.

HARDWARE   Climbing equipment, as in "a rack of hardware." PITONS, NUTS, FRIENDS and CARABINERS are examples of hardware, though the expression originally referred to pitons that were repeatedly hammered in and out of cracks during a climb, and had to be hard to withstand the hammering.

HARGREAVES, ALISON   **(1962–1995) (Britain)**   The first woman to climb both Mount Everest and K2 without supplementary oxygen, Hargreaves died on her descent from K2 during a wind storm in 1995. Hargreaves grew up in Derbyshire, England with a great love for climbing. At 18 she dropped out of school and married Jim Balland. In the early eighties she pioneered a new route up Kantega in the Himalayas with Americans Jeff LOWE, Tom FROST and Marc Twight. She also became the first to scale all of the North Faces of the ALPS in one summer (the MATTERHORN, GRANDES JORASSES, EIGER, DRU, Badille and Cima Grande) solo. Hargreaves captured her experiences of that summer in her book *A Hard Day's Summer*.

HARLIN, JOHN ELVIS II   **(1935–1966) (United States)** Known for his ascents in the French and Swiss Alps, especially the EIGER, Harlin was president of the Stanford University Alpine Club, climbed in YOSEMITE and made first ascents in CANADA and Castle Crags, CALIFORNIA while in college. Graduating in Fine Art, he served as a fighter pilot in the U.S. Air Force, till 1963. When stationed in Bernkastel, Germany, in 1959, he took to ALPINISM, becoming the first American to climb the Eiger north face (1962). He developed a reputation as a leading alpinist and proponent of the DIRETTISSIMA approach to the problems of the era, climbing routes like Aiguille du Fou south face (with Tom FROST, Gary HEMMING and Stewart Fulton); Aiguille du DRU west face (with Royal ROBBINS); Monch north face (with Martin Epp); and Freney Pillar on MONT BLANC (with Chris BONINGTON, Don WHILLANS and others). After leaving the Air Force he moved his family to Leysin, Switzerland, where he taught at the American School and founded the International School of Modern Mountaineering (now International School of Mountaineering). He then began numerous attempts on a direct route on the north face of the Eiger, the first new route to be attempted since the 1938 route. His name became synonymous with the mountain—he once received a postcard addressed simply "Eiger John, Switzerland." In February 1966 he began what was to be a nine-day alpine-style ascent of the wall with partners Layton KOR and Dougal HASTON. Bad weather hampered the ascent, and soon a team of eight Germans set off with ambitions for the same route. With an element of competition and worldwide media attention the parties resorted to seige-style climbing, using FIXED ROPES to compensate for some of the worst weather in Eiger-climbing history. On March 22 the rope Harlin was ascending broke and he fell 4,000 ft (1,220 m) to his death. Harlin's partners and the Germans completed the route, naming it the John Harlin Route. Author James Ramsey Ullman wrote Harlin's biography, *Straight Up* (1967). Harlin himself was writing a book, *Introspection Through Adventure*, at the time of his death. His son, John Elvis Harlin III, became a climber, writer and editor of *Summit* Magazine (United States).

HARNESS

Or sit harness, seat harness. A WEBBING waist belt with integral leg-loops into which the ROPE is tied. In all climbing activities—FREE CLIMBING, AID CLIMBING, MOUNTAINEERING, GLACIER travel, RAPPELLING or PRUSIKING—a harness is the safest link between climber and rope. The harness is a comparatively recent innovation. As recently as the 1950s climbers simply tied the rope around their waist. The SWAMI BELT waist tie (several loops of webbing tied around the waist, but no leg loops) appeared during the 1960s, but this was only a slight improvement over the hazards of tying directly into the rope, as a climber hanging by the waist will quickly suffocate from the pressure the rope or swami exerts around the ribs. The appearance of separate leg loops solved that hazard, and by the 1970s the availability of wide webbing allowed climbers to tie their own harnesses. Early one-piece sewn harnesses, like the WHILLANS Harness, were a breakthrough, but they were heavy and uncomfortable during falls. Modern rock-climbing harnesses are light and comfortable.

A typical harness has a wide padded waist belt that either locks around the waist by means of a buckle, or tied together with a loop of webbing. Leg loops may or may not be padded, adjustable or detachable from the waist belt. On some harnesses, a strong WEBBING loop at the waist is used for clipping in belay or rappel devices, however the rope itself is directly attached to the waist belt and leg loops, with either a bowline or FIGURE-EIGHT KNOT. Harnesses for alpine climbing are usually lighter and simpler. Equipment loops are usually provided at points around the waist of a harness. A well-made, properly fitting harness distributes the load of a fall across the waist belt and leg loops. Strong sewing and materials make harnesses virtually free of structural failure. However, in some falls it is possible to be flipped backward or upside down, and to hit the head. A full body harness, or combined waist harness with chest harness, supports the climber in a more upright position and prevents the climber from being flipped backward. Though the safest type of harness, they are cumbersome and seldom used. Harnesses are built differently by each manufacturer. It is important to follow specific tie-in and buckle instructions provided with a harness.

HARPER, WALTER (1892–1918) (United States)

On June 7, 1913, Harper, a 21-year-old halfblooded Athabaskan Indian, became the first man to step atop DENALI. He was the only climber not sick that day and when he looked to the south, he began laying plans to climb Mount FORAKER. Unfortunately, while en route to medical school in 1918, Harper and his new bride drowned when their ferry sank. Hudson STUCK named the GLACIER above the Muldrow after Harper.

HARRIS, ALAN (1944–1981) (Britain)

Inspirational climbing companion whose Welsh cottage, Bryn Bigil near Llanberis, was a clubhouse to several generations of Welsh climbers. Harris's freewheeling, devil-may-care attitudes embodied the most intensely lived version of the radical spirit that informed and sustained British climbing from the end of World War II to the onset of the humourless philistinism and aggressive materialism of the 1980s. A technical rock-climber of exceptional natural ability and near-total indolence, some of Harris's boulder-problems at Fachwen were masterpieces years ahead of their time. On visits to Yosemite, he managed ON-SIGHT ascents of the hardest problems (Bacharcracker, for example) of his day as well as fast times on the classic routes on EL CAPITAN. But it is as the most joyful and vibrant instigator of fun and provider of hospitality—despite a life spent on the continual brink of poverty—that he will be remembered. His death, inevitably, was in a car crash on his way to a party on a wet autumn night, his funeral the biggest wake international climbing has ever seen.
Further reading: Jim Perrin, "Prankster, maniac, hero, saint and fool" in *On & Off the Rocks* (1986).

HARRER, HEINRICH (1912–) (Austria)

Harrer is best known for making the FIRST ASCENT of the north face of the EIGER (1938), and the seven years he spent in TIBET in the 1940s, where he befriended the young and 14th Dalai Lama. These and subsequent travels have earned him recognition as one of the great explorers and adventurers of the century. His best-known book, *Seven Years in Tibet* (1953) has sold 3 million copies in nearly 50 languages since publication. It recounts his escape from a British internment camp in INDIA (where he was placed in 1939 when war broke out while he was a member of a German reconnaissance expedition to climb NANGA PARBAT), his two-year TRAVERSE of Tibet with partner Peter Aufschnaiter, and his subsequent five years in Lhasa, where he became a ranked member of the Tibetan government. He left Lhasa in 1950 when Communist Chinese forces invaded Tibet. More recently Harrer wrote *Lost Lhasa: Heinrich Harrer's Tibet* (1992). This historical record contains 200 of his 3,000 photos taken in Tibet during his residency. Among mountaineers, Harrer is known as the author of *The White Spider: The History of the Eiger's North Face* (1958; revised 1989).

Before climbing the Eiger in 1938 Harrer made hundreds of first ascents in the DOLOMITES. After leaving Tibet he made first ascents of Ausengate (PERU), and Mounts Drum, Deborah and HUNTER (ALASKA), in 1954. He then pursued cultural exploration, journeying in the Congo (1957), making the first crossing of New Guinea (1961–62, considered by Harrer as his hardest expedition), traveling in Amazonia to study the Huka Huka people (1966), French Guyana (1969), GREENLAND (1970), Sudan (1971), the first north-south traverse of Borneo (1972) and many Himalayan journeys. He maintained his friendship with the Dalai Lama during the latter's exile from Tibet and worked for Tibetan rights. On Harrer's 80th birthday the Dalai Lama visited Harrer's birthplace, Huttemberg, in the Carinthian region of Austria to bless the Heinrich Harrer Museum. Harrer's extensive collection on Tibet is housed in the University of Zurich. His awards include the Gold Medal of the Eiger, the Great Cross of Honor of Germany, the Austrian Cross of Honor for Art and Science, the Alexander von Humboldt Award and the Explorer's Medal of the Explorer's Club (United States).

HASTON, DOUGAL (1940–1977) (Britain) Generally accepted as the finest British ALPINIST of the late 1960s and early 1970s, Dougal Haston was one of a gifted generation of Scottish climbers who came together in Edinburgh University (where he read philosophy) Mountaineering Club at the end of the 1950s. Initially overshadowed by Robin SMITH, after Smith's death in 1962 he blossomed into the most competent and forceful British mountaineer of his time, particularly after his dogged performance on the international EIGER Direct climb of 1966, on which John HARLIN II died. His conviction for causing death by dangerous driving (he served two months of a prison sentence) in 1964 appears to have had a galvanizing effect on his character, and after the Eiger climb Haston took over the high-profile role left vacant by Harlin's death as director of the International School of Mountaineering in Leysin, Switzerland. His ascent of the south face of ANNAPURNA with Don WHILLANS in 1970 was epoch-making, and was followed by expeditions in successive years to EVEREST's southwest face, on which he PERFORMED with

great skill and determination. He climbed CHANGABANG in 1974, and in 1975 he and Doug SCOTT were finally successful on the southwest face line—becoming, the first Britons to reach the summit of EVEREST. Five months later the same pair made a rapid ascent of the south face of DENALI, and plans were being made for trips to The OGRE and K2 when he was engulfed by a small snow-slide while out skiing near Leysin in January 1977. An intense and sometimes aloof character, he wrote three books, the last of them a novel (*Calculated Risk*), underpinned by a crass and jejune Nietzscheanism.

Further reading: Dougal Haston, *In High Places* (1972).

HASTON, STEVIE (1957–   ) (Britain) Precocious young Anglo-Maltese climber who developed into one of the outstanding rock-terrorists and alpine soloists of the 1980s. He made the first solo ascent of the north face of the Col du Plan in the winter of 1973 at the age of 16, had soloed the north face of the EIGER by the age of 20 and proceeded to reel off a string of first solo ascents, FIRST WINTER ASCENTS and first winter solos in the ALPS and elsewhere thereafter. On British rock he produced a remarkable clutch of technically desperate, outlandishly strenuous and appallingly serious climbs through the crumbling overhangs of Yellow Wall on Anglesey's South Stack—Isis Is Angry can stand for many of the same ilk—some of which are still unrepeated 10 years on, and none of which seem destined for widespread popularity.

HAUL BAG Or haul sack. A sturdy, large-capacity sack hauled up a big wall and used to carry food, water and BIVOUAC gear.

HAULING Or sack hauling. The odious task of dragging a pack or HAUL BAG up a climb. On multiday BIG WALL CLIMBS where hundreds of pounds of food, water and bivouac gear are needed, the Yosemite hauling technique is required. The system requires a strong ANCHOR. The haul rope is run through a PULLEY and clipped to the anchor. The leader clamps an ASCENDER directly into his HARNESS. The haul rope is pulled through the ascender which pulls all slack through the pulley. On the other side of the pulley a second ascender is clamped to the haul rope upside down and also clipped to the anchor. This ascender locks the rope from sliding back through the pulley. The leader hauls by standing in ETRIERS and pushing away from the cliff, using his weight to move the haul bag. When the bag is unweighted from the lower belay the SECOND unclips it and lowers it out on a trail rope. When the bag reaches the upper belay it is clipped to a sturdy anchor. Stresses on pulleys and anchors are considerable.

HAUTE ROUTE French for high level route. The original haute route was a long ski route connecting high mountain passes, GLACIERS, and huts in the ALPS, from CHAMONIX, France, to Zermatt, Switzerland. The route was first TRAVERSED in 1861 by members of Britain's Alpine Club.

Waist Hauling the Bag

HAUTE SAVOIE ALPS **(France)** This describes the large area between Lake Geneva and the north side of the CHAMONIX valley. The biggest mountains are the Dents du Midi (10,682 ft/3,257 m) above Champéry. The Brévent téléphérique from Chamonix carries tourists and climbers alike to the top of the range's other great attraction—the Aiguilles Rouges. The area also has a wealth of low-lying limestone crags that offer those with less inclination to climb in the mountains a significant challenge. The cliffs at Sallanches are over 656 ft (200 m) high.

HAY TOR AND **LOW MAN** **(Britain)** In contrast to the dramatic coastline of north DEVON, the granite tors of Dartmoor provide climbing similar to GRITSTONE. Hay Tor and Low Man lie in open moorland above the road between Widecombe and Bovey Tracey. At 150 ft (45 m), Low Man has the highest rock wall on Dartmoor while the west face of Hay Tor is especially popular. The rock is rough and compact and well protected.

The crags have a longer history than most in Devon and an early classic is Raven Gully (5.6), climbed in 1949 by W. A. and R. Higgins. The great Scottish climber Tom PATEY also climbed here while stationed with the Marines nearby, climbing Vandal (5.8) in 1959 on Hay Tor and on Low Man Outward Bound (5.7) in 1960. The other great route from this period is Aviation (5.9), climbed in 1961 by D. Bassett and H. Cornish. Modern climbs include Interrogation (5.10d), freed by Mick Fowler in 1980.
Guidebook: Pat Littlejohn, *South West Climbs* (1991).

HEAD LAMP Or head torch. An essential item for climbers, especially ALPINISTS, who need reliable light when climbing at night. Numerous head lamps that strap onto helmets are made. Power sources include carbon-zinc cells that are cheap but have a short charge-life; alkaline batteries (the most popular), which outlive carbon-zinc but are less productive in the cold, working at about 20% efficiency in 0 degrees F (-18 degrees C); lithium batteries, which are light and offer double the amp/hours per unit than alkaline, remain very efficient at 0 degrees F (-18 degrees C) but are costly; and rechargeable high-capacity Nickel Cadmium (Nicad) batteries, which though very expensive can be recharged hundreds of times and resist cold well. A battery pack that can be placed in the breast pocket for warming prolongs the life of any battery. Halogen, krypton or xenon bulbs are bright but drain batteries faster. Spare bulbs of appropriate voltage and spare batteries should be carried by a climbing party.

HEADWALL A steep vertical FACE at the top of a lower BUTTRESS or formation.

HEAT ILLNESS Heat illness and heat stroke are brought on by exercise in hot temperatures. It is not uncommon among trekkers and mountaineers in high mountain areas, where reflection of heat and sunlight off mountains and GLACIERS can result in high temperatures. Onset is rapid and characterized by confusion, incoordination, delirium and, in heat stroke, unconsciousness. Convulsions may also occur. Pupils may be dilated and unresponsive to light. The skin feels hot, possibly dry, and the body temperature is elevated. Pulse and respiratory rate are increased. Efforts to lower body temperature should be immediate, and include moving the victim to a

Heelhook

signals, bright clothing or lights. Landing areas should be as flat as possible, away from trees, boulders or cliffs, and preferably on a rise and not in a depression, as touchdowns on hills or cliffs place rotor blades perilously close to obstacles. Helicopters with winches can retrieve climbers from more difficult locations. Items like packs should be secured from the wind kicked up by rotor blades. Helicopters should be approached from the front, in a crouched position. Always stay in the pilot's line of vision.

HELMETS Helmets protect the head from rockfall and injury. They are made either of Fiberglass or plastic. Fiberglass helmets tend to fit snugly around the head but are slightly heavier than plastic ones. Fiberglass absorbs massive impact forces by the breaking of the outer shell. Plastic is lighter but not as strong, transferring impact force onto a webbing cradle surrounding the head, which stretches to absorb energy. Plastic helmets sit higher on the head because of the cradle that keeps an air space between the head and helmet. Helmets should be replaced after severe impact. Ventilation holes, elastic straps for retaining HEADLAMPS and adjustability are features of helmets.

HEMMING, GARY **(1934–1970) (United States)** This American alpinist cut a romantic figure through the French climbing scene in the 1960s, though he is little known in America. He guided in CANADA and the TETONS, and moved to France in 1960 where he combined precarious jobs and university studies with climbing. On MONT BLANC he achieved the first American ascent of the Walker Spur on the north face of the GRANDES JORASSES (1962, with Henry Kendall) and a new route, the American Direct on the Petit Dru, with Royal ROBBINS. In 1963, with John HARLIN, Tom FROST and Stewart Fulton, he climbed the FIRST ASCENT of the south face of Fou. These YOSEMITE-style BIG WALL ascents were a sensation in France, and Hemming's reputation grew further with solo ascents of the Couturier Couloir on the Aiguille Verte and the north face of the Triolet. In 1966, an epic rescue of two German climbers stuck on the Dru brought media attention to Hemming. French magazines like *Paris Match* lionized his hippie personality and climbing tenacity. Hemming committed suicide on the border of Jenny Lake in Grand Teton National Park. The novel *Solo Faces* by James Salter (1979) is based on Hemming's life.
Further reading: Mirella Tenderini, *Gary Hemming* (1991).

HERO LOOP A short SLING for tying off PITONS. Also called a TIE OFF.

HERR, HUGH **(1964–   ) (United States)** A noted rock climber as a teenager in the early 1980s, Herr returned to the cutting edge of the sport as a double amputee in the mid-1980s. A native of Pennsylvania, he was the best climber in the SHAWANGUNKS by age 17. There he made FIRST ASCENTS like the dangerous Condemned Man, 5.12, and almost FLASHED Super Crack (5.12c), which he climbed on his second try. At 17, Hugh and Jeff Batzer were lost for three days after completing the ice climb Odell's Gully

cooler spot, applying cool towels or bathing the victim in cool, but not icy water. During cooling, extremities should be massaged to direct cooled blood to vital organs. Hospitalization should be sought as soon as possible. Heat stroke can be fatal.

HEELHOOK A FREE CLIMBING technique where one leg is raised high and the heel of the foot is hooked over a HOLD, while the body is supported by the arms. Heelhooking can reduce the weight hanging on the arms and conserve strength.

HELICOPTER EVACUATION Injured climbers are frequently evacuated by helicopter. In areas like the European ALPS, helicopter rescue techniques for plucking climbers from mountains are advanced, but such rescues are dangerous. Helicopter rescue is made safer if landing areas are cleared of large debris, and are marked with hand on Mount WASHINGTON, NEW HAMPSHIRE. In a winter storm they floundered through deep snow in an area called the Great Gulf till a snowshoer found them near death beneath a boulder. On the other side of the mountain a searcher, Albert Dow, died in an AVALANCHE. Herr lost both legs below the knee due to FROSTBITE. He learned to climb again on artificial legs and eventually surpassed his former abilities. He climbed many 5.12s and some 5.13s, including the 5.13 crack City Park at INDEX, Washington. While majoring in physics and biomechanical engineering at M.I.T. he created different feet and shanks to alter his height for his climbing needs, and patented a socket to ease the pain of amputees.

Further reading: Alison Osius, *Second Ascent: The Story of Hugh Herr* (1991).

HERRLIGKOFFER, KARL MARIA, DR. (1916–1991) (Germany)

In 1934 Herrligkoffer lost his half-brother, Willi MERKL, on NANGA PARBAT (PAKISTAN). This loss pointed the way for his future, moving him to organize many expeditions to Nanga Parbat. His first Nanga Parbat expedition, in 1953, was a memorial to Willi. On this trip, Hermann BUHL made the FIRST ASCENT, solo from a high camp. Though he never actually climbed or led the way (he was tactical and financial leader only) Herrligkoffer returned frequently and productively to the mountain: In 1962, Toni Kinshoffer, Anderl Mannhardt and Sigi Loew climbed Nanga Parbat's Diamir Flank; in 1970 Reinhold MESSNER and his brother Guenther summited via the Rupal Face, followed next day by Peter Scholz and Felix Kuen; in 1982 Herrligkoffer's team on the east buttress placed Ueli Buehler on top. All were first ascents.

Though not a great climber himself, his eye for a LINE on the 26,240-ft (8,000-m) peaks, and his organization and financing of expeditions led many German and international climbers to high summits. Some of his expeditions had unpleasant repercussions: Buhl (1953) and Messner (1970) clashed with Herrligkoffer over publication of their books. Messner's case ended in court. Such incidents and his autocratic leadership made him a controversial figure in mountaineering. Herrligkoffer also led successful expeditions to EVEREST (1978), KANGCHENJUNGA (1980), GREENLAND and the Arctic. He helped found the German Institute for Foreign Research in 1954 and the Deutsche Himalaya Club in 1971. His medical practice operated in Munich, and several of his expeditions served medical research. He led some 25 expeditions, published numerous books and made many documentaries of his climbs.

HERZOG, MAURICE (1919–   ) (France)

Herzog, with Louis LACHENAL, was the first man to reach the summit of an 26,240-ft (8,000-m) peak, ANNAPURNA I, on June 3, 1950. Their epic climb, without supplemental oxygen, is familiar through his book *Annapurna* (1953), which became a best-seller. Trained as a lawyer, he served in governmental posts as High Commissioner for Youth and Sport (1958–1963) and Secretary of State (1963–1966). Elective offices have included Mayor of Chamonix and Deputy to the National Assembly from Haute Savoie.

HEXENTRIC

A type of NUT introduced in 1971 by Chouinard Equipment (United States), that was a breakthrough in PROTECTION for CLEAN CLIMBING. Hexentrics are variously sized asymmetric hexagons of extruded aluminum alloy, threaded with PERLON or WEBBING or swagged with wire cable. They are an example of a passive camming device. (See CRACK PROTECTION.)

HIEBELER, TONI (1924–1984) (Germany)

Hiebeler made a mark on European MOUNTAINEERING as a climber and equipment designer (he designed the Eiger Triplex triple-boot). He was also the author of 30 mountaineering books and editor of the German climbing magazines *Bergkamarad, Alpinismus, Bersteiger* and the Swiss *Berge*. His greatest ROUTES were the FIRST WINTER ASCENT of the EIGER north face (1961), and the northwest face of the Civetta (1963). He devoted much energy to safety practices, and was instrumental in the formation of the German Alpine Club's (DAV) Safety Council. As a mountain skier he opened new HAUTE ROUTES in the DOLOMITES, Engadine and Wallis ranges. He died in a helicopter crash en route to the Julian alps, with his wife Traudl and the Yugoslavian mountaineer Ales Kunaver.

HIGH-ALTITUDE CLIMBING

The term refers to climbing in the HIMALAYA and KARAKORAM, and also lower ranges like the ALASKA range, the ANDES and Pamirs. At what altitude does high altitude begin is difficult to say, but at 16,000 ft (4,878 m) the effects of oxygen lack render climbing more difficult. High-altitude climbing is also EXPEDITION climbing, involving elaborate preparation, special equipment and long journeys to remote regions. Himalayan climbing groups traditionally hire porters or SHERPAS to carry loads to a base camp beneath the mountain objective. HIGH-ALTITUDE PORTER or Sherpas may or may not be engaged to carry loads on the mountain. Oxygen is used increasingly less by climbers than in the past but is still a facet of many climbs above 26,240 ft (8,000 m). Modern ascents of Himalayan peaks are now sometimes made in rapid times, using solo or ALPINE STYLE tactics, however traditional seige-style tactics are still the norm. Ranges outside the Himalaya and Karakoram are smaller (below 22,960 ft/7,000 m) and may be climbed with less expense and logistics by LIGHTWEIGHT EXPEDITIONS. Alaskan expeditions to DENALI and surrounding peaks rely on BUSH PILOTS to land climbers and supplies on glacier landing strips. Andean expeditions traditionally use vehicles and mules to ferry equipment to base camp. Expeditions to the Pamirs and other Soviet ranges are helicopter supported. Other aspects of high-altitude climbing are discussed in ACCLIMATIZATION, ACUTE MOUNTAIN SICKNESS, ALTITUDE MEDICINE, CEREBRAL EDEMA, EIGHT-THOUSAND-METER PEAKS, OXYGEN APPARATUS, PULMONARY EDEMA, RETINAL HEMORRHAGE.

HIGH-ALTITUDE PORTER (HAP)

Not to be confused with the SHERPAS of NEPAL, HAP is the term for Pakistani or Indian climbing porters who are paid load-carriers on high-altitude peaks. Pakistani HAPs are mainly Hunza and BALTI village men. Most Indian HAPs are villagers of the GARWHAL HIMALAYA. Several Pakistani HAPS have summited 26,240-ft (8,000-m) peaks.

HIGH POINT   The highest point reached during an attempt on a rock climb or mountain.

HIGH TOR (Britain)   This spectacular sheet of white limestone lies just outside the town of Matlock above the A6 road to Buxton. It was once an AID-CLIMBING cliff but since the late 1960s it has become an impressive FREE-CLIMBING venue of the PEAK DISTRICT. Matlock provides services. Sheffield and Manchester are nearby.

It was the imaginative and controversial Ed DRUMMOND who illustrated the potential for harder routes here by climbing I Darius (5.9) with one aid in 1970. In the mid-1970s, Pete LIVESEY freed the fingery and bold Bastille, formerly A3 but now 5.12. The gritstone genius John ALLEN and his gifted partner Steve Bancroft freed the huge OVER-HANG of Castellan (5.12a). In the early 1980s the remaining major gaps were filled by, among others, Ron FAWCETT's Roadrunner and Dominic and Daniel Lee's Mad Max, both 5.12.

High Tor is 200 ft (61 m) at its highest. Protection is a mixture of small wires, former aid pegs and BOLTS. Pic Tor is a small and worthwhile limestone crag in the lee of High Tor.

Guidebooks: BMC, *Peak Limestone—South* (1987); Paul Nunn, *Rock Climbing in the Peak District* (1987).

HILL, LYNN (1961–   ) (United States)   The fore-most American female rock climber for a decade, and the world's leading female competition climber in the latter 1980s, Hill was co-winner (with Isabelle PATISSIER) of the 1990 World Cup title and was first in the 1989 ASCI (Association of Sport Climbers International) rankings. She has FLASHED hundreds of 5.12s, and some 5.13a routes. Her achievements include risky FIRST ASCENTS and BIG WALL CLIMBS in YOSEMITE, but she is best known for being the first woman to climb 5.14, in 1990, with her ascent of Masse Critique (8b+ or 5.14a) at CIMAI, France. The 75-ft (22.8-m) route took her nine days to RED POINT. She also made the hardest first ascent by a woman, Running Man, 5.13d, in the SHAWANGUNKS in 1989, and in 1980 did the first ascent of Ophir Broke (5.12d/5.13a) in OPHIR.

As of this writing, Hill has won 20 world competitions, including the Rockmaster at ARCO, Italy (perhaps the sport's premier event), four times and the Masters Invitational at Bercy three times. Among Hill's other wins are the Masters of Maurienne, a World Masters Tour event, in France in 1991; the International Escalade at St. Jean de Maurienne, France, in 1990; and world events in Germany at Munich, 1989; Nuremberg, 1989; and Stuttgart, 1991. In BUOUX, France, in 1989, Hill took an 82-ft (25-m) groundfall when she neglected to finish knotting her ROPE through her HARNESS. She dislocated her elbow and fractured her foot, yet recovered by autumn to win the World Cup at Lyon. Hill competed on the same route as the four men superfinalists, and her performance would have placed her third among them. The win also clinched her first place in

the overall ASCI rankings for the year. At a contest in Lyon, France, 1990, she flashed the women's superfinal route, which served as the men's final and from which all but two men fell.

Although in recent seasons other contestants have closed the ability gap, Hill won the 1991 World Cup at Barcelona, Spain. This final win created a tie between Hill and Patissier. The French federation protested that in the case of a tie, each woman's slated throw-out competition (worst result) should be counted, in which case Patissier would win. The American federation (the American Alpine Club) defended Hill's position. After a year of review, the UIAA announced that the tie would hold, confirming Hill and Patissier as co-champions.

HILLARY, SIR EDMUND (1920–   ) (New Zealand)   In 1953 Hillary became the first man to step atop Mount EVEREST, with Sherpa Tenzing Norgay. He also climbed high on MAKALU, performed important high-altitude medical research and drove to the South Pole on a tractor. When a SHERPA said: "Our children have eyes, but they are blind," Hillary began building more than a dozen schools and hospitals throughout NEPAL. Most recently, he helped create Sagarmartha National Park, which surrounds Everest.

HIMALAYA   See ASSAM HIMALAYA, BHUTAN, CHINA, IN-DIA, KASHMIR, KISHTWAR HIMALAYA, KULU-LAHUL HIMA-LAYA, KUMAUN-GARWHAL HIMALAYA, LANGTANG HIMALAYA, MANSIRI HIMALAYA, PAKISTAN.

HINDU KUSH (Pakistan-Afghanistan)   This great KARAKORAM range contains 30 summits above 22,960 ft (7,000 m) and is shared by PAKISTAN and Afghanistan. It was popular among small expeditions during the 1960s and 1970s, but since the Soviet invasion of Afghanistan in 1979 and the subsequent turmoil, mountaineering ceas ed in the western Hindu Kush of Afghanistan. The eastern Hindu Kush of Pakistan remained open. The HinduKush is divided into several subsections: the Northern Hindu Kush (the highest peak here being Koh-e-Urgend at 23,085 ft/7,038 m); the Saragharar Group (with the Saraghrar massif, 24,104 ft/7,349 m); the Noshaq Group (with Noshaq, 24,574 ft/7,492 m); the Istor-O-Nal Group (with Istor-O-Nal, 24,282 ft/7,403 m) and the Tirich Mir Group. These mountains run north to south, beginning on the west of the Karambar River in Pakistan. The Tirich Mir Group, near the town of Chitral, is perhaps the most frequented by climbers, with the massif of Tirich Mir (25,276 ft/7,706 m) the dominant mountain. This peak was first climbed via the south ridge in 1950 by Norwegians. Numerous other routes have been made to the five summits of this massif, which includes a steep northwest face. Before the Soviet invasion the Afghan Hindu Kush received much attention by Polish expeditions. Some early ALPINE STYLE ascents of technically difficult peaks occurred in the Hindu Kush. The northeast face of Koh-e-Bandaka (22,450 ft/6,845 m), climbed in 1977 by Wojciech KURTYKA, Alex MACINTYRE and John Porter is an example.

Further reading: Jill Neate, *High Asia* (1989).

HIRAYAMA, YUJI (1969–   ) (Japan) Hirayama learned to climb in Japan, then moved to France to climb in 1986 at the age of 17. He ON-SIGHTED Orange Méchanique (8a or 5.13b) in CIMAI at the age of 19, and two years later made what remains rare, an on-sight of an 8a+, 5.13c, Les Néophytes in the VERDON. His hardest RED POINT is Le Rage de Vivre (8b+, 5.14a) at BUOUX. He has also done Les Spécialistes (8b/c, 5.14a) in the Verdon. Hirayama has a relaxed, natural, smooth style. Largely unknown, he surprised the crowd at a World Cup competition in Nuremberg in 1989 when he snagged the win from the top climbers there. In 1990, he won an invitational in Tokyo attended by the top climbers, and was second at a World Masters Tour invitational in Briançon and at the 1990 World Cup at Nuremberg. In 1991 he won the invitational Rockmaster at ARCO, Italy, and the World Cup at Tokyo, placing second overall in the World Cup standings.

HISPAR MUZTAGH   (Pakistan) This range of lofty KARAKORAM peaks begins at the gorge of the Hunza River (near the village of Nagar), extends north past the Hispar Glacier and ends at the head basin of the BIAFO GLACIER. Some of the highest peaks of the Greater Karakoram lie in this range. Among them are Trivor (25,348 ft/7,728 m), first climbed via the north ridge by the 1960 British-American expedition that included Don WHILLANS; Disteghil Sar (25,863 ft/7,885 m), climbed via the south face and west ridge by Austrians in 1960; and Disteghil Sar East (25,243 ft/ 7,696 m) climbed by Poles in 1980. Khunyang Chhish (25,754 ft/7,852 m) was climbed via the south face in 1971 by Poles; Pumari Chhish (24,574 ft/7,492 m), via the north ridge in 1979 by Japanese, Yukshin Gardan Sar (24,698 ft/7,530 m), via the south ridge by Austrians in 1984; and Kanjut Sar (25,453 ft/7,760 m), was climbed via the south ridge in 1959 by Italians. The area is heavily glaciated. The Hispar Glacier with its connection to the *Biafo* Glacier (over the 16,892-ft/5,150-m Hispar Pass) forms a passage of ice 76 miles (122 km) long.

HOAR FROST Delicate feathery ice crystals that cling to rocks and trees in moist, freezing conditions. Hoar frost is seldom a problem to climbers unless covered by a crust of snow, in which case the hoar frost and the snow may form an unstable, AVALANCHE-prone layer.

HOLD Any rock edge on a rock climb on which fingers and toes are placed or gripped.

HOOD, MOUNT   (United States) Until the 1980 eruption of Mount SAINT HELENS, this 11,239-ft/3,426-m volcano was probably the most frequently climbed glaciated peak in North America. Located 50 miles (80 km) east of Portland, OREGON, Mount Hood presides over the Columbia River Gorge and most of northwestern Oregon. Although it had some volcanic activity during the 1800s, there has been little visible activity since 1907. Nonetheless, it is one of the more active CASCADE RANGE volcanoes, with several fumaroles within its eroded crater, and it is considered by some geologists as very likely to erupt.

The first accepted ascent of Mount Hood was by W. S. Buckley, W. L. Chittenden, James Deardorff, H. L. Pittock and L. J. Powell in 1857. Thomas Dryer, publisher of *The Oregonian* (who made the FIRST ASCENT of Mount Saint Helens) claimed the ascent in 1854, but later parties proved he had not reached the summit. Thousands of people climbed the mountain prior to 1900. The Mazamas club of Portland, Oregon, (see Appendices) was formed on the summit in 1894, when 193 climbers made the ascent. The climb has been made by a woman wearing high heels, a gibbon, dogs, children and disabled persons. However, despite its easy climbing, Mount Hood has claimed many lives. Weather is a frequent factor, along with AVALANCHES, rockfall and falls from its steeper slopes. During poor weather and WHITE-OUT conditions, climbers regularly become temporarily lost in the "Mount Hood Triangle" while descending the south side to historic Timberline Lodge. Many of Hood's routes can be climbed in one day from the lodge. Routes on the north face are steeper and more challenging. Yocum Ridge is Mount Hood's most difficult route, and it must be climbed when it is covered in ice because of Hood's loose rock. A year-round ski lift is in operation from Timberline Lodge on Mount Hood's south slope. Climbing parties are encouraged to register before their climb.

Further reading: Jeff Smoot, *A Climber's Guide to the Cascade Volcanoes* (1992); Jeff Thomas, *Oregon High: A Climbing Guide to Nine Cascade Volcanoes* (1991).

HOOKING In AID CLIMBING, to use skyhooks. (See SKYHOOK.)

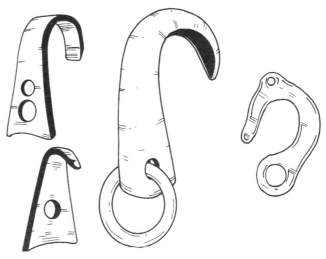

Types of Hooks

HORN A rock spike, like a BOLLARD.

HORNBEIN, THOMAS F., DR.   (1930–   ) (United States) Raised in St. Louis, Hornbein started climbing in the COLORADO Rockies while a student at Colorado University in BOULDER in the 1950s and pioneered many FIRST ASCENTS in the Estes Park and LONG'S PEAK area. During his medical training, he turned his attention to the HIMALAYA, climbing MASHERBRUM (1960), and EVEREST (1963) on which he and Willie UNSOELD made a bold first ascent of the west ridge. While descending they met Lute Jerstad and Barry Bishop who had just summited via the original route, and the four bivouacked at over 27,880 ft (8,500 m) before reaching the south col the next day. It was the first TRAVERSE of the peak and was a bold adventure. Hornbein's medical career later took precedence in his life. At the University of Washington in Seattle he has been professor and chairman of the Department of Anesthesiology. He wrote *Everest: The West Ridge* (1965).

HORSETOOTH RESERVOIR   (United States)   West of Fort Collins, COLORADO lie extensive OUTCROPS of Dakota sandstone. These short cliffs and boulders offer excellent BOULDERING and TOP ROPING. John Gill created many extreme short climbs here. They can still be identified by small painted arrows at the foot of steep and sometimes impossible looking faces. (See FRONT RANGE.)
Guidebook: Bob Horan, *Front Range Bouldering* (1990).

HOUSE, WILLIAM   (1913–   ) (United States)   An American climber active during the 1930s and 1940s, House first climbed in Switzerland as a teenager, then in Connecticut and NEW HAMPSHIRE with the Yale Mountaineering Club while a forestry student. He also took to ice climbing, leading the second full ascent of Huntington Ravine's Pinnacle Gully in winter 1934. His mettle as a technical climber attracted the attention of Fritz WIESSNER, and together they made the FIRST ASCENTS of Mount WADDINGTON (CANADA, 1936), and DEVILS TOWER (WYOMING, 1937). In 1938 House joined Charles HOUSTON's expedition attempting the first ascent of the southeast ridge of K2, the world's second-highest mountain. The expedition was unsuccessful but the party pioneered much difficult climbing. One PITCH led by House—a fissure penetrating a rock wall at 22,000 ft (6,707 m)—is still called House's Chimney, and stood for many years as one of the most difficult pieces of technical climbing achieved at high altitude. During World War II House helped the Army develop cold weather and mountaineering equipment. In winter 1946 he made a 3,400-mile (5,471-km) TRAVERSE of the Canadian north by tractor. In 1947 he returned to the field of forestry, and became prominent in that profession.

HOUSTON, CHARLES S., DR.   (1913–   )   Respected by climbers and doctors around the world as the grandfather of high-altitude medicine, Houston wrote, *Going Higher* and *K2: The Savage Mountain*. In addition to two early attempts on K2 in 1938 and 1953, Houston made the first ascent of ALASKA's Mount FORAKER in 1934, and would have summited on INDIA's NANDA DEVI in 1936 but for a can of tainted meat. In 1950, while accompanying his father and friends, Houston and Bill Tilman became the first westerners to reconnoiter EVEREST's south col route.

HUANDOY   (Peru)   In myth, Huandi was an Indian princess, executed by her own people for loving the prince of an enemy tribe. Petrified, both lovers became the mountains Huandoy and HUASCARAN. Huandi is a crown of four peaks, three of which are visible from the Santa valley where Huandoy is steepest. Farmers named them Tulparaju, "The Herd." Austrian-Germans and Americans have divided the FIRST ASCENTS among them. The men in the famous Austrian expedition, Erwin Heln and Erwin SCHNEIDER climbed in 1932 the highest, Huandoy Norte (20,981 ft/6,395 m). They did so trusting to their good luck that a huge SERAC above their route would not fall that day. It did not, but when the climbers returned a few weeks later it had crashed down. In 1952, four Americans under Allen Steck climbed the symmetrical Huandoy Este (20,000 ft/6,097 m). The key to reaching the main group of Huandoy is to reach the ice plateau at 19,000 (5,793 m) among the three western peaks. Americans did this in 1954 to climb Huandoy Oeste (20,853 ft/6,356 m). In 1955, the German Huber expedition also reached the plateau and climbed Huandoy Sur (20,210 ft/6,160 m). New routes on Huandi's mountains have always meant steep ice faces. Since 1955, 18 new routes have appeared and have been described in guidebooks, as well as in the *American Alpine Journal*. The boldest was the work of Frenchman Nicholas JAEGER, who in 1978 soloed the southwest side of Huandoy Oeste overcoming, always alone, near-vertical ice walls.
Guidebooks: Jim Bartle and David Sharman, *Trails and Climbs of the Cordillera Blanca of Peru* (1992); John Ricker, *Yuraq Janka* (1981).

Evelio Echevarria
Colorado State University

HUASCARAN, NEVADO   (Peru)   The name of PERU's highest mountain literally means "purple," possibly for the reflection of its snows at sunset. But Indian legends also refer to Huascar, a local prince executed on the spot where the mountain now stands. It is a spectacular mass rising more than 10,000 ft (3,049 m) above the floor of the Santa Valley in northern Peru. Its granite rock, crowned by GLACIERS, culminates in two DOMES: Huascaran Sur (22,205 ft/6,769 m) and Huascaran Norte (21,831 ft/6,654 m), respectively the fourth- and the ninth-highest peaks in the New World. The name was also given to the Parque Nacional Huascaran, actually the national park of the CORDILLERA BLANCA. The mountain first entered mountaineering history when the American Annie PECK, vowing to outdo men, launched several attempts to ascend it. On September 2, 1908, she and her two Swiss guides won the summit of Huascaran Norte. Huascaran Sur was climbed on July 20, 1932, by the Austro-German Borchers expedition. Ascents to both summits became commonplace in the late 1950s, but new routes, frequently sought, have represented long and difficult work. On Huascaran Norte, French climbers have monopolized the exposed RIDGES and BUTTRESSES of the north wall (1966, 1972, 1973; Italians in 1974), while Renato CASAROTTO soloed the awesome north wall itself. On Huascaran Sur Americans led by Leigh Ortenburger climbed in 1958 the southwest glacier. In 1961, Spaniards went over the long northeast ridge and in 1961 Canadians ascended the west ridge, apparently less laborious and the shortest, safest route of all. The first TRAVERSE was accomplished in 1971 by New Zealanders, while Australians were climbing the southeast face. In 1977, four Austro-Germans went up the east-southeast ridge. But the ample east face is now the main price and may remain so for some time. Two very exposed routes were opened in 1972 by Austrians under E. Koblmuller and in 1991 by two Americans. Much remains to be done on this spacious face, a veritable curtain of rock crowned by ice, but few will be willing to brave a combination of near-vertical walls and a bombardment of rocks. The mountain also acquired a sinister reputation for the mud avalanches it released in 1962 and again in 1970, burying towns and killing no less than 21,000 people.

Guidebooks: Philippe Beaud, *The Peruvian Andes* (1988); John Ricker, *Yuraq Janca* (1981).

HUECO TANKS (United States)

Regarded as one of the world's most aesthetic free-climbing areas, this complex plug of syenite porphyry is located on a 4,000-ft (1,220-m) desert plateau in Texas, 30 miles (48 km) east of El Paso. A wide range of climbing is found here, including CRACKS, ROOFS, SLABS, steep faces and BOLTED sport routes, but it is the plentitude of strenuous, technical BOULDERING—mostly pioneered in the 1980s and onward by locals Bob Murray, Mike Head and John Sherman—that has garnered Hueco's reputation as an international FREE-CLIMBING destination. So famous is Hueco rock—especially its unique spherical POCKET holds—that the term *hueco* is used worldwide to define any deep, incut jug. In Hueco's arid climate rainfall is minimal, winters are cold, summers are hot but not humid. The prime climbing season is November through March. Placement of bolts or PITONS is strictly controlled here by Hueco Tanks State Park. Roped climbing was banned altogether in the park in 1988, but restored in 1989, with the following stringent restrictions governing fixed protection and bew routes:

All routes, lead or top rope, must be applied for.

Only one application per applicant can be submitted during a review period (one month).

Only the applicant will be eligible to place the gear on the route, if approved.

Applicant with an approved route is ineligible to submit another application until the previous one is led by applicant.

All gear (ropes, quickdraws, etc.) left on climbs more than 24 hours is subject to confiscation by the park.

All routes under 30 feet (nine millimeters) will be considered as top rope problems only.

All gear will be painted brown to match the rock color.

Applications will be processed on a first come, first through basis.

Guidebooks: John Sherman, et al, *Hueco Tanks, A Climber's and Boulderers Guide* (1991).

HUNT, LORD JOHN (1910–   ) (Britain)

John Hunt, then a colonel in the British Army, was leader—appointed amid controversy—of the British expedition to Mount EVEREST in 1953 which succeeded in putting the SHERPA Tenzing Norgay and his New Zealander companion Ed HILLARY on top of Everest. This success was the culmination of a campaign fought, with breaks for war and political secession, over more than 30 years. "I was able to supply an element of military pragmatism," Hunt wrote of his own part in the proceedings, aptly summing them up.

Elder son of an Indian Army officer who was killed in the first months of World War I, Hunt's career in the army and public service was most distinguished. He went to Everest in 1953 with impressive credentials, despite having been outside the mainstream of Himalayan and alpine climbing in the preceding decades. His attempt on Peak 36—Kangri Peak in the SALTORO RANGE—in 1935, when he reached 24,500 ft (7,470 m) and then sat out a storm for three days in a high camp was among the more audacious Himalayan exploits of the 1930s and, but for an adverse medical report, would have earned him a place on the Everest expedition of 1936. Even at the age of 42 on the 1953 expedition, he still felt himself to be in contention for the summit. With the Sherpa Da Namgyal he carried loads, in poor weather, to 27,500 ft (8,384 m) three days prior to Tenzing and Hillary's ascent of the mountain. In the course of a mountaineering career which continues into old age, he has climbed widely in the Alps (where he was a potent force in the renaissance of British ALPINISM in the late 1940s and early 1950s), the Caucasus and the Pamirs (to which regions he led Anglo-Soviet expeditions in 1958 and 1962, which contributed to better relations between the two nations in that period), the Polish Tatras, the Pindos Mountains of Greece, the SAINT ELIAS Mountains of ALASKA and the Staunings Alps in GREENLAND.

Further reading: John Hunt, *Life Is Meeting* (1978).

HUNTER, MOUNT (United States)

This broad, elongated peak, due south of DENALI, just outside of Denali National Park wilderness boundaries, in Alaska, is probably the most difficult 14,000-ft (4,268-m) mountain in North America. The north peak (14,570 ft/4,442), central peak (13,450 ft/4,100 m), and south peak (13,966 ft/4,258 m) span a 3-mile (4.8-km) summit plateau. The Indian name for the mountain, Begguya, meant "Denali's child." Early prospectors referred to it as Mount Roosevelt. Its present name was given to the peak in 1903 when Robert Dunn was leading the way to a high pass. Dunn said, "There's the hell of a high mountain over there." He was actually pointing at Kahiltna Dome, but in 1906 government surveyors mistakenly gave Dunn's aunt's name to the present-day Mount Hunter, which Dunn never saw. When Dunn finally discovered this error in 1950, he took consolation upon learning that Hunter was a more magnificent peak than Kahiltna Dome.

At least twelve routes have been climbed on Mount Hunter. The FIRST ASCENT route, the west ridge, climbed by Fred BECKEY in 1954, is the most popular. The routes of greatest difficulty and easiest access are found on the north face, first climbed in 1981. John WATERMAN's 148-day solo first ascent of the southeast spur in 1978 remains an unequalled feat of endurance. It is uncommon for more than a half dozen climbers to reach Hunter's summit each year, due to difficult snow conditions. The mountain was first climbed in winter via its direct Kennedy-Lowe route in 1980.

Guidebooks: Steve Roper and Allen Steck, *Fifty Classic Climbs of North America* (1979); Jonathan Waterman, *High Alaska; A Historical Guide To Denali, Mount Foraker and Mount Hunter* (1989).

Further reading: Glenn Randall, *Breaking Point* (1983).

HUNTINGTON, MOUNT (United States) One of the most arresting peaks in the ALASKA RANGE, Mount Huntington (12,240 ft/3,732 m) rises sharply from the Ruth and Tokositna glaciers. Since 1957, there have been more attempts on Huntington than on any 12,000-ft (3,659-m) mountain in ALASKA. In 1964, French alpinist Lionel TERRAY led the FIRST ASCENT of the mountain by its northwest ridge. The difficult west face was established in 1965 by Dave ROBERTS and team. Numerous variations have been added to the west face, which is the mountain's most popular route. Otherwise, more than a dozen difficult LINES have been added to the mountain.

Guidebook: Steve Roper and Allen Steck, *Fifty Classic Climbs of North America* (1979).

Further reading: David Roberts, *Mountain of My Fear* (1990).

HUTS In some alpine regions of the world, systems of huts dot the mountains. Huts offer communal shelter to mountain travelers, usually for a fee. At some there are resident wardens or guardians. Huts range from tin shacks to elaborate buildings with cooking facilities. They are an institution in the European Alps, especially on the French side. The Canadian Rockies and New Zealand Alps also have hut systems. Often huts are placed strategically along high route tours (see HAUTE ROUTE).

HYPOTHERMIA Hypothermia or exposure is a potentially fatal condition in which the core body temperature cools after exposure to cold, wind, rain, snow or water immersion. The condition should be avoided by adequate dressing and shelter, as hypothermia can render a party helpless. A poorly protected body loses heat through convection, conduction, evaporation and radiation. Mechanisms of the body for reducing heat loss include shivering and redirecting blood flow from legs and arms to the body core. If core temperature drops to 90 degrees F (32 degrees

C) mild hypothermia sets in. Symptoms include feelings of cold and numbness, impairment of muscle coordination, difficulty walking and talking, and apathy. Though one may be able to walk in this state, warming and shelter are essential because if core temperatures drop further severe hypothermia will set in. In this case one cannot walk and must be evacuated. Symptoms include cessation of shivering, stiffness and muscular incoordination, incoherence and confusion, worsening to semiconsciousness, muscular rigidity, dilation of pupils and inapparent heartbeat or breathing. Below 82 degrees F (28 degrees C) unconsciousness and death can be rapid. Mild hypothermia may be treated by providing shelter, adding clothing (especially to the head where much heat is lost), warming by any means from fire to body heat, eating, and exercising large muscles like legs. Severe hypothermia has no easy cure, as the victim is incapacitated and rapid rewarming can cause heart and organ failure when chilled blood flows back into the core. Helicopter evacuation and hospitalization offer the best chance of survival, but in remote settings this can be impossible. However, the metabolism of a severely hypothermic person is so slowed down that many have survived four to six hours while a rescue was mustered. Otherwise, slow rewarming in the warmest shelter possible, adding clothing and sleeping bag and hot water bottles or warmed padded stones to the neck, chest and abdomen are advised. Legs and arms should be insulated but not warmed or rubbed or cold blood may travel from them to the core. Warm fluids can be given when the victim is conscious. (See also FROSTBITE, INSULATION, WIND CHILL.)

Further reading: J. Wilkerson, C. Bangs, J. Hayward, *Hypothermia, Frostbite and Other Cold Injuries: Prevention, Recognition and Prehospital Treatment* (1986).

HYPOXIA All high-altitude climbers suffer some degree of hypoxia, which is a deficiency of oxygen reaching the tissues of the body. The higher the altitude the more acute the hypoxia. Symptoms resemble ACUTE MOUNTAIN SICKNESS, and include breathlessness, lethargy, headache, confusion and pale or bluish skin color. At high elevations hypoxia may weaken a climber during sleep, when a normally decreased rate and depth of breathing produces a drop in oxygen saturation of arterial hemoglobin. AMS and lethargy during the day are believed to be linked to sleep hypoxia. Nutritionists endorse an iron-rich diet before and during an expedition, to aid transportation of oxygen in hemoglobin. Gradual ACCLIMATIZATION is the proven method of combating hypoxia.

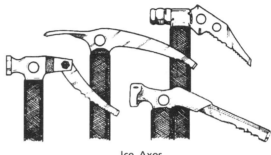

Ice Axes

ICE AXE The basic tool for climbing snow and ice, consisting of a shaft ending in a spike, or ferrule, and a head consisting of a pick and adze, or sometimes a hammer. A wrist loop tied to the axe head secures the axe in the climber's hand. Hickory or laminated bamboo were once popular as axe shafts but modern axes are made of aluminum, carbon fiber or titanium. Picks are made of either stamped steel or are forged and welded. The ice axe probably evolved from peasant implements used in the European ALPS beginning in the 1870s.

Specialization has divided the modern ice axe into loose categories: The ice axe, or piolet is a multipurpose tool for general mountaineering. It has a gently curved pick and an adze, or spade-shaped blade for chopping snow or ice. Ice axe shafts come in five cm (two-inch) increments from 55 to 75 cm (22 to 30 inches), or longer. Ice tools have shorter shafts (45–60 cm/18–24 inches) and sharply pointed, steeply drooped picks for hooking into steep ice. These tools are for technical ice such as WATERFALL CLIMBING. Picks can be curved, reverse curved (banana picks), straight or tubular. In modular ice tools picks are interchangeable and adjustable. Picks are specialized for different ice conditions. Thin picks shatter ice less. Tubular picks are effective in cold, brittle water ice because they also shatter ice less, though they are delicate and sometimes snap. Curved or reverse curved picks are favored on MIXED CLIMBING where rocks may break other picks. Each style of pick requires a slightly different technique for placement, but in general the swing should come from the elbow and be finished with a forward wrist movement to hook the pick into the ice. Some ice tool shafts are bent at the hand grip to avoid striking the knuckles when swinging the tool. Ice hammers are ice tools with a hammer head instead of an adze, for placing ice screws or pitons. The illustration shows a variety of ice axes and their features. (See ALPINE CLIMBING TECHNIQUES, ICE AXE BELAYS, SELF ARREST.)

ICE AXE BELAYS Belays using and incorporating ice axes (including buried-axe anchor, T-axe anchor, vertical-axe anchor, boot-axe belay and standing-axe belay) are discussed and shown in SNOW AND ICE ANCHORS.

ICE AXE BRAKE Another term for ice axe SELF ARREST.

ICE BOLLARD A horseshoe-shaped trough hacked into ice, over which a SLING or the ROPE may be draped to create an ANCHOR for BELAYING or RAPPELLING. The technique is discussed in SNOW AND ICE ANCHORS.

ICE CAP A thick, flat mantle of permanent GLACIER ice covering a land mass. Unlike a glacier, which carves a riverlike path out of a mountain range, an ice cap is a sprawling mass. Antarctica is a continental ice cap of some 5 million sq miles (13 million sq km), three miles (4.8 km) thick. The Greenland ice cap is approximately 600,000 sq miles (1,560,000 sq km) and two miles (3.2 km) thick. The Patagonian ice cap in Argentina is a smaller, inland ice cap.

ICE CLIMBING A general term for any climbing on ice. (See CRAMPONS, ICE AXE, SNOW AND ICE BELAYS, SNOW AND ICE CLIMBING TECHNIQUES, WATERFALL CLIMBING.)

ICE DAGGER TECHNIQUE Originally, the ice dagger was a short, pointed-hand tool (often a drive-in ice screw) stabbed into ice as a handhold, and used in conjunction with an ICE AXE. Now the term refers to an ice-climbing maneuver of holding the ice axe by its head and thrusting it at waist height into ice or NEVE. It is a quick way to climb moderate-angled snow. Two axes can be used. When using one axe, the palm of the other hand is placed against the slope for balance.

ICE FALL A steep, dangerous section of a GLACIER where rapid glacial movement has created a chaos of ever-changing CREVASSES, SERACS and ice debris that collapse periodically with surges in the glacier. Traveling around the edge of an ice fall is generally safer and easier than climbing through one.

ICE FIELD A large area of relatively flat glacier ice. The COLUMBIA ICE FIELD in Canada is an example.

Ice Climbing

into and chopped out of ice. Modern ice screws are threaded tubes 15 to 30 cm (six to 12 inches) long, with teeth or a sharp tip to penetrate ice, and an eye for clipping a CARABINER. Two main types are used: hammer in/screw out, which are driven in by hammer and retrieved by twisting them out of ice (examples are Snargs and Warthogs), and screw in/screw out, which require screwing for both placement and retrieval (such as Chouinard, Salewa, and Charlet screws). A modern improvement on the latter type is the self-ratcheting screw, which allows one-handed placement because of an inbuilt ratchet-end (examples are Lowe rats).

Different screws perform better in different types of ice. Waterfall ice climbers prefer hammer-in screws, which are easier to place on vertical ice. On frozen turf a Warthog works well. Climbers in the Canadian Rockies have developed a technique for making cheap rappel anchors out of metal conduit slotted into holes bored out by an ice screw, rather than abandon costly screws. Ice screw strengths vary, but a screw is only as strong as the ice in which it is placed. Furthermore, cold affects metal strength. The UIAA standard for ice screw strength under specific test conditions is 2250 lbs (10 kN) before bending and failure. Pull-out strength of an ice screw depends on the threads (coarser threads resist greater pull-out force) and the angle of placement. The correct angle for an ice screw is at 100 degrees to the slope, though in soft ice it is common to chop out deep benches and place screws vertically. Ice screws are generally placed under difficult conditions. Cold-surface ice may shatter into "dinner plates" when struck. This brittle layer must be chopped away to solid ice beneath. Ice may clog the tubes of screws, jamming them in place and forcing them to be hacked out of ice. Clogged ice must then be tapped or melted out, otherwise it will cause further placements to jam. An effective way of ridding ice from inside ice screws is to coat the tube with graphite. (See also SNOW AND ICE ANCHORS, SNOW AND ICE CLIMBING EQUIPMENT.)

ICE HAMMER A type of ICE AXE with a hammer head instead of an adze. Sometimes called a north wall hammer.

ICE MUSHROOM The unique ice formations found on CERRO TORRE in PATAGONIA. (See also RIME.)

ICE PITON Also ice peg, warthog. A PITON designed to be hammered into ice. (See ICE SCREWS.)

ICE SCREW RATCHET A ratchet wrench adapted to fit the head of an ice screw and more easily twist it into ice. On steep ice it offers the climber the option of placing conventional screws with one hand, rather than the usual two.

ICE SCREWS Peg-like shafts of metal used to penetrate ice, to protect and assist climbers ascending ice walls. As used today, ice screws are tubular aluminum alloy, or stainless steel, or titanium pegs placed in ice as PROTECTION or ANCHORS. Early ice screws were long PITONS hammered

ICE TOOLS See ICE AXE, ICE HAMMER.

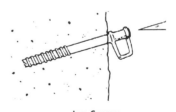

Ice Screw

IDAHO (United States) A dry climate and mountainous topography affords climbing opportunities in all seasons in Idaho. Granitic formations predominate in north and central Idaho. Here, mountain crags include the southern tips of Canada's Purcell and SELKIRK ranges, Bitteroot Mountains, SAWTOOTH mountains and Bighorn Crags. Of the alpine crags in the glaciated Selkirk Crest, CHIMNEY ROCK is the main formation. CITY OF ROCKS is the state's premiere FREE-CLIMBING area. Other granite crags, like La Clede Rocks (12 miles/19 km west of La Clede), Schweitzer

Rocks and Granite Point (both near Sandpoint), are popular among free climbers. Steamboat Rocks is a 400-ft (122-m) quartzite crag 20 miles (32 km) from Kingston. Numerous basaltic crags have been developed around Boise. The granite batholith from which the aforementioned areas spring is surrounded by sedimentary and metamorphic ranges. These offer the highest peaks in the state, Borah Peak, 12,662 ft (3,859 m), in central southern Idaho near the town of Mackay being Idaho's highest. This attractive peak is frequently ascended by several routes.

Guidebook: Randall Green, *Idaho Rock: A Climbing Guide to the Selkirk Crest and Sandpoint Areas* (1987).

IGLOO   A domed shelter of snow blocks, traditionally used by Eskimo Indians. Igloo construction is time-consuming, making igloos impractical as emergency shelter (in which case a SNOW CAVE is better), but igloos are efficient in base camps on snow. They are built by gathering large, thick blocks of wind-packed snow. A SNOW SAW shapes blocks easily. A circle (about 10 ft/3 m in diameter) is then marked on stamped-down snow. One technique is to lay blocks in concentric circles; another is to lay blocks in spiral form. In either case, overlap joints like brickwork, and overhang or slant each row to a taper. Seal the top with a flat block and gaps with snow. Ventilation holes are essential, but shouldn't be cut on the side of prevailing wind, or so low that drifting snow covers them. Smooth the interior to avoid drip points, as stove and body heat create considerable interior warmth. An entrance can be dug under the igloo, cut into the wall or built as blocks are laid. Igloos are subject to weakening from wind and warmth.

ILKLEY   (Britain)   These crags dominate the skyline above the town of Ilkley to the northwest of Leeds, and they dominate the history of YORKSHIRE gritstone climbing as well. The crags are a disused quarry, 60 ft (18 m) high. The climbs are naturally protected.

Climbing began at Ilkley in the late 1800s, but following World War II, Arthur Dolphin and Allan Austin, recognized as the fathers of modern gritstone climbing in Yorkshire, developed the crag. In the 1970s John Syrett, a student from Leeds University whose brief but tragic career inspired a generation of Britons, climbed Propeller Wall, grading it 5.7. It is now rated 5.12. A year later Pete LIVESEY climbed Wellington Crack (5.11a), a route that proved a national milestone, and later Guillotine (5.11d). Ron FAWCETT's strenuous crack Milky Way (5.12a), from 1978, reportedly left him too exhausted to untie the rope at the top. The 1980s were dominated by British wunderkind John Dunne, who at the age of 17 in 1986 climbed the bold Countdown to Disaster (5.13c). In 1987 he amazed the British climbing scene with his poorly protected, elegant ARETE, The New Statesman (5.13d), which remains unrepeated.

Guidebook: Yorkshire Mountain Club, *Yorkshire Gritstone* (1989).

ILLAMPU   (Bolivia)   Illampu, 94 miles (151 kms) north of La Paz, marks the northern reach of the CORDILLERA REAL. It is possible its name means "The Shining One" from the Aimara verb "to shine." This white massif of 20,887 ft (6,368 m) rises above the tropical town of Sorata (8,820 ft/2,690 m). With its higher but somewhat tamer brother Ancohuma ("White Head," 21,082 ft/6,427 m), Illampu forms the Sorata massif. On June 7, 1928, the northwest face was climbed by alpinist Hans Pfann, accompanied by E. Hein, H. Horeschowsky and H. Hortnagl, Austrians. Illampu's reputation as the hardest Bolivian giant is partly due to cold temperatures (usually −13 degrees F/−25 degrees C). Regensburgers climbed the north ridge in 1982 and TRAVERSED the twin summits of Illampu. French guide-writer Alain Messili and his team opened the east face direct (1969), the northeast and the southeast sides (1973); Germans climbed the east BUTTRESS in 1973; and in 1991 Yugoslavs scaled two direct routes on the west face. In 1935 and 1987, the German Alpine Club issued an excellent map of the Sorata massif, scale 1:50,000.

Guidebook: Alain Messili, *La Cordillera Real de los Andes, Bolivia* (1984).

Evelio Echevarria
Colorado State University

ILLIMANI   (Bolivia)   "Tell a Bolivian that Illimani is 7,000 m [2,960 ft] high and you will earn his gratitude," wrote a traveler early this century. Nevertheless Sajama (21,424 ft/6,520 m) and Ancohuma (20,958 ft/6,351 m) both in Bolivia, are either higher than or almost as high as Illimani, but Illimani is a Bolivian symbol. At sunset its glaciers are a celebrated sight for the inhabitants of La Paz, world's highest capital (12,163 ft/3,708 m). Illimani, the "Shining Condor" of the Aimaras, marks the southern end of the CORDILLERA REAL and is 21,005 ft (6,402 m) high. The first known ascent was by Martin CONWAY and his guides Aime Maquignaz and Louis Pellissier in 1898. There were sporadic ascents afterward. In 1940 three Germans hoisted the Nazi flag on the top, and a Briton and a Bolivian rushed to remove it. New things were done after 1950. Hans Ertl and Gert Schroeder climbed the steep north peak (ca. 20,926 ft/6,380 m) and claimed, wrongly, that it was higher than Conway's southern one. Bolivians climbed the central peak (20,828 ft/6,350 m) in the 1960s. German ace W. Kuhm perished in 1941 when attempting to TRAVERSE all peaks, a feat performed only in 1969 by the strong party of Rudolf Knott. In 1977, Italians under Cosimo Zappelli climbed two outlying peaks on the northeast side of Illimani. The southeast side is unknown and is one of the great precipices of the world, some 14,500 ft (4,420 m) high. Illimani has claimed many lives, partially due to the incredible firmness of Bolivian snow and ice.

Guidebook: Alain Messili, *La Cordillera Real de los Andes, Bolivia* (1984).

Evelio Echevarria
Colorado State University

ILLINOIS   (United States)   In southern Illinois lie an expanse of 60- to 100-ft (18- to 30-m) sandstone cliffs offering FACE routes on POCKETS and crystals. Most climbing surrounds the university town of Carbondale and lies within state parks of Shawnee National Forest. In Giant City State Park there is a complex of popular crags with both bolted and naturally protected routes. Similar climbing lies on Makanda Bluffs and Devil's Standtable. Two miles (3 km) south of the town of Marion is 120-ft (36-m) Draper's Bluff, the state's tallest crag. Nearby Cedar Bluff offers similar climbing. Ferne Clyffe, near Gore (with a 60-ft/18-m waterfall that has been climbed in winter); Dixon Springs near the eponymous town (with severe BOULDER-ING left by John Gill); and Stoneface, near Harrisburg, are frequented sandstone areas. SPORT CLIMBING is found at the premiere crag, Jackson Falls, an 80-ft (24-m) crag with some free-standing towers, 25 miles (40 km) northeast of Marion. This area has produced over 100 routes up to 5.13. In the north of the state, by the Mississippi River near Savanah, within the Mississippi Palisades State Park are limestone bluffs. Charles Mound, 1,235 ft (376 m), near the town of Galena is the state's high point.

Guidebooks: Mike Simpson, *Jackson Falls Guidebook* (1991); Jim Thurmond, *Southern Illinois Climbing Routes* (1990).

INCUT　A positive, sharp-lipped handhold behind which one can get the fingers.

INDEPENDENCE PASS　(United States)　This collection of crags just east of Aspen, COLORADO, offers steep FACE and CRACK CLIMBING on roadside granite crags, with many SPORT CLIMBS. Its high elevation makes it an ideal summer destination.

Guidebooks:　Larry Bruce, *Rock Climber's Guide to Aspen* (1989); Molly Higgins, *Aspen Rock Climbs* (1989).

INDEX　(United States)　A FREE-CLIMBING area above the town of Index, WASHINGTON, 60 miles (96 km) east of Seattle. The area comprises the Upper and Lower Town Walls and several OUTCROPS. The Upper Wall has routes up to five PITCHES. This area is not to be confused with Mount Index (5,979 ft/1,822 m), which lies within sight of Index, across the Skykomish River (alpine routes on this peak are described in Fred Beckey's *Cascade Alpine Guide: Columbia River to Stephens Pass* [1973]). The Lower Wall has popular cracks like Godzilla and Slow Children (5.10). City Park, a 5.13 tips crack, climbed by Hugh HERR, remains unrepeated. For power, Andy de Klerk's ARETE, Amandella (5.13b) is unmatched. Steep and very textured granite has made the Upper Wall the Northwest's leading face climbing crag. Notable sport climbs are Young Cynics (5.13a) by Collum, Heart's Desire (5.12c) by Keith Lennard, Child Abuse (5.12d) and Rise and Fall (5.12a) by Greg Child, Technicians of the Sacred (5.12b) by de Klerk and Sisu (5.11c) by Karl Kaiyala. June through September are the prime months for climbing here.

Guidebook:　Jeff Smoot, *Washington Rock Climbs* (1988).

INDIA　Though foreign mountaineers have visited India since the early 1900s, Indian-led mountaineering did not come of age till the 1960s, and rock climbing only arrived in India in the mid-1970s. Indians have summited most of their own major peaks, as well as giants like EVEREST and KANGCHENJUNGA. Clubs like the Himalayan Club and its *Himalayan Journal* (Oxford University Press, P.O. Box 31 Oxford House, Appollo Bunder, Bombay 400001), and the journal *Himavanta* (63E Mohanirban Rd., Calcutta 700 029) chronicle alpinism in India.

Like other Himalayan nations, in India mountaineering (though not the visiting of low-lying crags) for foreigners requires payment of peak fees. The Indian Mountaineering Foundation (Benito Juarez Rd., Shanti Niketan, New Delhi 110021) issues permits for mountaineering, at the following rates (1990 figures): $600 for peaks below 6,000m (19,680 ft); peaks 6,001 to 6,500 m (19,683 to 21,320 ft), $900; 6,501 to 7,000 m (21,323 to 22,960 ft), $1350; 7,001 m (22,963 ft) and higher, $1800; Nun and Kun in Kashmir, $2250; peaks in the East Karakoram, $3,000. Indian mountains discussed in this work are CHANGABANG, KAMET, NANDA DEVI, NUN KUN, SHIVLING. Ranges of India discussed here are ASSAM HIMALAYA, GANGOTRI REGION, GARWHAL, INDIAN KARA-KORAM, KAMET, KASHMIR, KINNAUR HIMALAYA, KISHTWAR HIMAL, KULU-LAHUL, PAMARI HIMAL, PERI HIMAL, RIMO MUZTAGH, SALTORO RANGE, SASER MUZTAGH, SIKKIM HIMAL, SPITI HIMALAYA, ZANSKAR HIMAL.

As for pure rock climbing, foreign alpinists en route to the Gangotri have long noticed the orange granite and big walls of the Gangotri Gorge, which is now seeing exploration. South India also contains rock climbing. The so-called City of Rocks forms a ring of crags around populous Bangalore. The areas, from six to 37.5 miles (10 to 60 km) from the city, are granite domes up to 984 ft (300 m), reminiscent of TUOLOMNE MEADOWS. Savandurga, Rama-nagram and Kabbaldurga offer friction and crack problems. Turalli and Raogudlu are boulder fields. An unusual feature of these areas are the many ancient Hindu temples near the climbing. The huge slabs are often bolt protected. Bangalore's climbing club is KINSROC, c/- K. H. Raju, 121 8th Main, 3RD Block, Jayanagur, Bangalore, 560011.

In central India climbing is found at Pachmarhi (Madhya Pradesh State), Mount Abu (Rajasthan State) and Pavagda (Gujarat State). The Western Ghats are an escarpment of central India but the rock is loose. Dhauj, 31 miles (50 km) Southwest of Delhi in the north, is steep quartzite. It is the only Indian crag served by a guidebook, which lists 250 climbs.

Due to the heat, the best time to rock climb in southern India is between September and January. Even so, temperatures can reach 86 degrees F (30 degrees C). In the north, October through February offers cool weather. Indian climbers have developed fairly traditional ethics, especially around Dhauj. Grades have been pushed to 5.11 in most areas, but easier climbs are the norm. Rock climbing is in a fledgling state in India and has been compared with that in BRITAIN in the 1950s.

INDIAN CREEK CANYON　(United States)　Located in UTAH, 56 miles/90 km from Moab, Indian Creek is the undisputed center of desert CRACK CLIMBING. The area sports some 500 crack routes of every width, ranging from 5.9 to 5.13. Cracks are frequently parallel and require considerable endurance. Protection is from CAMMING units, and large selections must be carried. Descent from the routes is generally by RAPPEL. SPORT CLIMBING has not found a niche here. The rock is abrasive, and taping is advisable. Cracks penetrate many types of sandstone, the lowest layer being Moenkopi, followed by Chinle, Wingate, Kayenta, Navajo, Carmel and Entrada. Camping is found on a variety of U.S. Bureau of Land Management sites and in nearby Newspaper Rock State Park. The cliffs of Indian Creek are on private land and access is a sensitive issue. Climbing at this area in summer is inconceivable due to heat. September through May is the prime season. (See COLORADO PLATEAU.)

Guidebook: Eric Bjornstad, *Desert Rock.*

INDIAN KARAKORAM (India) This region lies southeast of the K2-GASHERBRUM area of PAKISTAN, between the Shaksgam and Shyok rivers. It is considered separate from KARAKORAM because permission to climb is obtained from INDIA, not from Pakistan. The Siachen GLACIER, the largest in the Karakoram, drains much of the area, which includes five major groups of 22,960-ft (7,000-m) peaks. Tom LONGSTAFF first established the extent of this glacier and its peaks in 1909, and subsequent expeditions from Britain, Italy and the United States made rudimentary maps. G. O. DYHRENFURTH led the first serious climb here, of Sia Kangri (24,344 ft/7,422 m), in 1934.

During the 1960s and 1970s (after the 1947 India-Pakistan partition) Japanese teams entered the area via Pakistan and climbed Saltoro Kangri (25,393 ft/7,742 m), K-12 (24,364 ft/ 7,428 m), Teram Kangri (24,482 ft/7,464 m), Sherpi Kangri (23,954 ft/7,303 m), Apsarasas I (23,764 ft/7,245 m) and Singhi Kangri (25,423 ft/7,751 m). In 1973 the Indian Army climbed Saser Kangri (25,164 ft/7,672 m) and, in 1981, Saltoro II and Sia Kangri. Both Pakistan and India have used the authorization of mountaineering expeditions to support claims about this disputed territory. A high-altitude shelling war began in 1984 between India and Pakistan and continues as of 1994. In 1984 the Indian Army advanced up the Siachen Glacier and also authorized the first joint foreign-Indian climb in the area, resulting in the climb of Mamostang Kangri (24,652 ft/7,516 m) by a Japanese team. Joint foreign-Indian expeditions come under close scrutiny going to the Saser, Rimo and Mamostang groups in the southeast. British teams climbed Rimo II and III, and a Japanese and Indian team climbed Rimo I (24,223ft/7,385 m) in 1988. There seems to be fewer political difficulties for climbers on the Pakistan side of the Kar-

IN SITU Equipment left in place on a climb, such as an in situ PITON.

INSTEP CRAMPONS Short four-pointed CRAMPONS worn under the instep of the boot for walking on icy ground. They are not used for climbing, but are useful for GLACIER walking.

INSULATION Insulating materials (natural and synthetic), and the properties of thermal insulation, are discussed under SLEEPING BAGS AND INSULATED CLOTHING. (See also CLOTHING FOR MOUNTAINEERING.)

INTERIOR RANGES (Canada) In the southeast quadrant of BRITISH COLUMBIA, between the ROCKY MOUNTAINS and the COAST RANGES, are four smaller ranges—the Cariboos, the Monashees, the SELKIRKS, and the Purcells—which are known as the Interior Ranges and offer fine climbing and beautiful scenery. These ranges are home to peaks like the Premier Range of the Cariboos, the SIR DONALD group in the Rogers Pass area of the Selkirks, and the BUGABOOS in the Purcells. The geology of these ranges is varied, with granite appearing in the Bugaboos and Adamants ranges, gneiss in the Gold Range, quartzite in the Sir Donald range and in some places limestone. Rogers Pass, with its lush valleys, was the birthplace of Canadian climbing in the 1880s. There are 18 mountains over 11,000 ft (3,354 m) in the Interior Ranges. Many areas are remote and only the very hardy would deny themselves the use of a helicopter. The towns of Golden, Revelstoke, Cranbrook, Radium, Valemont and Nelson surround the Interior Range, and Glacier National Park and Bugaboo Provincial Park protect some area of the ranges.

Guidebooks: Bruce Fairley, *Guidebook to Hiking and Climbing in British Columbia* (1986); R. Krusznya and W. L. Putnam, *Climber's Guide to Interior Ranges of British Columbia, South* (1977); Krusznya and Putnam, *Climber's Guide to Interior Ranges of British Columbia, North* (1975).

ISPO TRADE FAIR (Germany) An annual trade show in Munich, at which manufacturers of climbing gear and climbers from all over the world convene.

ITALIAN HITCH Another name for the friction hitch or MUNTER HITCH used for belaying. (See BELAYING TECHNIQUES.)

J

JAEGER, NICOLAS (–1980) (France) A guide and medical doctor, Jaeger burst upon the world-class climbing scene in 1977 with a string of five remarkable solo ascents in PERU: the fourth ascent of Taulliraju (by a partial new route), a new route on the east face of Abasraju, a new route on Santa Cruz, the southwest face of Huandoy Oeste, and a new route on Chacraraju Este. The next year he was a member of the successful first French team to ascend EVEREST, and from 26,896 ft (8,200 m) descended on skis. Back in PERU he did another amazing string of solos and lived for 60 days, studying high-altitude symptoms, on the summit of Nevado Huascaran (21,976 ft/6,700 m), experiences he turned into a film and a book. In 1980 Jaeger attempted a solo of LHOTSE. After climbing strongly, he was pinned to the side of Lhotse Sar at 26,500 ft (8,079 m) for eight days by a storm and was never seen again.

JAMMING In FREE CLIMBING, to jam hands, fingers or feet into a crack; hand jamming. (See CRACK CLIMBING.)

JANAK HIMAL (Nepal, Sikkim, Tibet) This small range is bounded in the east by the Jongsang La Mountain Pass on the Nepal-Sikkim border, and by the Kangchenjunga Glacier and the Ghunsa Khola. The western boundary runs south from the Ghang La. There are five peaks above 22,960 ft (7,000 m) in this range: Jongsong, Peak 24,472 ft (7,461 m); Dome Kang, Peak 23,104 ft (7,044 m); and an outlying peak called Janak. Jongsong (24,472 ft/7,461 m) is the highest. It was first climbed by two members of the 1930 International Kangchenjunga expedition. One of the climbers was G. O. DYRENFURTH, who led the expedition. This ascent set an altitude record at the time.
Further reading: Jill Neate, *High Asia* (1989).

JAPAN Though Japan is a mountainous country, its peaks and cliffs seldom attract international visitors. Fuji Yama, or Mount Fuji (12,388 ft/3,777 m), with a road halfway to the summit is Japan's highest. While arduous, it is not challenging. Perhaps the most infamous peak of Japan is Mount Tanigawadake (6,440 ft/1,963 m), with an imposing east face and ridge and a reputation for wild weather and avalanche. Nonetheless, Japanese climbers are among the most active in the Himalayan expedition scene. They have launched many of the biggest, most lavishly funded expeditions ever, and won some of the hardest routes done in the great ranges, like K2 north

ridge (1982), on which alpinists Naoe Sakashita and team summited without oxygen. Japanese mountaineering is covered by two journals that cover world climbing; *Iwa to Yuki* and *Climbing Journal*. Both offer English summaries of their texts. Freeclimbs of 5.10 only appeared in Japan in 1980, and 5.12 in 1981. The main rock-climbing areas of Honshu Island lie west of Tokyo. Because of heavy traffic, travel to Japanese crags is slow. Areas include: Jogasaki, a volcanic cliff rising out of the sea on the Isu Peninsula; Maku Iwa, a granite crag in the Okuchichibu Mountains, with the famous testpiece, Spiderman (5.12a); Ogawa Yama, an area of steep granite pinnacles with the 5.13a and b climbs Excellent Power and Ninja, both created by visiting German Stefan GLOWACZ; and Nippara, a limestone crag. Japanese rock-climbers who have climbed world-class routes include Yuji HIRAYAMA and Hidetaka Suzuki.

JARDINE, RAY (1949–) (United States) The aerospace engineer and climber who invented the FRIEND, the SPRING-LOADED CAMMING DEVICE that revolutionized FREE CLIMBING. Jardine began developing his device in 1973 and after many prototypes a final version was released commercially in 1979. The invention has become standard equipment on every climber's rack. Jardine invented Friends to protect the parallel-sided cracks of YOSEMITE VALLEY. He was also among the first to climb 5.12. Famous Yosemite cracks that he made FIRST ASCENTS of include Seperate Reality, Crimson Cringe, Rostrum Roof, Hangdog Flyer and Phoenix, all climbed during the 1970s. Jardine was also one of the first free climbers to HANGDOG or work on routes by hanging his weight on protection in order to solve specific moves before leading the PITCH in RED POINT style, without hanging on any protection. This brought him criticism from many climbers who regarded this as cheating, but by the 1980s most of his critics had adopted this tactic and today it is commonplace in SPORT CLIMBING.

JOHNSON, BEVERLY (1947–1994) (United States) Johnson was one of the first women climbers in YOSEMITE VALLEY's most prolific period. By 1970 Johnson had climbed such Valley testpieces as the Steck-Salanthe route on Sentinel, Rixon's East Chimney, the left side of Reed Pinnacle and the Crack of Doom. She soloed the Leaning Tower and was a member of the first all-woman team to climb EL CAPITAN. Her most publicized climb was the first woman's and third solo ascent of El Capitan in September 1978, over an eight-day period. The event was covered by TV, radio and newspapers. In 1994 she died in a tragic helicopter crash while filming with her husband, Mike Hoover, and Disney Company chairman Frank Wells.

JORDAN Jordan's main climbing area, the sandstone massifs of Wadi Rum, lie 217 miles (349 km) from the capital, Amman. Tony Howard (Britain), one of the area's first climbers described Wadi Rum as, ". . . 500 square miles [1,300 sq km] of desert and mountains with red, yellow and purple sandstone towers and walls rising steeply and windworn into arabesque loops and whorls with tier upon tier of overlapping slabs melting into space." Climbs begin at an elevation of 3,000 ft (915 m). The highest summits are Jebel Rum (5,760 ft/1,756 m) and Jebel Um'ishrin (5,759 ft/1,756 m), which face each other across the valley of Wadi Rum. Further east lie the pyramidal Barrakhs, and south of Wadi Rum are smaller sandstone domes. Many summits have been scaled by local Bedouins, but many major summits guarded by huge vertical rock walls remain unclimbed. Climbers report excellent adventure climbing on what is at times soft rock.

The area was first visited by climbers in 1953 when Charmian Longstaff and Sylvia Branford (wife and daughter of Tom LONGSTAFF) climbed Jebel Rum by Sheikh Hamdan's Route. In 1984 the Jordanian Ministry of Tourism invited a British group to assess the area's trekking and climbing potential. Since then, visitors have regularly climbed in the area.
Guidebook: Tony Howard, *Treks and Climbs in the Mountains of Rum and Petra* (1987).

JOSHUA TREE (United States) One of America's best-known rock climbing destinations, this vast desert area of CALIFORNIA offers suitable climbing weather year-round, though Mojave Desert summers are hot and winters can bring snowstorms. Located 125 miles (201 km) east of Los Angeles, "JT" has nearly 2,000 short routes and extensive bouldering on hundreds of coarse granite outcrops.

Climbers first came here in the 1950s and 1960s to escape bad weather in YOSEMITE and TAHQUITZ. Among them were Royal ROBBINS, TM Herbert, Mark Powell and others. In the mid-1960s a group including Woody Stark, Dick Webster, Bill Briggs and others began developing JT as a destination of its own. By 1972 climbers like John LONG, Tobin Sorenson, Richard Harrison and John BACHAR brought the FREE-CLIMBING revolution to JT, putting up scores of high standard routes, especially cracks. Herb Laeger first climbed in the Wonderland of Rocks, a vast area of OUTCROPS still barely developed. Randy Vogel, Randy LEAVITT, Tony YANIRO, Alan Nelson and others have continued adding new routes here, especially steep face climbs.
Guidebook: Randy Vogel, *Joshua Tree Rock Climbing Guide* (1988).

JUG An extremely large, secure handhold found on a rock climb. Also called a BUCKET.

JUMARS Trade name for the original mechanical rope ascender, made in Switzerland. Numerous ascenders are made today, and Jumar is often used generically in reference to any type. Jumaring is the act of climbing a rope on ascenders. (See ASCENDERS.)

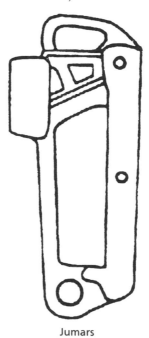

Jumars

JUNGFRAU AND MÖNCH (Austria) The Jungfrau (13,638 ft/4,158 m) is best seen from the north where it rises impressively from the Lauterbrunnen Valley. It was first climbed in 1811 by Johann Meyer and Hieronymous Meyer in a four-day expedition. The construction of the mountain railway to the Jungfraujoch, the pass between the Jungfrau and the Mönch, has shortened this time considerably but led some to complacency. Had World War I not intervened, the railway would have been continued to the summit. Apart from the usual route up the east side of the mountain, notable climbs include the Guggi Route climbed in 1865 by H. B. George, Sir G. Young with C. and U. Almer and A. Baumann—a TRAVERSE up the north face and still a serious proposition. Equally, the northeast ridge offers a considerable if venerable challenge at D+, first climbed in 1911. The Mönch (13,445 ft/4,099 m) is even more accessible, usually climbed from the south via the Mönchsjoch Hut—an ascent of only 1,640 ft (500 m). The Mönch Nordwand, climbed by Hans Lauper in 1921, is a more taxing affair at TD, taking 10 to 12 hours. (See RATING SYSTEMS for explanation of French ratings.)

K

K2 (Pakistan, China) At 28,250 ft/8,611 m, K2 is the world's second-highest mountain, and perhaps the most difficult 26,240 ft (8,000-m) summit. From the first attempts in 1902 to 1991, nearly 70 expeditions have attempted K2 but its steepness, lofty altitude and wild weather have let only 20 succeed. Ninety-three climbers have summited K2, 33 have died in the attempt.

Located on the Sino-PAKISTAN border in the KARAKORAM Range, K2's west, south and east flanks lie in Pakistan, above the Godwin-Austen Glacier, which flows into the BALTORO Glacier. K2's northern flanks rise above the North K2 Glacier in Xinjiang, CHINA. The Sino-Pakistan boundary runs along the northeast and northwest ridges. K2's 12,000-ft (3,659-m) faces and ridges of granite, limestone and metamorphics give the mountain a striking pyramid shape. Its northerly latitude—35 degrees north—subjects K2 to harsh winters that linger into spring. June to August is the usual climbing season for K2.

Although K2 is taller by 1,800 ft (549 m) than surrounding peaks, it remained unknown to Europeans until Captain T. G. Montgomerie of the British Survey of INDIA surveyed it in 1856, from 128 miles (205 km) distant. He allotted it a provisional name, with K standing for Karakoram, followed by a reference number. Native names replaced provisional ones, but because BALTI villagers never ventured to sites where K2 was visible, the name K2 stuck. The name Mount Godwin-Austen (after the first Surveyor-General of the Survey of India), appears on many maps, but is erroneous. The Chinese name, Qogir, has no local usage, being a corruption of Chogori, a name invented by western explorers in the early 1900s from the Balti words *chhogo,* "big," and *ri,* "mountain."

W. M. CONWAY first stood before K2 after trekking up the 35-mile (56-km) Baltoro Glacier in 1892. The first climbing attempt was made in 1902 by a team under the direction of Oscar ECKENSTEIN and including British occultist Aleister Crowley. They reached 21,400 ft (6,524 m) on the northeast ridge. In 1909 the Duke of the ABRUZZI's expedition reached 19,600 ft (5,976 m) on the southeast ridge and identified the most feasible route.

In 1939 German-American Fritz WEISSNER and Pasang Dawa Lama (Nepal) reached over 27,230 ft (8,302 m) without oxygen equipment, but American team member Dudley Wolfe and three SHERPAS later disappeared.

In 1953 Charles S. HOUSTON's seven-man team reached 24,600 ft (7,500 m), but storm and thrombosis in team member Art Gilkey forced a retreat. While they were lowering Gilkey, a multiple fall dragged five of the men toward a precipice, but remarkably, Pete Schoening arrested their fall with an ICE AXE BELAY. Gilkey however, disappeared.

The first successful ascent came in 1954. A large Italian expedition led by Ardito Desio placed nine camps on the southeast, or "Abruzzi" Ridge. Achille Compagnoni and Lino Lacedelli summited on July 31.

In 1976 a Polish expedition reached 27,600 ft (8,415 m) with oxygen on Eckenstein's northeast ridge. This route was completed in 1978 when Jim WICKWIRE, Louis REICHARDT, John ROSKELLEY and Rick Ridgeway became the first Americans to summit K2. Ridgeway and Roskelley made the first OXYGENLESS ascents. The Americans followed the ridge then traversed beneath the summit pyramid at 25,250 ft (7,698 m) to the Abruzzi Ridge.

In 1977 a gargantuan expedition was launched by a 42-member Japanese team that used 1,500 porters to base camp to make the second ascent of the Abruzzi Ridge. Six Japanese and the first Pakistani, Ashraf Aman, summited using oxygen. The west ridge was completed in 1980 by Japanese, who placed Eiho Ohtani and Nazir SABIR (Pakistan) on top. The stupendous and difficult north ridge succumbed to a Japanese party in 1982. After an approach by camel via the Shaksgam River, seven climbers summited without oxygen, but one, Yanagisawa, fell from 26,200 ft (7,988 m) while descending.

1986 was an active yet tragic year on K2. Although 27 climbers summited and two new routes were made, 13 climbers died. New routes were the lightweight ascent of the south face by J. KUKUCZKA and T. Piotrowski (Poland), and the exceptionally difficult south-southwest ridge climbed by a Polish-Czech summit team of P. Bozik, P. Przemyslaw and W. Wroz. Notable among the 22 ascents of the Abruzzi Ridge in 1986 were the first women's ascents by Wanda RUTKIEWICZ (Poland), Lilianne Barrard (France) and Briton Julie TULLIS; the first British ascents by Alan ROUSE and Tullis; and a rapid ascent by Benoit Chamoux (France) in 22.5 hours from Advance Base Camp to summit.

However, two Americans were killed by AVALANCHE, and the Italian soloist Renato CASAROTTO perished in a CREVASSE near base camp after reaching 27,200 ft (8,293 m) on the south-southwest ridge. Barrard and her husband, Maurice, fell while descending Abruzzi Ridge, as did Piotrowski and later, Wroz; a Pakistani HIGH-ALTITUDE POR-

K2

TER was killed by rockfall; and a catastrophic storm in a high camp led to the deaths of Rouse, Tullis and three others.

In 1990 a large Japanese expedition climbed the northwest face North K2 Glacier in China. This team solved a problem faced by expeditions in 1982 and 1986 that approached from Pakistan. The Japanese route joined the north ridge at 25,200 ft (7,683 m). Two climbers summited using oxygen. In 1991 Frenchmen C. PROFIT and P. BEGHIN summited in very light fashion via a variation of this route, climbing from the Savoia Glacier.

K2's height was questioned in 1986 when a survey by an American scientist suggested that K2 might be higher than Everest by 36 ft (11 m). A re-survey of K2 and Everest in 1987 by Italians led by Ardito Desio found that this was incorrect, though Desio's team surveyed both summits as being higher than previously thought—Everest, 29,108 ft/8,872 m; K2, 28,268 ft/8,616 m. K2 is still second highest, and the original height of 28,250 ft/8,613 m is still accepted by cartographers.

Further reading: Jim Curran, *K2: Triumph and Tragedy* (1987); Kurt Diemberger, *K2: The Endless Knot* (1990); Charles S. Houston and Robert Bates, *K2: The Savage Mountain* (1955); Andrew Kaufman and William Putnam, *K2 Diary, 1939: The Unanswered Questions* (1992); Rick Ridgeway, *The Last Step* (1980).

KAIN, CONRAD (1883–1934) (Austria) Austrian mountain guide and early developer of the Canadian ROCKIES. Kain came to CANADA in 1909, hired to guide for the Alpine Club of Canada. In 1910 he was a guide with Arthur Wheeler and Tom LONGSTAFF on a survey expedition into the Purcell Mountains of southeast BRITISH COLUMBIA when the Spillimacheen Peaks (now called the BUGABOOS) were first charted. In 1911, while assisting a survey team in the Mount ROBSON area, Kain made the FIRST ASCENT of Mount Whitehorn. Many doubted his success on this peak until his summit record was discovered years later. In 1912 he worked as a trapper for a Smithsonian expedition to Siberia, visited the European ALPS again, and then returned to Canada in 1913 to climb the first ascent of the Rockies' highest peak—Robson—with ACC members Albert MacCarthy and William Foster. Their northeast face route was unrepeated for 11 years, till Kain himself climbed it again. Robson cemented Kain's reputation as a guide. From 1913 to 1916 he spent three seasons guiding in NEW ZEALAND, where he made 29 first ascents including the first TRAVERSE of New Zealand's highest peak, Mount COOK. He returned to Canada in 1916, married the maid at the MacCarthy ranch in British Columbia, and worked as a farmhand, trapper and horsepacker. That year he soloed Jumbo Mountain in the Purcells in winter, on snowshoes, and in summer in the Bugaboos made the first ascents of North

Howser Tower with MacCarthy and his wife, Bess, and Bugaboo Spire with the MacCarthys and John Vincent. For some time, the 5.5 rock climbing on the latter peak stood as Canada's hardest. Kain regarded this climb as his finest achievement. Five peaks in Canada's Rockies and one in New Zealand bear Kain's name, as does a hut in the Bugaboos.

Further reading: Conrad Kain, *Where the Clouds Can Go* (1979).

KAMET (India)   Although this peak of the Central Garhwal Himalaya is seldom visited by westerners today, its 1931 FIRST ASCENT by a British team was a milestone in lightweight Himalayan climbing. Kamet (25,443 ft/7,756 m) rises near the Indo-Tibetan border. Its western GLACIERS feed the Saraswati River, and it is 19 miles (30 km) from the Hindu shrines of Badrinath. Kamet, or Kang-Med to Tibetans, means in Tibetan "Glacier Fire," because as the highest peak in the region its icy summit catches the first and last rays of the sun. Kamet received attention from British expeditions prior to World War I. Tom LONGSTAFF and others tried it from the east in 1907. From the west, C. F. Meade and A. M. Slingsby made five attempts between them, reaching 24,310 ft (7,412 m) on Meade's Col in 1913. In 1931 Frank SMYTHE led an expedition supported by 10 SHERPAS, and which included Eric SHIPTON and Raymond Greene (writer Graham Greene's brother). From Meade's Col they climbed a route up the northeast face, placing Smythe, Shipton, R. L. Holdsworth and Sherpa Lewa on the summit on the 21st of June. Even today, few expeditions approach high-altitude peaks in such lightweight style as theirs. Since the Chinese invasion of TIBET and the INDIA-CHINA war of 1962, the Indo-Tibetan border has been restricted to foreign expeditions. As such, westerners have had little input into Kamet's development, but Indian expeditions have been prolific, climbing the north ridge in 1955, the east face in 1979, and the difficult west ridge from the south by an Indian-French army team in 1986. Kamet and its neighboring peaks comprise the Kamet Group. The highest of these are Abi Gamin (24,130 ft/7,355 m),Mana (23,858 ft/7,272 m) and Mukut Parbat (23,759 ft/ 7,242 m).

Further reading: S. Mehta and H. Kapadia, *Exploring the Hidden Himalaya* (1990); Frank Smythe, *Kamet Conquered* (1932).

KANGCHENJUNGA (Nepal, Sikkim)   The third-highest mountain in the world is a 3-mile (5-km)-long complex of high ridges that form an X-shape around four summits: Kangchenjunga Main (28,201 ft/8,598 m), central (27,866 ft/8,496 m), south (27,801 ft/8,476 m), and Yalung Kang (west summit, 27,618 ft/8,420 m). It is hard hit by winds and monsoon snow, and it's SERAC barriers send down great AVALANCHES. Early explorations from 1850 to 1929 were mostly British, and the first climbing attempt in 1905 was led by Aleister Crowley, the flamboyant British occultist. Three expeditions by Germans and Austrians led separately by Paul Bauer and G. O. DHYRENFURTH culminated at 25,256 ft (7,700 m) on the northeast spur in 1931.

The faces of the massif have been approached via three GLACIERS: the Yalung on the southwest in Nepal delivered Britons George Band and Joe BROWN to the main summit in 1955 on their FIRST ASCENT. Poles used the start of this route in 1978 to climb the south and central summits. The south summit's southwest ridge became a dramatic alpine-style new route for two Slovenes, Andrej Stremfelj and Marko Prezelj (1991). The Zemu Glacier in Sikkim brought the 1977 Indian Army expedition to the northeast spur placing Major Prem Chand and Naik Sherpa on top. The Kangchenjunga Glacier gave Britons access to the main summit from the north in 1979 for a new route, alpine style, by Doug SCOTT, Peter BOARDMAN and Joe TASKER. Japanese achieved a direct route through huge seracs right of this route in 1980. This glacier also led Slovenes to the first ascent of Yalung Kang north face, by Borut Bergant and Tomo CESEN (Slovenia), in 1985.

The main, central and south summits were TRAVERSED by a large Japanese expedition in 1984, but in 1989 10 Soviets, including Sergei Bershov and Vladimer Balyberdin, made the traverse of all four of the massif's 26,240-ft (8,000-m) summits from opposite directions, achieving a superlative in high-altitude climbing. Other achievements include the first solo ascent by P. BEGHIN (1983, southwest face), and the first WINTER ASCENT (1985) by Poles Jerzy KUKUCZSKA and Kryzysztof Wielicki who endured −35 degree F/−37 degree C cold. Their partner, the great Czech climber Andzej Czok, died on the descent from high-altitude PULMONARY EDEMA.

KANGCHENJUNGA HIMAL (Nepal, Sikkim)   A range in eastern NEPAL, extending into Indian-controlled SIKKIM. Because of its size, it is subdivided into the northern and southern sections. The northern section is bounded in the north by Lhonak Peak near the Tibetan border, and in the south by the Zemu Glacier. Its eastern edge is the Tista River in Sikkim, and on its western edge are the Kangchenjunga Glaciers and the Tamur River. The southern section is also called the Kumbhakarna Section, and its boundaries are the Kumbhakarna Glacier in the north, and the Yalung Glacier in the south and east. The northern section is dominated by the world's third-highest mountain, KANGCHENJUNGA (28,168 ft/8,586 m), and by Yalung Kang (27,903 ft/8,505 m) and Kangbachen (25,927 ft/7,903 m). The main peak of the Kumbhakarna Section is Kumbhakarna, formerly called Jannu (25,294 ft/7,710 m). First climbed in 1962 by the south ridge, Kumbhakarna has long been regarded as a challenging massif, especially its rocky north face which New Zealanders made a concerted effort to climb in 1975, and Japanese completed in 1976. Frenchman Pierre BEGHIN and Eric Decamp made an ALPINE-STYLE ascent of this route in 1987, but the solo FIRST ASCENT of the direct north face by Slovene Tomo CESEN in 1989 remains an outstanding feat.

Guidebook: Jan Kielkowski, *Kangchenjunga and Khumbhakarna Himal,* (Polish text) (1988).

KARAKORAM RANGE (India, Pakistan, China)   Also Karakorum. The name of this range is derived from the historic Karakoram Pass, which leads to Central Asia. The word is an old Tibetan dialect and means black rubble. The term has come to cover a vast mountain region comprising many ranges in INDIA, PAKISTAN and CHINA. It is distinct from the HIMALAYA, being further north and west and divided by the Indus River. Nonetheless, the term Himalaya is often used to describe all the ranges of Asia.

The Karakoram is bounded by the Lower Shyok and Indus rivers on the south, and the Shaksgam tributary of the Yarkand River on the north. The Ishkoman and Karumbar rivers form the western boundary, and the Upper Shyok the eastern. Between the Lower Shyok and Upper Indus lies the Ladakh Range; west of the Karumbar River lies the HINDU KUSH; between the Shaksgam and Yarkand rivers lie the Aghil Mountains. The principal ranges of the Karakoram are the BATURA MUZTAGH, HISPAR MUZTAGH, PANMAH MUZTAGH, Baltoro Muztagh, Siachen Muztagh, RIMO MUZTAGH and SASER MUZTAGH, which form the Greater Karakoram. The RAKAPOSHI Range, HARAMOSH RANGE, MASHERBRUM Range and SALTORO RANGE form the Lesser Karakoram. Muztagh means ice mountain in the local languages.

The region has many long glaciers: The Batura (36 miles/58 km); the Hispar and Biafo that link together to form a 76-mile (122-km) passage of ice; the BALTORO (36 miles/58 km); and the Siachen (45 miles/72 km). In the Karakoram lie some of the world's highest peaks: K2 (28,250 ft/8,613 m) the second highest; the GASHERBRUM peaks, four of which are above 26,000 ft (7,927 m); BROAD PEAK (26,400 ft/8,049 m) and others like CHOGOLISA (25,147 ft/7,667 m), MASHERBRUM (25,660 ft/7,823 m), RAKAPOSHI (25,550 ft/7,790 m), Disteghil Sar (25,871 ft/7,889 m) and Saltoro Kangri (25,400 ft/7,744 m). In addition to peaks of lofty altitude, there is solid granite and BIG WALL CLIMBING in the Lower Baltoro Glacier, around Paiju Peak and the peaks of the TRANGO TOWERS, along the Biafo Glacier, and in the nearby LATOK Group.

Unlike the Himalaya of Nepal, which enjoys a high rainfall from the MONSOON, the Karakoram is less affected by the monsoon and is comparatively dry. Thus, climbers are active in the area from the frigid beginning of May till September, with June through August offering the best weather. At its best, the Karakoram offers warm cloudless days; at its worst, multi-day blizzards.

The Karakoram is frequented by many expeditions, especially in the Baltoro Glacier area. The mountain people are of many tribes and race mixtures, but the BALTI and Hunza of Pakistan are the best known due to their services as porters and high-altitude porters. A border way between India and Pakistan has made access into the Siachen region problematic.

The earliest western explorers to make the long trek into the Karakoram to climb and survey were H. H. Godwin Austen, W. M. CONWAY and Francis YOUNGHUSBAND, in the 1800s. Later, Sir Filippo de Filippi, C. Visser and the Duke of the ABRUZZI explored here, as did the Duke of Spoleto, Eric SHIPTON and Bill TILMAN. The climbing era began in the 1930s, with attempts on K2 by the likes of Fritz WIESSNER and Dr. Charles HOUSTON. Most of the

highest summits were climbed during the 1950s and 1960s by expeditions of many nationalities, and development continues today. Authorities granting permission for climbing in the Karakoram are listed under China, Pakistan and India. See also INDIAN KARAKORAM, KASHMIR.

Further reading: Greg Child, *Thin Air: Encounters in the Himalaya* (1988); Fosco Maraini, *Karakoram: The Ascent of Gasherbrum IV* (1961); Kenneth Mason, *Abode of Snow* (1987); Jill Neate, *High Asia* (1989); Galen Rowell, *In the Throneroom of the Mountain Gods* (1977, 1986); *American Alpine Journals*.

KARN, JIM (1966–   ) (United States) Karn was the first American man to win a World Cup event, in LaRiba, Spain, in 1988. He achieved the best showing ever for an American man when he placed third in the overall World Cup standings in 1990. A very talented, powerful boulderer, Karn won a world title at L'Open des Ecrins, a BOULDERING contest in L'Argentière, France, in 1991, and he placed 12th in the 1991 World Cup standings. In the U.S. national competitions Karn has made five straight wins in annual events from 1989 to 1990. On rock, he has ON-SIGHTED numerous hard SPORT CLIMBS to 5.13b and a possible 5.13c, High Water at AMERICAN FORK, though he disavows the credit, suggesting that the climb is overrated.

KASHMIR (India) This is the northern panhandle state of INDIA, and includes sections of the HIMALAYA and KARAKORAM. The mountains of Kashmir refers to the Kishtwar and Zanskar Himals, which are the northwest-southeast ranges east of the city of Srinagar. The highest peaks are in the northern Zanskar Himal, NUN KUN (23,403 ft/7,135 m and 23,213 ft/7,077 m, respectively). Nun, a huge snowy DOME, was first climbed in the 1950s by a French team, and now sees regular ascents. Above GLACIERS five to 10 miles (eight to 16 km) long, the highest Zanskar peaks, Z1–Z6 reach 19,680 ft (6,000 m). The Z peaks and many of their neighbors were first climbed in the early 1980s, when a road was built up the Suru River over the Pensi La Pass, making access from the east side of the range quite short. The Kishtwar Himal is an extension of the Zanskar Himal. It includes many 19,680-ft (6,000-m) peaks, and dozens of 16,400-ft (5,000-m) peaks. Like those of the Zanskar Himal, many are unclimbed. Prominent peaks here are Brammah, Kishtwar Shivling, Sickle Moon and White Sail. Most approaches take two to four days along narrow western canyons. The mountains of Kashmir receive westerly storms but only a weak midsummer MONSOON. Climbers visit these ranges May through September.

KATAHDIN, MOUNT (United States) This 5,267-ft (1,606-m) mountain, in northernmost Maine was first climbed in 1804 by the surveyor Charles Turner. Most northeastern mountaineers eventually visit Katahdin, if only to hike its superb knife EDGE, climb the renowned Armadillo rock ROUTE, or challenge themselves on difficult ice GULLIES. Baxter State Park requires winter climbers to make advance applications, with climbing resumes and equipment inspections.

Guidebook: Rick Wilcox, *An Ice Climber's Guide to Northern New England* (1982).
Further reading: Guy and Laura Waterman, *Forest And Crag* (1989).

KAUK, RON (1958–   ) (United States)

A leading American rock-climber since the 1970s, Kauk's name is synonymous with YOSEMITE FREE CLIMBING. After attending Yosemite Mountaineering School at the age of 14, he moved into CAMP FOUR at 16 to climb and made an early FLASH of the Yosemite testpiece BUTTERBALLS (5.11d). On multipitch Yosemite free climbs, he was on FIRST FREE ASCENTS of Geek Towers (5.11) in 1974, Astroman (5.11d, with John BACHAR and John LONG) in 1975, the Rostrum (5.11+), and the Lost Arrow, (V 5.12). On EL CAPITAN, with Dale BARD, he made the first ascent of Iron Hawk, (VI 5.10 A4+). With John Bachar he introduced 5.12 to Yosemite, freeing Hotline in 1975. Kauk lifted crack climbing standards to new highs with his routes in 1977 and 1978, Tales of Power (5.12c) and Separate Reality (5.12a). In 1977 he made the second ascent of Steve WUNSCH's Super Crack (5.12c) in the SHAWANGUNKS. Transplanting his finesse on long routes to the Karakoram he made the first ascent of Uli Biaho, a spire of the BALTORO Muztagh in Pakistan. This big wall, climbed with John ROSKELLEY, Kim Schmitz and Bill Forrest, was the first wall rated VII. His dedication to BOULDERING is witnessed by his successful climbs of two boulder problems, among the hardest in Yosemite: Midnight Lightning and Thriller (both B2). Kauk influenced a generation of American rock-climbers with traditional climbing ETHICS that eschewed RAPPEL BOLTING and weighting PROTECTION. But in 1987 a new Kauk emerged after a visit to Europe that instilled in him an appreciation of gymnastic SPORT-CLIMBING. He pursued rappel bolting, and clashed with his erstwhile partner John Bachar over the bolting of routes in Yosemite and Tuolomne. In sport climbing Kauk has FLASHED to 5.13a, has placed high in competitions and RED POINTED To Bolt or Not to Be (5.14a) at SMITH ROCKS.

KENNEDY, MICHAEL P. (1952–   ) (Canada) .

Born in Windsor, Ontario, Canada, April 15, 1952, he moved to the United States in 1964. After a period attending Antioch College, Ohio, 1969–1970, he dropped out to come west to climb. He has lived in Colorado since the summer of 1971 and has been the editor and publisher of *Climbing* magazine since 1974.

He pioneered many new rondes on big wilderness peaks and frozen waterfalls in North America. These include the North Face, Capitol Peak, Colorado (winter 1973) and Ames Falls (aka the Ophir Ice Hose).

His best successes were in Alaska, though. They include the "Lowe/Kennedy" route en MOUNT HUNTER, and INFINITE SPUR: Mount Foraker in 1977, with George Lowe. Also on Mount Hunter, in 1994 he climbed the very difficult Wall of Shadows, (first ascent, 1994, with Greg Child).

Significant attempts and ascents (foreign): Oddly, his best-known attempt is an unsuccessful attempt on the north ridge Latok I, to within 200 meters of summit (1978) with George Lowe, Jeff Lowe, and Jim Donini. In Nepal he made a fine winter first, with Carlos BUHLER, in 1985, on Northeast Face, Ama Dablam.

KENTUCKY (United States)

Sandstone climbing is found at Greencastle Bluffs, a 60-ft (18-m) CRAG near Bowling Green. The boulderer John Gill climbed here in Pennyrile Forest, on Gill's Bluffs and Indian Bluffs, located in southwest Kentucky. RED RIVER GORGE is the most extensive area of Kentucky. Black Mountain (4,145 ft/1,263 m), a hill in Harlan County, southeast Kentucky, is the state's high point.

KENYA

A small but active community of resident climbers have developed a wealth of rock and mountain climbing across this equatorial African nation. The climbing season falls between two wet seasons, which are from April to June, and from November to December. Alpine conditions are prime between June and October. Mount Kenya (17,032 ft/5,191 m), rising out of highland forests in central Kenya, is the country's best-known climbing landmark. This peak lies within a national park, and is commonly approached from either the town of Naro Moru on the west, or Nanyuki on the north. Guides and porters may be hired in Naru Moru. HUTS on the mountain offer accommodation to climbers. Thirty ROUTES lead to the main summits of Mount Kenya, the two highest of which are Batian (17,058 ft/5,199 m, first climbed in 1899 by Mackinder, Ollier and Brocherel) and Nelion (17,022 ft/5,188 m, first climbed in 1922 by Eric SHIPTON and P. W. Harris). Among the most famous climbs are The Diamond Couloir, a 14-pitch ice route, and The Standard Route, a 15-pitch 5.7 rock route. Most routes on this mountain take two days. Surrounding the moorlands around Mount Kenya are numerous rock spires of volcanic syenite, with summits of up to 14,000 ft (4,268 m). Of these, Point Pigott, Tereri and Sendeyo have significant rock climbing on solid rock. Because of the high elevation, Mount Kenya offers milder temperatures in summer.

Extensive rock climbing lies just 24 miles (38 km) southeast of the capital, Nairobi, on the gneiss of Leukenya. But Kenya's most famous rock-climbing area is in the west, at Hell's Gate, a volcanic gorge offering fine crack climbs. Wild African big game roam the grasslands beneath this crag. In remote northern Kenya, barely explored mountain ranges, volcanoes and rock spires rise above arid acacia scrublands. Significant formations here include the towering rock walls of Mount Poi in the Ndoto Mountains, and the 2,000-ft (610-m) face of Ol Doinyo Sabachi, near Marsabit. Other significant climbing areas of Kenya include Ndeyia, Nzaui, Soitpus and Kitchwa Tembo. The Matthews Range and the Aberdares contain easier mountain routes. The Mountain Club of Kenya (see Appendices) provides information about these areas.

Guidebooks: Iain Allen, *Guide to Mount Kenya and Kilimanjaro* (1981); Allen, *A Rock Climbing Guide to the Main Wall and Selected Routes at Hell's Gate* (1977); M. C. Watts, *A Climber's Guide to Leukenya* (1973); Andrew Wielochowski, *East Africa International Mountain Guide* (1986).

KERNMANTLE The standard type of modern climbing rope, consisting of a multistrand nylon core (kern), surrounded by a tightly braided nylon sheath (MANTLE). (See ROPES, PERLON.)

KHUMBU (Nepal) The upper section of the Solu-Khumbu district of NEPAL. It is famous as the land of Mount EVEREST and SHERPAS, who for centuries have raised crops and animals in this high-altitude region. Khumbu is generally thought of as the land above about 9,000 ft (2,744 m) in the three headwater valleys of the Dudh Kosi river. The Khumbu Himal is a subsection of the MAHALANGUR HIMAL, and includes Everest's neighbors LHOTSE, PUMORI, and Gyachung Kang and CHO OYU on the main east-west divide. South of the divide are spectacular lower peaks such as Taweche and Cholatse. North of the divide the peaks of Khumbu include Changtse, Palung Ri and others completely in TIBET.

KICHATNA SPIRES (United States) More correctly called the Kichatna Spires of the Cathedral Range, the Kichatna Spires is a range of granite peaks 85 miles (136 km) west of Talkeetna, in the southwest tip of the ALASKA RANGE. The range covers eight sq miles (21 sq km) and although its highest point—Kichatna Spire—is only 8,985 ft (2,739 m) high, the relief varies from 2,000 to 4,000 ft (610 to 1,220 m), generally as sheer walls. The area suffers from severe storms that often coat the spires in Patagonia-like ice encrustations, while the rock climbing presents challenges on the scale of YOSEMITE big walls. The area is usually reached by aircraft, which fly from Talkeetna and land on the GLACIERS. The first climbs were made in 1965, Kichatna Spire receiving its FIRST ASCENT a year later by Art Davidson and Rick Millikan, up the east couloir and north ridge. This peak has since been ascended by three major BIG WALL routes, one up the northwest face (J. BRIDWELL, A. Embick, J. Bouchard) in 1979 and two on the east face in 1982 (S. Woollums and B. Denz, and D. Black, M. Graber, G. Schunk). Other impressive peaks of this remote range are Gurney Peak, Mount Jeffers, The Citadel and North and Middle Triple peaks.
Further reading: Allen Steck and Steve Roper, *Fifty Classic Climbs of North America* (1979); *American Alpine Journal* (1982) and AAJs (1965–92).

KILIMANJARO, MOUNT (Tanzania, Kenya) Africa's highest mountain is 19,340 ft/5,895 m and lies three degrees south of the equator. This volcano's snow-capped summit is frequently mistaken for clouds floating above the arid plains. Its sprawling base measures 50 miles by 25 miles (80 km by 40 km) and is surrounded by lush equatorial alpine forests and African wildlife. Kilimanjaro is actually comprised of three summits: Kibo is the highest (19,340 ft/5,894 m); Mawenzi is a rocky summit (16,890 ft/5,148 m); and Shira is an easy angled slope leading to a 13,000-ft (3,900-m) top. January and February offer the best chances for climbing Kilimanjaro. Although Kilimanjaro lies on the Tanzanian and Kenyan borders, most climbing is done from the Tanzanian side. From either the capital Nairobi in KENYA, or from the Tanzanian capital Dar es Salaam,

Kilimanjaro is reached via road or air, to Kilimanjaro International Airport between the Tanzanian towns of Moshi and Arusha. The climb is commonly approached from Marangu, where guides and porters may be hired for ascents of the easy Standard Route. HUTS provide shelter on this route. Of the 14 other routes to the summit, the most popular non-TECHNICAL routes are the Barafu Route and the Western Breach Route. More challenging snowfields are found on the Heim Glacier. Kilimanjaro's hardest route is the Breach Wall, or Breach Icicle, first climbed by Reinhold MESSNER. (See TANZANIA.)
Guidebooks: Iain Allen, *A Guide to Mount Kenya and Kilimanjaro* (1981); Andrew Wielochowski, *East Africa International Mountain Guide* (1986).
Further reading: Harald Lange, *Kilimanjaro: White Roof of Africa* (1985); John Reader, *Kilimanjaro* (1982).

KILNSEY CRAG (Britain) This 160-ft (49-m) limestone CRAG lies a few miles north of Skipton in the Wharfe Valley of the Yorkshire Dales. Kilnsey's "rock umbrella" is severely overhanging and at one end sports a monstrous ROOF. The rock is sound but the angle offers little for middle-grade climbers. There is a pub in the tiny hamlet just south of the crag and a campsite nearby.

Early development at Kilnsey was dominated by AID CLIMBING. The Rock and Ice Club arrived in 1953 to climb the Main Overhang but both Joe BROWN and Ron Moseley retreated before the main roof. Moseley finally summoned the nerve in 1957, spending 11 hours in his ETRIERS before succeeding.

The arrival of Pete LIVESEY in the early 1970s produced FREE ASCENTS like The Diedre (5.9), Central Wall (5.11a) and, after chiseling holds, Claws (5.12a). In the 1980s Ron FAWCETT produced Deja Vu (5.11c) and Pete Gomersall opened Relax and Zero Option, both 5.12, and Martin Berzins snatched the arete of Dominatrix (5.12c) in 1984. Extreme additions include Gomersall's Show Time (5.13a) from 1989 and Dave Pegg's The Yorkshire Ripper (5.13b), but the most important, at least psychologically, was Mark Leach's free ascent of Main Overhang (5.13d), 31 years after Moseley's first ascent.
Guidebook: Yorkshire Mountain Club, *Yorkshire Limestone* (1992).

KINNAUR HIMALAYA (India) A small range of northern INDIA near the Indo-Tibetan border. Leo Pargial (22,280 ft/6,791 m) is the tallest peak. It was first climbed in 1933 by Marco Pallis and C. B. M. Warren. Numerous Indian parties have climbed the major summits, but many opportunities for new climbs exist. Access is easy into this region, as the Hindustan-Tibet road, which follows the Satluj River, penetrates the range, but being close to TIBET the area falls within a restricted zone called the *Inner Line*, making access for foreign expeditions somewhat difficult.
Further reading: S. Mehta and H. Kapadia, *Exploring the Hidden Himalaya* (1990).

KIRKUS, COLIN (1910–1942) (Britain) Colin Kirkus is one of the two defining presences—the other being

Menlove EDWARDS—of British rock-climbing in the 1930s. Liverpool-born, he began climbing in North Wales in his teens, surviving hair-raising solo escapades beautifully described in his classic instructional book of 1941, *Let's Go Climbing*. As a youth just turned 19, his leads of Lot's Groove on Glyder Fach and Central Climb on Tryfan, on consecutive days in 1929 announced his presence forcibly to the climbing world, and were followed by a series of great climbs on CLOGWYN DU'R ARDDU, Dinas Mot, Craig Cwm Silyn and Craig yr Ysfa, which are now considered to be among the medium-grade classics of the area. A couple of them—Bridge Groove on Clogwyn Du'r Arddu and West Rib on Dinas Mot—mark a distinct TECHNICAL advance, as do many of Kirkus's routes on the sandstone OUTCROP of Helsby, near Chester. Most of his climbs are characterized by openness and, for their day, exceptionally long run-outs. On his one trip to the Himalayas, in 1933, he made the FIRST ASCENT of the difficult 22,000-ft (6,707-m) Central Satopanth Peak in the GANGOTRI REGION of Garhwal.

Kirkus's pioneering virtually ended when, in 1934 at the age of 23, he and his companion, Maurice Linnell, fell from The Castle, a winter climb on the north face of Ben Nevis. Linnell was killed, Kirkus badly injured, and though he recovered, he never climbed as intensively as from 1929 to 1932 again. He died in September 1942, when the Wellington bomber of which he was navigator failed to return from a night raid on Bremen.

Further reading: Stephen Dean, *Colin Kirkus: A Biography* (1992); Colin Kirkus, *Let's Go Climbing* (1941).

KISHTWAR HIMAL   See KASHMIR.

KISHTWAR HIMALAYA   (India)   Indian Himalayan chroniclers Soli Mehta and Harish Kapadia wrote in their book *Exploring the Hidden Himalaya* (1990): "Kishtwar is the small party's hunting ground—there are innumerable valleys which are yet to be visited and the sheer variety of rock and ice formation is enough to satiate the most ardent alpinist, even if he ignored the prominent summits." The Kishtwar rises above the northeast bank of the Chenab River, with KASHMIR to the north and Chamba-Lahul to the south. In the northwest corner of the range is the region's highest peak, Sickle Moon (21,563 ft/6,574 m), climbed in 1975 by an Indian High-Altitude Warfare School expedition. Brammah I (21,044 ft/6,416 m), first climbed by Britons Nick Estcourt and Chris BONINGTON in 1973, and Brammah II (21,074 ft/6,425 m), climbed by Japanese in 1975, rise on the western edge of the range. The attractive peak Kishtwar Shivling, in the southeast corner of the range, had a fine route added to its north face in 1983 by Britons Stephen Venables and Dick Renshaw. This climb is described in Venables's book *The Painted Mountains* (1989). Other parties have found the granite of the area conducive to rock routes up to 15 pitches.

KITCHENER, MOUNT   (Canada)   This peak (11,500 ft/3,480 m) forms the north rim of the COLUMBIA ICE FIELD of the ROCKY MOUNTAINS in ALBERTA. While the southwest slopes provide a gentle ski ascent, the northeast face, rising above the Ice Fields Parkway, poses several of the great mountaineering challenges in North America. The FIRST ASCENT was made from the ice fields in 1927 by A. J. Ostheimer and H. Fuhrer. The northeast face was first climbed by Chris Jones, Graham Thompson and Jeff LOWE via the Ramp Route, in summer 1971. This route received its first WINTER ASCENT from John Lauchlan and Jim Elzinga in 1977. The main gully of the face became known as Grand Central Couloir, due to the regularity of debris rumbling down it, a name inspired by the steady clamor of trains at New York City's Grand Central Station. It was first climbed by Jeff Lowe and Mike Weiss in 1974, who rated it 5.9 VI grade 5. It received a first winter ascent from Tobin Sorenson and Jack Roberts in 1979.

Guidebook: Sean Dougherty, *Selected Alpine Climbs in the Canadian Rockies* (1991).

KLETTERSCHUHE   Or Klets. Light rock-climbing boots with stiffened soles, manufactured in Europe and popular until the late 1960s. No longer manufactured.

KNOTS   The following knots are used by climbers.
Bowline: A strong knot (breaking strength 70 to 75% of rope) that is easy to undo after knot is tightened but is unsafe if wrongly tied. It should be finished with a stopper knot.
Bowline on a coil: The end of the rope becomes the waist harness in this knot. Only useful if harness or webbing to make a harness is unavailable. This knot uses much rope, and one cannot rappel since one is connected to the rope.
Butterfly knot: The strongest mid-rope knot. Undos easily after being loaded with a force, which is advantageous.
Clove hitch: Useful for backing up the figure eight, but by itself offers only 60 to 65% breaking strength of the rope. However, its quick adjustability makes it the best knot for equalizing the rope to anchors.
Double fisherman's (or grapevine) knot: The common knot for linking two ropes, even of different diameter. Several inches of rope should be left as a trail on each strand in case of slippage. Offers a breaking strength of 65 to 70% of the rope. Difficult to untie after knot is tightened. A variation by tying a reef knot between the locking knots is sometimes used to alleviate tight knots.
Double-knotted bowline: An extra loop makes this a stronger, more failproof knot than the bowline.
Figure eight: The basic climber's knot and the strongest (breaking strength 75 to 80% of rope), even if incorrectly tied (usually resulting in an overhand knot). The main rope should lie outside the first bend in the knot.
French Prusik:
  Autoblock: A friction knot for crevasse rescue that supplies greater friction than the Prusik and locks a rope off.
Frost knot: For tying a loop within a webbing sling, as required when finishing ETRIERS.
Mariner's knot: In rescue operations, used for connecting the rope to an anchor where it may be necessary to later release the rope when weighted.
Overhand figure eight: Like the figure eight, only tied on a

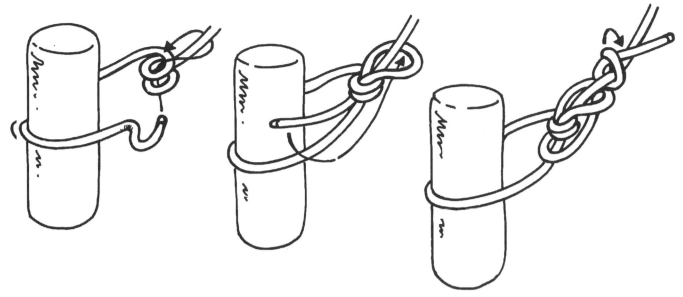

Double Knotted Bowline

blight of rope. Can be quickly tied anywhere along a rope. Used to connect the climbing rope to the main anchors.

Overhand knot: Also useful for quickly clipping in to anchors, this bulky knot will jam in rappel devices and prevent a climber inadvertently sliding off a rope end.

Prusik knot: A friction hitch that slides up a rope but locks when weighted. Even though an ASCENDER is more functional than a PRUSIK, the knot is essential for crevasse rescue operations.

Stopper knot: A simple hitch tied around the main rope to finish the main knot and prevent unraveling.

Tape knot (or water knot, ring bend): The common knot for joining webbing. Must be weighted to cinch the knot; otherwise, unraveling is possible.

KNOTTED SLINGS   An old technique using knotted slings of varying diameters of rope to jam into constrictions in cracks. The technique is still used in the ELBSANDSTEIN-GEBIRGE region of Germany. Modern NUTS have replaced this method.

KOGAN, CLAUDE (CLAUDETTE) TROUILLET (1919–1959) (France)   Himalayan expeditionary mountaineer Kogan began climbing while a teenager living in Belgium. She moved to Nice, France, during the early years of World War II and climbed with the Alpes Maritime section, Club Alpine Française. She led routes such as the Pueterey Noir on MONT BLANC with Georges Kogan, owner of a sportswear factory, whom she married in 1945. Attracted to the Peruvian ANDES by Erwin SCHNEIDER and Hans Kinzel's book *Cordillera Blanca—Peru* (1950), the Kogans organized the 1951 Franco-Belgian expedition, which made the FIRST ASCENT of Pisco (18,406 ft/5,612 m), and attempted HUASCARAN and ALPAMAYO. The climb of Alpamayo was thought to be a first ascent, until a German party climbed the peak in 1957 to find that the true summit, obscured by clouds in 1951, was beyond the Franco-Belgian

high point. Claude, with Nichole Leininger, made the first ascent of Quitaraju (19,520 ft/5,951 m). Georges died shortly after their return to Nice in 1951 and Claude took over the sportswear business of Nice-Tricot. She continued making expeditions: a return to Peru with a Franco-American team for the first ascent of Salcantay (1952); in the Himalaya with Swiss Pierre Vittoz, the first ascent of NUN KUN (1953); an attempt on CHO OYU, with Swiss Raymond Lambert, to 25,600 ft (7,805 m) in 1954; and a successful ascent of Ganesh I (24,298 ft/7,408 m) in 1955. She spoke at an Alpine Club meeting in London in 1955, the first woman to address the club in its 98-year history. She then climbed in Greenland (1956); returned to the CORDILLERA BLANCA (1957); went to the Caucasus (1958) for ascents of Elbrus, Ushba and Chatogan; and led an international expedition of women to Cho Oyu (1959). She, with Belgian Claudine van der Straten-Ponthoz and Sherpa Ang Norbu, were buried in an avalanche at the expedition's highest camp at 22,720 ft (6,927 m).

Further reading: Claude Kogan and Raymond Lambert, *White Fury,* translated by Showell Styles (1956).

KOR, LAYTON (19??–   ) (United States)   His drive and enthusiasm, combined with natural ability on rock, made him one of the best climbers in the world throughout the 1960s. He started climbing around BOULDER, COLORADO, in the early 1960s and with Pat AMENT, Larry Dalke, Bob Culp and others made many FIRST ASCENTS in ELDORADO CANYON. BIG WALL ascents in YOSEMITE during the mid-1960s, several in record time, brought him recognition as perhaps the fastest aid climber in the world. He also made big wall ascents in the BLACK CANYON OF THE GUNNISON. He was a master of climbing loose rock and pioneered many climbs of this fragile nature in Glenwood Canyon (Colorado) and the Southwest desert. His alpine achievements include the FIRST WINTER ASCENT of the DIAMOND on LONG'S PEAK, when temperatures dropped to −40 degrees F (−40 degrees C) and his role in the 1966 EIGER direct route. His autobiography is *Beyond the Vertical*.

KOSCIUSKO, MOUNT (Australia) Although only 7,328 ft/2,229 m, as the highest mountain in Australasia Kosciusko has the distinction of being one of the SEVEN SUMMITS, which are the seven highest points of the seven continents. However, because the definition of Australasia is not restricted to the Australian continent but also includes a large group of Pacific land masses, there is disagreement as to whether Kosciusko or CARSTENZ PYRAMID (16,532 ft/5,040 m) in New Guinea is the true high point.

Kosciusko lies in the Snowy Mountains, south of the city of Canberra, in the state of New South Wales. More of an alpine hill than a mountain, Kosciusko presents no TECHNICAL difficulties. Hikers in summer and cross-country skiers in winter make frequent ascents of the peak.

KUKUCZKA, JERZY (1948–1990) (Poland) Though Reinhold MESSNER was the first to complete ascents of all the 26,240-ft (8,000-m) peaks in 1986, Kukuczka was never far behind him, completing all 14 himself in 1988. Kukuczka, an electrician with a small family, overcame the difficulties of launching expeditions out of the Eastern Bloc where hard currency was virtually unobtainable. First climbing in his native Tatra Range, he added new routes in the Alps (on Petit DRU, GRANDES JORASSES, Torre Trieste and Torre del Bancon), and repeated DENALI south face in 1974. In the mid-1970s he climbed Koh e Tez (22,960 ft/7,000 m) in the HINDU KUSH, and a new route on Tirich Mir (24,934 ft/7,602 m), the north ridge. He began "collecting" 26,240-ft (8,000-m) peaks in 1979, with LHOTSE (regular route). EVEREST in 1980, via a new line, the Polish south face, was the only climb on which he used supplementary oxygen. On MAKALU in 1981 he reached 25,912 ft (7,900 m) on the west face (with Alex MACINTYRE and Wojciech KURTYKA), then soloed the peak by a new variant of the original route. In 1983 he and Kurtyka climbed new routes, ALPINE STYLE on GASHERBRUM I (southwest face) and GASHERBRUM II (southeast ridge). In 1984 they made an alpine-style TRAVERSE of BROAD PEAK's three summits, a new and committing route. The year 1985 saw him add a new route on NANGA PARBAT. The winter of 1985 gave him DHAULAGIRI and CHO OYU, and then KANGCHENJUNGA in winter 1986. His new alpine-style route up the south face of K2 was sensational but marred by the death of his partner, Tadeusz Pietrowski, who fell while descending. He made an alpine-style WINTER ASCENT of MANASLU with Artur Hajzer (Poland) the same year, summiting via a new route up Manaslu east-northeast face. In 1987 he climbed ANNAPURNA I and SHISHAPANGMA (regular routes). Not content to stop after his 14th eight-thousander, he participated on a new route on Annapurna south face (1988). In 1990, after reaching the summit ridge of the last great problem of the Himalaya—Lhotse south face—he fell, snapping his quarter-inch (6 mm) rope and plunging to his death. The climbing world lost its toughest Himalayan climber.

Further reading: Jerzy Kukuczka, *My Vertical World* (1992).

KULU-LAHUL HIMALAYA (India) Located at the headwaters of the Beas and Chenab rivers in northwest India, this range of modest altitude is popular with trekkers and climbers because it is accessible via a road penetrating lush valleys beyond the mountain towns east of Pathankot and around Manali. Here, smaller peaks offer opportunities for ALPINE-STYLE ascents. Out of the Kulu Valley rushes the Beas River, and around the river rise peaks like Deo Tibba (19,683 ft/6,001 m), Indrasan (20,405 ft/6,221 m), the attractive granite spire Ali Ratna Tibba (18,007 ft/5,490 m) and Dharamsura (White Sail) (21,143 ft/6,446 m). North of the Chandra River and bounded by its great curve is Lahul, with peaks of the Chandra Bhaga and Mulkilla groups rising up to 20,664 ft (6,300 m). Peaks up to 21,320 ft (6,500 m) lie above the Parbati River. The region was climbed in mainly by British and European climbers, from the 1930s through the 1960s.
Further reading: S. Mehta and H. Kapadia, *Exploring the Hidden Himalaya* (1990).

KUMAUN-GARHWAL HIMALAYA (India) A confusing term, as modern climbers usually refer to the Indian Himalaya as the Garhwal, yet geographers and early climbers called it the Kumaun. Joining the two terms to describe the entire Indian Himalaya has been accepted, though geographers disagree on boundaries of the ranges.

The eastern boundary of the Kumaun is the Kali River and its tributaries, separating INDIA from NEPAL. The western limit is the Kangribingri La, over the Unta Dhura, through the town of Milam and down the Ghori Ganga River. The northern boundary is the Zaskar Range, which forms the ill-defined Indo-Tibetan border. Several massifs rise in the Kumaun, such as the five-summited Panchchuli massif, with peak II the highest (22,645 ft/6,904 m); the peaks around the Ghori Valley, with Chiring We (21,514 ft/6,559 m, first climbed by Britons Snelson and de Graaf), and Nanda Kot (22,504 ft/6,861 m, first climbed by Japanese), Tirsuli (23,203 ft/7,074 m, first climbed by Indians) and Hardeol (23,455 ft/7,151 m, also by Indians), the latter three often included in the Nanda Devi Group.

West of the Ghori Ganga lies the most famous Himalayan region of India, the Garhwal Himal, which contains the NANDA DEVI group, KAMET group and GANGOTRI group. It is bounded by the Tibet border and the Kumaun region, which lies 50 miles (80 km) northwest of the Nepal border. The Garhwal Himal is 150 miles (241 km) long and includes scores of peaks aligned in northwest-southeast ranges. This region is revered by Indians as a spiritual center, because in it lies the headwaters of the Ganges River. As the westernmost Himalaya it receives a strong monsoon. Expeditions are generally active May through September.

The highest peak in India is twin-peaked Nanda Devi (25,545 ft/7,788 m), in east Garhwal Himal Nanda Devi is surrounded by a ring of peaks including Trisul (23,360 ft/7,122 m), Dunagiri (23,184 ft/7,068 m) and the precipitous

CHANGABANG (22,520 ft/6,869 m). Some forty miles (64 km) northwest of Nanda Devi the huge massif of Kamet reaches 25,447 ft (7,758 m). Southwest of Kamet the Gangotri region has attracted much attention since the 1980s because roads up the canyons put climbers two to four days from many objectives. Satopanth (23,212 ft/7,077 m), Brigupanth (22,220 ft/6,774 m), Kedar Dome (22,410 ft/6,832 m) and others offer moderate routes, while SHIVLING (21,467 ft/6,440 m), Bhagirathi III (21,175 ft/6,353 m), Meru (21,850 ft/6,545 m), and Thalay Sagar (22,650 ft/6,905 m) are dramatic peaks of ice and granite. Further west Kalanag (20,956 ft/6,389 m) and Banderpunch (20,720 ft/6,317 m) dominate westernmost Garhwal.

Further reading: S. Mehta and H. Kapadia, *Exploring the Hidden Himalaya* (1990).

KUNLUN RANGE (China, Tibet) Extending eastward from the Pamirs into Xinjiang and running for 2,486 miles (4,000 km) along the northern limit of the Tibetan Plateau is the Kunlun, a range little-known to modern climbers, presenting many unclimbed peaks. On its Tibetan and Chinese side the range rises abruptly from high dry plains and deserts. One peak—Amne Machen—enjoyed notoriety as possibly being higher than Everest when Joseph Rock (United States) estimated it at 27,880 ft (8,500 m) in 1928. An article in *National Geographic* magazine shored up this claim, and American pilots in World War Two reported seeing a mountain bigger than EVEREST. Then in 1949 Leonard Clark (United States) claimed to have surveyed the peak at 29,651 ft (9,040 m). After a Chinese survey in 1960 came up with a figure of 23,485 ft (7,160 m), a subsequent survey fixed the height at a modest 20,605 ft (6,282 m). The peak was climbed via the northeast ridge in 1981 by Americans Galen ROWELL, Harold Knutsen and Kim Scmitz. The highest peaks are Kongur Tobe Feng (24,912 ft/7,595 m), first climbed by Chinese in 1956; Kongur Shan (25,318 ft/7,719 m), climbed via the south ridge by British in 1981; MUZTAGATA (24,751 ft/7,546 m),

an often-climbed peak near the Sino-Russian border; and Ulugh Muztagh (22,917 ft/6,987 m, previously 25,331 ft/7,723 m) first climbed from the east in 1985 by an American-Chinese expedition that re-surveyed the peak.

Further reading: Chris Bonington, *Kongur: China's Elusive Summit* (1982).

KURTYKA, WOJCIECH "VOYTEK" (1947–) (Poland) One of the great modern proponents of ALPINE-STYLE climbing in the HIMALAYA, Kurtyka appeared on the high-altitude scene in the mid-1970s, on large, unsuccessful Polish attempts on K2 and LHOTSE. Thereafter he operated in small teams, alpine style, traveling overland from Poland on low-budget, big-ambition trips for new routes. In the HINDU KUSH he made FIRST ASCENTS on Acher Chioch north face (23,042 ft/7,025 m), Koh-e-Tez north ridge (23,009 ft/7,015 m), in 1972, and in 1977, with Alex MACINTYRE and John Porter (United States), Koh-e-Bandaka northeast face (22,527 ft/6,868 m). In INDIA in 1978 he climbed the big wall of CHANGABANG south face, with Porter, MacIntyre and Krzystof Zurek (Poland). With MacIntyre, Rene Ghillini (France) and Ludwick Wilczynski (Poland) he pioneered DHAULAGIRI east face (1980). From 1982 to 1984 Kurtyka teamed with Jerzy KUKUCZKA, opening new routes on GASHERBRUM I, GASHERBRUM II and a committing TRAVERSE of BROAD PEAK. Kurtyka received acclaim after his and Robert Schauer's bold ascent of GASHERBRUM IV west face (1985), a multiday climb that brought them close to death. They missed the summit, traversing at the top to descend the northwest ridge and save their lives. With Erhard LORETAN in 1988 he opened the vertical east face of Nameless Tower in the TRANGO TOWERS, then those two, with Jean TROILLET, made new routes on SHISHAPANGMA and CHO OYU in 1989. When asked why he and his fellow Poles have had such an impact on Himalayan alpinism he once remarked, "in the end we are better at the art of suffering, and for high altitude this is everything."

L

LA A word used in Himalayan countries that means pass.

LACHENAL, LOUIS (1921–1955) (France) Lachenal was one of the fastest and most graceful rock and ice climbers of his generation. A Chamonix guide, Lachenal did all of his best routes alongside Lionel TERRAY. From the beginning their partnership was marked by a huge advance in climbing speed. In 1946 they were the first to do the north spur of Les DROITES in less than a day. Their first big achievement, however, was a new ROUTE on the GRANDES JORASSES. Next they did the second ascent of the north face of the EIGER in 1947. At that time little was known about the route pioneered by the victorious German-Austrian party that had vanquished the "Killer Mountain" in 1938. So Lachenal and Terray improvised a partially new route, weaving through the legendary rock falls buffeted by several storms. They also foresaw the greater safety of making a winter ascent, the first on the Eigerwand taking advantage of the stable, frozen cliffs. In 1950 the pair did the first one-day ascent of the north east face of the Piz Badille, the route pioneered in 1937 by Ricardo Cassin and joined a French expedition to Annapurna. Like many of the French team, Lachenal's highest point had been MONT BLANC. He was sensitive to his lack of high-altitude experience and often expressed anxiety about the possibility of losing his hands and/or feet to frostbite. But he climbed brilliantly, endured incredible hardship, and finally became, along with Maurice Herzog, the first to summit a 26,240-ft (8,000-m) peak. He fell on the descent during a storm—losing hat, gloves and crampon—and became incapacitated with FROSTBITE. After some 16 operations on the stumps of his feet, Lachenal appeared to undergo a character change: the old charm and ebullience was replaced by a pronounced death wish. After a hundred narrow escapes behind the wheel of a car, he died accidentally by falling into a crevasse while skiing unroped. "Lachenal was by far the fastest and most brilliant climber I have ever known on delicate or loose terrain," wrote Terray in his autobigraphy *Conquistadors of the Useless.* "His dexterity was phenomenal, his vitality like that of a wild beast. On his day he was capable of something very like genius . . ."

LAKE DISTRICT (Britain) This is the birthplace of British rock-climbing, with gentle lakeside and rugged mountainside rouses. The number of significant ascents achieved both before and after World War I illustrate the level of exploratory skill that came to typify British climbing. After the World War II development turned to elsewhere in Britain, though there was a renaissance in the mid-1970s. See BORROWDALE; CASTLE ROCK OF TRIERMAIN; DOVE CRAG; DOW CRAG; ESK BUTTRESS; GABLE CRAG; GIMMER CRAG; NAPES, THE; PAVEY ARK; RAVEN CRAG; SCAFELL; SCAFELL EAST BUTTRESS; WHITE GHYLL CRAG.

LAND'S END (Britain) CORNWALL's Land's End, the most westerly point in England, is a tourist attraction as well as a SEA CLIFF. ROUTES are short, but they have tremendous atmosphere and are subject to the full force of the Atlantic. Land's End has three main areas—Cormorant, World's End and Longships promontories. Facilities are located in nearby Penzance.

Cormorant Promontory has some easier routes, but the main attractions of the area are Last Dancer, a technical RIB rated 5.12b, and Day Tripper, a 5.11 CRACK climb. Both these routes were the work of Rowland and Mark Edwards. Pat LITTLEJOHN's Voices (5.10a), is regarded as the most worthwhile climb at World's End.

Longships Promontory is a sea-swept crag with sound rock and excellent climbs. The outstanding LINES are Atlantic Ocean Wall, a technical and intimidating wall over 200 ft (61 m) high climbed by the Edwardses in 1981 and the BOLTED 5.12c Titanic.
Guidebooks: Pat Littlejohn, *South West Climbs* (1991); Pete O'Sullivan, *West Penwith* (1983).

LANGTANG HIMAL (Nepal, Tibet) The heart of this Himalayan range, which lies mostly in NEPAL, is just 45 miles (72 km) as the crow flies from Kathmandu. The Langtang and the Jugal Himal are felt by some geographers to warrant combining. The whole range extends from the Sun Kosi River in the east to the Trisuli-Bhote Kosi rivers in the west. The highest peak of the Jugal section—SHISHA-PANGMA (26,398 ft/8,046 m)—lies wholly within TIBET. Ten mapped peaks above 22,960 ft (7,000 m) and 49 peaks above 19,680 ft (6,000 m) lie within the range. Among these, the impregnable-looking Langtang Lirung (23,734 ft/7,234 m) was the scene of many attempts and five deaths between 1961 and 64 before it was climbed by the east ridge in 1978 by a Japanese expedition.

LAPSE RATE The drop in air temperature with increased altitude. Depending upon humidity levels, this rate is approximately four degrees per 1,000 vertical ft (305 m). (See also WIND CHILL.)

LATOK PEAKS (Pakistan) This chain of rarely climbed, fanglike KARAKORAM peaks comprise Latok I (23,441 ft/7,145 m), Latok II (23,319 ft/7,108 m), Latok III (22,798 ft/6,949 m) and Latok IV (21,180 ft/6,456 m). Like the OGRE, they are approached via the BIAFO GLACIER, or via the Panmah Glacier to the Choktoi Glaciers. The proudest of these peaks is Latok I. Japanese expeditions in 1975 and 1976 and Italians in 1977 tried and failed to force a way up this peak from the south. Americans Jim Donini, Michael KENNEDY, Jeff LOWE and George LOWE tackled the stupendous 8,000-ft (2,439-m) north ridge in 1978. They climbed in ALPINE STYLE, to 23,000 ft (7,012 m), but were then trapped in a five-day storm during which Jeff became ill from altitude, forcing a difficult retreat. They reached base camp after 26 days. Several expeditions have tried to complete this route but none have equalled the Americans' high point. In 1979 a Japanese team returned to the southern side and summited via a difficult BUTTRESS above the Baintha Lukpar Glacier. Latok II was first climbed in 1977 by Italians on the southeast buttress.

Further reading: Jill Neate, *High Asia* (1989); *American Alpine Journal*, (1979).

LAUCHLAN, JOHN (1954–1982) (Canada) Lauchlan was a leading climber of the CANADIAN ROCKIES during the late 1970s and early 1980s. He contributed as a cragger, a BIG WALL climber and an alpinist. His achievements include the rock climb The Maker, the first 5.10 in the Rockies, climbed in the early 1970s; FIRST ASCENTS of the FROZEN WATERFALLS Takakaw Falls, Professor Falls, Pilsner Pillar and Carlsberg Column; alpine climbs like Slipstream (on Snow Dome) and the FIRST WINTER ASCENT of the Ramp route on Mount KITCHENER. He also participated in expedition-style undertakings on Yukon peaks like Mount Vancouver west face (15,850 ft/4,832 m, 1977) and Mount LOGAN's south southwest buttress (1979), and, in the HIMALAYA, Gangapurna south face (24,457 ft/7,456 m, 1981). He was active in Canadian mountaineering organizations and founded the predecessor of Yamnuska Mountain School. He died while soloing the frozen waterfall route, Polar Circus.

LAW, MICHAEL (1958–) (Australia) This Sydney-based climber opened hundreds of rock climbs across AUSTRALIA during the 1970s and 1980s that were visionary for boldness and difficulty, and in the 1990s he led the trend toward Australian SPORT CLIMBING. But it is Law's theatrical presence on the cliffs and his humorous guidebooks that made him a legend in Australian climbing.

In 1974, while a schoolboy, his FIRST FREE ASCENT of Janicepts (Blue Mountains) produced the nation's first (see RATING SYSTEMS) 21. In 1978, his FREE ASCENT of Undertaker (Mount ARAPILES), with Greg Child, was Australia's first 25. He opened radically unprotected routes also, such as

his 1976 lead of No Holds Barred (Mount Buffalo), 21. In 1983 he extended the grading system with several routes that went unrepeated for years; Rent-a-doddle (Ben Cairn, VIC), Pain and Frequency (You-Yangs, VIC) and Space Junk (Blue Mountains) were all grade 28 (5.13). In the 1980s he plumbed the potential of the Sydney Sea Cliffs, opening dozens of routes, both hard, like SKP, 29, and bold, like Housemaid's Knee, 24.

LAYAWAY A single layback move. (See LIEBACK, LAYBACK.)

Layaway

LAYERING The principle of wearing multiple layers of clothing to adapt to the varying temperatures in the mountains.

LEADER The climber who ascends a PITCH first.

LEADING THROUGH Another term for ALTERNATE LEADS.

LEAVENWORTH (United States) Surrounding this Bavarian-style village of eastern WASHINGTON, 80 miles (128 km) east of Seattle, are some popular rock-climbing areas. Because Leavenworth lies in the rainshadow of the Cascade

Leading Through

Range, the climate is quite dry. Granitic formations along the Tumwater Canyon, like Castle Rock, and CRAGS in the Icicle Creek Canyon offer hundreds of moderate FREE CLIMBS, from BOULDERING to several PITCHES. ROUTES are frequently slabby, but steeper climbs can be found. In Tumwater Canyon waterfalls like Drury Falls and The Pencil sometimes freeze in winter, but temperature inversions and marine air make fickle ice conditions. East of Leavenworth is Peshastin Pinnacles, a cluster of sandstone pinnacles that are popular with middle-grade climbers. Access problems closed this area to climbers for five years, but it was reopened to climbing in 1991 after being bought by the Trust for Public Land. Leavenworth is a hub for trailheads leading into the CASCADE RANGE alpine areas. Fine granite peaks are found here, such as Mount STUART, and Prusik Peak in the Enchantment Lakes region.
Guidebooks: Fred Beckey, *Cascade Alpine Guide, Columbia River to Stevens Pass* (1979); Victor Kramar, *Leavenworth Rock Climbs* (1991); Kramar, *Topo Guide to Icicle Creek Rock Climbs* (1991); Jeff Smoot, *Washington Rock Climbs* (1989).

LEAVITT, RANDY (1960–   ) (United States) This Californian made two unusual contributions to American climbing: In 1981 he linked BASE jumping parachute tech-

niques (BASE being an acronym for Building, Antenna, Span and Earth) with BIG WALL CLIMBING, by climbing the EL CAPITAN route Excalibur, then descending the 3,000-ft (915-m) wall by parachute. He called this combination sport CLIFFING. Earlier, with Tony YANIRO, he developed the OFFWIDTH technique called Leavittation, which employs hand and fist stacking, alternating with knee locking to efficiently ascend difficult wide cracks. Otherwise his many big wall aid ascents of El Capitan in YOSEMITE VALLEY are notable, such as the first solo ascent of Aurora, A5; FIRST ASCENTS of Lost in America, A5, with Greg Child; and of Scorched Earth, A5, with Rob Slater. In the BLACK CANYON OF THE GUNNISON he made the FIRST FREE ASCENT of the Painted Wall via a 30-pitch variation called Stratosfear, 5.11c, with Leonard Coyne. in the late 1980s he opened scores of hard SPORT CLIMBS in the Wonderland of Rocks area of JOSHUA TREE (CALIFORNIA), perhaps the hardest of these being La Machine, 5.13d.

LEDGE A flat area on a cliff or mountain.

LEEPER A PITON with a Z-shaped cross-section.

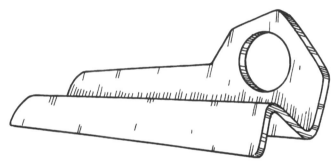

Leeper Z Piton

LEGRAND, FRANÇOIS (1970–   ) (France) The most dominant male climber in world competitions since 1990, Legrand has consistently won most World Cup titles. Ironically, in early 1990 Legrand was not a member of the French national team and was obliged to enter world events through open competitions. He was relatively unknown when he won his first World Cup, at Madonna de Campiglio, Italy, in 1990. That year he also attained several second places, and won the World Cup at Nuremberg, Germany, and the invitational at ARCO, Italy. Other wins include the Masters de Maurienne, in France, and a World Masters Tour event at Serre Chevalier, both in 1991; World Cups at Nuremberg and in Clusone, Italy, in 1991; and the 1991 UIAA World Championships in Frankfurt, Germany. On rock, he has climbed up to 8a (5.13b) ON SIGHT, and worked routes up to 8b+ (5.14a).

LE MENESTREL, MARC (1967–   ) AND ANTOINE (1968–   ) (France) The talented Le Menestrel brothers have raised world FREE-CLIMBING standards with SPORT CLIMBS in France and Switzerland. In 1983, Marc and another Frenchman, Fabrice Guillot, broke the 8a (5.13b) barrier separately in France on the same day, Marc with the ROUTE Reve d'un Papillon and Guillot with Crepinette at the CRAG Eaux Claires. Antoine followed soon after with the 8a routes Elixir de Violence at BUOUX and Salle Temps in the VERDON. The first French 8a+ (5.13c) went to the brothers and J. B. TRIBOUT, at SAUSSOIS, with La Bidule. The first 8b (5.13d) was Chouca by Marc, and the first 8b+ (5.14a) La Rage de Vivre by Antoine. Both are at Buoux. In Switzerland Antoine climbed Ravage (8b+). The latter two routes were possibly the hardest gymnastic routes in the world at the time. Antoine also put up Silence (8b/c, or 5.14a) at Troubat and he ON-SIGHTED Samizdat (8a) at CIMAI, both in 1987. Marc put up Le Minimum (8b+ 5.14a) in Buoux, and there made an early in 1987 repeat of Le Spectre Du Surmutant (8b/c). There is some question as to whether it was Marc Le Menestrel or Jerry MOFFAT who first did the Buoux 8b/c trilogy, all three routes of that grade. Antoine went on to combine climbing and dance in performance art, and is a COURSE SETTER for world sport climbing events.

LEMMON, MOUNT (United States) A popular rock-climbing area near Tucson, ARIZONA, consisting of short, usually OVERHANGING granitic crags along the Catalina Highway. The cliffs are on Mount Lemmon, which is from 2,000 to 9,000 ft (610 to 2,744 m) in elevation, offering year-round climbing at crags of different elevation. Crags on the upper sections of Mount Lemmon reach up to four PITCHES. Windy Point, on the east side of Tucson, is the most SPORT CLIMBING–oriented crag. It lies at 6,500 ft (1,982 m) and boasts several hundred extreme climbs. Beaver Wall is a landmark crag here, famous for its dense concentration of high-quality sport climbs that have attracted many world-class climbers.
Guidebooks: Eric Fazio-Rhicard, *Supplement to Climbers Guide to Sabino Canyon and Mount Lemmon Highway* (1989); John Steiger, *Climbers Guide to Sabino Canyon and Mount Lemmon Highway* (1985).

LHOTSE (Nepal, Tibet) The world's-highest peak (27,892 ft/8,501 m) is a ridge that doesn't fall below (26,240 ft/8,000 m) for 2.5 miles (four km). Along this ridge lie two other distinct summits: Lhotse Shar (27,514 ft/8,386 m) and the unclimbed Lhotse Middle (27,657 ft/8,430 m). Lhotse means "south peak," and it stands immediately south of EVEREST, separated from Everest by the south col. Its FIRST ASCENT (1956) was by Ernst Reiss and Fritz Luchsinger, whose Swiss expedition marched up the KHUMBU icefall and climbed the northwest face. Lhotse Shar fell in 1970 (east ridge) to Austrians S. Meyerl and R Walter.

Until 1990 Lhotse's 11,000-ft (3,355-m) south face stood as the last great problem of Himalayan climbing. Expeditions focused on two main LINES on this steep face, one beneath Lhotse and the other beneath Lhotse Shar, with a possible TRAVERSE from Lhotse Shar to Lhotse. In 1983 Lhotse Shar succumbed to an 18-man Czech seige, which used 16,500 ft (5,030 m) of FIXED ROPE. But all attempts to reach Lhotse by the south face ended in failure, often with loss of life. Efforts were both by seige tactics, as with the 1985 and 1987 Polish attempts, and by ALPINE STYLE, as

with the lightweight and solo efforts of Frenchmen Vincent Fine (1985), Marc Batard and Christophe PROFIT (1989). The great Jerzy KUKUCZKA perished on this face, in a fall just 650 ft (198 m) from Lhotse's summit. In 1990 Tomo CESEN claimed that he soloed the south face to the top in two days, with BIVOUACS at 24,600 and 27,000 ft (7,500 and 8,231 m). Considerable doubt has been placed on his claim. A 25-man Russian team did, however, climb the face in October 1990. Sergei Bozhov and Vladimer Karataev were the ones to reach the top.

LIBERTY BELL (United States) Rising above the Washington Pass Highway, Liberty Bell (7,720 ft/2,353 m) is the steepest of a cluster of granite spires, consisting of Concord Tower, Lexington Tower and the North and South Early Winter Spires, of which South Early Winter is highest, at 7,807 ft (2,380 m). They are located in the North Cascades, near the town of Mazama, in WASHINGTON. The area has ROUTES from easy fifth-class scrambles to extreme multi-PITCH FREE and AID routes. On Liberty Bell's east face, Liberty Crack is famous and popular. The 12-pitch route was first climbed as a BIG-WALL aid climb in 1965 by northwesterners Steve Marts, Fred Stanley and Don McPherson. Later parties freed the route except for the Lithuanian Roof, which remained aided until 1991, when Brooke Sandahl freed it at 5.13. Many free routes with a mix of BOLT protection and standard equipment are scattered over the towers. Fall is the main season, with mosquitoes being troublesome in summer. Minor WINTER ASCENTS have been made here also.
Guidebook: Fred Beckey, *Cascade Alpine Guide, Rainy Pass to Frazer River* (1991).

LIE BACK, LAYBACK Lie back is the U.S. spelling, and layback the British. A FREE CLIMBING technique for climbing CRACKS or ARETES in which the hands grip an edge and pull in one direction, while the feet press against the rock in the other direction. A LAYAWAY move uses the same principle, but usually for a single move. See CRACK CLIMBING, FACE CLIMBING.

LIGHTNING In mountainous regions lightning storms present hazards for climbers and claim several lives each year. Because peaks and ridges are natural targets of lightning strikes, immediate descent from a summit is often the best course of action at the first sign of electrical storm. Though RAPPELLING is dangerous during electrical storms, it may be preferable to remaining high on a peak.

Towering cumulonimbus clouds and associated cold air, rain, hail or snow, lightning flashes, and rolling thunder indicate an approaching electrical storm. Sound travels at approximately six-tenths of a mile (one km) per three seconds, so by timing the interval between flash and thunder one can estimate one's distance from the storm.

Air is a good insulator but in the presence of electrical activity air ionizes and becomes a conductor. Lightning seeks the shortest line from the cloud, through the air and into the earth. Peaks and projections, including climbers standing on a ridge, are likely targets. Rocks, earth, trees, humans and metal are conductors of electricity, more so when wet. Current from a lightning strike radiates down and out, decreasing rapidly with distance. Ridges, cracks and chimneys are natural pathways for current and should be avoided in electrical storms. Indicators of electricity in an area at risk of strike include crackling sounds caused by small sparks around a projection, the odor or taste of ozone, the phenomena of one's hair standing on end, tingling skin, hum and spark of metallic equipment and a bluish glow around a projection (a corona, or Saint Elmo's Fire).

The main lightning hazards are from direct strike, ground currents and induced currents in the vicinity of a strike. Direct strikes can cause serious burns, shock, unconsciousness and organ failure, yet are not always fatal because strikes are often partial or enter the victim through ground currents. However, because the victim may be disoriented, risks such as falling off a mountain increase. Induced currents are small currents attracted by metallic equipment. These currents add to ground currents. However, ice axes or pitons do not attract lightning strikes, and discarding such items—even if they are humming and sparking—may be disastrous when faced with descent. Instead, place them a few feet away.

Although a climber's instincts might dictate seeking shelter from an electrical storm and its attendant rain or hail in caves or beneath overhangs, this is not advisable action. Caves, overhangs and large boulders are often associated with natural cracks or fissures and present pathways for ground currents that can spark across a gap and into the climber. Caves also may hold water, which conducts electricity. Some experts endorse caves as safe shelter only if they have at least 10 ft (three m) of headroom and three ft (one m) on either side of the climber. Sheltering snugly against walls below a mountain top is dangerous because of ground currents shed from the summit. Depressions are also at risk as they are natural conduits for ground current.

The safest course of action in a lightning storm is to seek places on broken SCREE, away from the crest of a ridge, or behind the "shadow" of a peak or projection yet away from any cliff face by six to 10 ft (two to three m). The middle of a ridge is better than the ends or the shoulder. Sit on top of an insulating object like a dry rope or pack, or atop a small rock. Crouch with knees up and hands in lap. Do not sit on hands or lean against cliffs. This procedure minimizes one's points of contact with ground current, and ensures that current passes through nonvital parts of the body. On a cliff face, sit on the outer edge of a ledge, if possible away from deep cracks.

LIGHTWEIGHT EXPEDITIONS A general term used in recent years to describe small, low-budget expeditions to the great ranges. The number of climbers and hired PORTERS is small, and impact on the environment is minimal compared to that of large expeditions. Tactics used on the mountain may or may not employ FIXED ROPE, or seige tactics, though ALPINE STYLE is common. Lightweight expedition style has been used on trekking peaks and 26,240-ft (8,000-m) peaks.

LINE The path of a ROUTE on a mountain or cliff, usually the LINE of least resistance following some natural weakness like a crack system or line of handholds on a cliff, or a COULOIR or RIDGE on a mountain.

LITTLE COTTONWOOD CANYON (United States) Because of its proximity to Salt Lake City, UTAH, the GLACIER-scoured granite SLABS and FACES of this canyon are well developed with climbs. ROUTES are one to several PITCHES long, and are often steep slabs protected by BOLTS, but some difficult CRACKS and SPORT CLIMBS are here too. One remarkable feat is George LOWE's bold face route Dorsal Fin (5.10+), on the formation called the Fin, which he climbed in mountain boots in 1965. The endurance crack Fallen Arches (5.13a), is also significant. Spring and fall are the best seasons for this cliff. A parallel canyon to the north, called Big Cottonwood, has sport climbing on quartzite.
Guidebook: Stuart Ruckman and Bret Ruckman, *Wasatch Climbing North* (1991).

LITTLEJOHN, PAT (1951–) (Britain) The major explorer of British SEA CLIFFS over the last 20 years, Littlejohn began climbing on the cliffs near his hometown of Exeter in 1965. Under the tutelage of two very gifted local climber, Frank Cannings and Peter Biven, he soon became known as something of a teenage prodigy. The roll-call of his resonantly named ROUTES in DEVON and CORNWALL, CHEDDAR, PEMBROKE and ANGLESEY over the last two decades is outstanding: Il Duce, Crow, Deep Space, Hunger, Pagan. His climbing style also has long been celebrated for a consistent ethical purity and stringent "from the ground up, no inspection, no aid" ethos. A mountain guide, he is currently director of the International School of Mountaineering in Leysin, Switzerland.
Further reading: Jim Perrin, "The Craftsman," in *On & Off the Rocks* (1986).

LITTLE SWITZERLAND (United States) An area of a dozen granite peaks within the ALASKA RANGE, contained by the great bend of the Kahiltna Glacier on the west, and the Kanikula Glacier on the east. Peaks such as Crowned Jewel, the Throne, Dragons Spine, The Tower, and Triple Crown (8,610 ft/2,625 m, the highest), offer high standard climbing on spectacular FACES, RIDGES and ice routes. Some climbers fly into Little Switzerland's Pika Glacier, although most prefer the several-day walk in from the end of the Petersville Road. The Talkeetna ranger station offers route information.

LIVESEY, PETER (1943–) (Britain) A Yorkshireman who inspired the British climbing world. He was in his late twenties when he came to prominence in climbing was the most rigorous of trainers—he virtually introduced the concept of training along athletic lines to the climbing world. Livesey was also the slyest of tacticians—question marks often crowded in his routes. His legacy is a stunning roll-call of the great routes that stimulated

British climbing's mid-1970s revolution: Face Route, Footless Crow, Claws, Right Wall, Cream, Fingerlicker, Downhill Racer, Wellington Crack—all of them still testpieces for the aspiring extremist. Livesey also played an important part in the development of FREE CLIMBING in the VERDON gorge and was a frequent visitor to YOSEMITE.

When he deemed himself no longer competitive at the leading edge of British rock climbing, he retired summarily and took up orienteering, at which he also excelled. One of climbing's wittier writers, he contributed a column to the British magazine *Climber* for many years, and his essays have been much anthologized. Professionally, he lectures in outdoor activities at a college of education and also runs a cafe at Malham, Yorkshire.

LIZARD, THE   (Britain)   This area, the most southerly in mainland BRITAIN, has provided modern climbers with fresh areas for exploration. There are three principal areas, the remote Vellan Head and its Hidden Buttress close to Predannack Wollas Farm, Lizard Point near Lizard village and Bass Point to its east. One of Vellan's finest LINES is Pat LITTLEJOHN's Beauty and the Beast, with two PITCHES at 5.12a, climbed in 1987. Lizard Point has easier lines including The Goldrush and Limelight, both 5.7s from Iain Peters. Cull Wall at Bass Point sports one of the hardest routes in CORNWALL, Littlejohn's Lazarus a 5.13a, climbed in the mid-1980s.
Guidebooks: Pat Littlejohn, *South West Climbs* (1991); Iain Peters, *North Devon and Cornwall* (1988).

LLANBERIS PASS   (Britain)   Every British climber recognizes the craggy view looking northwest from the head of the Llanberis Pass along the valley toward the villages of Nant Peris and Llanberis. On either side are CRAGS whose rhyolite walls contain records of the major players who left some record of their climbs. The villages themselves contain pubs and a café, Pete's Eats, as famous as the cliffs themselves. Major crags include, on the south side, Dinas Mot and Cyrn Las, and on the north side Clogwyn y Grochan, Carreg Wastad and Dinas Cromlech. The valley is five miles (eight km) long and campsites lie below the crags and at Nant Peris. The ROUTES are protected by NUTS and are no more than three PITCHES in length.

The first significant ascents here were by Colin KIRKUS and J. Menlove EDWARDS in the 1930s. After the war, working-class heroes Joe BROWN and Don WHILLANS added LINES that were harder than anything that had gone before, often in adverse conditions. These routes include Cemetery Gates at 5.9 in 1951 and Cenotaph Corner (5.10a) in 1952 on Dinas Cromlech. Brown added the outstanding The Grooves (5.9) in 1953 on Cyrn Las. Ron Moseley aided the Cromlech's Left Wall in 1956. It was freed in 1971 by Andy Garlick at 5.10b.

The next major advance occurred in the 1970s when Pete LIVESEY climbed the imposing Right Wall of the Cromlech in 1974. At 5.11d it remains a testing lead with long falls a regular event. Ron FAWCETT, then added Lord of the Flies, also on the right wall of the Cromlech, a bold 5.12a. The

ascent was filmed for television and included Fawcett's now famous remark "Come on arms, do your stuff!"

John Redhead climbed the fiercely TECHNICAL Cockblock in 1980 on the Grochan, a 5.12b wall climb. Climbing in the Pass lost its impetus in the 1980s as lines were exhausted. Nonetheless, Craig Smith solved the obvious ARETE left of Grond on Dinas Cromlech at 5.13a to give Rumblefish.
Guidebooks: Paul Williams, *Llanberis* (1987); Williams, *Rock Climbing in Snowdonia* (1990).

LLANBERIS SLATE   (Britain)   The slate quarries around LLANBERIS PASS produced hundreds of new ROUTES in the mid-1980s. The quarries have been given names like Australia, California, Dali's Hole, Serengeti, Vivian and Rainbow Slabs, Twll Mawr and Bus Stop Quarry. They dry quickly and are very accessible.

The first recorded climb was by the legendary party-creator Al HARRIS with Pete Crew. Slate's period began though in 1981 when Stevie HASTON climbed Wendy Doll (5.10b) on the Vivian Slab. In 1982 he applied cutlery from Pete's Eats café to excavate the crackline Comes the Dervish (5.10c), perhaps the best known slate route of all. Andy Pollitt then climbed the bold Flashdance (5.11c), again on the Vivian Slab. In 1984 the Rainbow was discovered, a smooth sheet of rock climbed with minimal BOLTING. John Redhead and Dave Towse climbed Cystitis by Proxy (5.12b), and Redhead also added Raped by Affection (5.12b) which required SKYHOOKS and a RURP to protect its 80 desperate ft (24 m).

In 1985, Johnny Dawes added the terrifying Dawes of Perception (5.13a) to the Lower Vivian Quarry. By 1986 bolting was commonplace on slate, with Bob Drury's Quarryman (5.13c), a famous example. Hold manufacture also appeared, with Misogynist's Discharge and Manic Strain, both 5.13a. In 1990, Dawes added Big Things, Little Things, a 5.14b slab. On slate, routes are as bold as the first ascensionists wish them to be.
Guidebooks: Paul Williams, *Llanberis* (1987); Williams, *Rock Climbing in Snowdonia* (1990).

LLIWEDD   (Britain)   This north-facing cliff reaches 1,000 ft (305 m) high above Llyn Llydaw and forms part of the Snowdon chain. A rambling CRAG with easy ROUTES, it is approached from Pen y Pass. Its interest lies in its history. Since before World War I it was BRITAIN's most fashionable place to climb. George MALLORY's Slab, for instance, is a 900-ft (274-m) 5.5 climbed in 1908.
Guidebooks: Harold Drasdo, *Lliwedd* (1972); Paul Williams, *Rock Climbing in Snowdonia* (1990).

LOCKING   CARABINER   A   CARABINER with a threaded sleeve that, when twisted into its locking position, prevents the spring gate from opening.

LOCHABER   (Scotland)   Grouped under this heading are a number of CRAGS that aren't strictly within the district of Lochaber, but which for convenience are included here. There is a great diversity, from the granite slabs in Glen Etive, to the rhyolite of Glen Coe, to the lofty walls of BEN

NEVIS. The area is well served by transport, with the A82 from Glasgow running through Glen Coe to Fort William. One prominent crag near Fort William is the Etive Slabs, a huge, sweeping slab of granite below Beinn Trilleachan, near Glen Etive. They offer outstanding FRICTION CLIMBING between 5.8 and 5.10 with routes to 650 ft (198 m) in length. Famous here is the 1957 classic Swastika, which was freed of its few aid points by Willie Todd 20 years later at 5.10b. Rab Carrington and John Jackson added Etive's most famous route, Pinch Direct, a sustained 5.10c.

Other rock-climbing areas are Buachille Etive Mor (pronounced "Bookle Etiv Mor"), a three-mile (five-km) ridge that rises at its eastern end to the peak of Stob Dearg (3,403 ft/1,038 m). This overlooks the eastern end of Glen Coe. The Rannoch Wall is the best known of the Buachille's attractions, being in a spectacular position with good holds on steep rock. On its north buttress lies Robin SMITH's Shibboleth, an adequately protected 500-ft (152-m) 5.10a climbed in 1958, two years before anything equivalent appeared in North Wales.

Creag A'Bhancair is located in Coire na Tulaich and is approached from the Lagangarbh Hut. In recent years the crag has become famous for its Tunnel Walls, which sport BOLTED routes of a fierce difficulty.

Another crag, Aonach Dubh, lies on the south side of Glen Coe. It is dominated by Bidean nam Bian, at 3,795 ft (1,157 m) the highest mountain in the area. The east buttress on Aonach Dubh's west face has a number of excellent routes of over 450 ft (137 m). The Big Top is one of Robin Smith's finest efforts, taking the left ARETE of the east buttress's right wall. Rated 5.9, it was climbed in 1961 with Jimmy Gardner.

Stob Coire nan Lochan is an impressive andesite crag with striking columnar structure. It is reached by the path that climbs into the Coire under the east face of Aonach Dubh in two hours.

Bidean nam Bian is a cliff near the summit of Bidean at an altitude of 3,000 ft (915 m). Garbh Bheinn is a crag in Ardgour, an area to the west of Loch Linhe, below the summit of Garbh Bheinn. It is reached via the Corran ferry. Most climbers make day trips from Glen Coe or Fort William. Notable routes here are Great Ridge, which bounds the eastern side of the crag, a 1,000-ft (305-m) 5.5 climbed in 1897 by J. H. Bell and W. Brown. D. D. Stewart climbed Scimitar in 1952 to give a 300 ft (91 m) 5.7. Up the center of the wall is a brilliant addition from Pete Whillance, whose explorations have sometimes been underestimated in Britain. White Hope follows a thin vein of quartz at 5.11a.

Glen Nevis is a small series of crags situated beneath the large mass of Ben Nevis. The glen runs south and then east from Fort William. There is a wealth of small (120 ft/36 m) OUTCROPS scattered throughout its length. Most are clean and rough mica-schist, better climbed in the spring. Buzzard Buttress has a number of modern testpieces, all climbed in the 1980s, like Dave "Cubby" Cuthbertson's, The Handred Effect (5.12a) from 1983. He also added the area's most daunting route, Exocet, taking a ROOF and

magnificent PROW at 5.12c. On the Polldubh, major routes include a number of 5.6s like Pine Wall, from Jimmy Ness, who was the earliest explorer here, and also some classics from Ian Clough, whose Storm is the best 5.8 in the area. Other crags here include Whale Rock and Galaxy Buttress, on the flanks of Meall Cumhann.

Guidebooks: Rab Anderson, et al., *Glen Coe, Glen Etive and Ardgour* (1992); Donald Bennet, *The Munros* (1991); Ed Grindley, *Glen Nevis and the Lochaber Outcrops* (1985); Kevin Howett, *Rock Climbing in Scotland* (1990).

LOCK OFF   In RAPPELLING or BELAYING, to tie off a loaded ROPE to stop it from slipping through a belay or rappel, so the belayer or rappeller can take both hands off the rope to proceed with other tasks. Also, in FREE CLIMBING, to hold an arm in the bent position.

LOGAN HOOK   A type of SKYHOOK.

LOGAN, MOUNT   (Canada)   At 19,524 ft (5,952 m), Logan has the distinction of being the largest mountain massif in the world, with its 16,000-ft (4,878-m) summit plateau spanning 30 sq miles (78 sq km). The massif contains eight summits and two satellites, King and MacArthur peaks. Otherwise, Logan's Central Peak is the highest in CANADA (second-highest point in North America), located in the Yukon Territories, 60 miles (96 km) from the Pacific Ocean, 21 miles (34 km) from ALASKA, in the heart of the SAINT ELIAS Range. It is the most extensively glaciated, non-polar region in the world. The mountain was first climbed in 1925 by Albert McCarthy and his six companions under atrocious conditions after a 140-mile (224-km) approach. Their epic climb up the King Trench route and their journey back to civilization were heralded by that year's *Alpine Journal* (BRITAIN) as "the greatest tour de force in the history of mountaineering." The mountain's second ascent was made in 1950 by Norman Read, who was also on the 1925 ascent, and Andre ROCH. The knife-edged east ridge, first climbed in 1953, is a safer and challenging alternative to the King Trench. The Hummingbird Ridge, a six-mile (10-km) treachery of CORNICES and rotten rock, was first climbed in 1965 and, despite many attempts, has only had one successful repeat. Eight other demanding routes exist on Logan. Because of its proximity to the ocean, Logan has heavier snowfall than most Alaskan peaks. Consequently, AVALANCHE mishaps and cornice collapses are commonplace. The area is administered by Kluane National Park, in Haines Junction.

Guidebook: Steve Roper and Allen Steck, *Fifty Classic Climbs of North America* (1979).

LONG, JOHN   (1955–   ) (United States)   This Californian founded the Stonemasters, a clique of rock climbers devoted to hard climbing and hedonism in YOSEMITE and other California crags. Bestowed with a powerful build, Long brought an athletic attitude to American climbing, especially in BOULDERING which, on a few problems, he perfected two-handed dynamic moves. In addition to opening many routes at JOSHUA TREE, he probably established the first 5.12 in America, Paisano Overhang at Suicide Rock (1973), and the first 5.13, Hangover, at TAHQUITZ (1976). On Middle Cathedral Rock Long's Stoner's Highway (1973) was a breakthrough with almost every PITCH at 5.10. On the same wall in the mid-1970s he climbed variously with Mark Chapman, Kevin Worral and Ron KAUK to produce Black Rose (5.11+), Central Pillar (5.11+) and Mother Earth (5.12 A4+). Some of his FIRST FREE ASCENTS shaped American climbing like Astroman (5.11d) in 1975 on Washington Column, with John BACHAR and Kauk, and the Chouinard-Herbert on Sentinel in 1976 with Pete LIVESEY. He joined in on the first one-day ascent of The Nose of EL CAPITAN (1975) with Billy Westbay and Jim BRIDWELL, and on Mount Watkins made the FIRST ASCENT with Bridwell and Dale BARD of the Bob Locke Memorial Buttress (5.11 A4), in 1977. In the late 1970s he took to jungle exploration, making the first coast-to-coast traverse of Borneo and discovering the world's biggest cave chamber, in the Gulf Province of Papua New Guinea. His adventure stories are collected in *Gorilla Monsoon* (1989) and he is the main author of the *How to Rock Climb* series. (2nd ed., 1993).

LONGLAND, SIR JACK (1905–) (Britain)

In the years between the wars, as an all-round mountaineer Jack Longland was without equal in BRITAIN. Along with his younger contemporaries, Colin KIRKUS and John Menlove EDWARDS, he elevated the standard of British rock-climbing between 1927 and 1932, and while the number of his FIRST ASCENTS on British cliffs did not equal theirs, those he did make were of great significance. His climb of 1928 on the west buttress of CLOGWYN DU'R ARDDU was the first true breach in the defenses of this forbidding cliff. Purgatory on Lliwedd (1929) and the Javelin Blade in Cwm Idwal (1930) equally were milestones in British climbing history, the latter remaining perhaps the most difficult lead on a mountain CRAG until the immediate postwar period.

Short, muscular and agile, he was both academically distinguished and an Athletic Blue at Cambridge, his event being the pole-vault. Under the influence of Geoffrey WINTHROP YOUNG, he pioneered British guideless climbing in the Alps, and achieved some formidable feats of ridge-traversing and peak-bagging in successive alpine seasons of the late 1920s and early 1930s. He was a natural choice for Hugh Ruttledge's EVEREST expedition of 1933, which was plagued by atrocious weather. Longland's action in bringing down eight SHERPAS from Camp 6 at 27,400 ft (8,355 m), in a storm and WHITE-OUT conditions that obliterated all traces of the route, displayed skill and responsibility, and saved the Sherpas' lives. His last major expedition was to East Greenland in 1935, professional and political concerns occupying his attention thereafter. He continued, however, to establish climbs on the Northumberland and Derbyshire outcrops, and while director of education for Derbyshire he set up Britain's first outdoor pursuits center. Knighted for his services to education in 1970, his cultured and robustly humorous presence graced all the high offices of British climbing in the postwar period.

Further reading: Jim Perrin, "The Essential Jack Longland," in *Yes, to Dance* (1990).

LONG'S PEAK (United States)

At 14,255 ft (4,346 m), this is the high point of ROCKY MOUNTAIN NATIONAL PARK, COLORADO. It is located near the town of Estes Park. A long approach and high altitude make an ascent of Long's a challenge. Popular scrambles such as the Keyhole Route, and mountaineering routes, such as Keiner's Route, are found on the easy-angled north face, but rock climbers are drawn to the precipitous east face, called the DIAMOND, a 2,000-ft (610-m) big wall with free and aid routes. The first recorded ascent of Long's Peak was in 1868, by John Wesley Powell and party, though it is believed that Indians climbed the peak on hunting excursions. During the 1930s the first professional mountain guides service in Colorado began taking people up the north face.

Guidebooks: John Harlin, *Rocky Mountain Rock Climbs* (1985); Paul Nesbitt, *Long's Peak: Its Story and a Climbing Guide* Richard Rossiter, *Climbers Guide to Rocky Mountain National Park* (1991).

LONGSTAFF, THOMAS GEORGE (1875–1964) (Britain)

Though he had a medical degree, Longstaff never practiced. Instead he devoted his life to travel and climbing, and became the leading mountain explorer of his era. His memoir, *This My Voyage* (1951), describes his journeys across the mountains of the northern hemisphere, from CANADA to the HIMALAYA, over a period of 25 years. He pioneered LIGHTWEIGHT EXPEDITIONS and was quick to take advantage of the latest equipment. After a successful, guideless visit to the Caucasus in 1903, he paid his first visit to the Himalaya in 1905, where he attempted to penetrate the NANDA DEVI Sanctuary in INDIA, by way of a col that bears his name, south of Nanda Devi East. In the same year he reached 22,960 ft (7,000 m) on Gurla Mandhatta in TIBET and visited the Api region in northwest NEPAL, on the trail of Henry Savage-Landor. Two years later he became the first man to summit a 22,960-ft (7,000 m) peak when he climbed Trisul near Nanda Devi. In 1909, in the KARAKORAM, he traversed the Bilafond Glacier, crossed Saltoro Pass and explored the Siachen Glacer, discovering the peaks of Teram Kangri. Longstaff participated in the 1922 EVEREST expedition and explored in arctic Spitzbergen, GREENLAND and BAFFIN ISLAND. He served as honorary secretary of the Royal Geographical Society, receiving the Founder's Medal in 1928. He was president of Britain's Alpine Club between 1947 and 49.

Further reading: Jill Neate, *High Asia* (1989).

LOOKING GLASS ROCK (United States)

One of the largest cliffs in North Carolina, located 50 miles (80 km) south of Asheville, in the Appalachian Mountains. The cliff is a granite DOME up to 400 ft (122 m) high, with many moderate CRACK and SLAB routes, and harder routes to 5.11+. The most renowned route of the area was established in 1966, The Nose (5.8), by B. Gillespie, S. Longenecker and B. Watts. Free climbing on this cliff is marked by use of an unusual feature called "eyebrows," which are horizontal flared POCKETS. On the north face are long AID CLIMBS as hard as A5. Some require BIVOUACS. Climbing is possible year round, especially July through November, though the area has high rainfall.

Guidebooks: John Harlin, *Climber's Guide to North America, East Coast Rockclimbs* (1986); Thomas Kelley, *Climber's Guide to North Carolina* (1986).

LORETAN, ERHARD (1959–   ) (Switzerland) Following the tradition of OXYGENLESS alpine-style Himalayan climbing set by Reinhold MESSNER, this mountain guide and cabinet maker has "collected" many 26,240-ft (8,000-m) peaks, in fast times. His Himalayan career began with NANGA PARBAT's Diamir Face in 1982. Then, in 1983, he and several Swiss team members became the first to climb three 26,240-ft (8,000-m) peaks in one season: GASHERBRUM I and II, and BROAD PEAK. In 1984, with Joss Norbert, he made the first TRAVERSE of ANNAPURNA; 1985 earned him K2 (Abruzzi Ridge), and that winter, DHAULAGIRI east face with P. A. Steiner. His penchant for speed was shown in 1986, when he and Jean TROILLET climbed the Japanese Couloir of EVEREST's north face in 41 hours. He pioneered a new route up Nameless Tower's vertical east face (in the TRANGO TOWERS), with Wojciech KURTYKA in 1988. In a marathon enchainment in winter 1990 in the BERNESE Oberland in Switzerland, he and Andre Georges climbed 13 major north faces (including the EIGER) in 13 days. In 1990 he, Kurtyka and Troillet made new routes on CHO OYU (southeast face) and SHISHAPANGMA (south face), and in 1991 he climbed MAKALU.

LOST ARROW   A type of PITON.

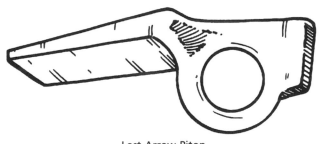

Lost Arrow Piton

LOUBIÈRE AND TÊTE DE CHIEN (Monaco) This SPORT-CLIMBING cliff is located above the palace of Monaco. Close to the coast and facing south, it is one of the best wintertime CRAGS around France. The crag has three main areas. The Loubière cliff is at the far left. La Tête de Chien in the center reaches 328 ft (100 m) in height. On the right is a 230-ft (70-m) cliff. There are hundreds of well-protected routes on these crags. The cliff flourished in the 1980s when climbers focused on short climbs, known as *couennes* in French. It has become famous in Europe from dramatic magazine photos of climbers in spectacular positions, sometimes at night, silhouetted against the city lights.

LOWE, GEORGE (1944–   ) (United States) In 1990 Lowe was awarded the AMERICAN ALPINE CLUB's Robert and Miriam UNDERHILL Award for outstanding MOUNTAINEERING achievement. A physicist from Golden, COLORADO, he has established over 20 remote and technically difficult alpine routes in North America, such as the north faces of ALBERTA and NORTH TWIN in CANADA, the Lowe/Kennedy (Mount HUNTER) and the Infinite Spur (Mount FORAKER) in ALASKA. His Himalayan climbs include the east face of Mount EVEREST, and most recently, a solo of DHAULAGIRI. He has over a hundred FIRST ASCENTS to his rock-climbing credit, and is the cousin of Jeff LOWE. He continues to climb and establish new routes to this day.

LOWE, GREG (1949–   ) (United States) Climber and inventor of revolutionary ice and rock equipment, Lowe climbed a FROZEN WATERFALL near Ogden, UTAH, Mahlens Peak, in 1971 using custom-made drooped ICE AXES and tubular ICE SCREWS to cope with ice for which existing tools were inadequate. The axe became the Hummingbird, the screw the Snarg, both now modern alpinists' mainstays. Yvon CHOUINARD called Lowe's ascent of Mahlens Peak "the first really important waterfall to be climbed." At the age of eight Lowe climbed the GRAND TETON with his father, then in 1968, with others including cousin George LOWE, made the FIRST WINTER ASCENT of its north face, the hardest alpine effort in America at the time. Lowe specialized in WINTER ASCENTS: on the north face of HALF DOME (1972) his lurp tent was the first hanging wall tent. He is regarded as the most gifted on rock of the Lowe family of climbers (Jeff LOWE is his brother), with many severe routes around Utah and IDAHO to his credit. He regards his hardest FREE CLIMB to be the 600-ft (183-m) Macabre Wall near Ogden, perhaps 5.12. He founded Lowe Alpine Systems in 1969 and designed the parallel-stay frame system of modern rucksacks. In 1967 he began experimenting with SPRING-LOADED CAMMING DEVICES, and in 1971 built the precursor to the devices used today. Not long after, Ray JARDINE introduced his own camming device, the FRIEND. Lowe and the manufacturers of Friends both made legal claims on this patent. Other Lowe inventions include stainless-steel subsheathed ropes, waterproof breathable fabrics, candle-powered heaters for sleeping bags and camming pulleys, winches and nuts. Film-making earned him a nomination for an Academy Award, for the skiing film *Fall Line*. He is cousin to George Lowe, brother of Jeff Lowe.

LOWE, JEFF (1950–   ) (United States) Lowe has long been hailed as America's foremost ice climber. In the early 1970s he established such winter climbs as the west face of the GRAND TETON and Bridal Veil Falls in COLORADO, as well as innumerable rock climbs and mixed routes throughout the West. For a long period, altitude sickness made Lowe beat epic retreats from the highest Himalayan peaks. Finally, he secured his fame by soloing Ama Dablam's unclimbed south face, climbing the difficult north face of NEPAL's Tawoche, FREE-CLIMBING TRANGO TOWER (while making a commercial TV film), and soloing a direct new winter route up the north face of the EIGER, in winter.

LOWER OFF   To lower down a climb on a rope, from an ANCHOR or point of PROTECTION.

LOWER SHARPNOSE (Britain) Probably the best CRAG on the Culm Coast of DEVON, with unique rock architecture, comprising three fins of rock projecting from the coastline. The middle fin is 130 ft (39 m) high, 200 ft (61 m) long and only six ft (1.8 m) thick. Such unusual formations provide natural windbreaks, dry quickly and can be climbed on both sides. The rock is solid, compact and steep and in situ pegs are common. Climbing here focuses on hard routes, like the 1986 and 1987 efforts The Devonian (5.12a) and Coronary Country (5.13a), both by Steve Monks. The latter is a bold and technical climb with a groundfall possible from 50 ft (15 m). Pacemaker (5.12a) from Pat LITTLEJOHN is also famous. The crags are six miles (9 km) north of the coastal town of Bude.
Guidebooks: Pat Littlejohn, *South West Climbs* (1991); Iain Peters, *North Devon and Cornwall* (1988).

LUMPY RIDGE (United States) A cluster of easily accessible, coarse-grained subalpine granite CRAGS located in ROCKY MOUNTAIN NATIONAL PARK, just north of Estes Park, COLORADO. SLABS, FACES and CRACK routes of one PITCH to 800 ft (244 m) abound. The main formations are the Twin Owls, the Book and Sundance Buttress.
Guidebook: Scott Kimball, *Lumpy Ridge and Estes Park Rock Climbs* (1986).

LUNDY (Britain) This area has unique climbing and awkward access. Lundy is an island 12 miles (19 km) off the DEVON coast and is reached by boat. Comprehensive access restrictions during sea bird nesting times mean that a popular "short season" has arisen for climbers, starting in August and ending in October when sailings from Bideford and Ilfracombe become less regular. Accommodation and visitor information can be obtained from the Landmark Trust, in Maidenhead. An anti-BOLT ethic has evolved at Lundy. ROUTES can reach over 400 ft (122 m).

Lundy is thin and finger-shaped, running north to south. Its western edge falls steeply into the Atlantic and presents many BUTTRESSES, ZAWNS and coves. Cliffs include Arch Zawn, Torrey Canyon, The Diamond, Devil's Slide, Egyptian Slabs and Deep Zawn. Development began with Admiral Keith Lawder's visit in 1961, which produced the island's most famous route, The Devil's Slide, a 400-ft (122-m) 5.6 SLAB running into the sea and offering four friction pitches. Later additions to this cliff were Peter Biven's Albion (5.7) in 1963 and Paul Fatti's Satan's Slip (5.9) in 1970.

In the early 1970s a number of climbers pioneered excellent climbs. Pete Thexton, partnered by *Mountain* magazine founder Ken Wilson, climbed Immaculate Slab (5.8) on the Egyptian Slabs and Wolfman Jack, a brilliant crack climb that now goes free at 5.10d. Pat LITTLEJOHN exposed Formula One (5.8) in Landing Craft Bay; The Promised Land (5.10d), on the Devil's Chimney Cliff; and in the Deep Zawn, Supernova, now free at 5.12a. Keith Darbyshire, often Littlejohn's partner at this time and tragically killed in 1974 while exploring in south CORNWALL, climbed the 5.10 Quatermass, a popular route in Deep Zawn.

In the early 1980s Gary Gibson emerged as a prolific explorer of Lundy, opening hundreds of new routes. His efforts include two LINES on the Diamond, the finest granite wall in BRITAIN. They are Watching the Ocean (5.12b) and A Widespread Ocean of Fear (5.11d).
Guidebooks: Gary Gibson, *Lundy Rock Climbs* (1985); Pat Littlejohn, *South West Climbs* (1991).

LUNGE See DYNO.

M

MACARTNEY-SNAPE, TIM (1956–   ) (Australia)
Probably the best-known climber to Australians, Macartney-Snape achieved national recognition in 1984 when he and fellow-Australian Greg MORTIMER summited EVEREST without oxygen via a new route on the north face, and again when he returned to Everest in 1990 to ascend from sea level.

Born in Tanganyika, he began climbing as a student at the Australian National University in Canberra. After seasons in NEW ZEALAND, he climbed Dunagiri (23,182 ft/7,068 m) in INDIA with Lincoln Hall (1978). This experience, though grueling, revealed his unique tolerance for altitude. All his ascents have been made without oxygen and in small teams. Ama Dablam (NEPAL, 1981) and a new route on 19,684-ft (6,001 m) Anyemaquin (CHINA, 1981) presaged his part in the First Australian Everest Expedition. As training for Everest, he climbed the difficult unclimbed south spur on ANNAPURNA II (26,039 ft/7,939 m) in Nepal (1983) with team members Lincoln Hall, Andy Henderson and Mortimer. After Everest came GASHERBRUM IV (26,000 ft/7,927 m) northwest ridge, a new route in PAKISTAN in 1986, with Greg Child (AUSTRALIA) and Tom Hargis (United States). In 1990 he reclimbed Everest, solo and without oxygen, by the south col route, taking a unique approach based on the notion that a mountain is unclimbed unless scaled from its lowest point, which is sea level. He marched 1,500 miles (2,414 km) from the Bay of Bengal through India and Nepal, traveling entirely on foot, even swimming across rivers rather than use mechanical assistance. His expedition films include: *Australians on Everest* (1984), *Gasherbrum IV: Harder than Everest* (1986) and *Everest: Sea to Sky* (1990).
Further reading: Greg Child, *Thin Air: Encounters in the Himalaya* (1990); Lincoln Hall, *White Limbo, The First Australian Climb of Mount Everest* (1984).

MACINNES, HAMISH (1931–   ) (Britain) Resident inventor and sage of Glencoe. Clydeside hard man of the Creag Dubh mountaineering club, writer, rescuer, photographer, and co-ascensionist with Tom PATEY of Zero Gulley on BEN NEVIS, MacInnes is one of the presiding characters in the last 40 years of British climbing. He took part (with John Cunningham) in the two-man Creag Dubh EVEREST Expedition of 1953, and was Chris BONINGTON's deputy on the Everest Southwest Face Expedition of 1975.

He is solely and entirely responsible for metal ICE AXES, MacInnes stretchers and curve-picked ICE TOOLS.
Further reading: Hamish MacInnes, *Look Behind the Ranges* (1979).

MACINTYRE, ALEX (1954–1982) (Britain) This audacious climber was the pick of the 1970s generation of British Himalayan mountaineers. MacIntyre rebelled against the Leeds University tradition of rock-climbing excellence, and instead took to the Alps, where he shone, making the first one-day ascent of The Shroud (1975), stealing the LINE that Chris BONINGTON had tried on the north face of the GRANDES JORASSES in 1976, and making the first ALPINE STYLE ascent (with Tobin Sorenson) of the John HARLIN route on the EIGER (1977). The same year he climbed the northeast face of Koh-e-Bandaka (HINDU KUSH) as member of a small international team. In 1978, with Polish companions (including Wojiech KURTYKA), he made a big wall route on the south face of CHANGABANG. He also attempted the west face of MAKALU (1981), succeeded on the south face of SHISHAPANGMA (1982), and died on the south face of ANNAPURNA the same year, when he was struck by a stone while climbing unroped. All his routes were alpine style. MacIntyre was individualistic and dismissive of the large nationalistic expeditions of the period, and served as national officer of the British Mountaineering Council from 1978 to 1980.
Further reading: Alex MacIntyre and Doug Scott, *The Shishapangma Expedition* (1984).

MAESTRI, CESARE (1929–   ) (Italy) This controversial climber is regarded by some as a visionary mountaineer who made the first and second ascents of CERRO TORRE (ARGENTINA), in 1959 and 1970, and by others as a fraud who never set foot on the summit and who desecrated this striking Patagonian peak by BOLTING the mountain into submission with a gasoline-powered drill. (See COMPRESSOR ROUTE.)

Maestri began climbing in the Italian DOLOMITES around his birthplace of Trento after World War II. During the war he fought as a partisan against the Nazis, and described his first climb as scaling a wall to rob a German barracks of food. As a climber he built a reputation in Italy with early solo ascents of the Solledar Route on the Civetta and the Solda Route on the Marmoletta, then later with new routes on the Roda di Vael and on the Farfalla. He seldom seconded a pitch, always insisting on taking the lead.

In 1957 the mountain Cerro Torre entered his life when he attempted the FIRST ASCENT with a team from Trento, at the same time as the Italians Walter BONATTI and Carlo Mauri were on the mountain. Both teams climbed from the west, but neither were successful. Maestri returned in 1959, to the east face, with Toni Egger, a skilled ice climber, and Cesarino Fava, both Italians. Ultimately Maestri and Egger set out together up the 2,500-ft (762-m) ice-encrusted granite wall above the col between Cerro Torre and Torre Egger. In three days, Maestri claims, they summited, but on the descent a thaw began to cause ice AVALANCHES all around them. On the fifth day, while descending, an avalanche swept Egger away. Maestri descended alone, and was found exhausted at the foot of the mountain by Fava.

Maestri's claim that two men had succeeded on Cerro Torre was treated with skepticism when other climbers attempting the peak (British on the southeast ridge in 1968, and Mauri's 1969 attempt on the west face) brought back tales of foul weather and technical difficulty. Many found Maestri's account implausible. He stopped expedition climbing after Egger's death, but the criticisms urged him to return to Cerro Torre in 1970 to defend his credibility as a climber.

On the 1970 ascent of the southeast ridge, funded by the Italian engineering firm Atlas Copco, a helicopter was used to dump a prefabricated hut at the foot of Cerro Torre, and Maestri's team hauled a 300-lb (135-kg) compressed-air drill to place 300 to 400 BOLTS on the peak. The route required 54 days of climbing from winter 1970 to three days in spring 1971. After bolting the final headwall Maestri did not stand on the true summit, an ice mushroom 150 ft (46 m) higher, which he dismissed as ". . . a lump of ice, not really part of the mountain—it'll blow away one of these days." Furthermore, he chopped the final bolts of the route so others would be forced to experience the difficulties of drilling in such a place (the feat was accomplished by Jim BRIDWELL in 1979).

Though Maestri regarded his tactics on the southeast ridge as the forefront of climbing techniques, he was condemned by subsequent teams (like the Anglo-Swiss team in 1971–72) for desecrating Cerro Torre with bolts and abandoning the compressor on the headwall. This criticism and doubts about his 1959 ascent appeared in many magazines. Nonetheless, he maintains that he climbed Cerro Torre in 1959, and the question remains unsolved. He is credited with the first ascent in Argentina.

MAGNETIC VARIATION   Or declination. The difference on a compass between true north and magnetic north (to which a compass needle naturally points) expressed in degrees. (See COMPASS.)

MAHALANGUR HIMAL   (Nepal, Tibet)   Within this great range of the HIMALAYA lie some of the world's highest peaks, including EVEREST, LHOTSE, MAKALU and CHO OYU. Its eastern boundaries are the Popti La (Popti Pass) and the Arun River. On the west it is bounded by the Gyabrang Glacier, the Nangpa La, and the Dudh Kosi River. It extends north into TIBET. It is subdivided into three sections. The Makalu Section is dominated by Makalu (27,766 ft/8,463 m) and Chomo Lonzo (25,558 ft/7,790 m), the latter being entirely in TIBET. The Barun Section, contains Chamlang (24,012 ft/7,319 m) and Baruntse (23,390 ft/7,129 m) and extends southwest toward the Lhotse Shar Glacier. The huge KHUMBU Section contains four 26,240-ft (8,000-m) points—Everest (29,028 ft/8,848 m), Lhotse (27,940 ft/8,516 m), Lhotse Shar (27,559 ft/8,400 m) and Cho Oyu (26,906 ft/8,201 m), as well as 22 summits above 22,960 ft (7,000 m), including NUPTSE (25,771 ft/7,855 m), PUMORI (23,494 ft/7,161 m), Gyachung Kang (26,089 ft/7,952 m) and Changtse (24,869 ft/7,580 m). The latter peak lies in Tibet near Everest. Dozens of challenging 19,680-ft (6,000-m) peaks, frequent fair weather and the services of SHERPAS as guides, HIGH-ALTITUDE PORTERS and porters make the Khumbu Section a playground for alpinists.

MAINE   (United States)   The best-known rock climbing in Maine is SEA CLIFF climbing, in Acadia National Park on the central Maine coast. There, Mount Desert Island offers solid granite, which is the predominant rock of the state. Maine's mountainous areas are in the north and west. Maine's high point is Mount KATAHDIN, on which there is rock and alpine climbing. The North Basin of Baxter State Park offers large walls in alpine settings. Frequented rock-climbing areas include Eagle Bluff, Big Chick, Little Chick and Parks Pond Bluff near Clifton; Tumbledown Cliff north of Dixfield; Barrett's Cove and Maiden Cliffs near Camden; The Pinnacle north of Livermore; Payne Ledge north of Norway; Bucks Ledge near Bryant Pond; Bear Mountain and Hawk Ledge near South Waterford; Rock-A-Dundee near Oxford; and small CRAGS around Portland like Rocky Hill and Fort Williams Park.
Guidebook: John Harlin, *Climber's Guide to North America, East Coast Rock Climbs* (1986).

MAKALU   (Nepal, Tibet)   A striking hulk of granite and ice, the fifth-highest summit (27,818 ft/8,481 m) in the world, and one of the hardest 26,240-ft (8,000-m) peaks. It is remote and lies at the end of a long trek through jungle and over high passes into the Barun Valley of NEPAL. The original route followed the snowy northeast ridge, from the col known as Makalu La, beside the peak Kangchungtse (25,059 ft/7,640 m) and was taken by a French team that placed nine men on top, the first of them Jean Couzy and Lionel TERRAY. In 1981 Jerzy KUKUCZKA soloed a variant route beside this line. In 1970 Japanese made the second new route by climbing the long southeast ridge. The eye-catching prize however was the west pillar, a rocky fin between both ridges, that fell to French climbers in 1971. Bernard Mellet and Yannick Seigneur summited. Right of the west pillar, the south face was climbed by Yugoslavs 1976; in 1989 Pierre BEGHIN made a more direct route up this wall, summiting alone. Beginning in 1981, several attempts to climb a direct route up the vertical west face failed to get higher than the ice fields that begin it. Its big granitic wall at 26,240 ft (8,000 m) remains a problem. However, in 1982, a Polish-Brazilian team climbed a rib on the left side of the wall which connected with the French route to the summit. Andrzej Czok summited. Further left, Romolo Nottaris climbed another line on the west face, in 1984. A Japanese expedition made the FIRST ASCENT through TIBET, in 1982, eventually joining the slopes of the first ascent.

MALHAM COVE (Britain) Regarded as YORKSHIRE's finest limestone CRAG, this cliff forms an impressive backdrop to the village of Malham. The crag was, in prehistory, an enormous waterfall on the scale of Niagara Falls. In its present form it is a huge white bowl. Modern routes at Malham are heavily BOLTED, making it the foremost SPORT-CLIMBING crag in Britain.

Climbing began here in 1959. Allan Austin was a major contributor then, with routes like Scorpio (5.8) and the brilliant Kirkby Wall (5.8). The Barley brothers also made major additions, Crossbones (5.10b) being just one of their outstanding routes. These routes followed lines on the right wing of the crag. In the middle of the crag, impressive aid lines formed the basis for a FREE-CLIMBING boom in the 1980s.

In the 1970s, as on so many crags in Britain, Pete LIVESEY and Ron FAWCETT dominated development. Livesey climbed the imposing wall of Doubting Thomas (5.12a) with one aid and Fawcett added, among others, Slender Loris (5.11). A host of fit young 1980s climbers, like Pete Gomersall, Neil Foster and Martin Berzins, used the shoulders of the previous generation to push standards further. Fawcett, however was far from finished, with FREE ASCENTS of Yosemite Wall (5.12a) and the stunning New Dawn (5.12c) in 1984. Ben MOON freed part of the Superdiretissima and Rob Gawthorpe freed the first PITCH of MAIN OVER-HANG (5.12c).

Perhaps Malham's greatest contributor was the muscular John Dunne who in 1987 and 1988 added routes like Austrian Oak (5.13c), Local Hero (5.13c), Zoolook/Well Dunne Finish (5.13c), Magnetic Fields (5.13c), Predator (5.13c) and the awesome Superdirect, which climbs the height of the crag, some 240 ft (73 m), at 5.14b. Dunne has in subsequent years suffered from the punishing training required for such demanding routes. Cry Freedom (5.14a), by Mark Leach, is another testpiece.

Guidebook: Yorkshire Mountain Club, *Yorkshire Limestone* (1985).

MALLORY, GEORGE LEIGH (1886–1924) (Britain) Archetypal romantic hero from MOUNTAINEERING history. George Leigh Mallory came from a line of Cheshire squire-parsons and was himself intended for Holy Orders before the secular world of Cambridge diverted him. Introduced to ALPINISM by R. L. G. Irving, a master at his public school of Winchester, it quickly became the dominating passion of his life. At Cambridge he met Geoffrey Winthrop YOUNG, who introduced him to the Easter parties at Pen y Pass, North Wales. During his attendance at those, Mallory made a number of significant new climbs in the region, but his assured fame rests with the role he played in the three British EVEREST expeditions of the 1920s. On Howard-Bury's reconnaissance of 1921 all the serious climbing fell to Mallory, while on Bruce's expeditions of 1922 and 1924 he reached 27,000 ft (8,232 m) on the north ridge with Norton and Somervell on the first, and his name has become indissociable from the second. Stormy weather early in the season necessitated two retreats to base camp, but in early June two summit bids were made. On the first, Norton and Somervell climbed to within 900 ft (274 m) of the summit before descending. On the second, Mallory and the tyro Andrew Irvine were last seen by ODELL, moving "expeditiously" upward 800 ft (244 m) below the summit. They disappeared, and the rest is romance and 70 years of speculative babble—did they make the summit? Personally, Mallory was a man of cultured taste who wrote a critical study of James Boswell, taught at Charterhouse for most of his working life, and whose good looks were much admired by the affectionate literati of his day.

Further reading: David Robertson, *George Mallory* (1969).

MANAGULA (Nepal) The eighth-highest mountain rises to 26,780 ft/8,163 m. It lies in the Mansiri (or Managula) Himal, bounded on the west by the Marysangdi River and on the east by the Budhi Gandaki River. Managula is a treachery of AVALANCHE slopes and steep rock walls. Indeed, Managula's flanks are hazardous. In 1972 an avalanche onto the Managula Glacier killed 15 Korean climbers. A Japanese team abandoned their expedition before base camp in 1954 when the villagers of Sama barred their passage, believing that Japanese who had nearly summited the previous year had offended mountain gods and caused the gods to destroy the village's Buddhist temple with an avalanche. The FIRST ASCENT finally came in 1956 when a Japanese Alpine Club expedition climbed the northeast side, and placed T. Imanishi and Sirdar Gyaltsen Norbu (NEPAL) on top. Japanese also succeeded on the steep northwest ridge in 1971. The 1972 Tyrolean expedition led by Wolfgang Nairz climbed a mixed route on the south and west flanks. However, though Reinhold MESSNER summited, two climbers disappeared in a blizzard on the summit plateau. An expedition in 1989 led by Benoit Chamoux climbed a variation to this route. The west face of Managula, at the head of the Dudh Kosi River, remained hidden until four French, including Pierre BEGHIN, climbed it in 1981. H. W. Tilman had judged this wall "impossible without wings." Poles climbed the south ridge in 1984, while another Polish group (including Jerzy KUKUCZKA) made a new route on the northeast face in 1986. The east ridge was climbed in 1988 by Swiss.

MANK A colloquialism for bad weather, mist, cloud or snow, as in "manky weather." Mank is also sometimes used like CHOSS, to describe dirty, vegetated rock. The term originated in Britain.

MANSIRI HIMAL (Nepal) Also called the Manaslu Himal. The 26,240-ft (8,000-m) peak MANASLU is the highest point in this range of west-central NEPAL, west of Kathmandu and east of Pokhara. The range is bounded on the east by the Gya La, which crosses into TIBET, and the Budhi Gandaki River. The northern limit starts at the Larkya La and descends the Dudh Khola. The western boundary is the Marsyangdi River. Besides Manaslu, several great peaks rise here, most notably Himal Chuli (25,889 ft/7,893 m), first climbed from the west by Japanese in 1960, and Ngadi Chuli (Peak 29) (25,817 ft/7,871 m), perhaps first summited via the east ridge by two members of a 1970 Japanese expedition who fell from high on the peak. However, the Polish climbers who ascended the difficult west buttress in 1979 dispute the Japanese ascent. Many outliers of Manaslu and Himal Chuli rise above and near to 22,960 ft (7,000 m).

MANTLE, MANTLESHELF In FREE CLIMBING, a move used to gain a ledge. A mantle begins with the climber gripping the edge of a ledge, then pulling through as if on a chin-up bar. When the ledge is at shoulder level, the struggling begins: Palms are placed flat on the ledge, and arms are gradually straightened until the ledge is at waist level. A foot is then cocked onto the ledge and weight is balanced onto it until the climber is standing.

MARMILLOD, DORLY (1914–1978) AND FREDERIC (1909–1978) (Switzerland) A major figure in women's Andean MOUNTAINEERING, Dorly Marmillod (née Eisenhut) has gone largely unnoticed, perhaps because she was not an outspoken feminist and always climbed with her husband, Frederic. Married in 1934, they came to South America when Frederic went to work for Sandoz Laboratories. In central CHILE, they made the second ascent

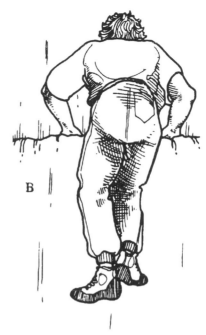

Mantle 2

Mantle 3

TYPES OF MANTLES
Mantle 1

of Nevado Juncal (20,046 ft/6,110 m) and the first of Alto de los Leones (17,866 ft/5,445 m). The latter, believed to be an impossible mountain, was climbed with a Chilean in 1939. In 1942, Dorly became the first woman to climb in VENEZUELA, ascending Pico Bolivar, 16,410 ft/5,002 m. In 1943 in COLOMBIA, she was also the first woman alpinist, climbing with Frederic six major peaks, including the previously unclimbed Sintana (18,570 ft/5,660 m), and with Erwin Kraus, FIRST ASCENTS of important peaks, like Castillo (16,807 ft/5,123 m). In PERU, the couple climbed Rajuntay (18,003 ft/5,488 m) and explored the northern

CORDILLERA BLANCA. Without Dorly, Frederic was in a 1948 Swiss party that seized the summits of Santa Cruz (20,463 ft/6,241 m) and Pucaranra (20,199 ft/6,156 m). Their last Andean exploit together was the first ascent of the southwest ridge of ACONCAGUA, in 1953 with two Argentinians. After resettling in Switzerland, they were caught in a storm during a descent of the Dent d'Herens in the Alps. They perished after a night in the open in −22 degrees F (−30 degrees C) temperatures. In South America, the Marmillods are ranked among the most accomplished ANDINISTAS.

Evelio Echevarria
Colorado State University

MARTINEZ, NICHOLAS G.   (1874–1934) (Ecuador)
From the sportive viewpoint, Martinez is the forerunner of South American ANDINISTAS. Living in the Andean city of Ambato he became fascinated by the mountain Volcan Tungurahua (16,420 ft/5,005 m) and by vulcanology. He climbed Tungurahua alone in 1900 and returned to research its crater repeatedly. In 1904, with three friends, he climbed Antisana (18,716 ft/5,705 m) and in 1906, Cotopaxi (19,350 ft/5,897 m). In January 1911, he and the Indian Miguel Tul, whom he had equipped and trained, made the third ascent of CHIMBORAZO (20,563 ft/6,267 m). To mark the ascent, Tul hoisted his pants on a pole . . . and left them there! In 1912, Martinez and F. Hiti made FIRST ASCENTS of the east face of Cotopaxi and of the rock peak of Illiniza Norte (16,733 ft/5,100 m). Bronchial pneumonia killed him a year later. Martinez published mountaineering books and coined such Spanish mountaineering terms as *piolet, crampones, andinista* and *andinismo.*

Evelio Echevarria
Colorado State University

MARYLAND   (United States)
Along the Potomac River, near Washington, D.C., are two popular 70-ft (21 m) TOP ROPING and BOULDERING areas, Carderock and Great Falls. Backbone Mountain (3,360 ft/1,024 m) in Garrett County, western Maryland, is this state's nontechnical high point.
Guidebook: James Eakin, *Climbers Guide to the Great Falls of the Potomac* (1985).

MASHERBRUM   (Pakistan)
At 25,661 ft/7,821 m, this KARAKORAM peak overlooks two great watersheds: the BALTORO Glacier to the north, and the Masherbrum Glacier and Hushe Valley on the south. Masherbrum La, a rugged high pass east of Masherbrum, is an old trade route once used by BALTI villagers of the Hushe and Braldu/Baltoro valleys. Although access is straightforward from the Hushe Valley, Masherbrum is rarely climbed. Attempts to climb the vast snowy slopes that are embraced by the southeast and east ridges thwarted a British team in 1938, and New Zealanders in 1955. In 1957 another British team from the Rucksack Club tried the southeast face. This expedition was fraught with bad weather and then bad luck when climber Bob Downes died of pneumonia (or possibly PULMONARY EDEMA). A final British attempt in August by Don WHILLANS and Joe Walmsley came maddeningly close to

the summit. In 1960 an American-Pakistani team, including Nick CLINCH, George Bell and Willi UNSOELD, finished the route, placing those three climbers and Jawed Akhter Kahn (Pakistan) on top. In 1985 two expeditions climbed difficult and hazardous routes on the northern side: First, from the Yermanendu Glacier, a Japanese expedition weaved up the northwest ridge and face, dodging SERACS and AVALANCHES. On the 24th of July, a day after the Japanese success, three Austrians completed a steep rock and ice route up the northwest face that began on the Mundu Glacier. The first ascent of Masherbrum's southwest summit, via the southeast face, was by Poles, but two of the three summiters died in a forced BIVOUAC on the descent.

MASSIF   A mountain mass of great size.

MATTERHORN   (Switzerland, Italy)
At 14,688 ft (4,478 m) the Matterhorn is roughly half the height of EVEREST, yet few mountaineers can resist her charms. Strangely isolated between Cervinia and Zermatt, the Matterhorn epitomizes what a mountain should look like, with four distinct ridges and four faces that meet in a knife-edge summit ridge 262 ft (80 m) long; the Italian or west Summit is 3.28 ft (one m) lower than the Swiss. The most usual method of ascent is that taken by Edward WHYMPER in 1865 with Hudson, Hadow, Douglas, Croz and the Taugwalders—the Hörnli Ridge (AD). On the descent Hadow slipped, pulling Croz off and Douglas and Hudson swiftly followed. Whymper and Peter Taugwalder Sr. hung on to the rope but it snapped and the four men fell to their deaths. Until the disappearance of George MALLORY and Irvine, it was the best-known mountaineering accident. Jean Carrel, who had wanted the mountain climbed first by Italians, watched Whymper succeed from the Swiss side after the former had broken an agreement and set out from the Cervinia (or Breuil as it was then) side with a group of Italian mountaineers. Whymper had thrown rocks down the Italian Ridge (not recommended) to attract Carrel's attention, which prompted him to retreat. Carrel returned a few days later to complete his ascent. The two men patched up their differences and climbed the mountain together in 1874.

Other notable ascents include the first by a woman in 1871, Lucy Walker, a member of the famous mountaineering family and lifelong friend of Melchior Anderegg. In 1879 Albert MUMMERY, the brilliant guide Alexander Burgener, A. Gentinetta and Johann Petrus climbed the Zmutt Ridge (D). In 1911 the final ridge, the Furggen, fell at D/TD—a fine achievement by Piacenza, Carrel and Gaspard. The west face was climbed in 1879, but the great north face, one of the classic four in the Alps, fell in 1931 to the brothers Franz and Toni Schmid. It was soloed in 1959, climbed in winter 1962 and by a woman, Yvette Vaucher in 1965 before Walter BONATTI climbed the north face direct solo in the winter and put an end to the matter. The mountain has become something of a stunt arena, with Jean-Marc BOIVIN skiing down the east face, soloing the north face in four hours and hang-gliding off the summit. Nevertheless, new hard routes have continued to arrive, most notable being the Zmutt Nose Couloir climbed in 1989 by Cogna and Cerutti.

There have been well over 400 deaths on the Matterhorn. Most occurred on the Hörnli Ridge, often due to stonefall caused by overcrowding on the route. Great care should be taken and the climbing not underestimated. There is a hut below the Hörnli Ridge and a bivouac shelter at 13,120 ft (4,000 m). On the Italian Ridge at 12,559 ft (3,829 m) is the Rifugio Carrel.

MCCARTHY, JAMES P. (1934–) **(United States)** Lawyer Jim McCarthy was one of the chief climbers to increase rock-climbing standards in the East during the 1960s. He played a major role in the SHAWANGUNKS making many of the CRAG's earliest 5.10 ascents. Some of the better-known routes include Retribution, Nosedive, Tough Shift, Transcontinental Nailway, Try Again and Coexistence—the last two with Richard Goldstone. McCarthy was also a member of a loose federation of irreverent and antisocial climbers who called themselves "The Vulgarians." McCarthy's ambitious nature took him into expeditionary climbing. Here his greatest successes were in the Logan Mountains of Canada's Northwest Territories. A party he led did the second ascent of Mount Probosis, the first by the southeast face, in 1963. A few years later McCarthy was back in the Logans and along with Tom FROST and Sandy Bill climbed a first ascent in the CIRQUE OF THE UNCLIMBABLES, called the Lotus Flower Tower, a peak 7,872 ft (2,400 m) from bottom to top, shaped like the Petit Dru, split by a series of nearly continuous fine cracks.

MCKINLEY, MOUNT **(United States)** Another widely used name for DENALI, North America's highest peak, in ALASKA.

MENLUNGTSE **(Tibet)** See ROLWALING HIMAL.

MERKL, WILLI **(1900–1934)** **(Germany)** Merkl's name is inseparable from the climbing history of NANGA PARBAT. He began climbing in 1916 on the Hoernwald in the Chiemgau Alps, near his birthplace at Kaltennordheim, Thuringen. From 1920 to 1925 he opened routes in the Berchtesgaden Alps, the Northern Kalkalps, the DOLOMITES and the ice of the Westalps. In 1929 in the virtually unexplored Caucasus Mountains, with Fritz Bechtold and Walter Raechl, he accomplished many firsts such as Koshtantau north ridge, and also the third ascent of Uschba south peak. While holidaying in Chamonix from his job as a railway superintendant in Munich, he and Willo WELZENBACH became trapped in frigid conditions on the Grandes Charmoz north face. They were believed dead, but their resourcefulness enabled them to survive and claim a FIRST ASCENT.

In 1932 Merkl led an unsuccessful attempt on Nanga Parbat, but discovered the route that Hermann BUHL would eventually climb in 1953. In 1934 Merkl returned to this route well equipped and with well-trained SHERPAS. The team placed Camp Eight at 24,534 ft (7,480 m), when a MONSOON storm struck in mid-July. During the terrible storm, Merkl, Uli Wieland, Willo Welzenbach and six Sherpas died from cold and exhaustion, and entered the legends of German climbing.

MESSNER, REINHOLD **(1944–)** **(Tyrol, Italy)** Messner is the Tyrolean mountaineer who, between 1970 and 1986, became the first person to climb all 14 26,240-ft (8,000-m) peaks. He is the most influential Himalayan climber of the century. His fast OXYGENLESS ascents of Himalayan peaks and his writing—his books number over 20—have inspired a generation of climbers.

Though born in the South Tyrol of Italy, Messner is of German stock. He began climbing with his father and brother Gunther, and by his late teens had climbed many hard routes in the ALPS and DOLOMITES, often by new lines, such as the northeast pillar on the EIGER (with Toni HIEBELER, 1968), and often solo, such as the north face of Les DROITES (1969). Later, he made a 10-hour ascent of the Eiger north face with Peter HABELER. The previous best time had been three days.

During the 1970s he expressed strong ETHICS about climbing. In an article titled "The Murder of the Impossible" he decried (like Walter BONATTI) the "killing of adventure" by the use of artificial aids like BOLTS. His books *The Seventh Grade, The Challenge* and *The Big Walls* (1974, 1977, 1978) consolidate his philosophy, which also regarded bottled oxygen as "unfair means" to climb a mountain. His more recent philosophy, which he terms "White Wilderness," calls for setting aside mountain areas protected from human access.

Messner's first Himalayan expedition was in 1970, to the Rupal Flank of NANGA PARBAT. This KARAKORAM face is among the world's largest. After a long seige he and Gunther reached the summit, but while descending to the Merkl Couloir they had a bad BIVOUAC and Gunther was overcome with altitude illness. A misunderstanding with their teammates had prevented them from obtaining a rope. The route of ascent was too hard for Gunther to descend, and they descended the opposite side of the mountain—the unexplored Diamir Face. After a 24-hour struggle they reached the GLACIERS below, but here Gunther disappeared in an AVALANCHE. Messner, given up for dead by his expedition, was found by villagers who helped him back to his team. The ordeal of losing Gunther and suffering amputations of his toes from FROSTBITE caused an emotional and physical hiatus in his career, but in 1972 he was back at altitude, on MANASLU. Though he summited via a new route—the south face—tragedy struck again, when two members of the expedition disappeared in a storm.

Messner's next eight thousander was in 1975, on GASHERBRUM I. This time he broke with FIXED ROPE tactics and, with Habeler, made the first ascent of the northwest face in three days of climbing. The ascent was nothing short of audacious: two men climbing ALPINE STYLE on a Himalayan peak, with no fixed ropes, no support and no oxygen. The climb is described in *The Challenge* (1977).

In 1978 the same pair made the first oxygenless ascent of EVEREST. At the time, many thought it impossible for anyone to survive such heights without bottled air. The pair were part of a larger group on the south col route that helped prepare the way, but nevertheless, the ascent was a breakthrough. *Everest: Expedition to the Ultimate* (1979) describes this climb. A few months after Everest, Messner returned to Nanga Parbat alone, making the first ascent of a new route on the Diamir Face in a 12-day roundtrip from base camp. Many regard this as his finest climb: a new route on 26,240-ft (8,000-m) peak solo, without oxygen or support climbers. *Nanga Parbat Solo* (1980) has been called the high point of his writing.

After repeating the Abruzzi Ridge of K2 (1979), Messner returned to Everest in 1980. In what can only be described as a visionary climb, he soloed the northeast ridge from the north col (in Tibet), in a three-day push during the MONSOON. His book *The Crystal Horizon* (1988) describes this ascent.

After SHISHAPANGMA (1981, north face), in 1982 he climbed three eight thousanders in one year—KANGCHEN-JUNGA north face, GASHERBRUM II and BROAD PEAK (by the regular routes). In 1983 he climbed CHO OYU via a variation on the southwest face. In 1984 he made another break-through when, with Hans Kammerlander, he TRAVERSED two 26,240-ft (8,000-m) peaks—Gasherbrum II and Gasher-brum I—by a major variation in poor weather.

By 1985 the so-called "race for the 8,000-m peaks" was his announced goal. Two others—Jerzy KUKUCZKA (Poland) and Marcel Ruedi (Switzerland)—were hot on Messner's tail, but when Messner climbed ANNAPURNA via a new route on the northwest face, and DHAULAGIRI (regular route) in 1985, then MAKALU and LHOTSE (regular routes) in 1986, the race was won and Messner's 16-year odyssey was over. *All 14 Eight-Thousanders* (1988) describes this quest. Messner shifted his focus from the Himalayas in 1989 to ANTARCTICA, making a new traverse across the South Pole. His autobiography is *Free Spirit* (1991).

MEXICO   Mexico is best known to climbers for its volca-noes. They rise in a sporadic east-west chain at about 19 degrees north of latitude, east of Mexico City. The highest and most-climbed are called by their Aztec names: Citlal-tepetl (18,700 ft/5,701 m, also called El Pico de Orizaba), Popocatepetl (17,887 ft/5,453 m) and Ixtaccihuatl (17,342 ft/5,287 m). The elevation gain from the plains is 4,000 to 5,000 ft (1,220 to 1,524 m). They are nontechnical climbs. Climbers the world over come to experience the moderately high altitudes during the dry winter season November through March. The southernmost GLACIERS in North America cling to these volcanoes. The glacier on the cone of "Popo" often has long slopes of 30 to 40 degree bare ice, but Citlaltepetl's north flank supports the largest.

Elsewhere, on rock, the YOSEMITE-scale granite forma-tions of El Gran Trono Glanco have been climbed on since the 1970s, and offer big wall routes. SPORT CLIMBING has also appeared in Mexico, on the limestone of Huasteca Canyon and El Potrero Chico, both in the state of Nuevo Leon, near the town of Hidalgo across the border from Laredo, Texas.

Guidebook: R. J. Secor, *Mexico's Volcanoes* (1981).

MICHIGAN   (United States)   A sandstone TOP-ROPING crag called Grand Ledges, near the town of Grand Ledges, is this midwestern state's main rock-climbing area. Another area lies on the Keweenaw Peninsula, 25 miles (40 km) north of Houghton. It is an extensive basalt escarpment up to 300 ft (91 m) high. Mount Arvon (1,979 ft/603 m), in the Upper Peninsula of the state, is Michigan's highest point. It is nontechnical.

MICRO NUT   A tiny wired NUT or STOPPER fitted into thin cracks. (See CRACK PROTECTION.)

MILLSTONE   (Britain)   This is a disused quarry above the village of Hathersage 5 miles (8 km) from Sheffield. Millstone has limited aesthetic charm but its routes have a significance beyond their size. Facilities are in Hathersage, Stanage Grindelford and STONEY MIDDLETON.

History at Millstone began in the 1950s with aid-climbs up its blank walls. Joe BROWN broke the aid monopoly with a FREE ASCENT of Great North Road (5.8), a huge corner. In the late 1960s Al Evans freed Great West Road (5.9) and Tom Proctor tiptoed up the unprotected corner of Green Death (5.10d), which remained unrepeated for several years. In 1974 Richard McHardy climbed the unprotected ARETE left of Green Death, Edge Lane (5.11a). He returned a year later to climb the Great Arete, another unprotected 5.11a. Such achievements made Millstone a crucible of Peak climbing, and were enforced with ascents like John ALLEN's lead of London Wall (5.12a), a steep peg-scar crack.

In 1982 Ron FAWCETT climbed the fiercely technical Scritto's Republic (5.12d), and in 1986 he solved the Mas-ter's Edge (5.13a), a poorly protected line that requires the SECOND to run backward at speed to save his LEADER from the ground if he falls from the final hard move.

Guidebooks: British Mountain Club, *Stanage/Millstone* (1983); Paul Nunn, *Rock Climbing in the Peak District* (1987).

MINNESOTA   (United States)   Numerous short cliffs dot this midwestern state, and harsh winters offer some ice climbing. Rock in this state is mainly basalt, rhyolite and anthrosite. On the north shore of Lake Superior, north of Duluth are lakeside CRAGS such as Palisade Head. CHALK use has been discouraged on these crags. Duluth has many small OUTCROPS: southwest of Duluth, Ely Peak, a 100-ft (30-m) wall, is the town's main crag. Taylor's Falls, a steep FACE and CRACK CLIMBING area, lies on the Wisconsin border, on the St. Croix River near Minneapolis. Fine, 75-ft (22.5-m) quartzite cliffs are found in Blue Mounds State Park, in the state's southwest corner. Eagle Mountain (2,301 ft/701 m) is a hill in Cook County, northeast Minne-sota, that constitutes the state's high point.

Guidebooks: D. Hynek and E. Landmann, *Blue Mounds-Prairie Walls: Climber's Guide to Minnesota's Blue Mounds State Park* (1989); Dave Pagel, *Taylor's Falls*; Pagel, *Superior Climbs, A Climber's Guide to the North Shore* (1985).

MINYA KONKA   (China)   An isolated range on the border of the Tibetan Plateau and Sechuan Province in CHINA, Minya Konka takes its name from a steep granite peak of 24,895 ft (7,590 m). Minya Konka's AVALANCHE-prone slopes have killed many climbers since the FIRST ASCENT by Americans in 1932. The mountain was erroneously surveyed in 1929 at far greater height by Joseph Rock (United States), who also erroneously surveyed Amne Machen in Sechuan at a height exceeding EVEREST.

In 1932 Terris MOORE, Richard Burdsall, Arthur Emmons and Jack Young arrived at Minya Konka serendipitously, after failing to receive permission to climb EVEREST. Their ascent via the northwest ridge was the highest summit reached by Americans until 1958.

Other peaks of the area include Jiazi (21,451 ft/6,540 m) and Zhong Shan (22,586 ft/6,886 m), which was climbed via the east ridge by Swiss in 1981.

Further reading: R. Burdsall and A. Emmons, *Men Against the Clouds* (1935, 1980).

MISCHABEL, THE (Switzerland) The northern Pennines, that area between the Saas and Matter valleys that runs south into the frontier crest, has a large number of 13,120-ft (4,000-m)-peaks. Its northern part is called Mischabel, and, unlike the MONTE ROSA group or the MATTERHORN, there are few cableways and so the climbing is correspondingly adventurous.

The most northerly of these peaks is the Dürrenhorn (13,235 ft/4,035 m), but because of the long approach to do any of the routes to its summit, it is usually included with an ascent of the neighboring peaks, the Hohberghorn (13,838 ft/4,219 m) and the Stecknadelhorn (13,910 ft/4,241 m). This was first done in 1892 by the guide Christian Klucker. The complete Nadelrat that takes in the dominating Nadelhorn (14,193 ft/4,327 m) and the Lenzspitze (14,084 ft/4,294 m) as well as the former peaks offers an outstanding day's sport and was first done in 1916 by Adrian Mazlam and Josef Knubel. All these mountains are accessible from the Mischabel huts, which are reached from Saas Fee.

The highest mountain wholly within Switzerland, Dom (14,908 ft/4,545 m) does not offer an overwhelming presence, not least from the south where it is dominated by the Täschhorn (14,727 ft/4,490 m). From the east it appears as the highest gneiss pyramid on a crest of them, but the usual mode of ascent is a tedious snow-plod up the north face from the Dom Hut above Randa on the edge of the Festi Glacier. A more interesting option is the northwest ridge, also the line of the FIRST ASCENT made in 1858 by J. L. Davies and his guides Johann Kronig et al, often called the Festigrat (PD+). The northeast ridge offers a harder alternative at TD. The south ridge linking Dom with the Täschhorn is a very long route at altitude although not difficult.

The south face of the Täschhorn is an exceptional mountain aspect. It was first climbed by Franz and Josef Lochmatter with V. J. E. Ryan and Geoffrey Winthrop YOUNG with Josef Knubel in 1906. When you consider that this is still graded TD+, takes 10 to 15 hours to complete and is ferociously dangerous, you can appreciate the true scale of their achievement. There are no easy routes to the summit of the Täschhorn. The first ascent was made in 1862 and

while it is not technically demanding, there are dangers presented by its ice sections. The southeast ridge climbed in 1876 by the Christian and Ulrich Almer with J. Jackson has become, with the construction of the Mischabeljoch, the usual route of ascent.

MITTENS A glove that covers the four fingers together and the thumb separately. (See GLOVES.)

MIXED CLIMBING A route with different types of climbing, such as FREE with AID, but more usually applied to alpine climbs with ICE CLIMBING and ROCK CLIMBING interspersed in the same PITCH.

MODULAR ICE AXE An ICE AXE offering interchangeable picks, adzes, hammer heads and sometimes ski pole–type baskets to replace the spike at the end of the shaft. They may also offer adjustable shaft lengths. Bolt and screw systems hold the parts in place. Modular ice axes are advantageous for replacing broken picks or modifying an ice axe for specific conditions.

MODULAR HOLD See CLIMBING HOLDS.

MOFFAT, JERRY (1963–   ) (Britain) This top British rock climber is known for power, endurance, bouldering skills, FLASHING, RED POINTING and bold FIRST ASCENTS. Moffat's most famous routes include the very dangerous Masters Wall (E6, 6b) at CLOGWYN DU'R ARDDU in 1983, with its death fall potential from a technically demanding crux of 7b+, 5.12b/c. Also in 1983, on STANAGE Edge, he opened the equally hard and dangerous Ulysses' Bow. Revelations (5.13c, 8a+), on RAVEN TOR, was one of the hardest routes in the world when done in 1984, and Liquid Amber, at Lower Pen Trwyn in 1990, was Britain's first 8c (5.14b).

Moffat, of Sheffield, made his mark at the age of 18 with Little Plum at STONEY MIDDLETON (7c), then the hardest route in Britain. In 1982 he made the first ON SIGHT of SuperCrack in the SHAWANGUNKS (5.12d), and the second ascents of Genesis (5.12c), which had been unrepeated since its FIRST FREE ASCENT by Jim Collins in 1979, and Psycho Roof (5.12c/d). He repeated Genesis days later in his tennis shoes. In 1983 he put up Germany's first 9+, Eckel (7c+ or 5.13a), and its first 10−, The Face (8a or 5.13b), in the FRANKENJURA. In 1984 he made the first ON SIGHT ascents of Phoenix in YOSEMITE and Equinox in JOSHUA TREE, both 5.13a cracks. That year, on his 21st birthday, he made the first FLASH of Chimpanzodrome, in Saussois (7c+ or 5.13a). In 1984 in the VERDON Gorge, he made the first free ascent of Papy Onsight (7c+) and on-sighted Pol Pot, 7c. Previously the hardest on-sight, by Patrick, had been 7b+.

After a two-year layoff due to injury, Moffat repeated the Rose and the Vampire, Le Minimum and Le Spectre, BUOUX's three 8b+s (5.14a) in France in 1986. In 1988, Moffat visited SMITH ROCKS, United States, and climbed all that crag's hardest routes: To Bolt Or Not To Be (third ascent), Scarface and White Wedding, all held then to be 5.14a.

His first big competition win was the World Cup at Leeds, England, in 1989. He was second at a World Cup at Lyon and third in the overall World Cup standings that year. He won an invitational at Briançon; the International Escalade at St. Jean de Maurienne, France; and an invitational at Madonna di Campiglio, in Italy, all in 1990. Although he placed second at the LaRiba Masters Invitational in Mont Blanc in Italy, in 1990, he was the unofficial co-winner.

Moffat and his countryman Simon NADIN had agreed before the final that if—as happened—both flashed their route, and were given no superfinal but judged on speed, they would split the prize and consider themselves equal winners. At the 1990 World Cup at Nuremberg, he was the only contender to flash both qualifying routes, though he erred in the final and placed fifth. Moffat was second overall in the ASCI rankings in 1990. He also won the Masters Invitational at Bercy, France, in 1991.

Moffat is also a top boulderer. In 1992, in HUECO TANKS United States, he did the second ascent of the area's hardest problem (V10 on the area's bouldering scale, which begins at V1) in an hour and a half, and added a new TRAVERSE of the same grade, called Nobody's Ugly After 2:00 A.M. On an earlier U.S. visit, in 1991, he did two boulder problems that, by comparison to the ones in Hueco, he estimates at V12. Harder still is a boulder problem in England, Superman Meets the Hulk.

In YOSEMITE he has established the hardest boulder problems, notably After Midnight.

MONO-DOIGT   French word used in FREE CLIMBING, meaning a one-finger POCKET, as found in limestone. A bi-doigt is a two-finger pocket.

MONSOON   The life-giving wet season of the Indian subcontinent. It wells up out of the Bay of Bengal and flows northwest, traditionally arriving in the SIKKIM HIMALAYA around June 5, reaching western NEPAL 10 days later, and arriving in KASHMIR by early July. The monsoon is mild in the drier KARAKORAM Mountains of Ladakh and PAKISTAN, though a strong monsoon in Nepal suggests unsettled weather in the Karakoram. Nonetheless, climbing in the Karakoram is comparatively uninterrupted from May till September. The Tibetan plateau, in the shadow of the Himalaya, also remains comparatively dry during the monsoon. For trekkers, the monsoon means muddy trails, mist, cloudbursts and leeches. In Nepal, BHUTAN, Sikkim, ASSAM and INDIA the monsoon divides climbing into two seasons: premonsoon and postmonsoon. The premonsoon, or spring season, is from March till May. Stifling heat below 5,000 ft (1,524 m), winter snows on peaks and passes, and early season thunder and electrical storms characterize this period, yet calm spells in the mountains offer warm, settled weather. Little climbing is done in the Himalaya during the monsoon, from June till September. However, some climbers have noted that the ceiling of the monsoon is low, and that above approximately 22,000 ft (6,707 m) temperatures and weather can be moderate. Reinhold MESSNER climbed EVEREST from TIBET during the monsoon of 1980. The postmonsoon, or autumn, climbing season spans September and October. Clear, cold weather and favorable snow conditions characterize this season, though by late October or November high winds and winter cold set in as jet stream winds descend. Most postmonsoon expeditions approach their objectives during the monsoon.

MONTANA   (United States)   Western Montana is covered in mountains and cliffs. Blodgett Canyon in the Bitteroot Mountains is among the more developed areas. The area is granite, requires a hike in of about two hours and has ROUTES ranging from short FREE CLIMBS to grade V BIG WALLS. Rock climbing abounds around Bozeman. Within a 10- to 30-mile (16- to 48-km) radius from the town are Gallatin Towers, Hyalite Canyon, the Madison River cliffs and the limestone of Bozeman Pass. Homestake Pass, 80 miles (128 km) east of Butte, is another popular free-climbing area. Winter ice abounds in southwest Montana, at Pine Creek (near Yellowstone), Hyalite Canyon and within Yellowstone. Granite Peak (12,799 ft/3,901 m), requiring modest mountaineering skills, is the state's high point. It lies 45 miles (72 km) southwest of Columbus, near the Wyoming border.

Guidebook: Bill Dockins, *Bozeman Rock Climbs* (1987).

MONT BLANC RANGE   (France, Switzerland, Italy)
This range is surprisingly small in area, considering its fame and popularity, and lies on the borders of France, Switzerland and Italy. The principal mountain is Mont Blanc 15,767 ft (4,807 m) but there are a number of others above 13,120 ft (4,000 m) and a great number of smaller but equally dramatic peaks. There are thousands of routes, some of them climbed by the great names in ALPINISM, and a MOUNTAINEERING career should not be considered complete without tasting a few of them. Téléphériques make the range immediately accessible, occasionally with disastrous results as inexperienced climbers can get themselves into dangerous situations very quickly.

Worthwhile peaks in the Mont Blanc Range with excellent routes include the Aiguille d'Argenitère (12,799 ft/3,902 m) with several classic lines and excellent views of the Courtes-Droites chain. Mont Dolent (12,539 ft/3,823 m) sits at the head of the Argentière Glacier and also has its share of excellent views. To the right of Dolent is the Aiguille du Triolet (12,694 ft/3,870 m) and its precipitous north face climbed in 1931 but still a demanding outing. Above the Albert Premier Hut is the Aiguille du Tour (11,617 ft/3,542 m) with its striking feature of the Table de Roc and the Aiguille du Chardonnet (12,602 ft/3,842 m), also above the Tour Glacier, where the Forbes Arête is especially well known.

The principal center for climbers is CHAMONIX, France, connected by railway to Montenvers, a hotel complex above the Mer de Glace, and the Aiguille du Midi by cable car. The valley itself, which runs west to east on the northern side of Mont Blanc, contains a number of villages, including Le Tour, Montroc, Argentière, Les Praz, Les Bossons and Les Houches. There is a cable car at Argentière giving access to the Grands Montets, a chair lift at Le Tour and one at Les Houches that gives access to the mountain railway that leads to the Nid d'Aigle and the start of the Voie Normale of Mont Blanc.

Chamonix is reached easily from Geneva, 54 miles (86 km) to the west, via the autoroute, and there is a vast array of hotels, bunk houses, campsites, restaurants, snack bars, supermarkets and cafés. In the past, the Bar National near the Post Office and the out-of-town campsite Snell's Field were popular with English-speaking climbers. For those with little money and some patience, Argentière offers an excellent base with cheap restaurants, a good campsite and an excellent bar.

The principal center on the south side of the range is Courmayeur, reached from Chamonix via the Mont Blanc tunnel. It is also connected by road to Aosta. At nearby Entrèves is the start of a cable car system that leads over the top to the Chamonix valley. The peaks are described roughly west to east.

Further reading: Walter Bonatti, *The Great Days* (1974); Riccardo Cassin, *50 Years of Alpinism* (Italian text 1977, translation 1981); René Desmaison, *Total Alpinism* (1982); Richard Goedeke, *The Alpine 4000m Peaks* (1991); Lindsay Griffin, *Mont Blanc Massif Vols I and II* (1990; 3rd ed., 1991); A. F. Mummery, *My Climbs in the Alps and Caucusus* (2nd ed., 1895); Michel Piola, *A Topo Guide to the Rock Climbs of the Mont Blanc Area*; Gaston Rébuffat, *The Mont Blanc Massif*.

MONTENEJOS (Spain) Standing above the Mediterranean coast, 44 miles (70 km) from Valencia, is this important Spanish limestone FREE CLIMBING area. Most ROUTES here are BOLTED in the SPORT-CLIMBING style, and the proximity to the coast makes it an all-year area. The principal area is a gorge of fluted 394-ft (120-m) walls (compared by some to the gorge of VERDON) that plummets into the Rio Mijares. Montenejos is divided into several areas, or sectors. La Presa and La Verda sectors offer moderate climbs, while Los Professionales sector and the Estrechos have steep walls and hard routes to 8a. Areas are easily accessed by road. A *refugio* (hut) and the eponymous village provide services.

MONTE ROSA MASSIF (Italy, Switzerland) This is the biggest mountain massif in the Alps. The highest summit in the Massif is the Dufourspitze (15,199 ft/4,634 m). Lying between Zermatt and Macugnaga, the 10 summits of Monte Rosa offer some rock climbing, most famously on the Cresta Rey and Cresta di Caterina, and ICE CLIMBING on the east face of the massif, the Marinelli Couloir, for instance, climbed in 1872 by the Pendlebury brothers et al. But the mountain is chiefly known for long mixed ridge climbs linking the various tops. These are, from north to south, Nordend (15,118 ft/4,609 m), Dufourspitze, Grenzgipfel (15,147 ft/4,618 m), Zumsteinspitze (14,967 ft/4,563 m), Signalkuppe or Punta Gnifetti (14,937 ft/4,554 m), Parrotspitze (14,537 ft/4,432 m), Ludwigshöhe (14,238 ft/4,341 m), Schwarzhorn or Corno Nero (14,176 ft/4,322 m), Pyramide Vincent (13,825 ft/4,215 m) and Punta Giordani (13,271 ft/4,046 m). There are a number of huts in the area; the Monte Rosa Hut above Zermatt on the Monte Rosa Glacier, the Rifugios Gnifetti and Mantova below the Pyramide Vincent, the Valsesia Hut to the southeast of the Parrotspitze and others.

MONTSERRAT (Spain) Located on the Iberian Peninsula in Catalonia, 25 miles (40 km) from the city of Barcelona, the Montserrat complex of conglomerate spires is among Spain's major rock-climbing areas. The spires—up to 984 ft (300 m) high—cover 16 sq miles (40 sq km) and contain some 600 summits. Three principal areas offer different styles of climbing. Zona del Camping and Tochos are SPORT-CLIMBING crags offering shorter, BOLTED athletic routes on which pebbles and POCKETS comprise the handholds. St. Benet is the higher area, with multi-PITCH routes, some involving aid. The best seasons are spring, summer, and fall. Mediterranean storms make most winters too cold for climbing.

Guidebooks: Toni Jimenez, *Guia de Escalada Libre: Montseratt*; Nico and Leuehsner Mailander, *Sun Rock*.

MOON, BEN (1966–) (Britain) Known for his power as a FREE CLIMBER, and for breaking difficulty barriers, Moon made the FIRST ASCENT of Agincourt, the world's first 8c, at BUOUX and put up Maginot Line (8c or 5.14b) a 25-ft (7.6-m) ROOF that had resisted many attempts, at VOLX in 1989. In 1990 he established Hubble, considered the world's first 8c+ or 5.14c, at RAVEN TOR, England. At age 18, at Lower Pen Trwyn, he made the first ascent of Statement of Youth, Britain's hardest route at the time and its second 8a. It took him five days. In 1987, he climbed Zeke the Freak, the first 8b in Britain.

During the next several years, he made early ascents of French testpieces, such as La Rose et La Vampire (8b, or 5.13d) and, during a two-week period, La Rage de Vivre, Le Spectre and Le Minimum (all 8b+ or 5.14a). Moon also did the second ascent of Jerry MOFFAT's testpiece at Lower Pen Trwyn Liquid Amber, Britain's first 8c (14b) in five days in 1991. It is said to be harder than Agincourt. In the United States, in 1991, he visited BOULDER, COLORADO, and FLASHED or on-SIGHTED routes to 5.13a and put up a new route, The Undertaker (5.13d).

In 1986, at 18, Moon placed second at the second Sport-Roccia, the premier European competition held at ARCO and Bardoneccia, Italy. He has racked up many top 10 finishes, such as fourth at Madonnadi Campiglio, Italy, in 1989; seventh at Arco in 1989; sixth at the World Cup in Lyon in 1990; and second at the World Cup at Madonna di Campiglio in 1990. In 1991, he attended some World Cup competitions, and placed second (tied) in Innsbruck, Austria; 10th at Vienna; and fifth at finals in Birmingham, England. He placed eighth in World Cup standings in 1990 and 1991.

MOORE, TERRIS (1908–1993) (United States) Moore's ascents in the ANDES, ALASKA and the HIMALAYA made him one of the most accomplished U.S. mountaineers of the 1930s. Moore began climbing in 1929 during a zoological expedition in ECUADOR when, as a comparative novice, he led the FIRST ASCENT of the volcano Sangay (17,500 ft/5,335 m), and later made the fourth ascent of CHIMBOR-AZO (20,551 ft/6,265 m). The same year, while at Harvard Business School studying economics, he joined the Harvard Mountaineering Club. In 1930 Moore teamed up with Alan Carpe to climb Mount Bona in the Wrangell Range of Alaska. The same year he teamed up with Noel ODELL, of EVEREST fame, who was on the geology faculty at Harvard, and another Everest climber, C. G. Crawford, to make the first guideless ascent of Mount ROBSON. In 1931 Moore returned to Alaska with Carpe to make the first ascent of the south face of Mount FAIRWEATHER, a 10,000-ft (3,049-m) TECHNICAL route climbed in virtual ALPINE STYLE. In 1932 Moore planned an expedition to Everest. However, when the party was refused entry into NEPAL and TIBET, the team shifted its goal to MINYA KONKA (24,892 ft/7,587 m)—then rumored to be 30,000 ft (9,146 m) high—in CHINA. Avoiding the Sino-Japanese war of 1931 and traveling through largely unknown territory, the team made the first ascent of the peak. Moore then reentered Harvard, married and became a pilot. During World War II he was assigned to the U.S. Army Quartermaster Corps Research and Development Project on DENALI. While stationed there he made the third ascent of the peak with other climbers in the research team. During his 1949–53 tenure as president of the University of Alaska at Fairbanks he helped revolutionize Alaskan aviation, developing light plane wheel-skis, and establishing a high-altitude landing record of 16,237 ft (4,950 m). With Bradford WASHBURN, Moore made an aerial reconnaissance of Denali, identifying the glacier aircraft runway now known as Kahiltna International. He also provided air support for Washburn's successful first ascent of the west buttress of Denali in 1951.

MOORE'S WALL   (United States)   Twenty miles (32 km) from Winston-Salem, North Carolina, within Hanging Rock State Park, and rising out of the forested North Carolina Piedmont are the Sauratown Mountains, which include Hanging Rock, Pilot Mountain and Sauratown Mountain. In this area is Moore's Wall which, along with Sauratown Mountain, is an important FREE-CLIMBING area of meta-quartzite. The cliffs overhang up to 15 degrees, making for strenuous leads. The bulk of routes lie in the 5.11 and harder category, but quality easier climbs (5.4 to 5.10) are also found. Most routes have been established from the ground up, with abundant NATURAL PROTECTION from tied-off CAMMING DEVICES in horizontal cracks, but in recent times, difficult RAPPEL-BOLTED routes (from 5.11 to a possible 5.14, Hercules, on the Hanging Garden Cliff) have also appeared. Due to the humid southeast climate, early spring and fall are the best seasons for this area.
Guidebook: Thomas Kelley, *Climbers Guide to North Carolina* (1986).

MOOSES TOOTH, THE   (United States)   At 10,335 ft (3,151 m) the Mooses Tooth lies in the main ALASKA RANGE, rising 5,000 ft (1,524 m) above the spectacular Gateway to the Ruth Glacier Gorge. Its first successful climb took place in 1964. Germans climbers Welsch, Bierl, Hasenkopf and Reichegger raced Fred BECKEY and two other Americans

across the west ridge. While the Americans retreated after the west summit, the Germans continued for 22 continuous hours across intricate CORNICING to the higher main summit. In the intervening years, many west ridge climbers have reached the west summit, but the German performance is seldom repeated. In 1981, the imposing east face, after years of attempts, was finally climbed as an early-season ice route by Mugs STUMP and Jim BRIDWELL. Other interesting rock and ice routes have been climbed on both the north and south faces.
Guidebook: Steve Roper and Allen Steck, *Fifty Classic Climbs of North America* (1979).

MORAINE   The mass of boulders, mud and old ice deposited in banks at the snout (terminal moraine), sides (lateral moraine) or along the center (medial moraine) of a glacier. As glaciers retreat, large moraine mounds may remain. Older, compact moraines provide easy travel along glaciers. Fresh moraine may be unstable. Moraine provides the basis for alpine plant and animal ecosystems. (See GLACIERS.)

MORROW, PATRICK (1952–   ) (Canada)   Morrow achieved international fame in 1986 when he became either the first or second person to climb the SEVEN SUMMITS (the highest summits on each of the seven continents). Dick BASS also claims the title. Morrow's climbs include DENALI (North America) in 1977, ACONCAGUA (South America) in 1981, EVEREST (Asia) in 1982, ELBRUS (Europe) in 1983, KILIMANJARO (Africa) in 1983, Mount VINSON (ANTARCTICA) in 1985 and CARSTENZ PYRAMID (Australasia) in 1986. He received the Order of Canada in 1987 for this achievement, and wrote *Beyond Everest, Quest for the Seven Summits* (1986). A respected mountain photographer, Morrow helped found the Adventure Network, a company that specializes in guiding in Antarctica.

MORTIMER, GREG (1952–   ) (Australia)   Mortimer summited on the first Australian ascents of the earth's highest and second-highest mountains, first in 1984 with Tim MACARTNEY-SNAPE (AUSTRALIA) on EVEREST via the Great Couloir on the north face—a new route; then in 1990, with Greg Child (Australia), on K2 north ridge. His principal new ROUTES include the first TRAVERSE in 1973 (with Australian Keith Bell) of Balls Pyramid, an 1,800-ft (549-m) tower rising in the Pacific Ocean off the Australian east coast; in NEW ZEALAND, the Hidden Balfour Face of Mount Tasman (1977) and the FIRST WINTER ASCENT of the east ridge of Mount COOK (1982); in the ANDES of PERU the south face of Chacaraju, southeast face of Artesonraju and east face of Kakakiru (1980); the FIRST ASCENT of the south face of ANNAPURNA II in NEPAL (1983); and in ANTARCTICA, the first ascent of Mount Minto. In 1987 and 1990 he climbed the Sydney Opera House and Centerpoint Tower, two Sydney buildings, as protest actions to support Greenpeace policies against nuclear-powered and -armed ships in the Pacific and against atmospheric ozone depletion.

MOUNTAINEERING The aspect of climbing that involves climbing mountains such as those found in the ALPS and the HIMALAYA. Distinguished from ROCK CLIMBING AND ICE CLIMBING, although mountaineering may involve sections of rock and ice climbing. (See EXPEDITIONS.)

MOUNTAIN SICKNESS Another name for the altitude-induced malady ACUTE MOUNTAIN SICKNESS.

MOVE One of a series of motions or body positions that make up a FREE CLIMB. Moves are linked together in sequences.

MOVING TOGETHER Another term for SIMULTANEOUS CLIMBING, meaning to climb together over easy rock or snow.

MUIR, JOHN (1838–1917) (United States) This mountaineer active in the 1800s left indelible marks on America's views of mountains with his writing and conservation efforts. Though born in SCOTLAND and raised in WISCONSIN, he is identified with the SIERRA NEVADA of CALIFORNIA, which he roamed from 1860 to 1890. He climbed Mount WHITNEY by a new route and made the first ascent of Mount Ritter and made early ascents in the CASCADES. He often climbed alone with no equipment. His strong beliefs in wilderness preservation were influential in the establishment of YOSEMITE National Park, and his statements on wilderness are often quoted. In 1892 Muir founded the Sierra Club.

MUMMERY, ALBERT FREDERICK (1855–1895) (Britain) Perhaps the greatest of late-Victorian mountaineers, his ascent of the Grepon with Alexander Burgener in 1881 was a landmark in 19th-century ALPINISM. In the 1889 season he began guideless climbing, and his ascents thus over the next few seasons were to exert a considerable influence over the future course of alpinism. He disappeared on NANGA PARBAT with two Gurkha companions in 1895, leaving ready for publication a book that was quickly recognized as ranking, along with Leslie Stephen's *The Playground of Europe* and WHYMPER's *Scrambles Amongst the Alps,* as one of the three classics of Victorian mountain literature.
Further reading: Albert F. Mummery, *My Climbs in the Alps and Caucasus* (1895).

MUNDAY, WALTER (1890–1950) **AND PHYLLIS MUNDAY** (1894–1990) (Canada) This husband and wife team were among the first to explore the COAST MOUNTAINS, discovering Mount WADDINGTON in the process, which they called Mystery Mountain. Their dream of climbing this mountain was never fulfilled, though they got as far as Waddington's adjoining, lower northwest summit. Phyllis was a capable mountaineer who, guided by Conrad KAIN, made the first female ascent of Mount ROBSON (1924). Between 1925 and 1936, Walter (Don) and Phyllis made 11 expeditions into the Coast Mountains. They explored the Waddington Range, the Homathko Icefield, the Sil-

verthrone, Mount Queen Bess and a mountain later named Mount Munday. Don was a fellow of the Royal Geographic Society, and an honorary member of the Appalachian Mountain Club. Phyllis was an honorary member of the Alpine Club of Canada, American Alpine Club, Ladies Alpine Club (England) and Appalachian Mountain Club. She served as honorary president of the Alpine Club of Canada and in 1973 was awarded the Order of Canada.
Further reading: Phil Dowling, *The Mountaineers* (1979); Don Munday, *The Unknown Mountain* (1948, 1975).

MUNRO BAGGING In British MOUNTAINEERING and hill-walking parlance, the practice of climbing to the tops of all of SCOTLAND's 543 high points and 276 mountains above 3,000 ft (915 m). Hugh Munro published his "Munro's Tables and other Tables of Lesser Heights" in 1891 (revised in later years), ushering in a craze of "bagging" or collecting ascents of the peaks. The term is used less frequently today.

MUNTER HITCH Another name for the Italian hitch or friction hitch, used for belaying. The hitch is named after its inventor, the Swiss climber Werner Munter. (See BELAYING TECHNIQUES.)

Munter Hitch

MURRAY, W. H. (1913–   ) (Britain) Bill Murray is author of what are generally accepted as the two finest books ever written about British hills—*Mountaineering in Scotland* (1947) and *Undiscovered Scotland* (1951). The first title was written under remarkable conditions, on toilet paper in German prisoner-of-war camps between 1942 and 1945 after his capture in the western desert by Rommel's Panzer Divisions. An initial draft of the book was confiscated by the Gestapo and Murray interrogated about its contents. It was published in 1947, and since then has never been out of print.

Murray was typical of a disadvantaged Scots generation growing up between the wars, in that he sought equality and release among the Scottish hills from the beginning of the 1930s onward. In 1936 he began a campaign that was to revitalize the laborious pastime of Scottish winter climbing and turn it into a recognizable version of the efficient and speedy modern sport. The revolution he led in what, since World War I had been a stagnant activity, was founded on the use of three items of equipment: tricouni-nailed boots "allowed much neater footwork than crampons on snow and ice-bound rock, and allowed too an occasional 'miracle' to be pulled off on thin, brittle ice"; Murray's own innovation, the short-handled slater's pick, scoffed at by his older contemporaries, eased the wrist strain consequent on hold-cutting for protracted periods with the old long-handled ICE AXES, and enabled climbing times to be halved; while head-torches "proved invaluable on the longer climbs when conditions would otherwise have stopped an ascent."

Thus equipped, Murray and his partners, through the winter seasons before the Second World War, notched up a tally of ascents now rated as the major inter-war achievements in Scottish winter climbing. Crowberry Ridge by Garrick's Shelf on the Buachaille Etive Mhor in 1937, and Deep-cut Chimney on Stob Coire nam Beith in 1938 were outstanding—and for their time outstandingly difficult—among many climbs of near-comparable quality. Nor were Murray's exploratory urges confined to winter. First to make the greater TRAVERSE of the Cuillin Ridge on SKYE, he led the FIRST ASCENTS of Glencoe's Clachaig Gully and the Great Gully of Gars Bheinn in Ardgour in 1938. His

ascent of Twisting Gully on Stob Coire nan Lochan in 1946 took up where the prewar campaign had left off, and in the early 1950s he was a member of two Himalayan expeditions—to Garhwal and Almora in 1950, and as deputy leader on Eric Shipton's 1951 EVEREST reconnaissance expedition. Subsequently, uncertain health restricted his climbing, and he wrote widely on Scottish themes.

Further reading: W. H. Murray, *Mountaineering in Scotland* and *Undiscovered Scotland*, republished in one vol. (1947 and 1951; 1979).

MUZTAGATA (China) This frequently climbed gently angled mountain of the KUNLUN RANGE in Xinjiang Province, western CHINA, is a popular trekking peak. Rising from arid plains to 24,757 ft/7,546 m, Muztagata lies 15 miles (24 km) east of the Sino-Russian border, and 155 miles (248 km) from the city of Kashgar. It is southwest of the massif of Kongur. Many expeditions reach Kashgar via the Karakoram Highway and the Kunjerab Pass between China and PAKISTAN. Muztagata is a rounded snow DOME, easy on all sides except for the precipitous east side. Muztagata (also incorrectly written as Muztagh Ata) has two summits, the lower northerly summit being 24,366 ft/7,427 m. Efforts to climb Muztagata were made by such notable explorers as Sven Hedin in 1894, Sir Aurel Stein in 1900

Muztagh Tower, Pakistan

and Eric SHIPTON and Bill TILMAN in 1947. A large Sino-Russian expedition climbed the west face in 1956, placing 31 members on top. The northwest ridge and southwest face were climbed in 1982, and the north ridge to the north summit was climbed in 1981. The mountain was skied in 1980 by Americans led by Ned Gillette.

MUZTAGH   A term used in the KARAKORAM to refer to a range of peaks, often named after the GLACIER the peaks surround, such as BALTORO Muztagh.

MUZTAGH   TOWER   (Pakistan) This precipitous black rock pyramid (23,861 ft/7,273 m) of the BALTORO Muztagh has an inviolable appearance. To date there are only two ROUTES to its twin summits, of which the east summit is higher by 10 ft (three m). Both routes were made in 1956, one by British, the other by French expeditions, who engaged in a "race" from different sides of the mountain. The first to summit were the British, who approached the northwest ridge from the Chagaran Glacier. Ian McNaught Davis and Joe BROWN reached the lower summit but failed to cross a treacherous knife-edge to the true summit, 1,000 horizontal ft (305 m) away; John Hartog and Tom PATEY, some hours behind them, overcame this difficulty but spent a frigid night out, in which Hartog froze his feet. The French, led by Guido Magnone, summited by the equally challenging southeast ridge a week later, then joined in the evacuation of Hartog. The expedition is recounted in Joe Brown's *The Hard Years* (1967) and Tom Patey's classic "One Man's Mountains" (1971). The second ascent of the mountain, via the British route, was not until 1984.

N

NADIN, SIMON (1965–   ) (Britain) Nadin won the first overall World Cup title in 1989. A high rigger in the construction industry from Buxton, England, Nadin was little known outside his local CRAGS when he entered his first competition in spring 1989. He qualified for the World Cup at Leeds, England, and ended up in a superfinal round with Didier RABOUTOU and Jerry MOFFAT. Nadin placed third. He also won the LaRiba Masters, an invitational in Mont Blanc, Spain, and the North Face World Cup at Berkeley, California, in 1990. On the rocks, he has ON-SIGHTED many routes up to 5.13c.

NAILING Another word for AID CLIMBING. A nailup is an aid route.

NAMCHE BARWA See ASSAM HIMALAYA.

NALAKANKAR HIMAL (Tibet, Nepal) Straddling the border areas of central NEPAL and TIBET, this range is bounded on the east by the Lapche La, and on the south and southwest by the Humla Karnali River. Much of the region has terrain typical of the Tibetan Plateau, which is high, dry and barren. The greatest massif of the range is that of Gurla Mandhata (25,348 ft/7,728 m, or 25,236 ft/7,694 m according to a recent Chinese survey), a mountain famous in old Tibetan Buddhist literature. Such notable explorer-climbers as Tom LONGSTAFF in 1905, and Herbert TICHY in 1936 tried to climb Gurla Mandhata. Longstaff and Swiss guides Henri and Alexis Brocherel climbed to over 22,960 ft (7,000 m) on the western spur and narrowly escaped disaster when they were avalanched 2,952 ft (900 m). The mountain was not climbed again until 1985, by a Japanese-Chinese expedition that found a route above the Zaromalangpa Glacier.

NAMIBIA Climbing in this southern African nation has been developed by South African climbers. Principal areas include Spitzkoppe, a 1,600-ft (488-m) extruded granite DOME 190 miles (306 km) southwest of Windhoek on the edge of the Namib Desert, and Pondoks, a small "wonderland of rocks," surrounding the Spitzkoppe, offering granite domes and boulders up to one PITCH long. The Mountain Club of South Africa, Transvaal Section (see Appendices), records information on Namibian climbing.

NANDA DEVI At 25,545 ft (7,788 m) the twin-peaked Nanda Devi is the highest peak in INDIA. The rivers approaching the mountains surrounding Nanda Devi in the GARHWAL HIMAL are rugged and difficult to cross. After a number of different attempts by others, Eric SHIPTON and William TILMAN became the first people to visit what is now known as the Nanda Devi Sanctuary in 1934. In 1936, with an Anglo-American expedition, Tilman and Noel ODELL made Nanda Devi's first ascent. In 1984 the Indian government closed the sanctuary because of ecological concerns.

NANGA PARBAT (Pakistan) The history of this snowy massif is clouded by spectacular tragedies. At 26,658 ft/8,125 m, it is the ninth-highest summit in the world. Nanga Parbat means, in Sanskrit, "naked mountain," and its long summit outline has been likened to the profile of a sleeping woman. Being the most westerly EIGHT THOUSAND METER PEAK (26,240 ft) it bears the brunt of westerly storms, and is notorious for AVALANCHES and fierce storms that dump deep snow. It is bounded on the north and west by the Indus River. Three great glaciated faces flow from its summit: the Rakhiot on the north, the Diamir on the west and the Rupal on the south.

Many famous climbers have tackled Nanga Parbat. C. G. BRUCE and Dr. J. N. COLLIE, G. Hastings and Alfred MUMMERY made the first attempt in 1895, and while trying to cross a pass between the Rakhiot and Diamir glaciers, Mummery and two Gurkhas disappeared. In 1932 came the first of many German attempts. The first included Willi MERKL, Peter Aschenbrenner and Fritz WIESSNER and reached 22,960 ft (7,000 m); in 1934 a strong team including Aschenbrenner, Merkl, and Willo WELZENBACH climbed over Rakhiot Peak, but they and six other Germans and SHERPAS died in a terrible storm; in 1937 on the same route 16 Germans and Sherpas died in an avalanche; the 1938 attempt claimed no lives but Merkl's body was found with a letter in a pocket begging for help; on the 1939 German reconnaissance Heinrich HARRER and Peter Aufschnaiter discovered relics of Mummery's attempt. Later, when war broke out, they were interned in India by the British and began a saga of escape and travel through the Himalaya. Finally, in 1953, an expedition led by Dr. Karl Maria HERRLIGKOFFER overcame the Rakhiot Face, and Hermann BUHL made a final solo climb to the summit. Herrligkoffer (Merkl's stepbrother) went on to lead many expeditions to Nanga Parbat, including the second (1962, Diamir Face) and third (1970) ascents. On the 1970 expedition Reinhold

Nanga Parbat

MESSNER and his brother Gunther summited via the difficult Rupal Face, but on the descent Gunther disappeared. Messner later returned to solo a new route on the Diamir Face in 1978. The southwest ridge, called the Kinshofer Route, was climbed in 1976 by a team led by Hanns Schell. Other routes have been forced up the three great faces, with the loss of additional lives.

Further reading: Hermann Buhl, *Nanga Parbat Pilgrimage* (1956); Karl Maria Herrligkoffer, *The Killer Mountain, Nanga Parbat* (1954); Reinhold Messner, *Nanga Parbat Solo* (1980).

NAPES, THE   (Britain) This famous LAKE DISTRICT cliff on the south flank of Great Gable is reached from Wasdale Head via the Sty Head Pass. The obvious feature is Tophet Wall, with the famous Napes Needle nearby. Walter Haskett-Smith created a legend in 1886 with his ascent of the Needle, although this 5.5 classic is now horribly polished. He is generally seen as the founder of rock climbing not because he was the first to climb rock, but because he pursued the activity for its own reward and not as a means to reaching a summit.

On Tophet Wall is H. M. Kelly's eponymous 5.6, an exposed line up a 250-ft (76-m) sheet of rock, which in 1923 must have been terrifying. In 1940 Jim Birkett added Tophet Grooves to the left of the wall, a sustained route

that probably deserves 5.9. Birkett made an enormous contribution to Lakeland climbing and his family continues to do so. Forty-four years later another local, Pete Whillance, and Dave Armstrong filled the gap between these two older classics with Incantations (5.12b).

Guidebooks: Bill Birkett, et al, *Rock Climbing in the Lake District* (1986); FRCC, *Gable and Pillar* (1989).

NATURAL LINE   An obvious feature in a cliff or peak presenting the logical weakness for climbers to follow. The weakness would typically be a crack system in a cliff, or a snow COULOIR in a mountain.

NATURAL PROTECTION   The term to indicate PROTECTION other than BOLTS. Includes PLACEMENTS in CRACKS (see ANCHORS, FRIENDS, NUTS, PITONS, STOPPERS, TRICAM, TUBE CHOCKS); and includes placements of SKYHOOKS, SLINGS around HORNS and CHICKENHEADS, and other CLEAN points of protection.

NEEDLES, THE   (United States) This group of spectacular granitic towers and DOMES in the southern SIERRA NEVADA of California lie at 6,000 to 8,000 ft (1,829 to 2,439 m) in the Kern River canyon. Climbs are from one to 12 PITCHES long, and are often steep, clean cracks, although knobby FACE CLIMBS are found too. Fred BECKEY pioneered climbing here in the early 1970s when he climbed the south face of Warlock Needle. In the late 1970s Herb Laeger climbed many classic routes, especially on Witch Needle. In the 1980s Mike Lechlinski, Tony YANIRO, Dick Leversee, Tom Gilje and Ron Carson were active. Currently there are over 100 routes.

Guidebook: Salley Moser, Greg Vernon and Patrick Paul, *Southern Sierra Rockclimbing: Vol. 2, The Needles Area* (1992).

NEEDLES, THE   (United States) An historic American FREE-CLIMBING area in the Black Hills, near Custer and Rapid City, South Dakota. The Needles are an extensive area of boulders, pinnacles and outcrops up to 200 ft (61 m) high, composed of eroded, coarse granite and pegmatite. FACE CLIMBING on chunky quartz crystals characterizes the cliffs, which are among the last U.S. areas to cling to traditional free climbing ETHICS. AID CLIMBING is eschewed for free climbing from the ground up. BOLTING is done on lead, by hand, and from natural stances only. RAPPEL BOLTING or BOLTS placed from SKYHOOKS are not condoned. This ethic makes for bold climbs with long RUNOUTS and has preserved many FIRST ASCENTS for future climbers with exceptional boldness. Another unique facet of Needles climbing is the tradition of summit registers on the 300-plus ft (91 m) summits for recording ascents.

Climbing in the Needles began in 1936, when Fritz WIESSNER led a party into the area. From 1947 to 1960 Herb and Jan Conn made 215 first ascents there, and mapped the region. Technically difficult climbing came during the 1960s, when Bob Kamps, Dave Rearick, and especially John Gill discovered the area. Gill's boulder problems, especially his B1 route on the Thimble, remain significant today. The difficulties of protecting Needles routes—by bolting from delicate stances—suppressed development of the area in the early 1960s, but in 1967 a breakthrough came when Pete Cleveland led his virtually unprotected 5.11 routes on the Super Pin and Hairy Pin. The 1970s and 1980s were active years in the Needles, with Paul Muehl, Bob Archibold, Kevin Bein and Barbara Devine active in pushing ratings toward 5.13. July and August are the best months for climbing.

Guidebooks: Horning and Marriott, *Black Hills Needles: Selected Free Climbs*; Paul Piana, *Touch the Sky: The Needles of the Black Hills of South Dakota* (1983).

NEPAL   The heartland of the HIMALAYA. Mountaineering here is done only by permission from the Nepal Ministry of Tourism (Mountaineering Section, Tourism Building, Kathmandu). Fees must be paid on all mountains. In 1992 these fees soared, with a fee of $50,000 for Everest, though other peaks were less affected. International climbing associations are negotiating reductions in these fees. For all but trekking peaks, a military or police liaison officer accompanies a party to the peak. Rules also govern travel of foreign climbers, the route of ascent assigned to an expedition and the hiring of porters and SHERPAS. The mountaineering season in Nepal is divided by the MONSOON into premonsoon (spring) and postmonsoon (autumn) seasons. Expeditions all begin from the capital, Kathmandu, where they commonly employ the services of trekking agencies to handle the hiring of base camp staff and permit matters. Aircraft, buses and arduous walks to the highlands are necessary to reach the mountains. Several prominent Nepalese peaks are described in this volume. (See ANNAPURNA, CHO OYU, DHAULAGIRI, EVEREST, KANGCHENJUNGA, LHOTSE, MAKALU, MANASLU and PUMORI. The Nepalese ranges are divided into many sections. See DHAULAGIRI HIMAL, GANESH HIMAL, GURANS HIMAL, JANAK HIMAL, KANGCHEN-JUNGA HIMAL, LANGTANG HIMAL, MAHALANGUR HIMAL, MANSIRI HIMAL, NALAKANAR HIMAL, PAMARI HIMAL, PERI HIMAL, ROLWALING HIMAL, SERANG HIMAL.)

NEVE   A French word often used in English. Neve describes a state of snow with a firm surface hardened by freeze and thaw action, excellent for climbing with ICE AXE and CRAMPONS. Also, the upper reaches of a snow or ice slope on a mountain that feeds a GLACIER; *firn* in German.

NEW ENGLAND ICE CLIMBING   (United States) New England offers the most accessible and diverse selection of ice climbs in the continental United States. North Conway is the hub for the popular NEW HAMPSHIRE routes on CATHEDRAL and Whitehorse ledges, Crawford Notch, Mount WASHINGTON and CANNON CLIFFS. In Vermont, Lake Willoughby has a host of difficult one- to five-pitch climbs, while Smugglers Notch has shorter, moderate routes. The New England ice season starts in early December, and depending upon the frequency of thaws, roadside ice lasts until early March, while mountain ice stays cool even later into spring.

Guidebook: Rick Wilcox, *An Ice Climber's Guide to Northern New England* (1982).

NEW HAMPSHIRE   (United States) Called Granite State because of its abundance of granite outcrops, New Hampshire has cliffs up to 1,000 ft (305 m) like CANNON Mountain, CATHEDRAL LEDGE and Whitehorse Mountain that lie in the White Mountains, around North Conway. SPORT CLIMBING at areas like Rumney, an overhanging metamorphic crag near Plymouth, came into vogue during the 1980s. New Hampshire is also a center of ICE CLIMBING (see NEW ENGLAND ICE CLIMBING). The state's high point is Mount WASHINGTON.

NEW JERSEY   (United States) An area of quartzite cliffs bordering the Delaware River on both the New Jersey and PENNSYLVANIA sides, called the Delaware Water Gap, provides rock climbs up to two PITCHES. The main areas are Mount Tammamy (New Jersey) and Mount Minsi (Pennsylvania). These cliffs have a tradition of climbing since the 1950s and are within a national recreation area. The highest point of New Jersey is called High Point (1,808 ft/550 m), 60 miles (96 km) northwest of New York City.

Guidebook: Mike Steele, *Climbing Guide to the Delaware Water Gap* (1988).

NEW MEXICO   (United States) This dry, desert state has notable climbing. At Cochiti Mesa, eight miles (13 km) northwest of the town of Cochiti Lake, is SPORT CLIMBING on POCKETED welded tuff on the Pajarito Plateau. This CRAG gained popularity in the 1980s, as did Box Canyon, a short porpyritic andesite crag seven miles (11 km) west of Socorro. Enchanted Rock, a welded tuff crag lying at 8,000 ft (2,439 m), near Socorro became a sport-climbing center in the late 1980s. These routes contain climbs up to 5.13. White Rock is a small basalt crag. Cochise's Stronghold is a spectacular granite area. The SANDIA MOUNTAINS are an uplifting of granite cliffs up to 10,600 ft (3,232 m) (the summit of Sandia Mountain) above the city of Albuquerque. While the cities 5,000 ft (1,524 m) below in the Rio Grande Valley swelter, the crests of the Sandias enjoy a mild climate. The area lies on National Forest Service land and some cliffs are periodically closed due to nesting peregrine falcons. Cliffs average 600 ft (183 m). Limestone caps the crest of the Sandias. The climbing is typified by long traditional mountain routes following discontinuous crack systems. Elsewhere, a stiff hike gains the 13,161-ft (4,012 m) high point of this state, Wheeler Peak, in Taos County, near Arroyo Seco. Perhaps the state's best-known formation is SHIPROCK.

Guidebooks: John Harlin, *Climbers Guide to North America, Rocky Mountain Rock Climbs* (1985); Mike Hill, *Hikers and Climbers Guide to the Sandias* (1983).

NEW RIVER GORGE   (United States) On the upper rim of the New River Gorge in southern West Virginia, 30 miles (48 km) from Beckley and near Fayetteville, is a band of fine-grained quartzose cliffs that extend for miles. These 50 to 150-ft (15 to 45-m) cliffs have become the most important FREE-CLIMBING and SPORT-CLIMBING center of the southeast United States. Though the area was initially popular due to its CRACKS, steep bolted faces became the focus in the 1980s. Horizontal breaks and vertical fractures combine to give many edges, cracks and ROOFS up to 50 ft/ 50 m. The area is divided into several cliffs, the major ones being Bridge Area Crags (by the New River Gorge Bridge, a 3,030-foot/924-m-long bridge that is the scene of an annual base-jumping celebration), Beauty Mountain, Endless Wall, Bubba City and Kaymoor. These cliffs form unbroken walls up to four miles long. They are well developed with 1,300 climbs from 5.7 to extreme routes in the 5.13 category. **Guidebook:** Richard Thompson, *New River Rock* (1987).

NEW ZEALAND   The North and South Islands of this southern island nation are mountainous and have given rise to a hardy breed of mountaineer. In fact, one of the best known mountaineers of all time—Sir Edmund HILLARY—is a New Zealander.

High glaciated peaks with tall faces and a weather pattern dictated by the moist westerly airstream means high precipitation and at times savage storms. The North Island has some large volcanos, like Mount Egmont (8,259 ft/2,518 m) and Mount Ruapehu (9,174 ft/2,797 m), reached from the cities of Wellington and Auckland.

Several major groups of peaks rise along the mountainous spine of the South Island. The Spenser Mountains near the city of St. Arnaud offer moderate alpine terrain. Further south more serious peaks arise. In Mount COOK and Westland National Parks 17 peaks rise over 9,840 ft (3,000 m) along a main divide that stays consistently above 6,560 ft (2,000 m). Mount Cook (12,346 ft/3,764 m) is the highest of these, and the highest in the country. The 48-mile (30-km) Tasman Glacier—the longest in New Zealand—is a major feature of the region and above it are many imposing peaks, Like Mount Elie de Beaumont (10,197 ft/3,109 m), Douglas Peak (10,102 ft/3,080 m) and Mount Haidinger (10,056 ft/3,066 m). The long triple-summited snowclad shape of Mount Cook dominates the region though, and it has been likened to Himalayan mountains for its size and severe weather, though it lacks such great altitude. North of Cook are Mount Tasman (11,473 ft/3,498 m) and Mount Dampier (11,283 ft/3,440 m), second and third highest in New Zealand. To the east, the steep faces of Mount Hicks (10,548 ft/3,216 m) present some of New Zealand's hardest alpine climbing. Rock tends to be of poor quality in the New Zealand Alps, though alpine rock routes lie in the Malte Brun Range on the east of the Tasman Glacier. The valleys west of this range are subject to rainfall up to 200 inches (5,000 mm) per year. Ten climbing huts spread through Mount Cook Park, a guiding service situated in the Hermitage, a village 37 miles (23 km) from Cook itself, and ski-plane service make this region a popular alpine destination.

Further south, 29 miles (47 km) from the town of Wanaka, another group of important mountains appear around Mount Aspiring (9,929 ft/3,027 m). Further south again, above Milford Sound, are the Darrans Mountains. It is a wet and lush area, but in the highlands are imposing cliffs of diorite where big wall routes have been made.

Rock climbing areas, on small outcrops of limestone and volcanic rock, are scattered throughout the country.

NICHE   A small recess in a cliff.

NIEVE PENITENTES   Snow or ice columns formed by the action of bright sun melting out deep pits and leaving tall ice pinnacles. They are common on snowfields and glaciers at higher altitudes, and may be very tall and present sometimes insurmountable obstacles to travel. (See GLACIER.)

NOEL, CAPTAIN JOHN BAPTIST LUCIUS "JACK" (1890–1989) (Britain)   Noel's long life gave modern climbers a link to the Golden Age of Himalayan exploration that took place in the decades around the First World War. Born in Devon, Noel received his schooling in Lausanne where the abiding interests of his life—mountaineering and photography—were kindled. With a school friend, he made guideless ascents of alpine peaks at a time when to do so verged on the unthinkable. A military career led to his assignment to India in 1909. When garrisons retired from the heat of Calcutta and the plains, Noel explored border valleys of INDIA and TIBET, studied native lifestyles, and immersed himself in the obsession of the British Army in India, that of reconnoitering the approaches to EVEREST.

In 1913, with three hill tribesmen he headed out across the mountains behind KANGCHENJUNGA to the Arun Gorge, and thence to Everest's eastern GLACIERS. His party was armed, and Noel was disguised as a native. The escapade ended with an exchange of fire with Tibetan soldiers on the Tibetan-Nepalese border, and Noel's retreat back to India. But he had come closer to Everest than any European. When he returned to his regiment two months overdue from his leave, the explanation he offered his colonel was that his calendar had been swept away during a river crossing. The colonel merely advised him to take two calendars next time.

Noel married an actress, and then survived two years on the Western Front in World War I. At Mons, 600 men of his battalion were wiped out in 20 minutes: "It was very exciting," he reminisced in his eighties.

On the 1922 Everest expedition, Noel was appointed official photographer. George MALLORY objected to this, saying the he "did not wish to be an actor on a film." Nor did the film of the 1922 attempt made by Noel receive much critical acclaim. George Bernard Shaw opined that it had all the appearance of "a picnic in Connemara surprised by a snowstorm." Nonetheless it made a profit and ensured Noel's opportunity to film the next Everest attempt in 1924. This expedition turned out to be one of the great heroic sagas of mountaineering history, and Noel was perfectly placed to capture it on film. His professionalism in spending long periods at altitude, and developing thousands of feet of film under adverse conditions, was remarkable. He captured the mood of events by being there at the right time. Even Mallory's last note before he and Andrew Irvine disappeared on the summit bid was addressed to Noel and recorded on film.

The ensuing film, much of it hand-tinted by Noel, was a commercial success that Noel exploited to the utmost by bringing a group of Tibetan monks to Britain to tour with it. This action upset the Dalai Lama and ensured there were no further British expeditions through Tibet for the next nine years. It also severed Noel's links with prewar mountaineers, though he enjoyed a honeymoon with postwar Everesters, who flocked to see him and rifle through his archives as he lived in retirement in Romney Marsh.

Further reading: John Noel, *Through Everest to Tibet* (1927).

NORGAY, TENZING (1914–1986) (Nepal) Norgay and Sir Edmund HILLARY were the first summit team to climb EVEREST. He was the 11th of 13 children born to Tibetan parents either in KHUMBU, NEPAL, or in Tingri, TIBET. As a youth he went to Darjeeling to find work, and was hired by Eric SHIPTON for his 1935 Everest reconnaissance. He was on Everest attempts in 1936, 1938 (Bill TILMAN's trip on which Norgay reached camp seven at 27,191 ft/8,290 m), 1947 (a clandestine attempt by Canadian Al Denman), and on the 1952 Swiss Everest attempt from the south, on which Norgay achieved an altitude record— 28,191 ft (8,595 m). When John Hunt hired him for the successful Everest climb Tenzing had more Everest experience than any man alive. He visited many peaks; among them NANGA PARBAT (1950) and KANGCHENJUNGA (1951); the same year he made the second ascent of NANDA DEVI East (24,383 ft/7,434 m). He climbed Kedarnath during Andre ROCH's Swiss expedition to the GARHWAL in India. In 1954, at the invitation of India's Prime Minister Nehru, he headed the Indian Mountaineering Institute in Darjeeling, training Indian and Nepali climbers. Some 4,600 students learned climbing under his directorship till his retirement in 1976. Tenzing's image upgraded SHERPAS from mere load bearers to supporting and leading climbers. As president of the Association of Sherpa Mountaineers he worked to improve the lot of Sherpas and to preserve Sherpa culture. He died of tuberculosis.

NORTH CAROLINA (United States) The Appalachian Mountains traverse this southern state, and on the hillsides are numerous rock formations. Linville Gorge, in the state's northwest corner, is the deepest canyon in the eastern states. Its 500-ft (152-m) quartzite walls are well developed with routes. The 600-ft (183-ft) exfoliated granite SLABS of Stone Mountain, in the Blue Ridge Mountains near Elkin, are popular, as are the similarly huge granite slabs LOOKING GLASS ROCK and Whitesides Mountain near Cashiers. MOORE'S WALL is a steep quartzite CRAG of interest to hard climbers. Other areas are Crowders Mountain, near Gastonia, and the Devil's Courthouse near Asheville. Mount Mitchell (6,684 ft/2,037 m), 35 miles (56 km) northeast of Asheville, is the state's high point and the highest point east of the Mississippi River. It is nontechnical.

Guidebooks: John Harlin, *Climber's Guide to North America, East Coast Rockclimbs* (1986); Thomas Kelley, *Climber's Guide to North Carolina* (1986); Roid Waddle, *Dixie Crystals: A Climber's Guide to Stone Mountain North Carolina* (1983).

NORTH CASCADES (United States) A range in Washington State's Cascade Range. (See CASCADE RANGE.)

NORTH TWIN (Canada) The east slopes of this peak of the Canadian Rocky Mountains (12,085 ft/3,730 m) rise gently from the COLUMBIA ICE FIELD, but its fearsome north face drops 5,000 ft (1,524 m) into what is known locally as the Black Hole. North Twin (more correctly, North Face of Twins Tower) is the third-highest summit in the Rockies and was first climbed by W. S. Ladd, J. M. Thorington and Conrad KAIN in 1923, from the ice fields. It was not until 1974 that the north face was climbed by Chris Jones and George LOWE. The ascent, in bad weather and with dwindling gear, was made famous by Jones's article in the 1976 edition of the mountaineering journal, *Ascent*. In 1985, Dave CHEESMOND and Barry BLANCHARD climbed the north pillar route, left of the Jones-Lowe effort. The climb took five days. At the time of this writing neither route has been repeated, and they are regarded as the most challenging routes in the Rockies, if not in North America.

Guidebook: Sean Dougherty, *Selected Alpine Climbs in the Canadian Rockies* (1991).

NORTH WALES LIMESTONE (Britain) These SPORT-CLIMBING crags can be split into three main areas, Great Orme and Little Orme, which lie at either end of the Llandudno promenade, and Craig y Forwyn, found one mile (1.6 km) inland from the village of Llanddulas. Most climbers use LLANBERIS as a base for visiting the crags.

Limestone climbing in North Wales took off in the early 1980s, though at Craig y Forwyn routes like the huge ROOF of Mojo (5.9), freed in 1975 by Rowland Edwards and Great Wall (5.10d), freed by Pete LIVESEY also in 1975 had been established. Edwards also climbed, in 1976, the ferociously steep New Dimensions (5.11a) on Castell y Gwynt, part of the Great Orme.

The new generation pushed standards in the 1980s. Andy Pollitt climbed Moonwind (5.12a) at Craig y Forwyn in 1981. (This crag was later closed to climbers.) On Craig Pen Trwyn on the Great Orme a host of routes appeared. Of note are Marc Griffith's popular Axle Attack (5.12a), Jerry MOFFATT's Oyster (5.12c) and Masterclass (5.13a), John Redhead's The Disillusioned Screw Machine (5.12b) with one aid, later removed by Andy Pollitt. Ron FAWCETT climbed Central Pillar (5.12c) on Castlell y Gwynt. Ben MOON made his Statement of Youth (5.13a) in 1984 on Lower Pen Trwyn, and in 1988 Pollit climbed Over The Moon and Café Libre, both 5.13a. Finally, Moffatt topped them all in 1990 with Liquid Amber (5.14b).

Guidebooks: Andy Pollitt, *North Wales Limestone*; Paul Williams, *Rock Climbing in Snowdonia* (1990).

NORTH WALL HAMMER An ice-climbing tool consisting of a gently curved pick with a hammer. (See ICE AXE.)

NORWAY Granite peaks rising virtually from sea-level fjords to 6,560-ft (2,000-m) summits, BIG WALLS, and some of the longest FROZEN WATERFALLS in the world characterize climbing in Norway. In addition, in recent years dozens of small crags have born hard FREE CLIMBS. Romsdal, 400 miles (643 km) northwest of Oslo, is the best-known granite region. In this valley, peaks like Romsdalshorn, TROLL WALL, Vengetind and Kvandalstind dominate the area. The nearby Isterdal Valley also bristles with big walls and peaks. A damp climate makes for decidedly alpine conditions on many cliffs. Nonetheless, Troll Wall is a celebrated 6,560-ft (2,000-m) wall that has drawn big wall alpine climbers from around the world. The water cascading over the Norwegian cliffs, coupled with the cold winters, makes Norway as impressive for waterfall climbing as the Canadian Rockies. Waterfall climbing got underway in 1977 when Henry BARBER and Rob Taylor climbed Vettifossen, an 886-ft (270-m) vertical icefall (Norway's longest) in the Laerdal region. Other waterfall areas are Hemsedal, Valdres, Oslo and Telemark; to Oslo's north are Otta and Drivdalen and, of course, Romsdal.

NOSE   A prominent protrusion of rock, like a buttress. Also the name of the most popular route on EL CAPITAN, YOSEMITE.

NOVAK, JIRI (1945–   ) (Czechoslovakia) This rock climber and alpinist has pioneered very technical FIRST ASCENTS in the High Tatra and Czech sandstone areas, the ALPS, Caucasus and HIMALAYA. His major mountain routes in Europe include Speckkarspitze north face (1979) and Piz Cengalo north face (winter 1982). In the Caucasus he climbed the north faces of Adyr-Su and Tjutju-Basci (1981). Among his seven expeditions in Himalayas he led successful first ascents of DHAULAGIRI west face (1984) and southwest pillar (1988). Since 1976 he has been active in the presidium of the Czechoslovak mountaineering association.

NUNATEK   A protuberance of rock or a rock island poking out of a GLACIER.

NUN KUN MASSIF   (India) This compact range of the western HIMALAYA rises about 62 miles (100 km) east of Srinagar in KASHMIR. The main peaks are the pyramid-shaped Nun (23,403 ft/7,135 m), Kun (23,242 ft/7,086 m) and the smaller Pinnacle Peak. Nun and Kun are separated by a high ice plateau surrounded by GLACIERS. Kun was

climbed via the northeast ridge in 1913 by a team of Italians led by Mario Piacenza. Other routes on Kun include the southeast face (1978, Czech) and west ridge and face (1981, Japanese). Nun remained unclimbed till 1953 when Frenchmen led by Bernard Pierre climbed the west ridge. Otherwise the east ridge (1971, Indian), northwest ridge (1976, Czech), west face (1977, American) and north ridge (1978, Indian) are Nun's principal routes.

NUPTSE   See EIGHT-THOUSAND-METER PEAKS.

NUTS   A broad array of metal wedge-shaped or hexagonal devices hand-placed into cracks as PROTECTION. (See ANCHORS.)

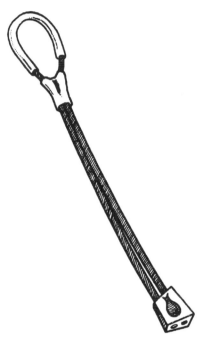

HB Nut

NUT TOOLS   Or nut keys. Devices for loosening NUTS that have become stuck in cracks. (See ANCHORS.)

O

OBJECTIVE DANGER Usually a mountaineering term, describing hazards beyond the climbers' control, such as STONEFALL, AVALANCHE, SERAC fall, LIGHTNING and CREVASSES. A climb with high objective danger is hazardous. One with low objective danger is comparatively safe.

ODELL, NOEL (1890–1987) (Britain) Odell was witness to one of mountaineering's most resonant catastrophes, as he was the last person to see George MALLORY and Andrew Irvine before their disappearance on EVEREST in 1924. He was also the butt of a famous joke of British climbing, namely H. W. TILMAN's sly jibe about Odell's formal demeanor on the occasion of the FIRST ASCENT of NANDA DEVI: "I believe we so far forgot ourselves as to shake hands on it." Odell's heyday was the period immediately after World War I, when he made first ascents of two classic British rock climbs—Tennis Shoe, on the Idwal Slabs in North Wales, which he climbed solo, and The Chasm on Glencoe's Buachaille Etive Mor. His most successful expedition performances were on Everest in 1924, when he twice climbed to 27,000 ft (8,232 m) in search of clues to the fate of Mallory and Irvine (he was convinced they had reached the summit after his final glimpse of them making "expeditiously" for the top), and the 1936 achievement on Nanda Devi—the highest summit climbed before 1950. A geologist by profession, he lived to extreme old age as a fellow of Clare College, Cambridge, where he was much sought after by delvers into the mystery of Mallory and Irvine's disappearance.

OFF HAND In CRACK CLIMBING, a crack wider than finger-width but too tight to HAND JAM. This size is approximately one-and-a-quarter-inches (3.18 cm) wide, and is an awkward size to climb.

OFFWIDTH Offwidth CRACKS are cracks too wide for HAND JAMS and narrower than CHIMNEYS. (See ARM BAR.)

OGRE, THE (Pakistan) More correctly known by its BALTI name, Baintha Brakk, this complex 23,900-ft/7,285-m KARAKORAM mountain of granite walls interspersed with steep RIDGES and ICE FIELDS is approached by the BIAFO GLACIER for the west side, and by the Panmah and Choktoi glaciers for the east side. Both routes are accessed from the Braldu Valley, as is the approach to the BALTORO Glacier. Baintha Brakk should not be confused with Con-way's Ogre, which is the highest of the nearby Baintha Spires. After several attempts by British and Japanese expeditions during the 1970s, a British expedition led by Chris BONINGTON reached the summit in 1977. The saga of this climb is one of the epics of mountaineering. The British climbed the west ridge via the Uzun Brakk Glacier, following the start of a Japanese attempt which reached 21,000 ft (6,402 m) in 1976. After Bonington and Doug SCOTT summited the final tower, Scott fractured both ankles in a RAPPELING mishap. After a forced overnight BIVOUAC on a ledge, the pair were helped by team members Mo ANTHOINE and Clive Rowlands. Scott could only crawl on his knees. During the descent the four were trapped for several days by a storm and ran out of food. When they pressed on, Bonington sustained injuries in a second rappeling accident. Seven days after Scott's accident, the group reached base camp. Scott was by this stage crawling across the glacier on shredded knees. Base camp was deserted, but the remaining team members returned with Balti porters who carried Scott and Bonington to safety. This is the sole ascent. Bonington's account is described in *The Everest Years* (1987), Scott's in *Himalayan Climber* (1992).

OGWEN AND CARNEDDAU (Britain) Running northwest from the village of Capel Curig to Bethesda, the A5 highway cuts through the Ogwen Valley of North Wales. To the north are the Carnedds, to the south the craggy slopes of Tryfan and the Glyders, all mountain ranges. The latter offer middle-grade climbers traditional routes that were climbed during the earliest period of rock-climbing in Britain. There are campsites and services in Bethesda.

The two CRAGS in the Carnedds are Llech Ddu and Craig yr Ysfa. Llech Ddu, over 400 ft (122 m) high, is approached from Gerlan. Three classic routes are The Great Corner (5.10), The Groove and The Great Arete (5.11a). First ascensionist Ed DRUMMOND described the latter route from 1975 as "a route of utter exposure and difficulty in a position of great cheek."

The two BUTTRESSES of Craig yr Ysfa face northeast from the flanks of Carnedd Llewelyn. Notable climbs include Amphitheatre Buttress, a 900-ft (274 m) 5.5 climbed in 1905 by the Abraham brothers and team. Pinnacle Wall, a 5.6 soloed by Colin KIRKUS in 1931, is also of interest.

Ogwen's crags include the Milestone Buttress, Idwal and the Gribin Facet which are low-lying, and Glyder Fawr and the east face of Tryfan, which are mountain crags. The area is rich in history. On the Milestone Buttress lies Superdirect, a 5.7 climbed in 1910 by G. Barlow and H. Priestly-Smith. John Menlove EDWARDS added Procrastination Cracks and Grey Slab (5.7) on Glyder Fawr in 1932. Tennis Shoe, on Idwal Slab was climbed in 1915 by Noel ODELL, who was the last to see George MALLORY and Andrew Irvine on EVEREST in 1924. Jack LONGLAND climbed Javelin Blade on Idwal's Holly Tree Wall in 1930 and at 5.9 a feat way ahead of its time. Colin Kirkus was also a major force and among his routes is Lot's Groove (5.8) on Glyder Fach climbed in 1929.

At the end of World War II, Chris Preston added iSuicide Wall (5.10) on Idwal's east wall. Exploration moved to the LLANBERIS PASS and CLOGYN DU'R ARDUU in the 1950s, but there have been notable modern additions, principally Martin BOYSEN's Capital Punishment (5.11a) from 1971, which boldly climbs the wall to the right of iSuicide Wall. In 1980, John Redhead climbed the Wrinkled Retainer (5.12b) on Milestone Buttress.

Guidebook: Paul Williams, *Rock Climbing in Snowdonia* (1990).

OJOS DEL SALADO (Chile, Argentina)

After ACONCAGUA, it is the highest mountain in the American continent. It is also the highest volcano on earth, active or otherwise, and the highest point in CHILE, which shares the mountain with ARGENTINA. Nevado Ojos del Salado means in Spanish, "Snow Peak at the Sources of the Salty River." It rises above the high desert locally called the Punade Atacama. Its fumaroles erupt at around 21,400 ft (6,500 m). The mountain was discovered in late 1904 by the surveyors of Luis RISO PATRON, head of the Chilean Boundary Commission. Its height (now fixed at 22,534 ft 6,870 m by Chileans and 22,566 ft/6,880 m by Argentinians) has caused much controversy, as ALTIMETER readings were pushed by various mountaineers to place Ojos del Salado above Aconcagua. In 1956, H. Adams CARTER's American expedition resurveyed the mountain at 22,590 ft (6,885 m), the height accepted nowadays. Two Poles made the FIRST ASCENT of the mountain in February 1937. They used the long, but not waterless, Argentinian (south) side. A Chilean army team climbed the north (waterless) side in 1956. Other events of note are the first female ascent by Lucia Rojas (Chile) in 1968, first ascent of steep north and northwest ridges in January 1979 by Austrians, Germans and a Chilean guide; and FIRST WINTER ASCENT in 1982 by three Germans. The Refugio (hut) Murray on the north side of the mountain greatly facilitates ascents from Chile. The hut was named after a passenger killed in a helicopter crash on the summit.

Further reading: H. Adams Carter, "Ojos del Salado," *American Alpine Journal* (1957).

Evelio Echevarria
Colorado State University

OKLAHOMA (United States)

Throughout this generally flat midwestern state are granite and limestone OUTcrops that climbers have developed since the 1970s. In northeast Oklahoma, overlooking Tulsa, are the steep POCKETED 40-ft (12-m) limestone CRAGS of Chandler Park, where the state's BOULDERING heritage is rooted and which some Oklahoman climbers call "the Fontainebleau of the high plains." One hour south of Tulsa is Lake Tenkiller, a sandstone SPORT-CLIMBING area. Oklahoma's most extensive areas are in the southwest, in the Quartz Mountains and Wichita Mountains, between the towns of Altus and Lawton. Of these areas, Mount Baldy, a complex of 70-degree coarse granite DOMES rises above the plains in a region known as Quartz, 20 miles (32 km) northwest of Mount Park. Other areas of weathered granite are scattered nearby, and within Wichita Wildlife Refuge—which contains the popular 300-ft (91-m) crags of The Narrows—and the easy SLABS and steeper FACES of Desperate Dome, Mount Scott and Elk Mountain. Crab Eyes, also in this area, is a CRACK CLIMBING cliff. Oklahoma's hardest climbing is also in the Wichita Mountains, on private land in a granite quarry called Rock of Ages. Colossus, led by Duane Raleigh, is a potential 5.14, while Poseidon was confirmed at 5.13b/c by visiting Shawagunks hard man Jeff Gruenberg. In southeast Oklahoma, east of McAlester is Robber's Cave State Park, a short crag with steep climbing. A nontechnical hill called Black Mesa (4,973 ft/1,576 m) in northwest Oklahoma is the state's high point. Spring, fall and early winter are the prime months for climbing in Oklahoma.

Guidebooks: Bo Mosel, *Tulsa Rock, '90* (1990); Jack Wurster and Jon Frank, *Oklahoma on the Rocks* (1989).

OLD MAN OF HOY (Scotland)

Off the northeastern tip of SCOTLAND are the Orkney Islands, and Hoy is the second-largest of the group. The Old Man, the king of sea stacks, is a 450-ft (137-m) pile of sandstone off St. John's Head on the west coast of the island. St. John's Head is the third-highest cliff in the British Isles at 1,141 ft (348 m) and there are routes on it, though not recommended. The Old Man was connected to the mainland as recently as the 19th century by an arch of rock but sadly this lies at the base of the stack necessitating a perilous and dampening approach. Hoy is reached from Scrabster, near Thurso, on a ferry that takes two hours. Flights are also available. Stromness provides stores and gas and there is a youth hostel at Linksness, or a campsite at Rackwick, a mile (1.6 km) southeast of the Old Man.

The Old Man's reputation, while deserved, was largely made by a television spectacular in 1967, which starred Dougal HASTON, Chris BONINGTON and Tom PATEY. The latter pair, together with Rusty Baillie, climbed the east face route, a 460-ft (140-m) 5.9 with only one technically demanding PITCH. The descent is another matter, and a FIXED ROPE must be left to facilitate the ABSEIL, which is imposing to say the least. Other routes have followed, including A Few Dollars More from Murray Hamilton, Tut Braithwaite and Pete Whillance. This takes a LINE on the stack's north face at 5.10c. There are other lines, including a 5.12.

Guidebooks: Geoff Cohen, *The Northern Highlands*, Vol. 1 (1991); Kevin Howett, *Rock Climbing in Scotland* (1990).

ON SIGHT   In FREE CLIMBING, to climb a route without prior knowledge or experience of the moves. (See A VUE, FLASH, STYLE.)

ONTARIO   (Canada)   The Niagara Escarpment is a major rock-climbing area in Ontario. It is a 400-mile (644-km) ridge of dolomitic limestone extending from Niagara Falls to Tobermory at the tip of the Bruce Peninsula in Georgian Bay. Thirty one-pitch-long cliffs bearing 1,500 climbs up to grade 5.13 surround Toronto. The rock offers CRACK CLIMBS and SPORT CLIMBS on POCKETS. On the Bruce Peninsula major areas like Lion's Head and White Bluff are Ontario's premiere crags, with the 33-ft (10-m) ROOF crack The Monument (5.12). In the Beaver Valley and the Blue Mountains south of Owen Sound and west of Collingwood are small sport-climbing crags like Metcalfe Rock, Old Baldy, Devil's Glen and Berlin Wall. Milton, 30 miles (48 km) from Toronto, is the escarpment's most visited area. Crags here include Mount Nemo and Rattlesnake Point. Granite is found at Bon Echo Provincial Park, in the form of a 350-ft (107-m) cliff rising from Mazinan lake. Farther west near the Manitoba border are the granite Gooseneck Cliffs, 200 ft (61 m) high and popular with Winnipeg climbers. John Turner (Britain) began exploring the potential of Ontario's cliffs in the early 1960s. Following him, Helmut Microys and more recently Rob Rohn, Mike Tschipper, George Manson, Tom Gibson, Steve Dimaio, and the Smart brothers pioneered Ontario climbing. WATERFALL ICE CLIMBING became popular in the 1980s around Thunder Bay and Orient Bay on Lake Superior (near the towns of Nipigon and Beardmore). Over 100 ice climbs have been discovered and an ice climbing festival is held annually. There are three Alpine Club of Canada chapters in Ontario: Toronto, Thunder Bay and Winnipeg (Manitoba).
Guidebooks: Chris Oates, Barnes, and Bracken *Climber's Guide to the Niagara Escarpment* (1991); Shaun Parent, *Climber's Guide to the Ice of Orient Bay* (1987); Parent, *Climbing Guide to Thunder Bay* (1987); David Smart, *Climbing on the Niagara Escarpment* (1985); Smart, *Ontario Limestone* (1988).

OPEN BOOK   Another term for a CORNER or DIHEDRAL.

OPHIR WALL   (United States)   In the San Juan Range, between Rico and Telluride in southwestern COLORADO lie the solid granite CRAGS of Ophir Wall and Cracked Canyon. Ophir Wall is up to 1,000 ft (305 m) high, and offers steep CRACK and FACE CLIMBING. At 9,500 ft (2,896 m) of elevation, the area is popular in summer.
Guidebook: Allen Pattie, *Climber's Guide to Ophir Wall.*

OPPOSITION   RUNNERS or ANCHORS set up in opposition consist of NUTS, STOPPERS or FRIENDS linked together with SLINGS or the ROPE and held in place by opposing forces. For example, in the diagram showing a BELAY, the nut in the crack is good for downward force only, and would pull out in the event of a fall. However, the nut placed beneath it accepts an upward force. When set up in opposition, this anchor can hold downward and upward loading. Also, as a principle of FREE CLIMBING, opposition

refers to physical climbing moves where opposing forces complement each other, as in STEMMING, where the pressure of hands and feet pushing outward against a CORNER create a stable position.

OREGON   (United States)   During the 1980s, SMITH ROCKS put Oregon on the map as a major international SPORT-CLIMBING crag. Lesser known rock-climbing areas entertained climbers here since 1917, beginning with Beacon Rock and Broughton Bluff, basaltic crags beside the Columbia River, east of Portland. Today they are well developed with CRACK and FACE routes. Among the snow-clad peaks and volcanoes (like Mount HOOD) of the CASCADE RANGE are rock formations like Mount WASHINGTON's south face (7,794 ft/2,376 m); the Menagerie (a collection of terrifying rock spires in the central Cascade foothills); and Wolf Rock (a 900-ft/274-m basalt monolith). These areas were sought-after challenges from the 1950s to the 1970s. They lie nestled between Salem, Eugene and Bend. Eastern Oregon has climbing areas like High Valley, a basaltic crag near the town of Union, and granitic peaks around the town of North Powder. These peaks—Gunsight, Van Patten Butte and Lee's Peak—are of the Elk Horn and Wallowa Mountains, which rise above the Anthony Lakes area. Oregon is home to one of the oldest mountain clubs in America: the Mazama Mountaineers. Developers of Oregon climbing from the exploratory days to the modern era include Pat Callis, Willi UNSOELD, Kim Schmitz, Tom and Bob Bauman, McGown, Jeff Thomas and Alan WATTS.

OROLATRIC MOUNTAINEERING   It is commonly believed that MOUNTAINEERING began with the FIRST ASCENT of MONT BLANC in 1786. Superstition prevalent among the alpine peoples of Europe was decisive in delaying the birth of the sport. But if the Europeans were fearful of mountains, peoples of other mountain lands were not. Centuries earlier than the birth of ALPINISM, people not only had been climbing mountains higher than anything found in Europe but even inhabiting some very high summits. Reasons for ancient mountaineering varied according to area and the needs of the population. In the Atlas and the Simien mountains of Africa, hunters for the indigenous goat reached summits up to 15,000 ft (4,573 m). The heights of southern Asian islands were ascended by caravans of natives who hurled living offerings—goats—into craters in order to propitiate their restless volcanoes. Fujiyama in Japan was already being routinely ascended by pilgrams in the 11th century and the 10,000-ft (3,049-m) high peaks of the Eastern Range of China were known to both hunters and worshippers in the 12th century. There are remnants of ruins of some age unknown on the summits of Mount Hermon (9,232 ft/2,815 m) in Syria and of Mount Taygetos (7,940 ft/2,421 m) in Greece. Before the soldiers of Cortes climbed the Mexican ice volcano of Popocatepetl (17,815 ft/5,430 m) in 1519, Aztecs had attempted its ascent several times and left a buried offering of precious stones on the lower knob of Ventorrillo (16,400 ft/5,000 m). And several mountains in the American Rockies, like Blanca Peak (14,338 ft/4,371 m) have Indian stone walls on their summits. But the most sensational climbing endeavors of the ancients took place in the ANDES. In a remarkable book, Argentinian Antonio Beorchia surveyed 107 peaks between 16,000 and 22,100 ft (4,878 and 6,739 m) that were ascended for religious purposes by the Incas and their subjects. The summits of Llullaillaco (22,100 ft/6,739 m), Antofalla (21,129 ft/6,440 m), El Toro (20,953 ft/6,386 m) and Licancabur (19,426 ft/5,921 m) are the highest archeological sites in the world. Incidentally, Europeans could not surpass the Incas' world altitude record until 1853, when the brothers Schlagintweit reached in the HIMALAYA a height greater than Llullaillaco's. Five Andean summits have yielded a mummy, a sacrificial offering to the gods that probably took place around the end of the 14th century. Other mountaintops display a complex of huts in whose interiors bedding and some desiccated food have been found. Mountain worship was no doubt the main reason for those ambitious achievements of the past, but that form of worshipping may have had many other aims: the cult of the sun; adoration of water (represented by snow on the summit); propitiation of the mountain gods; the need to enlist the favor of the genii that governed cold, snow, mountain sickness and thunder; and perhaps even a semipractical reason, such as recognizing mountains as the source of minerals. In South America, Chileans, Argentinians, Poles, Italians and the American anthropologist-climber Johan Reinhard have assiduously excavated summits and studied incredible findings. In San Juan, Argentina, local climbers have founded the Center for the Investigation of High Mountaineering Archeology (CIADAM).

Further reading: Antonio Beorchia, *El Enigma de los Santuarios Indigenas de Alta Montana* (1985); Edwin Bernbaum, *Sacred Mountains of the World* (1990); Evelio Echevarria, "The South American Indian as a Pioneer Alpinist," *Alpine Journal*, No. 316 (1968); Johan Reinhard, "Highest Archeology and Andean Mountain Gods," *American Alpine Journal*, Vol. 25 (1983); Patrick Tierney, *The Highest Altar* (1982).

Evelio Echevarria
Colorado State University

ORTLER ALPS **(Italy)** The Ortler Group is situated in northern Italy near the borders of Austria and Switzerland. It is most accessible from the north and Landeck in the Inn Valley or by traveling west from the Italian side of the Brenner Pass. Being in the South Tyrol, it is a German- as well as Italian-speaking area and many mountains have names in both languages. The Ortler or Cima Ortles (12,808 ft/3,905 m), Königspitze or Gran Zebru (12,631 ft/3,851 m) and Monte Cevedale (12,362 ft/3,769 m) are the principal peaks in the area. Rock types vary wildly from crumbly limestone to hard gneiss. The region's chief attraction is its snow and ice climbs. Sulden offers an excellent base. (See ALPS.)

ÖTZTAL ALPS **(Austria, Italy)** Also on the Austro-Italian border, this area offers excellent ski-mountaineering and hut-to-hut tours as well as harder MOUNTAINEERING. The Ötztal are located south of the Inn at Imst, which offers a good base. The principal mountain is the Wildspitze, the

highest in the Tyrol, and has a dramatic northern aspect above the Taschach Glacier. There are four huts to choose from for an ascent. Other peaks in the area include the Fluchtkogel (11,470 ft/3,497 m), the Weisskugel (12,260 ft/3,738 m) and the Similaun (11,804 ft/3,599 m), the latter offering a good introduction to the higher peaks of the Eastern Alps.

OUTCROP A general term meaning a small *cliff* or CRAG that juts out from a mountain or hillside. Crag and edge have the same meaning in British climbing jargon, *klettergarten* in German.

OUTRAM, SIR JAMES **(1864–1925) (Britain)** In only two seasons (1901 and 1902), this baronet made the FIRST ASCENTS of 10 notable peaks in the CANADIAN ROCKIES. He was educated at Cambridge and ordained in the Church of England (1889). In 1900 he experienced a breakdown in health and went to CANADA. In 1901 he made first ascents of Mount Vaux, Mount Chancellor and Cathedral Mountain. His finest achievement that year was the first ascent (and TRAVERSE) of Mount ASSINIBOINE with guides C. Bohren and C. Hasler. In 1902 he continued to make first ascents of challenging peaks in the Rockies, climbing Mounts Bryce (with guide C. Kaufmann), Columbia, Forbes and the lesser peaks Lyell, Alexandra and Freshfield. He settled in Calgary, Canada, and was elected an honorary member of the Alpine Club of Canada.

Further reading: Sir James Outram, *In the Heart of the Canadian Rockies* (1905).

OVERBOOTS Insulated, waterproof and windproof coverings worn over mountain boots and lower legs for cold weather mountaineering. Overboot insulation may be made of Neoprene rubber, closed- or open-cell foam, Thinsulate or other synthetic fibers, or fiber pile. The mukluk is a traditional overboot of Eskimo design made from seal or reindeer skins, and used by Eskimos and polar explorers.

OVERHANG On rock, a rooflike feature. Any wall beyond the vertical is said to overhang. ROOF or ceiling (specifically, the smooth underside of an overhang), overlap (smaller than an overhang, sometimes formed by one flake of rock laying over another) and bulge (a rounded protuberence of rock) have similar meanings for climbers. *Surplomb* is the French equivalent, *strapiombo* the Italian.

OVERLAP Yet another type of OVERHANG, this one formed by downward-pointing bedding in the rock.

OWENS GORGE **(United States)** This recently developed and popular cragging area lies a few miles north of Bishop, California. A few locals probed here in the 1960s and 1970s, but rumors of crackless, steep, rotten rock kept most away. As placing BOLTS from hooks and on rappel became popular, rediscovery and an explosion of new routes came to The Gorge in 1989, when Tony Puppo, Gary Slate and John BACHAR found the lowermost band of

Climbing Overhang

rhyolite firm and well salted with edges. Besides many high-standard FACE CLIMBS, there are excellent CRACK CLIMBS among the 200 one- and two-pitch climbs extending on either side of a seven-mile (11-km)-long corridor of the Owens River. Fine easy routes (5.8) coexist with severe climbs like Conquistadors without Swords (5.13b) and Shocker (5.13c).

Guidebook: Marty Lewis, *Owens Gorge Rock Climbs* (1990).

OXYGEN APPARATUS Attempts to carry supplemental oxygen on Himalayan peaks have been made since early in the 20th century. By the 1970s all the highest peaks had been climbed without extra oxygen, but most expeditions still carry tanks of oxygen for climbing and/or medical purposes. The major deterrent to these systems is their weight and expense. The tanks must hold high pressures of gas and, therefore, must be made of strong, lightweight substances (aluminum, titanium). Government regulations, which vary from country to country, also limit the amount of pressure in tanks.

The delivery system includes a regulator that limits the flow of oxygen through low-resistance tubing to the mask. There are two basic climbing masks: demand (Blume-Robertshaw) and reservoir (Hornbein). The former consists of a valve that opens only during inhalation, which conserves the amount of oxygen used, while the latter delivers a constant flow of oxygen to a reservoir bag. The oxygen in the bag is mixed with ambient air as the climber breathes. The demand valve system has been criticized because of occasional freezing of the valve. The older Hornbein system is still popular, because it is simple and reliable. Supplemental oxygen can physiologically "lower" the altitude 3,280 to 6,560 ft (1,000 to 2,000 m) while climbing. Typical flow rates are two to six pints one to three liters per minute.

During sleep, supplemental oxygen can be delivered with a simple plastic face mask or nasal prongs with flow rates of one to two pints (one half to one liter) per minute. These masks are commonly used by respiratory therapists in hospitals and are readily available.

OXYGENLESS CLIMBING Throughout the first half of the 20th century climbing above 26,240 ft (8,000) m without supplemental oxygen (02-Sup) was thought to be neither prudent or possible. To summit EVEREST without oxygen became the mountaineering challenge of the 1970s, and was realized in 1978 by Reinhold MESSNER and Peter HABELER. Since then, many ascents above 26,240 ft (8,000 m) have been accomplished without 02-Sup, but the feat carries risks both during and after the climb. Not all high-altitude climbers function well above 26,240 ft (8,000 m) without supplemental oxygen. Medical research conducted on extreme-altitude climbers in the United States and Europe and on the 1981 American Medical Research Everest expedition suggests that the brain seems to be the organ most sensitive to the lack of oxygen, and that at least transient neuro-psychometric alterations occur at high altitudes. Additionally, it is believed that many deaths on peaks where the availability of oxygen is precariously low for human existence are a direct result of the physical and mental deterioration caused by prolonged HYPOXIA.

Using supplemental oxygen on Himalayan expeditions carries substantial financial and logistic burdens. Porters and SHERPAS often bear much of the physical encumbrance and are often put at additional risk above BASE CAMP. Consequently expedition members using supplemental oxygen are increasingly assuming the risk and burden of carrying the oxygen on the mountain. (See EIGHT-THOUSAND-METER PEAKS.)

PACKS Also called backpacks, rucksacks. Packs for climbing fall into three main categories: external-frame, internal-frame and frameless packs. Each type suits distinctly different climbing activities.

External-frame packs excel for carrying large loads, such as on expeditions or on long approaches, but their bulky frames are cumbersome when climbing steep rock or ice. A frame pack rests against one's back on a rectangular frame of tubular aluminum or molded nylon onto which a large pack-bag (up to 3,000 to 6,000 cubic inches) and carrying harness is fixed. Fabric and foam stretched across the frame to cushion the back offers the advantage of letting air circulate freely between one's back and the load. However, external-frame packs are heavy (about eight lb/three-and-a-half kg), and the frame restricts arm movement when skiing and climbing. Because the load is carried high, they create a top-heavy center of gravity.

Internal-frame packs are the choice of most alpinists. They keep a load close to the back. The pack is as close to being a part of the body as possible, which is advantageous for maintaining balance in skiing and mountaineering. They typically carry 3,000 to 7,000 cubic inches, and weigh three to seven lbs (one to three kg), making them big enough yet light enough for most alpine activities. A typical internal-frame consists of two parallel aluminum stays (or sometimes a nylon sheet) held in place inside the foam-padded back of the pack. The stays are contoured to the curve of one's back. Back-padding, hip belt and shoulder straps are designed to distribute the weight between the three strongest points of the back, which are the lumbar, hips and shoulders. Unlike external-frame packs, the hip belt and shoulder straps are sewn directly to the pack-bag itself. This allows the pack to move with the body. Internal-frame packs are extremely adjustable.

Frameless packs are also popular among mountaineers and skiers because they are lightweight two to four-and-a-half lbs one to two kg. They resemble an internal-frame pack without stays, using high-density foam as back-padding. In some models the foam pad in the back can be removed as an emergency sleeping pad.

Features that make a good climbing pack include:

A low profile without side pockets to prevent the pack snagging on rocks.

A zippered lid for storing small, frequently used items.

Hip belts and shoulder straps padded with high-density foam for support when carrying heavy loads.

Adequate tie-in points to fix ICE TOOLS, CRAMPONS and a FOAM PAD are essential for alpinists.

An extendable "throat" with a drawstring at the top will keep water out of the pack.

Well-sewn (bar-tacked) loops for HAULING.

Tough, coated and waterproof fabric, like cordura nylon or nylon packcloth.

PAINE GROUP **(Chile)** South of CERRO TORRE and FITZROY by 118 miles (188 km) lie the Towers of Paine—a small range of vertical-walled granite spires and peaks, some of which are capped by crumbling black slate. It is the black-capped Cuernos ("Horns") rising above Lake Pehoe that have appeared in calendars and books throughout the world. Other striking peaks include the Mummer (6,069 ft/1,850 m), Blade (6,397 ft/1,950 m), Sword (6,725 ft/2,050 m) and Fortress (8,858 ft/2,700 m) to the north, and the Cathedral (7,217 ft/2,200 m) and Shark's Fin (6,069 ft/1,849 m) to the northwest. The group's highest peak is the 10,006-ft (3,049-m) Paine Grande, first climbed in 1957 by an Italian expedition up the southwest side. The inviolable-looking walls of the Fortress see few ascents: The northeast buttress (British, 1979) and the east face (1989), named One Minute of Wisdom by its Yugoslav ascensionists, are extreme.

The actual Towers of Paine are three granite spires (South, CENTRAL, and North towers) on the east side of the range. Of these, the slender finger of the Central Tower is the most compelling, rising above the glaciers 4,000 ft (1,220 m) to a height of 8,070 ft (2,460 m). Don WHILLANS and Chris BONINGTON were the first to reach the summit in 1963 as part of a seven-man British expedition. A jealous Italian team climbed the mountain only 20 hours later, having lost the race to the British. Aside from this, the original route (northwest face), six other difficult routes ascend the Central Tower, but there is great scope for extreme additions. The south ridge of the nearby North Tower has been climbed a dozen times or more and is an excellent one-day ascent with FREE CLIMBING up to 5.10a difficulty. Weather is typically Patagonian, with vicious winds and storms.

Further reading: Chris Bonington, *The Next Horizon* (1973); Alan Kearney, *Mountaineering in Patagonia* (1992).

PAKISTAN Many mountains of the KARAKORAM, the HINDU KUSH and the Western Himalaya lie in northern Pakistan. The world's second-highest peak, K2 (28,250 ft/8,613 m), lies at the head of the BALTORO and Godwin Austen glaciers. GASHERBRUMS I and II, BROAD PEAK and NANGA PARBAT—four of the EIGHT THOUSAND-METER PEAKS—are also here, as are 129 other mapped peaks above 23,100 ft (7,043 m). Thus, climbing in Pakistan is high-altitude expeditionary climbing. There is virtually no rock climbing of a cragging nature, but recent expeditions to granite areas of the BIAFO GLACIER and TRANGO TOWERS have produced BIG WALL routes.

Journeys into the mountains are long, and inevitably entail caravans of hired porters. The major towns from which expeditions embark are Chitral for the Hindu Kush; Gilgit for the BATURA MUZTAGH, HISPAR MUZTAGH, RAKA-POSHI, Nanga Parbat and HARAMOSH RANGES; and Skardu for the Baltoro Muztagh, PANMAH MUZTAGH, and MASHER-BRUM RANGE. Due to a border war between Pakistan and INDIA, peaks of the Siachen Muztagh and SASER MUZTAGH, once accessed through Pakistan, are inaccessible.

Pakistan has few climbers, though several have distin-guished themselves, with ascents of K2 by Ashraf Aman and Nazir SABIR, and of Broad Peak and Gasherbrum I by Major M. Sher Khan and Karim Khan, all during the 1980s.

Like all Himalayan and Karakoram countries, the govern-ment regulates climbing in Pakistan and permission must be received before embarking on an expedition. Peaks below 19,800 ft (6,037 m) may be climbed without fees or liaison officers. Rules regarding the route of an expedition's approach, rates of pay, compensation and equipment issue for porters and liaison officers and conduct by an expedi-tion while in the mountains are established by the Ministry of Tourism. Applications are made to the Ministry of Tour-ism, Sector F-7/2, College Road, Islamabad, Pakistan.

The climbing season in the high ranges extends from May through September, with most summits reached from June till August. The MONSOON has only minor impact on northern Pakistan.

PALISADES, THE (United States) This is a high, ser-rated uplift of the SIERRA NEVADA crest west of Big Pine, CALIFORNIA. It is regarded as having some of the finest alpine climbing in California. The highest peak is 14,242-ft (4,342-m) North Palisade, while nearby rise at least four other "Fourteeners"; Split Mountain, Middle Palisade, Mount Sill and Thunderbolt Peak. The peaks are of dark granitic rock, and they shade the largest (up to one sq mile two and a half sq km) glaciers in the Sierra. Routes are typically 2,000 ft (610 m) high, and range from exposed class 3–4 to highly technical Grade V. COULOIRS above the Palisade Glacier, most notably the U-Notch and V-Notch, turn to hard GULLY ice by late summer.
Guidebook: Steve Roper, *The Climber's Guide to the High Sierra* (1976).

PALMING Similar to STEMMING, but concerned specifi-cally with the hands. This FREE CLIMBING technique uses OPPOSITION forces and the natural friction of skin by push-ing outward and pressing or smearing the palms of the hands against holdless rock. Palming is most often used to climb DIHEDRALS.

PAMARI HIMAL (Nepal, Tibet) A small and little-visited range of the main frontier chain of eastern NEPAL HIMALAYA. It is bounded in the east by the Tamba Kosi and in the west by the Sun Kosi, both great Himalayan rivers. The Himalayan explorer Erwin SCHNEIDER called the range the Lapchi Kang. The highest peak included in this area is Labuche Kang, also called Choksiam (24,164 ft/7,367 m, or 23,983 ft/7,312 m or 23,996 ft/7,316 on some maps). This peak lies in TIBET and was first climbed in 1987 via the west ridge by a Tibetan-Japanese expedition.

PANMAH MUZTAGH (Pakistan) This KARAKORAM range, east of the HISPAR MUZTAGH is dominated by the craggy and difficult peaks of the LATOK group and the OGRE. H. H. Godwin Austen first mapped this region and the BALTORO Muztagh in 1861, and both Ardito Desio (Italy) in 1929, then Eric Shipton on his 1937 "Blank on the Map" expedition, explored and mapped the Hispar, BIAFO, Panmah and Chogo Lungma GLACIERS. A unique aspect of the Panmah Muztagh's glaciers is the convergence of the Biafo, Sim Gang and, over the Hispar Pass, the Hispar Glacier, which forms a sprawling area of ice and snow called Snow Lake. Along the Biafo Glacier lie numerous smaller granitic spires on which climbers have found BIG WALL CLIMBING objectives, such as Lukpilla Brakk (17,650 ft/5,381 m), climbed by American parties in 1984 and 1987.

PARADISE FORKS (United States) A basalt cliff of ARIZONA, near Flagstaff. The CRAG was initially developed by Arizonan Scott Baxter in 1979. Traditional tactics includ-ing a ban on CHALK were enforced for several years, but mainstream tactics have won out here. In the 1980s searing CRACK CLIMBS were done, like Paul Davidson's excellent Paradise Lost. RAPPEL BOLTING arrived with controversy here, yet produced two of the area's most striking routes: John Mattsen's The Equalizer and Americans at Arapiles. Other difficult ascents were made at this time (traditionally and otherwise), like Dick Cilley's I Want Your Sex (5.12 +), Dan Michael's Talismanic (5.12c) and Johnny Woodward's Resistin Arete (5.13 −).
Guidebook: Mike Lawson, *Climber's Guide to Paradise Forks* (1986).

PARAPENTE A lightweight (10-lb/4 1/2-kg) Ram Air parachute modified to give a high glide ratio of up to 6:1, making it perform like a hang glider. Parapentes are "inflated" from a standing position and launched from a run. The parapente was initially experimented with in the United States in the 1970s, but it was the French in 1978 who first saw its application in climbing, using them for mountain descents in the ALPS, as an alternative to hours of RAPPELLING or hiking down a peak. Today, parapente descents are very common in Europe. During the 1980s in the Alps, the portable parapente made viable the idea of linking multiple summits by rapid solo climbs and aerial descents to the next objective. In 1988 Christophe PROFIT used a parapente in his attempt to climb the three great north faces—the EIGER, MATTERHORN, GRANDES JORASSES—in a day, in winter solo. Since then, parapente descents from climbs are a daily event in the European Alps. The French also took parapentes to the great ranges: In 1985 Pierre Gevaux made the first parapente descent of an EIGHT-THOUSAND-METER (26,240-ft) PEAK when he flew from the 26,351-ft (8,034 m) summit of GASHERBRUM II, dropping 6,500 ft (1,982 m) to Camp One in two minutes 45 seconds. In 1989 Jean Marc BOIVIN parapented from Everest's summit. Other major summits flown include Eiger north face, CERRO TORRE, ACONCAGUA south face and HALF DOME in YOSEMITE.

PARKA   A windproof, waterproof jacket, sometimes insulated.

PASS   A crossing over a mountain ridge connecting one valley to another. The crest of a pass is called a summit, and crossings may be subject to weather conditions and winter snow levels. In modern times many passes are drivable, but in the traditional sense of the word, a pass was a route opened for trade or access between mountain communities. In mountain areas like the HIMALAYA or ANDES, rugged passes of 16,000 to 18,000 ft (4,878 to 5,488 m) are still used for yak and mule caravans, and trekking. For climbers, pass describes a route over a high col or ridge, which may involve technical alpine climbing.

PATAGONIA   **(Argentina, Chile)**   The entire region referred to as Patagonia extends north from the Strait of Magellan for 1,100 miles (1,770 km) to the Rio Negro River in ARGENTINA. The region is within both CHILE and Argentina, and although there are hundreds of peaks, the principal and most striking summits are found in three groups and are between 8,000 and 22,000 ft (2,439 and 6,707 m) high. Though the Patagonian summits are of modest altitude, they are steep and technical, and Patagonian weather is formidable.

The first of these groups is the PAINE GROUP, or Towers of Paine in Chile. These include the South (8,202 ft/2,500 m), Central (8,070 ft/2,460 m) and North Tower (7,414 ft/2,260 m); the Fortress (8,858 ft/2,700 m); and Paine Grande (10,006 ft/3,050 m). The second group is in Argentina and contains CERRO TORRE (10,262 ft/3,128 m), Torre Egger (9,511 ft/2,899 m) and Cerro Stanhardt (9,183 ft/2,799 m). The last group, also in Argentina, is made up of FITZROY (11,289 ft/3,441 m) and Aguja Poincenot (9,960 ft/3,036 m).

The region's weather is primarily influenced by the North and South Patagonian Ice Caps. Warm moist westerly air from the Pacific Ocean cools, condenses and picks up speed as it passes over the 9,000-sq-mile (23,400-sq-km) ice caps and hits the mountains on the eastern edge with the tremendous winds and precipitation that make the success rate for Patagonian climbing very low. Just east of the mountins lies a windy but arid rain shadow of grasslands known as the pampas.

The first recorded climbing in Patagonia goes back to 1916 when Argentines Lutz Witte, Fritz Kuhn and Alfredo Kolliker probed the valley of the Rio Tunel and climbed Cerro Huemul, a peak due south of Fitzroy. In 1937, Germans Hans Tuefel and Stephan Zuck climbed Paine Chico in the Towers of Paine, and in 1952 a French expedition scaled Fitzroy in Argentina. The French climb inspired greater activity and from the late 1950s to 1988 the major summits were scaled.

Permission for climbing in the Fitzroy area is obtained from Servicio National, Parques National, Santa Fe 690, Buenos Aires, Argentina; for the Paine, El Director, Ministerio de Fronteral Y Limites del Estado, Santiago, Chile.
Further reading: Alan Kearney, *Mountaineering in Patagonia* (1992).

PATEY, TOM   **(1932–1970) (Britain)**   An Aberdonian Scot who began climbing in his native CAIRNGORMS in 1949. Tom Patey revolutionized Scottish winter climbing in the postwar period and gave it a stock of routes that rank among the great hard classics of that genre: Parallel B Gully and Eagle Ridge on Lochnagar, Zero Gully on BEN NEVIS, the Last Post on Creag Meaghaidh and the winter TRAVERSE of SKYE's Cuillin Ridge. On rock his explorations also produced routes of the finest quality. The Cioch Nose in Applecross and the OLD MAN OF HOY among them. In the ALPS his new routes included lines on the Plan, the Leschaux, the Aiguille sans Nom and the Cardinal, and he also took part in successful expeditions to the MUZTAGH TOWER and RAKAPOSHI. He was killed when his ABSEIL device became detached from the rope in the descent from a Scottish sea-stack. An utterly endearing character with a huge zest for life who seemed to be able to go for weeks on end without sleep, both in his work as a doctor serving a vast area of northwest Scotland and on his mountaineering forays, he left behind a body of writing that was collected and published after his death. Irreverent, kindly and comical, his essays give a sane, humorous perspective on mountain activity and are perhaps the best work in that form since those of John Menlove EDWARDS.
Further reading: Tom Patey, *One Man's Mountains* (1971).

PATISSIER, ISABELLE   **(1967–   ) (France)**   Patissier was co-winner, with Lynn HILL, of the 1990 World Cup, and winner of the 1991 World Cup after a decisive win in an exciting 11th-hour showdown (with Susi Good and Robyn ERBESFIELD) in Birmingham, England, at the series' final event. Patissier began climbing with her parents at the age of five. When professional competitions began, she was a regular second behind Catherine DESTIVELLE or Lynn Hill. Patissier had her first major win in Nimes, France, at the Grand Prix d'Escalade, and she has since won many world events, including the Sportkeller World Cup at Nuremberg in 1991; the Rockmaster in ARCO, Italy, in 1991; a World Masters Tour invitational at Serre Chevalier, France, 1991; a World Masters Invitational at LaRiba, Mont Blanc, Spain, in 1990; the third Master International d'Escalade du Prorel-Briancon, Briancon, France, 1991; and the World Cup at Madonna di Campiglio, Italy, in 1990. On the rock, she was the first woman to climb an 8b, Sortileges in CIMAI, France. She has ON-SIGHTED up to 7c+, 5.13a.

PATONES (Spain) This is the main limestone SPORT-CLIMBING area for Madrid climbers. It lies 31 miles (50 km) north-northeast of Madrid, among the rugged hills around the Rio Lozoya and the village of Patones. Routes run the gamut of limestone, from slabs to bulging strenuous routes. The area is high enough to be too cold for climbing in winter. Spring and fall are the prime seasons.

PAVEY ARK (Britain) This CRAG lies above the picturesque Stickle Tarn on the craggy flanks of the Langdale Pikes. It is a magnificent place, with views of the eastern side of the LAKE DISTRICT. Climbs are generally 200 to 300 ft (61 to 91 m) long.

On Pavey Ark's left wall are outstanding LINES like Rake End Chimney (5.4), climbed in 1898 by G. W. Barton. Arcturus is a good 5.8 climbed by Allan Austin in 1963, but the best route here is Cruel Sister, a 5.10b taking the hanging RIB right of Arcturus, climbed by Rob Matheson and freed by Jeff Lamb and Pete Botterill. The right wall, however, has the majority of fine lines. Cascade is a fine 5.8 SLAB climb climbed by Austin in 1957, but the most impressive route is Fallen Angel (5.11a), whose main PITCH is an exacting groove.
Guidebooks: D. Armstrong, et al., *Langdale* (1989); Bill Birkett, et al, *Rock Climbing in the Lake District* (1986).

PEAK DISTRICT (Britain) An area of many crags around Sheffield. (See CHEEDALE, DOVEDALE, GRITSTONE, HIGH TOR, RAVEN TOR, STONEY MIDDLETON, WATER-CUM-JOLLY.)

PECK, ANNIE (1850–1935) (United States) For a time, Peck was one of the foremost American mountaineers as well as a lecturer and teacher. Born in Providence, Rhode Island, her independent spirit and advocacy of women's rights led her to wear men's attire when climbing. While studying in Europe she gained renown after she climbed the MATTERHORN at the age of 44. She also climbed Popocatepetl (17,815 ft/5,431 m) and Pico de Orizaba (18,435 ft/5,620 m) in MEXICO, the latter peak being, in 1897, the highest point in the continent reached by a woman. In 1902, she became a founding member of the AMERICAN ALPINE CLUB. She then set out to scale "some height where no man had previously stood," thus combining mountaineering with women's rights and her own vocation for lecturing. Already in her fifties but full of stamina, she traveled often to the ANDES. She failed, like others, on 21,082 ft (6,427 m)-high Ancohuma as well as on HUASCARAN. The latter became her greatest ambition. Always lacking the support of determined men climbers, she failed several times on that mountain but made the FIRST ASCENT of a 16,300-ft (4,097-m) peak in the Raura range in central PERU. At last, after *Harper's* Magazine had given her financial backing, she and two Swiss guides climbed Huascaran Norte (21,830 ft/6,654 m) on September 2, 1908. While she

paid full compliments to Gabriel zum Taugwald, she greatly resented the behavior of her other companion, Rudolf Taugwalder, who, contrary to the custom of professional guides, unroped and set foot on the summit before his client. Taugwalder later suffered several amputations due to FROSTBITE on this climb and, seemingly in anger, and supported by European alpinists, he declared that Peck's team did not climb higher than the southern 19,700-ft (6,006 m)-high saddle. But Peck's photos verified her achievement for all time. She set out to climb Coropuna next, a chain of ice volcanoes in southern Peru then believed to be the highest point in the continent. In open competition with another American, Hiram Bingham, she and her team of Peruvian hillmen climbed the two eastern summits of Coropuna (20,524 and 20,680 ft/6,254 and 6,303 m) in 1911, on which she hoisted the flag of the suffragists, with the motto "Votes for Women." She was 61. She later became interested in aviation and flew over Latin America in a marathon journey between 1929 and 1930. Before she died of bronchial pneumonia, she published several books including *A Search for the Apex of South America* (1911) and *Flying over South America* (1932).
Further reading: Elizabeth F. Olds, *Women of the Four Winds* (1985).

Evelio Echevarria
Colorado State University

PEDRIZA (Spain) Located 25 miles (40 km) northwest of Madrid, the grainy granite CRAGS of this large area (similar in appearance to JOSHUA TREE) comprise dozens of domelike formations and boulders piled into massifs, some reaching 1,312 ft (400 m). Over 1,000 routes dot the crags. The crags Yelmo, Cancho los Brezos and Sector Tortuga offer friction slabs, the Labarinto offers edging routes and the Murralla Chana is a steep area of bolted FACE CLIMBS. The longest routes are found at the crag Pajaro.
Guidebook: Gallinero and Francata Tozal, *Escalades en el Parque Nacional de Ordesa* (1986).

PEEL A term meaning to fall off a climb.

PEG Another name for a PITON.

PEMBROKE (Britain) The limestone of the south Pembrokeshire coast offers some of the finest climbing in BRITAIN. Climbing has focused on the CRAGS south of the village of Bosherston, south of Pembroke. The weather in this area tends to allow year-round climbing. Pembroke is characterized by steep but positive climbing, from 5.5 to 5.13, on good, well-spaced gear, such as wires, threads and rusting PITONS.

Pembroke boasts hundreds of ROUTES, climbed in the last 20 years. The principal crags include (from the west), Mewsford Point, Crickmail Point, The Castle, Rusty Walls, Saddle Head, Bosherston Head, Huntsman's Leap, Stennis Head and Chapel Point. Some areas of Pembroke are periodically closed by the military and by bird-nesting bans in early summer. Negotiations are underway here to free the largest virgin climbing area in England and Wales.

Other Pembroke crags include Trevallen, St. Govan's Head, Mowing Word and Stackpole Head and several crags on Lydstep Head. The dramatic Mother Carey's Kitchen is one of these. Excellent climbing lies on the north Pembrokeshire coast as well.

On Mewsford Point Daydreams (5.10a) and Surprise Attack (5.9) are excellent forays up groove systems, the former from Ben Wintringham and Jim Perrin in 1980 and the latter from Steve Lewis a year earlier. On Crickmail, B-Team Buttress (5.9), climbed in 1979 by Gary Lewis, is recommended.

On The Castle in 1982, Nipper Harrison, a major contributor to the area, climbed Heat of the Moment (5.12a), a fiercesome overhanging crack. The brilliant Lucky Strike on Rusty Walls is, at 5.10a, one of the finest lines in Pembroke. On Bosherston Head Pat LITTLEJOHN's dramatic Ivory Tower (5.10b) explores stunning natural architecture. Huntsman's Leap offers an overhanging POCKETED wall that is riddled with 5.12s. Littlejohn's contribution to Pembroke climbing has been almost unparalleled.

Trevallen has many excellent FACE routes including Trevallen Pillar, a 5.11a by Jon de Montjoye from 1981 and Gary Gobson's bold Ships That Pass in the Night (5.12a) from 1983. On Mowing Word the groove of Chimes of Freedom (5.10a), climbed in 1976 by Jim Perrin, is striking, and on Stackpole the steep and exposed Swordfish (5.10c) was climbed in 1978 by Littlejohn. He also added the bold Hyperspace (5.11a) at Mother Carey's Kitchen. At 200 ft (61 m) it is one of the longer routes in the area.

Guidebook: Jon de Montjoye and Mike Harber, *Pembroke* (1985).

PENDULUM A rope maneuver for crossing blank, steep rock by means of rigging the ROPE so the leader may execute a swing. A pendulum point is made from a solid ANCHOR with CARABINER into which the LEADER's rope is clipped. The belayer lowers the leader below the pendulum point and the leader swings back and forth, running against the rock until the objective—a CRACK or FLAKE which allows normal climbing to resume—is reached. The leader then "climbs up" from the pendulum point until level with it. Protection should not be placed below the pendulum point or rope drag will be a burden. If the leader lowers too far, ASCENDERS or PRUSIKS can be temporarily placed on the rope to adjust height.

Following a pendulum is as difficult as leading one, especially on a single rope. Also, pendulum strategies for the second vary depending if the PITCH is AID (in which case ascenders are used on the rope), or FREE. A pendulum ending at a BELAY below the pendulum point is easily seconded by repeating the leader's swing and being lowered by the leader. But if the belay is high and off to the side, other methods are used. Ideally, the SECOND trails an additional rope for this purpose. It is threaded through the pendulum point and the second lowers or RAPPELS off it. However, if a single rope is used, the second must reach the pendulum point, pull sufficient slack from behind or from the belay above, thread it through the pendulum point, then BACK ROPE, lower or rappel. The rope is pulled

back through the pendulum point after lowering is completed. For safety, the second can be clipped directly into the pendulum point while adjusting rope, or can be belayed from above if double ropes are being used; if knot changes at the HARNESS are required during the procedure, the second should tie into a BIGHT of the lead rope before parting with the rope's end. Never second a pendulum by letting go of the pendulum point to swing across the face. This invites disaster. Equipment at the pendulum point is usually abandoned.

PENNINE ALPS (Switzerland, Italy) There are more 13,120-ft (4,000-m) peaks in the Pennine Alps than all other ranges put together and the region constitutes the central mass of the ALPS. While the Dufourspitze of MONTE ROSA is, at 15,199 ft (4,634 m), the third-highest mountain in Western Europe, pride of place is unquestionably reserved for the MATTERHORN, perhaps the most famous mountain-shape in the world. The Pennines stretch from the Grand Col Ferret in the west to the Simplon Pass in the east and separate Italy from Switzerland, the Aosta Valley from that of the Rhône. This frontier crest is crossed at right angles (i.e. north to south) by other crests and valleys, although it is what happens on the Swiss side of the border that is of greatest interest to the mountaineer.

The most important center for climbers is Zermatt at the head of Mattertal. Cars are not allowed in this traditional mountain village and must be left in Täsch and the journey completed by train. It offers a base for many of the four thousanders including the Matterhorn, the Weisshorn, Monte Rosa and Dom. The view of the former from Zermatt is well known. Other important bases are Saas Fee and Arolla, although for specific or isolated peaks there are other starting points that are less crowded than the more popular centers. The recommended climbs in the Pennines are largely mixed routes since the quality of the rock hardly compares to that of the CHAMONIX Aiguilles. The style of climbing in this respect has more in common with the BERNESE Oberland than MONT BLANC.

PENNSYLVANIA (United States) Many small CRAGS are scattered throughout rural Pennsylvania. Stoney Ridge, High Rocks and White Rocks have had long histories of FREE CLIMBING, the former being the main area of the state. The cliff is steep—110 degrees—and mainly offers hard routes. It is located near the town of Bowmanstown. Bellefonte Quarry, near the eponymous town, is one of numerous limestone quarries in central Pennsylvania. The tilted strata of these quarry walls are highly developed. Hugh HERR introduced 5.12 to the crag in 1981, while SPORT CLIMBING in the 1980s produced severe 5.13 climbs, especially by Eric Horst. Western Pennsylvania offers many gritstone outcrops desired by locals for BOULDERING. In Allegheny National Forest are several such areas: Jake's Rocks, Rimrock, Heart's Content and Minister Creek—all around the town of Warren. More gritstone is found around Pittsburgh, at McConnell's Mill and Dickson's Quarry, while in the Laurel Highlands are Kralack Rocks, Coll's Cove and White Rock.

A nontechnical hill, Mount Davis (3,213 ft/979 m), 10 miles (16 km) west of Meyersdale, is the state's high point.
Guidebooks: Jim Bowers, *Bellefonte Climbing Guide* (1987); Curt Harler, *Climb Pennsylvania* (1985).

PENTIRE POINT   (Britain)   The Great Wall of Pentire Point is a magnificent sweep of rock, the finest in North Cornwall. Despite being a SEA CLIFF, it is unaffected by the tide. It is close to Polzeath, a holiday resort.

Eroica, climbed in 1972 by Pat LITTLEJOHN and freed in 1975 by Pete LIVESEY, is a famous route, and at 5.10c is the easiest way up Great Wall proper. Black Magic, a more sustained 5.11d, was the work of Steve Monks in 1987. Another historic route is Darkinbad the Brightdayler, another Littlejohn classic that was finally freed in 1976 by Pete Gomersall at 5.12a. This route has become recognized as one the finest in Britain and is emblematic of Littlejohn's contribution to climbing in the southwest. Pentire Point is formed of pillow lava and is a north-facing crag.
Guidebooks: Pat Littlejohn, *South West Climbs* (1991); Iain Peters, *North Devon and Cornwall* (1988).

PERI HIMAL   (Nepal)   This large range of the Central Nepal HIMALAYA is bounded on the southeast by the Gya La or pass, the Larkya La and the Dudh Khola (valley) and the Marsyangdi River. Its western boundary runs along the Hulung Khola, Nar Khola and Phu Khola, between the peak Chako (in the Damodar Himal) and Peak 6687 (21,993 ft). There are five peaks above 22,960 ft (7,000 m) here: Peak 7139 (23,416 ft), Himlung (23,373 ft/7,126 m), Peak 7098 (23,281 ft), Peak 7038 (23,084 ft) and Ratna Chuli. Kang Guru was previously regarded as being 22,992 ft (7,010 m) but is now surveyed at 22,897 ft (6,981 m).
Further reading: Jill Neate, *High Asia* (1989).

PERLON   Another name for sheathed climbing rope, or KERNMANTLE. (See ROPES.)

PERU   Until the recent opening of the mountains of Asia, Peru was the world's favorite for expeditionary mountaineering. The CORDILLERA BLANCA alone took in more than 1,000 expeditions in less than 20 years. Peru is a vast country and to this day it offers large tracts of unsurveyed mountains. The Peruvian *cordilleras* always appear as a confusing array of peaks, and indeed, orographical chains are still not clearly determined. There are four major zones. The Northern ANDES are formed, north to south, by the small Cordillera de Conchucos (Nevado Rosco Grande, 16,790 ft/5,118 m the highest), followed abruptly by one of the most grandiose massifs of the world, the Cordillera Blanca with Nevado HUSCARAN Sur, 22,205 ft/6,769 m, highest in Peru. Then comes the lesser Cordillera Chaupijanca (Nevado Huallanca, about 17,717 ft/5,400 m is highest), which stands beside the Amazonian basin and the wild CORDILLERA HUAYHUASH (Nevado YERUPAJA, 21,708 ft/6,617 m). This first zone ends with the tangled massifs of Cordillera de Milpo and Cordillera Raura (highest, Nevado Santa Rosa, 18,722 ft/5,707 m). The Central Andes are quite diverse. The main one is the Cordillera de Yauyos (highest, Nevado Ticlla or Cotoni, 19,350 ft/5,896 m). Access is easy, by either railroad or highway, which here reach heights above MONT BLANC. The eastern ranges are subject to Amazonian weather and display a greater glaciation than other areas. The Cordillera Oriental (highest, Nevado Huancarunchu, 18,799 ft/5,730 m) is situated north of the large mining settlement of La Oroya, and the attractive Cordillera de Huaytapallana (Inca for "The Shelter of Flowers") is accessible from the town of Huancayo. Its highest peak is Nevado Lasontay (18,280 ft/5,572 m). To the southwest, the ANDES of Peru reach again great heights with the volcanic ranges radiating from Arequipa. This, the third zone, is generally called the Cordillera Occidental, and is quite extensive (highest, Nevados Coropuna, 21,076 ft/6,425 m the highest). East of Arequipa, volcanoes begin to disappear and the *altiplano* (high plateau) asserts itself. The giant peaks of southeast Peru now prevail. The grandiose cordilleras VILCABAMBA and VILCANOTA, Urubamba and Carabaya are all accessible from Cuzco, the former Inca capital. The Peruvian Andes come to an end with the ice peaks of the Cordillera de Apolobamba (Nevado Chaupi Orco, 19,830 ft/6,044 m the highest), sitting astride the Bolivian border. Such a vast mountain land offers variety in many respects: Northern ranges are unstable granite, southwestern ones are made of volcanic andesite; in the Huaytapallana, glaciers descend below 16,000 ft (4,878 m), but near Arequipa, volcanoes over 18,000 ft (5,488 m) can display only a few snow drifts. However the climbing season is uniform for the entire country: the dry winter months of May through August are usually very stable.

As everywhere in the lands of the former Inca Empire, Indians were the first on the summits. They left a mummy buried on the top of Chachani (19,855 ft/6,052 m) and stone constructions on Sara Sara (18,111 ft/5,520 m). In colonial times, Spaniards braved eruptions several times to ascend and investigate El Misti (19,098 ft/5,822 m), the volcano that is always threatening the city of Arequipa. By doing so, those Spaniards unknowingly set the Europeans' altitude record, a record that was to last almost 200 years. Sportive climbing expeditions came late to Peru. In 1908 the American Annie PECK reached the summit of Huascaran Norte (21,830 ft/6,654 m). However, the great year of Peruvian mountaineering is 1932. The Austro-German expedition led by Philip Borchers explored and mapped the Cordillera Blanca and climbed important peaks like Huascaran Sur, the highest. Expeditions of the same nationalities returned in 1936 and 1939 and did more and better. It was in the 1960s and 1970s that international expeditions of all sizes harvested hundreds of new peaks. The storming of the great ice walls of Peru began in the 1980s, but although incredible routes were inaugurated—sometimes at a price—the scope that remains is immense. Paradoxically, Peruvian mountaineering itself has been weak due to distances and political unrest. Before 1954, a Club Andino Lima, formed mostly by local Germans, existed in central Peru, but its accomplishments were left unrecorded. In 1954, the Club Andino Peruano was founded. Organs for local mountaineering have been the *Revista Peruana de*

Andinismo y Glaciologia, edited by Cesar Morales Arnao, and *Alturas*, a publication of the youthful Club de Montaneros Americo Tordoya, the latter being the name of Peru's foremost climber. No reading about the Andes of Peru can be complete without consulting the AMERICAN ALPINE JOURNAL, from 1952 to present.
Guidebooks: Philippe Beaud, *The Peruvian Andes* (1988); John Ricker, *Yuraq Janca* (1981).

Evelio Echevarria
Colorado State University

PETZOLDT, PAUL (1908–   ) (United States) Without previous experience, Petzoldt climbed the GRAND TETON in 1924 at the age of 16. After years of indigence, wandering and freight-train hopping, he returned to the Tetons and took up guiding. Thanks in part to exceptional route-finding abilities, he did many FIRST ASCENTS and new routes there, most notably the north face of the Grand in 1936, with his brother Eldon and Jack Durrance. He'd also made the FIRST WINTER ASCENT of this peak the previous year. In 1938 he joined the American expedition to K2, the first since the Duke of ABRUZZI's in 1908. Along with Dr. Charles HOUSTON, the group leader, Petzoldt reached 26,000 ft, (7,927 m) when their food gave out. He made a successful jaunt in Colombia's Santa Marta range in 1941, where his group did a couple of first ascents, and in 1947 was a member of the group that made the first ascent of Warbonnet, the most spectacular peak in the SAWTOOTHS.

PICKET Another name for a SNOW STAKE.

PICOS DE EUROPA (Spain) This limestone range of many peaks and walls in the Pyrenees mountains of western Europe offers easy summits, BIG WALL CLIMBING and SPORT CLIMBING. It is divided into western, central and eastern massifs by river valleys. The first climbs appeared in the 1850s, when Spanish surveyors bagged the major summits. The nobleman Comte de Saint-Saud, an expert on the Pyrenees, made many climbs here, including in 1892 the FIRST ASCENT of Torre de Cerredo (8,738 ft/2,648 m), highest in the Picos and also in the entire range known as the Cordillera Cantabrica, of which the Picos is a part. As climbers became technically adept, the larger walls of the Picos were climbed from the 1920s to the 1970s. An early classic of Spanish mountaineering was the direct route up the vertiginous 1,968-ft (600-m) south face of Pena Santa, by three Madrid climbers in 1947. The 1,640-ft (500-m) west face of El Naranjo de Bulnes attracted big wall climbers during the 1970s and 1980s, with the brothers Miguel Angel, Jose Luis and Juan Carlos Gallego making several multi-day routes involving hard aid. Jose Luis Gallego and Miguel Angel Dias Vives made something of a record for perseverance with their 1983 winter ascent of this face, which took 69 days. Altogether, about five dozen routes ascend the steep walls of El Narranjo. Long free routes have also been established on this wall. In lower valleys, sport climbing has been developed in the La Hermida Gorge, along the River Casano and the Pena Fresnidiello.

Guidebooks: M. A. Adrados, and J. Lopez, *Los Picos de Europa* (1980); Robin Walker, *Walks and Climbs in the Picos de Europa* (1989).

PIED D'ELEPHANT A short sleeping bag that covers the body to the waist, used in conjunction with a duvet. Rarely used in modern mountaineering.

PIKES PEAK (United States) Set into the flanks of this 14,410-ft (4,393-m) summit near Colorado Springs, COLORADO, are GULLIES containing outcrops of solid pink granite, up to 500 ft/152 m high. The mountain, named after a U.S. Army captain, was thought to be over 18,000 ft (5,488 m) high in the early 1800s. Modern rock climbing development began in the area during the 1970s. Largely a CRACK CLIMBING area, the main formations on Pike's Peak are the Sphinx Buttress and the Pericle.
Guidebook: John Harlin, *Rocky Mountain Rock Climbs* (1985).

PILLAR A tall, slender column of rock having a distinct summit and standing apart from the main cliff. However, it may be attached by a narrow neck. The German equivalent is *pfeiler*, the French *pilier*, the Italian *pilastro*.

PIN Another name for a PITON.

PINCH GRIP A FREE CLIMBING technique, in which the thumb and forefinger are used like a clamp to pinch small pebbles, nubbins (small bits of rock sticking out from a blank face and usually about the size of a pencil eraser) and RIBS on a rock face.

PINK POINT A SPORT CLIMBING term, meaning to lead a FREE CLIMB that has been preprotected, usually with BOLTS or preplaced equipment rigged with QUICK DRAWS. (See RED POINT, STYLE.)

PINNACLE A narrow, slender and steep-sided free-standing rock tower, usually of modest height. Larger free-standing formations are generally referred to as towers, such as the desert sandstone towers on the COLORADO PLATEAU in the United States.

PINNACLES NATIONAL MONUMENT (United States) Lying 140 miles (225 km) southeast of San Francisco, this area features numerous one to two-pitch CRAGS of knobby volcanic rock. Some of the rock is solid, some of it friable. The earliest TECHNICAL ascents here were those in 1933 of Condor Crags, North Finger and Tuff Dome by David BROWER, Hervey Voge and George Rockwood. These climbs were among the first ever to use BOLTS to protect FREE CLIMBING. In 1947 John SALATHE made BOLD leads here. By the 1960s San Francisco Bay Area climbers frequented the Pinnacles and established contemporary free-climbing standards. Steve ROPER and Jim BRIDWELL were most active, with Bridwell establishing some tenuous aid climbs. Tom Higgins, Chris Vandiver, and Bob Kamps established stiff ETHICS for traditional free climbing. As ethics stand today in this park, it is a National Park Service requirement that all new routes be established from the ground up. In the 1980s Paul Gagner, John Barbella and others established many routes up to 5.12, resting on HOOKS to place BOLTS.

Guidebook: Dave Rubine, *Climber's Guide to Pinnacles National Monument* (2nd ed., 1995).

PIOLET   French for ICE AXE.

PITCH   The route between two BELAYS. Climbs are divided into roped PITCHES of various lengths, those lengths being limited to the length of the climbing ROPE.

PITON   Also pin, peg. A metal spike with an eye, hammered into CRACKS in rock and used as an ANCHOR. The Austrian climber Hans Fiechtl probably designed the earliest pitons, called *Fiechtlhaken*. His crude spikes, which appeared around 1910, ushered in a new era of climbing that swept through the Eastern Alps and Italy, where climbers like Emilio Comici used pitons to AID CLIMB up the steep limestone of the DOLOMITES. Pitons reached the Western Alps too and by the 1930s the French foundry of Simond was pounding out soft steel pitons. Pitons remained relatively unchanged until after World War II, when in America John SALATHE saw the need for tougher pitons to cope with the hard granite of YOSEMITE VALLEY. To climb the Lost Arrow Spire he forged his own pitons

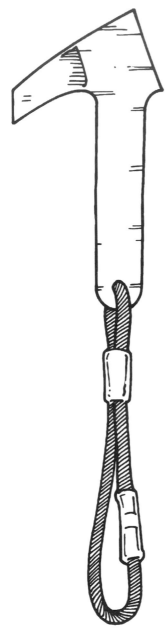

Birdbeak Piton

RURP (Realized Ultimate Reality Piton)

from car axles. Soon after, Chuck Wilts (United States) crafted the extremely thin knifeblade piton from chrome molybdenum steel. But it is Yvon CHOUINARD (United States) who brought pitons to the people, and in a range to fit any size crack, when he founded The Great Pacific Ironworks, in Ventura, California. Since the 1960s, Chouinard pitons have been the tool of choice on most of the world's hardest BIG WALL climbs. The introduction of lightweight titanium pitons into the West from the Soviet Union during the 1980s added an important dimension to LIGHTWEIGHT alpine climbing.

Of the three types of piton material, soft steel suits soft rock like limestone, by bending into irregular cracks; chrome-moly steel suits granite by withstanding the repeated hammering on aid climbs; and titanium, which weighs a fraction of steel, suits lightweight ALPINISM but is less durable than steel, and may break with over-driving.

The types of piton are usually referred to by trade names. The smallest pitons fit incipient cracks. They are the RURP, or "Realized Ultimate Reality Piton" (Chouinard), and the Birdbeak (A5 Products, United States). (See Appendices.) Knifeblades and Bugaboos (Chouinard) fit thin cracks; Lost Arrows (Chouinard) are of Salathe's original design and fit cracks up to 5/16-inch. They are sometimes called kingpins; Angles (or channel pitons made by many manufacturers) are rolled steel pitons fitting cracks one-half inch to one and one-and-one-half inches (one-quart to four cm); Bongs (Chouinard) are a larger, aluminum version of the angle, fitting cracks from two to six inches (five to 15 cm). They are archaic, and have been replaced by modern camming protection. The Leeper is a Z-section piton (Leeper, United States). A versatile piton, popular in Europe, is the universal, which has an eye aligned at an angle to the blade.

Although the use of modern CLEAN CLIMBING equipment has superseded the use of pitons for PROTECTION on FREE CLIMBS, they are still standard gear for AID CLIMBS. Subtleties like knowing whether a piton is well placed by the sound it sings when hammered (a solid piton rings like a tuning fork, a poorly placed or bottomed-out piton gives off a dull thud); techniques of tying off a piton not driven

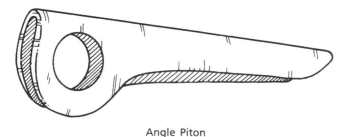

Angle Piton

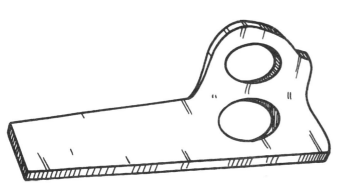

Knifeblade Piton

to the eye, to reduce leverage; the art of stacking, or nesting pitons together to fit irregular or expanding cracks; and removing pitons so as not to lose them (clipping an old CARABINER and SLING to the piton while hammering it out) are the product of much practice.

PLACEMENT   Any piece of equipment (NUT, STOPPER, FRIEND, PITON etc.) placed as PROTECTION on rock.

"Bomber," "BOMBPROOF," "AO" or "solid" refer to good placements. "Shaky," "marginal" or "A5" refer to bad placements.

PLASTIC   A term used in ICE CLIMBING to indicate a good condition of the ice. Plastic ice accepts ICE TOOLS more readily than ice prone to DINNER-PLATING.

Plastic Boots

PLASTIC BOOTS   Polyurethane-shelled mountaineering boots, which have replaced leather boots for serious mountaineering. (See BOOTS.)

PLUNGE STEP   A step used when descending snow without CRAMPONS, made by digging the heel sharply into the snow.

POCKET   A small hole in a rock FACE commonly formed in volcanic rock by gas pockets, or in limestone by erosion. Pockets are used as finger-holds. Pocket climbing places great stress on finger joints.

POINT OF AID   A single piece of PROTECTION used for AID CLIMBING on an otherwise FREE CLIMB.

POINT OF NO RETURN   Used in BIG WALL CLIMBING to indicate the point at which it is easier to continue ascending rather than begin descending.

POK-O-MOONSHINE (United States)   This FREE CLIMBING area of upstate New York, near Plattsburg, is the best and tallest of the cliffs of the ADIRONDACK Mountains. The rock is granitic gneiss, and the cliff is split by sweeping DIHEDRALS and clean CRACKS. Angle ranges from SLABS to vertical FACES and BULGES. The first routes on Pok-O-Moonshine were done in 1957, by Canadians from Montreal led by British expatriate John Turner, whose efforts included ROUTES like Cooler (5.8) and Bloody Mary (5.9). Development later was taken up by northeasterners. Multi-pitch classics of the CRAG include The Great Dihedral (5.9), freed by Richard Goldstone and Ivan Rezucha in 1976, and Summer Solstice (5.11) by Geoff Smith and Jimmy Dunn in 1977. Catharsis (5.6) is probably the cliff's most popular route; FM (5.7), Gamesmanship (5.8) and Fastest Gun (5.10) are notable. Due to its northerly position and the lingering winter snows, summer and fall are the prime seasons.

Pocket

Porta-ledge

Guidebook: Don Mellor, *Climbing in the Adirondacks* (1988).

PORTA-LEDGE   Literally, a portable, folding ledge or hanging tent platform for sleeping on steep cliffs. The porta-ledge originated in American BIG WALL CLIMBING during the 1960s, when Greg LOWE devised the Lurp tent. This rigid alloy frame with a nylon sheet strung across it and a tent fly built over it could be suspended from a single point of attachment and provided climbers with protection from bad weather on multiday aid routes. On EL CAPITAN, climbers also used heavy bunk frames from ships rigged with slings to sleep on overhanging walls. However, the weight and bulk of such platforms made them impractical, and climbers favored hammocks for sleeping on walls. When the eight-lb (three-and-a-half kg) collapsible Cliff Dwelling by Grammici Products (United States) appeared during the 1980s it changed big wall climbing, giving climbers stormproof shelter on long climbs. Grammici's two-man Porta-Ledge opened the way for big wall climbs in Himalayan conditions. The one- and two-man Porta-ledges by A5 Adventures, Inc. (United States) are the current state-of-the-art big wall bivouac systems.

PORTER   In Himalayan climbing and trekking, a local villager employed by an expedition to carry loads to base camp. Porter is a general term, describing peoples of many ethnic regions. The SHERPAS of NEPAL are the best known porters, and the term Sherpa is often wrongly attributed to all porters. PAKISTAN, INDIA and Nepal distinguish low-altitude porters from HIGH-ALTITUDE PORTERS, citing in the rules and regulations pertaining to expeditions that porters carrying loads above BASE CAMP must be paid increased wages and supplied with suitable equipment. An expedition commonly hires a head porter, or Sirdar, to manage the porters. Since the earliest explorations of the HIMALAYA and KARAKORAM, porters have been the backbone of expeditions.

PORTER, CHARLIE   (United States)   An Easterner, Porter appeared in YOSEMITE in 1969. From then till 1974 he created some of the finest BIG WALL routes on EL CAPITAN: he made solo FIRST ASCENTS of New Dawn and the Zodiac, and pioneered Tangerine Trip (with Jean Paul de St. Croix), The Shield (with Gary Bocarde) and Mescalito (with Canadians Hugh Burton and Steve Sutton). In the CANADIAN ROCKIES in 1974 he teamed up with Bugs McKeith and Adrian and Alan Burgess for the first ascent of the classic ice route, Polar Circus. In ALASKA in 1974 (with Bocarde, John Svenson and Mike Clark) he climbed the southwest wall of the MOOSES TOOTH, then in 1975 soloed the northwest face of Mt. Asgard on BAFFIN ISLAND. In 1976 he soloed DENALI, and in the KICHATNA SPIRES, with Russ McClean, climbed the west face of Middle Triple Peak, a huge wall. These remarkable achievements and his quiet, determined manner earned Porter a reputation as a big waller without comparison. Royal ROBBINS said of his ascent of the Shield, which reportedly involved a lead of 35 consecutive RURP pitons "Porter has gotten inside the RURP and is looking out." Enigmatically, he disappeared from climbing in the late 1970s after an attempt on the Fortress in the PAINE GROUP in CHILE. Climbing lore put him paddling a kayak into the sunset around Cape Horn, never to be seen again. In fact, he took up a career in Chile as a support researcher in scientific studies of marine biology, botany, archeology and glacial and tectonic geology.

POSITIVE In FREE CLIMBING, used to describe good, secure handholds.

POST HOLE A term meaning to climb or walk through deep snow, in a way that one's legs dig into the snow like posts are dug into the ground. Post-holing is arduous, and synonymous with drudgery.

POST MONSOON, PRE MONSOON The Himalayan climbing seasons. (See MONSOON.)

POWDER SNOW Fresh, cold and unconsolidated snow that is too soft to support a climber's weight and presents arduous difficulties when encountered on alpine climbs.

POWER DRILL Portable rotary hammer drills used for bolting. (See BOLTED CLIMB BOLTS, BOLT TO BOLT, BOSCH DRILL, ETHICS.)

PRATT, CHUCK **(United States)** From 1959 into the 1970s, Pratt was devoted to climbing new routes on the BIG WALLS of YOSEMITE VALLEY. His 1959 ascents with Steve ROPER and Bob Kamps of Middle Cathedral Rock's north face, and with Warren HARDING of Washington Column east face, established him as a big wall climber. Pratt's achievements on Yosemite's walls are many. His 1961 FIRST ASCENT of Crack of Doom, on Elephant Rock, was Yosemite's first 5.10. His later climb, Twilight Zone (5.10), on the Cookie Cliff, is still feared. Pratt's second ascent of THE NOSE of EL CAPITAN (1960), with Royal ROBBINS, Joe Fitschen and Tom FROST, was the first continuous ascent, in contrast to Harding's FIXED-ROPE siege on the first ascent. The first ascent of the Salathe Wall on El Capitan, with Robbins and Frost (1961), was the first big wall pioneered without extensive fixed ropes. In 1964 Pratt participated in two major routes: Mount Watkins south face, with Harding and Yvon CHOUINARD, and the first ascent of the North America Wall with Chouinard, Frost and Robbins. This route—the first to be rated A5—required nine days of

climbing and was the zenith of big wall climbing for many years.

PRE-INSPECTION In FREE CLIMBING, to inspect the HOLDS, MOVES and PROTECTION of a PITCH before leading it. Usually done on RAPPEL. Before the arrival of European SPORT CLIMBING tactics in the 1980s, pre-inspection in most areas was regarded as unethical and bad sportsmanship. Today, however, it is common play on both new routes and repeat ascents.

PRE-PLACED Gear placed as PROTECTION on a FREE CLIMB prior to a lead. (See PINK POINT, PRE-INSPECTION.)

PRESLES **(France)** Presles is a major SPORT-CLIMBING area on the extreme west of the Vercois plateau about halfway between Grenoble and Valence, and 78 miles (125 km) south of Lyon. Presles provides about 200 routes up to 984 ft (300 m) high, leading to a plateau at an elevation of almost 3,280 ft (1,000 m). It offers sustained routes comparable to VERDON's masterpieces. The south-facing cliffs allow year-round climbing. The limestone is generally excellent with plenty of *gouttes d'eau* (POCKETS). PROTECTION varies, with old routes having PITONS and one-third inch (eight mm) BOLTS while newer routes have stronger bolts. Some longer routes on the Choranche Cliff require NUTS and HOOKS. Presles's development took place in the 1970s when teams from Grenoble and Lyon competed for new LINES. Developers include J. M. Chapuis, A. Sebahi and Bruno Fara.
Guidebook: D. Duhaut, *"Presles"*.

PREUSS, PAUL **(1886–1913) (Austria)** Preuss was an uncompromising stylist who participated in one of the historic debates about climbing ETHICS. A Ph.D. from Munich University, he was dead set against the use of ROPES, even on RAPPEL, and also opposed PITONS which were then coming into style. Such technologies, he averred, violated the sacredness of mountains. One of his chief ideological opponents was Tita Piaz, the famous DOLOMITE guide, who argued forcefully for roped parties and DOUBLE-ROPED ABSEILS. In the end Preuss may have died for his uncompromising viewpoints: At the age of 27, in 1913, he fell on the kind of solo effort that was his trademark, the north face of the Manndlkogel in the Salzkammergut Range. He is credited with a total of 1,200 ascents—300 of them solo and 150 FIRST ASCENTS, many in the Dachstein, Gesause, Wilde Kaiser, Wetterstein, Silvretta and Dolomites. His most renowned exploit was in the Brenta Dolomites: the east face of the Campanile Basso (sometimes called the Guglia di Brenta), a first ascent that took just two hours. He also did difficult first ascents on the southern side of MONT BLANC, the first ski ascent of the Gran Paradiso and the first winter ascent MONTE ROSA.

PROFIT, CHRISTOPHE **(1961–   ) (France)** Introduced to the mountains by his parents, Profit took to hard ALPINISM at an early age. Ice routes like the famous Super Couloir on Mont Blanc du Tacul in winter, with D. Radigue; a solo of the Dru Couloir; and a new route on Les DROITES north face, established his alpine credentials. On rock, he FREE-SOLOED the American Direct on the DRU in just three hours. The careers of alpinists like Rene DESMAISON and Ricardo CASSIN inspired Profit to cultivate adventure, and he brought this creed into the 1980s mania for ENCHAINMENTS of the north faces. He linked the north faces of the MATTERHORN, EIGER and GRANDES JORASSES in summer 1985, then again in winter 1987. In the HIMALAYA, he tried the south face of LHOTSE three times, unsuccessfully. With Pierre BEGHIN, he scored his first 26,240-ft (8,000-m) peak in 1991 with an ascent of K2 via the northwest ridge and north face. Two films document his career: *Christophe* and *Trilogie Pour un Homme Seul*.

PRUDDEN, BONNIE (1914–   ) (United States) This American woman climber was active between 1937 and 1959, during which time she climbed in the SHAWANGUNKS, the CANADIAN ROCKIES, and the European ALPS and DOLOMITES. Prudden's introduction to climbing came on her honeymoon when her then-husband, Dick Hirschland, led her up the MATTERHORN (Switzerland). During the 1940s and 1950s Prudden became a driving force in Shawangunks rock climbing, establishing some 30 FIRST ASCENTS, on which she often shared leads with Hans Kraus, another major Shawangunks developer. Among her best 'Gunks routes are Bonnie's Roof (5.6 A1, later freed at 5.8), and Never Again (5.6 A1, later freed at 5.10). Prudden later established herself as an exercise instructor and a physical therapist, lecturing and writing books on the subject, as well as hosting a regular fitness-segment on U.S. TV's *Today Show*.

PROTECTION   ANCHORS and RUNNERS used to safeguard the leader. Protection may be hand-placed in CRACKS, using NUTS, STOPPERS or FRIENDS; may be hammered, in the case of PITONS; or may consist of BOLTS drilled into the rock. (See also NATURAL PROTECTION.)

PROW   A prominent rock feature or BUTTRESS, like a ship's prow.

PRUSIK   The sliding friction KNOT invented in the early 1900s by Dr. Karl Prusik of Austria. Originally used for repairing violin strings, the knot was adapted by Prusik to climbing because it can easily slide up a rope but locks tight when weighted with downward force. The knot is still a staple in emergency procedures like CREVASSE RESCUE, where it is used to ascend ropes or hold weighted ropes in place. Prusiking, or to prusik, is to ascend a rope by using this method. A prusik loop is a knotted loop of thin rope or webbing (usually eight mm diameter or nine-sixteenths-inch supertape). To ascend a rope, two loops are arranged into the prusik knots around the main rope. The climber then rigs SLINGS between the HARNESS and the prusiks, and suspends AIDERS from the prusiks. The procedure for movement—sliding the prusiks up the rope—is the same as for using ASCENDERS.

PSYCH OUT, PSYCH UP   The former means to lose psychological control on a climb and fail. The latter means to prepare mentally for a climb by visualization and positive thinking.

PULLEY   A miniature wheel adapted for climbing and clipping into CARABINERS. Used for HAULING and CREVASSE RESCUE.

PULMONARY EDEMA (HAPE)   Or High Altitude Pulmonary Edema. An extremely dangerous form of altitude illness that causes the alveoli or airsacs of the lungs to fill with fluid that has seeped through the walls of the pulmonary capillaries. As fluid smothers the alveoli, oxygen transfer from the air to the pulmonary capillaries is blocked. This results in a decreased concentration of oxygen in the blood, gradually causing cyanosis, impaired cerebral functions and death by suffocation. The disorder can occur even in acclimatized individuals who have climbed too quickly to high altitude, but it can occur as low as 8,000 ft (2,439 m). Early symptoms include a tight feeling in the chest, shortness of breath, fatigue, headache, loss of appetite, nausea and vomiting. Coughing is an early sign, and white frothy phlegm may be coughed up as the condition worsens. Rapid pulse rate, the sound of bubbling from the chest (called rales) and delerium are advanced symptoms. The best treatment is rapid descent to lower altitude. Bottled oxygen should be given if available. Researchers have used the drug Furosemide (Lasix) to remove moisture from the lungs, but this treatment is no longer popular. Drugs known to improve symptoms (though research in this field is ongoing) include morphine sulphate (this may suppress ventilation), Nifedipine and dexamethasone. The GAMOW BAG, a portable hyperbaric chamber, is a recent invention that has reversed the symptoms of pulmonary edema in many patients. The onset of pulmonary edema is rapid. Drugs are no substitute for long, slow acclimatization.

PUMORI (Nepal)   This steep-sided 23,494-ft/7,161-m peak near EVEREST receives many ascents, often in ALPINE STYLE, and quite regularly in winter, due to Pumori's easy access within the Solu KHUMBU region of eastern NEPAL. The mountain's name in SHERPA language means "unmarried daughter." It was named by George MALLORY, in honor of his own daughter. The first attempt on the peak was by Hamish MACINNES and John Cunningham, just after the British ascent of Everest in 1953. They tried the eastern side, but it was not until 1962 that a German-Swiss team reached the summit via the northeast ridge. Many elegant routes have been climbed on Pumori. These include the southwest ridge (1973), south face routes (1971 and 1986), west face (1974) and east face routes (winter 1981–82, 1983, 1984 and 1986).
Guidebook: Jan Kielkowski, *Pumori-Taboche Himal* (German text) (1988).

PUMPED   A term used to describe muscle exhaustion and loss of strength caused by difficult climbing or hard training. The term refers to the swelling, or pumping up, of the veins in the arm with blood laden with lactic acid.

Q

QOMOLANGMA The Tibetan name for EVEREST, meaning "Goddess Mother of the Snow."

QUEBEC (Canada) This vast province (595,048 sq miles/1,540,509 sq km) reaches from the 45th to beyond the 62nd parallel, or slightly above the southern tip of BAFFIN ISLAND. Much of this territory is unexplored in terms of climbing. Climbing development has centered around cities in the south, where most of Quebec's 6.5 million inhabitants live. Quebec has some 80 granitic rock climbing cliffs and some 25 ICE CLIMBING areas. The Laurentians are a collection of about 20 granitic cliffs, ranging in height from 66 to 443 ft (20 to 135 m), scattered 62 to 94 miles (100 to 150 km) northwest of Montreal. They are among Quebec's best crags. The most popular are Mount King, Mount Condor, Mount Cesaire, La Bleue and Les Fesses. These are commonly referred to as the Val David area, and the climbs challenge TRADITIONAL and SPORT CLIMBERS alike. Nearby Mount Nixon and Weir are both 62 ft (100 m) in height and offer solid rock. Along with Shawbridge, these three cliffs are where most of Quebec's ice climbing forms. Around Quebec City are about 15 granitic cliffs, from 33 to 1,312 ft (10 to 400 m) high, all situated from 16 to 125 miles (25 to 200 km) northeast of the city. The most popular areas are Les Pallisades, Stoneham and the three cliffs of the Parc des Grand Jardins—Mount du Gros Bras, Mount de l'Ours and Le Dome. Overlooking the Saguenay River, Cap Trinité's vertical walls are synonymous with Quebec BIG WALL CLIMBING history. This cliff is predominantly an AID cliff, but two long FREE routes exist. The Malbie River Wilderness area is home to La Pomme d'Or, a world-class 1,082-ft (330-m) steep ice climb. Good ice is also found in the Jacques Cartier Valley, and the 131-ft (40-m) free-standing pillars of the Pont-Rouge are breathtaking. The 262-ft (80-m) Montmorency Falls, beside the St. Lawrence River, are situated five minutes from Quebec City and offer ice climbing up to grade 5. In summer, climbers can be found BOULDERING near downtown at the Champlain and Pylone crags, and on the recently developed limestone sport-climbing crags of Kamouraska.

What the Estrie area lacks in quantity of cliffs they make up in quality. These three popular granitic cliffs, from 82 to 394 ft (25 to 120 m), are situated in a 31-mile (50-km) radius of Sherbrooke, east of the Appalachia Mountains and 94 miles (150 km) due east of Montreal. The Lac Larouche area offers traditional and sport climbing, while Mount Pinnacle with its 394-ft (120-m) walls has traditional rock routes and winter ice. The Gaspé Peninsula contains good SEA CLIFFS and spectacular ice climbing.

The names of a few Quebecois climbers stand out in the history of this province. Bernard Poisson and Claude Lavallee opened good routes in the Laurentians and the ADIRONDACKS from the 1950s to the 1970s. In the Charlevoix area, Jean Sylvain dominated the mid-1960s to the 1970s, while Claude Berube explored the Malbie Valley (he made an early, if not the first, all-NUT ascent of EL CAPITAN'S SALATHE WALL in YOSEMITE in 1976). But the most prolific climber residing in Quebec was an English chemist working in Montreal, John Turner, who, from 1956 to 1962 teamed up with Dick Wilmott and left hard routes in Val David and in SQUAMISH, the BUGABOOS, the Adirondacks, and NEW HAMPSHIRE. As a legacy to their skill, Turner's Repentance (5.9+) from 1958 waited more than 10 years before anyone had the gumption to repeat it.

Guidebooks: Bertrand Cote, *Escalade dans les Contons de l'Este* (1979); Julien Dery, *Escalade au Mont St-Hilaire* (1989); John Harlin III, *Climber's Guide to North America, East Coast Rock Climbs* (1986); Andre Hebert, *Alpinisme au Quebec* (1972); Alain Henault, *Les parois de Charlevoix, Palissades, St-Simeon,* Vol 1 (1988); Bernard Mailot and Charles Laliberte, *Guide d'Escalade en Estrie* (1990); Bernard Poisson, *Escalades Guide de Parois Region de Montreal* (1971); Jean Sylvain and Eugenie Levesque, *Parois d'Escalade au Quebec* (1978).

QUICK DRAW A sewn (usually with bar tack stitching) or knotted loop of WEBBING, 6 to 12 inches (15 to 30 cm) long, with a CARABINER clipped at either end. Used in FREE CLIMBING, especially SPORT CLIMBING, for quickly clipping BOLTS and PITONS to the leader's rope, or for extending the length of SLINGS to reduce ROPE DRAG.

QUIROS (Spain) Solid limestone up to 656 ft (200 m) high, of the type found at VERDON in France, is found in this popular FREE CLIMBING area. It is located 16 miles (25 km) south-southwest of Oviedo, in the province of Asturias in northern Spain. The well-BOLTED routes boast the POCKET-pulling style coveted by sport climbers, and grades extend from 5 to 8a. A hut near the village of Barzana de Quiros services the crag.

R

RABOUTOU, DIDIER (1962–   ) (France) Grand master of French competitive climbers, Raboutou has a powerful and precise style of climbing. He seems rarely to climb down; he just LOCKS OFF on a HOLD and reaches further. He narrowly lost the 1990 World Cup title to Simon NADIN of England in the season's last event. Before 1990, when François LEGRAND emerged, Raboutou was the most consistent winner of world events. His wins included the Rockmaster at ARCO, Italy, 1989; the Sport Roccia at Bardoneccia, Italy, 1988; and a World Cup at Lyon, France, in 1990, in which he FLASHED all routes with such unearthly strength and precision that people in the audience were actually laughing at his ease on the hardest moves. Raboutou was a potential winner at the first U.S. professional event, the 1988 International Sport Climbing Championship at Snowbird, Utah, but he stepped out of bounds and was disqualified. However, he won at Snowbird in 1989. On rock, he made the third ascent of the Maginot Line (called both 8c or 5.14b, and 8b+ or 5.14a) at VOLX, and the second ascent of Agincourt (8c or 5.14b) at Buoux, France. He has ON-SIGHTED a remarkable three 8a+ (5.13c) routes.

RACK A selection of gear for a climb, often "racked," or arranged, on a GEAR SLING. On a typical FREE CLIMB, NUTS, STOPPERS and FRIENDS, arranged in order of size on CARABINERS, as well as QUICK DRAWS and spare CARABINERS, make up a rack. AID CLIMBING racks may include multiple sets of the above as well as dozens of PITONS, COPPERHEADS, SKYHOOKS and TIE-OFFS.

RADIO COMMUNICATION Lightweight two-way radios are a valuable tool in rescue work and expedition logistics, but small radios have limited transmission capabilities. Forests, intervening land masses like ridges, distance and weather block radio signals, restricting most small radios to line-of-sight communication. Providing adequate battery power for long trips is also problematic. Solar-charging panels have been used successfully for recharging. Ham radios offer a more powerful signal, but are heavier.

RAINIER, MOUNT (United States) The highest of the CASCADE RANGE volcanoes and WASHINGTON's highest peak, standing 14,411 ft/4,392 m, with the largest single-mountain GLACIER system in North America outside of CANADA and ALASKA, consisting of 26 major glaciers covering over 35 sq miles (91 sq km). This impressive stratovolcano has been dormant during recorded history, but is not extinct. Fumaroles are still active in the summit craters. At its height, and due to its proximity to the Pacific Ocean (100 miles/160 km distant), Rainier experiences severe weather. Lenticular clouds often cap the summit, signifying high winds and heavy snowfalls. World-record snow accumulations have been recorded on Rainier–1,122 inches (2,850 cm) fell at Paradise (elevation 5,400 ft/1,646 m) in the winter of 1971–72.

Natives regarded the mountain as a great spirit that spewed smoke from a burning lake at its summit. The first recorded sighting of Mount Rainier was by Captain George Vancouver in 1792, who named the mountain after his friend, Rear Admiral Peter Rainier. That name was the subject of debate later on, because the Admiral had fought against colonists in the American Revolution. Local residents preferred the Indian name Takhoma, which means "high, snowy mountain," but the official name remains Rainier.

Colonel Benjamin Franklin Shaw, Sidney S. Ford and "a man named Bailey" may have climbed Mount Rainier in August 1854. Lieutenant August Kautz in 1857 reached over 12,000 ft (3,659 m) but turned back due to foul conditions and impending darkness. On August 17, 1870, Philemon Van Trump and Hazard Stevens made the FIRST ASCENT. They were benighted on top, and endured a night in the summit FIRN caves. When the pair returned to their camp the next day, their Indian guide Sluiskin believed they had died on the summit and their ghosts were returning to haunt him.

Of the 2 million visitors to Mount Rainier National Park each year some 4,000 climb the mountain, and almost twice that number attempt to climb it. About one-third of all climbers are guided, commonly via the Emmons Glacier or Disappointment Cleaver routes. Most routes are steep GLACIER climbs, but it has imposing TECHNICAL routes, including the Willis Wall and the Mowich Face that tackle steep walls of ice and crumbling basalt. Liberty Ridge, on Rainier's north face (first climbed in 1935 by Ome Daiber, A. Campbell and J. Borrow), is considered the mountain's best route. The highest point of the vast summit acreage and crater rim is called Columbia Crest.

Little Tahoma Peak (11,138 ft/3,395 m), a remnant of an older volcano, stands taller than most Cascade Range summits and is a popular climb. Snow conditions are their best on Rainier in July and August.

Further reading: Dee Molenaar, *The Challenge of Rainier* (1987); Jeff Smoot, *An Adventure Guide to Mount Rainier* (1991).

RAKAPOSHI (Pakistan) The earth's 31st-highest mountain is a huge massif of the Lesser KARAKORAM, situated in the northern district of Hunza. Rising abruptly to 25,552 ft/7,788 m from the low-lying Hunza River, its vast northern slopes drop from a long, triple-summited ridge crest, which dominates the skyline from the Karakoram Highway between Gilgit and Karimabad. Thunderous AVALANCHES rake these slopes, creating a spectacular roadside attraction. The principal problem with climbing Rakaposhi is its massive scale: From the meadows of the village of Minapin at the foot of the north face to the summit is a rise of 19,000 ft (5,793 m), though the horizontal distance is only seven miles (11 km).

Rakaposhi was first reconnoitered from the south by Martin CONWAY, on his 1892 expedition. Attempts to find a route up Rakaposhi began in 1938. Efforts concentrated on the southwest spur beginning with a 1947 attempt by a team that included H. W. TILMAN. Altogether, five expeditions attempted the southwest ridge before the successful ascent in 1958 by a British-Pakistani military expedition that placed Mike Banks and Tom PATEY on top. Summiting in a blizzard, both men suffered FROSTBITE.

Efforts then turned to the north. In 1979 a Polish-Pakistani expedition climbed the long northwest ridge. A massive avalanche destroyed their base camp on the Biro Glacier, but they persevered and placed eight climbers on top, including the Pakistani M. Sher Khan and the Polish women A. Czerwinska and K. Palmoswska. A Dutch team summited by a variation to this ridge in 1986. In 1979 a Waseda University expedition from Japan completed the difficult north ridge, attempted in 1971 and 1973 by German expeditions led by Karl HERRLIGKOFFER. This stupendous ridge is Rakaposhi's most difficult route. The Japanese E. Ohtani and M. Yamashita summited after a long seige. In 1984 a LIGHTWEIGHT ascent of the north ridge was made by Canadians Dave CHEESMOND, Barry BLANCHARD and Kevin Doyle.

Further reading: Mike Banks, *Rakaposhi* (1956).

RAKONCAJ, JOSEF (1954–   ) (Czechoslovakia) The most successful Czech high-altitude climber, Rakoncaj is the first climber to summit K2 twice, by the north ridge in 1984 and the ABRUZZI ridge in 1986. He also pioneered on sandstone hard rock climbs in Czechoslovakia. His mountaineering firsts include a TRAVERSE of Koschtan Tau-Dych Tau in the Caucasus (1975); FIRST WINTER ASCENTS of the TROLL WALL in NORWAY (1977) and in Italy of Monte Agner north face via the Messner route (1981); in the GARHWAL HIMAL, Kalanka north face (22,733 ft/6,931 m) (1978), and NANDA DEVI southeast ridge (1983); Pik Oshanin north face (20,730 ft/6,320 m) in the Pamir (1980); LHOTSE Shar south face (1984). He has also climbed ANNAPURNA south face, MANASLU southwest face and SHISHAPANGMA south face.

RANDKLUFT A German word meaning the crevasse between the snow slope and the rock of a mountain. Commonly called a BERGSCHRUND.

RANGE A series of mountains, usually with summits connected by COLS or RIDGES. In the nomenclature of mapping, mountains are grouped together in ranges.

RAPPEL ANCHORS When a climber rappels from an ANCHOR, great stress is exerted onto anchor components and the SLINGS or chains through which the ROPE is looped. Whenever the climber bounces, stops suddenly or swings around, dynamic loads of several times the static load, are exerted on an anchor. Sometimes, anchors and/or slings fail. Even when there are backup slings at an anchor, if one sling breaks a large dynamic load comes onto the rest of the anchor. The solution is to create the strongest possible anchor and to maintain existing anchors.

Several rules apply to creating and maintaining rappel anchors: First, always use at least two anchors that are equalized to share the weight of the RAPPELLING climber. That way, if one anchor fails, there is the chance the other will hold. Second, check the condition of existing anchors and slings at a rappel station. If old equipment appears unsafe, reset or replace it. Slings deteriorate in ultraviolet sunlight and weather. A stiff wad of old WEBBING that has seen an entire summer (or longer) of use can fail under loading and should be replaced with new webbing. Rappel rings should be at all anchors, but, if not, existing slings should be replaced, as the friction of pulling a rope directly through slings melts and dangerously weakens webbing.

RAPPEL BOLTING In SPORT CLIMBING, the tactic of BOLTING a route while hanging from a RAPPEL rope.

RAPPELLING Rappelling is a method of sliding down a ROPE, using friction devices, or "brakes" to control the speed of descent. It is an essential technique used in all forms of climbing. The word rappel comes from the French, but has been absorbed into North American usage. In Britain and Australia the equivalent term is ABSEIL.

Rappelling is called for on a descent when the terrain is too steep to safely climb down. All types of terrain may be descended by rappel, even overhanging cliffs. Although rappelling is easily learned, it can be dangerous. Inattention or incorrect use of equipment while rappelling has killed or injured even experienced climbers. Gravity is seldom forgiving.

The first thing to check in a rappel is that the ropes reach the next ANCHOR or the ground. If uncertain, tie a KNOT at the end of the ropes to avoid the chance of rappelling off the ropes' end. Even if a climber is certain the ropes reach their destination, the habit of knotting both ends together with an overhand knot is a safe one to prevent the climber from rappelling off the end of the ropes. However, knots must be undone before pulling the rope through the rappel anchor, or they will be impossible to retrieve.

Many rappelling methods exist. Some methods are regarded as safer than others. However the position one assumes for rappelling is essentially the same in all methods. To begin a rappel, the climber first checks that the rappel system is correctly set up, and that the climber is clipped to the rope. (Many accidents occur at this point, when climbers who think they are clipped in lean back on the ropes and find they are not.)

The climber stands facing the rappel anchor, with feet slightly apart. The rope between the rappel device and the anchor is gripped in the palm of the left hand. The rope trailing to the ground is held with the right hand. The right hand is the hand that controls the speed, the left hand acts only as a guide and for balance. By increasing or decreasing the grip on the rope with the right hand, or by tensioning the rope around the thigh, one increases friction and can adjust speed or stop. Rappelling begins by stepping backward toward the edge of the cliff and easing back on the rope until the angle of the body is roughly perpendicular to the cliff. One "walks" vertically down in this position, with feet slightly apart, easing oneself gently over roofs. Keep the head turned to the right, looking down at the rope and the terrain coming up. Novices should be BELAYED until they are confident with rappelling.

Whatever HARNESS system or rappel device one uses, it is safest to use a locking CARABINER clipped to the harness to hold the rappel system. Two carabiners with gates opposed is also safe. Climbing harnesses are the safest harnesses for rappelling, however in emergency situations slings may be arranged. The diaper sling and the figure-eight leg-loop sling with a waist tie offer two harness setups that may be quickly fashioned from slings.

It is helpful to know several methods of rappelling. The most basic rappel—the Dulfersitz—applies friction directly between the body and the rope, by wrapping the rope around the torso. It uses neither harness or devices. It is an essential technique for emergencies such as when a descent must be made without equipment. It is, however, highly uncomfortable and potentially dangerous as the climber is not clipped to the rope in any way. The technique was developed by Hans Dulfer (1893–1915), an Austrian climber who pioneered many alpine rock routes in the Eastern Alps.

All other methods of rappelling require a harness, carabiners and other equipment.

The shoulder rappel uses the body as a brake, by running the rope through a locking carabiner clipped to the harness then over the left shoulder and across the back to the right hand. A refinement of the Dulfersitz, this method is also uncomfortable and potentially hazardous as the rappeller is not clipped to a brake device. Also known as a Dülfersitz.

The twisted knot, or carabiner wrap, relies on one or more wraps (depending on the diameter of the rappel rope) around the carabiner. A locking carabiner should be used. This method is not recommended as it twists and tangles the rope.

The carabiner brake, or crossed-krab method, gains friction from the rope passing through an arrangement of carabiner brakes. It is very safe when set up correctly. The rope should never run over the carabiner gates (see diagrams). Non-carabiner brake systems, such as commercially made brake bars and angle PITONS are also used, but

are not as safe as crossed carabiners. The hazard with these non-carabiner methods is that they may swivel open, and that extreme force is applied to small areas of the brake bar, which may snap. For increased friction, brake bar sets can be doubled.

The FIGURE-EIGHT DESCENDER is the safest, most foolproof rappel device. It has achieved acceptance as the preferred method. The device consists of a pair of metal rings welded or cast together, shaped like the number eight. A BIGHT of rope is pushed through the larger hole, then passed over the smaller end and around the stem between the two holes. The smaller hole is then clipped into the locking carabiner attached to the harness. This method's major safety advantage is that the rope cannot come out of the device once it is set up. Its only disadvantage is that the device has a natural tendency to twist and kink the rope.

BELAY PLATES, or Sticht plates, can also be used for rappelling, although they do not always operate smoothly. A bight of rope (or ropes) is pushed into the slot (or slots) on the belay plate, then the loop is clipped to a locking carabiner properly attached to the harness. The "keeper leash" on the plate also is clipped into the locking carabiner. Ropes run smoother with this method if a carabiner is clipped into the loop of rope running through the locking carabiner (see diagrams). Care should be taken if using small-diameter ropes on belay plates with large diameter holes, as the friction will be reduced and the rappel will be fast. The problem with this system is that many belay plates consist of one opening for a one-third inch (nine-mm) rope and another for a half-inch (11-mm) rope. In practice, it can be almost impossible to squeeze a fat rope into a small hole. However, belay plates have the advantage of leaving the rope free of twists.

Numerous other devices and variations to those described above are made for rappelling, as well as belaying. Among the most successful is the Bachli Seilbremse, which is a variation of the belay plate. It offers two methods for rappelling. Unlike other belay devices, which are aluminum or alloy, it is made of steel and is more durable. The Lowe Tuber is a tube-shaped device set up like a belay plate. It offers smoother control, and the heat of friction is efficiently dispersed through the ribbed exterior surface.

Fatalities have occurred when rappelling climbers have been struck by rock or icefall and lost control of the rope. In wet conditions rope friction is decreased. Novices may become confused or intimidated and lose control. Aside from belaying a rapeller from above, which is practical only in novice situations, measures for adding safety include the use of a PRUSIK knot on the rope. Also a person on the ground can control the speed of a rappeller's descent by firmly pulling down on the rope. This causes the rappel device to bind and slows or stops the rappeller, however it must not be used in the Dulfersitz method. If a rappeller wishes to stop midway in a rappel, the rope may be wrapped around the right thigh two or three times, thus locking off the rappel. Figure-eights and belay plates can be locked off as shown in the diagrams.

Rappel devices accumulate considerable heat from rope friction, and may burn flesh or melt the sheaths on nylon rope. Hair and clothing should also be kept free of rappel devices. Finally, it is important before embarking on a rappel to ensure ropes are not crossed or that the knot will not jam in a crack or obstruction when it comes time to pull the rope down after the rappel. A visual check and a carabiner on a sling clipped to one strand of the rope and to the harness will separate ropes during the rappel. A jammed rope can be a serious problem. Often it is caused by pulling the wrong end and the knot locking in the rappel anchor (so always remember which end of the rope to pull). But if the rope is thoroughly jammed the only safe way is to tie off *both* ends of the rope to a strong anchor and prusik back up the rope.

RATING SYSTEMS   Various systems indicate the comparative difficulty of climbs. Separate rating systems are used for FREE CLIMBING, AID CLIMBING, ALPINE CLIMBING, and ICE CLIMBING. Several systems are in current use, each devised in different countries and at different periods during the climbing history of those countries.

All rating systems begin from a baseline rating of the easiest climb and progress upward. Some systems take into consideration technical difficulty only. Others consider factors like exposure, loose rock and poor protection. Though criteria exist to determine ratings, ratings are largely subjective and frequently contentious. For example, a free climb that may require a very long reach may be easy for a tall person and may be rated moderately, but for a short person the move may be several grades harder. Also, a 5.11 climb established during the 1970s may seem easy compared with a 5.11 established in the 1990s. Even within the same country, ratings often vary from one area to another. So also Appendix III: International Rating Systems comparison chart.

Free Climbing Rating Systems

The American System

The U.S. rating standard is the Yosemite Decimal System (YDS). This system evolved from the old Welzenbach System (see Willo WELZENBACH), used in Germany during the 1920s, which the Sierra Club in California began using in 1937. The American system divides mountain travel into six classes:

Class	Meaning
Class 1	Hiking.
Class 2	Easy scrambling. Hands used for balance on rocks.
Class 3	Steep scrambling. Handholds and footholds are used. Exposure is such that a beginner may require a rope for safety.
Class 4	Belayed climbing, with the need for equipment to ANCHOR the BELAY. A LEADER fall on class 4 would be serious, but the climbing is easy and PROTECTION is usually not necessary.
Class 5	Technical climbing requiring ropework, protection and belays and basis for American 5—ratings (such as 5.9 or 5.11).
Class 6	Too steep or featureless to climb without aid climbing techniques. Now replaced by A1–A5 system.

During the 1950s at Tahquitz Rock in Southern California, free climbs reached such a high level of technical difficulty that class 5 was divided into a closed-ended decimal system with 10 ratings from 5.0 to 5.9. However, this system proved inadequate as harder and harder climbs fell into the 5.9 category. In 1959 5.10 was established, but soon the problem of a top-heavy system rose again as harder routes were established. Then 5.10 was then divided into 5.10a, b, c, and d. The same divisions later arose within the categories 5.11, 5.12, and 5.13 during the late 1970s and 1980s. During the 1990s, 5.14 is in the process of expansion. Some areas append Yosemite Decimal System ratings with a note regarding the serious of a PITCH. A rating of 5.10× would indicate a 5.11 route with long stretches between protection and the risk of a long fall.

In areas like Yosemite Valley, with climbs between 100 and 3,000 ft (30 and 915 m) long, climbers found that an overall rating like 5.8 (free climbing rating) A1 (aid climbing rating) could include anything from a short outing of a few hours, to a multi-pitch climb lasting several days. In the late 1950s Mark Powell conceived a system using Roman numerals from I to VI to augment the Yosemite Decimal System (free climbing ratings) with a grading system that took length and time commitment into account. As used today, its principal function is as an indication of the amount of time a climb requires. Therefore typical Yosemite routes are given three grades or ratings: Grade VI (length), 5.10 (free climbing rating), A4 (aid climbing rating).

Grade	Duration
I	Several hours.
II	Half a day.
III	Most of a day for ascent and descent.
IV	A full day for ascent and descent.
V	The route requires one BIVOUAC en route.
VI	More than two days are needed. Several bivouacs on the climb may be required.

A U.S. system still used to rate the difficulty of BOULDERING problems is the B1–B3 system, devised by the boulderer John Gill. Gill developed this system during the 1960s and 1970s to rate boulder problems that at the time incorporated harder moves than the roped climbs of the day. B1 represents a move of extreme difficulty that may require repeated attempts; B2 is markedly harder; harder again, B3 is solved only after many tries, and traditionally designated a problem that has seen one ascent only and has resisted all attempted repeats.

Other rating systems have emerged from the United States over the years, but most are no longer used. Among these are the Teton Grading System, Appalachian Mountain Club System, American Classification System and Universal Standard System. Certain areas use other systems. The National Climbing Classification System (NCCS) is still used in some journals. This system rates difficulty only from F1 to F13.

The British System

Three systems have evolved in Britain. The original system is the Adjectival System. A numerical system developed in the GRITSTONE areas is used in conjunction with the adjectival system. The numerical system rates objective difficulty only, i.e., pure difficulty of a move. Because of the nature of British climbing, which traditionally incorporates loose rock, scant protection and an ethic of BOLDNESS, a system to indicate seriousness was necessary. In the early 1980s the E Grade System (the most extreme levels of the adjectival system) was devised to describe the seriousness of a pitch in terms of the difficulty of placing protection and runouts. The numerical system usually coexists with the E grades, ie E5 6c.

The Australian System

Also called the Ewbank System, after John Ewbank who devised it, this system is open ended and goes from 1 to 33.

The European Systems

In Europe, several systems exist. The UIAA system was developed in 1968 with the intention of its being adopted as the international standard for all areas. Though used in Europe alongside domestic rating systems, it did not gain acceptance in the United States or Britain.

Mountaineering Rating Systems

Alpine Rating System

Mountaineering ratings are hard to pinpoint due to the vagaries of mountain weather. For this reason alpine ratings apply largely to technical difficulty. An alpine route climbed during bad weather will always present a greater challenge than the same route climbed in perfect weather.

Used primarily in the European Alps, this system gives an overall rating to a mountain climb. The system uses six grades, I–VI, with the distinctions Sup. (Superior) and Inf. (Inferior) to add detail within a grade. Individual pitch ratings are indicated by the UIAA system.

An older French system still used in the European Alps uses adjectives to rate climbs.

French

F   Facile (easy)
PD Peu Difficile (slightly difficult)
AD Assez Difficile (more difficult)
D   Difficile (difficult)
TD Tres Difficile (very difficult)
ED Extremement Difficile (extremely difficult)

Ice Climbing Rating Systems

Because frozen waterfalls and ice formations are an ever-changing medium, dependent on the temperature, precipitation and weather of a given day, rating ice climbs has always proven difficult. Most systems are closely related to each other, and account for technical difficulty only. The Canadian System has added the grade VI for extremely long climbs found in the Rocky Mountains.

Scottish	New England Ice (NEI)	Canadian
I	I	I
II	II	II
III	III	III
IV	IV	IV
V	V	V/VI
		VI

Aid Climbing Rating Systems

The American aid rating system has dominated other systems. In the Welzenbach System, from which the Yosemite Decimal System sprang, all aid climbs are included in the grade 6, from which the American "A" system evolved. As American aid climbing developed during the 1950s and 1960s more specific ratings were found to be necessary. The Australian system is open ended. M stands for Mechanical.

American	Australian	Meaning
A0	M1	Extremely solid placements.
A1	M1	Very solid placements.
A2	M2	Less solid, more difficult to place.
A3	M3	Placements can hold short falls.
A3+	M4	Increased chance of longer falls.
A4	M5/M6	Placements hold only body weight.
A4+	M7	Numerous body weight placements.
A5	M8	Continuous A4.

RAVEN CRAG (Britain)   This roadside CRAG of Langdale is near the Old Dungeon Ghyll Hotel. It has a string of harder ROUTES appealing to modern climbers. Routes are between 150 and 300 ft (46 and 91 m) and are protected with NUTS and PEGS.

Easier classics include Pluto, a 225-ft (69-m) 5.8 whose hardest PITCH was added by Eric Metcalf in 1957. But the best LINES are steep, fingery walls in the upper grades. Examples include a 5.11c from 1979 by Jeff Lamb and Ed Cleasby called Trilogy, which takes a distinct corner on the crag's central wall, but the crag's centerpiece is Centerfold (5.12c) by Bill Birkett, a 1984 effort that takes the main challenge of the wall.

Guidebooks: Bill Birkett, et al., *Rock Climbing in the Lake District* (1986); D. Armstrong, et al., *Langdale FRCC* (1989).

RAVEN TOR (Britain)   This overhanging limestone CRAG 175 ft (53 m) high and 150 yards (137 m) long is home to a contender for the world's hardest route. Raven Tor is tucked into a hillside between CHEEDALE and WATER-CUM-JOLLY above the River Wye in Miller's Dale. The crag is popular with climbers from Sheffield, to the north. STONEY

MIDDLETON and Hathersage provide services. Most routes are protected by BOLTS although there are some bold, conventionally protected LINES.

Raven Tor was originally an AID CLIMBING cliff. Although a few FREE routes had been done before, 1982 was the first great year. Ron FAWCETT, who was then at the height of his powers, climbed Indecent Exposure (5.12a) and The Prow (5.12c), the latter a stunning route through the longest part of the crag. In 1984, Jerry MOFFATT, climbed Revelations (5.13a), a direct start to The Prow. Two years later Ben MOON added Pump up the Power (5.13a), which went unrepeated for three years. In 1987 Andy Pollitt added The Whore of Babylon (5.13c, with two aids to leave the ground), Boot Boys and Out of My Tree, both 5.13s. Martin "Basher" Atkinson capped a long and successful career with Mecca—The Mid-life Crisis (5.14a) in 1988, but in 1990 Moon went a step further with Hubble, which freed the aid moves of Pollit's Whore and was given the French grade of 8c+.

Guidebook: British Mountain Club, *Peak Limestone—Cheedale* (1987).

RAYBAUD, NANETTE (1962–) (France) Winner, by a long shot, of the 1989 World Cup title. Raybaud, of Marseille, emerged as an unknown at a competition in Marseille in 1988 to give the top women a run for their money, taking third. She had only been climbing for two years when she won a World Cup in Bardoneccia, Italy, at which Lynn HILL was absent, and then World Cups at Snowbird, UTAH, in 1989 and at Vienna, Austria, in 1990, in which she bested Hill. Raybaud also won the North Face World Cup at Berkeley, CALIFORNIA, in 1990, besting Hill just slightly, and was a decisive first in LaRiba, Spain, in June 1991, and in Innsbruck, Austria, in September of that year. On rock, she has ON SIGHTED grade 7c (5.12d) and climbed worked routes up to 8a (5.13b), including an early ascent of Samizdat (8a or 5.13b) in CIMAI in the late 1980s.

RAYNAUD'S DISEASE A condition in which the blood vessels in the extremities constrict in response to COLD. Climbers afflicted by Raynaud's Disease experience considerable discomfort on cold-weather climbs, especially ICE CLIMBS.

Under normal circumstances, the body responds to extreme cold by shutting off the blood supply to the extremities (fingers and toes), to concentrate blood flow to the body's core and vital organs. However, when the extremities get too cold (usually at an air temperature of around 50 degrees F/10 degrees C) the sympathetic nervous system signals the capillaries to reopen and circulation is restored. Among sufferers of Raynaud's Disease, the vessels remain constricted. Fingers and toes turn cold, appearing white or bluish, and feel numb. When circulation returns, a tingling, throbbing and pain may be severe. Sufferers of Raynaud's Disease may be at greater risk to FROSTBITE. Frequent exposure to cold may increase an individual's chances of getting Raynaud's Disease. The disease has a greater frequency among women.

Treatment and prevention for Raynaud's Disease include dressing warmly, covering the extremities with THERMAL UNDERWEAR (glove liners, mittens, socks, overboots, etc.), protecting the wrists and neck (where nerves controlling blood vessels in the hands are situated), reducing physical or emotional stress and avoiding consumption of caffeine or nicotine, which constrict blood vessels. Handwarming devices also help, as may the consumption of cayenne pepper, which causes body temperature to rise. In severe cases drugs such as vasodilators, prostaglandins, calcium channel-blockers, and thyroid hormones are sometimes prescribed to dilate blood vessels. U.S. Army cold-weather researchers have found that biofeedback treatment and conditioning to cold also alleviate Raynaud's Disease. (See CLOTHING FOR MOUNTAINEERING.)

REBUFFAT, GASTON (1921–1985) (France) Though he lacked formal education, Rebuffat penned 20 books about climbing, edited an ALPINISM column for the Paris daily *Le Monde*, directed a mountaineering book series for the French publisher Denoel and established his own publishing house. His films *Etoiles et Tempetes, Entre Terre et Ciel* and *Les Horizons Gagnes* won awards.

His first climbs were on the cliffs of the CALANQUES beside the Mediterranean, and on Sainte-Victoire in Provence. After graduating as a guide during World War II he became an instructor in the Ecole d'Alpinisme and the Ecole Militaire de Haute Montagne in CHAMONIX. He was accepted in the Compagnie des Guides in Chamonix in 1946. Already famous for the second ascent of the Walker Spur (GRANDES JORASSES) in 1941 and for hard new routes in the MONT BLANC massif, he played a key role in the first expedition to break the 26,240-ft (8,000-m) barrier, with the French on ANNAPURNA in 1950. He was one of the few to guide clients up all six major north faces in the ALPS.

Arthur King Peters wrote in a tribute after Rebuffat's death from cancer: "Rebuffat combined a mastery of modern climbing techniques with a romantic concept of the mountains rooted in the 19th century pioneers he so admired. His descriptions of ascents were never burdened with logistical trivia. He preferred to speak in more philosophical, even poetic, terms of what mountains do for man rather than what men do to mountains. . . . He felt the mountains should be open to everyone, and that each was free to learn the rules his own way."

Rebuffat's angular figure, climbing with poise up steep cliffs, embodied the climbing experience so perfectly that a photograph of him atop an aiguille and silhouetted against Mont Blanc was sealed inside a time capsule aboard the first American space probe.

Further reading: Gaston Rebuffat, *Mont Blanc to Everest* (1956); Rebuffat, *Starlight and Storm: The Ascent of Six Great North Faces of the Alps* (1956); Rebuffat, *Between Heaven and Earth* (1965); Rebuffat, *Men and the Matterhorn* (1967); Rebuffat, *On Ice and Snow and Rock* (1971).

RED POINT An English and French SPORT CLIMBING term meaning to lead a route without falls or weighting

PROTECTION. For a true red point, the climber must have placed protection on the lead. On very hard FREE CLIMBS the climber will usually lower off protection and rehearse moves (HANGDOGGING), working toward an eventual red point ascent. When protection is pre-placed by RAPPEL, and climbed without falls, the ascent is sometimes called PINK POINT. This distinction is somewhat blurry, as the world's hardest free routes are usually rigged with pre-placed protection anyway, yet no-falls ascents of them are still called red point. (See STYLE.)

RED RIVER GORGE (United States) Kentucky's premiere cliff. The rock is coarse, POCKETED conglomerate sandstone and the style of climbing is steep CRACK and modern FACE routes. It is located in the Appalachia of eastern KENTUCKY, on the west edge of the Cumberland Plateau, near Stanton and Lexington. Climbing began here in the 1960s. By 1985 20 different CRAGS were developed, bearing 300 routes up to 5.11. By the late 1980s SPORT CLIMBING reached the cliffs, and the area became highly regarded for its strenuous technical challenges. Table of Colors (5.13b), by Porter Jarrard in 1991, is one of the area's hardest routes. The cliffs are on Forest Service Land. Fall provides the best weather for climbing.
Guidebook: Martin Hackworth, *Climber's Guide to Red River Gorge* (1986).

RED ROCKS (United States) Located 20 miles (32 km) west of Las Vegas, Nevada, this 13-mile (20 km)-long, 2,000-ft (610-m)-high sandstone palisade rising above the Mojave Desert is situated in the Red Rocks National Conservation Area. The towering sandstone formations are indented by many canyons and offer multi-PITCH FREE and AID routes, CRACK CLIMBS, thin FACE and SLAB routes, and BOLTED, overhanging SPORT CLIMBS. Quality long routes are found on the walls of the Black Velvet Canyon, Oak Creek Canyon and Rainbow Wall. The sport-climbing areas are on short, deeply red crags in the Calico Hills, east of the main canyons. Spring and fall are the mildest seasons, but sport climbers flock to the sun-soaked smaller crags even in winter.
Guidebooks: John Harlin, *Climber's Guide to North America: West Coast Rock Climbs* (1986); Joanne Urioste, *The Red Rocks of Southern Nevada* (1984).

REICHARDT, LOUIS, DOCTOR (1942–) **(United States)** This professor of neurobiology at the University of California Medical Center in San Francisco is also one of America's great high-altitude climbers. He graduated from Harvard, attended Cambridge as a Fulbright Scholar and earned his doctorate at Stanford. At Stanford, he began climbing in the SIERRAS, YOSEMITE and ALASKA. In 1969 he joined an American expedition to DHAULAGIRI. Low on the route an AVALANCHE engulfed eight team members. Only Reichardt survived. He returned to the scene of the disaster in 1973 and participated in the first American ascent of the peak. After completing a postdoctoral fellowship at Harvard he participated in the first

American ascent of NANDA DEVI. The route was a new one, and he summited with John ROSKELLEY and Jim States. The next mountaineering sabbatical came in 1978, to K2. A storm pinned him and his teammates down at 25,000 ft (7,622 m) for a week. The weather cleared and he and three others became the first to summit K2 via the southeast ridge. Reichardt summited without supplemental oxygen. In 1981 he participated in an attempt on Mount EVEREST's steep Kangshung (east) Face, and returned in 1983 to complete this route and summit. It is one of Everest's hardest routes.

REICHERT, FRITZ (1878–1953) (Germany) Reichert is called "the father of our mountaineering" by southern South Americans. In Europe he earned a reputation for daring alpine climbs and ski TRAVERSES. On the *Rickmers expedition* to the Caucasus he made the FIRST ASCENT of Ushba (15,452 ft/4,710 m), the "Russian Matterhorn." His Andean career spanned from 1903 to 1940. While working for the government of ARGENTINA as a geologist he climbed peaks of over 19,000 ft (5,793 m) in the arid north of Argentina. From 1906 to 13 he explored and climbed in the central Argentinian-Chilean boundary. In 1908, he discovered the vast Plomo GLACIER system where he made first ascents of Juncal (20,046 ft/6,110 m) and Nevado del Plomo (19,850 ft/6,050 m) and the second of TUPUNGATO (21,490 ft/6,550 m). With Robert Helbling (Swiss) he mapped the area. From 1914 to 1940 he led eight expeditions to PATAGONIA, exploring the Upsala, Gaea, Leon, Huala and Viedma glaciers. In 1933, he discovered Volcan Lautaro (11,089 ft/3,380 m), an active Patagonian crater. Bad weather repulsed his three different attempts on San Valentin (12,697 ft/3,870 m), the highest peak in Patagonia. He produced many books, treatises and maps, and died in Santiago. The Chileans baptized a Cerro (peak) Reichert (17,946 ft/5,470 m) in the Santiago hinterland. The Argentinians have their own Cerro Reichert (16,897 ft/5,150 m) north of ACONCAGUA.

Evelio Echevarria
Colorado State University

RENAULT, THIERRY (1959–) (France) Renault is a multi-talented French climber with a strong grasp of ALPINISM and TECHNICAL rock climbing. He took part in the first competitions at Yalta, briefly held a record for climbing the Nose of EL CAPITAN in the 1980s (12 hours, with Pascal Etienne) and pioneered new FREE climbs in Thailand. Between working as a CHAMONIX guide, he and three other companions freed the American Direct on Les DRU (1981). He joined Alain GHERSEN on the 7c mountain route Divine Providence (1990). He also made the FIRST ASCENT of Digital Crack, the world's highest 8a, at 12,464 ft (3,800 m) on the Aiguille du Midi. In addition to climbing many north faces he pioneered FROZEN WATERFALLS in the Argentière region. His 1987 waterfall Shiva Lingam (IV, 6+) is respected. In winter 1992 at Le Fer a Cheval, a CIRQUE draped with ice-falls, he claimed the first grade 7 waterfall, La Lyre.

REST STEP A mountain walking technique useful on long uphill marches, intended to give respite to lungs and leg muscles. At each step the climber pauses, supporting body weight on the rear leg, which is straight and locked at the knee so that bones and not muscle support the weight, while the forward (uphill) leg is bent but unweighted. In this position muscle tension in both legs is briefly relaxed and breathing may be regulated before muscles are brought into play to carry the next step through.

RETINAL HEMORRHAGE Or high-altitude retinal hemorrhage. Bleeding of the blood vessels of the eye into the retina. This is a common symptom above 17,600 ft (5,366 m), but is rare below 14,000 ft (4,268 m). Most cases are so mild as to be barely noticeable, but in serious cases where the hemorrhage obscures vision, descent is advisable. However, no studies have linked this disorder to other altitude illnesses. Hemorrhaging is thought to be the result of blood being forced out of the blood vessels of the retina, due to higher pressure caused by reduced blood oxygen concentrations.

REVELATION MOUNTAINS (United States) A subrange of the ALASKA RANGE, located at its westernmost edge, approximately 150 miles (241 km) southwest of Denali National Park, and at the headwaters of three branches of the Kaskokium River. The range is not visible from inhabited land, and few climbing expeditions visit the area. There are 12 peaks over 9,000 ft (2,744 m) in the Revelations. David ROBERTS described an early climbing exploration here (1967) in the 1968 AMERICAN ALPINE JOURNAL. Mount Hesperus (9,828 ft/2,996 m), the highest peak in the range, was not climbed till May 1985 by Alaskans S. Spaulding and K. Swanson and New Zealander J. Lesuer. This ascent is described in the 1986 *American Alpine Journal*.

REVERSE To climb back down a section one has just climbed up, either to rest or compose oneself before a difficult move, or to retreat. (See DOWN CLIMBING.)

RHODE ISLAND (United States) This small state has a few TOP ROPING and BOULDERING areas. Best known is Lincoln Woods State Park, near Providence, which has a tradition of bouldering and short cragging on granitic rocks. Snake Den State Park, near the town of Johnston, also contains top-rope routes. In the Arcadia Management Center in the town of Exeter are aesthetic short CRAGS. Here on Mount Tom are some of the hardest top-rope routes in the state. A nontechnical hill, Jerimoth Hill (812 ft/248 m), 20 miles (32 km) west of Providence, is the state's high point.

RIB A small RIDGE or protuberance on a mountain FACE or cliff. The French equivalent is *nervure*, the German *rippe*.

RIDGE The crest where two mountain FACES meet; or a well-defined, often sharp PROW or BUTTRESS of a mountain, either of snow, ice or rock. The French equivalent is *arête*, the German *grat*.

RIDGEWAY, RICK (1949–) (United States) Ridgeway summited EVEREST (south col route) in 1976 on the second American expedition to that peak, and summited K2 on the 1978 American expedition. On K2 he was one of four who reached the summit by a new route on the northeast ridge. On this ascent of K2, Ridgeway and John ROSKELLEY made the FIRST ASCENT without oxygen.
Further reading: Rick Ridgeway, *The Boldest Dream* (1979); Ridgeway, *The Last Step* (1980); Ridgeway, *The Seven Summits* (1986).

RIFLE (United States) A thoroughly modern SPORT CLIMBING area consisting of several overhanging CRAGS up to 200 ft (61 m) high, lining a 2.5-mile (four-km) canyon. The area is near Rifle, 24 miles (38 km) west of Glenwood Springs. Rock is Mississippi Leadville limestone. Though Rifle is a recent discovery, it promises to be an important U.S. crag, already with several 5.13 routes and the looming Daydream Nation (5.14a). In winter several FROZEN WATERFALLS may be climbed.

RIMAYE French word for BERGSCHRUND.

RIME When snow crystals fall through air containing water droplets, these water droplets freeze onto the snow crystal as a rime deposit. As the rime encrusts the crystal, the crystalline shape is obscured and a rounded ball results. This form of snow is called GRAUPEL. Similarly, in the presence of wind, rime may form on rocks or mountain summits in the shape of large white feathery flakes and bulbous encrustations. (See ICE MUSHROOM.)

RIMO MUZTAGH (India) Some of the most shapely peaks of the Greater KARAKORAM lie in this range, which is east of the Siachen Glacier, north of the Saser Pass, and west of the Shyok River. The northern limit is approximately the Shaksgam River and the upper basins of the North and Central Rimo glaciers, which, combined with the South Rimo Glacier, form a trident-shaped glacial system comprising some 40 miles (64 km) of ice. The Rimo peaks are steep, reminiscent of K2 in their shape. However, their proximity to the Siachen Muztagh and the armed border conflict between INDIA and PAKISTAN have made access very difficult to these peaks. The main peaks are Rimo I (24,223 ft/7,385 m), first climbed via the west face by an Indian-Japanese team in 1988; Rimo III (23,724 ft/7,233 m), first climbed via the east-northeast ridge by an Indo-British team in 1985; Rimo IV (23,511 ft/7,168 m), first climbed via the southwest ridge by an Indian army team in 1984; and Mamostong Kangri I (24,652 ft/7,516 m), climbed via the northeast ridge by an Indo-Japanese team in 1984.

RING-ANGLE CLAW A large SKYHOOK made from a ring-angle PITON bent into a hook-shape. Used for hooking large flakes or ledges.

RISO PATRON, LUIS (1869–1930) (Chile) Nearly unknown outside the southern ANDES, Riso Patron is nevertheless the most important South American Andean explorer and surveyor. He was born in Valparaiso, became an engineer and a geographer and in 1895 headed the Chilean Boundary Commission to map the country's borders, at that time in dispute, with PERU, BOLIVIA and ARGENTINA. Between 1895 and 1910, Riso Patron directed the survey of the southern Andes, from Tacna to Cape Horn. He and his surveyors climbed all frontier passes and gaps, known and unknown, on which they erected a total of 488 benchmarks (10-ft three-m-tall iron pyramids). Many peaks were climbed for surveying purposes. Riso Patron himself discovered, named and climbed the active volcano Volcan Tupungatito (18,504 ft/5,640 m) in 1897 and again in 1901, as well as other peaks. In 1898 he participated in the first crossing of the Patagonian Ice Cap, traversing it up the Pascua Valley and Glacier to Lake San Martin. His team was also the first to determine exactly the height of ACONCAGUA (22,835 ft/6,960 m), the figure used today; they also discovered OJOS DEL SALADO (22,590 ft/6,885 m), second-highest mountain in the Andes and highest volcano in the world. Riso Patron produced many books methodically describing the entire Andes of CHILE and areas across the borders. In 1928, he published the *Diccionario Geografico de Chile*, providing an efficient description of each one of its 28,000 entries. For his work he received in 1928 the David Livingstone Centennial Medal of the American Geographical Society. German climbers named a Cerro (Peak) Riso Patron (18,865 ft/5,750 m) in the Santiago hinterland; and an Italian explorer christened a chain Riso Patron in PATAGONIA.

Further reading: Manuel Abascal, *Don Luis Riso Patron* (1942).

Evelio Echevarria
Colorado State University

RIVET Used in AID CLIMBING and BIG WALL CLIMBING as a fast method of overcoming blank rock. A rivet is a short metal stud (commonly one inch (2.5-cm)-long threaded machine bolt with a hex-head) tapped into a drilled hole. The thread deforms inside the hole to form a solid plug. When tied off with a short sling or a cable rivet hanger, a rivet will hold body weight, even in very shallow holes. (See BOLTS.)

ROBBINS, ROYAL (1935–) (United States) Royal Robbins is without question one of the most influential American climbers of the latter half of the 20th century. Born in WEST VIRGINIA, he moved to Los Angeles at the age of 5. As a teenager in the Boy Scouts, Royal was introduced to the mountains on a two-week camping trip in the SIERRA NEVADA, which sparked a lifelong commitment to the craft of MOUNTAINEERING in particular, and outdoor adventure in general.

After cutting his teeth on the sandstone crops of San Fernando Valley in CALIFORNIA, Royal spent his early years developing his skills at TAHQUITZ. He became one of the leading climbers in the area and made the FIRST FREE ASCENT of Open Book (5.9) which was identified at that time as the hardest FREE CLIMB in the country. In 1957, he, Jerry Gallwas and Mike Sherrick made the FIRST ASCENT in five days of the northwest face of HALF DOME, the first grade VI element in the country.

After a stint in the army, Robbins decided to devote his life to outdoor adventure. From 1960 to 1964 he worked at Sugar Bowl in California as a ski instructor in the winter, and spent the rest of the year traveling and climbing. During this period, he made the second ascent in seven days of the Nose route on EL CAPITAN (the first ascent by Warren HARDING took 45 days spread over a year and a half). He also climbed two new BIG WALL routes on El Capitan, the SALATHE WALL and the North American Wall, the latter considered the hardest big wall route in the world at the time. In 1964, Robbins climbed the first ascent of the southeast face of Proboscis, in the CIRQUE OF THE UNCLIMBABLES, the first time a major YOSEMITE-type big wall had been done in a remote setting.

In 1963 Robbins married Elizabeth Burkner, and in 1965 they moved to Leysin, Switzerland, where Robbins established many difficult routes in Europe, including the now CLASSIC American Direct on the DRU, at the time considered the hardest rock climb in the western ALPS.

They returned to the United States in 1967 where they set up a rock climbing school called Rockcraft, in Modesto, California, famous for its high level of instruction. In 1969, Robbins climbed Tis-sa-sack on Half Dome. In all Robbins climbed five new routes on Half Dome. He also made a solo ascent of the Muir route on El Capitan (named after John MUIR). This was the second ascent and the first ROPE SOLO of the great rock monolith, El Capitan. Robbins regards this as his most challenging climb.

In 1969, the Robbinses started the first of many successful business enterprises: Mountain Paraphernalia, which wholesaled and retailed imported climbing gear, many items of which helped to outfit the next generation of big wall climbers. In 1971 Royal wrote *Basic Rockcraft* and in 1973, *Advanced Rockcraft*, two books that inspired a generation of climbers to use clean PROTECTION. In 1979 Robbins founded Royal Robbins, a manufacturer of color-coordinated outdoor clothing which by 1988 had $10 million in sales. Ten percent of net profits are committed to projects to save the Earth.

Robbins learned to kayak in 1975 and has since kayaked down some of the most challenging rivers of the world, including many "first descents" (a term used by river runners to indicate the first time a particular section a river has been run) in California and Chile.

Further reading: Pat Ament, *Royal Robbins—Spirit of the Age* (1992).

ROBERTS, DAVID (1943–) (United States) This acclaimed American climbing writer wrote his first book, *Mountain of My Fear*, in 10 days during a semester break at college. It won smashing reviews in the climbing press and in literary circles. He has since written more than 50 mountaineering articles and a half dozen other books, including: *Deborah: A Wilderness Narrative, Great Exploration*

Hoaxes, Moments of Doubt, Jean Stafford, A Biography and, with Bradford Washburn, *Mount McKinley; The Conquest of Denali*. Roberts began his mountaineering career in 1963 when he and six other Harvard students climbed a dangerous new route on DENALI's Wickersham Wall; as of this writing, the route has not been repeated. Two years later, Roberts' magnum opus climb took place on the west face of Mount HUNTINGTON. Roberts participated in other notable Alaskan climbs such as KICHATNA SPIRE, Mount Deborah, and the east face of Dickey, but it was his honest and well-crafted prose that made his reputation.

ROBSON, MOUNT (Canada) This 12,972-ft (3,955-m) mountain lies in central BRITISH COLUMBIA, near the ALBERTA border. "The monarch of the CANADIAN ROCKIES" is renowned for a 9,742 ft (2,970-m) elevation rise from its Kinney Lake base. Because of storms, steepness and bad snow and ice conditions the mountain enjoys one of the highest climber failure rates in North America. Robson was first climbed in 1913 when Conrad KAIN brought two clients, Albert MacCarthy and William Foster, to the summit via the Kain Face. He said, "Gentlemen, that's as far as I can take you." In 1924 Kain pioneered what today is the standard route, iSSW Ridge and south face. Thence came Fuhrer Ridge (1938), Wishbone Arete (1955; though popularized in the Roper-Steck book *Fifty Classic Climbs of North America*, this route is serious and has claimed some lives); Emperor (or northwest) Ridge (1959); the elegant North Face (1963, by Pat Callis and Dan Davis); and hardest of all the Emperor Face. The latter was climbed by Mugs STUMP and Jim Logan in 1978. A variant left of this went to Dave CHEESMOND and Tony Dick in 1981. July to September is the climbing season. A HUT is found on the south-southwest ridge.

Guidebooks: Sean Dougherty, *Selected Alpine Climbs in the Canadian Rockies* (1991); R. Krusznuam and W. Putnam, *Rocky Mountains of Canada North* (1985).
Further reading: Chris Jones, *Climbing in North America* (1976).

ROCH, ANDRÉ (1906–   ) (Switzerland) The son of a mountaineer, André Roch took up the sport at the age of 12, and became an accomplished climber, skier, AVALANCHE expert and mountain photographer. In 1938 he led an expedition to GREENLAND's Schweizerland and did a number of significant FIRST ASCENTS there. The year following, Roch was in the GARHWAL HIMALAYA, where his party pulled off the first ascent of Dunagiri (23,184 ft/7,068 m). He also climbed and explored in the YUKON. Roch's lasting place in mountaineering history is deserved for a climb on which he did not succeed. In 1952 Roch led a Swiss expedition to Mount EVEREST that made the first serious effort up the Nepali side, finding a way through the treacherous KHUMBU icefall and on up to the south COL, where two successive teams were pinned down and weakened by storms and unable to climb the final 3,280 ft (1,000 m). Despite the intense national rivalry for this prize, the next winter Roch shared his priceless experiences and knowledge with the leaders of the British team, which put TENZING and HILLARY on the summit in 1953.
Further reading: André Roch, *On Rock and Ice—Mountaineering in Photos*; and Roch, *The Haute Route* (1949).

ROCK, TYPES OF Rock-climbing style is dictated by the type of rock on a cliff or mountain.

Sedimentary rocks like sandstone, gritstone, limestone or shale are made of tiny grains laid down by ancient water action. Sedimentary rocks erode to reveal their original bedding, and produce abundant EDGES and POCKETS. For this reason, sedimentary cliffs are often richly developed for climbing. Sandstone is variable. The sandstone of ELDORADO CANYON (United States) is solid, but the sandstone of the desert cliffs of the southwestern United States and the ELBSANDSTEINGEBIRGE (Germany) is soft and has weathered into bizarre formations.

Limestone tends to be wildly steep, and displays irregular erosion pockets from water action. The SPORT CLIMBING cliffs of France are classic examples of limestone. Dolomite is a magnesium limestone. Its most famous examples are found in the DOLOMITE Mountains (Italy).

Igneous rocks are solidified magma. Basalt and dolerite are dense igneous rocks that form regular columns and cracks. Rhyolite and porphyry are igneous rocks of granitic composition that form steep and rough-textured OUTCROPS. The welded tuff of SMITH ROCKS (United States) is solidified volcanic ash. It is characterized by small edges, gas pockets and steep relief.

Granite and gabbro are coarse-grained igneous rocks that are solid and give wide variety. In a single area such as YOSEMITE VALLEY (United States) one finds massive relief, a profusion of CRACKS, exfoliated flakes, GLACIER-polished SLABS, and FACE CLIMBING on intrusive bands of rock. Rock at higher elevations tends to be fractured through freeze and thaw actions.

Metamorphic rocks were originally sedimentary or igneous, but have been changed by heat and pressure. Gneiss, which is often shattered, is metamorphosed granite. Marble, which tends to be crackless, is metamorphosed limestone; slate is metamorphosed shale. Metamorphosed sandstone becomes quartzite. The solid rock of Mount ARAPILES (Australia), and the SHAWANGUNKS (United States), are examples of solid quartzite. Metamorphic rocks like schists and slate tend to fracture along horizontal and vertical planes.

ROCK CLIMBER One who climbs rocks, and vertical rock FACES. (See ICE CLIMBING, MOUNTAINEERING.)

ROCK HAMMER A hammer used to place PITONS and hand-placed BOLTS.

ROCKS™ The trade name of the first curved, tapered NUT, manufactured by Wild Country (Britain) during the 1980s. The design has virtually replaced the straight taper of the original STOPPER. The curve adds a camming element to the wedging action of the nut. (See NATURAL PROTECTION.)

Types of Rock Formation

ROCK SHOES Specialized footwear for rock climbing evolved out of the need for more sensitive soles than rigid mountain boots provided. From the 1930s to the 1950s climbers tried many types of boots and shoes. The first true rock shoes appeared in France in the 1930s, on the boulders of FOUNTAINEBLEAU. PAs, named after Pierre AL-LAIN, and EBs, named after Emile Bordenau, were tight-fitting, smooth-soled rubber boots with light canvas uppers designed for FRICTION CLIMBING and EDGING. EBs dominated climbing until the 1980s, when the Fire rock shoe from Spain swept the world with its innovative sticky rubber. The high-friction butyl rubber of Fires replaced the hard carbon-rubber sole of the EB, and paved the way for the specialization of rock shoes.

Modern rock shoes strive for a sensitive second-skin feel with no excess space between the foot and the rock. Different shoe styles suit different climbing styles: stiff-lasted soles suit precise edging climbs; flexible slippers give maximum feel on rounded HOLDS or on SLABS. The shape of a rock shoe's last dictates how a shoe performs. On a street shoe the toe point is symmetrical and centered, but rock shoes have asymmetrical toe points to bring the climber's weight onto the big toe and the inside edge of the shoe. The result may feel painful, but performance is enhanced.

High-friction rubber is a major factor in modern shoe performance. In reality, rubber is only one of up to 100 ingredients that make a rock climbing boot sole. Benzine

Rock Shoes

and resin are others. Sticky rubber sticks because it is soft and conforms to the rock, but overly soft rubber deforms and rolls off an edge. Rubber that has lost its sticky feel from adhered dirt may be rejuvenated by rubbing spit into the sole, or by removing a micro-layer with a file.

ROCKY MOUNTAIN NATIONAL PARK (United States)

This important playground for rock climbers and mountaineers is located in north-central COLORADO around the town of Estes Park. The park covers a tract of the Rocky Mountain Range. Deep glaciation cuts have revealed many rock OUTCROPS of high-quality granite, at relatively high elevations—8,000 to 14,000 ft (2,439 to 4,268 m). The principal peaks and formations within the park boundaries are LUMPY RIDGE, LONG'S PEAK, Hallett's Peak, Mount Alice, The Chief's Head, The Spearhead, Petit Grepon and Notchtop.

Guidebook: Richard Rossiter, *Climber's Guide to Rocky Mountain National Park* (1991).

ROCKY MOUNTAINS (Canada)

This range stretches 600 miles (965 km) along the ALBERTA/BRITISH COLUMBIA border, from the 49th parallel (U.S. border) to an intersection with the 120th meridian of longitude. There are 51 peak's over 11,000 ft (3,354 m) in the range. Mount ROBSON, the jewel of the range, lies in east-central British Columbia, near the Alberta border. FIRST ASCENTS on most peaks fell to British and American alpinists in the 1880s to 1920s, often with Swiss or Austrian guides, but a modern era of climbing since the 1970s brought more difficult ALPINISM to CANADA. The range is mainly limestone with POCKETS of quartzite. Rock is often loose, posing a hazard. Climbing in this range is characterized by unpopulated valleys, rarely climbed peaks, large game (elk, moose and bear), and frigid winters (see CANADIAN WATERFALL ICE CLIMBING). The national parks of Banff, Jasper, Kootenay, Yoho and Waterton, and provincial parks of Assiniboine, Hamber and Robson protect most of the Canadian Rockies. Facilities are found in the towns of Canmore, Banff, Lake Louise, Waterton and Jasper. The main range is transected from east to west by the Trans Canada and Yellowhead highways and lengthwise by the scenic Banff-Jasper (Ice Fields) Parkway. Within reach of these roads, in the southern end near Lake Louise and Jasper, Mounts TEMPLE and ASSINIBOINE rise up and rock-climbing areas abound. Nearby, the Wapta and Waputik ice fields contain the greatest concentration of mountain huts in Canada. The Highest peak here is Mount Balfour (10,732 ft/3,272 m). Mounts Baker (10,404 ft/3,172 m) and Collie (10,220 ft/3,116 m) offer moderate alpine routes. Northward and over Bow Pass lie glaciated eastern faces, from Mounts Patterson (10,486 ft/3,197 m) to Sarbach. Nearby, Howse Peak (10,791 ft/3,290 m) and Mount Chephren (10,712 ft/3,266 m) have moderate routes climbed in 1902 and 1913 respectively, and extreme alpine routes of the modern era, like the 3,608-ft (1,100-m) northeast BUTTRESS of Howse (1967, by Ken Baker, Lloyd Mackay, Don Vockeroth) and Chephren's northeast face (5.10 A3, winter 1987, by Barry BLANCHARD, Ward Robinson and Peter Arbic). West of Howse Peak, accessed via Golden, is the Freshfield Ice Field containing several 9,840-ft (3,000 m) peaks. The highest summit in Banff, National Park is Mount Forbes (11,847 ft/3,612 m). The regular route, the northwest face, is a snow and ice route (1971 by Chris Jones, Jeff LOWE and Graham Thompson). The nearby Lyell Ice Field and its penta-summited Mount Lyell dominates that ice field and bears a popular TRAVERSE. North of there lies the COLUMBIA ICE FIELD. Close to a road is the difficult Mount KITCHENER. Across the Sunwapta River lie the major peaks of Mounts Wooley (11,168 ft/3,405 m) and Diadem (11,056 ft/3,371 m), and the looming walls of Mount ALBERTA and NORTH TWIN. Thirty-one mile (50 km) north lies Brussel's Peak (10,368 ft/3,161 m) in the Fryatt Valley and the Sydney Vallance Hut, which is a base for climbers. Near Jasper lies Mount EDITH CAVELL.

Guidebooks: Glen Boles, R. Kruszyna and W. L. Putnam, *Rocky Mountains of Canada South* (1979); Sean Dougherty, *Selected Alpine Climbs in the Canadian Rockies* (1991); R. Kruszyna and W. L. Putnam, *Rocky Mountains of Canada North* (1985).

Further reading: Sean Dougherty, *Selected Alpine Climbs in the Canadian Rockies* (1991); Esther Fraser, *Canadian Rockies, Early Travels and Explorations* (1969); H. G. and P. E. Kariel, *Alpine Huts in the Rockies, Selkirks and Purcells* (1986); Murray Toft, *High and Dry, Alpine Huts in the Canadian Rockies* (1984); R. W. Sandford, *The Canadian Alps, History of Mountaineering in Canada* Vol. 1 (1990).

ROGNON

A French word, meaning a rock island, RIB or boulder protruding from a GLACIER. *Fluh*, in German.

ROLWALING HIMAL (Nepal, Tibet)

The Rolwaling Himal is bounded on the east by the Gyabrag Glacier, the Nangpa La (or Pass) and the Dudh Khosi River. The western boundary is the Tamba Kosi. Two impressive double-summited peaks, standing above a sea of 19,680-ft (6,000-m) peaks, preside over the GLACIERS and rhododendron forests of this region shared by NEPAL and TIBET: Gaurishankar (23,405 ft/7,134 m) on the border and, within Tibet, Menlungtse (23,560 ft/7,181 m). Gaurishankar's rocky west walls are visible from Katmandu on fine days, when evening alpenglow saturates the wall. The peak was first climbed via this steep FACE by an American expedition in 1979 that placed John ROSKELLEY and Dorje Sherpa on the summit after a long seige. The same year a British team led by Peter BOARDMAN climbed the southwest ridge. The Nepalese Rolwaling is usually accessed via the town of Barabise. Although Menlungtse lies close to Gaurishankar, because it is in Tibet and under Chinese control, expeditions are required to make a circuitous approach via the town of Tingri on the Tibetan plateau. Menlungtse is a

unique peak, isolated in a GLACIER basin. Eric SHIPTON, who was among the first to see it, wrote, "on every side its colossal granite walls were pale and smooth as polished marble." On a later trek, in 1951, Shipton photographed the now-famous set of purported YETI footprints on the Menlung Glacier. A British expedition to Menlungtse in 1988, led by Chris BONINGTON, climbed the lower west summit (23,042 ft/7,023 m), by the west face. Andy Fanshawe, who summited the lower peak with Alan Hinkes, described the climb in his book *Coming Through* (1990).
Further reading: Jill Neate, *High Asia* (1989).

ROOF   A rock OVERHANG that juts out horizontally.

Roof

ROPE COILING   The following five drawings show how to coil a rope without introducing kinks into the rope.

ROPE DRAG   Troublesome resistance to the movement of the ROPE as it is pulled through CARABINERS and over rock by a climber. (See ROPE TECHNIQUES.)

ROPED SOLO   A term to indicate climbing by oneself, generally used to distinguish from soloing, which often means climbing without ROPE or PROTECTION.

ROPER, STEVE (1941–   ) (United States) This CALIFORNIA writer and editor of the climbing journal *Ascent*

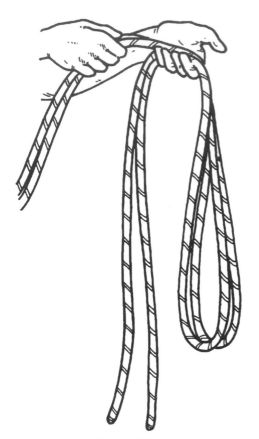

Types of Coils

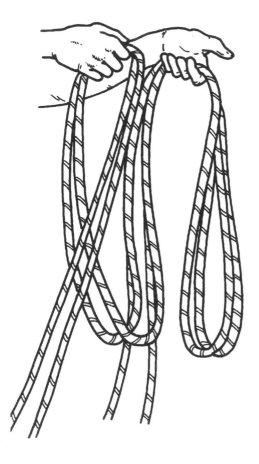

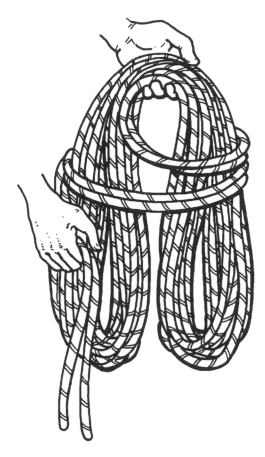

began climbing in YOSEMITE VALLEY in the late 1950s while a student at Berkeley, California. An avid speed climber, gifted on AID and FREE CLIMBING, Roper made the first one-day ascent of Half Dome, in 16 hours with Jeff Foott. He also made the first one-day ascents of Lost Arrow Chimney, with Yvon CHOUINARD in 1961, and the Steck-Salathe on Sentinel Rock, in eight-and-a-half hours, with Frank Sacherer. He made the FIRST ASCENTS of Middle Cathedral north face (VI, 5.9 A4), with Chuck PRATT and Bob Kamps in 1959, and EL CAPITAN west face with Layton KOR in 1963. Roper is best known for his carefully written guidebooks. His *Climber's Guide to Yosemite* (1971), though superseded by modern guides, is still regarded as a useful classic among American guidebooks. With Allen Steck he co-authored *Fifty Classic Climbs of North America* (1979), and, more recently, published *Camp Four,* a historical account of climbing in Yosemite.

Further reading: Chris Jones, *Climbing in North America* (1976).

ROPES Ropes for climbing and leading evolved from the natural hemp, or manila, used by climbing's pioneers, to the triple-strand laid nylon in the 1950s, to the nylon KERMANTLE ropes consisting of a core (kern) and sheath (MANTLE) used today. The maxim "the leader never falls" applied to early climbing partly because ropes and gear used in the early days of climbing were of dubious strength. However, falls are an integral aspect of modern SPORT CLIMBING, and the UIAA set standards for rope and equipment strengths.

The Composition of a Kernmantle Rope

Modern ropes come in many diameters and lengths. Ropes for leading are dynamic, meaning they elongate under impact to absorb a fall's energy. Static ropes have minimal elongation, and are used as FIXED ROPE, when RAPPELLING and ascending and as accessory cord (.2 to .32 inch five mm to eight mm) for threading NUTS. Single ropes are designed to be used as a single strand. They are between .39 and .44 inch (9.8 mm and 11 mm) in diameter. Double ropes are designed to be used in pairs, clipped alternately to protection. Double ropes are between .34 and .36 inch (8.5 mm and 9 mm). Twin-rope technique, which is not UIAA approved, uses two thin ropes of .36 inch (8.5 mm) in the same manner as a single rope. These options are discussed in ROPE TECHNIQUES. Lengths vary from 150 ft (45 m) to 165 ft (50 m), 181 ft (55 m) and 195 ft (60 m). Longer ropes are more versatile. A rope of 330 ft (100 m) (usually .36 inch/9 mm diameter, for double-rope technique) doubled, is useful in mountaineering, especially for long rappels where a continuous thread alleviates the problem of snagging a knot when two ropes are tied together.

In a fall, the rope stretches. Constant stretching reduces elasticity and over time a rope will fail to absorb this energy and break. Even short falls, if they are frequent, as on sport climbs, can damage rope. Ropes that have held a long fall, have flat or soft spots (a sign of core damage), or become stiff or worn, should be discarded. Lifespans for rarely used ropes should never exceed four years; for normal weekend use, two years; for multi-fall use, three to 12 months. Sunlight causes ultraviolet degradation to ropes, and oil and bleach damage nylon. Dirt penetrates rope and *cuts fibers*. Ropes can be cleaned by soaking them in lukewarm water with mild soap, and dried in a shaded area.

Ropes meeting UIAA test specifications are certified, and this information and related performance data is listed on tags accompanying ropes. UIAA-approved rope tests are rigorous, and UIAA-approved ropes are safe. The UIAA specifies that a climbing rope must survive a minimum of five consecutive drop tests. Manufacturers display this rating as the UIAA fall rating. Some ropes claim to hold up to 12 plus falls, but beyond the five falls required by the UIAA, the number of falls listed on a rope's label is a manufacturer's claim. A UIAA-certified rope in good condition won't break during a leader fall, provided it doesn't cut over an edge.

Maximum-impact force, or maximum load transmitted to the falling weight during a test fall (and to the leader during a fall) is an important factor in rope data. The UIAA sets the maximum-impact force at 2,640 lbs (1,180 kg) for single ropes, 1760 lb (792 kg) for double ropes (two ropes side by side). A rope with low maximum-impact force gives a softer-feeling "catch" in a fall and reduces the chances of pulling out protection. However, low-impact force also indicates high rope stretch, meaning that a falling leader will fall further due to elasticity, and may hit obstacles. The UIAA requires rope manufacturers to express maximum-impact force test results as measured on the first drop only, because impact force increases with successive falls on a rope as its elasticity reduces. Actual breaking strengths of dynamic ropes are in excess of what can be generated in a leader fall—approximately 5,000 lbs for .44 inch (2,200 kg for 11 mm), 3,500 lbs for .36 inch (1,575 kg for 9 mm). However, knots, edges and bends through which the rope passes weaken rope strength.

Static elongation measures rope elasticity. High-elongation makes rappelling and ascending ropes difficult. The UIAA maximum static elongation is 8% for a single rope, 10% for double ropes.

The UIAA determines rope diameter by measuring a sample of stretched, weighted rope. Larger-diameter ropes (.44, .42 inch/11 mm, 10.5 mm) last longer, are easier to grip and rappel on, and tangle less than smaller ones. Small-diameter ropes (.36, .4 inch/nine mm, 10 mm) have the advantage of being easier to clip into protection, and they produce less ROPE DRAG. Although small diameter suggests lighter weight, ropes can be made smaller by dense weaving and may not be lighter. To determine rope weight, the UIAA weighs one meter of stretched rope, then expresses the results as weight in grams-per-meter.

Ropes offer the option of "dry" coatings to reduce moisture absorption. Wet ropes are heavier, make belaying more difficult, and they abrade easily, lose strength, stretch more and may freeze. Manufacturer's terms for dry treatments include waterproof, dry, everdry and water-repellent. Silicon and Teflon are the most common water-repellent coatings. Paraffin may also be used, but it is sticky and attracts dirt. Dry coatings may be applied to individual fibers prior to weaving, or by bathing the finished rope in a solution. Dry coatings aside, ropes with tightly woven sheaths typically absorb less water than those with loosely woven ones. For ICE CLIMBING and MOUNTAINEERING the added freeze resistance of a dry rope is a safety asset, as ice crystals inside a rope can act as razors. For rock climbing, coated ropes are slicker than uncoated ones, so they produces less rope drag and are more abrasion-resistant.

Other UIAA criteria for ropes concern the rope's weave—interior knot diameter, sheath slippage, abrasion resistance—and affect handling quality. Soft, smooth-sheathed ropes knot better, produce less friction than coarse sheaths and last longer. They are more abrasion-resistant than stiff ropes. However, stiff ropes are easier to throw, tangle less often than soft ones and are easier when using ASCENDERS as they lift less, thereby easing the sliding action of ascenders. Kinks in a rope jam up belay and rappel devices. (Kinks are introduced into any rope by the twisting action that occurs when the rope runs through a figure-eight rappel device, and in certain methods of coiling such as the lap coil. Using BELAY TECHNIQUES like a Sticht plate and ROPE COILING by the "mountaineer's" or "pack" coil reduces kinking.) Kinks are removed from a rope by running the length of a rope through one's hands several times, or by hanging the rope over the cliff and allowing kinks to twist out.

Further reading: Helmut F. Micoys, "Climbing Ropes," *American Alpine Journal* (1977).

ROPE TECHNIQUES
There are three different rope systems for leading:

Single rope technique uses a rope of .4- or .44-inch (10 or 11 mm). It is light, presents simplicity in belaying, and suits climbs with straight LINES. SPORT CLIMBING and AID CLIMBING use this system. However, on climbs that weave a circuitous route, friction against PROTECTION can cause burdensome ROPE DRAG and may exert a sideways pull on hand-placed protection, levering protection loose. The solution is to extend protection with QUICK DRAWS and SLINGS so that the rope scribes as straight a line as possible.

Double rope technique uses two .36-inch (9 mm) half ropes that are clipped alternately to each piece of protection. The system is heavier than single-rope technique by about 30%, and rope management requires patience and dexterity as rope is constantly fed in and out of a BELAY device. However, this system, which is used in Britain for protecting complex CRAG routes, has advantages. First, two ropes allow long RAPPELS to be made. Second, protection can be CLIPPED in a pattern that keeps both ropes free from drag. Third, if trying to clip a rope into protection while in a tenuous position, double ropes allow the belayer to be ready to hold a fall on one rope, while the leader pulls slack through the other rope to make the clip. Should the leader fall while clipping, the fall will be shorter than if using a single rope, where the added slack will add to the fall. Arranging protection for the SECOND on TRAVERSES is also easier with double ropes. One tactic is for the leader to clip one rope to protection on a traverse, and rig the other directly overhead to give the second a belay from above. This eliminates the second's chances of swinging sideways in a fall. Finally, two ropes are less likely to cut over an edge or in a stonefall.

Twin rope technique is popular in Europe. Again, two ropes are used, but because each is lighter than .36 inch (9 mm) (usually .32 or .35 inch/8 or 8.8 mm) both ropes are placed through protection and treated as a single rope. Advantages are longer rope for descending, greater total surface area of rope, which is safer over an edge or in stonefall, and the option of switching to double-rope strategies in situations like difficult clips or traverses.

For other methods of using the rope as protection see BACK ROPE, PENDULUM, TENSION TRAVERSE, TYROLEAN TRAVERSE. See also ANCHORS, BELAYING TECHNIQUES, FALL FACTOR, ROPES.

ROPING UP
Also known as roping together or taking coils, roping up is a belay technique of tying climbers into a rope at intervals. It is the only sane method of travel on crevassed areas of glaciers. (See CREVASSE RESCUE.)

RORAIMA (Brazil, Guyana, Venezuela)
A remote plateau formation rising from jungles on the borders of BRAZIL, Guyana and VENEZUELA. The formation is 7 miles (11 km) long, 2 miles (3 km) wide and is cliffed all around by vegetated 1,500-ft (457-m) walls and waterfalls, save for a nontechnical route through jungle from Venezuela. Roraima became known to climbers after the 1974 ascent by Britons Mo ANTHOINE, Joe BROWN, Hamish MACINNES, Mike Thompson and Don WHILLANS. They climbed the cleanest section, the overhanging north PROW, in a BIG WALL seige effort, with difficulties to A3. Roraima inspired the Lost World saga by Sir Arthur Conan Doyle.

ROSIN
A sticky substance rendered from tree sap. Once used by European FREE CLIMBERS to increase friction for the fingers, rosin has been replaced by CHALK. Rosin leaves a permanent sticky layer on HOLDS, while chalk washes off easily.

ROSKELLEY, JOHN (1948–) (United States)
Roskelley is America's most successful HIMALAYAN and KARAKORAM mountaineer, and a native of Spokane, WASHINGTON. He has climbed many coveted summits, adding new routes to the 8,000-m (26,240-ft) peaks DHAULAGIRI (26,826 ft/8,178 m) in 1973 and K2 (28,250 ft/8,613 m) in 1978, and repeated the west pillar of MAKALU (27,790 ft/8,473 m) in 1980, all without oxygen. He also climbed Peak XIX in Russia (19,300 ft/5,884 m) in 1974, on the International Pamirs expedition, described in Bob Craig's book *Storm and Sorrow* (1980). He participated in technical ice and rock ascents on previously unclimbed peaks like Cholatse (22,128 ft/6,746 m) in 1982; Uli Biaho (20,000 ft/6,097 m) in 1979, which was one of the earliest high-altitude BIG WALL CLIMBS undertaken; and Great Trango Tower (20,650 ft/6,296 m) in 1977. His impetus on Gaurishankar (23,440 ft/7,146 m) in 1980 and on NANDA DEVI, via the north face and north ridge (25,250 ft/7,698 m) in 1976 contributed to successful American ascents. On Tawoche in Nepal's KHUMBU region, he and Jeff LOWE made a big-wall mixed route in winter 1989 that was visionary in its severity. He received the AMERICAN ALPINE CLUB's Underhill Award, for excellence in MOUNTAINEERING in 1983.

Further reading: John Roskelley, *Nanda Devi: The Tragic Expedition* (1987); Roskelley, *Last Days* (1991).

ROUSE ALAN (1951–1986) (Britain)
After becoming the first Englishman to climb K2, in 1986, Rouse was stranded by a blizzard for eight days in a camp near 26,240 ft (8,000 m) and died. Born and raised only yards away from a CRAG called The Breck—a ferociously fingery urban outcrop in Wallasey, Cheshire—Rouse used to joke that this early proximity meant that "I was doing 6a's before I started climbing. . . ." He developed into one of the most gifted rock climbers of his generation, astounding the Brit-

ish climbing scene of the early 1970s with solo ascents like Suicide Wall and The Boldest, and adding new routes, of which Gemini on CLOGWYN DU'R ARDDU and Positron on GOGARTH had fearsome reputations. In 1970 he studied mathematics at Cambridge, and teamed up with a Scottish student and climber, Mick Geddes, to form a strong winter-climbing duo. They made important WINTER ASCENTS in SCOTLAND, including the second ascent, 12 years after Robin SMITH, of BEN NEVIS's Orion Face Direct (1972). Other Scottish winter routes include: Right Hand Route on the Minus Face of Ben Nevis, and Left Edge of Gardyloo Buttress (both with Carrington); Central Buttress of Beinn Eighe's Triple Buttress (with Alex MACINTYRE); Route Two on Carn Dearg (with Geddes). Touchingly, Rouse was directed to his last major winter route in Scotland, only two months before his departure for K2, by the will of Geddes, who died of throat cancer in 1985. Rouse made 15 expeditions to the HIMALAYA and ANDES. He climbed five peaks over 25,000 ft (7,622 m)—Jannu, Nuptse, BROAD PEAK, Kongur and K2. Articulate and incisive, a raconteur and *bon viveur*, his death was a sad loss for British climbing society.

Further reading: Geoff Birtles, comp., *Alan Rouse, A Mountaineer's Life* (1987).

ROUTE The term given to a unique path of ascent of a rock face or mountain.

ROUTE FINDING The ability to follow a ROUTE either from a guidebook description or TOPO, or to find the best way up a cliff or mountain on new ground. In rock climbing, this may translate as the ability to "read the rock" and understand where natural features lead. On GLACIERS and mountains, knowledge of AVALANCHE conditions, CREVASSES and objective dangers must be "read" and a path picked through them. Practice, common sense, experience and some natural talent are the basis for this valuable skill.

ROWELL, GALEN (1940–   ) (United States) Rowell's rock climbing and MOUNTAINEERING were the inspiration for his well-known outdoor photojournalism. Born in Berkeley, CALIFORNIA, Rowell participated in the 1960s development of YOSEMITE VALLEY, making FIRST ASCENTS of difficult FREE CLIMBS and early repeats of BIG WALL routes. By 1970 he started making longer first ascents, including the south face of HALF DOME (with Warren HARDING), and scores in the SIERRA NEVADA. In ALASKA he climbed the first ascent of the east face of Mount Dickey, and in Asia he made first ascents of Great TRANGO TOWER (PAKISTAN) and Cholatse (NEPAL), and a 285-mile (458-km) ski TRAVERSE of the KARAKORAM. His books include *The Vertical World of Yosemite* (1974), *In the Throneroom of the Mountain Gods* (1977) and *Mountain Light* (1986).

RP The original wired brass micro-nut, named after its German-Australian inventor Roland Paulingk, and introduced in Australia in the 1970s. Paulingk's idea of soldering cable into drilled holes in the NUTS was widely adopted by many manufacturers. (See NATURAL PROTECTION.)

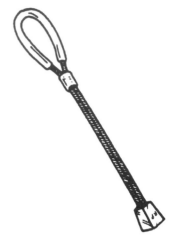

RP Nut

RUCKSACK Another term for a pack. (See PACKS.)

RUNNING BELAY An obsolete term for ANCHOR.

RUN OUT The distance between two points of PROTECTION. A ROUTE said to be "run out" is one that has sparse protection.

RURP Realized Ultimate Reality Piton, a tiny Postage-stamp-sized piton. Now generally replaced by the more versatile BIRDBEAK. (See PITONS.)

RUSHMORE, MOUNT (United States) This South Dakota SPORT CLIMBING area surrounds the presidential monuments at Mount Rushmore National Memorial, on the eastern edge of the Black Hills National Forest, 25 miles (40 km) from Rapid City. Steep, overhanging BOLT-protected FACE routes on crystals and knobs characterize the climbing in this area of heavily weathered and coarse granite/pegmatite spires. Fritz WIESSNER was among the first to explore here, in 1936, climbing the spire he named Olton's Shoulder (5.5), for the shoulderstand he made on Percy Olton to get up the last moves of the climb. As in the nearby NEEDLES area, summiting spires, rather than technical ROUTES, was the prime objective from the 1950s to the 1970s. Application of sport-climbing tactics during the 1980s was controversial—especially because of ground-up ETHICS in the Needles. However, locals agree that RAPPEL-BOLTING is permissable at Mount Rushmore, while the Needles preserve TRADITIONAL ethics. Difficult 5.12 sport climbs were established by local climbers in the late 1980s. Todd SKINNER's 5.14, called Lizzy Beam's Desire, is the hardest route in the area. The climbing seasons are summer and autumn.

Guidebook: Paul Piana, *Touch the Sky: Free Climbs in the Black Hills of South Dakota* (1983).

RUTH GLACIER (United States) This ALASKA GLACIER is rimmed by the most spectacular 3,000-ft (915-m) walls and ice-shrouded peaks of North America. The area is most commonly approached by ski planes out of Talkeetna.

Such peaks as the MOOSES TOOTH, Broken Tooth, Johnson, Dickey, Barille, HUNTINGTON, the Roosters Comb, Silverthrone and Dan Beard, and even DENALI, are all approached from the 7,600-ft (2,317-m) Ruth Glacier. The area is also popular with ski tourers.

RUTKIEWICZ, WANDA (1943–1992) (Poland)
Lithuanian-born mountaineer Wanda Blaszkiewicz Rutkiewicz led and participated in 22 expeditions to the HIMALAYA and Pamirs between 1970 and 1992. She reached the summits of eight 26,240-ft (8,000-m) peaks, the most yet attained by a woman, and dreamed of becoming the first woman to climb all 26,240-ft (8,000-m) summits.

Her first 26,240-ft (8,000-m) peak, EVEREST, on October 16, 1978, was the third ascent by a woman. Other 26,240-ft (8,000-m) peaks were NANGA PARBAT (1985), K2 (1986), SHISHAPANGMA (1987), GASHERBRUM II (1989), GASHERBRUM I (1990), CHO OYU and ANNAPURNA I (1991). She died in May 1992 while attempting KANGCHENJUNGA her ninth 26,240-ft (8,000-m) summit.

She skied, swam and did gymnastics and track and field while growing up in Warsaw. School friends introduced her to climbing in 1961 while she was training with the Polish women's volleyball team for the Tokyo Olympics. She remembered that her first rock climbs were with "great emotion" but "bad style." She progressed quickly and made her first trip outside of Poland to climb in the Austrian Alps in 1964. In 1968 she and Halina Kruger made the third ascent of the long and difficult Trollryggen East Pillar in NORWAY.

Her first high-altitude climb, in 1970, was Peak Lenin in the Pamirs, a month after she married fellow student Jan Rutkiewicz. They divorced in 1973, a year after her first Himalayan ascent (Noshaq), and the same year that Wanda, with Danuta Wach and Stefania Egierszdorff, made the second ascent of the EIGER's north pillar. Other expeditions followed: In the Pamirs, Korzenevyskya (1974); she co-led the first ascent of Gasherbrum III (1975). Her WINTER ASCENT of the MATTERHORN's north face with Irena Kesa, Anna Czerwinska and Krystyna Palmowska was a first for women. She took up rally driving and enjoyed it for the same reason she climbed—for the challenge and risk—following Everest. In spring 1981 a skier crashed into Wanda as she was coming down ELBRUS in the Caucasus and fractured her leg. She was on crutches for almost two years, during which she led an expedition to K2, married and divorced in 1984.

Educated as a computer engineer, she changed careers and began to lecture and make films of her climbs. Her first film, *Tango Aconcaqua* (1985), was of her ascent of the mountain's south face. In 1986 she produced *Requiem* about the tragic events on K2 that summer, and in 1987 a film of her all-women expedition to CERRO TORRE.

The Pakistani government presented her with the Star of Distinction in 1991 for contributing to the development of MOUNTAINEERING, and for encouraging Pakistanti women to climb.

RUWENZORI RANGE (Uganda, Zaire)
Known also as the Mountains of the Moon, the permanent snows of this 16,000-ft (4,878-m) equatorial range feed Lake Albert and the White Nile of Africa. The range straddles the Uganda-Zaire border. It is a perpetually misty range, with a 60-inch (62.4-cm) annual rainfall on the east side of the range and a 200-inch (508-cm) rainfall to the west. This climate and the high elevation has created verdant glacial valleys, though GLACIERS have receded dramatically in recent decades. The rainy seasons from March through May and September through December preclude climbing. These cloud-covered mountains were not seen by westerners until 1876. The Duke of the ABRUZZI explored the range in 1906, and climbed most of the main summits. The most common approach has been through Zaire, via Goma, but Uganda—the traditional route to the Ruwenzoris until Idi Amin's dictatorship—reopened to tourism in 1986. The ancient metamorphic rocks of this range are crowned by the Stanley Plateau, a half-mile (four-fifths km) cap of ice. The north group and south group lie at either end of this plateau. The highest peaks are in the north group. They are Mounts Margherita (16,763 ft/5,109 m), Albert (16,690 ft/5,087 m) and Alexandria (16,703 ft/5,091 m). Ice routes are found on the north face of Mount Albert and the west face of Moebius in the south group. McConell's Prong on Mount Luigi de Savoia sports difficult rock routes.

Further reading: Andrew Wielochowski, *East Africa International Mountain Guide* (1986).

S

SABIR, NAZIR (1955–) (Pakistan) Born in the Hunza hamlet of Dramanji in northwest PAKISTAN, Sabir began climbing as a HIGH-ALTITUDE PORTER but soon became Pakistan's strongest and most ambitious climber, and a partner of Reinhold MESSNER. After assisting foreign expeditions to Passu Peak and NANGA PARBAT in 1975, he learned technical climbing on the Pakistani Army's FIRST ASCENT of Paiju Peak in the BALTORO Muztagh, on which Allen Steck (United States) was an advisor. As a climber on the huge 1977 Japanese K2 expedition, he reached 26,900 ft (8,201 m) on the ABRUZZI Ridge, and his colleague Ashraf Iman became the first Pakistani to summit K2. Sabir was determined to return to K2, but his plans were delayed after his brother, a climber with the Pakistani Army, perished in an AVALANCHE while attempting Dhiran Peak, near RAKAPOSHI. Sabir accomplished a new route on K2 west face, with Japanese climber Eiho Otani in 1981, and received national recognition in Pakistan. In 1982, with Messner and Major M. Sher Khan (Pakistan) he climbed GASHERBRUM II and BROAD PEAK, ALPINE STYLE in the same season. Following a near-fatal avalanche on Nanga Parbat (1983) he concentrated on Nazir Sabir Expeditions, a business specializing in organizing adventure travel in Pakistan.

SADDLE The gap between two peaks or hills.

SAGARMATHA Nepalese name for EVEREST, and the name of the national park in which Everest lies. (See also QOMOLANGMA.)

SAINT ELIAS, MOUNT (United States, Canada) At 18,008 ft (5,490 m), Mount Saint Elias is unique in that its GLACIERS calf directly into the sea. Lying 20 miles (32 km) off the storm-lashed Pacific Ocean, its SERAC-strewn south face has 15,000 ft (4,573 m) of vertical relief. The first observation of Mount Saint Elias as "a high volcano" was recorded in 1741, when Vitrus Bering named a point of land Cape Saint Elias, in honor of the patron saint of July 20. In 1778, Captain James Cook bestowed the name on the mountain. Because of the ease of access for sailing ships, the mountain was nearly climbed twice in the late 19th century. Finally, in 1897, the Italian Duke of ABRUZZI and guides utilized American porters (laden with, among other items, the Duke's iron bedstead) and the famous photographer, Vittorio Sella, on a Himalayan-scale expedi-

tion. They reached the summit after weeks of toil. Their climb was not repeated until 1964. Although frequently climbed, the approach to the Abruzzi Ridge is AVALANCHE prone. Many parties prefer the safer south ridge, established in 1946. Otherwise, the most notable routes are the intricate east ridge (1972) and the ALPINE-STYLE ascent of the south face by Politz and Gove (United States) in 1984. As of this writing, a WINTER ASCENT has not been completed.
Guidebook: Steve Roper and Allen Steck, *Fifty Classic Climbs of North America* (1979).

SAINTE-VICTOIRE (France) This limestone cliff is nine mile (15 km) east of Aix-en-Provence. The most popular CRAGS are Les Deux Aiguilles and Saint-Ser both located at the bottom of the south slopes of Montagne Sainte-Victoire. There are more than 100 ROUTES on each crag. Steep, technical SLABS on micro edges and shallow *gouttes d'eau* typify these crags. Most routes require excellent footwork. Les Deux Aiguilles used to be infamous for its spectacular RUN OUTS, sometimes protected on SKYHOOKS, especially on Guyomar's routes. At Saint-Ser PROTECTION is excellent. Black arrows painted at the base of the routes indicate run-out climbs while pink ones show well-protected ones. Most routes are two PITCHES. It is an excellent spot for winter climbing except when the Mistral is blowing. In 1985, Patrick EDLINGER put up a famous 8a+ here, La Poule. Other testpieces include Levitation, Medius and Barnett from 6c to 7a+.
Guidebook: D. Gorgeon, *Escalade à Sainte Victoire*.

SAINT HELENS, MOUNT (United States) The WASHINGTON State CASCADE RANGE volcano that blew its top in a massive eruption in 1980. Prior to the eruption, St. Helens' 9,677-ft/2,930-m summit was frequently ascended by several nontechnical ROUTES, the FIRST ASCENT being via the south slopes in 1853 by the party of Thomas J. Dryer, the editor of the Portland newspaper *The Oregonian*. The famous eruption occurred on May 18, 1980, after two months of heavy seismic activity. The eruption was preceded by an earthquake that caused the north face of St. Helens to slide away, allowing pent-up pressure in the volcano to release in a lateral blast that wiped out everything in its path for 17 miles (27 km). Then, the summit exploded, sending an ash plume 60,000 ft (18,293 m) into the sky. The eruption was estimated to have a force comparable to 500 Hiroshima-sized nuclear blasts. The south side of St. Helens was reopened to climbing and winter ski ascents in 1987. After the 1980 eruption, the summit is 8,365 ft/2,549 m. The mountain, located 50 miles (80 km) northeast of Portland, Oregon, is expected to erupt again someday.

Guidebook: Chuck Williams, *Mount St. Helens National Volcanic Monument* (1988).

Further reading: *American Alpine Journal* (1981).

SALATHE, JOHN (1899–1992) (Switzerland-United States) A Swiss-born rock climber who pioneered routes in YOSEMITE VALLEY between 1946 and 1950, Salathe also designed rock-climbing equipment. He occupies a special place in American climbing as an inventor, a bold climber and a much-loved eccentric. A blacksmith living in San Francisco, CALIFORNIA, Salathe found himself discontented and plagued by illness in his forties. Harking back to the tranquillity he remembered as a youth in the Swiss mountains, and influenced by readings on vegetarianism, he dispensed with doctors and prescribed his own cure of a diet of fruit and climbing. At the age of 40, Salathe joined the San Francisco Bay Area Rock Climbing Section of the Sierra Club. Because of his age, he was less of a boulderer and more of an AID specialist. He quickly noticed the inadequacies of soft iron PITONS in the hard granite of Yosemite and manufactured hand-forged pitons using high-strength carbon steel from the axle of a Ford Model A car. His pitons were manufactured in a range of sizes under the trademark of the Peninsula Iron Works, a P enclosed in a diamond.

In 1946 the major features of Yosemite Valley were still unclimbed. Salathe was enchanted by the Lost Arrow, a striking spire beside Yosemite Falls. On his first attempt he roped into the notch between the spire and the valley rim and used an innovative self-protection solo system to get 100 ft (30 m) from the top before retreating. A week later he returned with a partner, but halted 40 ft (12 m) from the top when his bolt drills blunted. Soon after, Salathe was beaten to the summit of the Lost Arrow by a rival team who threw a weighted line over the summit from the valley rim, 150 ft (45 m) away, and ascended the hanging rope. Salathe turned his attention then to the imposing southwest face of HALF DOME, climbing it in two days with Anton "Ax" Nelson. The climb was among the most difficult done in America. Although the Lost Arrow had been summited, it had not really been climbed, and amid competition from other teams, Salathe and Nelson completed the first true ascent of the Spire over five days in 1947 via the 1,200-ft (366-m) Lost Arrow Chimney. Salathe and Nelson devised special tactics for the ascent. These included leading on a single rope rather than the usual two ropes, and following a PITCH by PRUSIKing up the rope rather than clipping into every piton placement. In addition to his special pitons, Salathe forged a SKYHOOK which the LEADER could perch on rock platforms and hang from in SLINGS. He also used smaller-diameter BOLTS and tempered drill bits for faster drilling. These innovations became standard practice for the modern BIG WALL CLIMBS

of the 1960s. In addition, the climbers trained themselves to climb on only one pint of water a day to save weight.

In 1950 climbers began probing the unclimbed north face of Sentinel Rock. With an experienced young Bay Area climber named Allen Steck, Salathe climbed the face. The Steck-Salathe route is popular even today. Salathe eased out of climbing soon after. He returned to Switzerland where he lived alone in a mountain chalet and subsisted on native plants. During the 1960s he returned to America, but he rarely visited Yosemite Valley, disturbed by the crowds and camping regulations that he regarded as an imposition on his freedom. The SALATHE WALL on Yosemite's EL CAPITAN, climbed in 1961, is named in his honor.

SALATHE WALL (United States) A route on EL CAPITAN in CALIFORNIA; established by Royal ROBBINS and named in honor of John SALATHE, an early pioneer in YOSEMITE.

SALEVE (France) Located six miles (10 km) from Geneva, Switzerland (but in France), this limestone cliff has been climbed on for over 100 years. Saleve is a huge climbing area with a major cliff, 492 ft (150 m) high above the village of Collonges, plus half a dozen other cliffs. The whole area is a mountain culminating in a summit at over 3,936 ft (1,200 m). The Saleve is mostly vertical, providing excellent FACE CLIMBING on rounded EDGES. The rock is polished on the popular ROUTES. Climbing is possible year round, though often cold in January and February. Climbers in fall or winter often look down on a thick sea of cold clouds covering the Geneva basin. Until the 1970s, Saleve was considered a training ground for ALPINISTS, and the cliff earned a reputation for RUN OUT multi-PITCH routes, like the 1976 Arc-en-ciel on the west face. Better-protected routes include Le Fil d'Ariane (7a). The hard short climbs are concentrated in an area called the golden triangle. They include Action et Meditation (7b +), Potion Magique (8a +), Dandy (7c) and Géant Jones (8a +).

SALTORO RANGE (Pakistan, India) Like the nearby Siachen Range, the ownership of this region of the Lesser KARAKORAM has been the object of a border war between INDIA and PAKISTAN. The Saltoro Range rises west of the Siachen Glacier and the Nubra River. It is bounded in the north by the Kaberi Glacier. In the east the range drops toward the Shyok River along which lie numerous BALTI villages like Khapalu. Access to peaks, GLACIERS and passes within Indian-held and Pakistan-held territories in the Saltoro area is restricted due to the armed conflict that has raged since 1984. The principal peaks here are Sherpi Kangri (24,206 ft/7,380 m), climbed via the west ridge by a Japanese party in 1976; Saltoro Kangri (25,394 ft/7,742 m), climbed via the southeast face by a Japanese-Pakistani team in 1962; and K12 (24,364 ft/7,428 m), climbed via the northwest ridge in 1974 by Japanese, and also via the west ridge in 1984 by an Indian army expedition.

Further reading: Jill Neate, *High Asia* (1989).

SANDBAG A colloquial rock-climbing term meaning to deceive a climber into attempting a ROUTE that is harder than it appears. The result of sandbagging is that the climber will fail and be humbled, generally to the amusement of those watching. A climb said to be a sandbag is one having a reputation for causing climbers to fail.

SANDIA MOUNTAINS (United States) This uplifting of granite cliffs rises to 10,600 ft (3,232 m) (the summit of Sandia Mountain) above the city of Albuquerque, in central NEW MEXICO. While the cities 5,000 ft (1,524 m) below in the Rio Grande Valley swelter in 100 degree F (37 degree C) heat, the crests of the Sandias enjoy a mild climate. The area lies on National Forest Service land and some cliffs are periodically closed due to nesting peregrine falcons. Cliffs average 600 ft (183 m), but the Shield is a 1,200-ft (366-m) wall. A limestone band caps the crest of the Sandias. The climbing is typified by long routes following discontinuous CRACK systems.
Guidebooks: John Harlin, *Climbers Guide to North America, Rocky Mountain Rock Climbs* (1985); Mike Hill, *Hikers and Climbers Guide to the Sandias* (1983).

SAN NICOLO (Italy) This valley located in the foothills of the DOLOMITES offers limestone walls and boulders from 70 to 600 ft (21 to 183 m) high. Climbers frequent the area, which lies near the village of Meida in northern Italy, when the summer heat of Italy's lowland CRAGS becomes intense. The area was a SPORT CLIMBING destination of the 1980s, and some extreme landmarks include Heinz Mariacher's Kendo (8b) and Luisa Jovane's Come Back (8a), one of the earliest 8a ROUTES put up by a woman.

SAN VALENTIN (Chile) The highest mountain in PATAGONIA, it is located at 46° 36' South and 73° 20' West in the Hielo Patagonico Norte (Northern Patagonian Ice Cap). Its height was placed at 12,717 ft (3,876 m) by Chilean surveyor Luis RISO PATRON in 1905, but explorers and climbers strove to make it over 13,124 ft (4,000 m). The new official Chilean figure is 12,828 ft (3,910 m). In the 1940s, large German, Chilean and Swiss parties attempted San Valentin but were repulsed by storms. It was finally climbed in 1952 by an eight-man expedition from the Club Andino Bariloche, Argentina, by the west route, (which starts at the government's Hotel by the San Rafael GLACIER). Subsequent ascents were, and still are, sporadic and are made in the Chilean summer (December through February). But in August 1989, a tough Italian party led by Casimiro Ferrari made the FIRST WINTER ASCENT, skiing to the top and back in bad weather. San Valentin is also called San Clemente, but the Chileans call it "Santo Blanco," the White Saint. Information about the mountain can only be found in mountaineering journals like the AMERICAN ALPINE JOURNAL.

Evelio Echevarria
Colorado State University

SARMIENTO (Chile) The most conspicuous and famous, but not the highest, mountain in Tierra del Fuego, southernmost CHILE. Its situation is 54° 28' South by 70° 48' West. It is a massive mountain, 7,369 ft (2,235 m) high,

crowned by two giant ice cathedrals, about one mile (1.6 km) apart. Its GLACIERS descend to the ocean. In 1580, the mountain was christened Volcan Nevado by Sarmiento de Gamboa (there are no volcanoes in Tierra del Fuego), but it was later named after the navigator himself. W. M. CONWAY and Alberto de AGOSTINI attempted it in 1902 and 1913 respectively, but the notorious Fuegan storms defeated both. In 1956 de Agostini returned with Italian alpine guides Carlo Mauri and Clemente Maffei and climbed the main (eastern) peak. In the 1980s, Italian expeditions returned in four successive years to attempt the slightly lower western peak. Only in December 1986 did they succeed. All other expeditions have failed, often without even sighting the mountain.
Further reading: Aldo Audisio, *Ai Limiti del Mondo* (Italian) (1985).

Evelio Echevarria
Colorado State University

SASER MUZTAGH (India) Like the Siachen Muztagh and SALTORO Muztagh, this arm of the Greater KARAKORAM is a region of territorial dispute between INDIA and PAKISTAN, though it is controlled by India. Since 1984 a large Indian military presence, checked by Pakistan forces 30 miles (48 km) west, has restricted climbing here. The area lies south of the Siachen Muztagh and Rimo Glacier, and between the Upper Shyok and mighty Nubra rivers. The Saser Pass, just north of this massif, is on the old Central Asian trade route. The compact range is dominated by four 22,960-ft (7,000-m) peaks that were among the last Karakoram giants to be climbed: Saser Kangri (25,164 ft/7,672 m), climbed via the south ridge by an Indo-Tibetan border police expedition in 1973; Saser Kangri II (24,659 ft/7,518 m), climbed via the northwest ridge by a Japanese party in 1985; Saser Kangri III (24,584 ft/7,495 m), climbed via the northwest face by an Indo-Tibetan border police expedition in 1986; and Saser Kangri IV (24,324 ft/7,416 m), climbed by an Indian and British army expedition in 1987.

SASTRUGI A Russian word referring to wind-sculpted snow formations that are rippled or wavelike in shape. Sastrugi occurs on low-angle snow slopes prone to constant wind. It presents difficulties for the mountaineer or skier because of its crusty consistency and irregular shape.

SAUSSOIS, LE (France) These steep SPORT CLIMBING cliffs are in a canyon, overlooking the river Yonne, 19 miles (30 km) from Auxerre, and 119 miles (190 km) southeast of Paris. There are three main areas: la Grande Roche, Le Paic and Le Renard, all up to 198 ft (60 m) high. The climbs are strenuous and technical, and notorious for their slick, rounded POCKETS which make for hard ON SIGHT ascents. Many great figures of French climbing like Rene DESMAISON in the 1950s and 1960s, Jean Claude Droyer in the 1970s and Jean Baptiste TRIBOUT in the 1980s have established ROUTES on this cliff. Famous routes include Super Loco (6a), Le Super Jardin (6b) and Dudule (7a). The exposed L'Ange established in 1980 was one of the first 7b's of France. Jean Paul Bouvier's famous route Chimpanzodrome (7c +), done in 1981, has since been SOLOED, DOWN CLIMBED, done naked and blindfolded.

SAWTOOTH RANGE (United States) A jagged mountain range in central IDAHO. Most climbing lies within a wilderness area, and access to this alpine area requires long hikes. Rock walls offer remote BIG WALL routes and atmospheric alpine ridges and snow COULOIRS lead to high summits. Forty-two peaks exceed 10,000 ft (3,049 m), with Thompson Peak (10,776 ft/3,285 m) the highest. The solid granite has attracted many pioneers, beginning with Robert and Miriam UNDERHILL in 1934, who climbed spectacular Mount Heyburn (10,229 ft/3,119 m) in 1935, then later Jack Durrance, Paul PETZOLDT and Fred BECKEY in the 1960s, thence modern climbers like the LOWE clan. Other prominent peaks include Elephant's Perch. This peak's west face, originally by Beckey and more recently freed at 5.11, is guarded by a 1,200-ft (366-m) sheet of granite on the south and west. Warbonnet Peak has a French Alps appearance and many alpine rock routes. The Sawtooths are reached via routes 75 or 21. No guidebook exists, but climbing outfitters and guiding services in Ketchum and Stanley, a town on the northeast edge of the range, provide information.

SCAFELL CRAG (Britain) The climbing around Wasdale is of the finest quality found anywhere in remote and impressive surroundings. Scafell is reached from either the coast road and the villages of Gosforth and Santon Bridge, or via Ambleside. Scafell is rhyolite, with plenty of CRACKS for nuts.

The four BUTTRESSES on the north side of Mickledore known as Scafell Crag contain many easy ROUTES with historical appeal. The buttresses, from left to right, are Central and Pisagh Buttresses, Scafell Pinnacle and Deep Ghyll Buttress with three obvious GULLIES between them. One of these, Moss Ghyll, was climbed in 1892 by John COLLIE, Geoffrey Hastings and John Robinson. Collie was required to cut a step in the rock with an ICE AXE to facilitate progress, the "Collie Step," during the FIRST ASCENT of this 415-ft (127-m) route. This route is rated 5.4, but with imagination, no gear and a wet day, their achievement can be better appreciated. A jump in standards came in 1898 by Owen Jones, who led Jones' Route Direct from Lord's Rake, a 215-ft (65-m) 5.6. Another step forward came from Yorkshireman Fred Botterill, who climbed the eponymous slab on Central Buttress in 1903 at an unprotected 5.7. He paused during his historic ascent to doff his cap to a lady before continuing. But the biggest achievement in the prewar period came from Siegfried Herford and G. Sansom in 1914 with Central Buttress a 500-ft (152-m) 5.8, the hardest rock-climb in BRITAIN for many years. Herford was killed at Ypres in 1916.

Post World War I highlights included H. M. Kelly's 5.7 from 1926, Moss Ghyll Direct on Moss Ghyll Buttress. Among the finest routes of the 1970s are Nazgul (5.10d), on the Central Buttress, Saxon (5.10b) by Ed Cleasby and J. Eastham, and Chris BONINGTON and Nick Estcourt's White Wizard, later freed at 5.10d by Martin Berzins.

Guidebooks: Bill Birkett, et al, *Rock Climbing in the Lake District* (1986); Al Phizacklea, *Scafell, Dow and Eskdale* (1988).

SCAFELL EAST BUTTRESS (Britain) This formidable Lake District CRAG stretches southeast from Mickledore and offers steeper, more difficult ROUTES than nearby SCAFELL. The routes reach over 300 ft (91 m) in some places, and PROTECTION is natural. It wasn't until the 1930s that exploration began in earnest. Two figures dominate that era, Colin KIRKUS, whose Mickledore Grooves (5.7) is one of the finest routes on the crag, and Maurice Linnel, who climbed outstanding LINES like Great Eastern Route, up the highest part of the crag, and Overhanging Wall (5.8).

After World War II Peter Greenwood and Arthur Dolphin climbed the magnificent Hell's Groove at 5.9. Don WHILLANS contributed Trinity (5.8) in 1955. By the end of the 1950s the crag had reached maturity, with Geoff Oliver's celebrated Ichabod, 5.10.

Modern climbers have also found new routes here. Pete Botterill and Jeff Lamb climbed Midnight Express in 1979 at 5.10d, a serious and exposed SLAB. In 1976 Pete LIVESEY and Jill Lawrence added Lost Horizons, an overhanging groove that now goes free at 5.11d. Ed Cleasby and Rob Matheson added iShere Khan (5.12a).

Guidebooks: Bill Birkett, et al, *Rock Climbing in the Lake District* (1986); Al Phizacklea, *Scafell, Dow and Eskdale* (1988).

SCHNEIDER, ERWIN (1906–1987) (Austria) Before 1940, Schneider had climbed more peaks over 19,680 and 22,960 ft (6,000 and 7,000 m) than any one else. By profession a surveyor, he incorporated photography into map-making and map-making into expeditionary climbing. In 1928 he joined the Austrian-German-Russian Pamir expedition, collecting numerous peaks over 18,000 ft (5,488 m), including Pik Lenin (23,384 ft/7,127 m). In the 1930 International Himalaya expedition he and Hans Hoerlin climbed Jongsong Peak (24,550 ft/7,483 m), an altitude record at the time. In the 1932 Austrian-German expedition to the CORDILLERA BLANCA he made the first ascent of HUASCARAN Sur (22,208 ft/6,768 m), the highest summit in PERU. While attempting NANGA PARBAT in 1934, a ferocious storm killed nine team members but Schneider survived. He returned to Peru in 1936 and surveyed and climbed in the CORDILLERAS HUAYHUASH and Blanca. After winter-climbing in the ALPS in 1939, he suffered amputations of several toes. During and after World War II, Schneider devoted himself to map-making. He directed the German survey of 8,368 sq yds (7,000 sq m) of East NEPAL (1959–74), during which time he climbed Palung Ri (23,005 ft/7,012 m), in TIBET. At age 77, he finished his last great survey, of the Mount Kenya GLACIERS, in Africa.

Further reading: Hans Kinzl and Erwin Schneider, *Cordillera Blanca* (1950).

Evelio Echevarria
Colorado State University

SCOTLAND Scottish climbing had the reputation for many years of involving huge walk-ins to greasy CRAGS where the visitor would invariably be eaten alive by bugs

(or midges as they are known locally). In reality, Scotland has as wide a range and certainly quality of climbing as elsewhere in BRITAIN, but without the crowds of the south. Its winter climbing is far superior. Scotland's tradition is as old as England's. It is only recently that the grading system has been reviewed, before which time demanding ROUTES were all rated 5.7. Tom Prentice's *Climbing Guide To Scotland* (1992) lists every crag in Scotland and is full of useful source information. Other recommended reading includes the trilogy *Extreme Rock, Hard Rock* and *Classic Rock* compiled by Ken Wilson. (See ARRAN, BEN NEVIS, CAIRNGORMS, CENTRAL HIGHLANDS, LOCHABER, OLD MAN OF HOY, SKYE, TORRIDON. See also SCOTTISH ICE CLIMBING.)

SCOTT, DOUG (1942–   ) (Britain)
After 30 HIMALAYAN expeditions, beginning with a lightweight ascent of Koh-e-Bandaka (Afghanistan) in 1967, Scott is, like Chris BONINGTON, among the last survivors of a generation of postwar British Himalayan ALPINISTS that included Dougal HASTON, Alex MACINTYRE, Peter BOARDMAN, Joe TASKER, Roger Baxter Jones, Alan ROUSE and Don WHILLANS. An early practitioner of ALPINE STYLE climbing, Scott made expeditioning and OXYGENLESS ascents of high peaks a way of life.

Following the FIRST ASCENTS of CHANGABANG (1974), and the British Spur on Pik Lenin (1974) in the Soviet Pamirs, Scott summited with Haston on EVEREST southwest face in 1975. The climb–a high point of British Himalayan climbing—cemented Scott's reputation as a high-altitude climber, and the pair's forced BIVOUAC without oxygen near the south summit exemplified Scott's commitment to a climb. After the FIXED ROPE siege of Everest, Scott moved toward alpine-style ascents. His alpine-style high-altitude climbs include the Scott-Haston route on DENALI in ALASKA (1976), and in the Himalaya and KARAKORAM, KANGCHENJUNGA north ridge (1979), Nuptse north face (1979), SHIVLING east pillar (1981), SHISHAPANGMA west face (1982), Lobsang Spire southeast face and a repeat of BROAD PEAK west face (1983), new routes on Chamlang and Baruntse (1984) and Jitchu Drake in BHUTAN (1988). However, his best-known climb is his first ascent with Bonington of The OGRE (1977) in PAKISTAN. Breaking his legs near the summit Scott crawled down the mountain and survived 13 days without medical help. Scott's failed climbs are often as significant as his successes, like his multi-day alpine-style attempts on MAKALU southeast ridge (1984) and K2 south face (1983), which tackled huge peaks with small, self-sufficient teams climbing with no prior preparation of the route. His books include *Big Wall Climbing* (1974) and *The Shishapangma Expedition* (1984).

SCOTTISH ICE CLIMBING
The chief location for ice climbing in the United Kingdom is Scotland, where the generally higher elevation and colder weather ensures reasonable ice in most years. Probably the best known ice-climbing area in Scotland is the northwest face of BEN NEVIS, at an elevation of over 3,000 ft (915 m). The Scottish grading system begins at 1, which would be a straightforward gully, to 6 and even 7, which indicates a highly technical mixed route requiring a strong faith. Scottish ice spawned the modern ICE TOOLS used today when in the 1960s, Hamish MACINNESS introduced short metal axes and inclined picks. In the 1970s and 1980s more and more climbers were becoming involved in what had been an esoteric sub-sport. Improvements in equipment, publicity and past achievements launched a host of Scottish and English climbers to a rapid exploration of remaining LINES, adding the first grade 6s. In recent years, debate has raged about what constitutes a WINTER ASCENT, indeed, whether snow and ice have to be involved at all.

Other major areas include Buchaille Etive Mr near Glen Coe, to the south of Ben Nevis. Here, Crowberry Gully, is a 1,000 ft (305-m)-long climb rated at Grade 3. To its right is Raven's, a deep forbidding gash that goes at Grade 5, even in good conditions, climbed in 1953 by Chris BONINGTON.

Between Spean Bridge and Newtonmore lies the spectacular Coire Ardair on Creag Meagiadh, which was largely undisturbed by earlier pioneers until after the Second World War, partly because of Raeburn's swift, avalanche-aided expulsion from the gully of Centre Post in 1896. Smith's Gully, named after Robin SMITH, was climbed by Jimmy Marshall and Graham Tiso in 1959, a steep and sustained Grade 5. The gully to its right is taken by The Fly, an equally good 5 of some 600 ft (183 m). Climbed in 1976 over a three-day period, the siege tactics of the first ascensionists, A. Wielochowski and D. Nottidge, were controversial. Further right is North Post, climbed in 1960 by Tom PATEY, a Creag Meagaidh devotee, and "Zeke" Deacon. An awkward Grade 5, it is 1,500 ft (457 m) long. Patey added the direct to South Post in 1962. Right of the Post Face is Staghorn Gully, a long Grade 3 with awkward BELAYS. The whole breadth of Coire Ardair is traversed by Patey's girdle The Crab Crawl, an 8,000-ft (2,439-m) grade 3/4 soloed in 1969.

There are a number of excellent climbs in the northern corries of Cairn Gorm, Coire an Lochain and Coire an t-Sneachda, and its height and location mean that they come into condition earlier than many areas. On the summit of Cairn Gorm the bleakness of the area adds considerably to its dangers during a WHITE-OUT.

The CAIRNGORMS jewel, is the north-east corrie of Lochnagar. The Parallel Gullies A and B are excellent, an outstanding 700-ft (213-m) grade 5 climbed by Jimmy Marshall and Graham Tiso in 1958. The buttress between, another grade 5, was climbed by Patey, Jerry Smith and Bill Brooker in 1956. To the right again is Raeburn's Gully, climbed in 1932 by A. Clark and W. Ewen at grade 3. In 1966 Ken Grassick and party did a winter ascent of Pinnacle Face, then a hard rock climb, at grade 5. The route illustrates the direction winter climbing would take in the 1980s. Finally, the 5.6 Eagle Ridge goes in winter at about grade 5, first climbed by Tom Patey and Bill Brooker.

SKYE and Beinn Eighe, where Mick Fowler has made committing contributions, also offer outstanding winter climbing.

Further reading: Donald Bennet, ed., *The Munros* (1991); Ken Wilson, et al, *Cold Climbs* (1983).

SCRAMBLING   Easy, nontechnical climbing of an ungraded standard, and usually too easy to warrant use of a ROPE.

SCREE   Loose rocks and boulders covering a slope below a cliff or mountain.

SCREE RUNNING   A technique for rapidly descending SCREE slopes in which one runs through fine, loose scree by alternating one's weight from heel to heel, creating a sliding motion. The technique works only on scree slopes comprised of small stones.

SCREW-GATE CARABINER   Another name for a locking CARABINER.

SEA CLIFF CLIMBING   Rock climbing on coastal cliffs facing the ocean is called sea cliff climbing. This aspect of rock climbing presents special difficulties. Ocean swells and tides make access to the base of sea cliffs difficult. Many sea cliff climbs require approach from above by RAPPEL. Decayed rock, poor PROTECTION and territorial behavior by nesting sea birds may also present problems. Sea cliffing began in BRITAIN during the 1880s, when the terrifyingly loose chalk cliffs of St. Kilda, Sark and Beach Head were climbed by Aleister Crowley and Alfred MUMMERY. These cliffs were so loose that the climbers cut steps into them with ICE AXES. During the 1980s British climbers like Mick Fowler returned to these areas and ascended the chalk walls with CRAMPONS and ice axes, using ICE SCREWS for protection. These feats are rarely, if ever, repeated. However, most sea-cliff climbing is on relatively solid rock. British sea cliffing blossomed during the 1950s and in the 1960s when areas like CORNWALL, LUNDY, Great Orme, Little Orme and Craig GOGARTH in Anglesey were developed. The climbs and the reckless personalities of the climbers contributed much to the folklore of British rock climbing. Sea-cliff areas in other countries include the CALANQUES in the French Mediterranean, Jogosaki in JAPAN and the Sydney sea cliffs in AUSTRALIA.

SEARCH AND RESCUE (S&R)   The search, rescue and recovery of climbers and hikers.

Rescues can be categorized as technical lowers, raises and trail carries. In any rescue the first priority is the safety of the rescuer. A rescuer must be BELAYED or tied in at all times. In a lower or raise, an anchor system, rather than a single anchor, should be used. The system should be made up of at least two anchors, connected so that there is a backup if one fails. Avoid excessive slack between anchors. A brake system controls the rope during lowering.

The litter is the best way of evacuating a patient, but improvised litters can be made from a combination of slings. This system cradles the patient in a semi-sitting position. The patient is rigged to hang at the waist level of the rescuer. When using the harness for handles the patient can be pulled away from the cliff and brought smoothly down the face. The "tragsitz" is a back-carrying system rigged from a rope or slings.

Lowering operations are the most complex and dangerous rescues. First, solid anchors are established, then a brake system is attached to the anchor. The belayer is tied in to the anchor. The rope is tied to the rescuer and patient. Clear communications during lowering are important: "Down" is a call to be lowered, "Down, Down" means lower faster, "Stop" means cease lowering. If the operation halts for an unknown reason either person can call "Stop, stop, why stop?"

SEA STACK   A free-standing PINNACLE rising out of the ocean, usually a short distance from a SEA CLIFF. Rock climbing on sea stacks presents similar problems as sea cliff climbing, with the additional difficulties of descending from a summit. As with sea cliffing, the origins of sea-stack climbing are British. From the 1930s onward, the sea stacks of Scotland and the Isle of Man became a focal point for British climbers. The OLD MAN OF HOY, a spectacular sea stack in SCOTLAND is one of BRITAIN's most famous. Areas outside Britain containing significant sea stacks are Tasmania in AUSTRALIA, where the Candlestick and the Totem Pole present steep challenges. The world's tallest sea stack is 1,800-ft (549-m) Ball's Pyramid, off Australia's east coast.

SECOND   The climber who ascends a PITCH after the LEADER.

SEDONA   (United States)   A cluster of sandstone and basalt areas around the town of Sedona, ARIZONA. Areas are known to climbers as Oak Creek Canyon and Red Rocks. Where it is sandstone the rock is soft and the climbing is best characterized as adventurous. Oak Creek Canyon is 16 miles (26 km) long, 2,500 ft (762 m) deep. Around Oak Creek Overlook is a basalt band. Below Oak Creek Overlook is a sandstone area called Pumphous Wash, which sports a searing CRACK, The Ultimate Finger Crack. Elsewhere, west of route 89A are the cliffs of the West Fork. Two classic climbs often repeated here are The Book of Friends and Dresdoom. Around Sedona are many PINNACLES, best seen from a vantage spot called Airport Mesa Vortex where climbing formations of red rock buttes and white Cococino sandstone abound. Among these formations are historic towers called the Mace, Chimney Rock, Earth Angel and Church Spire, some 600 ft (183 m) high. Climbers like Bob Kamps, T. M. Herbert and Dave Rearick first climbed here beginning in 1957. Their route on the Mace is the most popular climb in Sedona. Other climbers who tackled the difficult cracks and soft rocks to scale the major summits during the 1970s were Geoff Parker, Scott Baxter and Ross Hardwick. Spring and autumn offer a moderate climate.
Guidebook: Tim Toula, *A Cheap Way to Die: Climber's Guide to Sedona and Oak Creek Canyon.*

SEILBREMSE   Or Bachli Seilbremse. A compact combination belay-rappel device made of steel, manufactured in Switzerland and marketed in the United States by Black Diamond. (See BELAYING TECHNIQUES and RAPPELLING.)

SELF ARREST   Or ICE AXE brake. A technique for slowing and stopping a fall down a snow slope. The technique depends on the climber retaining the ice axe during the fall. A wrist-loop helps. Whether the fall is head first, feet first, on the back or the belly, the climber must quickly grip the axe in the braking position, which is to hold the head of the axe in one hand and the end of the shaft with the other. The axe is held across the body with the pick pointing outward. During the slide the pick is pressed into the snow, causing the climber to pivot around on it from whatever position to face the slope. The adze is now firmly pressed into the torso just below the collar bone and the weight and pressure of the torso is used to drive the pick into the snow. Care should be taken that CRAMPONS do not catch in the snow and flip the climber out of control again. Slides over ice are hard to stop. On ice, the pick may bite into ice and rip the axe out of the climber's hands. Quick judgement as to how much pressure to exert on the pick is essential. Practicing self arrest on a slope with a safe RUN OUT is advisable for novices.

Braking without an axe is difficult, but essential for survival. Hands and feet can be used to dig into the slope. Assuming a position of pushing outward from the slope on hands and toes can be effective. In a tumbling fall the ice axe is a potentially deadly weapon. Tumbling can be controlled by assuming a spread-eagle position, with the axe held by the hand, away from the body. Once in control, the brake position can be assumed. (See also GLISSADING, SNOW AND ICE CLIMBING TECHNIQUES.)

SELKIRK RANGE   (Canada)   This wilderness range is tucked into the great arc made by the Columbia River as it flows first north and then back south into the United States on its way to the Pacific Ocean. The rugged peaks above Rogers Pass (now easily accessed by the Trans-Canada Highway) in the center of this range formed the birthplace of Canadian mountaineering. When the Canadian Pacific Railway crossed CANADA in 1885, it opened half a continent of mountains to the climbers of the world. The railway chose to cross the Selkirks at Rogers Pass. Soon after its completion, the Glacier House Hotel was built in the shadow of Mount SIR DONALD, the area's most dramatic peak, first climbed in 1890. By 1896 the hotel was a popular destination for climbers. Here, Reverends Swanzy and Green made Canada's first TECHNICAL mountain climb, that of Terminal Peak in 1888. Mount Sir Sandford (11,580 ft/3,530 m) is the Selkirk's highest. It was first climbed in 1912 by E. Holway, H. Palmer, R. Aemmer and the guide Edward FEUZ. The Selkirks are comprised of many mountain groups: the Adamant group (with Mount Sir Sandford) lies north of Rogers Pass and present big granite walls and snow and ice routes; to the south are the Dawson group and, further south, the Battle Range. Glacier National Park protects the Selkirks. Access is difficult, and fraught with areas of dense under brush. In winter, Rogers Pass can receive up to 75 ft (23 m) of snow.
Guidebook: W. L. Putnam, *A Climbers Guide to the Interior Ranges of B.C.* (1975).

Further reading: J. F. Garden, *The Selkirks, Nelson's Mountains* (1984); H. G. and P. E. Kariel, *Alpine Huts in the Rockies, Selkirks and Purcells* (1986); W. L. Putnam, *The Great Glacier and Its House* (1982).

SENECA ROCKS   (United States)   This famous rock-climbing area of the southern United States, in northeast West Virginia, is 37 miles (59 km) from Elkins. The cliffs are quartzite, uplifted so that formations are in the form of 300-ft (90-m)-high fins (ribs of rocks that stick out from the main formation) and SPIRES with vertical strata. CRACK and FACE CLIMBING techniques are typically combined on ROUTES, and loose rock and RUN OUTS are common on the steep walls. Recorded climbs here date back to the 1930s, by Washington, D.C., climbers. During World War II the TENTH MOUNTAIN DIVISION trained on Seneca Rocks. One guidebook relates that during this period soldiers made some 75,000 PITON placements in the rocks. The area was important for pushing standards in America: An early (1960) 5.8 still popular is the DIHEDRAL Triple S, by Jim Shipley and Joe Faint. Several early hard routes of 5.9, 5.10 and 5.11 standard also went up at Seneca. The first 5.12 appeared in 1982. A major formation, the Gendarme, which had seen thousands of ascents, collapsed in 1988.
Guidebook: Bill Webster, *Seneca Rocks, A Climber's Guide* (1985).

SENNEN   (Britain)   Although short in stature, the granite SEA CLIFFS of Sennen provide gymnastic problems. They are located west of Sennen Cove, just off the A30 close to Land's End, in CORNWALL. Among the easier LINES are Demo Route (5.6), Joe Barry's 1943 classic, which is in a uniquely photogenic position. At the other end of the scale is the horizontal roof-crack of Superjam (5.12a), a route more reminiscent of YOSEMITE than England. Climbs at Sennen rarely exceed 70 ft (21 m).
Guidebooks: Pat Littlejohn, *West Climbs* (1991); Pete O'Sullivan, *West Penwith* (1983).

SENTRY BOX   A short, shallow, chimneylike recess in a rock face.

SEQUOIA-KINGS CANYON NATIONAL PARK (United States)   This park, 50 miles (80 km) east of Fresno, contains some of the finest climbing in CALIFORNIA'S SIERRA NEVADA high country. The eastern park boundaries include the west-draining facets (water drains from a peak's west faces) of nearly 100 miles (160 km) of southern Sierra crest peaks. Mount WHITNEY, highest peak in the contiguous United States, stands at the southern end. Summits along the northern crest are generally 13,000 to 14,000 ft (3,963 to 4,268 m) high. Most are granitic. The PALISADES dominate the northern section of the divide for 15 miles (24 km), and to the north they meet the peaks of the Evolution group. All climbing is in designated wilderness, and requires long approaches. The east-west divides branching from the main Sierra Crest also hold prominent peaks, most notably the Glacier Divide at the park's north boundary, and the Kings-Kern Divide some 15 miles (24 km) north of Whitney. The numerous 12,000-ft (3,659-m) peaks of the Great Western Divide run north-south for 20 miles (32 km), northwest of Whitney. Many walls and DOMES up to 2,000 ft (610 m) have yielded technical routes. Notable climbing areas lie in the Kings River Canyon (often termed "another Yosemite"), Charlotte's Dome and Tehipite Dome (on the forks of the Kings River), on the remote Angel Wings, at Castle Rocks, in the Kaweah Canyon and on the Watchtower, near Lodgepole. Moro Rock, a multi-PITCH granite fin 70 miles (112 km) east of Fresno offers spectacular features to climb. In recent years areas in the west of the park, like Courtright Reservoir and Tollhouse Rock, have produced SPORT CLIMBING CRAGS, but they are better known for traditional granite FACE ROUTES.

Guidebooks: Steve Roper, *Climber's Guide to the High Sierra* (1976); Greg Vernon, Sally Moser and David Hickey, *Southern Sierra Rockclimbing: Vol 3, Courtright Reservoir, Sequoia/Kings Canyon* (1992).

SERAC A French word meaning a tower or pinnacle of ice in an ICE FALL or on a glacier edge, formed by the breaking away of ice due to glacial movement. Seracs may be immense, and may collapse suddenly. See GLACIER.

SERANG HIMAL (Nepal) Also called the Sringi Himal, this remote range is located in the central NEPAL HIMALAYA. It is bounded on the east by the Taple La and the Shyar Khola (rivers), on the south by the Shyar Khola and the deep gorge of the Budhi Gandaki (river), on the west by the Tom Khola (river), and north by the Tibetan border. The principal peak is Chamar (23,573 ft/7,187 m), a jagged peak first climbed via the northeast ridge by New Zealanders in 1953.

SEVEN SUMMITS The highest summit in each of the seven continents. They are:

Asia: EVEREST (29,028 ft/8,850 m) in Nepal.
South America: ACONCAGUA (22,621 ft/6,897 m) in Chile.
North America: DENALI (20,324 ft/6,196 m) in Alaska, United States.
Africa: KILIMANJARO (19,563 ft/5,964 m) in Tanzania.
Europe: ELBRUS (18,480 ft/5,634 m) in Russia.
Antarctica: VINSON MASSIF (16,863 ft/5,141 m).
Australasia: KOSCIUSKO (7,318 ft/2,231 m) in Australia, or CARSTENSZ PYRAMID (given both 16,023 ft/4,885 m or 16,503 ft/5,031 m) in Irian Jaya.

Many climbers have "bagged" the seven summits since the first complete ascent in 1985, however, there exists disagreement as to who first gained the seven summits and whether Kosciusko or Carstenz Pyramid constitutes the highest summit in Australasia. Who was first depends on whether AUSTRALIA is regarded as a continent, or whether the islands of the Pacific should be included in Australasia. The highpoint of Australia is Kosciusko, a hill

with no mountaineering challenge. On the nearby island of New Guinea (in Indonesian-controlled Irian Jaya) is Carstensz Pyramid, which requires a major expedition.

When Dick BASS (United States) completed the seven summits with Everest on April 30, 1985, he became the first seven-summiter by the Kosciusko method; when Patrick MORROW (CANADA) completed the list with Vinson Massif on November 19, 1985, he became the first by the Carstensz Pyramid method. Bass's account of the quest is told in *Seven Summits* (1986).

SHAKE OUT A resting place on a strenuous PITCH where one can relieve the stress on the arms and "shake out" the accumulated blood in the muscles of the arms.

SHASTA, MOUNT (United States) This twin-summited volcano of the southern CASCADES rises to 14,162 ft (4,318 m), which is over 10,000 ft (3,049 m) above its Northern CALIFORNIA surroundings. Seven GLACIERS flow off it, including California's largest, the 4.5-mile (seven km) Whitney Glacier. Shasta's moderate ROUTES and southerly location attract thousands to its large-scale and potentially serious alpine climbing. Routes average 6,000 ft (1,829 m) in length, and range from nontechnical snow slopes to steep ice HEADWALLS, crevassed glaciers and class-4 RIDGES. Indian legends and latter-day religious cults surround Shasta in a nebula of mysticism.

Guidebook: Andy Selters and Michael Zanger, *The Mount Shasta Book* (1989).

SHAWANGUNKS (United States) Beside the town of New Paltz, in New York State, is one of the most historic FREE CLIMBING cliffs in the United States. The flawless 200-ft (60-m) quartzite walls of the 'Gunks were discovered by the climbing legend Fritz WIESSNER, in 1935, who with friends (like Hans Kraus, Bonnie PRUDDEN and Bill Shockley) climbed landmark ROUTES like High Exposure (5.6) and Minnie Bell (5.8). Even 5.4 routes of this era remain popular today, due to the clean rock and steep terrain. The Appalachian Mountain Club dominated development during the 1940s and 1950s, and out of this club arose breakaway groups like the infamous VULGARIANS. Routes of 5.9 and 5.10+ were established in the area by climbers like Jim MCCARTHY and Richard Goldstone, whose Retribution and Coexistence (both 5.10, and done in the 1960s) were ahead of their time. John STANNARD emerged as an influential climber in America with FREE ASCENTS of ROOF routes like Foops (5.10+) in 1967. His Persistent (5.11) in the area Lost World was another landmark from 1971. John Bragg's Kansas City (5.12) from 1973 was visionary, but Steve WUNSCH's Supercrack (5.12c) from 1974 eclipsed all as probably the hardest route in the country for many years. Lynn HILL brought 5.13 to the 'Gunks in 1983 with the bold Vandals, and recent years have seen extreme additions by New Yorkers like Scott FRANKLIN and Jeff Gruenberg. The main cliffs—The Trapps, Near Trapps, Uberfall and Skytop—are protected by the Mohonk Trust, and visitors pay a day-use fee. A ban on BOLTING has kept TRADITIONALISM relatively intact in this area, and creative PROTECTION and bold leads are typical. About 1,200 climbs dot the crags. Spring and fall are the prime climbing seasons.

Guidebooks: Todd Swain, *The Gunks Guide* (1990); Dick Williams, *Shawangunk Rock Climbs* (1980).

Further reading: Dick Dumais, *Shawangunk Rock Climbing* (1985).

SHELF ROAD (United States) Important SPORT CLIMBING area located north of Canon City (near Colorado Springs) in southcentral COLORADO. Shelf Road rock is POCKETED limestone. Cliffs are between 50 and 120 ft (five and 36 m) high. Heavily developed since 1986, this was the first area in Colorado to embrace the European sport-climbing ETHIC. ROUTES are established from the top down, power-drills are used for BOLTING, routes are bolt-protected. There are some 400 recorded routes, many in the 5.12 category. Its mild climate make it a popular year-round destination. Most cliffs have untroubled access, being on Bureau of Land Management property.

Guidebook: Mark Van Horn, *Shelf Road Rock Guide* (1990).

SHEPHERD, LOUISE (1958–   ) (Australia) Shepherd was probably the first woman to climb 5.12, with leads like Tales of Power, 5.12b, in YOSEMITE VALLEY (CALIFORNIA), Lord of the Flies, 6b (BRITAIN) and Trojan, 25 (AUSTRALIA), between 1981 and 1985. She also opened dozens of hard routes in Australia. Inspired by women climbers of the 1970s like Coral Bowman (United States), Shepherd began rock climbing at the age of 20 in Australia. She was, in her own words "one of a growing body of women climbers worldwide for whom a part of the pleasure of climbing was challenging some male assumptions about women's place in rock climbing." During the 1990s, disturbed by mining and environmental mismanagement that threatened the cliffs and surrounding land near Mount ARAPILES, she took an active role in the Wimmera Branch of the Australian Conservation Foundation.

SHERPAS (Nepal) This clan of Tibetan-stock people inhabit the KHUMBU and surrounding regions of NEPAL, near Mount EVEREST. Sherpas have become the preeminent porters and assistants on high-altitude expeditions, and thus the term Sherpa is often erroneously used as a generic term for any Himalayan native who works as a HIGH-ALTITUDE PORTER. Sherpas started playing a role in Himalayan expeditions throughout the 1930s. Eric SHIPTON praised them for "their natural mountaineering ability, their constant cheerfulness and their wonderful sense of loyalty . . ." Sherpas of that era include Ang Tharkay, who accompanied Shipton on many Asian explorations, and who played key, unsung roles in the first ascents of ANNAPURNA, CHO OYU and Everest; Pasang Dawa Lama, who in 1938 climbed high on K2 with Fritz WIESSNER; and, perhaps best known, Tenzing NORGAY, a Tibetan who worked with Shipton and who made the FIRST ASCENT of Mount Everest with Sir Edmund HILLARY.

Sherpa help is significant in giving modern Everest expeditions a greater success rate from the Nepal side. Besides carrying loads, Sherpas often lead ahead, establish camps, and are consulted about weather conditions and logistics. Few have advanced climbing skills, but their strength at altitude is unequalled. Often they spend more time in dangerous places than expedition members, most notably the Khumbu ICE FALL below Everest. While earning money has always been the primary incentive for Sherpas, they also share in the sense of adventure. Accomplished modern Sherpas include Pertemba, Sundare and Sambhu Tamang, all of whom have summited Everest repeatedly; Ang Phu, who climbed the complete west ridge of Everest; and Ang Rita Sherpa, one of the great mountaineers of all time, who has summited Everest six times, DHAULAGIRI four times, Cho Oyu and MANASLU, always without supplemental oxygen.

SHERPA TENZING See NORGAY, TENZING.

SHIPROCK (United States) A captivating formation visible for 50 miles (80 km) across the featureless desert, 10 miles (16 km) south-southwest of the town of Shiprock, NEW MEXICO. It is named for its resemblance to a full-rigged ship, and is the peak on which American desert climbing began. Wrote Robert Ormes in a 1939 *Saturday Evening Post* article, "A Piece of Bent Iron," about an unsuccessful attempt on Shiprock, "There is something unbelievable about a rock that could be set within the boundaries of a few city blocks, yet rises more than a third of a mile in height. In the evening you can see a shadow from it as long as Manhattan." Its ascent via the west face in 1939— by David BROWER (of Sierra Club and Friends of the Earth fame), John Dyer, Raffi Bedayn and Bestor Robinson—was a breakthrough in American climbing because it employed technical FREE and AID CLIMBING, complex ROUTE finding on crumbling rock, FIXED ROPE and PITONS on a scale not previously seen in America. This ascent also saw the first use of BOLTS in America. Today, nine routes lead to the summits of this complex peak of volcanic tuff-brechia and basalt. This and other sites throughout the southwestern desert have important religious and cultural significance to the Navajo Indians. Visiting climbers should respect the Navajos' wishes regarding access to climbing areas. In early spring and fall climbs avoid the blistering heat of summer and the sub-zero winter cold. (See COLORADO PLATEAU.)

Guidebook: Eric Bjornstad, *Desert Rock* (1988).

Further reading: Christopher Jones, *Climbing in North America* (1979).

SHIPTON, ERIC (1907–1977) (Britain) Along with H. W. TILMAN, Eric Shipton is one of the two great names in British HIMALAYAN exploration in the 1930s. Born in Ceylon (now Sri Lanka) in 1907, his MOUNTAINEERING career began in 1924 and was consolidated through four successive alpine seasons from 1925 to 1928. His FIRST ASCENT of Nelion, one of the twin summits of MOUNT KENYA, with Wyn Harris in 1929, and of the same mountain's west ridge with Tilman the following year (one of the major achievements of prewar mountaineering), brought him an invitation to join Frank Smythe's expedition to KAMET in 1931. Shipton distinguished himself on this trip, being in the summit party on 11 of the 12 peaks climbed, including that of Kamet itself, which at 25,447 ft (7,758 m) was the highest then attained. His performance in 1931 led to an invitation to join Ruttledge's 1933 EVEREST expedition. Thereafter, continuous activity: the Rishi Ganga 1934; Everest Reconnaissance 1935, which he led; Everest and another sortie to NANDA DEVI, 1936; the "Blank on the Map" expedition to Shaksgam with Tilman, Auden and Spender in 1937; EVEREST 1938; KARAKORAM 1939—virtually the whole decade was spent in Himalayan travel, and the extent of his exploratory achievement perhaps even now lacks full recognition.

He spent the Second World War in government service in Sinkiang, Persia and Hungary; went back for a further spell in the former from 1946 to 1948; and was consul-general at Kunming in southern CHINA from 1949 to 1951. On his return to England he was asked to lead an expedition to reconnoiter the southern approaches to Everest, in the course of which he and Ed HILLARY plotted out the eventual line of ascent up the western CWM to the south COL from a vantage point on the slopes of Pumori. The following year he led a tense and unsatisfactory expedition to CHO OYU. In the late summer of 1952, Shipton having been urged to lead a further expedition to Everest in 1953 and having accepted, the joint Himalayan Committee of the Alpine Club and Royal Geographical Society performed an astonishing about-face, appointing the then virtually unknown John Hunt as leader, and accepting the inevitable consequence of Shipton's resignation.

This sorry episode effectively marked a watershed in Shipton's life. After the break-up of his marriage and loss of his post as Warden of the Outward Bound School at Eskdale, which occurred shortly after the events of 1952–1953, he lived for a time in the rural seclusion of Shropshire, working as a forestry laborer. He was enticed back for a last trip to the Karakoram in 1957, and thereafter developed a new grand obsession with travel in the southernmost regions of SOUTH AMERICA, which absorbed most of the next decade of his life. He died of liver cancer in 1977.

Less interested in technical climbing than mountain exploration, Shipton and Tilman's influence on the modern LIGHTWEIGHT EXPEDITION was seminal. It came about of necessity:

"'Why not spend the rest of my life doing this sort of thing?' . . . The most obvious snag . . . was lack of private means; but surely such a mundane consideration could not be decisive . . . I was convinced that expeditions could be run for a tithe of the cost generally considered necessary. . . . The small town of tents that sprung up each evening, the noise and racket of each fresh start, the sight of a huge army invading the peaceful valleys, it was all so far removed from the light, free spirit with which we were wont to approach our peaks."

When he describes the result of putting his belief into practice in his first book, *Nanda Devi*, the result is a revolutionary text, the tenets of which made him and Tilman, in David ROBERTS's phrase, "retroactive heroes of the avant-

garde." Shipton's later books all share a spare dignity ideally suited to descriptions of sagas from the heroic age of Himalayan exploration, and are classics of the literature. **Further reading:** Jim Perrin, ed., *Eric Shipton: The Six Mountain Travel Books* (1985).

SHISHAPANGMA (Tibet) The 13th-highest of the 26,240-ft (8,000-m) peaks, Shishapangma (also Xixabangma) is 26,398 ft/8,046 m. Its Tibetan name means "the crest above the grassy plain." Its Sanskrit name, Gosainthan, means "home of the gods." Although Shishapangma lies 10 miles (16 km) from the Nepalese border (and 100 miles/160 km west-northwest of EVEREST) the mountain was little known to westerners until 1952, when the first close-range photographs were recorded by Toni Hagen. However, the political climate in TIBET under the occupation of communist CHINA, kept western mountaineers out for many years. The FIRST ASCENT was in 1963, by a 195-member Chinese team who placed 10 men on top, via the north ridge. This route is frequently ascended, and is one of the most popular routes of any 26,240-ft (8,000-m) peak. In 1982 Britons Doug SCOTT, Alex MACINTYRE and Roger Baxter Jones made a new route in ALPINE STYLE up the 7,000-ft (2,134-m) southwest face. This climb was a major breakthrough for alpine style tactics on big peaks. In 1987 an international expedition climbed the northwest ridge and the north face. Left of the British route, the southwest face accommodated two more alpine-style routes, one by Yugoslavs in 1989, the other by Jean TROILLET, Erhard LORETAN and Voytek KURTYKA in 1990. **Further reading:** Doug Scott, *The Shishapangma Expedition* (1984).

SHIVLING (India) Though this MATTERHORN-shaped peak of the GANGOTRI REGION is, at 21,467 ft/6,543 m, comparatively low, a network of difficult ROUTES—many climbed in ALPINE STYLE—cover it. Shivling lies near the holy town of Gangotri at the end of the Bhagirathi arm of the Ganges. The north ridge, east and south faces, look toward the Gangotri Glacier; the west face rises above the Meru Glacier. Flawless granite and steep ICE FIELDS characterize climbing on Shivling. Its name in Hindi refers to the God Shiva's lingam, or penis. The peak has two summits, the southwest summit (first climbed by Chris BONINGTON and Jim Fotheringham in 1983) is slightly lower than the main northeast summit. A large Indo-Tibetan border police expedition made the FIRST ASCENT of the northeast summit via the icy west face and ridge in 1961. The north ridge was climbed in 1980 by a Japanese expedition, who fixed much rope over a circuitous route. The east pillar was climbed in alpine style in 1981 by Doug SCOTT, Georges Bettembourg, Rich White and Greg Child, who traversed the peak via the west face. LIGHTWEIGHT EXPEDITIONS continued to focus on Shivling, with TRAVERSES down the original route usual. Most routes were the product of numerous attempts by other parties. In 1984 a Spanish group climbed the rocky south BUTTRESS; in 1986 Australians climbed the southwest ridge to the southwest summit; the dramatic direct northeast face was climbed by

Spaniards in 1986; the equally imposing northwest face fell to Czechs in 1987; also in 1987 Yugoslavs climbed the icy northeast face to connect with the upper east pillar.
Further reading: Greg Child, *Thin Air: Encounters in the Himalaya* (1990).

SHOULDER BELAY An outmoded belay in which the belayer takes in ROPE over the back and shoulder. Not recommended. (See BELAYING TECHNIQUES.)

SHUKSAN, MOUNT (United States) Rising to 9,127 ft (2,782 m) in western WASHINGTON STATE, east of the city of Bellingham, this is an impressively glaciated peak of sharp RIDGES with several challenging alpine ROUTES. Shuksan's FIRST ASCENT is given to Asahel Curtis and W. Montelius Price, in 1906. They climbed the far southwest face via the Sulphide Glacier. Most routes on Shuksan are climbed from camp to summit and back in a day. The routes are complex though, and GLACIER travel skills are essential as seven glaciers tumble down its green-schist rock spurs. Among the numerous routes on Shuksan, the Price Glacier on the north face is popular. Nooksack Tower, a craggy satellite summit of Shuksan first climbed by Fred BECKEY and C. Schmidtke in 1946, has some steep TECHNICAL routes to its summit.
Guidebook: Fred Beckey, *Cascade Alpine Guide, Rainy Pass to Fraser River* (1981).

SIDE PULL A vertical handhold which one leans away from.

SIERRA NEVADA (United States) This range forms an unbroken watershed for over 350 miles (560 km) in CALIFORNIA near the Nevada border, with summits up to 12,000 ft (3,659 m). The High Sierra country above timberline is well known for alpine granite climbing and fair summer weather, with ROUTES averaging 1,500 to 2,000 ft (457 to 610 m) high.

The 1863–70 California Geological Survey, headed by Josiah Whitney, first explored the high peaks, and of this party Clarence King was the most enthusiastic climber. John MUIR also made many early climbs, and the Sierra's benevolent beauty inspired his influential conservation ethic. His Sierra Club, formed in 1892, was significant partly for mapping and climbing the high country, with many trips led by Joseph N. LeConte. By the 1930s Robert UNDERHILL and especially Norman CLYDE were prominent climbers, with Clyde making more Sierra FIRST ASCENTS than anyone. Warren HARDING was probably the first to take YOSEMITE-style BIG WALL techniques to the mountains when he led the first ascent of the east face of Keeler Needle, near Mount WHITNEY, in 1960.

The most popular peaks can be grouped, from south to north, as follows:

1) The Mount Whitney group is capped by the highest peak in the contiguous United States, and includes at least six others over 14,000 ft (4,268 m), and at least 23 over 13,000 ft (3,963 m). Besides Whitney, prominent peaks include Mount Russell, Mount Williamson and Lone Pine Peak.
2) The Mount Pinchot-Kearsarge Pass area includes many peaks up to nearly 14,000 ft (4,268 m), including Mount Clarence King and popular Charlotte Dome.
3) The PALISADES raise the crest to over 14,000 ft (4,268 m) again, and are the most popular area for technical ALPINE CLIMBING.
4) The Evolution-Abbot group is best known for ice COULOIRS on Mounts Mendel and Darwin, though the area includes numerous rock routes on many peaks over 13,000 ft (3,963 m), including Bear Creek Spire and Mount Humphreys.
6) The Ritter Range, southeast of Yosemite, is made of surprisingly firm metamorphic rock. Its sharp summits rise to 13,157 ft (4,011 m), and include the popular Minarets.
7) The Conness-Matterhorn-Incredible Hulk peaks are the northernmost group of high peaks, with walls to 1,500 ft (457 m) high.

The Sierra's lower elevations hold innumerable granitic CRAGS and DOMES, those in Yosemite Valley being the most famous. Other areas include The NEEDLES in the far south, Domelands south of Mount Whitney, the Whitney Portal area, various in SEQUOIA NATIONAL PARK, walls of the Kings River and nearby Courtright Reservoir, domes in the San Joaquin canyon, TUOLUMNE MEADOWS northeast of Yosemite Valley and numerous accessible crags in the Lake Tahoe area.
Guidebooks: Salley Moser and Greg Vernon, *Southern Sierra Rockclimbing* Vol. 1 (1992); Steve Roper, *Climber's Guide to the High Sierra*.

SIKKIM HIMALAYA (India) This tiny, mountainous HIMALAYAN country wedged between NEPAL to the west, TIBET to the north and BHUTAN to the east is under Indian administration. Undoubtedly, the main peak of the region is KANGCHENJUNGA (28,169 ft/8,586 m), with its east face rising above the 15-mile (24-km)-long Zemu Glacier. Most ascents of this peak are from Nepal, but the 1977 Indian ascent of the northeast spur and north ridge from Sikkim is one of the high points in Indian MOUNTAINEERING. Sikkim's mountains are divided into the Dongkya Range to the northeast; the Chorten Nyima Range sharing the Tibetan frontier in the north; the KANGCHENJUNGA HIMAL, which lies in Nepal and Sikkim; and the Singalila and Western Sikkim regions along the Nepal-Sikkim border in the southwest. Although these ranges are easily accessible through INDIA, geographical restrictions arising from CHINA's 1950 invasion of Tibet and the India-China war of 1962 hamper entry for westerners. Sikkim was popular with western climbers in the first half of the century. Among them, Eric, SHIPTON, H. W. TILMAN, and G. O. DHYRENFURTH explored Sikkim during the 1930s. Two of the more significant peaks climbed during this period were Kabru (24,125 ft/7,353 m), by C. R. Cooke, and Kirat Chuli (formerly Tent Peak; 24,165 ft/7,365 m), by Germans. Since the closure of Sikkim to foreign climbers, Indian police and

military expeditions have made many FIRST ASCENTS in Sikkim. Most expeditions favor the post-MONSOON season for climbing.
Further reading: S. Mehta and H. Kapadia, *Exploring the Hidden Himalaya* (1990).

SIMU-CLIMBING   Also simultaneous climbing, meaning climbing together or moving together. On easy rock or alpine terrain experienced climbers sometimes forsake BELAYS and climb together. Simu-climbing is not soloing, because the climbers are connected by the ROPE with PROTECTION between them, placed by the LEADER and removed by the SECOND. Moving like this, confident parties may climb great distances rapidly.

SINGLE ROPE TECHNIQUE   The technique of using one lead line. See ROPE TECHNIQUES.

SIR DONALD, MOUNT (Canada)   This striking peak of 10,818 ft (3,298 m) towers above the Rogers Pass in the heart of the SELKIRK Mountains. The rock is good quality quartzite, and is the centerpiece of what was the birthplace of Canadian MOUNTAINEERING. The mountain was first climbed in 1890 by visiting Swiss alpinists Emil Huber and Carl Sulzer. The northwest ARETE, pioneered by E. Tewes with guides C. Bohren and Ed FEUZ, Jr., has now become the classic ROUTE. The FIRST WINTER ASCENT was done by Fred BECKEY, O. Beckstead, A. Bertulis and D. Liska in 1965. The mountain was originally referred to as Syndicate Peak but was named to honor Donald A. Smith, Lord of Strathcona, who organized the financing for the Canadian Pacific Railway.
Guidebook: W. L. Putnam, *A Climbers Guide to the Interior Ranges of B.C. South* (1975); Steve Roper and Allen Steck, *Fifty Classic Climbs of North America* (1979).

SIURANA   (Spain)   This cluster of steep limestone CRAGS, 19 miles (30 km) west-northwest of Torragona, is regarded as among northern Spain's best rock-climbing areas. Just a few of its many short crags are developed. The steepest walls offer EDGES and seams through BULGES and ROOFS, with very TECHNICAL moves. Most crags are south-oriented, making the area best for late fall and early spring climbing. Two of the premiere areas are Can Rebotat, a 229-ft (70-m) pillar with routes up to 8a, and Can Gans Dionas. A *refugio* (hut) lies near the crags.
Guidebook: Nico and Leuehnser Mailander, *Sun Rock.*

SKINNER, TODD   (1958–   ) (United States)   Born into a family of professional outdoorsmen, in WYOMING, this sometime hunting guide, horseshoer, cowboy and fulltime rock climber was one of the first American climbers to break with TRADITIONALIST styles and use SPORT CLIMBING tactics to create FREE CLIMBS in the early 1980s. Skinner has climbed hundreds of new ROUTES—some of them 5.14—across the world, and was among the first Americans to compete in CLIMBING COMPETITIONS, in 1986 and 1987, in Russia and Italy. He was a major activist at crags like HUECO TANKS, Mount RUSHMORE and Wild Iris in Wyoming.

However, his best known accomplishment is the FIRST FREE ASCENT of the SALATHE WALL, on EL CAPITAN in YOSEMITE VALLEY, in 1988, with Paul Piana. On this climb, the pair combined siege and sport climbing tactics to work each PITCH of this BIG WALL route free, even descending from the top to work on some pitches. Also with Piana, Skinner made the first free ascent of the north face of Mount Hooker in the WIND RIVER RANGE of Wyoming in 1990, and made free routes on Mount Proboscis (CIRQUE OF THE UNCLIMBABLES) and on HALF DOME in Yosemite.

SKVARCA, JORGE   (1941–   )   AND   SKVARCA, PEDRO   (1944–   )   (Slovenia/Argentina)   Born in Slovenia as Jure and Peter, the Skvarca brothers migrated to ARGENTINA, where they became leading Patagonian climbers by assimilating modern techniques of the 1960s to succeed on ice-encrusted, vertical rock walls that often defeated European experts. No less than 25 FIRST ASCENTS of peaks in PATAGONIA should be credited to them. Cerro "Pier Giorgio" (unofficial name, 8,414 ft/2,565 m) (1963) is the Skvarcas' most technical exploit. Other Patagonian climbs from 1976 include active Volcan Lautaro (11,089 ft/3,380 m), climbed by Pedro and Luciano Pera (1964) and the difficult Cerro Norte (9,679 ft/2,950 m). In 1964, during the FIRST WINTER ASCENT of the east face of Mendoza's Cerro de la Plata (19,305 ft/5,850 m), they both suffered FROSTBITE that resulted in several amputations.

Evelio Echevarria
Colorado State University

Skye   (Scotland)   The Isle of Skye is beautiful, bleak and rocky with huge mountain CRAGS, OUTCROPS and atmospheric SEA CLIFFS. It is dominated in the south by the Black Cuillins. Although 60 miles (96 km) long, the island is heavily indented, and so a climber is never more than five miles (eight km) from the sea. There is lots of rain, so visitors are advised to go in spring and early summer.

Bla Bheinn (pronounced "Blaven" and meaning the blue hill) lies east of the main Cuillin range near Glen Brittle and Sligachen. Bla Bheinn, like the Cuillins, is formed of gabbro, an especially rough rock with unsurpassed frictional qualities.

One of the major cliffs here is Sron na Ciche, half a mile (415 km) long and 1,000 ft (305 m) high, at the heart of the Cuillins above Coire Lagan. It is one of the oldest rock-climbing areas in the world. It has a distinctive feature, the Cioch, a huge protuberance half way up the CRAG. The crag is approached from Glen Brittle and has Skye's hardest ROUTES. Vulcan Wall climbs a slabby face at 5.8, the work of Hamish MACINNES and Ian Clough in 1957, and in the same year these two also produced the classic Creagh Dhu Grooves (5.10b). Murray Hamilton and Mick Fowler took up the challenge in the 1970s, the former climbing Enigma to the right of Creagh Dhu Grooves at 5.10c and the latter adding Dilemma in the center of the Vulcan Slab, also at 5.10c. In the 1980s, Pete Hunter climbed a couple of excellent routes, Strappado Direct (5.9) and Spock, an outstanding 5.10 up the left ARETE of the Vulcan Wall. Routes on the east BUTTRESS vary between 250 ft (76 m) on the Vulcan

Wall and 500 ft (152 m) further right. The rock is gabbro and exceptionally rough.

The Cioch Buttress routes are generally easier and much longer, including a number from before World War I. The Cioch was ascended by Norman COLLIE and John Mackenzie in 1906, two men who dominated the early years of exploration when maps were unavailable. Ashley Abraham, the Keswick mountaineer and H. Harland climbed the immensely popular Cioch Direct (5.6) in 1907. George MALLORY, of EVEREST fame, climbed his Slab and Groove, a 900-ft (274-m) 5.5.

Kilt Rock is a roadside crag of columnular dolerite, located on the northeast coast of the island, north of Portree and a short distance south of Staffin. Neist is another dolerite crag on the westernmost tip of Skye, near Dunvegan. The area's chief attraction is An T'aigeach, the Stallion's Head, a huge PROW rising from the sea. The overwhelming attraction of Neist is Supercharger, a 380-ft (116-m) 5.10b on An T'aigeach climbed in 1981 by Ed and Cynthia Grindley with Noel Williams. Grindley's commitment to the route was impressive, involving rubber dinghy approaches and tyrolean TRAVERSES.

Guidebooks: Kevin Howett, *Rock Climbing in Scotland* (1990); John Mackenzie, *Skye* (1982/1990).

SKYHOOK

SKYHOOK Or CLIFFHANGER. A metal hook used in AID CLIMBING, which is placed over a flake or edge and hung onto. Edward WHYMPER used a metal claw device in the ALPS during the 1800s before modern aid climbers used skyhooks during the 1960s on BIG WALLS in YOSEMITE VALLEY, CALIFORNIA. Hooking represents tenuous, body-weight-only aid climbing. Multiple hook moves exemplify the hardest aid RATING, A5.

SLAB

SLAB A smooth sheet of rock that is less than vertical, usually between 45 and 70 degrees, and which lacks large holds. The body is held away from the rock in slab climbing. It requires balance and a fluid rhythm of movement, incorporating pure friction and smearing from boots, edging on tiny HOLDS, PALMING and MANTLING. The strength and power needed for steep faces or cracks are replaced by finesse in slab climbing. Important U.S. slab climbing areas are in CALIFORNIA: TUOLOMNE MEADOWS, Glacier Point Apron in YOSEMITE VALLEY and TAHQUITZ AND SUICIDE.

SLEDS

SLEDS A useful item of equipment for towing loads across snow and GLACIERS, used with good results in ALASKA and CANADA. Sleds used for this task may be cheap children's sleds, specially made sleds for expedition use, or even tapered sacks made from (polyvinyl chloride) or plastic. When towing sleds in crevassed areas the team should be roped up, with the safety rope trailing from the lead sledder to his sled, then to the anchoring sledder in the rear. Accidents have occurred in which a crevassed person has dragged the sled into the CREVASSE and on top of them, causing injury and complicating rescue.

SLEEPING BAGS AND INSULATED CLOTHING

Sleeping bags and insulated clothing retain warmth by placing a layer of insulation between the body and the elements, trapping a layer of still air among insulating (fill) material. If this insulation contains enough tiny pockets of dead air, then the convection currents that cause warm air to rise and pass toward cold air stop rising, leaving pockets of dead air that remain warm as long as we generate body heat. This property is known as thermal insulation. The construction techniques that make use of thermal insulation apply to all insulated clothing, such as sleeping bags, duvets and down suits.

The best insulators for climbing purposes are feather down (natural) and polyester fibers (synthetic) like Hollofil, Quallofill, Polarguard and Thinsulate. Down is lighter than synthetic fill by about 35%. It is more compressible and more durable, and it flows around the body more evenly than synthetics, meaning fewer cold spots. Down performs best in cold, dry conditions. On the other hand, synthetic fibers are largely nonabsorbent, nonallergenic and cheap. They retain insulating properties when wet and dry quicker than down. In damp conditions, down soaks up water like a sponge and loses thermal efficiency.

To retain thermal efficiency, insulation must be shielded from water both from outside elements and from the body. Waterproofing methods for sleeping bags include using BIVOUAC SACKS and/or shell material of waterproof/breathable fabrics like Entrant, GORE TEX, Supplex or Versatech to repel external moisture. VAPOR BARRIER LINERS placed inside a sleeping bag stop insulation from soaking water from damp clothing. VBLs, which can be used in clothing and sleeping bags, increase warmth by 15 degrees F (−9 degrees C), by trapping transpired moisture and raising humidity inside the bag until the liner is moist enough for transpiration to stop. VBLs can feel clammy, however. Sealing seams of waterproof shells with seam-sealing glue reduces water penetration. Removing damp clothes and replacing them with dry clothes before getting into a bag is also helpful.

Manufacturers rate bags in terms of warmth. This is not an industry standard, and manufacturers use different systems. People have different tolerances to cold. In general, lightweight bags suitable for spring, summer and autumn are rated at around 5 degrees F (−15 degrees C). Winter bags are rated at around 0 to −5 degrees F (−18 to −14 degrees C). Bags for extreme cold are rated around −15 to −25 degrees F (−26 to −31 degrees C). Bags and clothing covered in waterproof/breathable materials are warmer, as these fabrics are windproof and slow the loss of warm air through the shell. Another method of increasing warmth and reducing weight is the use of Radiant Heat Barriers (RHB, or fabric coated with metallic applications), which reflect body heat. Manufacturers claim RHB linings increase a bag's temperature by 10 degrees F (−12 degrees C).

Down has the greatest warmth-to-weight ratio of any insulator. Down bags and garments use tunnel-shaped compartments called baffles to contain the down. Sewn-through quilted baffles lose heat through stitching, but baffles form a barrier between the sleeper and the outside elements. Baffles may be box-shaped, slant-shaped or V-shaped. In sleeping bags, features like hoods, draft tubes and draft collars seal off zippers and the bag opening. Instead of using baffles, synthetic bags are layered across the body in batts, sometimes sewn-through, sometimes overlapping like shingles, sometimes layered. Streamlined cuts increase thermal efficiency by keeping insulation close to the skin. A mummy-shaped bag—a body-hugging design, narrower at the legs and wider at the torso—makes the best use of insulation by keeping it close to the skin.

Bags and insulated clothing should be stored so they can loft freely. Storing them inside a stuffsack will damage the insulation. The safest way to clean insulated garments is to soak and hand wash them in warm water with mild soap, then dry them in the sun. (See CLOTHING FOR MOUNTAINEERS.)

SLESSE, MOUNT (Canada) This 7,800-ft (2,378-m) sentinel of the NORTH CASCADE Range lies just north of the United States–Canadian boundary, in BRITISH COLUMBIA, near the town of Hope. It is among the hardest of the Cascades' peaks, due to its ROUTES being long rock climbs, on metamorphic phyllite and granodiorite. Steep FACES and BUTTRESSES, with pocket GLACIERS of diminishing size guard its northern aspect. The easier ways up are from the west. Slesse was first scaled via a northerly system of COULOIRS and LEDGES in 1927 by Stan Henderson, Mills Winram and Fred Parkes. In 1956 a passenger plane crashed into Slesse, killing 62. Wreckage is still visible below the east face. About seven independant routes reach its craggy summit, but the most famous route is the 2,200-ft (670-m) northeast buttress, climbed in 1963 by Fred BECKEY, Eric Bjornstad and Steve Marts. As a free route the buttress offers 5.10 climbing and is one of the finest in the Northwest. In winter the buttress is heavily iced. Its FIRST WINTER ASCENT was by Kit Lewis and Jim Nelson in 1985, though Slesse's very first ascent was in 1955, by Fips Broda and John Dudra.
Guidebook: Fred Beckey, *Cascade Alpine Guide* (1981).

SLIDER An item of NATURAL PROTECTION, combining aspects of the tapered wedge and the SPRING-LOADED CAMMING DEVICE. Developed by Metolius Mountain Products (United States) in the 1980s.

SLINGS A loop of either tubular WEBBING or ROPE, used for extending ANCHORS or RUNNERS, slinging BOLLARDS, and making PRUSIKS. Webbing slings are usually of half, nine-sixteenths, or one-inch (1.27, 1.52 or 2.54 cm) tubular or flat webbing, sewn with industrial strength bar tacks or knotted with a tape knot or double fisherman's knot (see KNOTS). Rope slings are .2 to .36 inch (five to nine mm) KERNMANTLE accessory cord, tied with a double fisherman's knot. For prusiking, .28 to .32 inch (seven to eight mm) rope or nine-sixteenths-inch (1.52 cm) tubular webbing works best. For runner or anchor slings, .32 to .36 inch (eight to nine mm), dynamic rope or one-inch (2.54 cm) tubular webbing is strongest.

SLOVENIA Climbing in Slovenia ground to a halt since 1991 with the civil war that has ravaged the former Yugoslavia and left the independent countries of Bosnia Herzogovina, Serbia, Croatia and, in the north, Slovenia, where most of the climbing is located. Slovenia has produced notable alpinists like S. Karo, J. Jeglic and Sveticic Slave and controversial ones like Tomo CESEN. The Julian Alps are in the north. The most famous rock-climbing area is Paklenica, a 984-ft (300-m) limestone gorge, compared to the VERDON in France. It lies two miles (three km) from the Adriatic Sea, in the wilderness of the Dinarique Mountains, near the village of Starigrad, and 28 miles (45 km) from the city of Zadar. The gorge originates at Velebit Mountain (5,763 ft/1,757 m). The main walls are called Bebeli Kuk and Anica Kuk. ROUTES are rated from 4 to 8c (French). Climbing began here in the 1940s. In the 1970s the Slovenian Francek Knez climbed many long routes here. By the 1980s FREE CLIMBING ETHICS arrived, and short hard SPORT CLIMBS, often established by German visitors, appeared alongside the long routes, which are often protected by rusting PITONS. The hardest sport climb currently is Il Maratoneta (8c) by Manolo (Maurizio Zanolla) in 1987. The Remy brothers have produced big wall routes up to 7c on the west face of Anica.

SMEARING Or FRICTION CLIMBING. A FREE CLIMBING technique where the boot is "smeared," or placed flat over a rounded or sloping HOLD that is gripped by friction from

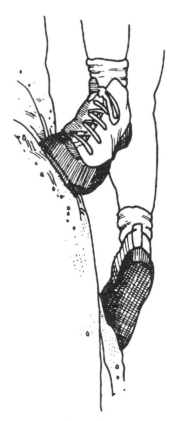

Smearing

boot rubber, as opposed to EDGING techniques that utilize distinct edges on rock. Smearing is used in SLAB climbing.

SMITH, ROBIN **(1939–1962) (Britain)** In the four years before his death, which took place while he was descending Pic Garmo in the Pamirs with Wilfrid Noyce in 1962, Robin Smith had established himself as the brightest, boldest and best of young Scottish climbers in whatever medium he chose to engage. On rock, his new routes include some of the major classics of the Highlands: Shibboleth, Yo-Yo, The Bat; on ice, Smith's Gully on Creag Meaghaidh and Smith's Route on Gardyloo Buttress, BEN NEVIS, give the measure of the man. His death cut short a career of richer promise than perhaps any other figure in British postwar MOUNTAINEERING possessed. A gifted, stylish and playful writer, his all-too-small output of essays has been much anthologized.

SMITH ROCKS **(United States)** This 100 to 300-ft (30- to 91 m) OUTCROP rising above farmlands and surrounded by extinct volcanic cinder-cones in west-central OREGON (20 miles/32 km north of Bend) is the area where American SPORT CLIMBING began, during the 1980s. Although the area is compact, an abundance of small EDGES and gas-pockets on the volcanic welded tuff and the artful eyes of first-ascensionists have resulted in a gymnasium of BOLT-PROTECTED FREE CLIMBING. Images of climbers on the orange walls and multi-hued SPIRES, like the 300-ft (91m) tower of the Monkey Face, have graced every international climbing magazine. In addition to the welded tuff walls, basalt CRACK and FACE routes rise above the Crooked River, facing the welded tuff CRAGS. The area is frequented by climbers year-round, with only midsummer being too hot for climbing.

Three undisputed 5.14 routes—To Bolt or Not To Be, and White Wedding climbed by J. B. TRIBOUT (France) and Scarface, climbed by Scott FRANKLIN (United States), are found in the Dihedrals Area. These routes of the latter-1980s are America's hardest sport climbs. But it was local climber Alan WATTS who first tapped the gymnastic potential of Smith Rocks. From 1980 to 1985 Watts was virtually peerless in his technical abilities and dedication to creating challenging routes. Through his influence 5.13 sport-climbing and EURO-STYLE tactics gained a footing in America—a fact that initially earned him criticism from TRADITIONAL-ISTS, but now is regarded as a great achievement.
Guidebook: Alan Watts, *Smith Rocks State Park Climber's Guide* (1992).

SMITH, W. P. HASKETT **(1859–1946) (Britain)** British rock-climbing is generally said to begin with Walter Parry Haskett Smith's ascent of NAPES Needle on Great Gable in Cumbria, Great Britain in 1886. As historical fact this is nonsense, but as evidence of a focused recreational approach to rock, it has some validity. The climb captured the public imagination and set rock climbing on course to develop as a separate sport from its parent one of alpine MOUNTAINEERING. In his *Alpine Journal* obituary for Haskett, Geoffrey Winthrop YOUNG wrote that "Haskett rocketed in

on his own, fascinated by the single adventure of climbing rocks," and added, "to the older mountaineers, of the wider view, English rocks were then still only a happy preparation for greater mountains, a pass-time in the off seasons." The *Alpine Journal* review of his first—and probably the world's first—rock-climbing guidebook, a marvel of playful erudition which appeared in 1894, underlines how revolutionary was Haskett's departure: "This little work . . . marks a distinct epoch in British holiday-making. It admits publicly, if not proudly, that there is a class of travellers who 'climb for climbing's sake . . .' "

Haskett Smith was born in Kent, went to Eton and Oxford (where he read law and in the long jump achieved a distance of nearly 25 ft/7.5 m—a leap that could not, however, be counted an official world record, because it was done in practice), after which he was called to the Bar at Lincoln's Inn, though he never practiced, being of ample independent means. In 1881 he "procured the Ordnance map of Cumberland, found that there was on it a sombre region thronged with portentous shadows; found that there was an inn at a spot which seemed the centre of all this gloom, and finally engaged rooms at Dan Tyson's for a month." The inn was at Wasdale Head, Haskett's stay of 1881 lasted two months, and from it the sport of rock climbing as we know it came about. For the next 10 years he had it his own way: Steep Ghyll in 1884, Napes Needle in 1886, Great Chimney on Pillar in 1887, the Cyfrwy Arete in 1888, north climb on Pillar Rock in 1891 and the Great and East Gullies of Craig y Cau in 1895.

Apart from British climbing, for which his enthusiasm continued lifelong, he traveled extensively: in the ALPS, in NORWAY, SOUTH AMERICA, the Pyrenees, MONTSERRAT, North Africa, Greece, the Balkans and the ROCKIES. In 1936, to commemorate the 50th anniversary of its first ascent, he climbed the Napes Needle again at the age of 77. His death came 10 years later, in March 1946 at Parkstone in Dorset, to which he had retired, little-visited, isolated and in failing health, after the bombing of his London house.
Further reading: W. P. Haskett Smith, *Rock Climbing in the British Isles* (1894, 1986).

SMYTHE, FRANK **(1900–1949) (Britain)** One of MOUNTAINEERING's great popularizing authors, Smythe wrote 25 books based on his prolific mountaineering career. Invalided out of the Royal Air Force in 1927 and cautioned to walk upstairs slowly for the rest of his life, Smythe's response was to head for the ALPS and, with Graham Brown, climb three new ROUTES on the Brenva Face of MONT BLANC. In 1929 he was with Jack LONGLAND on the FIRST ASCENT of the West Buttress of CLOGWYN D'UR ARDDU. In 1931 he led the expedition that climbed KAMET—the first 25,000-ft (7,622-m) peak to be climbed. Smythe reached the top. After that, his name became ubiquitous in the annals of HIMALAYAN mountaineering through the 1930s. He established a reputation as being tough at altitude, and reached 28,000 ft (8,537 m) on the north ridge of EVEREST in 1933. The first "professional" mountaineer, he made a living from lecturing, writing and photography on the subject. After the Second World War he made two fruitful forays to the CANADIAN ROCKIES, and was set to return to the Himalaya in 1949, but died of a brain hemorrhage on the eve of departure.

Further reading: Harry Calvert, *Smyth's Mountains* (1985).

SNAP LINK An old name for a CARABINER.

SNARG A type of drive-in ice screw. (See ICE SCREWS.)

SNOW AND ICE, PROPERTIES OF The shape and temperature of snow crystals influence the safety of a snow slope, the formation of ice and the ease or difficulty over which these surfaces may be climbed or skied. The density of snow or ice, or the amount of air between snow or ice crystals, also affects the ease with which a climber may travel. For example, powder snow has a lot of air between the crystals, making it fluffy, unconsolidated and arduous to break trail through. The denser FIRN snow, or NEVE, has been consolidated by compression and melting forces, and makes for easy CRAMPONING. When GLACIER ice or water ice is too dense, it is "bulletproof" to ICE TOOLS and shatters into DINNERPLATES when struck. Temperature affects snow both favorably and unfavorably. A sudden rise in temperature of four or five degrees C usually results in an unstable snow slope. But, a rise in temperature may also "clean" (AVALANCHE) a heavily laden snow slope and make it safe within a day, or a temperature rise may turn brittle ice PLASTIC, which produces an ideal ice-climbing surface. The strength of a layer of snow depends on the shape and size of interlocking snow crystals. Old snow is very strong, new snow is weak. Snow also creeps downhill like a liquid, moving as a mass, until a layer shears off. It may also be brittle, break and glide down a slope. The process of snow turning to ice is called FIRNIFICATION, and occurs when the air spaces between crystals seal off from each other and the mass becomes airtight. Ice changes constantly with temperature. FROZEN WATERFALLS form from seepage over rocks. Alpine ICE FIELDS are formed by meltwater and by snow compacting under pressure. Sublimation (the process of water molecules changing from ice to vapor and back again) hastens changes in snow and ice deposits. When a warm, dry wind blows over ice, water molecules are carried off without the ice turning to water. Great quantities of snow or ice may seemingly vanish overnight.

SNOW AND ICE ANCHORS See DEADMAN, ICE BOLLARD, ICE SCREW, SNOW BOLLARD, SNOW STAKE.

SNOW AND ICE BELAYS See ICE BOLLARDS, ICE SCREW, SNOW BOLLARDS.

SNOW AND ICE CLIMBING EQUIPMENT See ICE TOOLS.

SNOW AND ICE CLIMBING TECHNIQUES Finesse on snow and ice is a matter of balance, footwork and familiarity with ICE TOOLS, especially the ICE AXE and CRAMPONS. Even on gentle slopes that do not require crampons, the ice axe is a useful walking stick. Some climbers prefer holding the ice axe with the pick pointing backward, others prefer to point it forward. Either way, a leash tied to the ice axe and worn around the wrist makes the tool ready for SELF ARREST in the event of a slip. On crusty snow or NEVE, crampons may be unnecessary and steps may be kicked directly into the slope, with the ice axe acting like a third leg for balance. Steps into snow should be about a third of a boot deep. Whenever the angle of a slope steepens enough to cause consternation, crampons are necessary.

Before the invention of crampons, and even as recently as the 1960s, steep ice FACES were climbed by STEP CUTTING—hacking out footholds in the ice with the adze of the ice axe. Modern ice axes and crampons have eliminated step cutting; however, a few swings of the adze can quickly chop out a restful foot LEDGE when legs are aching from a long PITCH of FRONT POINTING. During the 1960s European climbers refined cramponing techniques. FRENCH TECHNIQUE (flat-footing) arose in this era, but contemporary alpinists agree that a combination of styles works better than adopting one to the exclusion of the other.

When cramponing on easy terrain, one should walk normally, mindful of the hazard of catching crampon points in clothing around the legs and ankles. The weight of the body should be centered over the foot, and shifted from one foot to the other. The flats of the feet should be as parallel to the slope as possible so that the maximum number of crampon points bite the snow. When climbing snow up to 55 degrees, the feet should sidestep across each other, with the toes angled across the slope or slightly downhill. The climber should avoid standing on the edges of his boots, and allow his ankles to roll so all points bite. When TRAVERSING, climbers walk sideways with the feet as flat as possible to the slope. Angling one foot slightly downhill compensates for a lack of flexibility in the ankles.

The ice axe is crucial for balance at steeper angles. It may be gripped in several ways, either by the head and held like a walking stick with the shaft thrust into the snow, or held braced with both hands.

On steep slopes climbing directly up is stressful on ankles, so a more comfortable zigzag diagonal path is struck. At changes in direction, care must be taken not to overbalance. The safest way to execute a switch from a right-trending path to a left-trending one, for example, is to sink the ice axe shaft (held in left hand while moving rightward) into the snow (or, if on ice or firm neve, into the slope); face the slope, kick the feet into the snow; change the left hand for the right on the ice axe head (perhaps bracing the freed hand on the shaft); then bring the inside foot (in this case right) forward to make the next step. The ice axe is always placed above the climber's path. Switches from one hand to another are made with care.

When climbing down, the choice of whether to face into the slope or face outward arises. The decision depends on how secure the climber feels. If facing outward, feet are kept flat and pointed downhill with the knees bent in a pronounced squat as the angle steepens. The ice axe is held to the side and behind, ready for self arrest. When the angle feels uncomfortable, face into the slope and front point down, digging the ice axe pick or shaft into the snow.

Technique Positions

Steep, hard ice is climbed largely by front pointing, and may require two ice axes. On moderate terrain this technique is rarely called for, but modern crampons and rigid mountain BOOTS make front pointing advantageous for many situations. True front pointing means climbing by kicking the tips of crampons into water ice. The ice axe(s) may be placed for balance, or, as in vertical ICE CLIMBING the climber may be literally hanging from the ice axe picks. On moderately steep alpine ice, American technique (called *pied troisème* in French technique) combines flatfooting with front pointing by front pointing with one foot while the other foot is placed flat. This method eases strain on the legs.

Further reading: John Barry, *Snow and Ice Climbing* (1987); Yvon Chouinard, *Climbing Ice* (1978); Jeff Lowe, *The Ice Experience* (1979).

SNOW BLINDNESS   (Photopthalmia)   Literally, sunburn of the eye. Because the cornea and conjunctiva absorb ultraviolet radiation like the skin, excessive exposure to the sun without eye protection can damage these tissues. Commonly, snow blindness occurs in mountaineers or skiers wearing inadequate eye protection on very bright days in areas where ultraviolet reflection from snow is extreme. Symptoms may take eight to 12 hours to develop. Initially, no sensation other than bright glare is felt by the victim. Irritation may be mild but as symptoms progress the eyes feel as if they are full of sand, and eye movement or blinking becomes excruciating. Eyelids can swell, and eyes may water and become red. Severe cases may be painfully debilitating for days, and may lead to permanent eye damage. Snow blindness is easily prevented by wearing GOGGLES or SUNGLASSES with lenses transmitting less than 10% of the erythemal band of sunlight. Side shields

are also helpful. Eye protection should be worn at all times, as even on cloudy days or during snowstorms reflection of ultraviolet light is severe.

Snow blindness heals within a few days. Pain may be relieved by cold compresses and a dark environment. Opthalmic ointments containing cortisone or other anti-inflammatory steroids ease pain and swelling, and may be enhanced by aspirin.

SNOW BOLLARD   Similar in shape to an ICE BOLLARD, this is a snow anchor that is fashioned by cutting a horseshoe-shaped trough in the snow, then draping the rope over the bollard. The softer the snow, the deeper the trough should be, and the greater the diameter of the bollard. The risk with snow bollards is the rope cutting through the snow. Packs, ICE AXE shafts, even clothing, can be used to pad the sides of a bollard.

SNOW BRIDGE   A bridge of snow spanning a CREVASSE. Snow bridges can offer ROUTES across otherwise impassable crevasses, but many accidents and deaths occur when unroped people collapse snow bridges. Temperature fluctuations, glacial movement and the stress of climbers crossing a snow bridge can weaken one that had previously supported climbers. ROPING UP and use of SNOW AND ICE ANCHORS should be mandatory when crossing all such glacial features. (See GLACIERS.)

SNOW CAVE   Any shelter dug into a snow bank, consisting of a chamber excavated by ICE AXE or shovel, with a doorway sealed with snow blocks or a pack. Snow saws are also helpful tools in snow cave construction. Snow caves are windproof, and can be built big enough to accommodate many people. Interior temperatures can rise to a comfortable level. Stoves and several people can lead to problems of ventilation, especially with fuel fumes, and the melting of the inside walls. A ventilation hole in the wall or ceiling, bored out with an ice axe shaft or ski pole, is essential to ventilate a snow cave. Such holes should be reopened regularly as drifting snow can clog them. In practice, doorways are hard to seal from fine wind-blown snow. Digging a dog-leg-shaped entrance can act as a baffle and prevent snow from penetrating a snow cave. Another construction technique is the two-door snow hole, which is dug by two persons who excavate a hole around a column. Once the chamber is tunneled out, the second door is sealed. Advantages of this shelter are that the column provides a strong structural support allowing a larger chamber, and that two persons may dig the shelter and share the work. A snow mound is a more fragile shelter built on terrain where there is only loose, powdery snow and no snow bank to tunnel into. It is made by shoveling loose snow into a large mound, letting it consolidate for two hours or more, then tunneling out the inside. An emergency shelter for flat terrain is sometimes called a snow grave. It is simply a trough cut into snowy ground and covered with carefully cut snow blocks. A bivi hole is a small, one-person emergency snow cave. After snow storms, snow caves and shelters blend into surrounding snow. Snow caves should be well marked by WANDS or with rope leading to entrances so they can be relocated, as well as to prevent climbers stepping through the roof.

SNOW CRYSTALS See SNOW AND ICE, PROPERTIES OF.

SNOW FLUKE Another name for a DEADMAN snow anchor.

SNOW-ICE Another name for NEVE, or hard snow formed by freeze-thaw.

SNOW LINE The altitude at which permanent snow is found.

SNOW PACK The total depth of snow on the ground.

SNOW PLOD Colloquial term for snow climbing, referring to the tedium of long uphill trudging.

SNOW SAW A compact saw with coarse teeth for cutting snow, useful for IGLOO and SNOW CAVE building.

SNOWSHOES Snowshoes consist of WEBBING stretched over a rigid frame on which a boot binding is mounted. Traditional snowshoes have hide thongs lashed to a curved wooden frame. Modern snowshoe frames are metal, and Neoprene is usually used for straps and bindings. Though slower and more cumbersome than skis, snowshoes are useful in situations where skis are impractical, such as in snowed-up and convoluted GLACIERS. For MOUNTAINEERING, snowshoes that allow CRAMPONS to be clipped to BOOTS are essential, as slips are common on snow slopes. Many snowshoes have inbuilt "claws" for this purpose. Lightweight "bearpaw" or "racket" snowshoes have a smaller surface area than full-size snowshoes, and sink deeper into soft snow. However, though larger snowshoes float well in powder, they are difficult to turn and are clumsy on slopes. A zigzag path is the most efficient way to travel uphill with snowshoes. A shuffling zigzag path is the best way to travel downhill. A long gliding gait travels best on flat stretches. Ski poles or ICE AXES are indispensable for maintaining balance with snowshoes.

SNOW STAKE Also picket. A T-shaped or V-shaped length of aluminum stock, two to three ft (.6 to .9 m) long, hammered into snow as an ANCHOR.

SOURDOUGHS, THE (United States) In Alaskan MOUNTAINEERING folklore Peter Anderson, Billy Taylor, Tom Lloyd and Charles McGonagall were the three unassuming miners, or "Sourdoughs" (a colloquialism implying familiarity with ALASKA), who made an unmatched 10-hour ascent from the Muldrow Glacier to DENALI's lower north summit. On April 3, 1910, the three miners set out with Thermoses and doughnuts. They wore steel creepers on their boots and carried "alpine poles," to prevent them from falling into CREVASSES. In addition, they dragged a 14-ft (four-m) spruce tree as they marched up the knife-edged RIDGE. At about 19,000 ft (5,793 m), they planted the tree in some rocks. Taylor and Anderson continued to

the north summit, 19,470 ft (5,936 m). While the Sourdoughs worked their mining claims back in Fairbanks, their *leader*, Tom Lloyd, bragged that they had climbed both the north and south summits. Alaskans had already been driven to a frenzy by Frederick COOK's fraudulent summit claim in 1906, and lacking photographs, no one believed the Sourdoughs. Finally, in 1913, while en route to the south summit, Hudson STUCK sighted the spruce tree still stuck in the ridge and set the Sourdough record straight.

SOUTH AFRICA An exceptionally benign, dry climate makes South Africa favorable for year-round climbing. Summer temperatures average around 86 degrees F (30 degrees C), winter temperatures average 68 degrees F (20 degrees C). Occasionally waterfalls freeze in the Drakensberg Mountains (elevation 9,800 ft/2,988 m) allowing limited ICE CLIMBING. The rock is predominantly steep, dense quartzite sandstone ranging in color from white to blood red. Some extruded granite DOMES offer climbing, and escarpments of dolerite and basalt lie in the interior of the country.

South Africa is divided into four provinces: The Cape, Transvaal, Natal and Orange Free State. Most climbing lies in the first three provinces and is centered around the cities of Cape Town, Johannesburg and Durban. The South African climbing community is small, isolated and closely knit, with only about 200 active climbers to develop acres of unexplored rock. The impetus of South African climbing has always come from Cape Town climbers, probably due to the proximity of Table Mountain rising above the city. Individuals like George Londt, Mike Mammacos, the Barley brothers, Tony Dick, Roger Fuggle, Ed FEBRUARY and Dave CHEESMOND pushed rock-climbing standards from the 1960s to the 1990s, with active new routing in traditional style during the 1980s. The SPORT CLIMBING wave arrived in the 1990s as climbers used roto-hammers to bolt protectionless walls. Sport climbing activists include Roger Nattrass, Kevin Smith and Jonathan Fisher. Climbs are rated according to a modified Australian RATING SYSTEM, first introduced by visiting Australian John Fantini in the 1970s. As of 1991, the hardest routes in South Africa are rated 30.

Principal areas of the Western Cape include: Table Mountain, a 650-ft (198-m) quartzite cliff above Cape Town; Elsies Peak, a SEA CLIFF on the Cape Peninsula; Paarl Rock, 300-ft (91-m) granite domes 30 miles (48 km) east of Cape Town. The cliffs around Cedarberg—Krakadouw, Tatelberg and Wolfberg—are regarded as the best climbing in the country. They are set in a wilderness area 125 miles (200 km) northwest of Cape Town. Montague (Lost World and New World crags) is a highly developed area of 300-ft (91-m) cliffs. The Country Areas, of the Du Toits and Hex River Ranges outlying the Cape Peninsula (including Du Toits Peak, Klein Winterhoek and Milner Amphitheater cliffs), offer multi-pitch aid climbs. On the Eastern Cape, near Port Elizabeth, lie quartz and basalt crags like Mary and the Hogsback Ranges.

Monteseel, a 200-ft (61-m) sandstone edge is Natal's premiere crag, with hut accommodation for climbers. Kloot Gorge (The Canyon, Boneyard, Winston Park cliffs) offers sport climbing. Drakensberg is a 9,800-ft (2,988-m) elevation escarpment of dolerite and basalt peaks in a remote region 250 miles (400 km) inland from the East Coast.

Principal areas of Transvaal include Magaliesberg "Kloofs," a complex of 260-ft (79-m) quartzite cliffs in narrow river canyons 56 miles (90 km) northeast of Johannesburg, and Blonberg, a highly developed 1,500-ft (457-m) AID CLIMBING wall rising out of thornbrush plains.

TOPOS and ROUTE descriptions are available through the Mountain Club of South Africa and respective sections of South African Climbers Club (see Appendices).
Guidebooks: Dave Cheesmond, *Fifty Classic Climbs of the West Cape* (1977); Andy de Klerk and Jeremy Colenso, *Western Cape Rock* (1989); Adrian Hill and Mike Roberts, *Climber's Guide to Monteseel* (1982); Mountain Club of South Africa, Transvaal Section, *Transvaal Climbing Guides Files*; Mountain Club of South Africa, *Guidebook series to Table Mountain, the Apostles and Du Toits Kloof* (1983).

SOUTH KOREA There are about 50,000 climbers in South Korea today. Han-Ra-San (6,399 ft/1,951 m) is the highest peak in South Korea but Mount Sul-Ak (5,760 ft/1,756 m) is the most shapely mountain. It is six hours from Seoul, the capital city, near Kan-Neung City. On it are Ul-San-Am and Chuck-Byuk, both major rock-climbing areas, with many PITCHES of 5.11. In winter, this peak offers vertical FROZEN WATERFALL CLIMBING up to 300 ft (91 m). To-Wang-Sung waterfall is the most popular ice climb (WI5), while Dae-Seung Waterfall (WI6) and So-Seung Waterfall (WI6+) are the hardest.

Korean rock climbing began in the 1930s with a secret climbing club called Back-Ryung-Whe, as it was illegal to organize clubs under Japanese military occupation. After World War II this club organized the Korean Alpine Club. Korea manufactures much of the camping and climbing equipment currently made.

Most South Korean rock is rough granite but southern Korea has sedimentry rocks. The main granite rock-climbing areas are within a 40-minute drive of Seoul: In-Soo Peak and "Sun-In" Peak. Most climbing is on friction SLABS, ranging in difficulty from 5.6 to 5.11. Also near Seoul is a steep SPORT CLIMBING area on Che-Ju Island, called Kwang-Young Valley.

July and August comprise the rainy season and it's best to climb in spring and fall (April to June 15th, September to October 30th). December 15th through February 15th is the ICE CLIMBING season.

North Korea's highest peak is Mount Baeck-Du-San (9,099 ft/2,774 m). Though this country has much climbing potential it is almost impossible to obtain climbing permits here.

South Koreans launched 92 expeditions to the HIMALAYAS in the 1980s. Kim Chang Sun and Huh Young Ho have both climbed four 26,240-ft EIGHT THOUSAND-M PEAKS, while Chang Bong Wan has climbed EVEREST and K2. Park Rae Kyung is a leading sportclimber.

The main climbing associations in South Korea are the Korean Alpine Federation (1663-5 Bong Chon 7-Dong, Kwan-Ak-Ku, Seoul) and Korean Alpine Club (110-610 CPO Box 1014, Kwang-Wha-Mun, Seoul).

A guide book to South Korean climbing is called *Ba-Wee-Kil* (Rock Trails). South Korea's climbing magazine is *San-Ak-In*. It has an English summary within the magazine.

SOUTH PLATTE (United States) This cluster of some 50 COLORADO CRAGS southwest of Denver and northwest of Colorado Springs is located where the forks of the South Platte River and its tributaries cut through the PIKES PEAK batholith. The rock is mostly solid, coarse granite with a high mica content, but some areas like TURKEY ROCK are comprised of very hard hornblende minerals. Many DOMES and walls from one PITCH to 1,000 ft (305 m) lie in this sprawling area where climbing ranges from GLACIER-polished SLABS to knobby FACES to soaring CRACKS. One of the area's pioneers was Albert ELLINGWOOD, a professor of science at Colorado College and Rhodes Scholar who, while studying at Oxford University in England, learned techniques of roped climbing and brought the techniques back to America. In 1924 his 5.7 FIRST ASCENT on the Bishop was one of the first instances of technical ropework in America. Modern ROUTES, both traditionally established and BOLTED sport climbs lie on prominent crags like The Bishop, Cathedral Spires, Cynical Pinnacle, Sphinx Rock, Turkey Rock and Big Rock Candy Mountain. Perennially good weather and a wealth of climbing makes this an important area.
Guidebook: Peter Hubbel and Mark Rolofson, *Rock Climbing Guide to the South Platte River Valleys and Garden of the Gods* (1988).

SOVIET REPUBLICS Until the dissolution of the USSR, foreign climbers sought permission to climb there through The Mountaineering and Rockclimbing Federation of the USSR, a government-funded body. This body no longer exists, and the various states do not fund the climbing organizations that now control climbing in their respective states. Instead, foreign climbers must deal with the many private companies, associations or clubs in each region to arrange commercial climbing tours. Typically, guiding companies in western countries have established relationships with the most capable of the groups now offering climbing tours. UIAA recognition-status of various state organizations is available from the UIAA.

For rock climbing, main areas of interest include Karelia, a granite area north of St. Petersburg (formerly Leningrad) in the Karelian Republic; St. Petersburg itself is a climbing capital, with many clubs and indoor CLIMBING GYMS; the Crimea of Ukraine offers a wealth of limestone SPORT CLIMBING around the towns of Yalta and Sudak, beside the Black Sea, and is a site for sport-climbing competitions; and in Russia, the granite pinnacles of Stolby, near Krasnojarsk. Alpine rock climbing is centered around the Pamirs of Kirgizia, in the Ak-Su and Asan-Usan mountains, with granitic BIG WALLS developed by Eastern-Bloc climbers and great potential on 13,120- and 16,400-ft (4,000- and 5,000-m) rock peaks. Alpine rock climbing and MOUNTAINEERING is also practiced in the Fanskiye Gory of Kirgizia. For mountaineering, within Russia itself are the Altai, Sayan and Caucasus ranges. The latter divides Georgia and Armenia and contains sought-after peaks like Mount ELBRUS

(18,589 ft/5,633 m), one of the SEVEN SUMMITS, and Ushba (15,543 ft/4,710 m). In the "Middle Asia" region rise the Pamir-Alay and Pamir ranges of Uzbekistan, Kirgizia and Tadzhikistan, with peaks up to 22,960 ft (7,000 m): Peak Communism (24,584 ft/7,495 m) and highest in the former USSR, Peak Lenin (23,400 ft/7,134 m) and Korzhenevskaya (23,304 ft/7,105 m). In the Tien Shan of Kazakhstan and Kirgizia the highest peaks are Pobeda (24,400 ft/7,439 m) and Khan Tengri (22,944 ft/6,995 m). Eastern mountaineers have climbed demanding ROUTES on these peaks since the 1930s. Those who climb all the summits are referred to as "Snow Leopards." In the far east of the land, in the wild Kurilskiye Islands, Sakhalin Island and Kamchatka Peninsula are active volcanos. The highest, Klyuchevskaya (15,580 ft/4,750 m), on Kamchatka, was climbed in 1788. On a 1931 ascent climbers were killed by debris exploding from the crater.

Information on climbing in these countries is hard to come by. The regional clubs have detailed route books of their efforts in the mountains. AMERICAN ALPINE JOURNAL (United States), ALPINE JOURNAL (BRITAIN) and magazines should be consulted.

Further reading: John Cleare, *Collins Guide to Mountains and Mountaineering* (1979); Robert Craig, *Storm and Sorrow in the High Pamirs* (1977); M. Kelscy, *Guide to the World's Mountains* (1990); Jill Neate, *High Asia, An Illustrated History of the 7000 metre Peaks* (1989).

SPAIN   An abundance of rock and mountain climbing is scattered across this nation: A 1982 edition of the Spanish Climbing magazine *Desnivel* listed 403 separate CRAGS. MOUNTAINEERING in Spain evolved in the Pyrenees, while rock climbing has been carried out since the 1930s in MONTSERRAT and PEDRIZA. In the 1980s Spanish *escaladores* (climbers) absorbed techniques from France and America and the result has been an explosion in ALPINISM, SPORT CLIMBING and, in areas like PICOS DE EUROPA, BIG WALL CLIMBING. The most developed cragging lies around the Mediterranean coast from Barcelona to Leiva, around Madrid and also in the north. The RATING SYSTEM used is essentially the French system. Spain's benign climate assures year-round climbing, with *refugios* (huts) and camping conveniently located. Guidebooks are uncommon in Spain, but a useful overview of rock-climbing areas is contained in Nico and Leuehsner Mailander's *Sun Rock*. (See also CHULILLA, MONTENEJOS, PATONES, QUIROS, SIURANA.)

SPECTRA   Trade name for extremely strong WEBBING or cord fibers manufactured by Blue Water Ropes (United States). (See ROPES.)

SPEED CLIMBING   A competitive event in which climbers race head-to-head up identical ROUTES, moving as fast as possible. Each hits a bell at the top of the route and this sound signifies the finish. The contest is generally two or three rounds. Speed routes are technically easier than those in difficulty contests, and usually feature large HOLDS that climbers DYNO for. The sport originated in Russia decades ago, and was popular in Eastern Bloc countries.

Speed climbing events are held at some world and national contests. Champion speed climbers include Catherine DESTIVELLE and Jacky Godoffe (France) and Hans Florine (United States).

SPIKES   Archaic term for PITON.

SPINDRIFT   Extremely fine, dustlike powder snow that is airborne or sloughing down a slope. Spindrift may be propelled by wind or AVALANCHE and may be so fine as to be suffocating.

SPITI HIMALAYA   (India)   A small range between TIBET and INDIA, in the Indian state of Himachal Pradesh. Rivers flowing from these mountains feed the Spiti River, which flows into the Sutlej River. It was through Spiti that Heinrich HARRER (of EIGER fame) and Peter Aufschnaiter traveled during their escape from British internment during World War II. The peaks are popular among Indian mountaineers. Gya (22,289 ft/6,794 m) is the highest summit in Spiti.
Further reading: S. Mehta and H. Kapadia, *Exploring the Hidden Himalaya* (1990).

SPORT CLIMBING   A term of the 1980s that originated in France, and which describes the style of FREE CLIMBING

Sport Climbing

on BOLT-protected, technically difficult ROUTES. Climbing on ARTIFICIAL walls and COMPETITION walls is another facet of sport climbing. Also called EURO-STYLE.

SPOT   A BOULDERING term. A climber who calls for a spot, or calls "Spot me," is requesting a climber on the ground to break a possible fall and prevent a dangerous landing.

SPRING-LOADED CAMMING DEVICE   Or SLCD, active camming device. A broad term describing many brands of adjustable camming units for CRACK PROTECTION, such as CAMALOTS, FRIENDS and TCUS. They consist of three or four independently sprung cams mounted on an axle that is mounted on a stem of alloy or cable. A cabled trigger retracts the cams creating a range of widths, and coiled springs ensure that the cams are held in position before a load is applied. The cams have a constant angle curve, meaning they are in contact with the rock at the same angle at all times. Cams are held in place by friction against the rock. When a cam is pulled downward it reacts with a multiplied outward force, which pushes the cam face against the rock, creating friction to oppose the downward pull. These outward forces are large: a downward force of 1000-lb (450 kg) pushes outward on the rock with a 2,000-lb (900-kg) force. SLCDs placed behind loose blocks can lever them outward in the event of a fall.

SLCDs were introduced in the 1970s as "Friends," the brainchild of Ray JARDINE (United States). Since their introduction they have revolutionized crack protection, because of their speed and ease of placement in flared and parallel cracks that previously had been difficult to protect with passive camming devices such as HEXENTRICS and STOPPERS.

Other SLCD devices like Sliders, Lowe-Balls and Rock 'n' Rollers rely on the principle of two inclined planes sliding against each other, working in opposition. They fit very thin cracks. All SLCDs should be cleaned and lubricated to ensure camming efficiency.

Comparative Strengths of SLCDs (depending on size of unit):

Wild Country Friend: 2,860–3,300 lb (1,287–1,485 kg)

Wild Country Flexible Friend: 2,860–3,300 lb (1,287–1,485 kg)

Climb High (HB) Quad Cam: 3,080 lb (1,386 kg)

Colorado Custom Hardware Alien II: 1,600–3,000 lb (720–1,350 kg)

Metolius TCU: 1,600–2,400 lb (720–1,080 kg)

Liberty Four Cam: 2,500 lb (1,125 kg)

Liberty Tri Cam: 2,000 lb (900 kg)

Liberty Spider: 2,700–3,000 lb (1,215–1,350 kg)

Chouinard Camalot: 2,420–3,300 lb (1,089–1,485 kg)

Yates Big Dude: 3,500 lb (1,575 kg)

Wired Bliss TCU: 2,800 lb (1,260 kg)

SQUAMISH   (Canada)   The jewel of BRITISH COLUMBIAN rock climbing is located 60 miles (96 km) north of Vancouver. The YOSEMITE-scale granodiorite cliffs rise behind the town of the same name and overlook Howe Sound. The 2,000-ft (610-m) Squamish Chief initially attracted climbers in 1961 when Ed Cooper and Jim Baldwin climbed Grand Wall in BIG WALL style. This eight-PITCH CRACK classic is now virtually free (5.11) and is typically done in a day. During the 1960s and 1970s major AID routes were added to this and surrounding walls by climbers like Darryl Hatten, Steve Sutton, Hugh Burton and Eric Weinstein, but in the 1980s climbers began pushing long tree climbs up the featured rock. One major breakthrough from this time was the Peter CROFT-Hamish Fraser-Greg Foweraker FREE ASCENT of the crack route University Wall (5.12). Other local climbers responsible for new routes are Robin Barley, Dave Lane, Scott Flavelle and Perry Beckham. Squamish is famous for moderate climbing on the SLABS of the Apron and the Smoke Bluffs. SPORT CLIMBING is found on Petrifying Wall, where Jim Sandford has pushed Canadian ratings to 5.13d. Land development led to degradation of the climbing environment in the Smoke Bluffs in the 1980s, and to the formation of The Squamish Rockclimbers Association, which provides a voice regarding access and development there. The climbing season runs from June to September.
Guidebook: Kevin McClean, *Squamish Rockclimbs* (1992).

STAFFORDSHIRE GRIT   (Britain)   This region of the PEAK DISTRICT comprises several warty CRAGS northeast of the village of Leek, namely Hen Cloud, Five Clouds, The Roaches and Ramshaw. The Roaches are set in an exposed position 1,500 ft (457 m) up with magnificent views of the countryside. Camping is found beneath Hen Cloud, while Upper Hulme provides services.

In 1946 Peter Harding climbed the superb Valkyrie (5.7), now enormously popular, and Joe BROWN climbed Saul's Crack (5.8). With Don WHILLANS's arrival, they set about cleaning the crags' CRACK LINES and on a winter's day in early 1954, Whillans set out across the huge ROOF of The Sloth (5.9), a daunting challenge even today.

John ALLEN left his mark here in the 1970s with Caricature (5.11d). But this period was dominated by Johnny Woodward, who in 1977 climbed Wings of Unreason and Piece of Mind, both hard 5.12s. Visiting American climber Ray JARDINE led Ray's Roof at Baldstones, which he graded 5.11c. It is probably closer to 5.12c.

In the 1980s Simon NADIN climbed such brilliant ROUTES as roof Paralogism (5.13b) and B4 XS (5.13a), Against the Grain and Thing on a Spring, both 5.13d. Nick Dixon, another bold local climber, climbed the equally serious Doug (5.13c).
Guidebooks: British Mountain Club, *Staffordshire Gritstone* (1989); Paul Nunn, *Rock Climbing in the Peak District* (1987).

STANAGE   (Britain)   The centerpiece of PEAK DISTRICT gritstone, Stanage is a unique CRAG, stretching for three miles (five km) along the moorland on the outskirts of Sheffield. Gritstone proved more amenable to early pioneers than limestone, and so the traditions established here spurn BOLTS. Stanage sported 824 ROUTES in the last published guide. Its rough, weathered rock offers everything from SLABS climbed on pebbles to arm-pumping OVERHANGS, usually around 50 ft (15 m) in length. PROTECTION is with NUTS and CAMMING DEVICES. Camping is possible beneath the crag at the North Lees site.

As at many gritstone crags near Sheffield, it was J. W. Puttrell who explored first, climbing Hollybush Gully (5.4) in 1890. Colin KIRKUS put up Kirkus' Corner in 1934, one of the hardest of the era at 5.9. Peter Harding's Goliath's Groove (5.8) was a notable post-World War II route, but it was Joe BROWN and Don WHILLANS who pushed standards. In 1952 Whillans jammed his way up The Unprintable (5.9). Two years later Brown climbed the neighboring CRACK to give The Dangler (5.10b), a brutish climb.

Activity was less frenetic in the 1960s, although Jim Perrin's Censor (5.10c) was a bold exception. In 1973 John ALLEN, aged 14, solved an often-tried climb at High Neb BUTTRESS when he climbed Old Friends (5.11a). Ed DRUMMOND added the elegant ARETE of Archangel (5.10b) and Wuthering (5.9), climbed in 1971 and 1973. Another important contribution was Gabe Regan's terrifying Calvary (5.11a), a heart-stopping FACE route climbed in the heat wave of 1976.

In the 1980s the newest generation also cut their teeth on Stanage. Jerry MOFFATT solved a long-observed problem with Ulysses (5.12b), and Johnny Dawes, one of the finest gritstone climbers ever, added Sad Amongst Friends (5.12c). Ron FAWCETT also contributed with his technically fiendish Careless Torque (5.13a).

Other crags lie nearby, including those around Burbage Moor that contain fine routes.

Guidebooks: British Mountain Club, *Stanage* (1989); Paul Nunn, *Rock Climbing in the Peak District* (1987).

STANNARD, JOHN (1942–   ) **(United States)** John Stannard's career reflects important trends in U.S. rock climbing in the 1970s. He was an early example of a great climber who limited his activities to a single region, or CRAG—in Stannard's case the SHAWANGUNKS. A physicist by profession, Stannard assiduously trained to build the upper-body strength demanded by the Gunks' ubiquitous OVERHANGS. This paid off in 1970, when he was the first to FREE CLIMB the 8-ft (2-m) Foops ROOF, now rated 5.11. Along with Henry BARBER, Steve WUNCH and John BRAGG, Stannard established the 5.12 grade at the Gunks. Some of the routes they freed were: Crack of Bizarre Delights, Kligfields Follies, Open Cockpit, Sling Time, P.R., Kama Sutra, The Throne, Kansas City and To Have and Have Not. Stannard also played a big role in shaping climbing ETHICS: In his privately published newsletter, *The Eastern Trade*, he propagandized use of the then novel STOPPERS and NUTS instead of PITONS. His attacks on the use of CHALK—a common peeve of climbers of his generation—were less influential.

STATIC MOVE In FREE CLIMBING, to move between HOLDS in a controlled, graceful sweep, rather than with lunges. Requires considerable strength and the ability to rigidly LOCK OFF the arms.

STATIC ROPE Low-stretch rope used for FIXED ROPE, PRUSIKing and threading through NUTS. Not suitable for use as the main leading rope, which should a high-stretch DYNAMIC ROPE. (See ROPES.)

STEMMING Or BRIDGING, PALMING. A FREE CLIMBING technique for ascending featureless DIHEDRALS (inside CORNERS). The stemming stance is made by exerting outward pressure with the palms of the hands and the feet against the walls of the dihedral. In this position, small depressions or edges may be utilized for friction and balance. Flexibility of hips and legs is a distinct advantage in stemming situations.

Stemming

STEP CUTTING Using the ICE AXE to hack out foot steps in ice. The technique was used extensively for climbing ice faces in the European ALPS, before the advent of modern CRAMPONS. Guides would swing their axes and cut steps for nail-booted clients for hundreds of feet. Advances in ice axes and crampons and the advent of FRONT POINTING in the 1950s, eliminated the need for step cutting.

Step kicking is the process of kicking the boot into snow or NEVE.

STICHT PLATE   The original belay plate, invented by Franz Sticht. (See BELAYING TECHNIQUES.)

STICK CLIP   A technique popular in SPORT CLIMBING for clipping the first BOLT or piece of PROTECTION above the ground so the leader may TOP ROPE the first moves. The method involves taping a QUICK DRAW or CARABINER to the end of a long stick after the ROPE has been clipped through the carabiner, then reaching up and clip the carabiner into the bolt. The stick is removed with a sharp pull that releases the tape. A small twig positioned to hold the gate open helps the procedure.

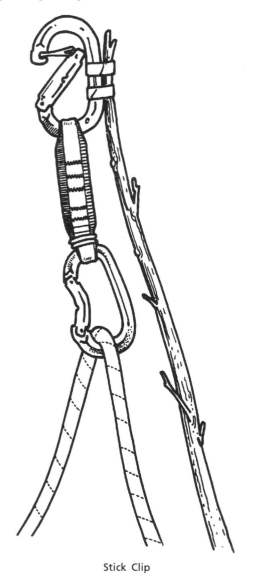

Stick Clip

STIRRUPS   Another name for ETRIERS.

STONEFALL   A common and potentially serious cliff or mountain hazard caused by random erosion, or by the daily freeze/thaw action of snow melt seeping into cracks around rocks, then freezing by night and expanding as ice. The resulting fractured rock eventually breaks away from the mountain face when sunlight warms the surroundings and clatters down at great velocity. Stonefall may also be caused by climbers dislodging loose stones. Cover should be taken when the call "below" or "rock" is heard, and the call should be given when stones are dislodged. Alpine FACES, GULLIES and COULOIRS are at most risk of stonefall; RIDGES, ARETES and BUTTRESSES are safest. Flanks of mountains that see little or no sun, such as north faces, or mountains in winter, are often at less risk of stonefall due to their nearly permanent state of freeze. Since sunlight causes stonefall, climbing in the warmth of day is dangerous on some ROUTES. Guidebooks usually advise of notoriously hazardous stonefall areas. Stonefall evasion requires fast reflexes to find shelter behind rock OUTCROPS. Helmets afford essential protection and should always be worn on mountain routes.

STONEY MIDDLETON   (Britain)   Stoney Middleton Dale is one of the less attractive areas within the PEAK DISTRICT National Park because of the intensive quarrying for limestone there, but the old quarry on its north side became a crucible of British climbing in the late 1960s. The CRAG is 10 miles (16 km) from Sheffield and an hour's drive from Manchester. The café in the nearby village remains a legendary meeting-place for climbers. There are numerous campsites in the area, and near Hathersage, to the north.

In the mid-1960s, climbers realized that the steep limestone crags they used for AID in the winter months could yield FREE routes too. The prodigiously strong Tom Proctor in 1967 produced a cluster of mold-breaking routes, including Our Father (5.10d), Wee Doris (5.10c) and Dies Irae (5.10b). At a stroke, Proctor's attention ensured the crag's popularity and a new generation found a launching pad for the new, athletic approach. Proctor, 10 years after his debut, climbed the imposing Circe (5.12a).

In the early 1980s, a group started serving what was termed their Stoney apprenticeships. Among these was the gritstone specialist Gabe Regan, who added Bitter Fingers (5.11a). Another student of the fiercely overhanging was Jerry MOFFATT who climbed Little Plum (5.12c) and Andy Pollitt who in 1984 added Easy Shanking (5.12c).

Climbing at Stoney is characterized by steep, fingery climbing on generally sound rock. The routes, around 70 ft (21 m) in length, are usually protected by wires and the occasional in situ PEG. Unfortunately, the crag's popularity has meant that the well-known climbs have become very polished.
Guidebooks: British Mountain Club, *Peak Limestone—Stoney* (1987); Paul Nunn, *Rock Climbing in the Peak District* (1987).

STOPPER   Trade name for the wedge-shaped NUT introduced in the 1960s. Though a registered trade name of Chouinard Equipment (United States), stopper has become a generic word describing any wedge-shaped nut. (See NATURAL PROTECTION.)

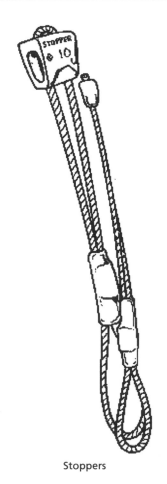

Stoppers

STORM See WEATHER.

STOVES AND FUEL Stove and fuel choices depend on the environment and type of climbing. Stoves for winter or alpine use must burn hot to melt snow for drinks; high-altitude stoves must cope with cold and low oxygen; stoves in Third-World countries should be multi-fuel burning; stoves for BASE CAMP must be durable for prolonged cooking.

Fuel options are:

White gas, or Shellite, is a clear, clean, volatile gasoline derivative formulated for stoves. It is efficient in cold weather. Though readily available in the United States, it is less popular in Europe and unavailable in South America or Asia.

Kerosene, or paraffin, burns hotter than white gas, butane or propane. It has a high weight-to-energy ratio, good cold weather performance and is cheaply available worldwide. Low volatility makes it safe, but it requires priming with hotter fuel or priming paste. Kerosene odor penetrates food, and it should be filtered. This is the usual fuel for Asian or South American expeditions.

Butane is liquified compressed gas that vaporizes when released. It is packaged in disposable metal canisters which should be brought back home from a trip. Though butane performs poorly in cold weather (it doesn't vaporize in

extremely cold temperatures) it is popular for low-altitude MOUNTAINEERING in Europe and the United States because of its light weight, and non-leak convenience. In Asia it is found only in markets that resell expedition equipment.

Propane is similar to butane, but vaporizes in cold more readily. Though available worldwide it is unsuited to climbing because it is contained in heavy, refillable metal cylinders. It is sometimes used in base camps but not on climbs.

Butane-propane mix in disposable canisters solves the problems of butane or propane alone. It burns hot in cold weather and is safe. It is the best fuel for high altitude. However, airlines will not ship pressurized-flammable containers with accompanied cargo and this fuel is difficult to find in the Third World.

Alcohol, or methylated spirits, is clear, clean and low volatile, though hard to find in the Third World. Its heat-to-weight ratio and cold performance is poor.

Solid chemical fuel is small cubes of chemical/fiber mix burned in a special stove. It is light, but heat output is insufficient for serious cooking. It is useful as an emergency wood-fire starter.

Automobile gasoline: This is readily available worldwide, burns hot and performs well in cold temperatures. However, few stoves run on gasoline; it clogs stove burners and fills a tent with harmful fumes. It is explosive and requires filtering before use. Unleaded gasoline only should be used, and as a last resort.

Four general types of stove include:

Multi-fuel stoves: Mountain Safety Research's expedition and high altitude-proven MSR XGK stoves burn gasoline, white gas and kerosene. The MSR Internationale and Coleman Peak 1 Multi-fuel burns white gas and kerosene. The Optimus 111 Hiker burns white gas, kerosene and alcohol. The Swiss-made Phoebus is also multi-fuel. The MSR-XGK boils water quicker than other stoves.

White-gas stoves include MSR Whisperlite, Coleman Feather 400 and Optimus's 123R Climber and 8R Hunter. Such white gas stoves make good winter stoves.

Gas stoves include the Camping Gaz Bluet, EPI Gas, the alcohol-burning Trangia system with its butane-canister attachment, and the MSR Rapid Fire. Bluet and EPI gas stoves are the choice of Himalayan mountaineers. Gas stoves consist of a fuel jet with an on-off control that clamps onto a canister.

Alcohol stoves are light but inefficient. The Trangia is popular for low-altitude hiking. A cup-shaped fuel container is filled with alcohol and ignited. Fuel vaporizes in a compartment within the cup and produces a flame.

Hanging stoves are combined potsets and windshield to which a burner (usually gas) is attached. The system hangs from a light chain. They are useful in BIVOUACS.

STUART, MOUNT (United States) Sound granite, lofty elevation (9,415 ft/2,870 m) and a variety of passages from the many easy-angled routes of the southeast and northeast side, to the steep, technical flanks on the northwest and southwest make this one of the most challenging peaks in the CASCADE RANGE of WASHINGTON STATE. A few miles from the town of Leavenworth, the peak sees many ascents. A possible FIRST ASCENT dates back to 1873 and one Angus McPherson, who left a carved and dated stick on the summit. The west ridge is a popular moderate route, but the technical interest lies with the long rock PROW of the north ridge (Rupley and Gordon, 1956) and the FACES and COULOIRS to either side, on which are about 10 routes, some involving 5.11 climbing. Stuart's northern flanks support three small GLACIERS, and winter ascensionists find true alpine conditions on this side.

Guidebook: Fred Beckey, *Cascade Alpine Guide* (3 vols) (1979).

STUCK, HUDSON (1863–1920) (United States) The archdeacon of the Yukon, Stuck led the FIRST ASCENT of DENALI in 1913 with Harry Karstens. He worked with and developed a fondness for the native peoples of the north and fought fervently for the mountain to be restored to its original Tanaina Indian name, Denali. As he explained in his book, *The Ascent of Denali*, Stuck was "no professed explorer, or climber or scientist, but a missionary." Nonetheless, he climbed in Great BRITAIN, COLORADO, the CANADIAN ROCKIES, and reached the summit of Mount RAINIER in Washington. After seeing Denali from Fairbanks, he wrote, "I would rather climb that mountain than discover the richest goldmine in Alaska."

Further reading: Hudson Stuck, *The Ascent of Denali (Mount McKinley): A Narrative of the First Complete Ascent of the Highest Peak in North America* (1989).

STUMP, TERRENCE "MUGS" (1949–1992) (United States) One of the America's strongest alpinists, Stump perished in a CREVASSE fall while guiding on DENALI. Prior to his climbing career, he played football at Pennsylvania State University and earned the nickname "Mugs" from his teammates. He began climbing in 1975, after a gaining note as an extreme skier in Utah's Wasatch Mountains. In 1977 he made the FIRST ASCENT of Merlin (5.10 A3) on the BLACK CANYON OF THE GUNNISON. Later BIG WALL ROUTES included a WINTER ASCENT of Hallucinogenic Wall there with John Middendorf, and the first ascent of Streaked Wall in ZION. His natural strength led him into ALPINISM; he made first ascents of the Emperor Face of ROBSON in the Candian Rockies (1978, with Jim Logan), and in his spiritual home of the ALASKA RANGE in 1981 he made first ascents of MOOSES TOOTH east face (with Jim BRIDWELL), and Moonflower Buttress on Mount HUNTER (with Paul Aubrey). In 1991 he made a visionary solo "loop" on Denali by beginning at the 14,200-ft (4,329-m) camp on the west buttress, descending to and climbing up the Cassin Ridge, then descending the west buttress, in 24 hours. He attempted new routes on Asian peaks like GASHERBRUM IV. Perhaps his finest efforts were his solo climbs in ANTARCTICA, while he was a safety consultant for the National Science Foundation. In the Ellsworth Mountains, he climbed the 7,000-ft (2,134-m) southwest Face of Mount

Gardner and the 8,000-ft (2,439-m) west face of Mount Tyree, each in a day.

STYLE Climbing style refers to FREE CLIMBING and SPORT CLIMBING methods of ascent. (See RED POINT, PINK POINT, A VUE, ONSIGHT, FLASH. For EXPEDITONS, see ALPINE STYLE, CAPSULE STYLE. See also ETHICS.)

SUBLIMATION The property by which snow or ice turns from solid to vapor and back again without going through the liquid stage. (See SNOW AND ICE, PROPERTIES OF.)

SUMMIT REGISTER A small container housing a notebook in which climbers record their ascents and visits to the summit of a peak. Summit Registers are placed atop a few peaks across the world. The practice was more common in the earlier half of the twentieth century. Summit Registers, when the notebooks are full, are generally kept in the libraries of mountaineering clubs as historical objects.

SUNCUP A cup-shaped pit in a snowfield or GLACIER caused by melting action. Suncup expanses may be deep and soft and present obstacles for travel over alpine terrain, but they sometimes form convenient natural steps.

SUNGLASSES Eye protection in bright sunlight and snow conditions is essential to prevent SNOW BLINDNESS. Prior to the invention of sunglasses, native peoples such as the Eskimo shielded their eyes from harmful snow glare by fashioning GOGGLES of driftwood or bone pierced with narrow slits. UV, or ultraviolet light, is responsible for sunburn and snow blindness. It is more intense at higher elevations, increasing about 15% per 3,000 ft (915 m) due to the gradual thinning of the atmosphere, which acts as a natural shield against UV light. At high elevations, the only safe eye protection is from sunglasses or goggles that deflect 100% of UV light. Tint on lenses does not deflect UV, but coatings of metal oxides do. Photochromic lenses, which react to sunlight by darkening, and polarized lenses, which have a polarizing filter sandwiched between glass, also effectively cut UV light. Visible light is also harmful. It is measured by the percentage of light allowed through a lens. Lenses for high altitude should transmit about 4% visible light, lenses for lower elevations approximately 15%. Sunglass material may be polycarbonate (a thermoplastic) or glass. Glass has the advantage of being more scratch-resistant, and retains eye-protecting coatings more effectively. Polycarbonate has absorbs UV rays and should be used in the lenses. There is some advantage in the tint of a lens: Brown and amber make objects appear sharper because these colors cut out red and blue, the colors in the spectrum that the eye has difficulty focusing on.

SUNSCREEN Or glacier cream. Sunscreen protects the skin from burning in extreme sunlight. Most applications use PABA (p-amino benzoic acid) to achieve sun protection. The amount of protection is measured by SPF, or Sun Protection Factor. Sunscreen and lip balms for MOUNTAIN-

EERING should be at least SPF 15. Zinc-oxide paste also affords good sun protection, and resists washing off in sweat. Sensitive areas like lips, the tongue, the roof of the mouth and the inside of the nose are susceptible to sunburn. Where sunscreen cannot be applied, a scarf, hat or face mask may give protection. Some sunscreens are medicated with mild analgesics to ease sunburn discomfort.

SUPER GAITORS A gaitor, or leg covering to keep out snow and water, that covers the entire boot upper, from ankle to knee, and is insulated for cold weather use. There are several methods of securing a super gaitor to the boot, such as cable or elastic tightened around the welt; straps; or moulded rubber bands that stretch over the boot to form a seal. Many climbers use glue to secure gaitors to boots.

SWAMI BELT A crude HARNESS consisting of a waist belt without leg loops. A swami belt can be made from four or six pieces of two-inch (five-cm) WEBBING wrapped around the waist and tied with a tape knot (see KNOTS). The climbing ROPE is tied directly into the swami belt. Swami belts are a better option than the old method of tying the rope around the waist, in that they distribute the forces of a fall more evenly around the midsection of the body. Without leg loops they are uncomfortable to hang or RAPPEL in, and can cause suffocation in prolonged hangs.

SWANAGE (Britain) These Jurassic limestone cliffs lie on the Dorset coast of southeast England, near Swanage village and the seaside town of Bournemouth. The rock is looser than other limestone areas, and its steep angle has slowed development until recent years. The three and a half miles (six km) of CRAGS include Subluminal, Boulder Ruckle, Cattle Troughs, Blackers Hole and Cormorant and Guillemot ledges. Where the sea and the passage of climbers have combined, the ROUTES are of a high quality.

Before the 1950s, the crags provided smugglers with hideouts, builders with stone and American Rangers with World War II training areas. Notable routes from the 1960s include Thunderball (5.8) on Boulder Ruckle, Philatus (5.9) at Subluminal and Squid on Fisherman's Ledge. Though Swanage lagged behind other United Kingdom climbing areas throughout the 1970s because many climbers believed that the loose rock prohibited technical climbing, bold LINES continued to appear, one notable example being Nick Buckley's Freeborn Man (5.11a). But in 1983 Martin Crocker added Relax and Swing, a 20-ft (six-m) 5.12 ROOF on Boulder Ruckle. This trend continued with Pete Oxley's route Seizure (5.12c), which climbs through multi-layered roofs on The Promenade. Crispin Waddy's Swordfish Trombones (5.11a) was also completed despite two 40-ft (12-m) falls into the sea while attempting a solo FIRST ASCENT. Most routes are naturally protected and rarely exceed 150 ft (46 m) high.

Guidebooks: Gordon Jenkin, *Swanage* (which includes other, less celebrated areas like Lulworth Cove and Durdle Door) (1986); Pat Littlejohn, *South West Climbs* (1991).

SWING LEADS Another term for ALTERNATE LEADS.

T

TABEI, JUNKO (1939–) (Japan) This Japanese mountaineer became the first woman to climb Mount EVEREST (29,028 ft/8,848 m) on May 16, 1975. The popular media at the time described her ascent as "Japanese housewife climbs Everest." Tabei has achieved recognition not only as a climber, but also as a stereotype-breaking individualist in traditional Japan, who has combined marriage and raising children with ascents of the highest summits in 32 countries. In 1992, at age 52, she became the first woman to climb the SEVEN SUMMITS—the highest peaks in Asia, Europe, Africa, South America, North America, Australasia and ANTARCTICA.

TAHOE, LAKE (United States) This massive lake, in the northern SIERRA NEVADA and the town of Tahoe, is surrounded by some of the most popular cragging in CALIFORNIA, with over a dozen granitic areas. Most well known and longest established is Lover's Leap, a cliff about a mile long (1.6 km) and averaging 400 ft (122 m) high, southwest of Tahoe near the town of Strawberry. Horizontal dikes layer "The Leap," allowing ROUTES up nearly vertical walls. Tom Higgins, TM Herbert, Royal ROBBINS, Frank Sarnquist and others opened this CRAG in the 1960s. Nearby, the Sugarloaf is famous for the bearing world's first 5.13, Grand Illusion, climbed by Tony YANIRO in 1977. Donner Summit, north of the lake, has numerous one-pitch routes of all difficulties, including many 5.12 SPORT CLIMBS, and extreme 5.13 routes on the radically overhung Star-Wars Wall. Among other OUTCROPS, Cave Rock on the east shore has gotten much recent publicity for a concentration of wildly OVERHANGING 5.13 sport climbs. The Emeralds, near Nevada City, is a gorge of metamorphic rock which is a popular sport-climbing area, boasting about 90 routes. During winter cold spells ICE CLIMBS form on some of these crags and elsewhere in the area.
Guidebook: Mike Carville, *Climber's Guide to Tahoe Rock* (1991).

TAHQUITZ AND SUICIDE (United States) These granitic CRAGS face each other across Fern Valley in the San Jacinto mountains of southern CALIFORNIA, 100 miles (160 km) east of Los Angeles, near the town of Idyllwild. ROUTES are one PITCH to 1,000 ft (305 m) high, and are known for their aesthetic quality. For decades these cliffs sported the highest standards of FREE CLIMBING in America. The "Yosemite" decimal system of RATING climbs originated here.

Glen Dawson climbed at least two 5.8 routes in 1936–37. After World War II Chuck Wilts led the scene, climbing 17 FIRST ASCENTS in a few years, and developing the knifeblade PITON to protect thin CRACKS. Royal ROBBINS climbed what might have been America's first 5.9 here in 1952, and Mark Powell put up possibly the first 5.10 in 1955. Tahquitz, with its sweeping cracks, became known as the best training ground for YOSEMITE, and in the 1960s Bob Kamps, TM Herbert, Tom Higgins and Tom FROST all developed routes here. Powell and Steve Altman put up an early 5.11 in 1964.

Attention soon switched to Suicide, a crag known for friction FACES. Pat Callis, Charlie Raymond and Larry Harrell led many new SLAB routes. By the early 1970s a new generation including Tobin Sorenson, John LONG, Rick Accomazzo, Gib Lewis, Mike Graham, John BACHAR and Jim Wilson climbed many 5.11 routes on both crags, often freeing routes previously aided. The crack Insomnia (5.11), when freed by Jim Erickson in 1972, was a breakthrough. Randy LEAVITT made his Leavittation wide-crack technique famous on the Paisano Overhang, a ROOF crack at Suicide. In the 1980s Kevin Powell, Darryl Hensel, John Long and Bob Gaines pushed standards here to 5.12.
Guidebook: Randy Vogel, *Tahquitz and Suicide* (1993).

TALUS Another term for SCREE.

TANZANIA Africa's highest peak, KILIMANJARO (19,340 ft/5,895 m), lies in this east African nation. Rock climbing and BOULDERING on granite DOME formations called *kopjes* is found amid the roaming big game of Serengeti National Park.

TAPE Another name for WEBBING.

TAPING UP Porous cloth adhesive tape protects hands and fingers from pain and abrasion during CRACK CLIMBING. Bonding compounds like tincture of benzoine applied before tape forms a sticky surface and gives tape better holding power.

TARN A small, steep-banked mountain lake. The word is of Scandinavian origin.

TASKER, JOE (1948–1982) (Britain) Tasker became one of the leading British alpinists and Himalayan mountaineers of the 1970s. Though not a dazzling rock-climber, his fierce will drove him up an impressive itinerary of alpine ROUTES—including the 1938 route on the EIGER in winter. In 1975 with Dick Renshaw, he made the FIRST ASCENT of the south ridge of Dunagiri in INDIA. Climbing ALPINE STYLE, they took 10 days to reach the summit, the last four of them without food or fuel. On the descent Renshaw sustained FROSTBITE. In 1976 Tasker and Peter BOARDMAN climbed the west face of the nearby CHANGA-BANG—one of the most technically advanced Himalayan climbs done that decade. Tasker tried K2 in 1978 and 1980, summited KANGCHENJUNGA in 1979, tried EVEREST west ridge in winter 1980, and summited Kongur in CHINA in 1981. He and Boardman died on the northeast ridge of Everest, in 1982.

Further reading: Maria Coffey, *Fragile Edge* (1989); Joe Tasker, *Everest the Cruel Way* (1981); Tasker, *Savage Arena* (1982).

TCU Abbreviation for tri-cam unit. A SPRING-LOADED CAMMING DEVICE with three cams instead of the usual four, and which fits thinner CRACKS and shallower POCKETS than other SLCDs. First developed by Metolius Mountain Products (United States) during the 1980s, and later by other manufacturers.

TECHNICAL CLIMBING Difficult climbing moves in FREE CLIMBING or ICE CLIMBING, generally of a level requiring use of ROPE or BELAYS.

TECHNIQUE STYLE, finesse and technical ability used to overcome climbing difficulties.

TEJAS, VERN (1953–) (United States) This Alaskan mountain guide gained prominence after a winter solo of DENALI in 1988. Tejas's winter climb was preceded by an outstanding MOUNTAINEERING career. Most notably, he made the first WINTER ASCENTS of Mount HUNTER and Mount LOGAN and the first ALPINE-STYLE ascent of Denali's northwest BUTTRESS. He singlehandedly rescued two dying Korean climbers from the top of Denali's Cassin Ridge, parasailed and mountain-biked down ARGENTINA's ACON-CAGUA, and soloed and parasailed Mount VINSON in ANT-ARCTICA. Tejas carried an aluminum ladder on his winter climb of Denali's west buttress and walked in the middle of it to prevent himself from falling into CREVASSES. He spent several weeks in an extremely stormy period on the west buttress, reached the summit, then descended uneventfully. Ultimately, Tejas showed the world that Denali could be climbed in winter without suffering any epic disasters or FROSTBITE.

Further reading: Lewis Freedman, *Dangerous Steps; Vernon Tejas and the Solo Winter Ascent of Mount McKinley* (1990).

TEMPERATURE INVERSION A weather condition in which cold air falls into a valley and warm air rises to occupy the high ground. This can lead to unstable snow and ice conditions high on a mountain. Because climbers may set out from the cold valley expecting to find a good

freeze higher up, they are at risk of AVALANCHE from the unstable ground above them.

TEMPLE, MOUNT (Canada) Mount Temple was the first 11,000 ft (11,636 ft/3,543 m) peak to be climbed in the CANADIAN ROCKIES. The peak is visible from the village of Lake Louise. The summit was reached in 1894 by S. E. S. Allen, L. F. Frissel and W. D. Wilcox via a scramble up the southwest slopes, now the normal ROUTE. The north face is sometimes called the "EIGER of the Rockies." On the north face, there are about a half-dozen distinct routes. They are typically done in a day, yet are serious, with risk from ICE FALL. Among the north face routes the 1966 Brian Greenwood–Charlie Locke (5.8 A2) route is said to be the safest. The east ridge, first climbed in 1931 by Stegmaier and Wittich, is a classic 5.7 route and was hard for the time.

Guidebooks: G. Boles, R. Kruszyna and W. L. Putnam, *The Rocky Mountains of Canada South* (1979); Sean Dougherty, *Selected Alpine Climbs in the Canadian Rockies* (1991); S. Roper and A. Steck, *Fifty Classic Climbs of North America* (1979).

TENDONITIS The inflammation of the membrane or sheath surrounding the tendons. In climbers, the tendons of the fingers, wrist, elbow and shoulder may be damaged during difficult climbing or training, especially on thin EDGES. Conservative training, warming up before climbs or workouts and avoiding extreme exertion on fingertips reduce risk of tendon damage. Dead hangs (or straight-arm hangs) from chin-up bars or fingerboards can strain tendons in the shoulder and elbow. A snapped tendon is very serious and requires expert medical treatment and long rehabilitation. Treatment for injured tendons is summed up as rest, because tendons need several weeks to heal. A damaged tendon is prone to re-injury. Taping the fingers between the knuckles, or around wrists or elbows, offers some support to tendons.

TENNESSEE (United States) Dotting the hilly southeast corner of Tennessee and the Cumberland Plateau are numerous cliffs of quartzite and sandstone, which extend in a "sandstone belt" from Sunset Rock on Lookout Mountain (a stronghold for Confederate forces in a Civil War battle) and Tennessee Wall outside the city of Chattanooga, for 70 miles (112 km) south to YELLOW CREEK FALLS in ALABAMA. The walls range from 80 to 200 ft (24 to 61 m) high, and feature CRACK and FACE CLIMBING. Tennessee Wall, a vast area in the Tennessee River Gorge, was selected for *Mountain* Magazine's series "The Ten Best Crags in America" for its unique quality of having the biggest free-climbable roofs in the world, like the route Celestial Mechanics (5.12+), a 35-ft (10.5-m) horizontal CEILING. A mild climate make year-round climbing possible on these cliffs. Many rock-climbing areas have been opened in this region since 1988; Buzzard Point near Dayton, Spider Rock and Hidden Rock, near Monterey. Older areas include Great Stone Door, a gorge in Savage Gulf State Natural Area near Monteagle; Fall Creek Falls near Pikeville (with a 250-ft/76-m waterfall which has frozen in winter); and

Fiery Gizzard Gulch Elizabethtown, Honey Creek, Colditz Cove, Ozone Falls, Piney Falls, Virgin Falls, Foster Falls and Bucksnort Bluffs. A nontechnical hill, Clingman's Dome (6,643 ft/2,025 m), in Great Smoky National Park, is the state's high point.

Guidebooks: Rob Robinson, *Underground Guide to the Tennessee Wall* (1990); Robinson, *Southern Sandstone, A Climbers Guide to Chattanooga, Tennessee* (1986).

TENSION TRAVERSE A ROPE maneuver where the LEADER or SECOND uses some tension from the rope through a point of PROTECTION or ANCHOR above. The rope takes some of the climber's weight, and by leaning into the rope, the climber may move sideways, pulling across on HOLDS. To follow a tension traverse, the second may have to rig a BACK ROPE to avoid a swing. (See also PENDULUM.)

TENTH MOUNTAIN INFANTRY DIVISION (United States) Although civilian climbing in the United States ground to a virtual halt during World War II, the army's Quartermaster Corps developed special equipment that was used by climbers in postwar years, such as aluminum CARABINERS, nylon ROPES and the first angle PITONS. In November 1941 the first mountain infantry troops began training near Mount RAINIER (WASHINGTON), and combat troops trained in climbing at SENECA ROCKS (WEST VIRGINIA). The Tenth Mountain Infantry Division was formed in July 1943. During autumn 1944 German troops dug into mountainous high ground at the foot of the Apennine Range and blocked the Allied advance through Italy. After two allied ground attacks failed, the Tenth Mountain Division was moved to the front. Under cover of darkness, their piton hammers muffled with cloth, they climbed the steep Riva Ridge and took the Germans completely by surprise. The attack by the the Tenth Mountain Division opened a hole in the German defenses that led to its fall within a week, and the allies continued their march into Europe.

Further reading: Rene Coquoz, *The Invisible Men on Skis* (1986).

TENTS Modern tents for various types of MOUNTAINEERING can be divided into several categories.

A-shaped tents have a pitched roof and a rectangular floor. The simplest designs use upright poles at either end and are staked at the corners and tensioned out with guy cords. Stronger designs use poles along the ridge and sides. Though most are suited for moderate climates, some very strong A-shaped tents are made. Aside from being heavy, the biggest drawback of such tents is their vulnerablity to being flattened by storms because of their broad, flat walls.

Pyramid tents use a central supporting pole, which is tensioned out by guy cords. Floor shape may be square or circular. They have similar advantages and disadvantages to A-shaped tents.

Tunnel tents or hoop tents have a curved cross-section, and use two or three poles to form curved ribs. This lightweight design deflects wind and sheds snow well due to curved walls and a curved roof, and is suitable for extreme weather.

Free-standing dome and modified-dome tents are built around the principle of the geodesic dome. These symmetrical tents stand upright due to their pole configuration. Wind is deflected equally from any angle, and they have good resistance to heavy snow-loading. They are usually rated for extreme weather use.

Hybrid tents, transverse hoop tents: There is a broad category of tents that derive their shapes by modifying aspects of the above designs.

Lightweight mountaineering or bivouac tents are simple shelters having two crossed poles. They are rectangular with a curved roof. Some models use one skin of GORE-TEX instead of the usual double nylon layer. They withstand winds by flexing with gusts. Rated for four-season use.

General findings of wind tunnel tests indicate that A-shaped tents collapse in winds beyond 30 mph (50 km/h); tunnel tents collapse at wind speeds between 72 and 75 mph (116 and 121 km/h) when pitched along the wind stream; 59 and 83 mph (94 and 133 km/h) when pitched across the wind stream; and dome-style tents collapse at speeds between 72 and 81 mph (116 and 129 km/h) when pitched along the wind stream.

Furthermore, tents with steep sides shed snow better than tents with low angles. An overnight snowfall can load a tent with 50 lbs (23 kgs) of weight, which can easily collapse a tent. Digging tents out of snow is essential during storms.

Most tents consist of two ceiling layers, one waterproof, the other breathable, and a waterproof floor. The outer ceiling layer, or "fly" is usually waterproofed ripstop nylon or Dacron. A few tents use treated canvas blends for the fly, which are strong but heavy. A fabric weight of 1.9 oz (53 g) ripstop nylon with a tear resistance of nine lbs (four kg) is strong enough for high-wind use. The waterproof coating on cloth is measured in PSI (pounds per square inch), to indicate the pressure needed before water penetrates the coating. Cloth of about 5 PSI is typical for fly sheets. The inner ceiling layer is protected by the fly. It is lightweight, breathable nylon with a light silicon coating to resist moisture but not the passage of air. Lightweight single-skin tents have a Gore-Tex ceiling. Tent-weight Gore-Tex is usually 3 oz (84 gr) per square foot. Seams contain about 10 stitches per inch, and these pinholes let rain in if they are not sealed. The tent floor is tough nylon taffeta or Dacron coated with polyurethane or PVC. A 15 PSI coating-weight is typical. Tents for serious use have "bathtub floors" that wrap up the wall of the tent.

Other than in low-humidity climates like a desert, condensation inside a tent is a fact of life. Two people sleeping in a tent put out over 1,000 mls (about 2.25 pints) of perspired and exhaled water vapor per night. Evaporation from clothing, steam from cooking and the natural humidity of air can double or quadruple this amount of moisture. This moisture stays airborne until the temperature inside the tent cools to "dewpoint." At that point droplets of moisture condense on the inside of the tent; if it's cold enough, the moisture freezes into a layer of frost. Either way, the result is water dripping onto sleeping bags and clothing. Condensation is controlled by introducing air into a tent. Mesh doors or panels act as vents to allow water vapor to pass to the outside, yet keep wind-blown snow out. Some tents have mesh ceilings for ventilation. The air space between double walls permits an even current of air to pass through open vents and remove water vapor that has passed through the inner tent.

Poles comprise the skeleton of the tent. They are segmented for portability and slot together during pitching. Poles of tubular alloy such as 7075 T9 or 7001 T6 aluminum, with a tensile strength of 96,000 PSI, are usual. Carbon fiber is lighter and as strong as aluminum. Fiberglass is strong but brittle under stress, and is subject to deterioration from age and exposure to ultraviolet sunlight. Tubular pole repair sleeves act as splints on broken poles. Tents that pitch quickly are advantageous in howling winds.

TERRADACTYL   A technical ICE TOOL developed in the 1960s by Scottish climber Hamish MACINNES. This tool was a radical departure from ICE AXES of the day because its pick was steeply angled at 55 degrees to the short-handled shaft, enabling a terradactyl to be swung and hooked into ice and allowing a climber to hang securely from the pick. This tool and the refinements it inspired made FRONT POINTING on vertical ice the natural way to climb, and virtually eliminated laborious STEP CUTTING.

TERRAY, LIONEL   (1923–1965) (France)   French ALPINISM made a giant stride forward in the decade after World War II. The stocky, energetic Terray was the master in this period. With Louis LACHENAL, Terray set new standards for speed and daring in alpine climbing. In 1946 they forged a new ROUTE on the Walker Spur of the GRANDES JORASSES, quickly followed by the second ascent of the EIGERwand in July 1947 by a new route, in atrocious winter weather. Their 1949 seventh ascent of the northeast face of the Piz Badille took seven and a half hours—nearly a third of the time of CASSIN's first ascent. The following year Terray narrowly missed being on the summit of the first EIGHT THOUSAND METER PEAK ever climbed, ANNAPURNA. Soon afterward, he made the first ascent of Cerro FITZROY in PATAGONIA, the first major rock route in a region of notoriously severe weather. Later he took two clients up the first ascent of Huantzan in PERU. And in 1955 he and Jean Couzy made a breezy first ascent of MAKALU, the fifth-highest peak in the world. Back in Peru in 1956 he made FIRST ASCENTS of two of the loveliest peaks of the Cordillera Vilcabamba: Chacraraju and Taulliraju. At this point in his life, Terray reckoned that in less than seven years he'd taken part in seven foreign expeditions, done approximately 180 ascents in the ALPS, given some 700 lectures and driven 9,000 miles (14,400 km). Though one side of him longed for a quieter domestic life, he could not stop his obsession with climbing. In NEPAL at the age of 40 he made the first ascent of Jannu on a second attempt in 1962. Back in Peru Terray led an expert French team up the first attempt on Chacraraju East, easily the hardest technical route then done in the ANDES. Two months later he was in Nepal again and climbed Nilgiri a neighbor of Annapurna. In the course of two and a half decades in the

sport, Terray had many narrow escapes on rock and ice. His legendary luck ran out one afternoon at the end of an ordinary climb on a limestone FACE. At the top of the cliff, either he or his roped partner slipped on a grassy slope and both plunged to their death.

TETONS   (United States)   The most famous mountains in the United States offer spectacular and diverse ALPINE CLIMBING on craggy peaks of gneiss. The Tetons abruptly rise 7,000 ft (2,134 m) above the plains of western WYOMING and culminate in 13,770-ft (4,198-m) GRAND TETON. Some dozen other prominent summits and two dozen or more subsidiary summits are clustered in a 40-mile (64-km)-long north-south chain within Grand Teton National Park. Prominent peaks include Mount Owen (12,928 ft/3,941 m), Middle and South Tetons (12,804 and 12,514 ft/3,904 and 3,815 m), Mount Moran (12,605 ft/3,843 m) and Teewinot (12,325 ft/3,758 m). At Jenny Lake, the AMERICAN ALPINE CLUB runs a climber's hut. Climbing centers on Grand Teton, a giant thumb with about three dozen significant ROUTES. Throughout the range the rock is blocky, angular and generally solid, although loose rock and natural rock fall can be expected. Routes on "The Grand" and other high Teton peaks may reach 3,000 ft (915 m) long. Routes range in difficulty from Class 4 scrambles to multi-day FREE and AID routes. Although most climbing is on rock, there are some small GLACIERS and ice COULOIRS. North-aspect routes can be coated in VERGLAS. The climate is generally dry, but summer thunderstorms are common.

The confirmed FIRST ASCENT of the Grand Teton was in 1898. The 1930s were dominated by climbers like Robert UNDERHILL, Kenneth Henderson, Phil Smith and Fritiof Fryxell, Jack Durrance and Paul PETZOLDT who made many first ascents up to 5.8 in difficulty. Underhill and Fryxell's north ridge of the Grand Teton was perhaps the greatest climb of this era. In the 1950s and 1960s many climbers developed the Tetons, such as Willie UNSOELD, Fred BECKEY, Leigh Ortenburger, Robert Merriam, Art Gilkey, Yvon CHOUINARD, Royal ROBBINS and John Gill. In the 1970s attention moved to the rock walls without summits. The walls of Death Canyon, Disappointment Peak, Symmetry Spire and the south ridges of Mount Moran yielded technical routes to climbers like Roger Briggs, Jim Ericson, Jim Donini, the LOWE family and Steve WUNSCH. Difficult routes continue to appear. During the 1980s Jim BEYER, Rennie Jackson, Charlie Fowler and Paul Gagner pushed BIG WALL alpine climbing to high levels in the Tetons.

Today routes to the prominent summits are popular and frequently guided. Numbers of overnight climbers are closely regulated by the National Park Service.
Guidebooks: Leigh Ortenburger and Reynold Jackson, *A Climber's Guide to the Teton Range* Vols. I and II (1965); Richard Rossiter, *Tetons Classics: Selected Climbs in Grand Teton National Park* (1991).

TEXAS   (United States)   Rock climbing in this state is dominated by legendary HUECO TANKS, yet other areas are highly developed. SPORT CLIMBING is practiced at New Wall, a limestone CRAG within Austin. Traditional ETHICS prevail at Gus Fruh, also limestone, also near Austin. Enchanted Rock State Park, 100 miles (160 km) from Austin, is a popular granite area with CRACKS and steep SLABS. Big Bend National Park is a deep limestone gorge with potential for long adventure climbs. Texas's high point is a craggy mountain that may be hiked up, Guadalupe Peak (8,749 ft/2,667 m) in Guadalupe Mountains National Park. **Guidebook:** James Crump, et al, *Enchanted Rock Austin TX* (1989).

THAILAND Cragging and bolted SPORT CLIMBING on limestone karst cliffs on the coastline and islands of southern Thailand has been developed by Europeans. The main area is Koh Phi Phi, a pair of islands, Phi Phi Le and Phi Phi Don, in the Andaman Sea, about 25 miles (40 km) from Pranang Bay. Access to cragging is by hired boat. The cliffs are regularly scaled by local swallow-nest hunters, who use bamboo poles and scaffolding to reach the nests, which are sold to Chinese merchants. The birds' saliva, which bonds the nests together, is believed to impart vigor. Even in the cool season, November to February, temperatures in southern Thailand may reach 90 degrees F (32 degrees C).

THERMAL UNDERWEAR Underwear for cold weather that absorbs minimal moisture and traps warmth by means of thermal insulation. (See CLOTHING FOR MOUNTAINEERS.)

THIN Refers to difficult FREE CLIMBING on small HOLDS. Thin ice refers to ice less than one inch (2.54 cm) thick. (See BLACK ICE, VERGLAS.)

THIRD CLASSING A term used in the United States, meaning to FREE SOLO without a ROPE. The term is derived from the U.S. RATING SYSTEM of classes one to six. Third classing typically means to scramble over easy "third-class" terrain without a BELAY, but it can also describe an ascent of a fifth-class climb, which requires rope and belaying, by applying third-class tactics to it.

THREAD A small natural tunnel through rock into which a SLING may be inserted, or threaded, and used as an ANCHOR or PROTECTION.

THREE POINT CONTACT A principle of FREE CLIMBING that states that at any time a climber should have three limbs in contact with the rock while one limb moves up for the next HOLD. The principle is meant to ensure stability.

TIBESTI MOUNTAINS (Africa) This range of volcanic peaks lies 600 miles (960 km) east of the Hoggar Mountains, in the Sahara of North Africa. Although the rock walls are huge, they are loose, and the area is devoid of water. One of the main formations is the 5,000-ft (1,524-m) volcanic crater wall of the north face of Tarso Tieroko, a 10,430-ft (3,180-m) peak.

TIBET See CHINA.

TIEN SHAN RANGE (Russia, China) This range extends for 1,000 miles (1,600 km) from the Russian city of Tashkent to Urumchi in Chinese Xinjiang. Some in CHINA call it the Celestial Range. Because of its northerly latitude the area can experience severe storms. Much of the mountain landscape here is characterized by barren terrain and undistinguished peaks, but along the Russo-Chinese border, southeast of Lake Issyk-kul, lie several peaks that are famous in the history of Soviet climbing. Khan Tengri (22,734 ft/6,995 m, formerly 23,593 ft/7,193 m) is a striking ice-clad pyramid of seemingly crackless marble, breached via a moderate ROUTE up the west ridge in 1931 by Ukranians. Some dozen routes up all aspects of this steep peak have been climbed by Soviets. On the Russo-Chinese border is Pik Pobeda, or, to the Chinese, Mount Tomur (24,400 ft/7,439 m). The huge ice wall of Pobeda was not climbed until 1956, when an expedition led by V. ABALAKOV climbed the northeast spur. Over 60 climbers have perished on this frequently ascended peak. The first Chinese ascent was in 1977, via the south face.
Further reading: Jill Neate, *High Asia* (1989).

TIE OFF Sometimes called hero loop. A short SLING (six inches to 12 inches/15 to 30 cm long) of thin WEBBING or thin ROPE (half-inch/1.27 cm or nine-sixteenths-inch/1.30 width webbing or six-m rope) used for tying off PITONS or RIVETS. Tie offs are commonly used on AID climbs for reducing leverage on protruding or stacked pitons. A slip knot, lark's head, or clove hitch are used to secure the piton. See KNOTS.

TIGHT ROPE Tension on the rope. A SECOND following a PITCH may call for tension from the BELAYER to assist in a difficult section. A TENSION TRAVERSE may permit a climber to cross blank rock by taking his weight on the rope. On a true FREE ASCENT of a rock climb, tension is not used. (See CLIMBING COMMANDS.)

TILMAN, H. W. (1898–1977) (Britain) The great romantic figure of mountain exploration this century, Harold William Tilman was 30 before his MOUNTAINEERING career began with the ascent, as a novice, of the west ridge of Mount Kenya in 1930. His life before then had been eventful enough. In World War I he was sent to the Western Front at age 17 and spent his 18th birthday—February 14, 1916—in a dugout on the Somme. He was wounded, won the Military Cross and bar, ended the war as a major, then went to plant coffee in British East Africa (now KENYA), where he met a fellow planter, Eric SHIPTON. Mountains dictated the course of his life for the next two decades. He traveled up the Rishi Ganga to the NANDA DEVI sanctuary with Shipton in 1934; was on the 1935 Mount EVEREST reconnaissance; he climbed NANDA DEVI, the highest summit climbed in the prewar period, with ODELL in 1936; he attended the 1937 "Blank on the Map" explorations with Shipton, Auden and Spender that contributed greatly to knowledge of the KARAKORAM; and finally led the 1938 Everest EXPEDITION.

In the Second World War he fought in the Western Desert and behind enemy lines in Albania and the DOLOMITES, for which he was awarded the DSO and made a freeman of the City of Belluno. After it he served as a British Consul in Burma before an extraordinary period from 1947 to 1952 of continual, often solitary, travel through CHINA, NEPAL, Sinkiang, Kashmir, the Gobi Desert and Afghanistan.

Finally, there are 23 years and 150,000 miles of sailing—in Bristol Channel pilot-cutters built at the turn of the century—to climb peaks and cross uncharted ICE CAPS in the ANTARCTIC, PATAGONIA, GREENLAND, Spitzbergen. He disappeared in his 80th year when the boat on which he was sailing as an ordinary crew member was lost without trace in November storms between Rio and Port Stanley.

His books, of which there are 15, are among the best in mountaineering literature, written with cultured clarity, detached irony, wit and self-effacement.
Further reading: Jim Perrin, ed., *H. W. Tilman: The Seven Mountain-Travel Books* (1983).

TINTAGEL HEAD (Britain) This imposing cliff on the north Cornish coast offers a few outstanding ROUTES in a formidable position. The CRAG 250 ft (76 m) at its highest point is separated from the mainland and its eponymous village and is reached via a footbridge. Tinatagel boasts one of the finest routes in southern England, Il Duce, a magnificent 5.11 up a huge groove above the sea. The route was climbed by Pat LITTLEJOHN and Keith Darbyshire in 1972 with one aid. To the right of Il Duce is King's Arete, a serious 5.11 climbed in 1982 by Andy Meyers and Mick Fowler.
Guidebooks: Pat Littlejohn, *South West Climbs* (1991); Iain Peters, *North Devon and Cornwall* (1988).

TICHY, HERBERT (1912–   ) (Austria) A lone adventurer and student of Buddhism, Tichy earned a place in MOUNTAINEERING legend because of one climb—the FIRST ASCENT of CHO OYU in 1954, the third EIGHT THOUSAND METER PEAK ever to be climbed. Whereas ANNAPURNA and EVEREST had been surmounted with large-scale EXPEDITIONS, the Cho Oyu effort was the work of a small team in which SHERPAS climbed as equals. The total complement was three Austrians and seven Sherpas, including the legendary Pasang. During the epic climb on Cho Oyu, Pasang was often the de facto LEADER. Halfway though the expedition, when he was down in the valley buying fresh provisions, Pasang heard of a Swiss expedition that had moved into position on their route on Cho Oyu. In just two days he and two other Sherpas travelled fully laden from 13,120 to 21,615 ft (4,000 to 6,590 m), and over 30 miles (48 km) of rough country. On the next day Pasang pushed up to Camp Four at 22,960 ft (7,000 m), and the day following made the 26,742 ft (8,153-m) summit, along with Tichy and Sepp Jöchler. Pasang's feat of endurance was paralleled by Tichy's strong determination and willpower to overcome a bad case of debilitating FROSTBITE and physical burnout. Of the summit, Tichy later wrote:

"The endless blue sky fell around us like a bell. To have reached the peak was glorious, but the nearness of the sky was overwhelming. Only a few men have been nearer to it than we were that day."

TOPO Short for topographic route description. A technique of graphically depicting a climb by using symbols instead of words to illustrate formations and climbing maneuvers. The technique originated in Europe. Topo guidebooks have gradually replaced written descriptions for most climbing areas of the world. The topo's principal advantage is that it uses universal symbols, alleviating problems of language and translation.

TOP ROPING A BELAYING method in which the climber is belayed from above. There are two types: From above, in which the LEADER has completed a PITCH and belays the SECOND from above; and from the ground, in which an ANCHOR is arranged at the top of the cliff. The ROPE is passed through CARABINERS (preferably a LOCKING CARABINER or doubled carabiners with gates in opposition) and connected to this belay. A belayer on the ground handles the rope as required.

TORBAY (Britain) This large bay surrounded by the towns of Torquay, Paignton and Brixham, offers rock climbers everything from SPORT CLIMBS to adventure routes, and the many south-facing limestone CRAGS allow activity to continue throughout the year. The principal areas are Long Quarry Point and Anstey's Cove, Daddyhole and Telegraph Hole Quarry, and Berry Head, which contains the frightening Old Redoubt Cliff.

On Long Quarry Point Slabs lie harder ROUTES like Pat LITTLEJOHN's Black Ice (5.10c) from 1973, and Nick White and Pete Bull's Renegade (5.11a), climbed in 1984. White's late-1980s routes Up the Styx (5.12a) and Shadow Beast (5.12c) are popular bolt-protected climbs. In contrast, the overhanging Sanctuary Wall has strenuous routes like Steve Monks' Call to Arms (5.10d), and Martin Crocker's Free the Spirit (5.12b). Finally in this area, Mitre Buttress in Anstey's Cove has great PITCHES like Nick White's 1988 classic, Empire of the Sun (5.12b).

Near Torquay, Daddyhole has easier routes. On the Main Cliff Gargantua is a steep and airy 5.9 climbed in 1967 by Frank Cannings, while the route that started interest in Torbay climbing is Gates of Eden, which has a wild position for its 5.6 grade.

The 300-ft (91-m) Old Redoubt Cliff at Berry Head is a serious proposition, from which escape at high tide is only achieved by swimming. Moonraker is a famous 5.8 route climbed by Peter Biven and Pat Littlejohn. More awesome is Caveman (5.12b), climbed in 1982 by Andy Meyers and Mick Fowler. It traverses a huge cave at the base of the crag. The route, almost 400 ft (122 m) long, was soloed by Dave Thomas in 1990.
Guidebook: Pat Littlejohn, *South West Climbs* (1991).

TORRE Spanish "Tower," used principally in South America.

TORRIDON (Scotland) Torridon stretches from Loch Carron in the south to Loch Maree in the north and is characterized by highly stratified sandstone peaks that are often too loose and dangerous to climb on, with some notable exceptions. The area is generally remote, being several hours drive from Fort William.

The cliffs of Sgurr a' Chaorachain, comprising six sandstone buttresses up to 500 ft (152 m) high, are only minutes from the Tornapass to Applecross road. Higher up the mountain is The Cioch, a dramatic promontory of rock whose tallest facet is almost 1,000 ft (305 m) high. Tom PATEY climbed an outstanding 5.5 here with Chris BONINGTON in 1960, described as "the Diff to end all Diffs" by the first ascensionists. The other classic LINE is the Cioch Super Direct and Cioch Corner combination, a 900-ft (274-m) 5.8. The routes were climbed in 1968 and 1970 by R. Hobbs and C. Rowland respectively.

Diabaig, near the village of Torridon, is a huge wave of slabby, crystalline gneiss. Elsewhere, Coire Mhic Fhearchair, pronounced (Korry-Vik-Erker) lies on the northern flanks of Beinn Eighe (pronounced Ben A). The rock has a lower tier of sandstone and an upper one of quartzite, the former being much harder to protect. The CRAG is approached from Torridon.

Carnmore Crag, lying between Gairloch and Ullapool, is in one of BRITAIN's few remaining wilderness areas. This is a fine, massive sweep of clean gneiss, lying on the south flank of Beinn a'Chaisgein Mor and overlooking Fionn Loch. The crag is remote and is approached from the village of Poolewe. Carnmore is nearly 900 ft (274 m) high and has some of the best routes in Britain. Famous is Gob, climbed by the partnership of Dougal HASTON and Robin SMITH in 1960. There are harder routes here as well.

The Old Man of Stoer, 7 miles (11 km) north of Ullapool near the village of Lochinver, is separated by a 25-ft (seven-m) channel from the mainland, a 200-ft (61-m) column of sandstone set on a more sea-resistant plinth. There are a large number of such stacks on the Scottish coast and they provide sport for climbers who enjoy traveling vast distances and making difficult approaches. Tom Patey's original route is an outstanding 5.6 that he climbed in 1966 on the stack's landward face. The stack's other facets have also been climbed. Descending sea stacks is usually more dangerous than climbing them.

An amazing cliff on the island of Lewis in the Outer Hebrides is Sron Ulladale. Tarbert, the port for the Skye ferry, is a good base for visits to Sron or Strone, as it is also known. The west face is continuous for half a mile (.4 km) and culminates in a huge overhanging wall.

There are easier routes, Eureka for instance, an excellent 5.7 climbed by J. Grieve and E. Jones in 1967, and a 5.6, Prelude, but the chief attractions are more demanding. Stone is a 670-ft (204-m) 5.11d of outstanding quality, freed in 1981 by Mick Fowler and Andy Meyers. Fowler has made a specialty of stealing the best routes from under Scottish noses. Undoubtedly the best effort occurred in 1987 when a team of Welsh hotshots, including Johnny DAWES and Paul Pritchard, descended on Lewis, freeing the Doug SCOTT 1969 A4 classic, The Scoop. This route

overhangs 150 ft (46 m) in its 500-ft (152-m) height, illustrating the nature of the enterprise. Every PITCH is 5.12+ and the route gets an overall classification of 5.13a.

Guidebooks: Donald Bennet, ed., *The Munros* (1991); Geoff Cohen, *The Northern Highlands* Vol. 1 and Vol. 2 (1991); Kevin Howett, *Rock Climbing in Scotland* (1990).

TRADITIONALIST A term used in reference to a climber who eschews SPORT CLIMBING techniques and prefers ROUTES with fewer BOLTS and more NATURAL PROTECTION.

TRANGO TOWERS (Pakistan) This cluster of steep granite spires is comprised of some of the highest walls in the world and exemplifies Himalayan BIG WALL CLIMBING. The Trango Towers rise near the lower BALTORO Glacier in the Baltoro Muztagh. They are bounded by the Trango and Dunge Glaciers and include Great Trango Tower (20,618 ft/6,286 m) and Trango Tower (also called Nameless Tower, 20,464 ft/6,239 m). On GLACIERS nearby are the spires of Uli Biaho Tower (20,042 ft/6,109 m), Grand Cathedral (19,120 ft/5,828 m), Lobsang Spire (18,723 ft/5,707 m) and, six miles (10 km) to the southwest, Paiju Peak (21,686 ft/6,610 m). The forepeaks of Great Trango, facing the Baltoro Glacier, are called Trango Castle, and have been climbed by French, Italian and Japanese EXPEDITIONS.

Great Trango's FIRST ASCENT was in 1977 by Americans Dennis Hennek, Jim Morrisey, Galen ROWELL, John ROSKELLEY and Kim Schmitz who climbed the mixed southwest face. The zenith of big wall climbing came in 1984 when four Norwegians spent 22 days on the 5,000-ft (1,524-m) vertical northeast pillar of Great Trango. During the ascent, two climbers descended to allow the others enough provisions to complete the climb, but after Hans Christian Doseth and Finn Doehli finished the route, they disappeared while RAPPELLING down. The same year, Andy Selters and Scott Woollums (United States) climbed a mixed route on the northwest face. In 1992 a route more demanding than the Norwegian effort was established in 18 days on the east face by John Middendorf (United States) and Xavier Bongard (Switzerland), and is now considered one of the most difficult big walls of the world.

Chris BONINGTON summed up the Trangos' allure when he said "Everest is the cake but Trango is the icing." He was speaking of Trango Tower, which Britons attempted twice before successfully climbing the south face. On the first attempt (1975) Martin BOYSEN nearly perished in a strange mishap when his knee became wedged in a CRACK for many hours. In 1976 Boysen, Mo ANTHOINE, Joe BROWN, and Malcolm Howells summited. Jim Curran's book, *Trango, The Nameless Tower* (1978), describes this climb.

On shapely Nameless Tower, Slovenians climbed a new route on the south face in 1987 (largely freed at 5.12 by Wolfgang GULLICH and Kurt Albert in 1988), and French-Swiss led by Michel Piola climbed the west pillar and PARAPENTED off the summit. In 1988 the east face went to Wojciech KURTYKA and Erhard LORETAN. In 1989 a Spanish team climbed the southwest face, and Gullich and Albert added a 5.12 free route, Eternal Flame, on the south face.

Trango Towers

In 1990 Takeyasu Minamiura (Japan) made a 40-day solo-ascent of the northeast face. When he attempted to para-pente from the top he became trapped on a LEDGE and was rescued a week later. In 1992 Greg Child and Mark Wilford added another route to the south face. An altogether differ-ent achievement occurred that year on Great Trango, when Australians Nic Feteris and Glenn Singleman BASE JUMPED from the northeast face.

Guidebook: Jan Kielkowski, *Trango Towers* (German text) (1989).

TRANSHIMALAYA (Tibet, China) A (625-mile 1,000-km)-long range of little-known, ill-defined peaks run-ning through TIBET. The southern edge of the range follows the curvature of the HIMALAYA, while the northern limit runs between Lake Pamgkong Tsho in the west and Lake Tengri Nor in the east. The range is usually divided into two sections. The Kailas Range, in which lies the sacred Tibetan peak Kailas above Lake Manasrowar, is the main part. Northwest of Lhasa is the Nyenchin Tangla Range. The range was explored in the late 1800s and early 1900s by a variety of explorers, the best known of whom was Sven Hedin. Little climbing has been done here, though Nigchin Kangsha (23,691 ft/7,223 m) was climbed by the

Tibet Mountaineering Association in 1986, and Nanchen Tangla (23,491 ft/7,162 m) was climbed by a Japanese team in 1986.

TRAPROCK (United States) The main FREE CLIMBING region in Connecticut, near New Haven. Though small, at 120 ft (36 m), the quality CRACK and FACE CLIMBING of these basalt rocks has caused them to be well developed, with some 2,000 ROUTES on a collection of CRAGS scattered through the wooded New England hills. Ragged Mountain, East Peak and Pinnacle Rock are the main areas. Traprock has an ETHIC that permits BOLTING to be done only free and on the lead, so bolts are rare. As a solution to otherwise unprotected leads here, a few local climbers devised a complex system of TIED-OFF SKYHOOK placements that en-abled some bold FACES to be led. This exemplifies the traditional heritage of the crags. During the early 1990s, local activist Ken Nichols, who climbed many Traprock routes in the 1970s and 1980s, became well known if not infamous in U.S. climbing magazines for removing RAPPEL-placed bolts in his own and other East Coast areas.

Guidebooks: John Harlin, *Climber's Guide to North America, East Coast Rock Climbs* (1986); Ken Nichols, *Trap-rock* (1982).

Proper Balance Traverse

TRAVERSE To climb sideways and up rather than straight up. (See BACK ROPE, PENDULUM, TENSION TRAVERSE, TYROLEAN TRAVERSE.)

TREMADOG (Britain) The CRAGS, Craig y Gesail, Craig y Castell, Craig Pant Ifan and Craig Bwlch y Moch, which lie above the A487 near Porthmadog, are popular areas of WALES. They are collectively known as Tremadog. The crags reach 200 ft (61 m), and are served by amenities such as the noted climber hangout, Eric's Café.

Trevor Jones was among the pioneers of the 1950s, climbing Great Western (5.7) in 1957. The Vector Buttress of Bwlch y Moch is a piece of rock that is as much part of British climbing folklore as any part of Wales. On this lies Joe BROWN's 1960 ROUTE Vector (5.10b), which sneaks through the large OVERHANGS and is one of BRITAIN's most famous routes. On the same crag is Peter Crew's Zukator, from 1964, undertaken for a bet with his SECOND, Al HARRIS, who followed in monk's cowl and winklepickers (men's shoes with extremely long toes). It was freed in 1974 at 5.11c. Hank Pasquill climbed the outstanding Silly Arete (5.10c) on Craig Pant Ifan in 1971. In 1975, Rowland Edwards added Void up the Vector Buttress headwall with one aid, which now goes free at 5.11a. Peter LIVESEY, at the height of his powers in 1975, climbed the strenuous CRACK of Fingerlicker on Pant Ifan at 5.11c.

John Redhead, a great contributor to Welsh climbing, added several excellent routes in 1980, including Atomic Finger Flake, on Vector Buttress, Sexual Salami and Sultans of Swing, all 5.11c. Also in 1980, Ron FAWCETT ventured out onto the Vector Buttress headwall up a thin crackline he called Strawberries (5.12b). Martin Atkinson added its direct finish four years later, Dream Topping, at a demanding 5.13b. Johnny Dawes solved one of the last LINES in 1987 with his Llanberries (5.13b).

Other notable crags south of the Snowdon massif are crags in the Cwellyn Valley, Craig y Bera on the north side of the Nantlle Valley, the Nantlle Ridge to its south and at the end of this CWM Silyn. Finally, there are the mysterious crags of the Lleyn Peninsula that have become increasingly popular in recent years.

Guidebooks: Mark Pretty, *Tremadog and Cwm Silyn* (1989); Paul Williams, *Rock Climbing in Snowdonia* (1990).

TRIBOUT, JEAN BAPTISTE (1961–) (France) This top French and world climber is the author of an abundance of hard climbs, including the first U.S. 5.14, To Bolt or Not to Be. Tribout established Le Spectre du Surmutant (8b/c or 5.14a) at BUOUX; Les Specialistes (8b/c) in the VERDON; Revanche, SAUSSOIS (8b/c or 5.14a). In 1982 he and Laurent Jacob established L'Autoroute du Soleiland and La Polka, both 7c, at Buoux. In 1983 he clocked in with an early 8a, Le Voyageur Imprudent at Mouries, near Avignon. He called Just Do It (8c+, or 5.14c) at SMITH ROCKS (United States), established in spring 1992, "the hardest thing I've ever done." In competitions, he has won many seconds and thirds, and for a long time a major win eluded him. By 1989 he appeared to be locked into second place. He was second at: the Masters' Invitational at Bercy, 1989; the Arco, Italy, Invitational Rockmaster in 1990; and the LaRiba Masters' Invitational in Mont Blanc, Spain, 1990. He was third in the overall World Cup and ASCI rankings in 1990. Finally, he won the third Master International D'Escalade du Prorel-Briançon in Briançon, France, in February 1991. This victory seemed especially due to him. He had outclimbed his peers in the finals at the Masters' Invitational at Bercy the year before, but that event was scored cumulatively, and he came in second overall.

TRI-CAM A passive camming NUT manufactured by Lowe (United States) and Camp (Italy). Tri-cams rely on the principle of a fulcrum point camming on one side of a CRACK and two rails camming against the other. They work well in horizontal cracks and irregular POCKETS. The fulcrum point tends to dig into soft rock, making it popular among desert sandstone climbers in the American Southwest. (See NATURAL PROTECTION.)

TRIG STATION Also trig point, triangulation point. A summit used by surveyors as a datum point. Maps show trig points as a triangle. On some summits a brass cap or a metal or wooden pyramid-structure mark the point for surveying.

TRINITY ALPS **(United States)** This "miniature High Sierra" lies in northwest CALIFORNIA. The concentration of highest peaks are granitic, up to 9,000 ft (2,744 m) high, with a few TECHNICAL routes up to 900 ft (274 m) high. A major complex of spires and DOMES near Mount SHASTA known as Castle Crags has the greatest potential for climbing. Pioneer climbers like John HARLIN and Fred BECKEY climbed in the Castle Crags as early as the 1940s, and new ROUTES up to 1,000 ft (305 m) high continue to be added, but difficulty of access and a history of nonreporting has kept this area in relative obscurity.

TROG British colloquialism for a mountain walk. Somewhat archaic.

TROILLET, JEAN **(1948–   )** **(Switzerland)** This Swiss guide climbed extensively in the ALPS, but it is on the EIGHT THOUSAND-METER PEAKS that he made his most significant contributions, climbing in a committing, new style, which he summarizes as "fast, light, non-stop day and night, with half a liter of water and a candy bar." Of the seven (26,240-ft) 8,000-m peaks he has climbed, most were made ALPINE STYLE and without oxygen, and six were climbed with Erhard LORETAN (Swiss). Troillet's eight thousanders include MAKALU (27,818 ft/8,481 m) climbed in 1982 by a new ROUTE on the north face, and again in 1991 by the west pillar; EVEREST (29,021 ft/8,848 m) in 1983 and 1986, both by the north face, the latter ascent via the direct Japanese-Hornbein Couloir and climbed up and down in the stunning time of 43 hours (with Loretan); ANNAPURNA I (26,538 ft/8,091 m) in 1984 by a new route on the west face; K2 (28,416 ft/8,611 m) by the southeast ridge; DHAULAGIRI (26,788 ft/8,167 m) east face in winter 1985, the first WINTER ASCENT of an eight thousand-meter peak; CHO OYU (26,903 ft/8,202 m) west face; and SHISHAPANGMA (26,391 ft/8,046 m) south face, both new routes, in autumn 1990.

TROLL WALL **(Norway)** A 3,936-ft (1,200-m) wall in the Romsdal Valley, of vertical and overhanging dark gneiss, that has drawn BIG WALL alpine climbers from around the world. The wall presents complex ROUTE finding and is often wet, despite its overhanging nature. The first probes of this wall began after Norwegians Arne Randers Heen and Ralph Hoibakk climbed Trollryggen East Pillar, a smaller wall beside Troll Wall, in 1958. The main wall, however, was first climbed in 1965, by British and Norwegians, climbing separate routes. The Norwegian route, which included Odd Eliassen, required 11 days, and climbed the left margin of the wall. The British team (John Amatt, Tony Howard, Bill Tweedale) tackled the main wall. This is now a popular FREE CLIMB. A French team in 1967 climbed an even steeper route. FIXED ROPES were employed on all these ascents, but several epic ascents and attempts in the early 1970s by Britons Ed Drummond, Ben Campbell-Kelly and Brian Wyvill produced ALPINE-STYLE ascents. Ward-Drummond's 20-day route in 1972, the culmination of three years of attempts to push a route up the FACE, became the subject of an inspired piece of climbing writing called "Mirror Mirror," published in the journal

Ascent. Polish climbers in the 1970s endured a WINTER ASCENT of Troll Wall.

TUBE CHOCK An item of PROTECTION for wide CRACKS. A section of tubular aluminum, four inches to eight inches (10 to 20 cm) in length and slung with cord or WEBBING through centrally located holes. Tube chocks are cut with a slight taper at the end and are simply wedged into constrictions in CRACKS. See NATURAL PROTECTION.

TUBER A belaying device consisting of a conical aluminum alloy tube through which the ROPE is fed, and clipped into a CARABINER. Manufactured by Lowe (United States). Discussed in BELAYING TECHNIQUES.

TULLIS, JULIE **(1939–1986)** **(Britain)** Tullis was BRITAIN's most accomplished female high-altitude climber and a co-founder of a documentary-making film team on K2 in 1983 with climber-cameraman Kurt DIEMBERGER. With the "Highest Filmteam in the World," she documented Himalayan climbing expeditions to NANGA PARBAT (1982, 1985), EVEREST (1985), K2 (1983, 1984, 1986) and BROAD PEAK (1984), and explored TIBET and NEPAL. She became the first British woman to summit Broad Peak and K2 (with Diemberger). She died on August 7, 1986 in a blizzard during the descent of K2. Her autobiography, *Clouds from Both Sides* (1986), appeared posthumously. Her film work includes *K2—The Elusive Summit, Under the Spell of Diamir, Tashigang—Tibetan Village Between Gods and Men* and *K2—Mountains of Dreams and Fate.* She also had black belts in judo and aikido. A campsite at Harrison's Rocks in Sussex, England, and a bar at the pub beneath High Rocks are named in her memory.

TUNBRIDGE WELLS **(Britain)** A loose term for the short sandstone OUTCROPS of southeast England, on the border between Kent and Sussex. Popular outcrops include Harrison's Rocks near Eridge Station, Bowles Rocks on the A26, High Rocks on the outskirts of Tunbridge and Stone Farm Rocks, south of East Grinstead. These areas—an hour's drive south of London—provide a TOP-ROPING playground with a high level of technicality.

Recorded climbing began at Harrison's in 1926, when Nea Morin observed the similarities between these rocks and those of FONTAINEBLEAU near Paris. She and others like Eric SHIPTON established some ROUTES at High Rocks that retain a 5.9 rating, including Unclimbed Wall at Harrison's and Steps Crack at High Rocks.

Technical standards shot ahead of the rest of England in 1945, when Clifford Fenner climbed 5.10s like The Niblick at Harrison's. In the late 1950s the Sandstone Climbing Club, of which Martin BOYSEN was a member, dominated development. In 1959, the SCC rediscovered Bowles, adding The Thing, still rated 5.12, and Digitalis and iHate, both 5.11.

While new climbs went up, including Guy McLelland's Crisis—What Crisis (5.13) at Harrison's, the modern era has been characterized by bold solos of established routes. Climbing on southern sandstone is unusual due to the slippery nature of the rock. Great care must be taken to avoid further erosion of this soft rock. CHALK is banned at Harrison's.

Guidebook: Dave Turner, *Southern Sandstone* (1989).

TUOLUMNE MEADOWS (United States) Located in the CALIFORNIA high country above YOSEMITE VALLEY, in the SIERRA NEVADA range, Tuolomne is famous for its varied and aesthetic rock climbing in a scenic sub-alpine setting. Warren HARDING and other Yosemite climbers first ventured northeast from their valley to Tuolumne's granite DOMES in the 1950s. In 1958 Chuck PRATT and Wally Reed initiated serious climbing here by completing a 10-pitch ROUTE on Fairview Dome. Bob Kamps went on to climb a legacy of TECHNICAL face routes here, with sparse BOLTS drilled only from available stances. Kamps' disciple Tom Higgins continued this trend into the 1970s, and became an out-spoken proponent of traditional ETHICS.

Tuolumne became popular during the 1970s, and scores of 1– 15-pitch FREE CLIMBS were established, up both CRACKS and FACES. Vern Clevenger was particularly active. In the early to mid-1980s John BACHAR put up numerous ROUTES, many legendary for their RUN OUTS on steep knobs. His famous Bachar-Yerian route brought to the fore the technique of placing bolts while standing on hook placements. Kurt Smith, Alan Nelson and Steve Schneider prolonged Tuolomne's ground-up reputation into the late 1980s. Today, TRADITIONAL routing tactics coexist with RAPPEL-BOLTED routes.

Guidebook: Don Reid and Chris Falkenstein, *Rock Climbs of Tuolumne Meadows* (1992).

TUPUNGATO (Chile, Argentina) This extinct, glaciated volcano on the Chilean-Argentinian border between Santiago and Mendoza is considered 21,490 ft (6,550 m) high by CHILE, 22,334 ft (6,807 m) by ARGENTINA. The peak lies within the Parque Provincial Tupungato. Access from either country entails three days on muleback and river fording. The Fitzgerald EXPEDITION won its summit via the north gap in April 1897. Stuart Vines and Matthias ZURBRIGGEN were the summiters. Some 15 other ROUTES have been opened since then. To the southwest Tupungato has a little brother aptly called Tupungatito (18,504 ft/5,640 m), which is continuously belching sulfurous steam. It was climbed in 1897 by Luis RISO PATRON. In 1934, several Chilean Germans camped at 17,000 ft (5,100 m) on the southwest FACE of Tupungato had to run down for their lives when the fumes of Tupungatito nearly choked them

to death during the night. In 1963, Argentinians climbed the south GLACIER. Germans climbed the eastern RIB in 1974 and Spaniard Francisco Garrido, alone, made the first WINTER ASCENT (October 1980) from the Chilean side.

Evelio Echevarria
Colorado State University

TURKEY ROCK (United States) A coarse-grained granite CRAG in COLORADO noted for difficult CRACKS, but also having knobby FACE CLIMBS. This complex of cliffs, up to 350 ft (107 m) high, lie 40 miles (64 km) northwest of Colorado Springs, 18 miles north of Woodland Park. Development began here in the early 1970s, with cracks like Brown Sugar (5.9), Quivering Quill (5.10) and For Turkeys Only (5.11 +).

Traditional ETHICS remain staunchly preserved here, yet bold face routes have appeared on the Turkey tail formation. Extreme routes include Charlie Fowler's Future Chic (5.13). The area lies at a cool 8,000 ft (2,439 m). A nearby formation called Sheep Nose also offers excellent granite cracks.

Guidebooks: Steve Cheyney, *For Turkeys Only: A Climber's Guide to Turkey Rock* (1989); John Harlin, *Climber's Guide to North America, Rocky Mountain Rock Climbs* (1985); Peter Hubbel and Mark Rolofson, *South Platte Rock Climbing and Garden of the Gods* (1989).

TYROLEAN TRAVERSE A method of crossing a deep gap with a ROPE, usually to gain the summit of a PINNACLE.

A rope must first be fixed between the pinnacle and the adjoining cliff. Most commonly a party climbing the pinnacle fixes a rope atop the cliff, and tows it up the pinnacle as they climb. Thus, the rope can be anchored across the gap. Otherwise, the pinnacle is lassoed with a doubled rope and the near end of the rope is anchored securely. The climber then clips his harness into the rope with a LOCKING CARABINER (as a self belay) and uses PRUSIK knots or mechanical ASCENDERS on one strand to cross the gap. BELAYING the traversing climber with a separate safety rope is recommended. The technique can be difficult to rig up and awkward to perform, especially if using DYNAMIC ROPES that stretch considerably. When retrieving the rope, it is pulled through the ANCHOR on the summit as for a RAPPEL. The Tyrolean is more fun than practical, but it can be helpful in rescue work. The name is derived from the mountains of the South Tyrol, in the Italian DOLOMITES, where the method was devised.

UEMURA, NAOMI (1941–1984) (Japan) Uemura's modesty and courage combined with exploits as diverse as rafting the length of the Amazon (1968) and becoming, with T. Matsuura, the first Japanese to summit on EVEREST (May 11, 1970) made him a national hero. Subsequent adventures included a return to Everest (1971) and a succession of solo trips: an 18-month-long, 7,500-mile (12,067-km) TRAVERSE by dog sled from GREENLAND to Kotzebu, ALASKA (1975), to the North Pole by dogsled (1978); and ascents of ACONCAGUA and KILIMANJARO. He died in February 1984 decending from the first solo ascent of DENALI in winter. He wrote of his solo exploits, "In all the splendor of solitude . . . it is a test of myself, and one thing I loathe is to have to test myself in front of other people."

UIAA Abbreviation for Union Internationale des Associations d'Alpinisme, the European organization that lays down specifications for climbing equipment and advises policy on matters of conservation and land use by climbers. Equipment marked "UIAA Approved" has met the standards of UIAA tests. See RATING SYSTEMS, ROPES.

UNDERCLING A FREE CLIMBING move in which the climber grips the underside of a flake or ROOF and applies upward force while exerting an opposite force with the feet directly below. Similar in principle to LIE BACKING.

UNDERHILL, MIRIAM O'BRIEN (1899–1976) (United States) One of America's finest woman climber, during the 1920s and 1930s, Underhill championed the cause of women's climbing in the United States and Europe. In an era when most ascents in the European ALPS were guided, she introduced guideless climbing and teaming with other women. Such ascents she called "manless," and in the company of women like Winifred Marples she climbed the Aiguille de Peigne in 1929, and with Alice Damesme the Grepon and the MATTERHORN. She was married to Robert UNDERHILL, and together they made many climbs in Europe and America. One of their finest routes together was the first TRAVERSE, in 1928, of the five PINNACLES of the Aiguilles du Diable, with guides Georges Cachat and Armand CHARLET. She wrote articles for *National Geographic* Magazine and an autobiography called *Give Me the Hills*.

UNDERHILL, ROBERT (1889–1983) (United States) During the 1920s and 1930s Underhill pioneered the ad-

, Undercling

vancement of technical roped climbing in the United States, which he learned while climbing in the ALPS. In the 1920s he climbed the Brenva and Peuterey Ridges of MONT BLANC, the Grepon, east face of the Dom, the MATTERHORN in a guideless ascent, the Piz Bernina, and in the DOLOMITES a guideless ascent of the Schmit-Kamin on the Funffingerspitze. He brought technical rope work and rock climbing to the Appalachian Mountain Club, and to CALIFORNIA climbers at the annual Sierra Club high camp in 1931. From 1928 to 1933 he opened early technical routes in the United States, on CANNON CLIFF, the Pinnacle Route on Mount WASHINGTON, east Ridge and north Ridge of the GRAND TETON, new routes in the WIND RIVERS, and, with Norman CLYDE, Jules Eichorn and Glen Dawson, the east face of Mount WHITNEY. In 1932 he married the American climber Miriam O'Brien, with whom most of his subsequent climbs were made. Their one-day TRAVERSE of the Aiguilles du Diable in the MONT BLANC area was a celebrated climb in its day. From 1928 to 1934 he edited *Appalachia*, the journal of the Appalachian Mountain Club, and he spent his life working on a book on logic. The couple is commemorated by the AMERICAN ALPINE CLUB's most prestigious honor, The Robert and Miriam UNDERHILL Award.

UNSOELD, WILLI (1926–1979) (United States) This legendary American climber is best known for his part in the FIRST ASCENT of EVEREST west ridge in 1963 with Tom HORNBEIN. The feat included the first TRAVERSE of Everest down the south COL, and forced BIVOUAC at 28,000 ft (8,537 m), on which Unsoeld was FROSTBITTEN and lost most of his toes. Otherwise, he was a well-known guide, lecturer, professor of philosophy and religion and an environmentalist who believed in the mystical aspects of life.

Unsoeld's first HIMALAYAN encounter was on a three-man trip to Nilkantha (21,640 ft/6,597 m) in the Indian GARHWAL HIMALAYA (1949). The EXPEDITION had such limited finances that it was only through the kindness of a holy man, Swami Jnanananda at the Hindu Temple at Badrinath, that the trio had even enough food to attempt Nilkantha. Their poor physical condition and avalanche danger halted the attempt at 18,000 ft (5,488 m), but Unsoeld's encounter with the Swami began a lifelong search to blend Hindu and Christian philosophies into his own system of religious beliefs. Unsoeld's words in the 1956 *American Alpine Journal* (on Nilkantha) indicate the spirit with which he approached the mountain experience:

". . . it is this writer's opinion that the benefits of such marginal-existence travel as this outweigh in many respects the rewards of a comfortably supported expedition. Certainly the impact of the country and its people is much more stark and provoking than when the traveller is insulated from its effects by a well-padded pocket book. The dangers of sickness and general deterioration of the health are greatly multiplied when one's funds are low; consequently, the chance of reaching many summits is much reduced. However, the quality of the mountain experience enjoyed by members of small expeditions has much to recommend it over that gained by the gigantic Himalayan task forces which have attracted so much popular attention in recent years."

In 1954 he attempted MAKALU, then in 1960 he made the first ascent of MASHERBRUM (25,660 ft/7,823 m) with the American-Pakistan KARAKORAM expedition. In 1976 in INDIA, he co-led the Indo-American NANDA DEVI expedition. Though the expedition succeeded on the north ridge, Unsoeld's daughter—named Nanda Devi—died of altitude and gastrointestinal illness high on the mountain. In 1979 while descending Mount RAINIER (WASHINGTON) with 21 students from Evergreen State College, he and a student died in an AVALANCHE at the site called Cadaver Gap. The play *Willi, an Evening of Wilderness and Spirit*, by John Pielmeier (1991) is reconstructed from Unsoeld's lectures.
Further reading: Laurence Leamer, *Ascent, The Spiritual and Physical Quest of Willi Unsoeld* (1982).

UTAH   (United States)   A rich diversity of FREE CLIMBING lies in Utah, from desert CRACKS in the sandstone of CANYONLANDS (Monument Valley, Arches National Park, Castle Valley, Fisher Towers), INDIAN CREEK and ZION, to limestone SPORT CLIMBING at AMERICAN FORK CANYON and Virgin River Gorge (in southwest Utah, at the intersection of the Virgin River and Interstate 15), to granite climbs in LITTLE COTTONWOOD CANYON. Utah's high point, Kings Peak (13,528 ft/4,123 m), is in the Uintas Mountains, Wasatch National Forest, in northern Utah. The Wasatch Range (in which lie American Fork and the Cottonwood Canyons) is famous for ICE CLIMBING. Provo Canyon is the most famous of Utah's FROZEN WATERFALL areas, but most canyons between Ogden in the north and south to Mona offer significant frozen waterfalls.

VALDEZ (United States) The densest concentration of FROZEN WATERFALL/ICE CLIMBING in North America lies around the Alaskan town of Valdez, 350 miles (560 km) west of Anchorage, via Glenallen and the Richardson Highway. There are one hundred sixty named and rated ice climbs along a 25-mile (40-km) stretch of road, 60 of them in a 2.5-mile (four-km) stretch of the Keystone Canyon. The waterfalls begin freezing in November and are fully formed by the cold of December, but optimal conditions come in March and April when warmer temperatures soften the ice into a PLASTIC consistency. Strong ADIABATIC WINDS descending from the surrounding CHUGACH MOUNTAINS commonly funnel down the north south-oriented canyons in which the waterfalls and seeps lie. Climbs are found of all difficulties, with the bulk lying in the middle-range of grade III. The Alaska Section of the American Alpine Club (see Appendices) sponsors an annual ice-climbing festival here over Washington's Birthday weekend.
Guidebook: Andrew Embick, *Blue Ice and Black Gold* (1989).

VAPOR BARRIER LINERS A waterproof lining in boots, gloves and sleeping bags, primarily for MOUNTAINEERING. Thought to increase warmth by maintaining all body moisture. See CLOTHING FOR MOUNTAINEERS.

VEDAUWOO (United States) Located equidistant (18 miles/29 km) between Laramie and Cheyenne, WYOMING, off Interstate 80, Vedauwoo is a FREE CLIMBING area comprised of coarse-grained, heavily weathered Sherman granite DOME formations. The area is noted for strenuous, sharp CRACK CLIMBING, but there are also FACE CLIMBS and SPORT CLIMBS, up to 5.13b. ROUTES are up to two PITCHES in length. Climbing development of the area began in the 1940s and is active still as climbers explore outlying OUT-CROPS. Vedauwoo offers a mild summer climate, but from May to October cold weather sweeps this 8,000-ft (2,439-m) high desert plateau. The area is on National Forest land.
Guidebooks: John Harlin, *Rocky Mountain Rock Climbs* (1985); Layne Kopischka, *Crack Country Revisited* (1982).

VENEZUELA The Venezuelan ANDES are shared by the states of Tachira, Merida and Trujillo, but Merida owns all the important heights. There are three ranges: Culata (with Pico Piedras Blancas, 15,623 ft/4,762 m), north of Merida city; Santo Domingo (with Pico Mucunuque, 15,328 ft/4,672 m), to the southeast; and Sierra Nevada de Merida, to the south. This range, the only one with glaciers, has Pico Bolivar (16,410 ft/5,002 m), the highest in Venezuela. All ranges are granitic; GLACIERS are small and retreating. In normal years, there is skiing on Pico Espejo (16,000 ft/4,878 m), near Merida. The higher moors (*paramos*) support high-tropical vegetation, with giant groundsels (*frailejones*) at 14,000 ft (4,268 m).

The Venezuelan Andes were surveyed by engineer Alfredo Jahn, whose map (1912) is still in use. Most MOUNTAINEERING has concentrated in the glaciated Merida range. Jahn initiated mountaineering by climbing El Toro (15,611 ft/4,758 m) in 1910 and Pico Humboldt (16,124 ft/4,942 m) in 1911. The Swiss Moritz Blummenthal made in 1922 climbs and TRAVERSES in all three ranges. Pico Bolivar was then beseiged by foreigners and nationals alike. In 1935, Venezuelans Enrique Bourgoin and Domingo Pena climbed to 22 ft (seven m) below the top. A year later German Fritz Weiss scaled the summit but he chivalrously awarded the FIRST ASCENT to Bourgoin. Italians climbed the north face, steep ice, of Pico Bolivar in 1953. In the 1970s, Jose Betancourt opened ROUTES on rock faces everywhere. Pico Bolivar's airy rock PINNACLES are a great attraction today. Two Venezuelan women, Rosa Pabon and Dora Ocanto, have done TECHNICAL climbing and expeditioned abroad. The history of Venezuelan climbing has been meticulously researched by the climbing surgeon Carlos Chalbaud. Venezuela has 15 mountain clubs, four rescue groups and two mountaineering associations (Caracas and Merida). The latter is the starting point for the heights.

Evelio Echevarria
Colorado State University

VERDON (France) One of the best climbing areas in the world, Verdon's sculptured limestone boasts sustained ROUTES up to 984 ft (300 m) high, extreme one-PITCH testpieces with tremendous exposure, FACE CLIMBS, spurs, CRACKS, ROOFS, and AID routes. The climbs are in an awesome gorge 44 miles (70 km) northeast of Aix-en-Provence, near the little village of La Palud. Routes are commonly, approached by RAPPEL. Most cliffs face southeast but a variety of sun exposures make climbing year round possible. At an elevation of about 2,952 ft (900 m) Verdon sometimes sees snow between December and March. Spring and fall are the mildest seasons. Due to the scale, climbing in Verdon is more serious than on most French CRAGS. Double 148- or 164-ft (45- or 50-m) ROPES are needed for rappels. A rack of NUTS is necessary on old crack routes, but SPORT CLIMBING is more typical. A typical Verdon practice is to TOP-ROPE a whole route using a 328- or 656-ft (100- or 200-m) static rope. The obvious crack LINES were pioneered between 1968 and 1975 by people like J. Coqueugniot, F. Guillot, G. Abert, P. Cordier, G. Heran and B. Gorgeon, who opened classics as La Demande, La Ula, Luna-Bong, Roumagaou and l'Eperon Sublime. At the end of the 1970s, the blank walls and pillars were explored by the Troussier brothers and others, sometimes on the lead, but more often on rappel. Today the heaviest traffic is at the top of the canyon with most climbers rappelling only one or two pitches or top-roping from the fence.

Guidebook: "Verdon," *Montagnes Magazine.*

VERGLAS A French word referring to a treacherous, thin, hard layer of ice over rock. Verglas forms when warmer daytime temperatures thaw snow fields and cause meltwater to ooze over the rock, then the cold snap of night freezes the water. Verglas presents difficulties in MOUNTAINEERING, as a verglased cliff may be too slick to rock climb, and the patina of ice may be too thin for CRAMPONS or ICE TOOLS to grip.

VERTICAL CLUB (United States) The first of many indoor climbing gymnasiums in the United States, established October 1987 in Seattle by Rich Johnson and Dan Cauthorn. With weight facilities, FINGERBOARDS, artificial walls made from stone glued to plywood surfaces, stucco sculptures, and walls set with climbing HOLDS, the Vertical Club created a controlled, safe atmosphere with TOP-ROPES and impact-absorbing landing sites for BOULDERING, training and climbing instruction. In February 1992 the Vertical Club expanded with a second gym in the city of Redmond.

VIA FERRATA Spectacular mountain paths using ladders to breach cliffs in the Italian DOLOMITES.

VIBRAM Trade name for the first molded-rubber boot sole used on climbing boots, introduced in the 1950s. (See BOOTS.)

VINSON MASSIF The highest peak in ANTARCTICA. See SEVEN SUMMITS.

VOLX (France) This short SPORT CLIMBING CRAG is notable only for its cave featuring some of the hardest OVERHANGING and ROOF problems in France. The cliff is just above the old castle in the village of Volx, between Aix-en-Provence and Sisteron. It is a new area mostly developed by J. M. Troussier and Robert Cortijo, and includes Maginot Line, the world's second 8c by Ben MOON, repeated by P. EDLINGER.

Guidebook: Regis Mulot, "Roc et Falaises."

VULGARIANS A group of climbers and pranksters who emerged in the SHAWANGUNKS in the late 1950s and early 1960s to challenge the then-dominant group, the staid Appalachian Mountain Club. The Vulgarians included Dick Williams, Elaine Mathews, Burt Angrist, Jack Hansen, Claude Suhl, Art Gran, Dave Craft and Al DeMaria. They published the ribald *Vulgarian Digest,* and created a mystique and a legacy of humor and extremism. Classic ROUTES put up by the Vulgarians include CCK, Limelight and Modern Times. They put up the first solid 5.9s and 5.10s in the area, including Never, Never Land; MF; and Tough Shift.

WADDINGTON, MOUNT (Canada) The highest summit of the COAST MOUNTAINS of BRITISH COLUMBIA and the centerpiece of the WADDINGTON RANGE, this mountain is a complexity of winding GLACIERS, jagged granite spires, cascading ICE FALLS and ice faces. There are no easy routes on Waddington (13,260 ft/4,043 m), called locally "the Wadd." Its discoverers were Walter and Phyl MUNDAY who made several attempts, climbing as high as the lower Northwest summit. They named it Mystery Mountain. It was renamed for Alfred Waddington, a pioneer surveyor. The mountain was first climbed via the south face by Fritz WIESSNER and William HOUSE in 1936, a remarkable achievement for the time. Waddington received its first WINTER ASCENT in 1969 by R. Culbert, Allen Steck and B. Hagen. The usual route is now the northeast flank (first climbed in 1950 by a Sierra Club group).

Further reading: Don Munday, *The Unknown Mountain* (1948, 1975); Steve Roper and Allen Steck, *Fifty Classic Climbs of North America* (1979).

WADDINGTON RANGE (Canada) A popular range of the COAST MOUNTAINS. The highest peak here is Mount WADDINGTON, but its 12,000-ft (3,659-m) neighbors—Mounts Combatant, Tiedeman, Asperity and the five Serra Peaks—are also targets of TECHNICAL alpinists. The range is characterized by steep COULOIRS and ice faces and sweeping BUTTRESSES of flawless granite. The area is heavily glaciated. Autumn offers the most reliable weather. Approach is generally made by helicopter from Bluff Lake, 125 miles (200 km) west of Williams Lake across the Chilcotin Plateau. Alternatively, the four-day march of early ascensionists from Knight Inlet up the Franklin Glacier is strenuous. Another option is to fly by float plane to the lakes on the eastern fringe of the range and walk. Bushwacking is arduous and grizzly bear encounters are not unheard of.

Guidebooks: R. Culbert, *A Climber's Guide to the Coastal Ranges of British Columbia* (1969, supplement 1974); Bruce Fairley, *A Guide to Climbing and Hiking in British Columbia* (1986).

WAIST BELAY Or body BELAY. A basic belay in which the ROPE runs around the waist and through a CARABINER on the HARNESS to keep it from parting from the belayer in the event of a fall. The rope is controlled, or paid out, by the hands. (See BELAYING TECHNIQUES.)

WALES (Britain) The Welsh countryside teems with atmospheric climbs steeped in the history of British climbing. (See CLOGWYN D'UR ARDDU, GOGARTH, LLANBERIS PASS, LLANBERIS SLATE, LLIWEDD, NORTH WALES LIMESTONE, OGWEN AND CARNEDDAU, TREMADOG.)

WAND A stick used to mark a trail, usually between camps on a GLACIER or snow slope. Wands are lightweight cane or plastic tubing, with bright tape or cloth fixed to the end as a flag. They are especially helpful as markers during WHITE-OUT, storm or low-visibility conditions. Depending on terrain and conditions, a wand every 100 to 200 ft (30 to 61 m) will define a ROUTE.

WASHBURN, BRADFORD (1910–) (United States) No person can surpass the contributions Washburn has made to Alaskan climbing. His climbing career began in the European ALPS and was followed by two intensive decades of pioneering ascents in ALASKA. Most notable was his 1933 climb of Mount Crillon, his 1937 TRAVERSE of Mount Lucania and Mount Steele, a mapping expedition through the SAINT ELIAS Range, his 1941 FIRST ASCENT of Mount Hayes and the opening up DENALI's west buttress in 1951. Thousands of climbers have since climbed this ROUTE. His wife, Barbara, accompanied him on all of his journeys and in 1947, she became the first woman to climb Denali. But Washburn's climbing was only a peripheral avocation for his photography and cartography. As director of the Boston Museum of Science, Washburn spent 14 years using laser technology to map Denali. This map was succeeded by his unerringly precise maps of the Grand Canyon and Mount WASHINGTON. In 1990, he received his third National Geographic award for spearheading the team that mapped Mount EVEREST. Washburn is also known for his selfless assistance to climbers. His unerringly precise photographs and his advice have inspired hundreds of first ascents throughout Alaska.

Further reading: Bradford Washburn, *Mt. McKinley; The Conquest of Denali* (1991).

WASHINGTON, MOUNT (United States) This New Hampshire peak is, at 6,288 ft (1,917 m), the highest mountain in New England, and is reputed to have the worst weather in the world. In 1934, a 231 mph (370 km/ph) wind was recorded at the summit observatory. The mountain was first climbed by Darby Field in 1842. Because of its accessible popularity and its sudden storms, nearly

100 of the many thousands who have climbed the mountain have died. Tuckermans Ravine, a snow-filled bowl halfway up the mountain, attracts thousands of skiers every spring. The rugged Huntingtons Ravine is cut by ice gullies and granite SLABS, drawing climbers from all over the East Coast. And the Alpine Gardens is a mecca for botanists, who come to examine rare, subarctic flowers.

Guidebook: Rick Wilcox, *An Ice Climber's Guide to Northern New England* (1982).

Further reading: Guy and Laura Waterman, *Forest and Crag* (1989).

WASHINGTON STATE   (United States)   The rugged CASCADE RANGE dominates Washington geography. LEAVENWORTH, a tourist town 100 miles (160 km) east of Seattle and east of the Cascades has been called the hub of the state's cragging and MOUNTAINEERING. Granite CRAGS here like Castle Rock and Icicle Creek Canyon and the sandstone of Peshastin Pinnacles offer diverse FREE CLIMBS of all levels, while the Enchantment Lakes and Stuart Range in the Cascades have long, TECHNICAL alpine rock ROUTES on diorite granite. The north ridge of Mount STUART, the north face of Dragontail Peak and the west ridge of Prusik Peak are among this area's classic alpine climbs. INDEX, 60 miles (96 km) east of Seattle is a granite FREE CLIMBING area, with CRACK and SPORT climbs. Darrington, 80 miles (128 km) northeast of Seattle, has free climbs on knobby granite up to 300 ft (91 m) long. The VERTICAL CLUB, in Seattle, is the first commercial climbing gym in the United States.

In general, climbing in western Washington is subject to the whims of damp marine weather that travels eastward across the Cascades, but Eastern Washington areas like the Tieton River Valley near Yakima, with its abundant columnar basalt cliffs, bask in the rain shadow. Cold winters in Eastern Washington often produce ICE CLIMBING, especially around the Columbia Basin areas of Banks Lake, the Palisades and numerous coulees.

Visible on the skyline west of Seattle are Mount Deception, Mount Constance, Mount Anderson and The Brothers—peaks of the Olympic Range. Mount Olympus (7,965 ft/2,428m) is that area's highest peak.

Four glaciated volcanoes—Mount Baker, Glacier Peak, Mount RAINIER and Mount Adams—offer high mountaineering within two hours drive from Seattle. These volcanoes have GLACIER walk-up routes and also TECHNICAL routes such as the Coleman Headwall (Mount Baker), Liberty Ridge (Rainier) and the Adams Glacier (Mount Adams). Since its 1980 eruption, Mount SAINT HELENS has become the most-often-climbed glaciated peak in North America, although it has no technical challenge.

In the North Cascades, mountains such as SHUKSAN, Fury, Challenger, Goode, LIBERTY BELL, Bonanza, SLESSE (in CANADA), and peaks in the North Cascades National Park are highly regarded by alpinists.

Guidebooks: Fred Beckey, *Cascade Alpine Guide, Climbing and High Routes* (Vol. I, II, and III) (1987); John Eminger and John Kittel, *The Washington Desert: A Climber's Guide* (1991); Jeff Smoot, *A Climber's Guide to the Cascade Volcanoes* (1992); Smoot, *Washington Rock Climbs* (1988).

WATER-CUM-JOLLY   (Britain)   This beautiful dale lies below the village of Cressbrook and downstream of CHEEDALE and RAVEN TOR. The chief attraction of the area is the overhanging Rubicon Wall, a 40-ft (12-m) BOLT-protected wall with a host of boulder-problem-style ROUTES. Like other CRAGS in this area, services can be found in STONEY MIDDLETON and Hathersage.

This crag experienced the same revolution in the early 1980s that occurred elsewhere on PEAK DISTRICT limestone. Ron FAWCETT made a number of contributions, including Piranha (5.12c) in 1981 on Rubicon Wall and The Vision (5.12c) on Vision Buttress in 1982. Daniel Lee's Whitebait, Tony Ryan's Caviar and Ben MOON's Hot Fun Closing are all 5.13. In 1987 Moon reclimbed Zeke the Freak (5.13c) after its HOLDS had been chiseled off by an irate AID-climber.

Guidebook: British Mountain Club, *Peak Limestone—Cheedale* (1987).

WATERFALL CLIMBING   Climbing on FROZEN WATERFALLS, cascades and water-seeps. Waterfalls are often vertical. The activity is limited to winter and cold weather. The most developed waterfall climbing areas are in Banff (CANADA) and areas of the United States such as NEW ENGLAND, UTAH and COLORADO. The largest waterfalls are found in NORWAY.

WATERMAN, JOHN   (1952–1981)   (United States)   Waterman assumed legendary status among Alaskan climbers for his 148-day solo FIRST ASCENT of the southeast spur on Mount HUNTER in 1978. Waterman was a very experienced ALPINIST, having completed a first ascent on Mount HUNTINGTON a few years before. His time alone on Mount Hunter—climbing difficult rock, straddling a knife-edge RIDGE that plunged thousands of feet on either side, dodging collapsing CORNICES—pushed him to the breaking point. In fact, he grew convinced that he would die on the mountain, until he safely TRAVERSED down the northeast ridge. Waterman (not to be confused with another active Alaskan climber, Jonathan Waterman) eventually disappeared carrying only a daypack while soloing up the east side of DENALI.

Further reading: Glenn Randall, *Breaking Point* (1983).

WATERPROOF CLOTHING   See CLOTHING FOR MOUNTAINEERING.

WATTS, ALAN   (1960–   )   (United States)   Watts was one of the U.S.'s leading climbers in the mid- and late 1980s. He brought 5.13 into its own, developing SMITH ROCK, OREGON, into a mecca for world-class climbers. Among the ROUTES he established are Vicious Fish (5.13c) in early 1988 and the East Face of Monkey Face (5.13c) in 1985. He made the prized second ascent of Scarface (5.14a) in 1988, and did the FIRST ASCENT of the originally envisioned Rude Femmes (5.13c/d). He has also RED POINTED To Bolt or Not to Be (5.14).

WEATHER More than any factor, weather determines the movements of climbers, but predicting it is never easy. In areas near civilization, synoptic weather charts in newspapers offer a good indication of current weather patterns. Time and date of a chart should be checked, as they are often several hours old. Normally, a high-pressure system or ridge of high pressure means stable conditions and good weather. Conversely, a low-pressure system, a trough of low pressure or a cold front indicates unstable conditions. Extreme lows may result in cyclones in certain regions. Knowing the direction that cold fronts travel from is also important. It varies from region to region. In general, cold fronts sweep down from polar regions, appearing out of the north in North America, and from the south in the southern hemisphere. It is also important to check where the prevailing winds are coming from, since this affects the amount of moisture in the air, picked up by the wind as it blows over the land or sea. On a synoptic chart, prevailing winds are indicated parallel to isobars, which are the contour-like lines marking high- and low-pressure systems. Wind flows in a counterclockwise direction around a low and in a clockwise direction around a high in the northern hemisphere. In the southern hemisphere the directions are reversed—clockwise around a low and counterclockwise around a high.

In mountain areas weather forecasts, printed or from radio, may not be readily obtainable. The climber can use clouds, or the lack of them, to judge the weather signs. There are four main groups of clouds: cumuliform, stratiform, nimbus and cirrus.

Cumuliform, described as heaped clouds, are often separated from each other by clear spaces formed by convection currents (the movement of air caused by heat). Cumulus clouds are common, normally appearing in the afternoon. The precipitation from cumulus is in the form of rain showers, the intensity being governed by the vertical height of the cloud. The higher the vertical growth of the cloud, the heavier the rain.

Stratiform clouds are sheets or layers covering large areas. They are formed by the gradual upward movement of moist air occurring in low-pressure systems. Stratus clouds will normally produce drizzle with overcast skies.

Nimbus is an extension of the previous two groups. This group produces heavy precipitation. Cumulonimbus clouds forewarn of thunderstorms, producing high winds and heavy rain, snow or hail accompanied by thunder and lightning. The easily recognizable anvil-shaped tops of these clouds may rise to over 40,000 ft (12,195 m). Although they produce severe conditions, these clouds generally pass within an hour. Cumulonimbus clouds are associated with cold fronts and related local conditions.

The other form of nimbus cloud is nimbostratus, which produces copious amounts of rain and snow. It is associated with intense low pressure.

Cirrus is a very high cloud of wispy, hairlike appearance that produces no precipitation. It indicates a change in temperature, and is pushed ahead of advancing fronts. Its appearance after a storm can signal the approach of a warm front. But, especially in the mountains, the sudden appearance of waves of herringbone-shaped high cirrus clouds generally signals the approach of low pressure and storm.

Frequently, cold fronts appear with little warning. Only a few hours may elapse between the sighting of a large buildup of cumulus and cumulonimbus clouds marking the surface position of the cold front, and its arrival. However, in mountain areas the warning time can be reduced considerably due to the terrain restricting the view of approaching cloud. With the approach of a cold front, winds often change and temperature rapidly decreases. Generally, the more intense the wind, the more severe the front. Knowing what sort of cloud is overhead can indicate present and future weather conditions. This is difficult to ascertain if the cloud base is low and higher clouds cannot be seen, particularly at night. But, because different precipitation falls from different clouds, if the form of precipitation is known the cloud can be determined. For example, drizzle falls from stratocumulus or stratus; intermittant to continuous rain or snow falls from altostratus; heavy precipitation falls from nimbostratus. Rain or snow showers fall from cumulus or cumulonimbus; hail falls from cumulonimbus clouds.

A high-pressure system provides the most stable weather—cloudless skies and warm, windless weather. Morning fog is associated with highs and is usually a good indication of fine weather ahead. Another indication of high pressure is reduced visibilty due to haze and smoke not being able to escape into the upper atmosphere. Local weather conditions, such as ADIABATIC WINDS, can lead to confusion when interpreting weather.

WEBBING Woven nylon tape, used for SLINGS and HARNESSES, and for threading through many items of equipment. It is extremely strong, especially the tubular, or hollow type: One-inch (2.54 cm) tubular tape has an approximate breaking strength of nearly 5,000 lbs (2,250 kg). Of the main widths, two-inch (five cm) webbing is used for waist harnesses, and one-inch, eleven-sixteenths-inch and nine-sixteenths-inch for slings and tying through equipment. Thin half-inch tape is used for TIE OFFS.

WEBSTER, ED (1956–) (United States) This prolific cragsman has established hundreds of new ROUTES throughout the United States. In the American desert Webster is responsible for such classics as Super Crack and Primrose Dihedrals; in NEW HAMPSHIRE, Women In Love; in the BLACK CANYON OF THE GUNNISON, the Hallucinogen Wall. In 1990, Robert Anderson, Steve Venables, Paul Teare and Webster battled up the technically difficult Kangshung Face of EVEREST, on a new route to the south COL. While Venables continued to the summit alone, Webster was badly FROSTBITTEN, and later lost portions of several fingers. He returned to climbing within two years.

WEISSMEIS GROUP (Switzerland) Situated on the eastern side of the Saas Valley, the Lagginhorn (13,153 ft/4,010 m) and the Weismeiss (13,195 ft/4,023 m) are two of the lowest (13,120-ft/4,000 m) peaks. Local villagers have tried to add the Fletschorn (13,097 ft/3,993 m), located just to the north of the Lagginhorn, to the list by piling stones on top of the summit. Ascents for both mountains start from the Weismeiss Huts above the Kreuzboden cableway station above the village of Saas Grund or from the Hohsaas cableway station. The most usual route of ascent up the Lagginhorn is via the west ridge, first climbed in 1856 by the Saas priest Johann Imseng with his servant, Joseph Andermatten, and a group of Englishmen. It is largely a rock ROUTE and fairly spectacular. There are two regularly taken options for the Weismeiss; the southeast ridge, which, without a cableway, is remoter, older and safer, and the northwest face and west ridge, which are accessible from the Hohsaas but more dangerous. The south side is rock, the north is snow and ice, but the mountain is uniformly beautiful.

Further reading: Robin Collomb, *The Pennine Alps* (3 Vols.) (1975, 1979); Richard Goedeke, *The Alpine 4000m Peaks* (1991); Edward Whymper, *Scrambles Amongst the Alps in the Years 1860–9,* (1986); Geoffrey Winthrop Young, *On High Hills* (1927); Young, *Mountains with a Difference* (1951).

WELLMAN, MARK (1960–　) (United States) After a climbing accident in 1982 that confined him to a wheelchair, Wellman made the first paraplegic ascent of EL CAPITAN in YOSEMITE VALLEY via the Shield Route in 1989. The 19-pitch AID climb was made over eight days. All PITCHES were led by Yosemite veteran Mike Corbett. To follow Corbett's leads Wellman used a system of AS-CENDERS clipped to a t-bar. His lower body was supported by a body-harness. The ascent involved 7,000 pull-ups by Wellman, and was Corbett's 42nd personal ascent of El Capitan. The U.S. media reported their spirited collaboration, and they were congratulated by President George Bush. Wellman and Corbett climbed Tis-sa-ack on HALF DOME in 1992. Wellman is a Yosemite Valley ranger and consultant on disability issues, Corbett a full-time Yosemite resident.

WELZENBACH, WILLO (1900–1934) (Germany) This Munich alpinist has been called the greatest German mountain climber of the post-World War I era. Welzenbach, a respected engineer who wrote his doctoral thesis on snow deposits and snow movements began climbing while studying at the Academic Alps Association of Munich (AAVM). His climbing journals recount ascents on 540 peaks, including 72 13,120-ft (4,000-m) mountains and over 50 FIRST ASCENTS. His modification of Hans Dulfer's RATING SYSTEM of technical difficulties (to which he added grade VI) became known as the Welzenbach Scale.

In Europe, his climbs spanned the rocks of the North ALPS, the ice of the Central Alps and the north faces of the Western Alps. His first ascent of the Weisbachhorn's Northwest Face, in 1924, was historic because it was the first use of the ICE PITON, invented by his partner, Fritz Rigele. Between 1924 and 1933, he opened ROUTES on north FACES like the Glockerin, Eiskogele and GrossGlockner in the Glockner Range, and in the West Alps, the Dent d'Herens, Fiesherwand, Lauterbrunner Breithorn and

Nesthorn. His efforts in the MONT BLANC Range are remembered by such routes as Pointe Welzenbach on the south ridge of the Aiguille Noire de Peuterey. He and partner Willi MERKL were celebrated in the European press when they survived a frigid spell of weather while making a first ascent on the Grandes Charmoz north face, in 1931. Though Welzenbach planned the unsuccessful 1932 German NANGA PARBAT expedition, Merkl led it when Welzenbach couldn't get leave from work. The pair returned to Nanga Parbat in 1934, but a catastrophic storm at 24,534 ft (7,480 m) killed them and seven others. A book of his climbing articles, *Willo Welzenbach's Climbing Expeditions* was published in 1935, by the AAVM. His biography is *Welzenbach's Climbs* by Eric Roberts (1983).

WENDENSTOCK (Switzerland) This large (up to 3,280 ft/1,000 m) south-facing mountain cliff of perfect limestone rises between the towns of Wassen and Innertkirchen. It became a popular BIG WALL FREE CLIMBING crag in the 1980s. The Wenden is actually a series of distinct walls and BUTTRESSES, which include the Mahren and Pfaffenhuet. The area known as Wenden is one massif of a chain that includes impressive formations such as the Tallistock and Titlis. ROUTES require an approach of an hour and a half, and involve 1,640 ft (500 m) of steep climbing, from French 6a to 7a. Routes are usually equipped in the European style, earlier ones with PITONS, later ones with BOLTS, though FRIENDS and NUTS are also used. One famous route, Vrenli, has 140 bolts in its 22 PITCHES. The wall was largely developed by Swiss climbers like Peter Lechner, Kaspar Ochsner and Claude and Yves Remy. Driest weather occurs in late summer and autumn.

WEST VIRGINIA (United States) The Appalachian Mountains run through this state, providing many rock-climbing areas. Among these are two important American CRAGS: SENECA ROCKS and the vast NEW RIVER GORGE. In northern West Virginia, Cooper's Rock, a sandstone crag 10 miles (16 km) east of Morgantown, is popular. A non-technical hill, Spruce Knob (4,863 ft/1,482 m), 25 miles (40 km) southeast of Elkins, is the state's high point.

WHILLANS BOX A custom-built heavyweight tent for HIMALAYAN expeditions designed by British climber Don WHILLANS. This roomy, rigid, metal-framed box-tent with heavy fabric was used at high camps on the successful 1975 British ascent of EVEREST southwest face. Abandoned Whillans boxes anchored to the southwest face with cable have survived AVALANCHES and high winds so well that the frames are still visible to climbers today. The tent is no longer used because of its weight, and has been replaced by PORTA-LEDGES. (See also TENTS.)

WHILLANS, DON (1933–1985) (Britain) Legendary Lancastrian mountaineer of diminutive stature, ferocious temperament and the build of a pocket battleship. Whillans and his partner, Joe BROWN, in the early 1950s were crucial in the development of the modern sport. Although his climbing career was perhaps overshadowed a little initially by that of the slightly older Brown, and in terms of his output of new ROUTES lasted for a much shorter period of time, his climbs have a uniquely aggressive imprint, and in their number are included some of the great OUTCROP and mountain routes of BRITAIN: The Sloth, Sentinel and Forked Lightning Cracks, Centurion, Surplomb, Taurus, Woubits and Grond.

He was born in the northern industrial town of Salford and began climbing on the Derbyshire and YORKSHIRE gritstone outcrops in 1950. From the outset, a natural gymnastic skill combined with great physical strength and an aggressive character soon brought him fame or even notoriety among his peers, and his routes and fists became feared in equal proportion. In the ALPS, his ascents in the 1950s culminated in the FIRST ASCENT of the central pillar of Freney in 1961. In South America he made the ascents of the Aiguille Poincenot in the FITZROY group, and of the Central Tower of PAINE, but in the HIMALAYAS, although he established a reputation as a very safe climber, success eluded him on expeditions to MASHERBRUM, Trivor and Gaurisankar. His climbing declined in the 1960s, but in 1970 he crowned his career by the ascent, with Dougal HASTON, of the British route on the south face of ANNAPURNA—the first of the really difficult Himalayan FACES to be climbed.

He continued to climb in Europe, Asia and America, and died in bed of a heart attack after riding his motorcycle back from the DOLOMITES in cold weather in 1985.
Further reading: Jim Perrin, *The Villain: A Life of Don Whillans* (1993).

WHITE GHYLL CRAG (Britain) This popular crag seven miles (11 km) east of Langdale and Ambleside appears as an obvious notch in the skyline three-quarters of a mile (one km) above the New Dungeon Ghyll. It offers steep ROUTES on good rock between 5.7 and 5.10. It is a blocky but largely sound rhyolite CRAG. Routes are generally 150 to 250 ft (46 to 76 m) high.

Jim Birkett was active here just after World War II with the excellent 5.7 Slip Knot and White Ghyll Wall (5.6). Joe BROWN climbed the corner of Laugh Knot, an underrated 5.8. There are more demanding climbs. Haste Not Direct (5.10b) is both delicate and strenuous and Paladin takes a forbidding groove at 5.10c.
Guidebooks: D. Armstrong et al., *Langdale* (1989); Bill Birkett, et al., *Rock Climbing in the Lake District* (1986).

WHITE-OUT A condition of low or zero visibility caused by falling snow that combines with snow-cover to obscure the horizon. The effect is an optical illusion in which the ground and sky merge together as a single white or gray sheet. Fog may also cause white-out. Even with objects close to a climber, perception of depth, of distance and even of up or down can become completely disoriented. White-out is a dangerous condition, causing climbers to become lost. Sitting tight until visibility returns is the safest option. Brightly flagged WANDS stand out like beacons in white-out and mark trails well.

WHITNEY, MOUNT (United States) At 14,495 ft (4,419 m), this California peak of the southern SIERRA NEVADA, rises higher than any other point in the contiguous United States. Whitney stands along a picket fence of granitic satellites, all with dramatic east FACES and gentle western slopes. After three years of attempts to reach these easy slopes, it was first climbed in 1873. Now Whitney has a trail to its summit. The mountain offers a variety of TECHNICAL routes, including the surprisingly moderate east face, first climbed in 1934 by Norman CLYDE, Glen Dawson, Robert UNDERHILL and Jules Eichorn. Harder routes include the east BUTTRESS (III, 5.7) and the east face direct (IV, 5.7, A3).
Guidebook: Steve Roper, *The Climber's Guide to the High Sierra* (1976).

WHITTAKER, JAMES (1929–   ) (United States) Whittaker achieved fame as the first American to summit EVEREST on the 1963 expedition led by Norman DYHRENFURTH, on which he and SHERPA Nawang Gombu repeated the south COL route on May 1. As part of the same expedition, Barry Bishop and Luther Jerstad followed the route on May 22, and Whilli UNSOELD and Tom HORNBEIN climbed the FIRST ASCENT of the west ridge the same day, descending via the south col. This expedition is described in the 1964 AMERICAN ALPINE JOURNAL and in Hornbein's *Everest: The West Ridge* (1965).

Whittaker and his twin brother, Lou, began as guides on Mount RAINIER (WASHINGTON) and DENALI (ALASKA) and founded Rainier Mountain Guides. They separately led HIMALAYAN expeditions in later years. Jim led the successful 1978 American K2 expedition, described in Rick Ridgeway's *The Last Step* (1980). In 1990 he led the large, controversial "International Peace Climb" on which 20 climbers from the United States, Russia and CHINA summited Everest from Chinese-occupied TIBET. Lou led successful American expeditions to Everest (1984) and KANGCHENJUNGA (1988).

WHYMPER, EDWARD (1840–1911) (Britain) At the age of 20 Whymper was sent to the ALPS on business, to prepare engravings for a book written by some members of the ALPINE CLUB. The tall, humorless artist was never the same: nor was the sport of MOUNTAINEERING. In a hectic couple of years he established himself in the front line of British alpinists, famous for his ambition, determination and technical ability. The conquest of the MATTERHORN became an obsession, but all his early attempts were dogged by frustration and failure. Finally in 1865 he managed to attach himself to a party led by Charles Hudson, one of the few of Whymper's equals, and the legendary guide Michel Croz. Joined by Lord Francis Douglas, Roger Hadow and the guide Taugwalders and his son, the party ascended the peak from the Zermatt side without much difficulty—beating out a rival team 1,500/457 m below on the Italian side. On the way down, the inexperienced Hadow slipped on worn-out shoes, striking guide Croz who was LEADING the seven-man ROPE. Croz lost his footing and the whole party fell. Between the fourth and fifth the rope snapped and four bodies sailed out over the north face—that of Lord Douglas never to be found. To Whymper's surprise, this accident became a *cause célèbre*, but he continued to climb. He repeated his Matterhorn route and wrote the classic book *Scrambles Amongs the Alps* a "book from which there still comes the thunder of the falling rocks and the voices of the old guides speaking of a distant mountain world" according to Ronald W. Clark in his *Six Great Mountaineers* (1956). In 1881 Whymper went to ECUADOR and did the FIRST ASCENT of the volcanoes CHIMBORAZO, Cotopaxi and Cayambe. At the age of 61 he made the first of three journeys to the CANADIAN ROCKIES and did a number of peaks. At 71 he died suddenly in CHAMONIX, where his tombstone has been the object of veneration for many generations.

WICKWIRE, JAMES (1941–　) (United States) This Seattle attorney was the first of four Americans to climb K2, the world's second-highest mountain, on the 1978 expedition led by Jim WHITTAKER. It was Wickwire's second attempt; he had failed on K2 in 1975. The route was the northeast RIDGE with a TRAVERSE above 24,000 ft (7,317 m) leading to the ABRUZZI Ridge. He was accompanied by Lou REICHARDT. On his way down, Wickwire survived a forced BIVOUAC a short distance below the summit. He also attempted EVEREST from TIBET twice, (1982, 1984). In the 1960s, he made many FIRST ASCENTS in the CASCADE RANGE, including a new ROUTE in winter on Mount RAINIER's treacherous Willis Wall with Alex Bertulis (1970).
Further reading: Rick Ridgeway, *The Last Step* (1979).

WIESSNER, FRITZ (1900–1987) (Germany-United States) Reinhold MESSNER called Wiessner the pivotal mountaineer of the 20th century. Wiessner began rock climbing at the age of 17 on the sandstone towers of the ELBSANDSTEINGEBIRGE, around Dresden, Germany. In the mid-1920s he was among the first to pioneer true FREE CLIMBING there. In the DOLOMITES, on ROUTES like the Southeast Face of the Fleischbank in the Tyrol and the FIRST ASCENT of the north face of the Grosse Furchetta he established himself as the best rock climber of the decade. In 1929 he immigrated to New York, took U.S. citizenship in 1939, and worked as a chemist. In 1935 he discovered the SHAWANGUNKS in New York, and established the cliff's first climb, Old Route, 5.5. Over the years, climbing often with Hans Kraus, he climbed futuristic routes like High Exposure, 5.6. The first ascent of DEVILS TOWER (1937), with William HOUSE and Lawrence Coveney, proved Wiessner was the best rock climber in America. In Canada he made the first ascent of the serious south face of Mount WADDINGTON, also with House. This peak had repulsed 13 attempts and is regarded as his finest success.

He attempted NANGA PARBAT (KARAKORAM) in 1932 with a German-American expedition. In 1939 he returned to the Karakoram, to try the coveted first ascent of K2, leading six Americans supported by 13 SHERPAS. On the southeast (ABRUZZI) ridge, the expedition placed camps to over 26,000 ft (7,927 m). On July 19, Weissner and Pasang Lama Sherpa made a summit bid, reaching approximately 27,560 ft (8,402 m) without oxygen. Wiessner intended to climb to the summit at night, but Pasang urged descent. During the descent to Camp IX they lost their CRAMPONS, making a second attempt next day impossible. The pair descended, meeting Dudley Wolfe at a high camp where Wolfe remained while the other two went lower to replenish supplies before another summit bid. Inexplicably, the camps below had been stripped. By the time they reached BASE CAMP Wiessner and Pasang were exhausted and Wolfe was, effectively, stranded. The camps, it transpired, had been stripped because the Sherpas believed an avalanche had swept the trio off K2, and Wiessner had been out of contact with base camp for many days. When Sherpas reached Wolfe he had so weakened from altitude that he refused to descend. Storms kept rescuers from reaching Wolfe again until August 1, when Sherpas Kikuli, Pinsoo and Kitar went up once more, but all disappeared. It was a tragic episode for Wiessner and for American climbing. The deaths were the subject of an investigation by the AMERICAN ALPINE CLUB and much acrimony ensued, with members of the expedition blaming each other for events leading to the tragedy. Wiessner resigned from the AAC in 1940, amid the anti-German sentiment of World War II. The burden of K2 remained with him forever, yet he climbed actively. In 1960 he completed all the 13,120-ft (4,000-m) peaks of Europe. Even at the age of 86 he climbed 5.6 in the Shawangunks. Wiessner died from complications arising from a stroke.
Further reading: Andrew Kauffman and William Putnam, *K2: The 1939 Tragedy* (1992).

WIND CHILL The effect of wind removing heat from the body and thus reducing the body's core temperature. Wind chill is a major factor in HYPOTHERMIA and FROSTBITE. Wind chill is experienced when riding a bicycle; at increasing speeds at a constant temperature the effect of wind on the skin feels colder. A thermometer mounted on the bike would not register a drop in temperature because wind chill does not effect inorganic objects.

WIND RIVER RANGE (United States) This wilderness range of west-central WYOMING is renowned for excellent climbing. The range trends southeast-northwest for 60 miles (96 km), and contains granitic peaks up to 13,000 ft (3,963 m) high that rise above high lake basins and plateaus. The northern peaks are of gneiss and other metamorphic rocks blending into granites further south. The region contains GLACIERS which, at up to three miles (five km) long, are the longest in the American Rockies. Routes range from hikes to very TECHNICAL, from 500 to 2,500 ft (152 to 762 m) high. Approach hikes range from five to 25 miles (eight to 40 km). Overall the climate is dry, but weather in "The Winds" is unpredictable, and thunderstorms are common during summer. Bitter cold is the norm during winter. Many peaks were first climbed from the 1920s to the 1940s.

The northernmost range has scattered climbing interest. Squaretop is an imposing stump with FACES up to 1,800 ft

(549 m) high. Just south is Gannett Peak, at 13,804 ft (4,208 m) the highest mountain in Wyoming. It is a DOME of snow and gneiss with five glaciers. Gannett was first climbed in 1922 by Arthur Tate and Floyd Stahlnaker. Further south the peaks remain above 13,000 ft (3,963 m) and they become more granitic. Mounts Woodrow Wilson, Helen, Sacagawea and Fremont Peak have faces and BUTTRESSES up to 1,500 ft (457 m) high, and ice gullies similar to those in the TETONS. Kenneth Henderson, Robert UNDERHILL and Albert Ellingwood pioneered many ROUTES in this area in the 1920s and 1930s.

The central Winds have more scattered climbing interest. Mount Hooker drops from a very broad, flat summit with steep walls over 2,000 ft (610 m) high. Hooker's north face has five Grade VI routes, the first done in 1964 by Dick McCracken, Charlie Raymond and Royal ROBBINS. Raid Peak, Roberts Peak and Musembeah have routes up to 1,700 ft (518 m) long.

The southern Wind Rivers are the most popular for climbers, especially the area above Lonesome and Cirque lakes known as the Cirque of The Towers. Wolf's Head, Shark's Nose, Pingora and Warbonnet rise among many 11,000- to 12,000-ft (3,354- to 3,658-m) peaks known for their distinctive shapes of clean rock, and spectacular yet often moderate routes. Orrin Bonney and Frank and Notsie Garnick first climbed many of these peaks in the 1940s.

Just south of the Cirque of the Towers are two notable peaks. Haystack Mountain has a mile-long (1.6 km) cliff with almost two dozen routes, more than any other peak in the range, from Grade I to V. East Temple Peak has significant walls, including the northwest face, where in 1961 Yvon CHOUINARD and Art Gran made an early YOSEMITE-style BIG WALL climb in a wilderness setting.

Further reading: Joe Kelsey, *Climbing and Hiking in the Wind River Mountains* (2nd ed., 1994); Allen Steck and Steve Roper, *Fifty Classic Climbs of North America* (1979).

WIND SLAB   Snow deposited by wind, usually blown onto lee slopes. Strong winds produce a crusty layer that may overlay softer snow and present avalanche danger. (See AVALANCHE.)

WINTER ASCENT   Or winter MOUNTAINEERING. The ascent of a climb made under winter conditions. First winter ascents are coveted. For a winter ascent to be recognized, it must fall within the official dates of winter.

WIRE   Another name for a NUT or STOPPER on wire cable.

WIRED   A modern FREE CLIMBING term. A climber is said to have a ROUTE wired when the moves and sequences of the route are thoroughly memorized after frequent attempts and rehearsal. The result is a seemingly effortless execution of the climb.

WISCONSIN   (United States)   One of the earliest areas in which American FREE CLIMBING was developed is the quartzite of DEVIL'S LAKE, the Midwest's most popular cliff, located near Madison, in Devil's Lake State Park. Most climbing here is TOP ROPED. In addition to this CRAG are

Wired

several sandstone cliffs such as Gibraltar Rock, which has been designated as a SPORT CLIMBING area. Taylor Falls State Park, on the MINNESOTA border, also has rock climbing. Ice is found around La Crosse. A nontechnical hill, Timms Hill (1,951 ft/595 m), 23 miles (37 km) west of Tomahawk, is the state's high point.

Guidebooks: Eric Landmann, *Climber's Guide to Gibraltar Rock* (1987); Widule and Swartling, *Climber's Guide to Devil's Lake* (1979).

WOOD, SHARON   (1957–   ) (Canada)   Wood became a celebrity in 1986 when, as a member of a large Canadian expedition using oxygen, she became the first North American woman to reach the summit of Mount EVEREST (via the west ridge from TIBET) with Canadian Dwayne Congdon. Notable climbs in her career are Mount LOGAN (1977), DENALI via the Cassin Ridge (1983), an attempt on the west pillar of MAKALU (1984), ACONCAGUA south face (1985), and HUASCURAN Sur via the Anquosh face (1985).

WOODSON, MOUNT   (United States)   Located in the hills northeast of San Diego, California, this area offers a myriad of granitic BOULDERING and TOP ROPE problems. Woodson is most famous for fierce CRACK CLIMBS of all widths and at all angles. Climbers visited Woodson as early as the early 1960s. Striking cracks inspired locals to achieve solid 5.11 standards by the early 1970s. In the early 1980s The Great Western Bouldering Championship, supposedly the world's first organized FREE CLIMBING competition, was held at Woodson.

WORKMAN,   FANNY   BULLOCK   (1859–1925) (United States)   AND WILLIAM HUNTER WORKMAN   (1847–1937) (United States)   The Workmans were an indefatigable and wealthy Massachusetts husband and wife who organized seven expeditions to the KARAKORAM between 1898 and 1912 and one to the SIKKIM HIMALAYA (1898). Their HIMALAYAN exploration began simply as a break from Indian heat while they were in Srinagar during a bicycle tour of INDIA. Hiring European guides and cartographers, they explored the Karakoram's BIAFO GLACIER (1899); the Chogolungma, with an attempt on Pyramid Peak (1903); the NUN KUN Massif (1906), when Mrs. Workman and guide Cyprien Savoye reached the summit of Pinnacle Peak (estimated then at 23,300 ft/7,104 m); the HISPAR Glacier (1908), and Siachen and Bilaphond glaciers (1911 and 1912). Mrs. Workman's claim to the highest point yet reached by a man or woman (Pinnacle Peak in the Nun Kun Massif in 1906) at 22,176 ft (6,761 m) stood for a year, until Englishman Tom LONGSTAFF climbed Trisul (22,784 ft/6,946 m). Fellow American Annie Smith PECK (1850–1935) challenged Mrs. Workman's claim for highest ascent by a woman with her September 2, 1908, ascent of HUASCARAN's north peak in the CORDILLERA BLANCA of PERU. Press reports inflated the elevation of Huascaran to as high as 26,000 ft (7,927 m). Mrs. Workman dispatched French surveyors to confirm or correct the height of the mountain. The team found Huascaran's south peak to be 22,187 ft (6,764 m) and the north peak 21,812 ft (6,650 ft), thus validating Mrs. Workman's claim until German-born Hettie Dyhrenfurth climbed Queen Mary Peak, or Sia Kangri (23,750 ft/7,241 m) in the Karakoram in 1934. The Workmans presented their observations in numerous illustrated lectures, articles and five large books. They prided themselves on the accuracy of their surveys and took previous expeditions to task for any apparent discrepancy with their findings.

Further reading: Fanny and William Workman, *The Call of the Snowy Hispar: A Narrative of Exploration and Mountaineering on the Northern Frontier of India* (1910); *Ice-bound Heights of the Mustagh: An Account of Two Seasons of Pioneer Exploration and High Climbing in the Baltistan Himalaya* (1908); *In the Ice World of Himalaya . . . : Among the Peaks and Passes of Ladakh, Nubra, Suru, and Baltistan* (1901); *Peaks and Glaciers of Nun Kun: A Record of Pioneer Exploration and Mountaineering in the Punjab Himalaya* (1909).

WORLD CUP This annual series of competitions sanctioned by the UIAA features climbers from numerous countries. Some six to nine contests, depending on sponsorship availability and organization, take place each year on carefully crafted courses on artificial climbing walls. The events are held in Europe, the United States and Japan. The UIAA World Cup is different from the World Masters Tour, a separate, private series. Also worth explanation are the two ranking systems used: UIAA permanent world rankings and the overall UIAA standings. The former includes both UIAA and non UIAA events, and the latter only UIAA events. The permanent world rankings are similar to ASCI (Association of Sport Climbers International) rankings, which include results from both UIAA and invita-

tional events. At this writing, however ASCI is in transition, and is not issuing rankings.

WRIST LOOP A SLING connected to an ICE AXE through which the wrist is passed. Used for support and attachment between the sling and the ICE TOOL, to prevent the ice tool from being lost while climbing.

WUNSCH, STEVE (1949–) (United States) Wunsch pushed FREE CLIMBING standards during the 1970s, especially in ELDORADO CANYON, COLORADO, and the SHAWANGUNKS, New York, and his climbing ETHICS helped shape the philosophy of American free climbing.

Between 1970 and 1975 Wunsch climbed mainly in Colorado. Among his best ROUTES from this period are the FIRST FREE ASCENT of the east ridge of the Maiden (5.10), a rock tower in the FLATIRONS above BOULDER, Colorado, and in Eldorado Canyon the first free ascent of PITCH one of The Naked Edge (5.10+), and the roof climbs Guenese (5.10), Kloberdanz (5.10) and Psycho (5.11). His lead of the fourth pitch of the FACE CLIMB Jules Verne (5.10) was a breakthrough—a BOLD free climb made with ground-up, clean climbing no-PITON ethics. The pitch, which was attempted frequently in the 1970s, involves thin face climbing with the risk of a 60-ft (18-m) LEADER fall onto small wired STOPPERS.

In 1973 Wunsch climbed extensively in the Shawangunks, where he was influenced by the climbing philosophy and tactics of John STANNARD. Prior to visiting the Shawangunks Wunsch had been conservative about falling while working on extremely hard climbs, regarding falling onto PROTECTION or lowering off of protection as a flaw in his concept of a free climb. Instead, Wunsch trained himself to down climb difficult moves. While in the Shawangunks, however, Wunsch observed Stannard achieve physically demanding routes by his willingness to push himself to the limit and sustain falls onto good protection. Wunsch adopted this philosophy to achieve routes like Super Crack (5.12+), which stood as the Shawangunks', and North America's, hardest route for many years.

WYOMING (United States) A glaciated peak of modest difficulty, Gannett Peak (13,804 ft/4,207 m), in the WIND RIVER RANGE, is Wyoming's high point.

The Bighorn Mountains are an impressive range of 13,000 ft (3,963 m). One of this range's dominant features is the 1,000-ft (305-m) east face of Cloud Peak, on which Steve Petro and Arnold Ilgner made a FREE ASCENT in 1983, opening the way for other BIG WALL free climbs in the area.

Abundant limestone has recently been discovered in Wyoming. SPORT CLIMBING on dolomite exists at Sinks Canyon (where there is also sandstone), nine miles (14 km) southwest of Lander. Within reach of the TETON RANGE, around Jackson Hole, are several limestone sport climbing areas, Blacktail Butte being the best known. Also around the Tetons, at Jenny Lake is significant granite BOULDERING.

YANIRO, TONY (1960–) (United States) Even at the age of 15, in 1975, this California FREE CLIMBER had established routes of 5.12, such as Gates of Delirium, at TAHQUITZ Rock (CALIFORNIA). He opened scores of hard routes up to 5.14 at the NEEDLES, JOSHUA TREE (California) and CITY OF ROCKS (Idaho), and is credited with one of the world's first 5.13 CRACKS, Grand Illusion, (5.13b), at the Sugarloaf, near Tahoe, California. His other cracks—Sphinx Crack, 5, 13b (SOUTH PLATTE, Colorado), and Boogieman, (City of Rocks) 5.13d/5.14a are famous for their difficulty, as are his FACE routes, like Remora (5.14), at City of Rocks. He was among the first climbers to embrace strength and endurance training specific to climbing, and to develop unique CRACK-CLIMBING techniques. One technique, Leavittation, which he developed with Randy LEAVITT, was a breakthrough in OFFWIDTH crack climbing, and enabled Yaniro's ascent of Paisano Overhang, 5.12c, at Suicide Rock (California).

YELLOW CREEK FALLS (United States) A 200-ft (61-m) sandstone cliff, located on the side of Lookout Mountain, nine miles from Collinsville, Alabama. It is noted for FREE CLIMBS through multi-tiered ROOFS and OVERHANGING FACES, some split by clean CRACKS. Due to the CRAG's steepness, RATINGS are predominantly high, from 5.9 and with a glut of routes in the 5.11 and 5.12 categories. SPORT CLIMBS and traditional climbs exist side by side. The crag is a canyon, with a north and south wall. On the north side Maneater (5.12c), from 1986, is one of the South's first sport climbs, by Mark Cole and Curt Merchant. Grand Dragon (5.12b), a crack compared to Supercrack in the SHAWANGUNKS, was freed by Rob Robinson in 1983. White Supremacy (5.10b/c), climbed by Chick Holtkamp and Rich Gottlieb in 1980, is hailed as one of the finest 5.10s in the eastern United States. Harder is Ayran Nation (5.13a), on the north side, by Jerry Roberts in 1989. Year-round climbing is possible, but high humidity in June through September makes climbing uncomfortable.
Guidebook: John Harlin, *Climber's Guide to North America, East Coast Rockclimbs* (1986).

YERUPAJA (Peru) The highest mountain in the CORDILLERA HUAYUASH of north-central PERU and one of the most ferocious South American peaks. Its name, originally Yarupaya, is related to the Yaru tribe of eastern Peru. Rather a RIDGE (a range of hills), its main peak rises to 21,708 ft/6,617 m and its southern point, some 300 ft (91 m) lower. It has also been called El Carnicero ("The Butcher") for its ever-defiant reputation. Austrians Hans Kinzl and Erwin SCHNEIDER made the mountain and its entire range known through picture books. In 1950, a group of American university students won one of the greatest triumphs in American MOUNTAINEERING: David Harrah and James Maxwell reached the precarious summit CORNICE (which collapsed shortly afterward) then descended the dangerous ridge. Harrah suffered amputations. Other ROUTES, all exposed and difficult, include: west face, N. Leif-Patterson (United States) and J. Peterek (ARGENTINA) (1966); west face direct, Germans (1977); northeast face, C. Jones and P. Dix (US) (1968); traverse north to south, Adcock's party (1968); and north ridge, Japanese (1968). The south summit has also received some routes. Several climbers have perished on Yerupaja's flanks, with the peculiarity that their bodies have never been found or sighted. Yerupaja is easily reached from the Andean town of Chiquian, but due to political unrest, no attempts have taken place since 1989.
Guidebook: Jim Bartle and David Sharman, *Trails and Climbs of the Cordillera Blanca of Peru* (1992).
Further reading: Beaud, Philippe, *The Peruvian Andes* (1988); John Sack, *The Butcher, The Ascent of Yerupaja* (1952).

Evelio Echevarria
Colorado State University

YETI Also, Abominable Snowman. A mythical creature with characteristics of man and ape said to inhabit high altitudes of the HIMALAYA, especially around the EVEREST region of NEPAL and TIBET, but also throughout mountainous ranges of Asia where the creature is known by many names. The legend was brought to westerners' attention by early Everest climbers. Bill TILMAN wrote an appendix about Yeti in his book about the 1938 Everest expedition, and Eric SHIPTON brought back the famous photographs of a purported Yeti footprint in 1951, which he found at 18,000 ft (5,488 m) on the Menlung Glacier in Tibet, during an Everest reconnaissance. This photo and others like it have been labeled as proof positive, as a hoax and as monkey tracks. Individuals like Sir Edmund HILLARY and Reinhold MESSNER have participated in unsuccessful expeditions to find the Yeti. Hillary and others have brought back the scalp and hand of what Buddhist monks claimed was a Yeti. They proved to be parts of a yak. Though no evidence exists, occasional photographs and sightings by mountaineers and trekkers continue to stir the imaginations of Yeti enthusiasts even today.

Further reading: Myra Shackley, *Yeti, Sasquatch and the Neanderthal Enigma* (1983).

YORKSHIRE (Britain) This region of England contains some important CRAGS, among them GORDALE, MALHAM, KILNSEY, BLUE SCAR and BRIMHAM, which are limestone, and ILKLEY, ALMSCLIFF, CALEY and BRIDESTONES, which are gritstone. Other grit crags bearing good climbing include Rylstone, Crookrise and Heptonstall, all of which are described in the Yorkshire Mountain Club guidebook, *Yorkshire Gritstone* (1989).

YOSEMITE DECIMAL SYSTEM (YDS) The FREE-CLIMBING decimal rating system used in the United States, conceived by climbers at TAHQUITZ in southern CALIFORNIA during the 1950s, later adopted and refined in Yosemite.

This system begins at 5.0 (5 for fifth class: rope required) and continues 5.1, 5.2, 5.3, 5.4, 5.5, 5.6, 5.7, 5.8, 5.9, 5.10, 5.11, 5.12, 5.13 and 5.14, the hardest. The top grades are often given a "+" or "−" rating, like 5.10+, or 5.12−, and sometimes the letters a, b, c and d, such as 5.10d (same as 5.10+) or 5.12a (same as 5.12−). (See RATING SYSTEMS.)

YOSEMITE VALLEY (United States) One of the world's premier rock-climbing centers since the 1950s. The steep, huge and accessible fair-weather walls of this west-draining canyon of the SIERRA NEVADA in CALIFORNIA have inspired climbers and demanded advances in techniques and equipment like no other rock-climbing area.

George Anderson was first to climb technically here when, in 1875, he ascended HALF DOME by drilling and standing on a ladder of BOLTS. In 1934 Bestor Robinson, Jules Eichorn and Dick Leonard, American pioneers of BELAY and tension/aid techniques, made a ground-breaking climb of Higher Cathedral Spire. David BROWER was another to climb new ROUTES after this, and his experiences helped form his influential conservation ethic. Swiss immigrant John SALATHE led the next advances in BOLDNESS, endurance and technology in the late 1940's. To ascend walls like the southwest face of Half Dome (1946), the Lost Arrow (1947) and the north face of Sentinel Rock (1950), he invented PITONS of hard steel from a car axle. Salathe also initiated the mental toughness to endure many days on a Yosemite wall with minimal food and water.

Allen Steck (Salathe's partner on Sentinel) and Mark Powell were top Yosemite climbers of the 1950s who committed to Yosemite to make climbing their principal life focus. Wally Reed led the drive to push FREE CLIMBING standards to 5.9. Royal ROBBINS led the push to climb the big walls, and in 1957, with Mike Sherrick and Jerry Gallwas, achieved the FIRST ASCENT of the 2000-ft (610-m) northwest face of Half Dome, America's first Grade VI.

Warren HARDING missed joining the Half Dome team, but immediately afterward he enlisted Mark Powell and Bill Feurer and began sieging Yosemite's greatest wall, 3,000-ft (915-m) high EL CAPITAN. An injury to Powell and

Park Service bans during the tourist season forced Harding to delay his efforts until the fall of 1958. Accompanied by Wayne Merry and international publicity, they completed the Nose Route in a final 12-day push.

After the big walls were climbed, Yosemite's firm rock and fair weather led climbers to see simple success on a wall as inevitable given enough engineering, and climbs came to be judged more by style. Yosemite climbers had a sense that their valley had made them into the strongest TECHNICAL climbers in the world. Further ascents of El Capitan, especially the Salathe Wall by Robbins, Chuck PRATT and Tom FROST (1961), and the North American Wall by the same three plus Yvon CHOUINARD (1964), gave credence to the Yosemite reputation. Pratt was especially strong at free-climbing Yosemite's CRACKS. Chouinard began a career of manufacturing hardware in response to the demands of Yosemite.

Charlie PORTER and the team of Hugh Burton and Steve Sutton were most notable for climbing new, seemingly blank El Cap routes using a minimum of drilling and a maximum of finesse with tiny pitons, malleable NUTS, HOOKS and CAMMING NUTS. Jim BRIDWELL then became the moving force in both AID and free climbing. He pushed the limits of A5 aid climbing with routes like Pacific Ocean Wall on El Capitan, and during the mid-1970s he inspired many young free climbers to push limits toward 5.12 and multi-pitch 5.11 routes. Most successful of this group were Ron KAUK, Dale BARD and John BACHAR.

Ray Jardine developed improved SPRING-LOADED CAMMING DEVICES (FRIENDS) in Yosemite in 1977–78, offering crack climbers fast, reliable PROTECTION. Bachar became well known for climbing difficult free routes unroped. By the mid-1980s a rift developed between climbers over whether to preserve the Yosemite tradition of ground-up climbing, preferably with no weighting of protection, or to place bolts on RAPPEL. Randy LEAVITT, John Middendorf John Barbella, Greg Child, Walt Shipley and others continued to find severe aid lines on El Capitan and Half Dome. Peter CROFT has led a recent trend toward dramatic free solo ascents and speed ascents of walls. He and Hans Florine climbed El Cap's Nose in four hours, 24 minutes.

Guidebook: George Meyers and Don Reid, *Yosemite Climbs* (1987).

YOUNG, GEOFFREY WINTHROP (1876–1958) (Britain) Son of one of the important figures in Victorian MOUNTAINEERING, "GWY" grew up in a household where all mention of the sport, after the death of a favourite uncle in its pursuit, was forbidden. The result of this was that he became the foremost British alpinist in the early years of the century, usually climbing with the great guide Josef Knubel. Two alpine RIDGES (the Younggrats on the Breithorn and Weisshorn) were named after him. He lost his leg in the First World War, but continued actively to climb thereafter, reaching the summit of the Zinal Rothorn as late as 1935. His salons in Cambridge and Easter parties at Pen y Pass in Snowdonia gathered together and encouraged many of the best mountaineers and rock climbers of his time, and continued until the outbreak of the Second

World War. His final legacy was probably the formation of a representative body for climbing in Britain, the British Mountaineering Council. A poet and writer, he was by profession an educationalist, and probably only robbed of the knighthood he deserved for work in that field by a scandal.

Further reading: Geoffrey Winthrop Young, *On High Hills* (1927).

YOUNGHUSBAND, SIR FRANCIS (1863–1942)

(Britain) Nephew of the eminent 19th-century Himalayan explorer Robert Barkley Shaw, Francis Edward Younghusband was born into an Indian Army family, educated at Clifton (where he was contemporary with Norman COLLIE) and Sandhurst, and commissioned into the King's Dragoon Guards in INDIA in 1882. Early travels in Turkestan (he was the first European to cross the Gobi Desert), Tien Shan and Shaksgam established his reputation as the foremost Central Asian explorer of his day, and led on to the crucial role allotted him in the "Great Game" played out between Russia and BRITAIN along the marches of Afghanistan, CHINA, India and TIBET. In 1903–1904 he headed the Mission to Lhasa. After his retirement from military and diplomatic life, his knowledge of the HIMALAYAS and enthusiasm for the project inspired the three British EVEREST expeditions of the 1920s. Small and wiry, with penetrating blue eyes and great physical courage, he became an essential point of reference for all prewar Himalayan ventures. His own bent in later life was religious, and he wrote several books on Hinduism, Buddhism and mysticism. His account of Asian travels from 1884 to 1894, *The Heart of a Continent* (1896), is the classic text of 19th-century Himalayan exploration.

Further reading: Peter Fleming, *Bayonets to Lhasa* (1961); George Seaver, *Sir Francis Younghusband* (1952).

YO-YO A FREE CLIMBING tactic in which the LEADER tries the MOVES of a ROUTE repeatedly, LOWERING OFF PROTECTION and TOP ROPING back up to the high point until eventually the PITCH is led past the high point. (See FLASH, ON SIGHT, PRE-INSPECTION, STYLE, WIRED.)

Z

ZANSKAR HIMAL   See KASHMIR.

ZAWADA, ANDRZEJ (1930–   ) (Poland) Zawada was the leader of Polish expeditions to the HIMALAYA, many in winter, and one of the most successful EXPEDITION leaders ever. Of the eight expeditions he led up to 1987, four were in winter and only two (LHOTSE and K2) failed. He began climbing at the age of 20 with the Polish Alpine Club, climbing in the ALPS, and making the first winter TRAVERSE (45 mile/72 km long) of all the Tatra peaks, in 1960. In 1971 he led and summited on the successful first ascent of Khunyang Chish southeast face and south ridge (25,755 ft/7,852 m). This Pakistani massif covers an area about three times greater than that occupied by K2. In winter 1973 he led the Polish Noshaq (24,574 ft/7,492 m) west ridge expedition in Afghanistan with T. Piotrowski. Back in Afghanistan in 1977, he summited Koh-e-Mandaras with Terry King (BRITAIN). In the winter of 1979–80 he directed the first WINTER ASCENT of EVEREST, and in spring 1980 directed the FIRST ASCENT of Everest's south pillar. In winter 1985 he directed the difficult 9,840-ft (3,000-m) southeast BUTTRESS of CHO OYU. His Polish-English-Canadian attempt on K2 in winter 1987 was unsuccessful.

ZAWN A British term describing a deep cliffed inlet on a SEA CLIFF.

ZION (United States) An adventure climbing area in southwest UTAH, in Zion National Park. Zion is a valley on the scale of YOSEMITE, but of red Navajo sandstone. The rock is generally sound yet soft, and most ROUTES follow distinct CRACK lines. The larger BIG WALLS are 2,000 ft (610 m) high, and sport numerous Grade V and VI routes, some FREE, others with much AID. Because of Zion's soft rock, PITONS quickly scar the rock, so modern routes are climbed hammerless when possible. A CLEAN CLIMBING RATING SYSTEM for aid is used here, as in other desert areas. C1–C5 functions the same as A1–A5, with the C informing climbers that pitons need not be used. BOLTS can be unreliable in the soft rock, and on some routes drilled holes are filled with angle pitons. To preserve the rock, pitons are usually left in place. Long climbs often end at a band of soft rock before the rim and descent is by RAPPEL.

Climbing began in Zion in the late 1960s with ascents of the major formations, like Great White Throne and Angel's Landing, by climbers like Jeff LOWE. Multiday routes like Touchstone Wall, Moonlight Buttress, Space Shot and Monkeyfinger Wall were established in the 1970s and 1980s, and difficult multiday routes like the Radiator on Abraham and the Swiss-American route on Angel's Landing were established in the early 1990s.

Guidebook: John Harlin III, *Climber's Guide to North America: Rocky Mountain Rock Climbs* (1985).

Z-PULLEY Also Z-hoist, or unassisted hoist. The hoisting technique offering a 3:1 mechanical advantage that is most often used in CREVASSE RESCUE.

ZURBRIGGEN, MATTHIAS (1855–1917) (Switzerland) This famous guide who worked in the Wallister Alps, MONT BLANC Group, and MONTE ROSA, on which he pioneered several new ROUTES, like Monte Rosa east face in 1886. From 1892 to 1902 Zurbriggen was a sought-after guide for the great ranges: He accompanied W. M. CONWAY to the KARAKORAM (1892), where they explored the HISPAR, BIAFO and BALTORO glaciers and set an altitude record with Pioneer Peak (22,599 ft/6,890 m). E. A. Fitzgerald took him to NEW ZEALAND (1894–95) and Zurbriggen led FIRST ASCENTS there on Mount Sealy, Mount Tasman, Mount Haidunger and Mount Befton, and soloed the second ascent of Mount COOK, the highest mountain in New Zealand. While with Fitzgerald in the ANDES (1896–97) he soloed ACONCAGUA and Tupungato. He accompanied the Americans Fanny Bullock and William Hunte WORKMAN to the Karakorum (1899, 1902), and Prince Borghese in the TIEN SHAN mountains (1900). His last 10 years, according to the climbing historian Benuzzi, were lived in "moral and material destruction." Zurbriggen's memoirs—*Von den Alpen zu den Anden (From the Alps to the Andes)*—appeared posthumously, after his suicide by hanging.

APPENDIX I

FEATURES OF MOUNTAINS AND GLACIERS : MUZTAGH TOWER

1 Summit
2 Ridge
3 Face or wall
4 Shoulder or col
5 Aiguille or pinnacle or tower
6 Gendarme
7 Snowfield, ice field
8 Serac, ice cliff
9 Couloir
10 Rib
11 Bergschrund
12 Cirque
13 Glacier
14 Icefall
15 Seracs
16 Medial moraine
17 Lateral moraine
18 Buttress
19 Chute

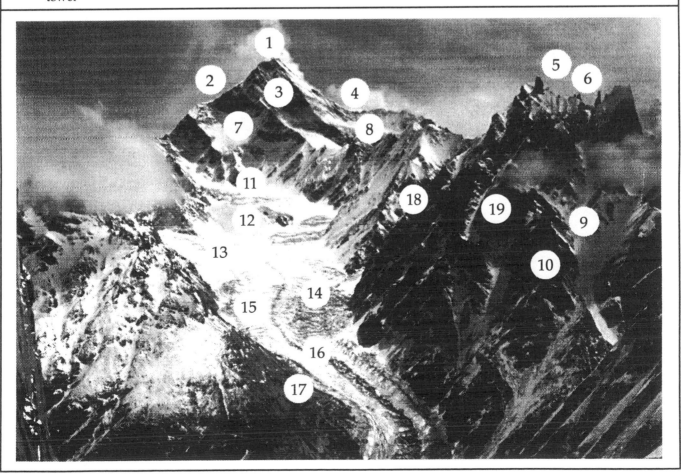

APPENDIX II

KEY TO STANDARD CLIMBING SYMBOLS AND ABBREVIATIONS

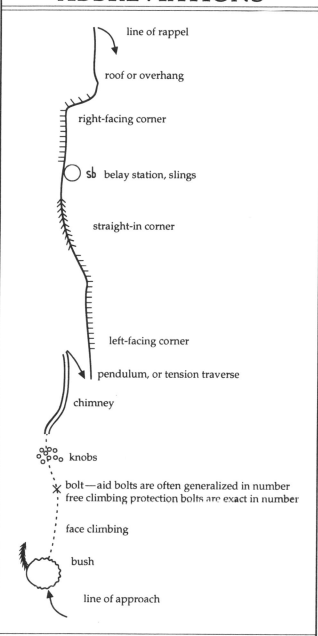

line of rappel

roof or overhang

right-facing corner

sb   belay station, slings

straight-in corner

left-facing corner

pendulum, or tension traverse

chimney

knobs

bolt—aid bolts are often generalized in number
free climbing protection bolts are exact in number

face climbing

bush

line of approach

OTHER ABBREVIATIONS

lb	lieback	**KB**	knifeblades
chim.	chimney	**LA**	Lost Arrows
ow	offwidth (3½"–8")	**pro.**	Protection needed beyond a standard rack
thin	thin crack (to 1½ ")		

INTERNATIONAL RATING SYSTEMS COMPARISON CHART (ROCK CLIMBING)

POLAND	BELGIUM	SCANDINAVIA	EAST GERMAN (ELBSANSTEIN)	GERMANY (UIAA)	FRANCE	U.S.A.	BRITISH		AUSTRALIA	SOUTH AFRICA	NCCS (U.S.A.)
I	I	1	I	I	1	Class 1	Easy (E)		1	1	F1
						Class 2			2	2	F2
						Class 3			3	3	
						Class 4			4	4	F3
						5.0	Moderate (MOD)		5	5	F4
						5.1			6	6	
II		2				5.2	Difficult (DIFF)		7	7	
	II		II	II	2	5.3	Very Difficult (VDIFF)		8	8	F5
III	III		III	III	3	5.4	Severe (S)		9	9	
IV		3	IV	IV	4a	5.5	4a	Hard Severe (HS)	10-11	10-12	
	IV		V	V–	4b	5.6	4b	Mild Very Severe (MVS)	12	13	F6
	IV+	4	VI	V	4c / 5a	5.7	4c	Very Severe (VS)	13	14	
V			VIIa	V+	5b	5.8			14	15	F7
	V–	5–	VIIb	VI–	5c	5.9	5a	Hard Very Severe (HVS)	15	16	F8
				VI	5c+				16	17	
						5.10a			17	18	F9
VI	V	5	VIIc	VI+	6a	5.10b	5b	E1	18	19	
						5.10c				20	
VI+	V+	5+	VIIIa	VII–	6a+	5.10d	5b	E2	19	21	F10
						5.11a			20	22	
VI.1	VI-	6–	VIIIb	VII	6b	5.11b			21	23	F11
		6	VIIIc	VII+	6b+	5.11c	5b	E3	22	24	
VI.1+	VI	6+		VIII–	6c	5.11d	5c		23		F12
VI.2		7–	IXa	VIII	6c+	5.12a		E4	24	25	F13
VI.2+	VI+	7	IXb	VIII+	7a	5.12b		E5	25	26	
VI.3		7+	IXc	IX–	7a+	5.12c	6a		26	27	
VI.3+	VII-	8–	Xa	IX	7b	5.12d			27	28	
		8			7b+	5.13a		E6		29	
VI.4	VII	8+	Xb	IX+	7c	5.13b	6b		28	30	
		9–	Xc	X–	7c+	5.13c		E7	29	31	
VI.5				X	8a	5.13d	6c		30	32	
		9		X+	8 a+	5.14a		E8	31	33	
		9+		XI–	8b	5.14b	7a		32	34	
				XI	8b+	5.14c		E9	33		
					8c	5.14d			34		
					8c+						
					9a						

BIBLIOGRAPHY

Ashton, Steve. *Rock Climbing Techniques*. North Promfret, Vt.: Trafalgar Square, 1991.

Barry, John. *Rock Climbing*. Mechanicsburg, Pa.: Stackpole Books, 1989.

Bridwell, Jim. *Climbing Adventures: A Climber's Passion*. Merrillville, Ind.: ICS Books, 1992.

Fyffe, Allen, and Iain Peter. *The Handbook of Climbing*. New York: Viking Penguin, 1991.

Gregory, John F. *Rock Sport: Tools, Training, & Techniques for Climbers*. Mechanicsburg, Pa.: Stackpole Books, 1989.

Italia, Bob. *Rock Climbing*. Minneapolis: Abdo & Daughters, 1994.

Johnson, Turlough. *Rock Climbing Basics*. Mechanicsburg, Pa.: Stackpole Books, 1995.

Livesey, Pete. *Rock Climbing*. Golden, Colo.: Fulcrum Publishing, 1990.

Long, John. *How to Rock Climb!* Evergreen, Colo.: Chockstone Press, 1993.

————. *Sport and Face Climbing*. Evergreen, Colo.: Chockstone Press, 1994.

Loughman, Michael. *Learning to Rock Climb*. San Francisco: Sierra Club Books, 1981.

Reidel, Arthur. *Fundamental Rock Climbing*. Cambridge, Mass.: MIT Outing Club, 1973.

Roper, Steve, and Allen Steck, eds. *The Best of Ascent: Twenty-five Years of the Mountaineering Experience*. San Francisco: Sierra Club Books, 1993.

————. *Climbers Guide to Yosemite Valley*. San Francisco: Sierra Club Books, 1971.

Scott, Doug. *Big Wall Climbing: Development, Techniques and Aids*. New York: Oxford University Press, 1974.

Skinner, Todd, and Jim McMullen. *Modern Rock Climbing: Beyond the Basics*. Merrillville, Ind.: ICS Books, 1993.

Strassman, Michael. *Rock Climbing: The Basic Essentials Of*. Merrillville, Ind.: ICS Books, 1989.

INDEX

This index is designed to be used in conjunction with the many cross-references within the A-to-Z entries. The main A-to-Z entries are indicated by **boldface** page references. The general subjects are subdivided by the A-to-Z entries. *Italicized* page references indicate illustrations.